The People's Clearing House:

Utilizing Democratic Principles to Restore the Genuine
Representation Envisioned by the Founders

Mark Eady

For Alex Moore, 1994-2010

Table of Contents

Introduction

An episode of "60 Minutes" entitled "Anonymous Inc." from January 2016 was partially utilized to take an in-depth look at how easily money is being laundered into America through the use of "anonymous shell companies." In order to better understand the degree of difficulty facing law enforcement officials in attempting to follow a money trail shadowed through dummy corporations and offshore banking accounts, correspondent Steve Kroft observed the work of an undercover investigator for Global Witness, a "social advocacy group that exposes corruption in the developing world."

Under the pseudonym of "Ralph Kayser," the private investigator sought the assistance of attorneys in Manhattan by pretending to be a "representative of a government official from a poor West African country who wants to move millions of dollars in suspicious funds into the U.S." Just one of the sixteen attorneys approached by Kayser rejected the idea of offering any form of advice or assistance.

Charmian Gooch, co-founder of Global Witness, told Steve Kroft that 300 billion dollars annually was being laundered into the United States through the use of practices highlighted in his report. Obviously, stricter laws and more meaningful regulations are needed to rein in the ability of a middle entity to inappropriately shield the identity of the actual owner, while at the same time being careful to maintain a balance of privacy.

Not surprisingly, efforts at passing meaningful legislation for garnering necessary transparency have failed to pass, with the American Bar Association providing some of the strongest pushback. This type of clientele often means big money for those providing the road map to legally conceal these transactions. Any attempt similar to those spearheaded by former Senator Carl Levin to require the name of the "real owner," the "beneficial owner," on the forms continues to be routinely rejected by legislators.

One of the attorneys who offered initial advice and a possible willingness to proceed during the preliminary hearing was actually a "former president of the American Bar Association." However, though disheartening in its own right, it's actually the reasoning articulated from one of the attorneys as to why he was never concerned about the potential of an investigation that is the most troubling and revealing.

As can be seen with the undercover work of Ralph Kayser, the attorney said, "They don't send the lawyers to jail, because we run the country." To further clarify his exact meaning, he added, "We're still the members of a privileged, privilege [sic] class in this country," before concluding with, "We make the laws, and when we do so, we make them in a way that is advantageous to the lawyer." Though many legislators expressed outrage over these words, most were actually being rather hypocritical in their judgment.

Beyond the fact that most politicians are lawyers, the arrogance and entitlement expressed by this attorney runs rampant in government. Many who possess similar feelings as the attorney may not be as forthright with the sentiments that lead them, but their consistent actions clearly identify them on both sides of the political aisle.

The political elite in both parties continue to disregard their constituency, as John LeBoutiller briefly summarized with his words from a July 2015 segment of "The Political Insiders" on Fox News. The former Republican lawmaker and dedicated activist for American POW/MIA summarized the times in saying, "The American people are alienated from the American leadership class… And I think the big thing is: what is America on the fourth of July? You know America the beautiful, land of the home and free and all that, but it's also the best example of—'of the people, by the people, and for the people.' And we have to ask ourselves: is our government any longer representing the people of the United States? And the American people, I think in most polls, are saying 'No it doesn't.' Republicans and Democrats and Independents are all saying it."

President Kennedy was once quoted as saying, "Mothers may still want their favorite sons to grow up to be President, but, according to a famous Gallup poll of some years ago, they don't want them to become politicians in the process." Legislators have created a genuine distrust among the electorate. The self-serving career politician who has consistently taken an opportunistic approach toward the current political system that is centered on money has only strengthened this broad-scale, negative perception.

Many of the disillusioned among the middle and lower classes have become convinced that they have no actual voice in government, witnessing that policy decisions often ignore them. Consistent negative polls should have provided evidence of how much of the country was realizing that the agenda was only being tailored for a select few—without rightful consideration to the common issues facing most Americans.

State and federal leaders have either chosen to ignore or failed to value the idea of serving their constituency. Their focus is on maintaining the status quo, which rewards them and the few they truly serve. However, their own personal failures in accountability do not hinder them in their self-righteous condemnation of others who project the same.

Most politicians pretend to be blameless, causing a number of Americans to actually give up on the concept of a republic-oriented government. These individuals have grown to realize the present notion of possessing representation is nothing more than a facade— with a few of those same individuals concluding that protests or disobedience to current laws are the only actual methods for being socially and politically acknowledged.

America is built on capitalism, but when representatives through corruption, self-interest, and a false sense of entitlement pervert its fundamental principles to such a degree that its values and benefits become increasingly unrecognizable, alternatives once unimaginable are widely entertained by more of the general electorate.

As noted on the "Real Story with Gretchen Carlson" of Fox News in an August 2015 episode, "In a Pew Research Center survey only 50% of Americans have a positive view of capitalism, and 40% have a negative response. Mix in the fact that 31% have a positive reaction to the word *socialism* and what does it all mean? When you factor in that 50% of 30 to 49-year-olds and 69% of 18 to 29-year-olds would say they would vote for a socialist, I think it showcases an alarming trend in this great country of ours."

These polls firmly indicate the level of frustration within the middle class and the poor that have for years pleaded for someone to fight for them to have a seat at the table—and each election cycle witnessed basically the same results. Even in the instances when some of their economic outcomes became better as the result of policy changes, waste and abuse in government remained. Genuine political equality remains hopeless as more power has been given to the wealthy to keep the political elite firmly insulated.

Simply directing those considering socialism to the results in countries like Venezuela, which has followed such a form of government, is not sufficient. This is especially true for young people, who have never experienced supply shortages and have only been educated through a liberal prism. Outrage over governmental failures in places like Flint, Michigan, and New Orleans, Louisiana, are only confined in scope to those specific cases for most. Both instances should be recognized as clear predictors of how life would be under a system more reliant on government for even basic needs.

After Ed Krayewski, associate editor of Reason.com, informed readers in late April 2016 that Venezuela had, in fact, run out of beer, he ended his article by displaying the depravity of socialism by writing: "In Venezuela, there have been shortages of: batteries, beef, birth-control pills, bleach, brass, bread, breast implants, butter, cheese, chicken, chocolate, clothes irons, coffee, coffins, condensed milk, condoms, corn oil, deodorant, detergents, diapers, eggs, fabric softeners, fish, flour, French fries, fruits, gauze, hops, ice cream, insecticide, jams, juice, lentils, margarine, Marie biscuits, makeup, mayonnaise, medical gloves, milk, mouthwash, mustard, napkins, sacramental bread, sardines, satin, shampoo, shoes, skim milk, soap, sodas, sugar, sunflower oil, tires, toilet paper, toothbrushes, toothpaste, varnish, vegetables, water, wine, and more."

However, the style of government in Venezuela, which is on the verge of a complete and utter meltdown, is actually viewed as a favorable alternative by some Americans. Such an absence in reasonable judgment falls squarely on the backs of those representatives who went to D.C. and sold out the people.

The heightened possibility for mass chaos, the proclivity for riots, and consistent migrations from one failed socialistic country to the next have done little to dissuade those Americans advocating a more socialistic approach to governing. The well-known words of past leaders like Margaret Thatcher resonate: "The trouble with socialism is that eventually you run out of other people's money." These thinkers are being disregarded or ignored by individuals desperate for the opportunity that they sadly believe socialism will bring.

This blind reconsideration for replacing capitalism is not just happening in America. Some British citizens who are new to politics are being lured into the democratic socialistic platform. Jill Lawless detailed a young man supporting Labour Party Leader and Democratic Socialist Jeremy Corbyn as stating, "it's a breath of fresh air." He articulated specific detestation for the financial crisis being placed on the backs of average citizens. Clearly, a number of young voters are beginning to determine that representatives are no longer being held accountable to the people. American leaders could eventually witness far-reaching implications if the young continue on this thought trajectory, as a 2015 U.S. Census Bureau found millennials to now be the largest group.

Those looking to democratic socialism join the ranks of other Americans who, by and large, are tired of an electoral system that maintains the same set of conditions that produces the same set of results. While most Americans still favor capitalism, they have grown increasingly weary of social and economic inequality; something that a system rooted in excess money seems hopeless to ever adequately address.

From how individuals become elected to the people allowed to gain access to them before voting, the entire political system in D.C. and most state legislatures across the country, which has increasingly become more unequal, has gained the attention of more Americans. Stagnant wages, rising poverty, difficulty in obtaining full-time work, consequential executive orders, and an inability of the legislature to properly provide checks and balances has caused great apprehension. Everywhere Americans look, their country seems to merely be placed on autopilot; as passengers, they have no one advocating for them. More importantly, the final outcome presents a unique uncertainty to previous voyages, in that the future destination no longer seems promising.

As Rick Newman pointed out in an article for Yahoo Finance in May 2015, "About half of Santorum's campaign budget in 2012 (not including the super PAC) came from individuals who contributed $200 or less. Just 18% of Romney's funding, by contrast, came from small donors." And though Democrats often rail against Republicans for the influence of money in politics, Kenneth P. Vogel of Politico reported that "the 100 biggest donors of 2014 gave nearly $174 million to Democrats, compared to more than $140 million to Republicans." Although non-disclosed contributions, commonly referred to as "dark money," were more heavily accredited toward the Republicans, the overall numbers clearly display that both major parties offer little resistance in taking large donations solely intended to perpetuate the game of politics.

Pat Caddell, Doug Schoen, and John LeBoutillier compose "The Political Insiders" on Fox News and provide a clear-cut analysis each week of key political issues facing the nation. Although the group is composed of two Democrats and a Republican, each of whom holds strong ties to their respective party, their overall conversations reflect an unfiltered perspective. On the Fourth of July weekend in 2015, the group offered a meaningful critique of the current political system and described to host Pattie Ann Browne what kind of presidential candidate is needed to help set things right in government. They already believed then that the voters were signaling a desire to embrace such a candidate.

Pat Caddell: "We have something here, which is a moment, you know. We have the voters, this thing about wanting everyone to get along which they do. They want to accomplish things. At the same time, they see these leaders as failed. The leaders will not admit that they have failed...."

John LeBoutillier: "The system, Pat; the system has failed."

Pat Caddell: "The system has failed, exactly, and they are being oppressed and they know it. They know these people are failures on both sides. Bernie Sanders is [sic] a socialist, is getting more votes because he is being authentic about what he views as the corruption of inequality and the banks and the control of money—and people are responding. The question is whether there will be a positive advocate for all of this who could both critique and offer the American people a way out."

Doug Schoen: "Pat, who is that person? We don't have such a person."

John LeBoutillier: "We don't have it. We don't have that, Pat. What we need is—"

Pat Caddell: "The name is Smith and I'm looking for him."

John LeBoutillier: "Smith, yeah!"

Pattie Anne: "Yes, that's what everyone is looking for: that Smith goes to Washington. So let's see if he is out there."

John LeBoutillier: "Right. Smith needs to be, Smith needs to be [sic] not a Socialist, but authentic, not a little crazy business man thing, but expressing the anger of the American people. And most of all he has to be someone that the public trust. You look back over history; the two Roosevelts and John Kennedy were from the aristocracy. They were rich. The public trusted them. The little man and little women [sic] trusted them because they said 'that guy's not out to rip me off. He's out to help the country.' Where is that candidate and who is going to help the country?"

Doug Schoen: "But you know what, the political, the political [sic] class has so rigged the game, John, so rigged the system. It's not that the people don't want such a person. Pat and you are exactly right. They have rigged the game so it's hard for such a person to emerge."

John LeBoutillier: "Hard, but not impossible."

Pattie Anne: "But you know the media, too, though, because the media decides who to focus on and who to just completely ignore."

Doug Schoen: "That's correct."

Mr. Smith Goes to Washington is an award-winning film from 1939 that centered on how an ordinary man, played by Jimmy Stewart, was able to successfully take on the negative forces of greed and manipulation within the nation's capital by providing clarity through a re-emphasis on the principles of democracy. While entirely agreeing with the assessment of "The Political Insiders" in regards to the type of candidate needed and desired to correct the flaws within the current political system, it would be naïve for viewers to misinterpret their words and falsely believe that it is possible for one person to single-handedly change things.

Even if you confined your analysis to 2016 Presidential candidates and took the intelligence of Ben Carson, the passion for income equality of Bernie Sanders, the business expertise of Donald Trump, the leadership of Chris Christie, the charisma of Marco Rubio, the resiliency of Hillary Clinton, the knowledge of Ted Cruz, the fiscal management of Gary Johnson, and the compassion and pragmatism of John Kasich, the task of re-affirming the ownership of the government by its people would be impossible to bear on the shoulders of one individual.

True change will require broad-scale unity.

New congressmen and congresswomen have entered office possessing the sentiments of hope and optimism from the people, only to increase the difficulty of their task ahead by adding additional layers to the foundation of neglect, waste, and inefficiency. Lawmakers cannot be trusted to change their ways without definite participation from those outside the political arena. Even if a champion emerged who spoke to the hearts of the people and somehow won within the current system slanted toward the political and social elite, he or she would still face the same uphill battle in governing with a representative body bought and paid for by special interests.

The lack of term limits, the power of lobbyists, and partisanship all help maintain the status quo. Building a coalition for achieving the change necessary would be impossible within the current environment because of greed and self-interest.

While the right individual can set the proper course, any genuine degree of success will require a number of Americans to act, as "The Political Insiders" seem to be indicating. The country has always been about more than one individual, regardless of title or socioeconomic position. This profound understanding is what formed the unique spirit for achieving personal freedom from an oppressive monarchy, established an inner guide for a set of ordinary men in establishing a new nation, fueled a conviction within citizens to consistently defend their freedoms, and reminded a sitting president that even he was not above the fundamental laws and principles which bind them together.

Each American has value and can contribute to restoring the equality the founders envisioned. Just as the soul is for a Christian, the country is not something that can be given away—although some politicians have certainly tried to sell theirs. Instead, it's the choices made which determine the fate of each. The country will always remain "of the people, by the people, and for the people," with the question of whether the people will decide to reclaim their ownership of it or allow others to unrightfully determine its fate.

The Founders conceived the greatest governmental system known to man. Though they were not perfect in their decisions, as witnessed in originally allowing only state legislatures to select U.S. Senators, there should be confidence that today they would take immediate action to eliminate the power of special interests, which manipulate fair representation. Although these men realized it was impossible to foresee all the specific and unique challenges that growth and ever-changing dynamics would bring, they placed their hope and faith in the Constitution providing an ample blueprint of ideas and principles to effectively address future issues.

In that spirit, what if adjustments could be made to the current political system, through the use of principles within democracy, to take on the task of securing the voice of the people in deciding the direction of the country as was originally envisioned? What if that outcome allowed elections to not provide new ways to divide us, but instead helped Americans come closer together for progress?

Imagine if election results were no longer viewed as the sole indicator of whether the country would move forward, but instead something that only added to what was being assessed every day within communities across the country. Think how refreshing it would be, within the current state of division and partisanship, to have faith in the fairness of the political system to provide genuine hope for setting things right in the next election. This atmosphere would allow the people to begin reclaiming their government, as well as create greater unity for rejecting those forces that deliberately attempt to mitigate their power by dividing them.

One of the most common requests of voters today is to simply call their legislator. While important, the people are capable of much more. All throughout history great changes have come from ordinary people who decided to reach for the extraordinary. The Founders were talented, but success was built on their resolve and willingness to believe in what they could achieve—despite coming from various backgrounds. George Washington entered the war as a farmer with limited education and a subpar military career, yet he would be the man who led and sustained the cause at every critical turn.

Author and award-winning journalist Stephen Kiernan—in his 2010 book, *Authentic Patriotism: Restoring America's Founding Ideals Through Selfless Action*—perfectly explained the significant potential in all of us by writing: "There is no them, no distant entity that will solve the nation's problems. In a democracy, there is only us, the people who elect the government, who live in the neighborhoods, who worship in our faith communities. Each one of us contains the same potential that the nation's Founders not only believed in but spent their lives demonstrating—the noble power of every individual to effect change. What the Founders knew, Americans must rediscover."

The success or failure of any movement depends on whether the leader can persuade others to act, although their individual role will most likely not be specifically recognized in history. These individuals are unmistakably driven by the considerations of "we," to that of "I," and are who form the bedrock of any successful change. As Martin Luther King, Jr. acknowledged in his 1963 book, *Why We Can't Wait*: "It was the people who moved their leaders, not the leaders who moved the people."

It's the little man and woman who become engaged because they simply share the same desire to see things corrected. Deciding to take action often places them against a backdrop of long-standing ideas and beliefs that involve a confrontation which requires determination and endurance. However, these individuals are willing to accept the burden whether they taste victory or simply serve to lay the groundwork for others who come after them—because they realize they are part of something greater than themselves. Genuine confidence in the necessity of change serves as adequate motivation.

What often makes major endeavors difficult is that there are no guarantees. This is especially true when working to change things for the better in areas where people have become resigned to follow a certain standard or practice. It is often forgotten that this is the circumstance that faced so many others before. The Founders, for a while, looked as if they would go down in history as those who led a failed rebellion. General Washington actually lost more battles than he won and if it were not for his heroics in sneaking his men across the Delaware River late in the war, the outcome may have been much different. Prior to those events, the Loyalists felt confident in their decision not to join a cause seeking more, possibly believing their families would be judged on the right side of history. Today, we can recognize them as nothing more than a segment of the first self-serving cowards who learned the fate of those who test the American spirit.

From women's suffrage to the battles waged to afford African Americans the civil rights they deserve, history is full of people who failed to act partly out of fear or cynicism toward the outcome. Others simply chose to cling to the status quo that benefited them. However, none of those unwilling to act kept others from traveling the road to justice by possessing an understanding of how high the stakes truly were.

This same type of resolve is needed to save the Republic.

Americans must be willing to take an active role in tackling the problems that few in D.C. and the legislative bodies across the country can be counted on to address. Boris Johnson understood that Winston Churchill clearly taught us this fact. In his book, *The Churchill Factor: How One Man Made History*, he wrote: "The difference between Churchill and others was that he acted on his insights. He not only meditated on what was happening; he tried to change it. Most politicians go with the flow of events. They see what seems inevitable, and then try to align themselves with destiny—and then [usually] try to present matters as well as they can and try in some feeble way to claim credit for whatever has occurred."

Representation from a place of weakness, which is built on the inappropriate influence of crony capitalists and lobbyists, will never provide adequate leadership. Within this environment, barriers are placed in front of common sense, as politicians, instead of simply seeking answers, are too often attempting to determine the most beneficial balance between passing what is right and still maintaining good standing with the influential few who play a significant role in keeping them firmly insulated in office. Just as some contend that any immigration reform would be inadequate until we seal the border, if the current political system is not corrected to provide the appropriate representation, it will not make much difference which party wins control of Congress, which candidates gain a seat in office, or which individual becomes President.

Only when representatives lead from a place of strength—built from and maintained by a newfound level of accountability—will they earn the necessary standing among the people to actually serve them effectively. The current lack of trust and the overwhelming aim of most legislators to maintain a good relationship with donors prevents them from having the ability to lay out all the variables in solving issues.

As President Kennedy was quoted as saying, "What does truth require? It requires us to face the facts as they are, not to involve ourselves in self-destruction; to refuse to think merely in slogans." The People's Clearing House could embolden representatives to courageously take on issues, without fear of speaking the truth in discovering answers; certain that they have proven to the people that integrity will guide their decisions.

Although The People's Clearing House provides the method for re-establishing the ownership of the country to the citizens, there has to be a willingness to act. A reform designed to garner support across areas of major divisions, as well as provide incentives to feed the needs of instant gratification, does not guarantee participation. As the nation continues to be snatched away from the people, the question remains whether enough citizens will choose to take action. What President Kennedy articulated in the 1960s still applies today, "For all America—its President and its people—the coming years will be a time of decision. We must decide whether we have reached our limit or whether, in the words of Thomas Wolfe, the true discovery of America is before us—the true fulfillment of our mighty and immortal land is yet to come."

One man in our country definitely believes that the best days for America lie ahead if the people choose to unite. Clay Higgins, former lieutenant and spokesman for the St. Landry Parish Sheriff's Department, resigned from his job at the end of February 2016, citing, among other things, his unwillingness to "kneel to bureaucrats from Washington, Baton Rouge, or anywhere else." Despite being widely admired and referred by some as the "Cajun John Wayne" for the tough, no-nonsense approach he took in his public messaging, others within the politically correct did not take kindly to his words.

Clay Higgins now serves as Reserve Deputy Marshal for the Lafayette City Marshal's Office. He released a video in May 2016 entitled "America United," which he utilized to describe what makes America great—as well as summarized the threats to America and what type of effort he believed it would take to set things right. Even without actually hearing him articulate them, anyone could recognize from the excerpts of his speech that what he offers comes directly from his heart. While there will be some who do not share all of his views, the necessity for the unity he advocates is undeniable if the people are truly going to reclaim the government that they own.

"American citizens work tirelessly across the globe to bring relief to the poor, to bring peace to the besieged, to bring stability to the shaken, and to bring freedom to the oppressed. Yet now, our own nation is threatened. America's in grave peril from threats across the seas, and also from within. The elected and appointed elitist few who have seized power in Washington have squandered our wealth, mortgaged our children's future, and betrayed our trust. America faces a twenty-trillion-dollar debt."

"Our veterans return to a nation almost unrecognizable, and are forced to battle the oppression of their own government. Our prisons overflow with poor men who have long ago paid their debt to society. Meanwhile, our nation is run by thieves—thieves in suits, career politicians who no longer represent 'we the people.' They represent strictly their own agenda: greed and ravenous hunger for power."

"I've often said in my career as a cop that a man's character shouldn't be measured by how he falls. It should be measured by how he stands back up. In many ways, our nation has fallen. I ask you to join me. I ask you to take the hand of your brother and sister of every creed as we magnify our strength by the power of our American spirit. I ask you to set aside our differences and stand together as one nation under God, to stand as one people beneath the glory of one flag, and to stand as a nation reborn as we face perils both foreign and domestic. Together, we can stand this thing back up. Our finest hour can yet lay ahead."

"The threats we face are menacing and real, but an American nation standing as one is a force the world's evils cannot defeat; a force that career politicians fear; a force that every peril dreads, that foreign horrors like ISIS tremble before. You are that force. We are that force."

The Accepted Culture of Waste

In January 2016, the national debt rose to $19 trillion, with an estimated $21 trillion around the corner. Of course, this projection is only valid when choosing to accept these numbers at face value. However, when actually accounting for future liabilities, the magnitude of debt could be around twenty times larger according to Stan Druckenmiller.

His observations are based on simple adherence to the arithmetic displaying a "fiscal gap" by 2029 that inevitably requires higher taxes and cuts in benefits to meet the upcoming demand of 11,000 new recipients joining the ranks of Social Security with each new sunrise. The ratio of workforce to recipients will simply be overwhelming, especially when allowing for some decline in additional jobs due to the strain of businesses searching for methods to fulfill their pension promises.

As Stan Druckenmiller emphasizes, those overseeing governmental finances are only focusing on the short-term as opposed to the long-term financial picture. That's probably not a surprise to most citizens. Lawmakers must commit to meaningful reforms for mitigating some of the catastrophe that looms in the imminent future.

Similar sentiments were to a degree echoed by the Congressional Budget Office in June 2015, and highlighted by Kasia Klimasinska of Bloomberg News. In her article, she documented some of the report by writing, "With debt 'already usually high' relative to the gross domestic product, 'further sustained increases could be especially harmful to economic growth,' the CBO said in a long-term fiscal report released Tuesday in Washington. 'To put the federal budget on a sustainable path for the long term, lawmakers would have to make major changes to tax policies, spending practices, or both.'" Although routinely disregarded by citizen and lawmaker alike, even some of the most ardent advocates to the Keynesian approach of basically disregarding the national debt and increasing governmental spending to stimulate the economy have begun to take notice of the inevitable in following similar logic within the current set of circumstances.

Former 2012 Republican Presidential candidate Herman Cain wrote on his website in December 2015, "The Congressional Budget Office announced last week that the deficit just for the first two months of the fiscal year (which starts in October of each year) had already topped $200 billion. In two months. That's $22 billion larger than the deficit racked up in the first two months of FY 2015." That same office, in June 2015, forecasted that the "U.S. government debt held by the public is expected to rise to 107 percent of the economy in 2040 from 74 percent this year." However, instead of breeding any sense of urgency within our leaders, the routine projections of cataclysmic proportions within these reports are viewed as more of a temporary nuisance for a number of them. If inaction allows them to retain more votes in the short run for political preservation, then why risk potential votes with necessary, but definite, unpopular action?

This dismal economic outlook for future generations comes as no surprise to anyone; yet, this fate which could have been alleviated, if not avoided all together with proper management of finances, has done very little in taming the general fraud, waste, and abuse within local, state, and federal governments. Lawmakers put about as much value and effort into solving past and current waste practices as they do in discovering facilitators for long-term financial sustainability. Agencies lack proper oversight, allowing governmental employees to mirror the half-hearted effort of many of our representatives in providing a genuine stewardship of finances.

Politicians on both sides of the political aisle directly increase the deficit at the cost of greater efficiency and opportunity for millions of Americans. Members of the U.S. Congress continue to ignore sequestration caps established by law in 2011, with very few believing they would actually hold true to them to begin with. Instead, members do what they do best: routinely kick the can further down the road. Lawmakers choose to rely on a stronger economy and a belief in future restraint to eventually offset current spending levels—blindly disregarding their previous failures in financial discipline. Obviously, some politicians believe past performance will not be indicative of future behavior; painting this group as naïve would be too kind.

Representatives simply go through the motions, regardless of the circumstances. Bills possess a mandatory thousand pages and are written to thwart any legitimate opportunity for other colleagues in Congress, much less the constituency, to scrutinize what is being spent until after the bill has already passed. On the state level, similar practices of neglect in stewardship of finances result in the people feeling the effects of cuts to critical agencies in the aim of ultimately achieving the balanced budget required by law. As for Congress, they are simply allowed to further insulate themselves and their special interests with another round of printed green paper.

As Herman Cain wrote in December, 2015, "The government thinks it can borrow and spend forever with no consequences because a) it can print money; and b) surely its creditors would never let the U.S. government collapse. And yet, things have gotten so bad that we have to borrow every month just to pay the interest on what we've already borrowed." Unfortunately, most of the American public chooses to prescribe to the same apathetic view of their leaders. The stories of Greece teetering on the verge of collapse and forced to accept unsatisfactory conditions as a result seem unlikely, if not impossible, to happen in America. Either much of the general public has become virtually numb to any discussion around the consequences of debt or they fear what is to come, but choose to focus on other things in their immediate control. Thoughts of debt only bring more stress to something they don't feel empowered to change.

Fewer and fewer citizens remain who lived through the Great Depression and actually value the worth of a dollar. The long lines at the gas pumps during the last years of the Carter Administration due to the instability within the oil market and rising inflation seem but a distant memory for most. Time marches on and people merely forget past difficulties. As for a majority of young people, the results of general debt and fights over policy decisions seem confined to which party will be in power. They don't yet understand what those a bit older are clearly recognizing as they attempt to save in an environment of greater unpredictability to the buying power of a dollar. It never seems to resonate with young people that easy access to goods and services could actually be reduced or eliminated if Congress continues to produce similar fiscal policy decisions.

Republican Presidential candidate and current governor of Ohio John Kasich appeared on "Meet the Press" in February 2016 and discussed how he and others within Congress were able to work with President Bill Clinton in actually passing a balanced budget—an accomplishment that today could almost be viewed as an urban legend. Since President Obama took office, neither major party has passed an actual budget that covered an entire year, regardless of which side controlled the Congress. However, Democrats are often attributed to the runaway spending, and John Kasich wanted to be candid with viewers about where the extent of the fault actually was. As he told Chuck Todd, "The dirty little secret is Democrats love to spend. And Republicans do, too. It's just that Republicans feel guilty. Look, if you don't have a leader that stands in the breach to restrain the spending of government, they'll always spend."

The truth is that a genuine commitment from the leadership in either major party for actually addressing the debt remains overshadowed by routine arguments concerning more domestic or military spending. Even in the case of legitimate need, little regard is actually given to how the funding is enacted on most occasions, with politicians instead remaining true to talking points that will most certainly resonate with their political bases at the polls. Immediate political survival comes before the long-term benefits to the country, something that may have been demonstrated best from current Chicago mayor Rahm Emanuel's treatment of the tragic murder of seventeen-year-old Laquan McDonald.

An officer is now being charged with murder after shooting the teen sixteen times. Many don't believe Mayor Emanuel when he says he was not made aware of all the details surrounding the incident until after he had successfully won his bid for re-election. Some of those same individuals are convinced his administration covered up the incident in a similar fashion to how the Obama Administration is thought to have downplayed the attack in Benghazi to preserve his bid for winning a second term. Of course, both conclusions are questionable and left to personal interpretation. However, both indicate the genuine possibility that those in leadership ultimately chose to delay facilitating human dignity and justice for the sake of maintaining their own political survival.

In the case of Laquan McDonald, I am reminded of how vital it is for all Americans to work together to improve race relations. This especially requires solidarity in instances of clear injustice. While most of the men and women in blue serve each day with integrity and honor, such a unified effort in purpose will send a resolute message to the few who abuse their sacred trust to serve and protect; communities will come together and utilize every available source to bring you to justice.

In specific relation to finances, one of the network political talking -heads actually attempted to add some credibility to Mayor Emanuel's assertion that he didn't know some of the details of Laquan's death.

The individual explained it was actually likely considering the settlement to Laquan's family was only five million. Placing any justified criticism aside in the mayor not knowing every aspect of what caused a teen's death, this rationale sums up exactly why the country is facing a monetary crisis. While a family cannot be given enough money to replace a son, the broader context of what this says about how money is being spent is indicative of the troubling reality toward the spending of taxpayer money. While not being naïve enough to believe that the mayors of major cities are not inundated with multiple concerns, they should know how every penny is being spent by those beholden to them. We need leaders who are truly driven to rein in spending. Although routinely forgotten by those in government who live in a separate land of entitlement apart from the rest of the general public, every dollar spent counts and should be justified.

Americans often wonder what the Founders would think of the current state of our country. What actions would they take to solve many of the chronic issues that face the nation? In regards to the massive accumulation of debt, one Founder offered a clear answer. During the Revolutionary War, the soldiers of the Continental Army met in Newburgh, New York, to discuss a revolt. The men no longer had faith in the Congress, which had consistently denied them the payment they had been promised. The war would have surely been lost if it had not been for General George Washington utilizing the immense standing he held among the men who admired and respected him for his personal integrity and sacrifice. The men knew he shared their grievances and were persuaded to abandon the idea of a revolt; instead, they trusted him to make their concerns properly known to Congress. Today, one could wonder whether anyone in government possesses the same degree of respect. However, there is little mystery as to how adamant George Washington would be today in his support of advancing measures aimed at garnering a greater degree of stewardship in national finances.

As Richard Brookhiser wrote in his 1996 book, *Founding Fathers: Rediscovering George Washington*, "Countries, like individuals, have reputations and Washington was as concerned for America's as he was for his own. 'We have now a National character to establish,' he wrote, three weeks after addressing the officers at Newburgh, 'and it is of the utmost importance to stamp favorable impressions upon it.'" Brookhiser went on to explain Washington's rationale in writing, "One way a country did this was by sound finances. Washington had a Virginia planter's horror of debt, made more acute by the fact that so many planters slid insensibly into it and compounded by his experience as commander of an ill-paid army. In one of his last letters to Jefferson, in a list of villainous types, he ranked defaulters and pickpockets behind the emperor Nero."

For those unfamiliar with Nero, he is considered one of Rome's worst emperors—specifically known for his brutality, as well as for his high taxation of the people to meet his own desires. Referring to the emperor in his final book, *The Decline and Fall of Practically Everybody: Great Figures of History Hilariously Humbled*, one of the great satirists, Will Cuppy wrote: "Since Nero's character leaves much to be desired, we are apt to forge his good side. We should try and remember that he did not murder his mother until he was twenty-one years old. Besides, he only did it to please his sweetheart, Poppaea Sabina, whom he later married and kicked to death while she was with child. It was her own fault, in a way, as she nagged him for coming home late from the race." Quite the company for America's first and beloved President to place those who foster debt as being closely akin. President Washington may have initially sided with Alexander Hamilton over Thomas Jefferson when it came to increasing the national debt, but it could never be assumed that he favored or advocated debt. The set of circumstances were unique and his decision came at a time when the new nation desperately needed a means for providing a foundation of finances to survive.

In February, 2012, Michael Snyder, publisher of "The Economic Collapse Blog" and author of the fiction novel, *The Beginning of the End*, documented many of the ridiculous ways the U.S. government is spending the peoples' money. Although the list he details is rather extensive and holds other items equally as troubling, just a few of the things he cites are: $750,000 on a new soccer field for detainees held at Guantanamo Bay; $239,100 to study how Americans use the Internet to find love; $3 million to researchers at the University of California at Irvine to fund their research on video games, such as World of Warcraft; $998,798 shipping two 19-cent washers from South Carolina to Texas; $293,451 sending an 89-cent washer from South Carolina to Florida; and last, but not least, $216,000 to study whether or not politicians "gain or lose support by taking ambiguous positions"— because discovering how to win the next election is of chief importance to a majority of members in Congress.

Much, if not all, of the list Michael Snyder provided on his website came from the report of former U.S. Senator Tom Coburn from Oklahoma. He began annually releasing a report to the American public to better enlighten them on the magnitude of waste that could be found in government. Senator Jeff Flake (R-AZ) has picked up the baton of the retired Senator in working to highlight some of the waste. In his first report, Senator Flake discovered $100 billion in overall waste, with just one example being $707,000 spent on a "shrimp fight club that included 34 bouts with mantis shrimp." Such a degree of waste, fraud, and abuse could be eliminated from the federal government if leaders would simply choose to dedicate themselves to the task. Until such a prioritization occurs, it appears special interests will continue to control much of the agenda, resulting in outcomes in which shrimp are given precedence over people!

When it comes to solving the problems of excessive waste in government, I am often reminded of *Dave*. For anyone unfamiliar with the movie, it is about a man who gains access to the presidency as a look-a-like due to unforeseen circumstances. During the brief time in which Dave actually serves as President, he is sarcastically told that the only chance of saving a program he supports from being eliminated is by finding savings within the budget to fully pay for it. The senior official within the White House only offers him this challenge with confidence in his failure. However, Dave takes up the task and enlists the services of a friend who is an accountant within the private sector. The friend is amazed at the incoherent records and even wonders out loud how any business could survive by following such counterproductive practices. Without being handicapped by special interests and purely political motives, Dave garners the encouragement of his friend and easily discovers what is necessary to save the program. As expected, his work places him at odds with those desperate to maintain the status quo.

While things are never as easy as they seem, it is obvious that any degree of common sense or devotion implemented by Dave for eliminating some of the excess in government is rarely being utilized by Congress. Romina Boccia, the leading fiscal and economic expert at The Heritage Foundation, penned an article on how to rein in governmental waste in October 2014. In her article, she cited a 2014 Gallup poll which reported that "Americans think the federal government wastes 51 cents of every dollar they pay in taxes." In direct relation to cents, Greg Richter, a freelance political writer, documented how Republican Presidential frontrunner Donald Trump had confirmed his support for utilizing the "Penny Plan" on all agencies throughout the federal government, except for the military, during an appearance on "Hannity." Richter explained what the basis of the original plan meant: "The Penny Plan," often touted by host Sean Hannity, would cut one penny from every dollar of government spending for five years, including the military, to eliminate the federal spending deficit.

However, if Ben Carson is correct, this plan could be at odds with a number of Democrats and make actual passage of a bill rather difficult. During an appearance on "Wolf," in clarifying his opposition to consistently raise the debt ceiling, Dr. Carson said, "We have 4.1 million federal employees. Do we really need 4.1 million federal employees? We have 645 federal agencies and sub-agencies. Do we really need that? I mean, we need to be looking at other things. I know that Nancy Pelosi said if you cut one penny, the whole system will collapse. You know what I say about that—it's not true."

In August, 2015, popular syndicated columnist Cal Thomas wrote an article in support of then Republican candidate for President Carly Fiorina's call for a "zero-based budgeting standard to force every governmental agency to justify what it spends." As a prelude to the discussion of some of her plans to correct the budget, Cal wrote, "This year the federal government is projected to take in a record $3.18 trillion, according to the Office of Management and Budget. And yet, for 45 of the last 50 years, the government overspent and had to borrow money to meet its spending addiction." The numbers he presents aren't surprising when considering that each agency operates with the goal of at least re-allocating the same amount of money the following year. Discovering savings is not important, but spending everything is vital to proving that the funds were necessary. Unfortunately, most state and local agencies operate with the same logic.

As if the practice of waste in itself was not enough to trouble the American people, the manner in which Congress often shamelessly spends taxpayer money definitely should. Although there are more than enough examples of contracts awarded within each agency to demonstrate the disregard many of our congressmen have for being good stewards of governmental finances, the work of one long-term U.S. Senator may offer one of the greatest insights. In regards to the award of a "contract worth up to $5 million for fancy crystal stem and barware for its embassies around the world" to a company within his own state, Patrick Leahy (D-VT) said, "It is wonderful to have such an exquisite example of Vermont craftsmanship on display and in use in our embassies around the world." While many Americans are making sacrifices in an attempt to provide for a financial future, instances of meaningless indulgences are commonly being distributed across government with little to no remorse. I doubt any of our diplomats at the American Embassy in Benghazi thought about the crystal before they were killed. Instead, I'm certain they wished our leaders would spend more time working to serve and protect their people, instead of reveling in awarding gifts to special interests.

This type behavior is especially true during the "use it or lose it" time period in which the company from Vermont was actually award-ed the crystal contract. Career politicians like Senator Patrick Leahy are far from alone in needlessly doling out taxpayer money. In her August 2013 article for Newsmax, "State Dept. spent millions on em-bassy crystal week before shutdown," Cathy Burke detailed the extent of spending during this timeframe by writing: "During the last week of September 2012, the government spent $45 billion on contracts and spending spiked by $100 billion." Akin to the popular TV show "Supermarket Sweep," federal agencies resemble contestants who feverishly work to buy enough expensive items to win. Winning game-show contestants secure a few grocery items. Governmental agencies secure similar future allocations.

Very few Americans realize that regardless of whether the federal government is shut down or not, it still provides more of the same in terms of useless spending. In fact, if Senator Rand Paul (R-KY) is correct, shutting down the government is actually more costly to the American taxpayer. During a 2015 appearance on Fox News Chan-nel's "Outnumbered," Senator Paul told the surprised panel, "When we had a shutdown a year or two ago, they had us fill out forms to say, 'Are your employees essential or unessential?' So we found that the I.R.S. said 90% of their employees were unessential and we thought, oh wow, maybe we're going to learn something here. But you know what it turns out? If you're unessential during a shutdown, you don't have to come in, but you still get paid. During the govern-mental shutdown we paid more money than we do than when it's open and we got no work done. So we had to pay all the people not to work."

While Rand Paul's insights toward the I.R.S. only add further fuel to the fire of some for eliminating that agency entirely, it only serves as a microcosm to the lack of accountability and oversight found within the federal government. In an article from March 2016, Cal Thomas reminded readers of the effort former House Speaker Newt Gingrich launched to keep his promise of auditing the federal govern-ment under the "Contract with America." He and other Republicans had campaigned on the pledge. However, those delegated to inde-pendently perform the audit quickly discovered that there were "no coherent records" in place to support their immense task; a sad truth actually referred to by White House Press Secretary Josh Ernest in his attempt to deflect criticism away from the Obama Administration setting the record for the number of times it had failed to produce files requested under the Freedom of Information Act.

In defending against close to 130,000 times in which nothing was actually given to those legally seeking federal information under the act, Josh Ernest reminded reporters that the U.S. records law had never been utilized on Congress since passed under the Johnson Administration; something he hoped the press would be as diligent in pressing the Congress to change. As he stated in March, 2016, and to which most anyone would agree, regardless of party affiliation, "Congress writes the rules and they write themselves out of being accountable." This definitely remained accurate despite the audit designed to lay the sufficient foundation of greater transparency instituted under House Speaker Gingrich. Cal Thomas clearly confirmed this in writing, "A Nov. 13, 2000 article by Edward H. Crane, president of the libertarian Cato Institute, said, '…the combined budgets of the 95 major programs the Contract with America promised to eliminate have increased by 13 percent." Obviously, the genuine commitment necessary to change government remains elusive in Congress. Much of this may result from the inaction of those who have the most power to change things, such as Senate Minority Leader Harry Reid. Although there is broad support within both parties, Reid continues to block the IG Empowerment Act which would give the Inspector General access to everything they need within agencies to raise accountability.

The I.R.S. seems to consistently place the agency at public odds with voters, such as in "[identifying] more than 1,000 cardholders who misused their travel cards during fiscal years 2010 and 2011" and still choosing to retain most of those involved. However, stats and figures have consistently displayed that the problem of waste and abuse is wide-ranging in nature. As award-winning journalist M.D. Kittle reported in an article for Watchdog.org in June 2013, "In fiscal 2012, about 95.6 million transactions were made and $29.32 billion was charged on SmartPay cards." Without even looking at a single report, a majority of the American public should wonder just how much opportunity this volume of transactions provides for fraud and misuse.

In studying the GAO report referenced by M.D. Kittle in an attempt to further detail some of the same areas of misuse, we discover that the findings were based on a sample that most likely only provided a snapshot of the actual mishandling. As stated directly in the report, "Using a statistical sample of purchase card transactions from July 1, 2005, through June 30, 2006, GAO estimated that nearly 41 percent of the transactions failed to meet either of these basic internal control standards. Using a second sample of transactions over $2,500, GAO found a similar failure rate—agencies could not demonstrate that 48 percent of these large purchases met the standard." Clearly, these numbers display that a general mistrust in government is not unfounded.

Some describe the abuses by governmental officials as essentially analogous to throwing a party on the backs of the general taxpayer who actually never receives an invitation. A view that could only be strengthened with the discovery that the U.S. Postal Service, the governmental agency often billions in the red, threw a 2006 party that barred no expense, totaling $13,500 on 81 dinners. "Further, USPS paid for over 200 appetizers and over $3,000 of alcohol, including more than 30 bottles of wine costing more than $50 each and brand name liquor such as Courvoisier, Belvedere, and Johnny Walker Gold."

If this is the reward given to employees within a failing agency, one can only imagine what the reward would be for those that show some degree of competence. Maybe the quality of the dinner would remain, with the only difference being other members from the middle class and poor being selected to serve everything to this elite class of governmental employees who obviously feel above them. While there are many admirable workers within the U.S. Postal Service, those who attended this party chose to mimic the sense of entitlement rampant in government. As they enjoyed their meal, a veteran housed at the Chicago Veterans Affairs hospital most likely finished another cockroach-infested dinner; a problem that looks to have gone on for years unaddressed.

In 1980, then Governor Ronald Reagan placed the idea of limited government as the cornerstone of his campaign for President, projecting a man driven by the words of a previous speech from 1964. In that speech entitled, "A Time for Choosing," in which he offered his support of the Republican nominee for President, Barry Goldwater, one of the most memorable things Reagan said was, "No government ever voluntarily reduces itself in size. So government's programs, once launched, never disappear. Actually, a government bureau is the nearest thing to eternal life we'll ever see on this earth."

Looking to convince the electorate he was the one who would trim off the fat in government, Ronald Reagan took direct aim at specific agencies within the federal government to demonstrate how things could be different once questions began being asked. Not surprisingly, his criticisms put him at odds with those embedded in Washington, who, in turn, sent out the mainstream media, or the outer edge of the establishment, to help discredit or at the least downplay the extent of his claims.

During a 1980 primary debate with his lone remaining opponent for the Republican nomination, George H.W. Bush, the moderator questioned some of the numbers Reagan was offering. When challenged on his claim that it "cost the government three dollars to provide one dollar's worth of benefits," by referencing the words of an official with the Health, Education, and Welfare (HEW) agency who said it actually only cost "12 cents for a dollar of benefits," Ronald Reagan without hesitation responded, "And I wouldn't believe HEW if they were here in the room saying that."

Reagan also went on to point out that a news network had been wrong in the narrative that he was misleading the public in the large amount of federal employees that had been added back under the Carter administration. The news report had centered on an interview with an official in government who said only 6,000 workers had been added, although the real number was actually over 60,000 (according to an article by Don Landrieu of UPI at the time). After citing the article, Reagan went on to inform the audience that this was just the tip of the iceberg, with millions of workers actually being paid by federal agencies despite not being counted as part of their official numbers.

Even today, a zero-based budgeting bill, which could offer some chance for a degree of clarity within our federal agencies, sits in Congress. Inaction on the bill has remained just as consistent, regardless of which party possesses congressional control. And although Reagan's heart was in the right place concerning limited government, his fortitude for remaining true to it was not. As Max Stier of *The Washington Post* noted in 2010, "Even during the Reagan administration, when small government was a political mantra, there were still between 2.1 and 2.2 million federal workers. In fact, there was an increase of about 95,000 federal employees between 1981 and 1989."

Even more ironic, Ronald Reagan raised the debt ceiling more times than any other President. He also ended the zero-based budgeting from the Carter Administration. Though much of the increase in the deficit was due to the ongoing effort to win the Cold War, it does not reduce the significance within the fact that no other President since Jimmy Carter has embraced the idea of instituting such a measure within government.

Zero-based budgeting would force federal agencies to justify everything they spend, as well as their very existence. Although it would still rely on a genuine commitment of legislators to utilize the system properly, putting forth the opportunity would be a start. If Doctor Veronique de Rugy is correct, one result maybe the elimination (or extensive downsizing) of the Department of Commerce. The research fellow at the Mercatus Center at George Mason University in an article from 2014 cited the former Commerce Secretary Robert Mosbacher in writing, "In a 1995 *Washington Times* article titled 'Trade Will Go On, Even without Commerce,' the one-time administrator called the agency 'nothing more than a hall closet where you throw in everything that you don't know what to do with.'" She further wrote, "The U.S. has enough debt problems without funding Commerce-style corporate welfare. American businesses managed to prosper and grow long before the department was created. In fact, Commerce's cronyist subsidies are a net drag on the economy because they undermine competition and drain productive resources." Although members from both major parties have offered support for its elimination in the past, the hold over the special-interests-led U.S Congress has prevented the formation of willpower necessary for achievement.

Instead of reining in waste within agencies to establish the necessary foundation of accountability for future economic stability and greater opportunity for meaningful allocation of finances, our representatives choose to maintain the status quo. Beyond this decision hurting the American people as a whole, the result is that the burden is often absorbed the most by those who deserve to carry it the least. In an appearance on "The Kelly File" in October 2015, former Navy Seal Brandon Webb demonstrated his frustrations with the absence of genuine support being given to the families of the valiant Americans killed in Benghazi. In his rebuke of the government, he mentioned other bills that also remain dormant alongside the zero-based budgeting bill in the Congress.

> "I mean, there's talk and then there's action. I mean, I can listen to politicians say, 'Oh, my heart goes out to the families,' but the fact is, one of the issues that came up, uh [sic], from all the attention from the Benghazi Committee is there is over fifty families of contractors since 1983 in the Beirut barracks bombing who have not been paid a death benefit, like my best friend, Glen Doherty, his family. So here we have an American hero, gives his life in Benghazi. His family goes to the White House. They, they [sic] get a bunch of lip service from Hillary and at the end of the day, the family is left holding the bag as far as not even getting a basic, uh [sic], death benefit to bury their family members. And you've got two initiatives held up in the House right now. You have an initiative called the, the [sic] Lynch Bill (H.R. 5721, the Overseas Security Personnel Fairness Act) under my friend Glen's name, uh [sic], that's held up in the House that's supposed to reform the Defense Base Act and provide relief for these families... The

C.I.A., Senate Intel Committee also held [it] up and these career politicians. I think Americans are just sick of of [sic] paralysis by analysis. It's time for action and to take care of these families."

While it is disgraceful that these bills have remained outside the congressional docket as a result of both parties, the notion one prominent Republican offered from November 2015 to alleviate some of the suffering on these families of lost federal contractors was beyond comprehension. In a brazen move, U.S. Rep. Bob Goodlatte of Virginia placed the heroes of 9/11 as the centerpiece of his political agenda by offering an alternative bill to replace the expired James L. Zadroga 9/11 Health and Compensation Act, the legislation which had temporarily provided medical care.

Although his bill provided funding to the families of federal contractors, there was already a standalone bill in place for the needs of the first responders; one which was supported by majorities in both parties. However, playing politics was more important, and the Republican leadership refused to simply bring the original bill up for certain passage. Waiting to place a similar piece of legislation for the first responders within the end-of-the-year spending bill was preferred for obtaining other desired bills.

U.S. Rep. Goodlatte put together a bill that was drastically smaller in financial size than what was being asked from the group. The prolonging of worry this needless delay caused for the first responders and their families as to the uncertainty of long-term care seemed to be of little concern. The reality that many of them had already been forced to come to the Capitol on numerous occasions to practically beg for more funding from Congress didn't matter. Instead, this was seen as just another bargaining chip for securing votes on something else that was more difficult to pass—a practice so often utilized regardless of the lives it negatively affects.

Never waste a chance to push another agenda could actually be the mantra of the U.S. Congress, although Jon Stewart, a vocal advocate for the men and women of 9/11, summed up things in another way. In a December 2015 return appearance on "The Daily Show," he told host Trevor Noah, "The only conclusions that I can draw is the people from Congress are not as good a people as the people who are first responders."

An article at the time from the staff at *News Leader* informed us that "permanently renewing the fund would require about $900 million more, according to a congressional staffer involved in the legislature." In regards to this funding, I doubt few Americans would have minded placing a small dent in the "25 billion dollars a year [used to maintain] federal buildings that are either unused or totally vacant." Although it may have seemed impossible for Republican leadership to look any more incompetent or foolish for rejecting the initial bill, this one nugget of waste alone looks to have proven otherwise. Maintenance of useless federal buildings is more acceptable in Congress than displaying appreciation to these courageous men and women. Although the families of federal contractors, such as Glen Doherty, are still unfortunately being denied benefits they deserve, public pressure and the need to pass the end-of-the-year spending bill provided the incentives to allocate permanent funding.

Sadly, men and women who have chosen to serve in the United States Armed Forces are all too familiar with the feeling of being underappreciated. Former Senator Tom Coburn put out a 2014 study entitled "Friendly Fire: Death, Delay, and Dismay at the VA" that documented the consequences of the mismanagement and fraud he discovered from his yearlong investigation. In terms of monetary loss, "the report [reviewed] VA spending and found that the VA paid $200 million to veterans' families for wrongful deaths, spent $5.1 million purchasing unused software licenses, spent almost $500 million on conference rooms and curtains, paid millions to department employees to perform union duties, and spent millions on lavish conferences and employee travel." In terms of human cost, a 2015 investigation by the VA Inspector General placed the number of military men and women who died while on the waiting list at 307,000.

Falsifying claims, implementing hidden waste lists, and spending needlessly while veterans fought for care was acceptable within the VA. Even when the extent of the scandals began surfacing, some things remained business as usual. Over $140 million in performance-based bonuses were doled out to close to 160,000 workers within the VA in 2014; some even going to areas that had been identified as perpetrating some of the worst instances of neglect and fraud. As Donovan Slack and Bill Theobald acknowledged in their *USA Today* article from November 2015, one such instance was the reward given to the incompetent "executives who managed the construction of a facility in Denver, a disastrous project years overdue and more than $1 billion over budget."

Despite the troubling pattern of misconduct within the Department of Veterans Affairs, the government chose not to enact any form of genuine punishment to some of the individuals most responsible for the failures. Danny Pummil, the head of the Veterans Benefits Administration, was suspended for a little over two weeks without pay for improper oversight. Under his watch, Kimberly Graves and Diana Rubens, two top VA executives, took advantage of their power to create new openings for themselves by forcing lower-ranking managers out of positions they wanted at other locations. They also took money associated with the move that was not justified. However, after a lengthy process, the result for all of their calculated manipulations was a measly punishment of 10% being taken from the over $350,000 the two made (combined).

No criminal charges were filed as a deterrent to future misconduct. Though Presidential Republican frontrunner Donald Trump often receives backlash from the remarks he makes, most would probably agree he summarized the problem of this case in a statement from November 2015, when he said, "Politicians in Washington have tried to fix the VA by holding hearings and blindly throwing money at the problem." The need for reforming the dysfunctional civil service system is actually highlighted best by the military hearings in front of the Merit Systems Protection Board run by special interests.

A newfound commitment from Congress to our military does not seem to be on the horizon anytime soon. Despite the documented list of failures within the VA, Democratic Senator Richard Blumenthal from Connecticut chose to block an "up or down" vote on the VA Accountability Act of 2015 when it was offered for immediate consideration by Sen. Marco Rubio (R-FL). However, Republicans are by no means blameless in the failure of the bill to pass. Dan Caldwell, Vice President for the Political and Legislative Action for Concerned Veterans for America (CVA), appeared on "Fox and Friends" in April 2016 and discussed what he described as the "complete lack of accountability" within the VA. The Marine veteran spoke about how appalling it was that no one at the hospital in Phoenix, the original site to receive public spotlight for abuse, had lost their job. Almost 300 veterans seeking care had died while on secret and typical waiting lists at the location. As part of his discussion, the Vice President for the CVA described the role prominent Republicans have also played in rejecting the bill.

> "Sadly uh [sic], Sen. Mitch McConnell (R-KY), the Majority Leader, won't bring it up for a vote. And then you have the Sen. VA Comm. Chairman, Sen. Isakson (R-GA) [sic] has refused to help in bringing the vote as well... What they want to do is they want to pass an easy bill. They want to do the the [sic] easy thing and Sen. Isakson is putting out an Omnibus VA Bill. Unfortunately, it looks like it's going to be a bunch of nice things that sound great, but actually don't fix the problem. It's going to be great to talk about on the campaign trail,

but it's not going to fix the problem. We hope Sen. Isakson does the right thing and advances the VA Accountability Act, but sadly it doesn't look like that is going to happen right now."

The American people are viewed as merely pawns by many of our legislators. Whether or not someone has served in the role of first responder or soldier doesn't change this view. If the VA Accountability Act of 2015 had been passed, it would have finally given the Department of Veterans Affairs' Secretary Robert McDonald the power to implement the broad-scale reform that independent assessments have concluded is warranted. However, even if the Senate had followed the lead of the House in passing the legislation, it may have been a moot point. As Morgan Chalfant of the *Washington Free Beacon* wrote at the time, "President Obama has threatened to veto the legislation, calling it 'counterproductive' and insisting that it would 'have a significant impact on the VA's ability to retain and recruit qualified professionals and may result in a loss of qualified and capable staff to other government agencies or the private sector.'"

As long as Congress and the President refuse to act, countless more of our veterans will suffer needlessly. Although the estimate of over 300,000 was finally given for those lost while on the waiting list, the VA still admitted that their "system that tracks veterans' applications for healthcare is so bad that VA officials have no idea how many former troops want healthcare." This is about as frustrating as knowing that while suicide rates among veterans receiving treatment at the VA are lower, it seems to take a desperate phone call to the national veterans crisis line to garner immediate attention. As Colleen Mastony of the *Chicago Tribune* confirmed in September 2015, "In those cases, the social workers become expediters, cutting through red tape and connecting people to service." Being proactive is as lost an art to the chambers of the U.S. Congress as it is to state legislatures across the country.

While better days could be ahead as 2016 Presidential candidates from both parties criticize the VA and promise to institute common sense reforms such as an identification card to provide more access to expedited care, no branch of government is blameless for the current state of low morale in the military. Beyond the inability of Congress to act decisively in passing legislation, the President continues his unprecedented purge of the military: high-ranking officials being forced out, rules of engagement crippling our troops, and new initiatives turning the military into a social experiment. Even when Congress almost completely acted in unison to pass the Stolen Valor Act of

2013, the courts ultimately decided that someone who never served a day in their life could falsely decorate their clothes with service medals as long as nothing of value was gained.

Though disheartening for most, the decision of the court may have been a sign of vindication for Rep. Justin Amash (R-MI), Thomas Massie (R-KY), and Rep. Paul Brown (R-GA)—the three lone representatives who opted to vote against the act. It is not as certain what the reaction was from the 40 representatives who chose not to cast a vote. There must have been something more important to them, like a fundraiser, than to protect the honor of those who have served in the military with distinction; while Rep. Brown chose to retire in 2015, the other two representatives remain in congress.

Beyond the scandal-ridden Department of Veterans Affairs generally displaying how massive and entrenched the tentacles of government have become, it specifically demonstrated how difficult it has become to fire federal employees; a set of workers that James Sherk of the Heritage Foundation argued in 2010 makes "22% more per hour, on average, than private sector workers." Although no group compares to the nearly $300,000 every member of Congress receives annually when combining salary and fringe benefits according to the report from Our Generation and the Taxpayers Protection Alliance, federal workers most likely feel just as secure in employment. As Kathryn Watson of *The Daily Caller* wrote in March 2016, "The embattled Department of Veterans Affairs said it will take no less than 275 days to take disciplinary action against a nurse charged with operating on a veteran drunk, due to the complex and time-consuming hoops administrators have to jump through, according to another DCNF (Daily Caller News Foundation) report." She further explained, "Federal workers have enjoyed incredible job security for a long time, thanks to layers of bureaucracy, complicated employment laws, well-funded and politically powerful government unions, and multiple incentives against firing anyone."

As troubling as it is to know that instilling genuine accountability within the federal workforce will be a difficult process, what should receive the most concern is the alleged treatment of those in a number of agencies who are trying to do what is right. Ron Nixon wrote a story for *The New York Times* in April 2016 about T.S.A. employees pointing to leadership that made it clear they were not sympathetic toward information about problems within the agency. Of course, T.S.A. officials denied their claims and said they actually value input. Among other things, Nixon cited Edward J. Goodwin, the former security director at Jacksonville International Airport in Florida, as saying, "There is a culture at headquarters that we do what we want, no one holds us accountable to the rule." Edward and others within the agency who voiced concerns found out the price of attempting to do what is right. As the article alluded to, the legal fees associated with restoring a lost career is enough to likely persuade others to second guess rocking the boat, regardless of whether it is in the best interest of the people.

The nation's southern border with Mexico, despite being crucial to maintaining national security, has definitely not been immune in recent years from similar criticism of manipulation of facts and intimidation of workers. Jack Davis of *Western Journalism* documented the Pinal County Sheriff, Paul Babeu, as saying this of President Obama in early 2016, "He has manipulated the data, had agents assigned to low-traffic areas, and attempted to quiet dissent by calling those who question his approach as misinformed without offering any evidence to support these allegations." A similar sentiment was articulated in February 2016 by Brandon Judd, the Border Patrol Union Chief who has many years of experience. Speaking in front of a House subcommittee on immigration and border security, Judd blamed the Obama administration's "priorities" program for problems at the border in saying, "Simply put, the new policy makes mandatory the release—without a [Notice to Appear]—of any person arrested by the Border Patrol for being in the country illegally, as long as they don't have a previous felony arrest and conviction; and as long as they claim to have been continuously in the United States since January 2014." He pointed out how ridiculous it is to believe such a system would work, basically pinning any hope of success on the honesty of those apprehended to know whether or not border agents can enforce the law.

As expected, Customs and Border Protection Commissioner R. Gil Kerlikowske testified in front of the House Committee on Appropriations and denied the "catch and release" depiction offered by Brandon Judd, assuring the committee that anyone over 14 encountered by border agents was properly placed within the database. He also made clear that if you're an agent and you don't want to follow the orders you have been told, "then you really do need to look for another job." However, Union Border Chief Brandon Judd said by the time information is processed, what is being received by those at the top is most likely not indicative of what is really happening on the ground; with the reality that all of these new restrictions are designed to lower morale. Although one could still choose to believe Customs and Border Protection Commissioner Kerlikowske, no one should overlook how increasingly difficult, if not impossible, it has become to find anyone actually willing to man all the open positions on the border. Something is obviously behind people choosing to leave or not join the ranks altogether.

While the debate and political wrangling over border policy continues, what cannot be forgotten is the finality of death. Reminiscent of Kate Steniel, Jas Shaw, and other Americans, the unfortunate death of twenty-one-year-old Sara Root can be indirectly tied to the unwillingness of U.S. Immigration and Customs Enforcement (ICE) to enforce immigration law. Sara was allegedly killed in January 2016 by Eswin Mejia, an undocumented alien who was street-racing while driving drunk. Mejia had basically made a complete mockery of the American judicial system before the January incident. However, he had remained below the threshold of the "priorities" focus of enforcement under the Obama administration and had never been taken into custody by ICE.

Americans must still drive with an even extra level of caution, as Eswin Mejia is still on the run as a result of ICE's refusal or claimed inability to pick him up. The March 2016 testimony of (ICE) Director Sara Saldana to a Senate Committee as to why Eswin was not apprehended following the murder charge was mindboggling, and actually seemed to include the rationale that Sara Root had not died soon enough to raise him to that threshold. As Chuck Ross of *The Daily Caller* pointed out at the time, her excuse seemed to go against what the facts presented, as Eswin Mejia was bailed out almost a week after Sara Root tragically succumbed to her injuries. Whatever the reasons, no excuse will bring back the Americans killed by the undocumented. Just as no excuse will be sufficient in explaining why ICE failed to use common sense discretion and fulfill the detainer request from the Omaha Police Department following the January incident.

It looks as though bureaucratic obstruction that has been publicly detailed by individuals like Union Border Chief Judd is being conducted to an even further extent behind closed doors. It definitely seems as if an environment of intimidation exists within CENTCOM, or the United States Central Command, where two senior analysts said they lost their positions after "[accusing] their bosses of manipulating intelligence reports about the U.S.-led campaign against ISIS in order to paint a rosier picture of progress in war." Obviously, their claims have received pushback. However, as part of their coverage in April 2016, Shane Harris and Nancy A Youssef of the *Daily Beast* highlighted an earlier report which found that "more than 50 CENTCOM analysts [had] said senior officials gave more scrutiny and pushback on reports that suggested U.S. efforts to destroy ISIS weren't progressing. Analysis that took a more optimistic view of the war effort got comparatively less attention from higher-ups."

Though the release of the "Pentagon Papers" was more emphatic in proving manipulation of facts in Vietnam, having more than a handful of employees offering similar accusations about the mistreatment of data as it relates to current intelligence is a revelation. Yet, how many workers will choose to risk their livelihood when they know first-hand how desperate some in government are for controlling the facts to implement their agenda. This is especially true when analysts witness many in the mainstream media disregarding their documented fear of bucking the system to focus more attention on the fear of a few college students seeing a basic campaign slogan written in chalk.

Phillip Haney, a fifteen-year veteran of the Department of Homeland Security (DHS), painted a bleak picture of U.S. counterintelligence in an article for *The Hill*. His article centered on the low morale of the DHS following the failed bombing attempt of an airliner in December 2009. His contention is that the vulnerability that existed that day, and now, comes as a direct result of the "political correctness" that was instituted under the Obama Administration. In his February 2016 article he wrote, "Just before that Christmas attack, in early November 2009, I was ordered by my superiors at the Department of Homeland Security to delete or modify several hundred records of individuals tied to designated Islamist terror groups like Hamas from the important federal database, the Treasury Enforcement Communications System (TECS)." Without having or reproducing files with similar information, the department was blinded. Fed up with the how the agency had been changed, Phillip Haney chose to retire in July 2015.

Taylor Johnson, a senior special agent with a division of the Immigration and Customs Enforcement, did not choose to retire. As Evan Gahr, an investigative journalist for *The Daily Caller*, summed up in a February 2016, article: "Special Agent Taylor Johnson—who had a storied career until she irked Senator Minority Leader Harry Reid by objecting to a visa program for foreign investors tied to the senator's son—says she declined to take a $100,000 severance package because it included a non-disclosure settlement." Johnson spoke about being ostracized when returning to work after testifying in front of the Senate Committee on Homeland Security and Government Affairs.

Beyond Evan Gahr writing that Special Agent Johnson was placed on administrative leave after Senator Reid's office contacted her superiors—beyond the Inspector General backing the claims she made that the U.S. Customs and Immigration Services (USCIS) Director Mayorkas had, in fact, played an improper role in approving the EB-5 visas that benefited the Senator's son—the past actions of Harry Reid project a man who feels entitled to do anything he desires. He is the same senator from Nevada who frequently appeared on Judicial Watch's "Ten Most Wanted Corrupt Politicians" list and just recently told the Federal Elections Committee (FEC) he did not need them to approve his use of $600,000 in campaign money for his personal retirement.

After withdrawing the original request for the approval he now views as unnecessary to do as he pleases, Sen. Reid's lawyer sent a letter to the FEC that, in part, read: "Had he not been in office, he would not need an assistant to manage correspondence, draft materials, or schedule appearances pertaining to his tenure in office. As a result, we now believe that no further opinion is needed." This is the type of entitlement that allows someone to place national-security concerns aside and bypass properly vetting visa applicants because it was deemed more important to satisfy your son. This is a similar level of self-interest that almost cost a woman to be separated from her child. As Special Agent Johnson told lawmakers on Capitol Hill, "When an adoption social worker tried to contact and verify employment, she was told that I had been terminated for a criminal offense." She added, "I almost lost my one-year-old child."

Of course, Sen. Harry Reid wasn't the only one who attempted to take full advantage of the visa system—nor did he engage in the most egregious entitlement. According to a report from the Inspector General of the Dept. of Homeland Security that distinction belongs to Virginia Governor Terry McAuliffe. As an article from *The Washington Post*'s Tom Hamburger and Rachel Weiner revealed, the "intervention on behalf of McAuliffe's GreenTech Automotive company by Alejandro Mayorkas, now the department's No. 2 official, 'was unprecedented,' according to the report."

The reporters made note of Mayorkas's description of the Virginia Governor's relentless effort, seemingly devoid of character: "I recall that over the course of many months I received several voice messages from Mr. McAuliffe complaining about USCIS's handling of the… case. The messages were caustic. I remember in particular one voice message that I played, as it was laced with expletives at a high volume. I recall one occasion on which Mr. McAuliffe complained to me directly over the telephone."

Governor Terry McAuliffe's dismissive attitude toward border safety in his desire to receive favors from self-interest groups shouldn't come as a surprise. This is the same man who used his power as governor to clear the way for around 200,000 felons to cast their vote in the upcoming election with the stroke of his pen in April 2016; many believe it was done to help his long-time friend Hillary Clinton secure the swing state.

Sara Horwitz and Jenna Portnoy of *The Washington Post* detailed some of the criticisms the order obviously received: "Republicans were particularly outraged that the policy doesn't take into account the violence of the crime, whether the person committed serial crimes, whether they've committed crimes since completing their sentence, or whether they've paid their victims back for medical bills." Even if most citizens agree with state laws that restore the rights of those who have paid their debt to society, families and victims deserve to have a petition process in place for each individual case, instead of a blanket order that eliminates the necessity.

Although the Virginia Supreme Court agreed and ruled the order unconstitutional, Governor McAuliffe has pledged to place his signature on all clemency orders to make them legal. *The Washington Post* writers summed up best what this likely political move means by detailing these words, "Murder victims don't get to sit on juries, but now the man that killed them will," said Del. Robert B. Bell (R-Albemarle), who is running for attorney general. "A murder victim won't get to vote, but the man that killed them will." It was revealed a month after signing the order that Gov. McAuliffe faced his own set of criminal charges from an investigation regarding campaign finance launched by the FBI.

In a time of unprecedented threats at home and abroad, the last thing the American people need is governmental officials who place themselves above the people. This is especially true within the Department of Homeland Security, which ISIS and other terrorist groups are hoping to exploit. Using the Freedom of Information Act, the act so often ignored by the White House, Complete Colorado discovered an internal document displaying that the "U.S. Department of Homeland Security (DHS) reported over 1,300 badges and credentials lost or stolen, and no fewer than 165 firearms lost or stolen over the course of 31 months." This isn't the first time firearms have been lost, with some of the previous weapons from the 2010 report ending up in the hands of gangs.

Yet, according to a DHS statement to Fox News following the public revelation that all these things had been lost since 2012, it would seem clear the agency is simply hanging its hat on reducing the number of lost or stolen items this time. Nothing would make Islamic terrorists happier than to hear the cries of American children similar to that of the crying baby heard amidst the immediate silence following the Brussels attack or the screams of children who were plowed over by a truck in Nice, France. The bar should be set much higher at DHS. Unfortunately, many within DHS are prescribing to the low standard of our representatives; one lost item from neglect is too many!

Is it possible that Philip Haney and others voicing concerns are painting a grim picture of the culture behind the scenes within various agencies out of disagreement with the Obama administration? Of course, and each individual must assess and make their own conclusions from the information before them. However, a number of individuals within various agencies have pointed to the same themes of manipulation of facts and intimidation by leadership for those unwilling to abstain from painting the administration or federal agencies in a negative light when warranted. General reports, internal documents, and testimony from those directly involved seem to confirm the claims made.

Neither retired DHS intelligence agent Philip Haney or Special Agent Taylor Johnson has ever been convicted of any wrongdoing. These two workers—along with others, including the more than 50 CENTCOM analysts—decided they could no longer blindly accept what appears to so often be the desired protocol for federal employees: don't worry about outcomes, work to keep the wheels spinning, know that incompetence is fine, clock in, clock out, don't ask too many questions, don't do anything to bring attention to issues, protect agency turf and agenda, and, above all, collect a pay check.

These federal workers who highlighted problems within agencies most likely also grew tired of the same old song and dance offered from agency officials when placed in front of the public for issues that stem from a clear lack of accountability: attempt to deny or downplay the severity of the problem, make an investigation difficult and time-consuming when possible, promise to place new policies in place to fix the mistake, perform a similar (or worse) offense, and simply repeat the cycle.

Something has to change.

Although plenty of documentation exists, common sense should tell anyone that waste and inefficiency is not an acceptable trait in government. While no earthly organization composed of humans will ever be perfect, the American people deserve better effort from their government. Put on a smaller scale, the question is how do the people make the federal government more accountable in regards to efficiency and justice? On a broader scale, the overriding question is whether citizens will unite to re-establish more of a constitutional republic again or will they allow the executive branch and a horde of ever-increasing, unelected bureaucrats to seemingly rule as a monarchy?

Despite a focus often being placed more on the recent issues of waste, fraud, and abuse in government, the current culture of a lack of accountability was not created overnight. Nor will it be solved in a day. The massive entrenchment of bureaucracy is similar to a cancer that representatives of government have allowed to metastasize over time.

The issue revolving around the undocumented provides one of the best examples. Both Republican and Democratic Presidents have taken direct actions to increase the perplexity in solving the issue. Major scandals involving the border have happened under both parties, long before the current allegations of obstruction by the administration: "Operation Wide Receiver" occurred under the George W. Bush Administration, while "Fast and Furious" happened during President Obama's tenure. Members from both sides of the political aisle hampered efforts in reaching a resolution, which, in turn, maintains a cheap labor force benefiting constituents who support each party.

Without proper representation, the American people should count on more of the same from the government. Chronic issues will persist as new problems emerge, while government consistently fails to meet the demands. It will take a set of leaders who are not only committed to solving the current problems within government, but also in laying the foundation necessary for long-term success. Bureaucracy, without consistent challenges of justification from lawmakers, virtually guarantees permanence and expansion. The people must take the lead in creating a new type of representation built on accountability.

America has accomplished some of the greatest feats in history and will always possess the potential for setting the world standard. However, few truly understand how an overreaching bureaucracy and a special-interests-led Congress limit what can be achieved. Matthew VanDyke, a Baltimore native and international-security analyst, founded Sons of Liberty International, which "provides free security consulting and training services to vulnerable populations to enable them to defend themselves against terrorist and insurgent groups." VanDyke says that SOLI "was created to enable those abandoned by the international community to take action in defense of themselves and their people, and to combat these forces that seek to harm and oppress them."

VanDyke's non-profit organization relies entirely on the generosity of the public. However, while our government was only able to produce five U.S.-trained Syrian rebels despite spending $500,000,000, Sons of Liberty International was able to train over 300 Christians to fight in the region for around $50,000. Despite changes to the governmental program that previously wasted nearly half a billion dollars on a handful of troops, not even 100 troops were ready as of July 2016. However, as is so often the case, the answer for legislators is to simply throw more money at the problem, with $416,000,000 already set aside in 2016 for another attempt. Although I was unable to discover the program I heard VanDyke interviewed on this past year, I do remember what his response was to the question of why the government has not found as much success as he has. He said it was because the decisions of government are "being made in cubicles."

It is often said that we can learn the most from children if we simply sit back and watch. Such is the case with Myles Eckert. As Steve Hartman of CBS News reported, "With his dad in mind, Myles wrapped the $20 in a note that read, 'Dear soldier—my dad was a soldier. He's in Heaven now. I found this 20 dollars in the parking lot when we got here. We like to pay it forward in my family. It's your lucky day! Thank you for your service. Myles Eckert, a gold-star kid.'" Myles father, Sgt. Andy Eckert, tragically died while courageously serving his country in Iraq shortly after Myles entered the world.

What Myles decided to do with the $20 he discovered in the parking lot of a Cracker Barrel that day ultimately sparked a movement. His one act of genuine kindness was the catalyst for The Myles Eckert "Pay It Forward" Challenge, which raises money for the Snowball Express, a charity for children who lose a parent to war. Imagine if our representatives were this dedicated in their service to the people. It's amazing how clear choices often become when actions are simply dictated by the desire to do what is right. For this to happen, many of our elected officials will have to learn the value of being selfless; something an eight-year-old clearly understands.

Truman Leads the Way

In November 2015, Neil Cavuto, host of "Cavuto: Coast to Coast" on the Fox Business channel, interviewed Keely Mullen, the national organizer of the "Million Student March," a rally in which students from over one hundred college campuses took part in protests for "free tuition at public universities, the cancellation of all student debt, and a $15-per-hour minimum wage for all campus workers." When asked who would provide the funding, Keely's entire argument centered on taxing the wealthy. Although taxing the one-percent garnered the most attention from Keely, she also expressed her unwavering support for eventually using a 90% tax on anyone making over $200,000 a year. Neil Cavuto seized the opportunity to inform the national march organizer of some basic arithmetic that had obviously been overlooked or ignored. "They've done studies on this, Keely. I don't want to get boring here, but even if you were to take the one-percent and tax all their money, tax it one hundred percent, do you know that couldn't keep Medicare, just Medicare, in this country going for three years?"

When presented with this information, Keely Mullen was noticeably stunned and chose to question the validity of the numbers being presented. Though she acknowledged that relieving student debt would cost over a trillion dollars alone, Keely firmly maintained her position on taxation. Neil Cavuto concluded the interview by asking one more significant question. "A lot of those college [sic] behind you, and institutions behind you, knowing that student debt is taken care of, it's forgiven and done; do you think any of those administrators, any of those schools, aren't going to leap at the opportunity to gauge even more, to raise tuitions even more, to raise room and board even more?" Despite presenting controversial policies for anyone outside the confines of her movement, Keely remained confident in the expansion of those joining the cause; the power of the group was seen as preventing such a response from educational institutions.

Part of this confidence in eventually gaining broad-scale support for the causes she supports may come from her own family's willingness to involve themselves in the movement, regardless of their socioeconomic stature. In the interview with Neil, Keely described her family as "an incredibly working-class family," which was "already on numerous forms of government assistance" and "basically scraping by in order to, you know, get her through school." However, Renee Nal, a writer for the *Examiner*, revealed that was highly questionable. Just shortly following the interview, she wrote, "Organizer for the 'Million Student March' Keely Mullen, who claimed to come from an 'incredibly working-class family' on Neil Cavuto on Fox Business News Thursday, turns out to have quite a comfortable existence as a member of the so called 'one-percent.'" Nal goes on to cite an interview Keely took part in for "The Privilege Project" in 2013, in which she described herself as "a white, upper middle-class family." Other documentation was given to suggest that it is almost certain that Keely was not being up front with viewers, or something in her circumstances had drastically changed.

Less than six months later, Darlette Scruggs, another prominent organizer of the "Million Student March," chose to speak with Neil Cavuto concerning why these things should be free. It is understandable that Darlette would come into the interview on the defensive after watching Keely's disastrous interview. However, she was very rude and condescending throughout the entire interview and consistently interrupted Neil. As I watched her demeanor, I thought of the words of Harry S. Truman: "I'll tell you one thing for sure. The only things worth learning are the things you learn after you know it all." Most viewers probably turned the channel rather quickly.

There are a number of reasons someone could choose to disregard what either of the young women said. Both obviously detest capitalism. Both are affiliated with the Socialist Alternative organization, with Darlette actually advertising the group with a t-shirt during her interview. Taken directly from a portion of the "about page" on the Socialist Alternative website, "We see the global capitalist system as the root cause of the economic crisis, poverty, discrimination, war, and environmental destruction. As capitalism moves deeper into crisis, a new generation of workers and youth must join together to take the top 500 corporations into public ownership under democratic control to end the ruling elites' global competition for profits and power." The next two lines are even more revealing: "We believe the dictatorship that existed in the Soviet Union and Eastern Europe were perversions of what socialism is really about. We are for democratic socialism, where ordinary people will have control over our daily lives."

Obviously, the young women wholeheartedly believe in this group that helped put together their march, with Keely stating, "The U.S. is like the bastion of, um [sic], of capitalism and its success"; while Darlette chose to say, "I'm a tax-paying citizen, a person, a young person that is seeking opportunities in a system that is unable to provide it regardless of what the argument is, and I say that this system of capitalism has proven itself illegitimate and it cannot provide basic things like education, shelter, and healthcare." However, as misguided as Darlette appears to be in her support of socialism, she did raise some valid points: the need for a re-prioritization, the failure of government to hold Wall Street accountable, and the immense amount of money that is always allowed to be spent on wars and nuclear proliferation, regardless of the debt. Attacking capitalism only serves to dilute the impact of the message that could resonate with a number of Americans who are also currently feeling disenfranchised; and there is a wide base of the electorate that is already primed to act if properly directed.

Regardless of who voters are choosing to back in the unique 2016 Presidential election, many share the similar characteristic of feeling they have no genuine voice in government. Peggy Noonan, former Presidential speechwriter for President Reagan and world-renowned author and columnist, wrote about how this feeling has led to the rise of Republican frontrunner Donald Trump. She broke down the country into the "protected," who set the rules for the country, and the "unprotected," who are simply forced to live by them. In describing the protected, she wrote, "They are figures in government, politics, and media. They live in nice neighborhoods, safe ones. Their families function, their kids go to good schools, they've got some money. All of these things tend to isolate them or provide buffers. Some of them—in Washington it is important officials in the executive branch or on the Hill; in Brussels, significant figures in the European Union—literally have their own security." Thus, she concludes: "Because they are protected they feel they can do pretty much anything, impose any reality. They're insulated from many of the effects of their own decisions;" only unity of the "unprotected" can change things.

As for capitalism, there is nothing wrong with the structure itself. Without even genuinely assessing the level of turmoil and ruin brought upon those who have supported other forms of government, such as socialism or communism, one merely needs to look outside the classroom to understand this truth. Education is vital, but it is the private sector, particularly through small businesses, that provides most of the actual employment opportunities. The unique American dream of success through entrepreneurship is still alive and well. It is the unequal representation dictating the structure that is causing the problems, with both major parties being bought and paid for by special interests. Many of our state and federal legislators have manipulated the principles of capitalism to such a degree that those discovering a more difficult path to upward mobility are beginning to question the system. Greed has far too long served as the catalyst for a majority of our lawmakers to disregard their duty to represent their constituency and work for fairness in opportunity. It makes no difference which party holds power, a system-wide lack in leadership and oversight remains a staple of D.C.

Most Americans do not agree with the assertion of simply giving away things for free without any personal responsibility attached. However, they have grown tired of lawmakers saying they cannot re-prioritize allocation of finances for more domestic initiatives because of the debt, and then immediately rubber-stamping a new round of defense spending without question. While debates over what tax policy or how to re-prioritize the budget will be more difficult and divisive, the goal of creating more accountability in how the government operates should provide an easy point of unity; all sides benefit from the opportunities created from maintaining greater efficiency in government. Currently, too many agencies are out of control, with too few attempting to man the ship for the people. Unifying to place pressure on members from both major parties to root out waste, corruption, and abuse remains elusive. Attempting to create long-term financial stability, which would benefit everyone, is being overshadowed by fights among factions over how to spend more borrowed money.

Most would agree that maintaining a strong military is vital to immediate and long-term national security. However, no other agency within the federal government requires a higher level of accountability. Funding the military always dwarfs all other aspects of the federal budget, accounting for 54% of discretionary spending in 2015. Beyond the money directly allocated to the base budget, Congress consistently circumvents the 2011 sequestration caps established by law––adding additional funds through the Overseas Contingency Operation (OCO) fund. As Eric Pianin, Washington editor and D.C. bureau chief of *The Fiscal Times* wrote in May 2015, "For a decade and a half, the White House, Congress, and the Department of Defense have played a deceitful game in funding the $1.7 trillion cost of the wars in Afghanistan and Iraq, keeping much of that spending 'off budget' even as it still added to the national debt."

Although the Overseas Contingency Operation fund was originally created only to provide more funding to the war efforts in Afghanistan and Iraq, it now serves as a "slush fund" for the Pentagon. "From 2001 to 2014, nearly $71 billion of non-war funding was provided through war appropriations, according to the Pentagon's own definition, the nonpartisan Congressional Research Service reported"; this reached $103 billion as of October 2015. In terms of funding for operations abroad, the OCO has provided the perfect method for the Pentagon to wage wars in the Middle East.

In a February 2016 article entitled "Inside the Pentagon's 'slush fund'," Paul D. Shinkman of *U.S. News and World Report* perfectly summarized the OCO by writing: "It's been called war planner's crack cocaine, a shifty accounting scheme or a habit-forming opiate imbibed government-wide. Barack Obama pledged to eliminate it at the beginning of his presidency, but its potency has only grown stronger since. Now, it accounts for the unregulated spending of $60 billion or more in taxpayer dollars per year, with no end in sight." Few are working to eliminate the dependence on it. "A road to nowhere" was the description given to OCO by Secretary of Defense Ash Carter.

President Obama initially vetoed the National Defense Authorization Act of 2016, specifically citing the inappropriate use of the Overseas Contingency Operation fund. It briefly looked as if some constraint was going to be placed on spending. However, in the end, his resistance only served to provide a blank check for both military and domestic spending. Beyond suspending the debt limit until 2017 and adding billions of dollars more to the OCO fund, Paul M. Krawzak, senior budget reporter for *CQ Roll Call*, detailed, "The budget portion of the deal would raise post-sequester base discretionary spending caps by $80 billion over two years—by $50 billion in fiscal 2016 and $30 billion in fiscal 2017. With the increase evenly split, the fiscal 2016 defense cap will rise to $548.1 billion while the nondefense cap will go up to $518.5 billion."

In their handling of the National Defense Authorization Act of 2016, Congress failed once again to offset some of the mandatory spending by displaying it could reasonably control discretionary spending, which makes up around one-third of the federal budget.

This pattern of reaching agreement by giving both sides what they want in domestic and military spending requests has become routine. Neither side ever displays the ability to look beyond the immediate, short-term goal of securing allocations to value the broader picture of necessary restraint for future national security.

During the time period in which President Obama was threatening to veto the initial $612 billion Defense Bill, Deb Reichmann of *The Associated Press* pointed out, "If Obama vetoes the defense bill, it would be only the fifth time that has happened in the past half-century. The bipartisan measure has become law every year for more than 50 years." This is an amazing truth when considering a 2013 report from Reuters which discovered that the 1996 Congress allocated 8.5 trillion dollars to the Department of Defense that "has never been accounted for." Various laws requiring audits going back to 1992 have essentially been ignored by the Department of Defense, when considering nothing of substance has been produced as a result. The latest 2009 law requiring an audit by 2017 is very unlikely to be followed, with little to no consequence.

As is so often the case, with other agencies throughout the federal government, the records in place were problematic and unreliable. Outdated accounting systems are being used within the most powerful country in the world. In-fighting among agencies was given as the reason genuine efforts have been thwarted—with billions being wasted on software attempts inundated with errors that failed to correct the problem. Of course, failures in software for greater accountability and efficiency have become a trademark of government. From the disastrous Obamacare rollout through the website to the mindboggling failure of the Department of Homeland Security to successfully digitalize more than one immigration form, despite spending over a billion dollars: software problems never cease to amaze.

In summarizing some of the findings within the 8.5 trillion unaccounted for, Jacqueline Leo and Brianna Ehley of *The Fiscal Times* wrote, "A scathing investigative report by Reuters in November 2013 described how an accountant at the DOD in Cleveland would face the same monthly problem: Missing numbers, wrong numbers—numbers with no explanation of where they came from or what they were for. To rectify the problem, the accountant was instructed to 'plug' in false numbers in the DOD's books." Yet, despite saying, "Let's make sure that we're able in a constructive way to reform our military spending to make it sustainable over the long term," at the press conference announcing his decision to veto the Defense Bill, President Obama did not make raising accountability in accounting a focus behind his tough stance. Instead, the desired additional funding for both sides was secured, with the military once again seeing no consequences for merely working within the same parameters of poor transparency.

The President may deflect criticism by referring to previous cuts in defense spending as a way he has held the department responsible. However, even verifying the actual magnitude of any cuts he cites is important. According to an article from factcheck.org in 2011, "President Obama's claim 'that we've already cut' $400 billion in defense spending is misleading. The President was referring to a Defense Department report that identified $178 billion in 'efficiencies' over five years—which the administration says will save $400 billion over 10 years. But only $78 billion of the $178 billion represents actual cuts; the rest of the identified efficiencies [would] be reinvested in other Pentagon programs." It is clear that the leadership out of D.C., whether from the White House or Congress, is failing in sending a message to the Defense Department that business as usual must change. The necessity of having a strong military is continuing to be utilized by the Department of Defense in basically presenting any numbers and figures they choose in achieving desired security. Waste, abuse, and fraud within this federal agency, consistently receiving the largest allocation of the budget, must be reined in.

Will Offensicht, a staff writer for scragged.com, was a previous employee of Gould, a federal contractor in the 1980s. In January 2010, he wrote an article entitled "Yes, Virginia, a $2.98 hammer really cost our government $100" in an attempt to clarify how the government can often spend exorbitant amounts of money on products commonly bought at low prices by the general public. He described the tedious task of accountants to search through poorly kept records to try and determine if these high prices were somehow legitimized on the contractor's side of the equation. He explained, "Accountants don't often use words like 'shock,' 'amaze,' or 'astound,' but they made it clear that they were quite surprised by government-required accounting principles. They found more than 20 cost categories associated with the hammer—marketing, travel, training, cleaning, general administration, facilities, and other overhead items were allocated to the hammer by formulas defined in the contract." All of the costs associated to the procurement regulations are legally binding. Despite the complete and utter ridiculousness of it, these separate item distinctions can reach the extreme cost provided.

Then you have "cost plus contracting" items, which involves attempting to achieve things that have never been done before. In these cases, the government seems to end up paying whatever the company says it will take to be successful. Dina Razor, a tireless advocate for reining in waste, fraud, and inefficiency in government, provided some insights as to how these figures can routinely reach such extraordinary proportions. In a 2010 article entitled "Solution: The Pentagon continues to overpay for everything; lets fix it," she wrote, "To understand how weapons and other costs keep overrunning and growing exponentially with each new generation of weapons, you have to first understand how the DoD looks at costs—what they paid for in the past and how they calculate what is reasonable to spend in the future. For much of the past 40 years, the DoD has used historical cost pricing to see what is reasonable to pay for future systems."

Her description would certainly shed light on officials reaching the estimate from the Government Accountability Office that now places the price tag at 1 trillion "to maintain and operate the JSF (F-35 Joint Strike Fighter) program over the course of its lifetime." Dina Razor went on to explain the result of routinely using such estimations by writing, "What will happen with most of these programs is that the DoD will pay for these weapons with their overruns anyway, and then those overruns will become part of the new baseline for new programs for new weapons. Essentially, this process magnifies the waste and makes it grow exponentially with every new weapons system."

Dina Razor's over thirty-plus years working on Capitol Hill to bring a greater degree of accountability within government has led to some major accomplishments. She has continued to consistently project what we are in great demand of in D.C.: an individual unwilling to be intimidated out of pursuing the noble task of reining in waste, fraud, and abuse. Nor will she allow others to be bullied for attempting to do what is right. Much of her work has been specifically aimed at instilling the confidence she has within others, founding the Bauman and Razer Group for whistleblowers. In 1981, she founded Project on Military Procurement (now POGO), which, among other things, helped discover numerous instances—such as the overpriced hammer. As with new weapons procedures, the hammer has witnessed consistent increases to the baseline formula, resulting in the price being $436 for the Navy. Almost all blame lies with government.

As for why the general public never hears as much in the media about similar overcharges for basic items, Will Offensich says it is in how things are disguised within allocation. He writes, "We the People still pay $100 for $2.98 hammers, but the accounting regulations make hammer-related overhead charges instead appear next to some other item so that the hammer doesn't seem so expensive. How do you, the voter, really know the difference between a $200 million fighter jet vs. one that's only $100 million?" Even if they knew what the cost of each item should reasonably be, do most Americans want (or have) the time to provide the sufficient oversight that members of Congress are elected to maintain? Then again, could it simply be that average American citizens just don't understand why these basic items are worth the additional cost?

In 1986, Jack Smith, a WWII veteran and one of the great reporters of the *Los Angeles Times*, wrote an article that centered on *The Pentagon Catalog: Ordinary Products at Extraordinary Prices*, a book by authors Christopher Cerf and Henry Beard. In describing why it is necessary to pay more for a military thumbtack, Jack cited the authors as writing, "That's because the good old American competitive spirit that brings us a dime-store item like a thumbtack for just a couple of cents is primarily concerned with keeping the cost down, not with making sure that it can take it out there on the battlefield where there are no shopping malls to get some more thumbtacks from. After all, if a defective thumbtack falls off your kitchen bulletin board, you may lose a recipe, but if a defective thumbtack holding an all-important battle plan falls off the situation display in a command bunker, that's a recipe for disaster, because we may lose a war...."

Regardless of who is presenting the information, some will question whether the military actually wastes money in the fashion described. Although a billion has become the new million, little things add up and just a few of the examples of waste I learned from a conversation with a former officer serves as a microcosm of the culture within government that consistently drives our national debt. The former officer was in the army in the 1970s and he told me a few stories about how he had personally experienced the results of serving within a system that rewards spending. In one instance, he and other servicemen were told to replace all the batteries in the jeeps on the base, despite the fact that all of them already had new ones. He decided to question the logic behind the order and quickly received a scolding from his superior officer. Later, he was told that it was about spending all the allocated money to receive the same the following year.

The same "spend it or lose it" rationale that is commonly utilized on the local, state, and federal level also dictated the treatment he received in the infirmary. Although his sickness could have been easily treatable with penicillin, the doctor on the base refused to give it to him. The doctor had more incentive to keep him confined to the medical ward for an extended period of time, not wanting to risk losing future allocations for housing a certain number of patients during a set timeframe. The nurse eventually told him how to adjust the thermometer reading and what to say to the doctor to be successfully discharged. It's ironic: as a soldier, he was forced to use tricks to get out of unnecessary care, while veterans are routinely fighting to receive the care they deserve.

Within an environment dedicated to spending, obviously some contractors take an opportunistic approach to maximizing profit. As former President Truman informed Merle Miller in an interview, "I've told you before, contractors and people who deal with government funds have very little respect for them." In an attempt to mitigate some of these unnecessary financial losses in contracts, Congress established the 2008 Commission on Wartime Contracting in Iraq and Afghanistan, with Sen. Jim Webb (D-VA), Sen. Claire McCaskill (D-MO), and Rep. John F. Tierney (D-MA) leading the way.

The commission was temporary and only lasted three years: "the report estimated that at least $31 billion, and possibly as much as $60 billion, [had] been lost to waste and fraud from the $206 billion spent on contracts and grants since U.S. contingency operations began in Afghanistan in 2001 and in Iraq in 2003—and that a similar amount could be lost due to unsustainable projects and programs." The extensive list of causes given for this waste was troubling: "poor planning, imprecise contract requirements, lack of competition, unnecessary purchases or overpayments, inadequate contract management and oversight, unsustainable projects, poor performance, weak enforcement, and a long-standing shortage of federal acquisition personnel."

Although the commission did identify some of the waste in government, one has to wonder whether it only achieved a small degree of actual success. It's obvious any number given from the Department of Defense must be scrutinized. Being unfamiliar with specifically how the investigation of the commission was conducted, it is reasonable to assume most of it was probably done by taking a sampling from the massive amount of military contracts to place under the microscope. This would be similar in nature to how the Government Accountability Office (GAO) conducts much of its work when it attempts to provide oversight through various audits on governmental agencies by statute or requests from members of Congress. Yet, actually getting a federal agency to implement many of the recommendations made by the GAO are often difficult, if not impossible, when considering that much of the wasteful practices have remained. Congressional hearings provide great soundbites for politicians, but it seems agencies rarely change as a result.

To make matters worse, the GAO also admitted in April 2016 to something that everyone else already knew: the numbers they project from the records provided by agencies cannot be taken at face value. Ali Meyer of the *Washington Free Beacon* wrote an article in April 2016 that detailed some of the latest findings from the GAO. Beyond close to $140 billion in improper payments being discovered, she wrote, "The audit also called into question the reliability of the government's financial statements. According to the report, if a federal entity purchases a good or service, that cost should match the revenue recorded by the federal entity that sold the good or service. The report found that this was not always the case and found hundreds of billions of dollars in differences between transactions between federal entities." She concluded her article by writing, "According to the audit, these weaknesses will eventually harm the government's ability to reliably report their assets, liabilities, and costs, and this will prevent the government from having the information to operate in an efficient and effective manner." Apparently, the government is the only entity left that needs to be told that the country is already there.

Of course, Harry S. Truman didn't need a governmental report to tell him the numbers were often cooked. From what the U.S. Senator at the time didn't already know from his own experience as the judge for Jackson County, Missouri, he learned from actually listening to his constituency—before personally going out to investigate. He started within his own state of Missouri and documented everything he discovered, which included: overpriced construction projects, equipment being ruined out of neglect, and hundreds of workers doing absolutely nothing on the job. After driving "twenty-five thousand to thirty thousand miles or so all over the country" and seeing the consistent waste of millions at each area he visited, he went back and reported his findings to the U.S. Senate. Can you imagine a sitting U.S. Senator or House Representative traveling in an old truck like he did without any of the luxury and security routinely offered to each member of Congress? Neither can I, not for even a second!

The report from Truman led to the formation of the Committee to Investigate the National Defense Program in 1941, later to be known as the "Truman Committee." Along with taking other senators with him to personally discover waste, he also oversaw the hiring of a number of trusted and accomplished investigators who understood that only the desire to find the truth should guide their work.

The investigators placed their faith in Harry Truman to protect them from any form of retaliation for what they might report. The investigation ran for seven years, with Truman leading the committee for the first three. One of the most memorable discoveries was locating hundreds of men hiding underneath a hangar trapdoor doing nothing but receiving a paycheck. The site had received advance notice and tried to make everything look fine by hiding things below.

Harry Truman's willingness to pry beneath the surface led to "one of the most successful investigative efforts ever mounted by the U.S. government: an initial budget of $15,000 was expanded over three years to $360,000 to save an estimated $10-15 billion in military spending, and thousands of lives of U.S. servicemen." For comparison, the entire cost of the Manhattan Project was $2 billion, at the time. Yet many say today that simply eliminating waste would not do much in alleviating the debt. More importantly, it was not about Truman making a name for himself, but instead about the people. As former President Truman explained in his post-presidency interview with Merle Miller, "Eventually, as I've told you, we saved the taxpayers fifteen billion dollars. And what frightens me... what I often think about: What if somebody hadn't been there looking after the interest of the taxpayers who were putting up all the money?" Sadly, the clearest answer to the question he poses can still be found within the Department of Defense.

General Dwight D. Eisenhower took time during his last Presidential speech to warn the nation against the military-industrial complex––or the mutually beneficial alliance between the military and industry. If left unchecked, the fear is that some will continue to place as much emphasis as possible on building up the military instead of investing more money into the people. Extraordinary profit is found in a permanent armament process. Waging wars abroad or highlighting national security concerns at home help legitimize the advocated demand for more weaponry. Few in the American public question the military contracts that are shrouded in the feeling of the moment.

Many politicians remain committed to bringing back defense contracts to their states while as a member of Congress; a role that remains, but transitions into a lobbyist upon retirement, partially explaining why earmarks still get buried within appropriation bills despite the moratorium passed into law in 2011. Citizens Against Government Waste highlighted in their 2016 Congressional Pig Book that "the number of earmarks increased 17 percent between FY 2015 and FY 2016, from 105 to 123, and the total cost jumped by 21 percent, from $4.2 billion to $5.1 billion." As for oversight, earmarks merely add an additional level of difficulty to properly scrutinizing federal contracts.

The broader consideration of national interest can easily become lost amidst the immediate concern of those seeking to simply secure a federal contract for political or business reasons. Maybe no better proof could be that the "D.C. metro area has seven of the top 10 wealthiest counties in the United States." Trillions spent on wars in the Middle East and abroad will only add more to the coffers of defense contractors, which might explain why decisions to follow the French into Vietnam or the Russians into Afghanistan were not viewed unfavorably by some. Although Vietnam served as a legitimate aspect of the "Containment Policy" against Soviet expansion, one could question foreign policy that continues to place the U.S. military within conflicts surrounding civil wars despite earlier history. It would be naïve to believe that great profits do not play some role in the decisions. Though trouble often arises in the absence of the U.S. Armed Forces in military conflicts abroad, entering into them without a clear strategy or foreseeable victory in sight seems ill conceived. Maintaining a presence in Afghanistan for fifteen years has left many Americans unable to remember why we're still there.

Eisenhower obviously believed a proper balance could be formed if the need for establishing adequate restraints was understood. Before warning against failing to comprehend the "grave implications" of the military-industrial complex he said, "A vital element in keeping the peace is our military establishment. Our arms must be mighty, ready for instant action, so that no potential aggressor may be tempted to risk his own destruction." However, above all, it was clear he was desperate for the American people to understand that the very essence of what placed America as the city upon a hill could be slowly taken from underneath our feet if we were not vigilant. He said, "We must never let the weight of this combination endanger our liberties or democratic processes. We should take nothing for granted. Only an alert and knowledgeable citizenry can compel the proper meshing of the huge industrial and military machinery of defense with our peaceful methods and goals, so that security and liberty may prosper together."

Just like Thomas Jefferson, former President Eisenhower placed his faith in the people to set things right. However, today that aim almost seems unachievable. The bureaucracy present in Washington is ever increasing, with elections not providing leadership from either party to aid the people in reining in the government. More and more appointed bureaucrats are making decisions that should be dictated by elected officials—at least through oversight that is currently almost non-existent. Even the small degree of control the Senate held to approve Presidential nominees to cabinet positions has now been thwarted through the ever-increasing appointments of czars. Although concerns have been raised by members from both sides of the aisle, no legislation has been passed to place a halt on the White House making them now and in the future.

Czars have been appointed by both Republican and Democratic Presidents since the first time the label was used to describe some of the New Deal team appointed under President Franklin Roosevelt. Similar to the current debate revolving around whether the Senate should take a vote on Federal Appeals Court Judge Merrick Garland, President Obama's nominee for the Supreme Court, the answer for each U.S. Senator typically depends on which party is in power. Although Democrats are currently complaining about the Republican-led Senate not performing their constitutional duty to offer advice and consent on the nominee, they have previously used a similar approach when Democrats held control of the Senate. While some Republicans have joined a few Democrats in the past in questioning the use of czars, many of the same Republicans had little problem with them when appointed under the presidency of George W. Bush.

In September 2009, then White House Communications Director Anita Dunn wrote a blog post entitled "The truth about Czars," in which she described the hypocrisy of certain Republicans. She wrote, "Sen. Robert Bennet has criticized czars as 'undermining the constitution,' but reportedly prodded President Clinton to appoint a Y2K Czar. She also wrote, "Senator Lamar Alexander has also criticized President Obama's 'czars,' calling them 'an affront on the constitution.' But during remarks delivered on the Senate floor in 2003, Sen. Alexander said 'I would welcome' President Bush's 'manufacturing job czar.' That same day in the Senate, he also expressed support for President Bush's AIDS czar Randall Tobias." As usual, the arguments look to be nothing more than a show for votes. Although they hold no actual legal authority, many czars act as if they do. Greater use of czars can either be seen as resulting from the obstruction of the Senate in not taking up a vote or as an easy method for the President to appoint someone they know will not be approved. Regardless, useless political squabbles do not solve the real problem of czars adding more power to the bureaucracy in D.C.

The growth in influence of the National Security Council provides a similar example of how the U.S. Congress fails to effectively address the matter due to rhetoric and votes being dictated almost entirely by the politics of the time. Although designed to hold no more than a little over seventy members, the composition of national security and foreign advisors to the President has ballooned under both Republican and Democratic presidents. Today, some estimates place the number of advisors to President Obama at over four hundred, convincing some that even more unwarranted power has been given.

Although Republicans, led by House Armed Services Committee Chairman Mac Thornberry (R-TX), are seeking to drastically reduce the number of advisors within the NSC, similar voices of concern from former administrative officials have been bipartisan in composition. Others believe the pushback simply comes as a result of the military not wanting to have an additional layer of management. Regardless, the inability of Congress to come together and discover the appropriate oversight for the NSC only further highlights how the deck continues to be stacked against the principles of a republic. Elected officials are the ones who should be setting the agenda through proper oversight of bureaucrats. The absence of such diminishes the power of the people.

The most recent annual report from the Competitive Enterprise Institute released in May 2016 estimated that federal regulation cost taxpayers $1.885 trillion, which broken down results in "a hidden tax that amounts to nearly $15,000 per U.S. household each year." What may be more revealing is that the report discovered that "in 2015, 114 laws were enacted by Congress during the calendar year, while 3,410 rules were issued by agencies." A heavy hand of regulation only pushes Americans further from creating the ideal capitalistic system that can supply the capital for investment and economic growth that the country has been desperate to produce.

The general growth of the federal bureaucracy is alarming in its own right. Agencies continue to expand and demonstrate their proclivity to confidently push the bounds of their power, with little fear of actual consequence. The failure of Congress to provide the level of oversight essential to maintaining the will of the electorate is threatening the sacred foundation of democracy. As Dov Zakheim, Pentagon comptroller under George W. Bush, said of the NSC, "It was designed as a small group that would provide the President the best set of options—but now the NSC makes the options, too." However, regardless of whether candidates for agencies are actually going through the vetting process, too much unchecked power is almost freely being granted. Heightened secrecy has made attempting to determine the extent of what aspects of Americans lives are actually being controlled or manipulated virtually impossible to genuinely assess.

President Kennedy made his share of mistakes in withholding information, such as the Diem Coup, which resulted in the death of the South Vietnamese President and two others, but he was very clear on the need for a balance between security and secrecy.

> "The very word 'secrecy' is repugnant in a free and open society; and we are as a people inherently and historically opposed to secret societies, to secret oaths, and to secret proceedings. We decided long ago that the dangers of excessive and unwarranted concealment of pertinent facts far outweighed the dangers which are cited to justify it. Even today, there is little value in opposing the threat of a closed society by imitating its arbitrary restrictions. Even today, there is little value in insuring the survival of our nation if our traditions do not survive with it. And there is very grave danger that an announced need for increased security will be seized upon by those anxious to expand its meaning to the very limits of official censorship and concealment."

Imploring the American people to harken back to the similar sentiments of President Eisenhower in his warning for the need to remain vigilant, President Kennedy understood the dangers of national-security concerns being used to casually limit necessary transparency and debate. Time after time, in modern history, we have witnessed the work of a few help illuminate a glimpse of what is truly going on behind the closed doors of government. The Pentagon Papers, WikiLeaks, NSA papers from Snowden, and the Panama Papers provided major sources of clarity to the American people about the need to hold the government accountable. Potential ties between politicians and the benefits of following certain decisions relating to war, such as President Johnson and Vice President Cheney's similar association with Halilburton, are disconcerting. Questions concerning a possible inappropriate relationship between the Clinton Foundation and access to the State Department under former Secretary Clinton are breathtaking.

Mass global surveillance and documented inconsistencies of facts from current and previous war efforts are troubling. There is a complete disregard for privacy as the government collects available information on Americans. This massive amount of recorded data could provide the federal government a ready available source for the purpose of intimidating anyone who threatens their desired agenda. It is an extensive surveillance few knew about and will most likely remain, as few officials fear prosecution. Sacred rights and liberties have practically been placed at the discretion of a set of bureaucrats to decipher and balance.

Today, the greatest threat of overreach clearly comes from departments and agencies directly associated with national security, which are, in many cases, displaying an almost unabridged level of power and influence. In an April 2016 article, William Jackson, a respected columnist with an extensive political background, summarized some of the catalysts behind this overreach in authority, "In the global war on terrorism, the checks and balances on power written into the Constitution have given way to a unity form of government under which several hundred unelected military and civilian bureaucrats—at the National Security Council, and in the C.I.A., Defense, State, and Justice departments—decide on the use of military force by the United States."

Mike Lofgren, a retired congressional staff member who spent more than half of his twenty-eight-year career as a senior budget analyst within both houses of Congress, also believes that inappropriate influence pervades the fabric of the Republic. Lofgren has utilized essays, interviews, and his latest 2016 book, *The Deep State: The Fall of the Constitution and the Rise of a Shadow Government*, to extensively address the subject and provide detailed examples concerning the unhealthy and permeable relationship that exists among Washington, Wall Street, and Silicon Valley—which signify the "Deep State," a coalition that willingly makes a mockery out of the principles of democracy to advance certain agendas. Interchanging positions between private industry and government provide the perfect incentive for many within various entities, inside and outside of D.C., to betray their duty to the people and work in collusion with the group.

It would seem to explain why the same faces are always seen at the heights of power. Wall Street is utilized to rein in any non-compliers possessing essential roles in government by providing political pressure through its immense concentration of money, while the reward of a golden parachute for unwavering obedience is often sufficient. Silicon Valley feeds the appetite of government with intelligence to keep consistent favor, with allocation of H-1B visas and former federal employees remaining in demand. As Philip Giraldi, executive director of the Council for the National Interest, explains: "In some cases the door revolves a number of times, with officials leaving government before returning to an even more elevated position. Along the way, those select individuals are protected, promoted, and groomed for bigger things. And bigger things do occur that justify the considerable costs, to include bank bailouts, tax breaks, and resistance to legislation that would regulate Wall Street, political donors, and lob-byists." It would definitely seem to explain the puzzling absence of genuine punishment for so many.

Despite instances in which a greater focus is placed upon the debt, the wheels of the defense industry keep churning, with national-security concerns being utilized as the trump card against any effort for changing the way things operate. In a February 2014 article enti-tled "Essay: Anatomy of a Deep State," Mike Lofgren highlighted much of how a certain aspect of the privatized portion of the Deep State came to be as strong and as entrenched as it currently is today. He wrote, "In a special series in *The Washington Post* called 'Top Secret America,' Dana Priest and William K. Arkin described the scope of the privatized Deep State and the degree to which it has metastasized after the September 11 attacks. There are now 854,000 contract per-sonnel with top-secret clearances—a number greater than that of top-secret-cleared civilian employees of the government. While they work throughout the country and the world, their heavy concentration in and around Washington suburbs is unmistakable: Since 9/11, 33 facil-ities for top-secret intelligence have been built or are under construc-tion. Combined, they occupy the floor space of almost three Penta-gons—about 17 million square feet. Seventy percent of the intelli-gence community's budget goes to paying contracts."

The depth and scope of the Deep State currently seems destined to remain firmly insulated within the country, as a virtually independ-ent entity unto itself, merely maneuvering through the ebb and flow of whichever party controls the Congress and the White House. Uti-lizing his veteran experience as an officer within the C.I.A. and Army Intelligence, Philip Giraldi summarized the stronghold of this concen-tration of power by explaining, "What makes the Deep State so suc-cessful? It wins no matter who is in power, by creating bipartisan-supported money pits within the system. Monetizing the completely unnecessary and hideously expensive global war on terror benefits the senior government officials, beltway industries, and financial services that feed off it. Because it is essential to keep the money flowing, the Deep State persists in promoting policies that make no sense, to in-clude the unwinnable wars currently enjoying marquee status in Iraq/ Syria and Afghanistan. The Deep State knows that a fearful public will buy its product and does not even have to make much of an ef-fort to sell it."

In March 2015, Scott Amey, General Counsel for the Project On Government Oversight (POGO), wrote an article about the numer-ous groups, at that time, joining the call for President Obama to sign an executive order forcing federal contractors to disclose political spending. He cited a 2014 Sunlight Foundation report which "found that between 2007 and 2012, 200 corporations spent a combined total of $5.8 billion on federal lobbying and campaign contributions. In return, these corporations received $4.4 trillion on federal business and support. In other words, for every $1 the companies spent on political influence and access, they got $760 from the federal government."

In January 2016, a number of Democratic Senators took great strides in renewing the push for Obama to actually take executive action on the matter by sending the White House a formal letter. As part of the letter, the Senators wrote, "The federal government spent approximately $460 billion in FY2013 on private sector contracts. Almost 40 percent of that total, roughly $177 billion, went to just 25 major companies. Since 2000, the top 10 federal contractors have made $1.5 trillion from the federal government." With less than a year left in office, despite demonstrating a past willingness to unilaterally decide major issues with a stroke of a pen, President Obama has yet to sign an executive order requiring federal contractors to disclose political spending.

Greater accountability through reasonable transparency remains nothing more than a talking point; something that is doubtful to change if former Secretary of State Hillary Clinton becomes President. It is inconceivable to believe that a candidate who displays an unwillingness to release the transcripts of her paid speeches to various private groups and businesses would ask for more transparency in the allocation of governmental contracts. As Stephen Braun of the Associated Press reported, "The AP review identified at least 60 firms and organizations that sponsored Clinton's speeches and lobbied the U.S. government at some point since the start of the Obama administration. Over the same period, at least 30 also profited from government contracts. Twenty-two groups lobbied the State Department during Clinton's tenure as secretary of state."

If federal contractors have an inside track that dilutes, if not eliminates entirely, competition from the process, and all but guarantees consistent work from government, then what is the incentive to offer the highest quality work? Take the case of Imperatis: "As of 2012, the firm had contracts worth almost $1 billion from U.S. government contracts." In July 2015, ABC News highlighted how "the company, formerly known as Jorge Scientific, was awarded the 'sole contract' to overhaul OPM's (Office of Personnel Management's) computer network last year after hackers believed to be from China stole the personal records of more than 22 million U.S. government employees." This decision seems to indicate that previous, questionable behavior in professionalism is not the variable that holds the most weight when allocating work vital to national security.

ABC News was already very familiar with Jorge Scientific before their report in 2015. [In 2012], "Jorge Scientific was the subject of an ABC News investigation that featured video from whistleblowers showing employees staggeringly drunk while working as security personnel for the U.S. government in Afghanistan." Despite the findings of the ABC News investigation and congressional hearings spearheaded by Senator Claire McCaskill (D-MO) and Jason Chaffetz (R-UT), which emphasized an audit from the Inspector General that revealed discrepancies of accountability for over 130 million dollars (which had already been paid to the group), the contract was awarded. A name change and the addition of more high-ranking former military officials seems to be the unbeatable combination for receiving more contractors like clockwork. Potential harm to the American people as a result of documented negligence appears secondary to money.

Although it's difficult to determine from the outside how secure the U.S. government truly is from cyber-attacks, recent history warrants serious doubt. Although the extent of the hack actually serving as a long-term threat to U.S. national security is questionable, it looks as though ISIS sympathizers did retrieve some data from the Centcom, the U.S. military's Central Command, in January 2015. It only adds to the unprecedented data breaches involving private and public entities across America, which actually allowed one group of teens to gain access to the emails of the directors of the C.I.A. and National Intelligence. One of the members of the group, who goes by the name of "Crackas With Attitudes," said of the hack, "Like a five-year-old could do it."

There has also been talk concerning the distinct possibility that world powers, such as Russia and China, are already capable of breaking into the network infrastructure. Ted Koppel, long-time former anchor of "Nightline" on ABC, knows full well what the consequences could be if we continue to be indifferent to facilitating the best available source for United States cybersecurity, writing a 2015 book, *Lights Out*, on the subject of cyber-attacks. In an interview back in October 2015, he described the possible magnitude of such an attack on the power grid by saying, "Potentially, it could cover many states—tens of millions of people—and last for weeks, if not months. Once a power outage lasts more than three to four days, you're in deep trouble. You have no flowing water, you have no waste disposal, and unless you have food supplies that can last without refrigeration, you're going to run out of food—and very, very quickly. Without electricity, we're essentially thrown back into the middle of the 19th century."

Later in the interview, when asked by Charles Green of AARP about what level of hope he held for his work actually making an impact on bringing more preparedness to American cybersecurity, he said, "Not very. It might cause a little bit of shouting back and forth. In the final analysis, those who say 'Koppel is wrong' will probably win because saying that I'm right requires action." Sadly his skepticism is shared by the vast majority of Americans as consistently seen in poll after poll on congressional job approval. The current world of rising threats does very little to change the culture in D.C.

Decisions have consequences and it seems that for too long human beings have simply been viewed as chess pieces to those in power. While there may be debate as to what actually fuels it, there is little doubt that there is always an underlining push for war when opportunities are presented. As President Obama told a group of veterans, and those who had lost loved ones to war, in October 2015, "Right now, if I was taking the advice of some of the members of Congress who holler all the time, we'd be in, like, seven wars right now"; a statement most likely close to the truth, considering the variable of war-profiteering alone. However, even if keeping a distance from the civil war in Syria was viewed as an instance in which President Obama correctly protected American interests, and despite allowing Syrian President Assad to cross the 2012 "red line" he imposed against using chemical weapons on his own people, it's almost certain that few Americans would agree with the President actually saying he "was right" on Syria.

How could Syria be rationalized as something to gloat about for anyone, much less a U.S. President, when considering the death and destruction that only continues to grow in the war-torn region? As of March 2014, "the total number of displaced people [was] comprised of over 2.5 million refugees who [were] living in neighboring countries and 6.5 million internally displaced persons (IDPs) within Syria, according to the UNHCR (the United Nation's refugee agency)." These figures only account for the war entering into its fourth year. Statistics, which have been presented from more recent reports like the one from October 2015, discovered that over 250,000 individuals have been killed as a result of the civil war, with over 115,627 of those being civilians, according to the Syrian Observatory for Human

Rights.

Beyond the numbers, the clearest indication of how callous President Obama was in his statement comes from the words of a young girl spotlighted in the "Children of Syria" film on PBS. Helen, who was ten at the time, and her family were trying to remain in Aleppo, Syria in 2013 as her father fought for the resistance against the two fronts of Assad forces and ISIS. She witnessed her younger sisters constantly worrying about being "shelled," even for some time after they finally escaped the region. Helen's family left after her father was taken by ISIS. Following his abrupt removal, this brave girl said, "I'm not scared of anything anymore. There's no need to be scared of anything, because there's nothing left in our lives." President Obama's illogical statement only serves as a microcosm of the failure within our leaders to truly grasp or value the real consequences attached to their choices. The disconnect that exists among our leaders to the domestic or international policy decisions they make is astonishing.

Long before the warnings of Presidents Eisenhower and Kennedy, Theodore Roosevelt underscored the necessity for addressing the hidden forces behind the scenes. Within the "Bull Moose Party" platform he helped form in 1912 is written, "Behind the ostensible government sits enthroned an invisible government, owing no allegiance and acknowledging no responsibility to the people. To destroy this invisible government, to dissolve the unholy alliance between corrupt business and corrupt politics is the first task of the statesmanship of the day." This is quite the task considering the permeable relationship among business and politics, the embedded career politicians who benefit from the status quo, and the unprecedented rule of money on the entire political system.

The only hope for creating the type statesman advocated by Teddy Roosevelt is when a new set of elected officials understand that a higher degree of accountability is expected from the people in their service. The people must come together and send our elected officials the same message the Sixth Circuit Court of Appeals sent the overreaching federal bureaucracy in March 2016. The Justice Department continued in its effort that day to shield the I.R.S. from accountability. When the DOJ cited 6103 of the tax code as the reason names of conservative groups that applied for non-profit status could not be released, "Judge Kethledge set the record straight and explained Section 6103 was 'enacted to protect taxpayers from the IRS, not the IRS from taxpayers.'"

By rooting out corruption through greater equality in representation, the excessive influence of federal contractors and insulated bureaucrats in dictating policy can be drastically reduced; providing a more genuine arena for achieving the balance between maintaining adequate security and also leaving in place sacred, fundamental rights. Only under these conditions will citizens begin trusting that their leaders are placing the most value on them.

Until such a time of newfound accountability, outcomes which should be viewed as unacceptable will continue to occur with little, if any, punishment attached. Like the DEA wasting $86 million on a plane to aid in the fight on drugs in Afghanistan, but never actually taking it to the region—missing deadlines until the mission became obsolete. The original price tag was $22 million. If the money was going to be wasted anyway, it seems the best-case scenario for the American taxpayer would have been for the Pentagon to place some of the funds instead toward the $43 million that was used to create a gas station in Afghanistan; "a rate far exceeding a similar Pakistan project that cost just $500,000." John Spoko, the Special Inspector General for Afghanistan Reconstruction, wrote, "One of the most troubling aspects of this project is that the Department of Defense claims that it is unable to provide an explanation for the high cost of the project or to answer any other questions concerning its planning, implementation, or outcome."

Why should the Department of Defense provide an explanation to the findings of the study conducted by John Spoko and his response team? There might be some inconvenience in sitting through the blistering words offered at a congressional hearing, but chances of anyone being held accountable are slim. If anything, any responsible senior official would probably either receive a slap on the wrist or choose to resign to a cushy private-sector position. More likely, blame would be assigned to a set of lower-level officers. This definitely looks to have been the case in the mistaken 2015 bombing of a Doctors without Borders hospital in Kunduz, Afghanistan—if we are to believe the passionate words of military officers who were actually on the ground that tragic day.

Although one "two star general" was among the men internally disciplined for the act, all the men receiving punishment were far below the military brass that always seem immune from receiving any consequence for failure. One Special Forces officer pointed to not receiving the information they needed on the ground, despite multiple requests. He was not pleased with the men on the ground who were, unsurprisingly, being utilized as scapegoats.

In his April 2016 article entitled "Green Beret officer blames 'moral cowardness' for strike on Doctors without border," Dan

Lamoth of *The Washington Post* details the written words of a Special Forcers officer who wrote that the enemies of the Kunduz operation demonstrated "moral cowardice" and a "profound lack of strategy." Within the declassified documents was also the soldier explaining how the military has lost its way. In listing what he believes are the root causes of the decline, he wrote, "I will tell you how. It is a decrepit state that grows out of the expansion of moral cowardice, careerism, and compromise devoid of principle exchanged for cheap personal gain. We owe the man on the ground more than that, because for him the decisions that he makes hopefully lands him somewhere between the judge's gavel and the enemy's bullet."

Those at the top are never the ones held accountable. Maybe it results out of the protection high-ranking officials receive from the "Deep State" or simply the lack in oversight provided by weak representation. There could also be a genuine consensus among all agencies in believing that Eric Holder was right in his "Too Big To Jail" doctrine, which assumes that holding those accountable at the top will bring too much collateral damage below. In March 2013, according to *The Hill*, then acting Attorney General Eric Holder told the Senate Judiciary Committee, "I am concerned that the size of some of these institutions becomes so large that it does become difficult for us to prosecute them when we are hit with indications that if you do prosecute, if you do bring a criminal charge, it will have a negative impact on the national economy, perhaps even the world economy." Though referring to the banking sector, his sentiments would seem to apply to all federal agencies when considering how difficult it is to hold anyone, much less those in high-ranking offices, accountable.

Regardless of why those at the top always seem shielded from actual consequences, the result is often that the little man is the one who suffers. A letter from Rep. Mac Thrornberry, Chairman of the House Armed Services Committee, attached with the Excess DOD Infrastructure Study, identified "22% excess capacity" and said, "As Department of Defense leadership has repeatedly testified, spending resources on excess infrastructure does not make sense. Therefore, we urge Congress to provide the Department of Defense authorization for another round of BRAC (Base Realignment and Closure)." It seems while the military is fine in maintaining a system of general waste, fraud, inefficiency, and lack of competition in federal contracts, it does have an issue with keeping open bases that the families of soldiers have learned to build a life around.

As is so often the case with government, there is a strategy centered on building a dependency within the system, so that eliminating what becomes necessary will be political. Military contractors are following suit in this smart strategy, such as sponsoring military magazines for a small amount of money—while behind the scenes they are making a tremendous amount of money with consistent contracts. Before the first base is eliminated or money is reduced from salaries and pensions of the men and women of the military, the government should actually work to eliminate broad waste in other areas such as in defense contracting—which is draining resources, heightening the general debt, and eliminating the chance to spend meaningfully. However, the military maintains practices such as piecemeal funding, which is shortsighted and does little to rein in excess spending.

While the government spends like there is no tomorrow on federal contracts, members within the military are suffering; some are actually even forced to spend their own money to buy needed equipment. This was the case for some members of Special Forces. Travis J. Tritten detailed this in an article for *Stars and Stripes* in February 2016, which documented Aaron Negherbon as saying, "Troops often buy their own medical equipment, such as tourniquets, and shell out about $1,000 each for their own helmets or $500 for a GPS device that they need for duty during a deployment."

Negherbon should know: he is the director of a nonprofit group called "Troops Direct," which provides these supplies while the U.S. government chooses instead to give an Afghanistan individual the best experience possible at the gas pump! When the House was made aware, Rep. Duncan Hunter, (R-CA) said, "It's been impossible for me to find out how the money is getting stopped and why it is not going down to where it's supposed to be."

Is anyone surprised by such a problem?

Of course, these soldiers aren't the first or, most likely, the last to directly be placed in harm's way as a result of the current system in place. This should be unacceptable; although, as always, politicians bear a bulk of the responsibility. Making speeches on the U.S. Senate and House floor about the military having to recycle parts from old equipment to service planes should be recognized, but wasteful spending that has remained out of control for years aids in these arguments falling on deaf ears. The speech should be centered on the lost art of being proactive in establishing a new standard of genuine accountability that doesn't place soldiers in this position again. Politicians need to quit making speeches for political points, and instead get their butts in the weeds to root out all the waste, corruption, and mismanagement of military funds.

Soldiers have died as a direct result of unopposed greed. Further relying on the interviews of former President Truman, we discover that some have paid the ultimate price as a result. Again, as part of his work with the Truman Committee, these are the words of Harry Truman directly found in Merle Miller's 1974 book, *Plain Speaking*:

> But dozens, hundreds of things like that and worse happened. They... Glen Martin was making B-26 bombers, and they were crashing and killing kids right and left. So I said to Martin, "What's wrong with those planes?" He said, "The wingspread isn't wide enough." So I said, "Then why aren't you making it wider?" And he said, "I don't have to. The plans are too far along, and besides, I've got a contract." So I said, "All right. If that's the way you feel, I'll see to it that your contract is canceled and you won't get another. "Oh," he says, "if that's the way it's going to be, we'll fix it," and he did. I just don't understand people like that. He was killing kids, murdering kids, and he didn't give a damn. I never will understand people who can do a thing like that.

As I read Truman's words, I immediately thought about all the members of my family who have chosen to serve in the military. From my father, as a helicopter pilot in Vietnam, to multiple members from both sides of my family who dedicated themselves to protecting America in Korea and the previous World Wars. I thought of my grandmother explaining to me how blue stars placed in a window signified having a child at war, while the replacement of a gold star meant their life had unfortunately been lost. During WWII, her family at one time had five stars in the window, with all, by the grace of God, remaining blue stars. I'm left to wonder how anyone who may have actually lost a family member to war would feel if they discovered that death had come as a result of something similar to what Truman described. What if the letter informing the Kennedy family of the loss of Joseph P. Kennedy, Jr. in a plane crash had also included a paragraph describing a similar instance of neglect being at the root of his death?

Something has to change to limit the greed in government.

Beyond specific domestic and military instances in which waste, abuse, and mismanagement are limiting the efficiency of government, fiscal neglect is placing national security at risk through debt accumulation. It is a consistent increase of unfathomable proportions, as Jerry Willis of Fox Business News revealed on "Shepard Smith Reporting" by saying, "The debt goes up by 2.5 billion dollars every day."

James Grant, founder and editor of *Grant's Interest Rate Observer*, offered a scathing review of federal fiscal policies in an article entitled

"The United States of Insolvency" for *Time* in April 2016. In summarizing how the Federal Reserve is inappropriately allowed to questionably dictate finances, he wrote, "Congress is the source of the Fed's power. The Constitution is the source of Congress' power. The parchment enjoins Congress to coin money and regulate the value thereof. The founders viewed money as a scale or yardstick, something that measures value. The Fed views money as a magic wand, something that creates value." Despite the current consequences or future implications, some on the Left dismiss the idea of a debt crisis.

In response to critics, including Jordan Weissman, the senior business and economics correspondent for *Slate*, scoffing at the article and indicating that simply paying off the interest of the debt would maintain sustainability, Tho Bishop of the Mises Institute pointed out that James Grant had adequately addressed those who share this logic. He wrote, "So, yes, Weismann is correct that at the current historically low interest rate, the United States has little problem in paying back the money it is owed—but there has been no serious effort by anyone in government to make the painful cuts necessary to start making a dent in the underlying debt obligations and no reason to believe that current interest rates have a never-ending shelf life."

James Grant highlighted how things could drastically change if the interest rate was heightened to previous levels when he wrote, "In the short term, the debt would no doubt be refinanced, but at which interest rate? At 4.8%, the rate prevailing as recently as 2007, the government would pay more in interest—$654 billion—than it does for national defense. At a blended rate of 6.7%, the average prevailing rate in the 1990s, the net federal-interest bill would reach $913 billion, which very nearly equals the year's projected outlay on Social Security."

More importantly, Thos Bishop cited an earlier article from Ryan McMaken, his colleague and editor of the Mises Institute, by writing, "Foreign governments are already reconsidering their holdings of U.S. securities." In the referenced March 2016 article entitled "Foreign regimes dumping U.S. debt—will the Fed just monetize the debt instead?" McMaken explained, "For years, the discussion over a possible debt-dumping scenario has focused on the possibility that the Chinese and others would dump U.S. debt and U.S. dollar holdings as part of the geopolitical scheme to bankrupt and destabilize the U.S. government."

As Tho Bishop sees it, the result could be that the rise in inflation would be accelerated by the Federal Reserve almost certainly trying to take up the load and, in the process, serving to lower more faith in

U.S. currency. He also noted that McMaken's article on foreign re-considerations to handling U.S. held debt even came before the 28 declassified pages of controversy surrounding 9/11 that resulted in the Saudi's quick threat "to dump U.S. debt." Eventually, you have to reap what you sow.

The sad reality is that the price of debt can also be witnessed in how it serves to place limits on the available options the United States has when dealing with other countries. Just as some cite this limitation with China, which holds the largest amount of U.S. debt, so must a Saudi threat to take 750 billion out of the U.S. economy if the American families of 9/11 victims are finally given the right to sue them over possible involvement.

In an April 2016 interview on "CBS This Morning," President Obama told host Charlie Rose, "If we open up the possibility that individuals in the United States can routinely start suing other governments, then we are also opening up the United States to being continually sued by individuals in other countries." One could wonder why President Obama never cites or values a similar concern when it comes to trade deals that allow foreign companies to sue governments, as witnessed with NAFTA. The Trans-Pacific Partnership (TTP) and Transatlantic Trade and Investment Partnership (TTIP), currently under consideration and advocated for by the President, would offer the same.

The families do not believe that the argument offered by President Obama to Charlie Rose in the "60 minutes" interview holds much credibility. As the head attorney for the families has been documented as saying, "We have had a sovereign immunity statute that creates broad exceptions for years and we have never seen the kind of retaliatory practice that they have suggested." The U.S. Senate obviously sided with the families, passing a bill in May, 2016, that placing them on the path of being able to sue. Time will ultimately tell whether the President will veto legislation if it reaches his desk.

Beyond the Senate legislation, the government strategically released "File 17" over the 4th of July weekend. It basically offers an overview of the question marks within the classified pages, as well as presents recommendations on how various federal agencies could further investigate. Considering the fight it took for the families to get anywhere almost fifteen years later, few citizens will be holding their breath.

The fact that the government did finally release the declassified 28 pages later in the same month shouldn't bring any newfound confidence in families receiving justice. Despite the troubling connections that possibly pointed to the Saudi government both funding and assisting the terrorists, many within the U.S. government have attempted to downplay the finding of the report. Should anything else be expected from a government that seemed to share the Saudis' vigor in delaying the release of the report for so long?

Regardless of the outcome, this type of controversy has only displayed more of why a newfound accountability in government is necessary in order to provide the proper oversight for rooting out the secrecy which continues to threaten the Republic. Re-establishing the ownership of the country depends on creating a tool for the people.

What confidence could anyone have in federal agencies being efficient and expedient in their dedication to serving the people? This is the same government with a State Department that can barely process email requests under the Freedom of Information Act. Agency officials offer the most basic errors as reasons behind the need for more time; the Obama administration requested that Hillary Clinton's emails—and, by extension, her State Department aides—not be released until two years after the 2016 election. In another request, the Deputy Secretary Spokesman for the State Department, Mark Toner, was all smiles—and could barely contain his laughter—as he explained to AP reporter Matt Lee that the 75-year projection of time necessary was actually reasonable.

Harry S. Truman understood what could happen if a government was left unchecked and to its own devices; he constantly advocated the need for keeping an eye out for potential overreach and abuse. As only he could, he summed up what must be done:

> "Now, as nearly as I can make out, those fellows in the CIA don't just report on wars and the like, they go out and make their own, and there's nobody to keep track of what they're up to. They spend billions of dollars on stirring up trouble so they'll have something to report on. They've become... it's become a government all of its own and all secret. They don't have to account to anybody. That's a very dangerous thing in a domestic society, and it's got to be put a stop to. The people have got a right to know what those birds are up to. And if I was back in the White House, people would know. You see, the way a free government works, there's got to be a housecleaning every now and again, and I don't care what branch of government is involved. Somebody has to keep an eye on things. And when you can't do any housecleaning because everything that goes on is a d**n secret, why, then we're on our way to something the Founding Fathers didn't have in mind. Secrecy and a free, democratic government don't mix. And if what happened at the Bay of Pigs doesn't prove it that, I don't know what does."

The Peoples' Clearing House could help determine which individuals can be trusted for rooting out corruption and maintaining proper oversight as advocated by Harry S. Truman. It is clear that without proper representation, the people will continue to suffer as a result of forces seen and unseen. As James Bovard wrote in a *USA Today* article, "Self-government is an illusion if politicians can shroud the most important details driving federal policy." Americans, by and large, must awaken to this truth.

Complexities in Migration

Kareem Abdul-Jabbar appeared on "Meet the Press" in January of 2015 to address the criticisms he and other Muslims were receiving for not being more active in confronting radical Islamic jihadists. Chuck Todd, the acting host of "Meet the Press" since September of 2014, actually led into the segment by asking, "Coming up, are we misunderstanding Islam when we talk about these terrorist attacks?" In his opening remarks, Kareem chose to remain consistent to the idea that "knowledge" offered the principle for "understanding," a theme that he had offered in an op-ed earlier in the month for *Time*. In that same article, he had also emphasized the idea that these type fanatics only "[wear] an ill-fitting Muslim mask" and "actually pervert the Qur'an through omission and false interpretation."

Although the segment introduction and Kareem's opening statements had seemed to indicate a meaningful dialogue was rather imminent, viewers quickly realized that they would get more of the same. His second public appearance in a month was used to speak in more generalities about the peaceful nature of Islam and further downplay the assertion that a necessity existed for him and other Muslims to actively speak out against terrorism.

Kareem's desire is for people to naturally assume that Islam is a peaceful religion that should not require a response to acts of terror. He believes these acts should already be understood as not belonging to a religion. However, with or without acts of terrorism, most Americans are not very knowledgeable about Islam and already have a foundation of suspicion about teachings which seems to allow various forms of oppression. If Kareem wants more people to make such an assessment, he should welcome any opportunity to help alleviate the doubts and fears surrounding the religion. Kareem alternatively chose to utilize all his publicity in January to merely point to a misunderstanding of Islam without offering any specifics for useful clarification. He chose to use his time to defend himself and others from the criticism of not taking a more firm stand—when he could have instead seized the moment to do just that by educating the American public on a few of the areas within the text which were being egregiously misused. By doing so, Kareem, a well-respected man, could have taught and offered a clear and understandable rebuke of the jihadist for many to rally around.

Although he received a heavy dose of criticism from the Left, Bill Maher used one of his "Real Time with Bill Maher" episodes from November of 2015 to stress this need for more dialogue in addressing all the truths and misconceptions revolving around Islam. The host strengthened his point by "citing a poll showing 53 percent of Americans [believed] Syrian refugees [had] values that [were] at odds with American values."

Beyond the backlash he received after the show aired, viewers witnessed plenty of pushback from within the program. One of his guests, Canadian author and politician Chrystia Freeland, countered his thoughts by saying that "you can't change [an] extreme Islamic perspective by broadly saying Muslim ideas are bad"; to which Mr. Maher retorted that "he was trying to stand up for moderate Muslims by having a debate about Islam's extremist ideologies." The host of the critically acclaimed HBO show, who's known for speaking his mind, went on to add, "Killing women for being raped, I would say, is a bad idea"—actually highlighting one of the most prominent areas of concern for many.

Some are confident that the cultural beliefs of some Muslims can be accredited with the growing number of rapes across Europe. This notion is especially true in regards to Sweden, which is referred to as "the rape capital of the west," with "77.6 percent of the country's rapists [being] identified as foreigners." Although Swedish governmental officials and national media have been accused of purposely attempting to downplay the severity of the acts and correlation with migration policy, similar allegations abound.

In Germany, "According to an editorial comment in the newspaper Westfalen-Blatt, police [were] refusing to go public about crimes involving refugees and migrants because they [didn't] want to give legitimacy to critics of mass migration." Although that article came from the summer of 2015, more recent allegations of sexual mistreatment by almost 200 women in Cologne, Germany this past New Year's Eve must have some credibility considering the police chief of the city ultimately resigned.

Although "the mayor of Cologne, Germany, blamed the victims of a mass sexual assault/rape, saying they should follow a 'code of conduct' to ensure they don't get raped again," Norway and other countries are now offering voluntary training to refugees in assimilating to their new culture. Officials are now teaching them that "to force someone into sex is not permitted in Norway, even when you are married to that person."

Media bias and the power of statistics to advance an agenda must always be accounted for, but correlations with migration to rape, paired with the current unrest from terrorist attacks, only confirm why Muslims like Kareem must actively speak out about their experiences with Islam. Just as Christians shouldn't be accountable for the actions of a few, such as those from Westboro Baptist Church—known for hateful harassment at funerals—they must be willing to stand up and offer a definitive rebuke.

As it specifically relates to the Westboro Baptist Church, Christians have been very active in opposing them by blocking the impact of their disgusting rhetoric through picket lines and newly established city ordinances. While no one is so naïve to believe that such a resolution will be as easy to advance in the realm of confronting radical Islam, moderate Muslims must work for a greater presence in a fractured religion.

President Obama, speaking in Turkey to an audience predominantly composed of Muslims following the horrific Paris attacks, re-emphasized this necessity by saying the "Muslim community" must "think about how [they] make sure the children are not being infected with this twisted notion that somehow they can kill innocent people, and that that [sic] it is justified by religion." He went on to say, "And to some degree, that is something that has to come from within the Muslim community itself. And I think there have been times where there has not been enough pushback against extremism."

Unfortunately, Kareem, a beloved sports legend, missed a golden opportunity to use his immense influence to better provide a foundation of information for helping many Americans begin to re-assess their partial or blanketed cynicism toward Muslims. However, Chuck Todd did not ask the type of questions for better facilitating responses that could have gone a long way in changing negative perspectives held by so many.

Where were the questions from the "Meet the Press" host concerning the harsh and oppressive treatment of women? What about his position on the implementation of Sharia Law? Does he ever favor any of the extreme punishments sometimes utilized? More importantly, where does Kareem believe the foundation of misinterpretations within the Qur'an and other foundational Islamic source materials are serving as the catalyst of justification by the actions of extremists? None of these questions were ever presented to Kareem in an attempt to illuminate any misunderstandings. Obviously, Kareem still provides an active voice, as well as continues the general humanitarian work that defines the great character that endears him to myself and so many others. However, any opportunity lost makes the task harder moving forward.

Since Kareem's visit almost a year ago, Chuck Todd has welcomed a number of guests, obviously including Muslims, who have provided real-time analyses of Islamic extremists and what they believe the role of the Muslim community should be in better confronting it. Among them, two well-known Muslim women appeared on the program in December 2015 and offered different perspectives on the role of modern Muslims. Dalia Mogahed, research director at the Institute for Social Policy and Understanding, took a stance that was similar to that of Kareem. She believes radical extremists should clearly not be considered as "true Muslims," as their actions in any shape, form, or fashion misrepresent the teachings of Islam. Dalia thought even engaging in a discussion of the sort would offer "propaganda" for them by feeding the "apocalyptic narrative of ISIS that wants to start a war between Muslims and everybody else."

Asra Nomani, on the other hand, advocated for a more active approach, which President Obama would also again advance only a few hours later in a speech designed to alleviate the fears of Americans following the San Bernardino shooting. Asra did not mince words in courageously saying that to succeed "Muslims need to take back their religion from ISIS." This same tone was also utilized by President Obama in emphasizing the significance of more Muslims to go beyond reacting to attacks by providing clarification:

> "This is a real problem that Muslims must confront, without excuse. Muslim leaders here and around the globe have to continue working with us to decisively and unequivocally reject the hateful ideology that groups like ISIL and al Qaeda promote; to speak out against not just acts of violence, but also those interpretations of Islam that are incompatible with the values of religious tolerance, mutual respect, and human dignity."

When Asra Nomani, the author of *Standing Alone: An American Woman's Struggle for the Soul of Islam*, was asked by Chuck Todd to specify how she proposed her fellow Muslims take back their religion, she answered by describing the steps that she and others had already taken to lay the foundation for more advanced activism.

> "On Friday, I stood with a group of brave and courageous Muslims. And we stood and we provided a declaration to the world of reform. We are calling ourselves the 'Muslim Reform Movement' and we are opposing a very real interpretation of Islam that espouses violence, social injustice, and political Islam. And what we did is walked through the gates of Islamic center of Washington here in D.C. that's very much run by a government of Saudi Arabia, and we posted our precepts on the door of that mosque because the problem is not simply in Syria. The problem is sitting in the birthplace of Islam, in Mecca, Saudi Arabia, where this interpretation of Islam has gone out into the world over the last four decades, creating militancy groups from Indonesia to, now, the San Bernardino, California, vicious attack. We have to take back the faith. And we have to take it back with the principles of peace, social justice, and human rights, women's rights, and secularize governance."

Asra Nomani is a realist willing to honestly lay out all the variables that must be recognized and addressed for any chance of success. She is willing to share some of her firsthand knowledge concerning the extremist rhetoric coming from mosques and communities, clearly indicating that defeating the spread of this ideology is going to require cooperation with Muslims from within America.

This is exactly why she and others "went to the mosque and took the risks on [their] own lives" by advancing such a proclamation. A Bloomberg Politics National Poll from just after the Paris attacks found that "64 % of Americans still agreed that Islam is an inherently peaceful religion, but there are some who twist its teachings to justify violence." Although, an entire year before the Paris and San Bernardino attacks could have been better utilized for diluting some of the present Islamophobia, Asra Nomani and others obviously understand there is still time to persuade many minds through bold steps for greater understanding.

The research of Seamus Hughes and Lorenzo Vidino of George Washington University underscores the need for cooperation with Muslims at home. In the study released in December 2015 entitled "ISIS in America: From Retweets to Raqqa," the men "[focused] on around 300 people who [had] been identified as American recruits or supporters of ISIS." When "looking at 71 people who've been indicted in the U.S. for ISIS-related activities, Vidino and his colleagues say that except for seven suspects whose legal residency status hasn't been determined, 'the vast majority of individuals charged as U.S. citizens (58) or permanent residents (6), underscoring the homegrown nature of the threat.'"

Despite a YouGov poll from early December 2015 following the San Bernardino attacks finding that "62% of Americans including 66% women, 55% of black Americans, and 63% of Hispanics believe the U.S. should not admit Muslim Syrian refugees," there should still be optimism among Asra Nomani and others for moving forward through cooperation. Though the poll clearly found that a majority of Americans desired to deny Syrian refugees further access at that time, Carrie Johnson of NPR highlights that only "about 40 percent of the cases George Washington reviewed involved converts to Islam, and a small fraction, about 1 in 10 are women." The ability of ISIS to influence the vulnerable and disillusioned is obviously not always dependent on religious beliefs and as the poll further reveals, there is a clear distinction in success of this message by gender.

While the San Bernardino attacks looked to have been uncommonly spearheaded by a woman, the absence of such attacks from the vast numbers of Muslims who have migrated to the United States, as well as findings of the study from George Washington University, should not be forgotten.

In direct relation to the Syrian refugee crisis, Canada seems to have accepted this correlation and in November 2015 moved to a resettlement plan that "will be limited to women, children, and families from now on after increased security concerns about single males." However, the same strategy has not been implemented in much of Europe. According to a report from the United Nations Refugee Agency (UNHCR) in September 2015, "of the European host countries, Greece takes on most of the arrivals, with 244,855 [to that point], followed by Italy receiving 115,000. In total, 75 percent of the refugees [were] reported to be men, 12 percent women, and 13 percent children." Videos of groups that seem to display a common uniformity of men walking in large groups verify the numbers.

All throughout history are examples of a preference being given to women and children in times of emergency, leaving questions as to why the migration practices of many countries involved in the Syrian migration have not been driven by such long-standing logic. If the statistics are even close to being accurate, then these European countries have overwhelmingly rejected such a notion. Although there are numerous demographics within populations that may somehow explain some of these discrepancies, one is still left to wonder what type of male would leave his immediate family or relatives behind in a war-torn country?

Is it possible that the male-driven Arab culture almost entirely explains why there is an absence of sufficient remorse for recognizing how unconscionable it is to leave women and children to their own devices in war for survival? It seems that honorable men would be given an additional incentive to fight harder to succeed in hopes of one day seeing their loved ones again. However, for those that have practiced extreme forms of oppression on their female counterparts, a sense of fear may drive them to believe, for good reason, that women may ultimately choose a different path than to return to them if given the chance.

President Kennedy once said, "When written in Chinese, the word 'crisis' is composed of two characteristics—one represents danger and one represents opportunity." Among all the discussions pertaining to additional security measures and the elimination of ISIS that demand the most attention, what should not be overlooked is the unique opening that has been created for America to liberate many who have lived for decades under oppression. Stories of girls like Malaya Yousafzai and Nujood Ali, two Muslim teens who courageously stood up against the unfair practices often accepted by those that profess to follow Islam, must be considered when making future policy decisions.

In the case of Malaya Yousafzai, she received the attention of the world after being shot in the head as a result of her contrasting views on education for women. Despite remaining a consistent target for assassination by the Taliban, Malaya has maintained her resolve and refuses to be silenced out of fear. She believes, as Americans do, that self-initiative and ambition should determine whether one fulfills their potential; not a set of discriminatory practices which limit them. If we allow fear and anger to blind us from such considerations, then we allow the divisive endeavors of ISIS to rob us of what has always designated us as the consistent hope of the rest of the world.

"Our emphasis is on admitting the most vulnerable Syrians—particularly survivors of violence and torture, those with severe medical conditions, and women and children—in a manner that is consistent with U.S. national security," a State Department spokesman told BuzzFeed News. "Military-aged males unattached to families comprise only approximately two percent of Syrian refugee admissions to date." American policy at the present time clearly seems to be driven by this desired emphasis of protecting women and children. Nevertheless, any policy requires a faith in the security process and much of the opposition concerning migration continues to revolve around legitimate doubts as to whether our government can serve as adequate gatekeepers.

Americans have reason to wage concerns as to whether their government can be trusted to protect them from terror. Skepticism seems to only expand in magnitude daily with additional lapses in judgment and accountability, which actually includes instances of incompetence within the White House detail. It may be legitimate to ask whether the government can be trusted to protect the people when the President has even been put at risk more than once.

The FBI and other agencies across the country stop more threats than most Americans could ever imagine each year, with many remaining unrevealed, but the list of mistakes in oversight that led up to 9/11, and now the San Bernardino attack, presents a justifiable reason for Americans to be concerned. These concerns are only confounded when learning that the government may have stopped an ongoing investigation within the State Department that could have possibly uncovered the San Bernardino attackers. However, hearing that profiling concerns from the top may have hampered officials within Homeland Security from accessing the social media of those seeking visas is alarming. The failure of Homeland Security to do so at the direction of those in Washington may partially explain some of the unprecedented uptick of gun sales.

Even if Americans ultimately have faith in the vetting process, can they trust Washington to remain consistent to the current percentages that keep single, military-aged males only slightly accounted for among the admitted refugees? Congress often disregards the voice of the people on significant matters, placing ideology before country. The President has made some decisions on a whim that were questionable at best in terms of being in the country's overall best interest.

International policy magnifies this distrust with fairly recent actions of the current administration, where it seemed acceptable to broker a deal with Iran built on public lies and backroom promises—while, on the other hand, stress the importance of having a legally binding tool on climate control. Both resulted in negative outcomes. Iran predictably violated the terms of the agreement and the non-ratified climate agreement will most likely only be unilaterally followed by the United States. Of course, this isn't the first time the President has placed his national security emphasis more on climate change than wrangling in the Middle East. Pulitzer-Prize-winner Charles Krauthammer explained this tendency by saying, "He lives in a world where people get together—reasonable, educated, Harvard

Law School people from all over the world—and agree on futuristic designs that mean nothing, like the League of Nations, like the U.N."

Once again, where is the foundation for establishing trust? Even though migration provides unique complexities, it is not immune from becoming yet another issue to which those in D.C. desire to move forward with complete confidence from the American public despite the absence of initial steps to earning any. Instead, they further build a record to create the opposite effect.

What about the unwillingness to adequately protect the southern border or uphold the laws in sanctuary cities? How should Americans feel when remembering the decision of some legislators to reject Kate's Law, which would have demonstrated that all sides to the heated immigration debate can at least come together in common sense in ridding our country of felons? Then there's the troubling tendency from our government to consistently shy away from labeling any acts as being Islamic terror or the apology tour to the Middle East with which President Obama began his presidency. So many failures in trust cannot easily be disregarded when some of the previous decisions continue to cost lives.

The confidence in leadership an administration or congressional leader seeks is not something that can simply be garnered from one well-spoken speech or the introduction of a rightly timed hashtag such as one from the White House which read "#RefugeesWelcome." This particular choice made assessing success impossible, which might have been wise considering the lack of any effectiveness found in others coming from the White House, such as "#BringBackOurGirls."

The kidnapped Nigerian girls to whom the First Lady was referring in that hashtag have still not been found almost two years later. The only individual who has possibly received less attention from the U.S. government is an actual American hostage, Robert "Bob" Levinson, who is possibly still alive and being held captive in Iran. In November 2015, Sanford D. Bishop, Jr., a Democratic U.S. House member from the state of Georgia, "[fought] back to bring the 219 Nigerian schoolgirls kidnapped by Boko Haram by co-sponsoring H.R. 3833, a bill requiring the United States to develop a strategy to defeat Boko Haram." Maybe another congressman will go beyond a resolution to bring back "Bob."

It seems the only way Nigeria may receive some meaningful support in fighting for the growing number of victims of Boko Haram is through a bill that would force the White House to act before another "JV team" grows in strength. Until such time, Boko Haram and his similar set of Islamist, militant thugs have proven they will simply continue to expand their reign of terror, which started in northeast Nigeria and has now reached into the neighboring countries. In this endeavor, it looks like those Nigerian girls not used as sex slaves will instead be used as suicide bombers if a report from a survivor of an attack from February 2016 is true. In that attack, Boko Haram not only utilized a few of these teen girls for quite possibly one of his most despicable acts, but found it comical to bring suffering to a new set of children in the process, as he and his followers chose to happily burn their young souls alive during the unprovoked village attack.

Although most Americans may never grasp the true magnitude of complexities involved in making decisions concerning foreign affairs, especially when considering most knowledge remains hidden due to national security, some conclusions remain rather clear. Apart from all of the variables involved with each decision, on the most simplified level, the international strategy that has been followed by the current administration continues to lack the defining characteristic of all championship teams: the ability to change course and make the necessary adjustments for victory. So often what ultimately separated football teams in maneuvering through their schedule of games during a championship run was being able to go into a game with a flexible strategy; one in which they entered the game confident in one set of beliefs on how to win, but possessed the depth and willingness in leadership to make the appropriate adjustments at the half to address unforeseen strengths. Sadly, the leadership coming from the White House today seems to remain too tied to former beliefs and ideology to recognize or value when it is necessary to make such changes.

In almost every aspect, great or small, from our prolonged strategy of failure in Syria to the mindboggling policy of continuing to release terrorists from Guantanamo who have and will continue to predictably rejoin the fight against us, the current U.S. foreign policy remains enslaved to a losing theme. The current administration confidently holds true to their initial policy assessments in the face of overwhelming criticism that often includes retired and seasoned generals; they believe, as with so many other issues facing the nation, that they know better than anyone what is best for America despite the mounting list of failures that say otherwise. However, this practice of disregarding the voice of the people has never been confined to the White House, but now more than ever plagues the bodies of elected officials that extend to legislative chambers nationwide.

Americans are fearful and though some have more than likely been rightfully accused of fear-mongering for pure political purposes, the threats we face demand a strong and united response that is expected from our divided set of leaders. Even in knowing that the vast majority of Syrian refugees seeking asylum only desire opportunity and pose no risk, we know the jubilation that would come from ISIS if they were able to carry out their cowardly plan of infiltrating America as they have done in Paris and across Europe.

Any eventual faith in security aside, fears cannot be expected to easily subside, or should they, with the knowledge that in some cases "ISIS fighters [were] reportedly shaving their beards and dressing up as women in order to flee Syria in the wake of Russia stepping up its military campaign in support of (Syrian) President Bashar al-Assad." This is the same Assad who was allowed to cross the "red line" established by President Obama in using chemical weapons on the Syrian people and resulted in producing the refugees who are now being used by the White House to lecture the American people on compassion.

In speaking at American University during the height of Soviet tensions, President Kennedy said, "For in the final analysis our most basic common link is that we all inhabit this planet. We all breathe the same air. We all cherish our children's future. And we are all mortal." Those commonalities described as applying to all mankind, regardless of our differences, no longer hold true. If they are not crucifying and torturing children to death or cowardly using them as a shield against attacks, ISIS and other Islamist militants, such as the Taliban, are actively recruiting them through propaganda and intimidation of their families.

A promising future for their youth is of little value as they pursue their heinous endeavors. This lack of empathy is what allows them to actively work to sway the minds of their youth to believe they are immortal for fulfilling the roles of suicide bombers. The individuals that compose these extremist groups only look as if they grasp the sanctity of human life when prompted to shed this tough demeanor to beg and weep for their own lives to be mercifully spared.

In his article "Afghan boy suicide bombers tell how they are brainwashed into believing they will survive" from January 2012, Ben Farmer of *The Telegraph* details how this process of mental training occurs. A senior Afghan intelligence official he spoke with told him about how they are manipulated through Islamic materials that persuade them to believe that: "When this explodes, you will survive and God will help you survive the fire. Only the infidels will be killed, you will be saved and your parents will go to paradise."

With such depths of depravity driving the soulless jihadists who are hell-bent on bringing their destruction and mayhem through infiltration of Europe and the West, Americans have the right to expect more of our leaders in defeating it. Lack of direction in policy strategy or inaction in regard to providing our authorities with the tools and powers they need is inexcusable. This is especially true when considering that ISIS may already have the foundation to build upon.

Speaking at a congressional hearing this past October, FBI Director James Comey added a sobering reminder concerning migration by saying that "federal authorities have an estimated 900 active investigations pending against suspected Islamic-State-inspired operatives across the country." However, what was more revealing and disheartening was when Comey said, "it is still unclear whether the bureau [has] the necessary resources to meet the demand."

The visa system is one program that has been placed under further scrutiny since the attack in San Bernardino, with the female gunman originally entering the country on a K-1 visa as the fiancée of her American boyfriend and counterpart in the attack. Americans had already displayed a heightened desire for raising the standards of security in admitting Syrian refugees after the Paris attacks, with a Bloomberg Politics National poll finding that "just 28% would keep the program with the screening process as it [then] existed."

Even without the polls, what's most troubling is that these types of considerations should have taken place a long time ago. "A 241-page report produced by the staff of the 9/11 and Terrorist Travel detailed numerous flaws in the visa program that allowed the hijackers to gain entry to and remain in the U.S. to carry out the attacks." More importantly, the report particularly shed light to the significant fact that "only two hijackers—Satam al Suqami and Nawaf al Hazmi, both non-pilots on the day of the attacks—overstayed their visas."

Everything we know points to the need for the entire system to be overhauled with the deficiencies not confined to just one set of visas. When just looking at the groups of hijackers who carried out the 9/11 attacks, you discover a diversity, with "only one of the 19 hijackers [coming] to the U.S. on a student visa. The rest arrived here on tourist or business visas." It took slightly over fourteen years after 9/11, in the light of new attacks, for Congress to even entertain a vigorous debate about trying to patch some of the flaws in the clearly broken visa system.

The only other aspect of procrastination that could possibly be more inexcusable as it relates to 9/11 is that many of the terrorists have still not been put on trial, leaving the families of the victims to suffer in limbo as to how to move forward without the loose ends of justice being brought together for closure.

So many challenges facing our country are consistently kicked down the road for future generations to address—adequately correcting the problems within the visa system is just the latest example of what results from inactivity. Even after 9/11, career politicians merely schooled each consecutive class of Congress as to how to safely cling to their political security through maintaining the status quo in such matters. This record of failure in our visa process was spotlighted by the latest terrorist attacks and served to reinforce the fears related to plans about expediting the migration of more Syrian refugees. This is especially true when considering the State Department could not even tell a congressional panel how many individuals were currently in the country who overstayed their visas, with Syrians being part of the list that was missing.

Following the lackluster speech of the President shortly after the San Bernardino attacks, Republican Presidential candidate Donald Trump issued a statement calling for a temporary ban on all Muslims entering the country. While his announcement drew a mixed result of support and alienation, it also served as a common reminder to almost all Americans of the exact reason they despise the culture in Washington. Beneath all the various denouncements remained the underlying truth that while members of both sides of the aisle would be more than willing to unite in condemning his proposal, few would be as prepared to put aside partisan politics for advancing legislation in the pursuit of a solution.

A bill designed to strengthen the visa program held enough support for passage, but was delayed by Democrats who chose to seize the time to further debate gun control. Procedural politics are normal, but employing them when knowing that an extended void in security could possibly cost more lives provides a clear window into the broken system in Washington. Even with the apprehension surrounding Trump's extreme proposal, the contrast between the "business as usual" tactics of Congress and President Obama's "pie in the sky" climate focus during such times convinced many Americans that in Trump they finally had someone who was listening to their often forgotten voices. They viewed him as one person, whether right or wrong, who seemed to clearly assess the magnitude of the threat and wasn't allowing any ideology or fears of political correctness to deter him from expressing his understanding of their concerns.

Following the Brexit vote, Steve Hilton appeared on Fox Business' "Varney and Company and addressed the similarity between British voters who chose to leave the European Union and those supporting

Donald Trump.

The former director of strategy for Prime Minister David Cameron, who had actively advocated for exiting the EU, said, "What you're seeing in this vote today, just as with support for Donald Trump, is people saying we've had enough of not being listened to; of being ignored by the elites and we want power back over the things that matter in our lives. And it's a revolt against the bureaucratic, centralization of power and the elites who think they know best and that they're the ones who can just push people around and tell them what to do. And people have had enough of it."

A majority of Americans do feel like second-class citizens within their own country because their voices seem to never be heard by those in state and federal government. This may be the reason that Donald Trump chose to specify the length of his Muslim ban with the words "until our country's representatives can figure out what the Hell is going on" to display that he also recognized that the lack of urgency in our representatives was not accounting for the fears of the people who could only feel more alienated from their unreliable leaders.

While some, including Democratic Presidential front runner Hillary Clinton, confidently point to the harsh rhetoric of Trump as providing the perfect recruiting material for ISIS—nothing could be more effective in bringing new people to the group than the genuine hope for success that the unwillingness of the United States to adequately destroy the group. It is also reasonable to assume that these individuals would have joined ISIS regardless of what Trump said if they are that sensitive to words, although the Benghazi incident taught Americans that our government seems to love to blame acts of terrorism on videos.

It's amazing how some of the same liberals who mock the idea that using the words "radical Islam" could be a meaningful acknowledgement in fighting terrorism are the same ones who consistently presented the argument that words from Trump alone could radicalize people. Many of the same ones who mocked his religious test being based on a question upon entering the country wholeheartedly supported allowing more refugees in the country with a process a former refugee admitted at one point involves a simple "yes" or "no" answer to whether you are a terrorist. Both instances are ridiculous and brimming with utter hypocrisy.

A number of debates concerning Syria will likely continue for some time into the foreseeable future. Should the United States advocate for the removal of President Assad of Syria despite his support from Iran and Russia and the complexities witnessed from the regime change in Iraq? Can the 34-nation Islamic Alliance from the Saudis aid in any transition in Syria or actually be trusted to pick up some of the slack in defeating terrorism in the region? Or will the group simply be more celebrated in name than in action? Would it be practical for the United States to actually pivot more toward containing the refugee crisis within the region than bringing it to our shores by establishing safe havens and no-fly zones in western Syria (which borders Jordan and Turkey)?

Regardless of the conclusions reached, the resettlement of Syrian refugees displays even more how the Obama administration underestimated the power of the private sector in helping provide the humanitarian aid necessary to meet the influx of undocumented immigrants across the Southern border. "About 70 percent of all refugees admitted to the U.S. [are being] resettled by faith groups, according to the U.S. State Department office for refugees." The legitimate question is why can the current administration only seem to have faith in the role of these groups when it is within our borders, sometimes not even informing the governors of the states that receive refugees?

While migration currently dominates discussions on American security, the real concern should be centered on the slow and further infiltration of our Congress since the founding of our country by special interests, career politicians, and crony capitalists that drive the status quo. Our national security has actually been in jeopardy since the day we started opening the door for massive amounts of money to enter politics and drive the agenda—to when we started accepting arguing over how high to raise the debt ceiling instead of truly working to address the underlying problems for solutions. And it continues as we ease oversight on governmental agencies that have resulted in a culture that lacks accountability and is taught from the top to simply point to the person beside you as the one responsible.

There is no need from outside forces to bring our demise when such an environment exists from within. As the iceberg continues to approach, the question remains as to how many more will be left to see the water rise above their heads while those on the top deck refuse to hear their cries and take steps to change their outcome.

Lack of genuine leadership may serve as a limiting factor to the things the American people can control, but it cannot take away the spirit that can drive us forward on the right path again. Underneath the focus placed on the fears of Americans to the desires of Islamic extremists exists stories of faith and generosity that have always defined us. Basim Ismail is one individual who discovered this truth.

He is actually a student at my beloved alma mater, Auburn University. As part of the "Blind Trust" experiment conducted by the Muslim Student Association on campus, Basim decided to stand blindfolded with a sign that read, "I am Muslim and I trust you. Do you trust me enough to hug me?"

Needless to say, Basim was overwhelmed and encouraged by the sheer amount of compassion through hugs he received in a strictly positive response that day. This small gesture, during a time of heightened skepticism, provided one Muslim student hope that the educational institution he attended will continue to strive to maintain an environment in which individuals will be assessed not by the color of their skin or what they wear, but by the character they possess.

Beyond being guided by patriotic spirit, those of the Auburn family—composed of students, fans, alumni, and city residents—are driven by a creed that produces good citizens at home and abroad, who desire to give back. The words even sustained Auburn University's most beloved football coach, Ralph "Shug" Jordan, through war, possessing a copy of it within his uniform as he joined the ranks of other heroes in storming the beaches of Normandy, France in WWII.

A portion of The Auburn Creed from George Petrie reads, "I believe in my Country, because it is a land of freedom and because it is my own home, and that I can best serve that country by 'doing justly, loving mercy, and walking humbly with my God.'" Regardless of religious affiliation, a wide range of diversity could be seen in those offering support as a Muslim trusted his community to display kindness. One father actually held up his son to also offer Basim a hug.

All gestures of acceptance seemed in line with the remarks President Reagan offered to members of the congregation of Temple Hillel and Jewish Community Leaders at Valley Stream, New York in October 1984. "We must never remain silent in the face of bigotry. We must condemn those who seek to divide us. In all quarters and at all times, we must teach tolerance and denounce racism, anti-Semitism, and all ethnic or religious bigotry wherever they exist as unacceptable evils. We have no place for haters in America—none, whatsoever."

The willingness presented at Auburn University that day to accept everyone will hopefully serve as a microcosm of what the rest of the country will ultimately choose to embrace as a proper balance between security and liberty. With a renewed trust in government, established from The People's Clearing House, a newfound hope for greater equality in opportunity will create a contagious spirit of optimism for finally moving forward with the desired progress.

Trade Policy for the People

In his book *America the Beautiful: Rediscovering What Made the Nation Great*, Ben Carson addressed the subject of trade by writing, "With all the intellect that exists in our nation, it should be easy for us to come up with bipartisan, business-friendly policies to encourage businesses and manufacturers to bring their factories and offices back to our land." Most Americans would agree with the former neurosurgeon and 2016 Republican Presidential candidate regarding the potential of a determined America.

Unfortunately, the formulation of trade policies is similar to any other decision facing our leaders, in that the process places limits on what can actually be achieved. The dialogue, debate, and eventual action taken results from attempting to strike a balance between the conflict of self-interest and what is best for the people.

Appearing on "Morning Joe" in June 2015, the eventual Republican nominee for president, Donald J. Trump, described what is driving the trade deficit in a manner that is unique to him. "We don't have our best and our brightest negotiating for us. We have a bunch of losers; we have a bunch of political hacks. We have diplomats. And China puts the people—hey, look. I know the smartest guys on Wall Street. I know our best negotiators. I know the overrated guys, the underrated guys, the guys that nobody ever heard of that are killers that are great. We gotta [sic] use those people."

While offensive to some, much of the appeal for Donald Trump is that he projects a clear confidence for soundly addressing many of the deficiencies that result from the counterproductive culture in D.C. For many Americans who have had their lives turned upside down through loss of employment as a direct result of policies abroad, hearing someone specifically talk about correcting trade negotiations is music to their ears.

In his book *The Squandering of America: How the Failure of Our Politics Undermines Our Prosperity*, Robert Kuttner writes, "Trade policy is the most striking area where America's true interests are obscured—and defeated—by a complex tangle of geopolitical objectives, ideology, and concentrated power of industry and finance. For more than three decades, the United States has promoted a series of trade policies whose end result has been a chronic structural deficit that has left us financially dependent on foreign banks, the near collapse of America's manufacturing sector, and the destruction of a high-wage social contract." Basically, in the area of trade, where the stakes couldn't have been any higher, those designated to speak for the American worker in the past have barely uttered a sound, bringing a devastating burden to families who feel forgotten.

Despite a record of failure that should offer some sense of pause in utilizing previous negotiating practices, the current administration has practically followed the same logic with the latest massive trade endeavor. The Trans-Pacific Partnership Trade Accord is an agreement between the United States and 11 Pacific Rim nations. If ratified, it "would eliminate duties on countless goods and establish uniform rules on intellectual property, labor rights, the environment, and other issues affecting trade and investment."

From the elimination of thousands of tariffs to gaining unprecedented further access to the influential Japanese market, a number of incentives have been given by advocates in hopes of seeing the deal realized. However, being a deterrent to the unfair trade policies of China is the significant reason presented for the historic trade measure.

Robert J. Shapiro, former economic advisor to President Bill Clinton, presents the Trans-Pacific Partnership as serving as a deterrent to unfair practices by providing a more refined effort similar to the type strategy the United States utilized in the 1950s to build unity for winning the Cold War. Whether it is cutting export prices and dumping products below the American market, or shutting down mid-day trading to control losses, China seems to currently hold uncontested power.

In a speech from October 2015, following the signing of the trade agreement to potentially be ratified by Congress, President Obama said, "When more than 95 percent of our potential customers live outside our borders, we can't let countries like China write the rules of the global economy." While previous behavior from the Chinese demands eventual action, not everyone agrees that securing control of the rising Asia-Pacific region requires proceeding with the Trans-

Pacific Partnership. Utilizing failed trade practices from the past to create the largest trade accord in history seems unwise.

Understanding that every good magician never reveals the secret of an act until he has fooled his audience, those opposed refuse to allow The Trans-Pacific Partnership Trade Accord to produce the similar outcome of the North American Free Trade Agreement. They haven't forgotten that many of the same reasons offered for supporting the TPP are similar to the ones echoed before the eventual signing of NAFTA: "An agreement signed by Canada, Mexico, and the United States. It [created] a trilateral rules-based [trading] bloc in North America" that has been in effect since 1994.

Lou Dobbs, long-time media personality, clarified why similar rhetoric shouldn't be listened to again in his book, *Exporting America: Why Corporate Greed is Shipping American Jobs Overseas*. He wrote, "U.S. companies and multinational corporations operating in the United States pushed hard for the Free Trade Area of the Americas in 2003, arguing that it would open new markets for the United States' $10 trillion economy. But we'd heard this specious logic before—one decade and nearly one million jobs ago. Proponents of NAFTA declared that the 1994 pact could create 170,000 U.S. jobs annually. Instead, at least 750,000 jobs were lost as a direct result of NAFTA."

The AFL-CIO, which identifies as an umbrella federation for U.S. unions with 56 unions representing 12.5 million working men and women, also posted a parallel sentiment on its website. "The AFL-CIO provided the Obama administration with ideas to improve U.S. trade positions so that they work for the 99%, not just the 1%. Unfortunately, it is becoming clear the TPP will not create jobs, protect the environment, and ensure safe imports. Rather, it appears modeled after the North American Free Trade Agreement (NAFTA), a free trade agreement where the largest global corporations benefit and working families are left behind." Obviously the negative effects of NAFTA have not been easily lost on the blue-collar workers the country was originally built upon.

The American people, by and large, seem to share a consistent view regarding the inefficiencies of our leaders in trade, especially in terms of NAFTA. As of 2011, "the nation [had] lost 3.1 million manufacturing jobs since 1994, and its trade deficit with Mexico and Canada had risen to $138.5 billion in 2007 from $9.1 billion in 1993." As Lori Wallach, director and founder of Global Trade Watch, informs us, "A 2012 Angus Reid Public Opinion poll found that 53 percent of Americans believe the U.S. should 'do whatever is necessary' to 'renegotiate' or 'leave' NAFTA, while only 15 percent believe the U.S.

should 'continue to be a member of NAFTA.'"

Although polls have fluctuated over time, they have remained consistent in an opposition to NAFTA and general practices utilized by America in establishing free trade. A National Pew Center Poll from 2010 found that "some 76 percent of respondents said they supported more trade with Canada, and 52 percent said they supported more with Mexico, but only 35 percent of those surveyed said they liked NAFTA."

Those unsatisfied with past performance in trade are diverse. A poll from 2012 highlighted that the "opposition [cut] across party lines, class divisions, and education levels, perhaps explaining the growing controversy over the proposed deepening and expansion of NAFTA model through the TPP," highlighting a trend of possible long-term unity against negative trade policies that don't meet proper standards. Although 2015 briefly saw Americans slightly change their negative views toward trade, this enthusiasm was quickly lost according to a set of Wall Street Journal/NBC polls from the spring and summer of 2015, with even the height of favorability never reaching above 37 percent.

Although there was also a Rasmussen poll in 2008 that showed American support for NAFTA failing to register beyond the teens, the late Tim Russert, former Washington bureau chief of NBC News and host of "Meet the Press," wouldn't have needed it to know the pulse of America. From his tireless work ethic in preparation, to insights he took from his dad, "Big Russ," who he often referred to as his "cheapest most accurate focus group," Tim always knew what questions the American people wanted posed to their leaders and never let them down in masterfully asking them for understanding.

"Plotting his interviews out like chess matches, he deploys aggressive openings, subtle feints, artfully constructed traps, and lightning offenses to crack politicians' phony veneer and reveal the genuine veneer beneath," wrote Jack Shaver in an article for *Slate* from 2003. The Democratic Debate he co-moderated that year between the two remaining candidates, Senator Barack Obama and Senator Hillary Clinton, would be no different. The actual beliefs held by both in regards to NAFTA held question marks and Russert wasted little time in bringing the necessary clarification.

> "Senator Clinton, Senator Obama said that you did say in 2004, that on balance, NAFTA has been good for New York and America. You did say that. When President Clinton signed this bill—and this was after he negotiated two new side agreements for labor and environment—President Clin-

ton said it would be a force for economic growth and social progress. You said in '96 it was proving its worth as free and fair trade. You said that in 2000, it was a good idea that took political courage. So your record is pretty clear."

Tim Russert then reminded Clinton that Al Gore had once informed Ross Perot of the option of opting out of NAFTA and questioned her about a possible willingness. Although confident she could successfully re-negotiate, Senator Clinton agreed that to opt out entirely would definitely be on the table. Beyond agreeing with his fellow debater, Senator Obama felt the need to add, "I think actually Senator Clinton's answer on this one is right. I think we should use the hammer of a potential opt-out as leverage to ensure that we actually get labor and environmental standards that are enforced."

Although popular when said at the time, with less than a year left in office, President Obama has never followed through with that hammer, although administration officials will point to the Trans-Pacific Trade Accord as offering an attempt to do so. As for Hillary Clinton, she followed the lead of the other 2016 Democratic candidates and made known this October 2015 that she opposed the TPP agreement, citing a failure in "meeting her standard for creating jobs, raising wages, and protecting national security."

With her past history of supporting NAFTA—from the years after her husband signed the accord to while serving as Secretary of State under President Obama—many immediately questioned her new-found opposition. Most remain convinced her resistance to these trade deals only came as a result of the pressure she felt to follow the lead of her primary challenger, Senator Bernie Sanders.

After what Virginia Gov. Terry McAuliffe said in an interview at the Democratic Convention from July 2016, many of Bernie's supporters remain skeptical of her commitment. Almost immediately following Sen. Sanders announcement to pledge all his delegates to Hillary Clinton as the nominee in a symbolic gesture of unity, McAuliffe, a long-time friend and colleague of the Clintons, said Hillary would definitely flip on TTP once she is elected.

Either way, in possibly looking at the lack of movement by President Obama in renegotiating NAFTA alone as just one example within a consistent pattern, Jimmy Fallon may have summed up the situation best in an opening monologue from January 2016: "I saw that the White House joined Snapchat yesterday. It's a great platform for the White House because moments after you make a promise it magically disappears."

Whether the President has broken his word in regards to NAFTA may be a matter of interpretation, but nothing is uncertain about the significant role Congress played in advancement of the bill. By granting the President Trade Promotion Authority, often referred to as the "Fast-Track" Authority, the executive branch can now tailor entire trade accords for the next six years, with Congress only allowed to take an up or down vote—but not amend or filibuster. Members from both major parties offered necessary support.

Republicans led the way in both houses of the U.S. Congress to set the stage for a vote on this trade agreement that would form a trade bloc "with an annual gross domestic product of nearly $28 trillion that represents roughly 40 percent of global GDP and one-third of world trade." In the House of Representatives, 190 Republicans and 28 Democrats voted to extend the Trade Promotion Authority to President Obama; while in the Senate, 13 Democrats joined Republicans in approving the measure. There were only five lone Republican senators who voted against the rest of their party: Susan Collins (ME), Ted Cruz (TX), Rand Paul (KY), Jeff Sessions (AL), and Richard Shelby (AL).

Although those favoring the Trade Promotion Authority renewal ultimately proved successful, the victory did not come easily, especially in the House of Representatives, with a number of Democrats arguing against the measure. As far as the Senate, where voices of opposition were scarcer, Senator Elizabeth Warren of Massachusetts led the charge of resistance. Previous history has proven that this executive power to unilaterally negotiate is vital to reaching agreements, but Sen. Warren simply attempted to establish a greater check on granting such authority to presidents.

Instead of blindly offering the President this power, Senator Warren's "bill would [have required] the President to release the scrubbed bracketed text of any trade agreement at least 60 days before Congress grants fast-track authority." In introducing the bill, she argued, "The Trade Transparency Act would ensure that the public, experts, and the press can engage in meaningful debate over the terms of trade deals before Congress reduces its ability to shape, amend, or block those deals."

Democratic Senator Joe Manchin from West Virginia, who co-sponsored the bill, expressed similar sentiments: "If this bill is as good for the American worker as proponents have claimed, then the Administration should let the American worker see the details before Congress is forced to grant the President Trade Promotion Authority."

The progression of the TTP may be viewed by some as merely

resulting from the arguments of those opposed simply falling on deaf ears within the routine debate of a model republic. However, Pat Caddell, long-time political consultant and member of the "Political Insiders" on Fox News, offered his assessment in July 2015 of what he believes actually allowed the trade deal to become positioned for a majority vote for passage.

"You have well over in the eighty percentile of Americans who believe that the system is rigged against them uh [sic] by the special interest and the wealthy and uh [sic] we see that in both parties—it's across the board... Look we just had a trade deal in which the Republican leadership and [sic] was ordered by, and let me put it bluntly, the strings are pulled by the Chamber of Commerce and other big businesses to get in bed with Barack Obama who's also on with them and to produce an [sic] parliamentary gymnastics after it (Trade Promotion Authority) was defeated to bring it back to life because that was the order and that's who they serve because a majority of Americans in both parties oppose the trade deal. It was secret anyway. It was all being done in secret... The corruption is overwhelming and it is defiance and a [sic] basically an absolute contempt for the people by the political class in both parties, whether it's John Boehner and Mitch McConnell, or Obama with Harry Reid and Nancy Pelosi."

Placing any questions of predominant motivations aside, the degree of general secrecy within the process of negotiation is small in comparison to the apprehension of what the text of the accord actually contains. Beyond the "more than 130,000 jobs" the Economic Policy Institute "estimates will be lost to Vietnam and China alone," Heather Gautney of *The Huffington Post* further highlights the dangers of how TPP "also threatens Internet freedoms and civil liberties, collective bargaining rights, public and environmental health, food safety, financial stability—and American democracy."

Some of these threats come as a direct result of the governing bodies created within the international system. Senator Warren and others, including Senator Jeff Sessions (R-AL), have focused most of their attention on this aspect for derailing the plan.

In a letter to the President from May 2015, Senator Sessions, among other things, took aim at a "living agreement" provision in TPP that allows the agreement to be changed after adoption—in effect, vesting TPP countries with a sweeping new form of "global governance authority" comprised within the "Trans-Pacific Partnership Commission." Six months after the Trade Promotion Authority had been granted to the President and the provision remained, Senator

Sessions said it was "really breathtaking" and an "erosion of sovereignty" in an interview with Breitbart News on Sirius XM. Perhaps the most well-known power of concern lies within the arbitral tribunal for facilitating Investor-State Dispute Settlements, which allow corporations greater power in dictating regulatory practices freely launching lawsuits against foreign governments.

In relation to these Investor-State Dispute Settlements (ISDS) provisions, a group of legal scholars from some of America's most distinguished law schools joined the Honorable H. Lee Sarokin in composing a letter of concern to the leadership in D.C. In the letter, which centered on the question of why the U.S. legal system was not preferred, the group contrasted the replacement of "judges" who "must follow legal precedent" for that of "ISDS arbitral panels," which are not held to "precedential" standards; "public servants" of the "independent judiciary" offer reviewable decisions for "ISDS private arbitrators" that make "decisions [which] are functionally unreviewable."

How can any American, much less a legislator supposedly invested in the interests of the people, look at these provisions and not understand that it is a mere enhancement of more power and influence to Big Business? Of course, a number of congressmen are more than aware, gladly allowing greed and self-interest to undermine due process to all American citizens as the letter specifies.

> "ISDS provides a separate legal system available only to certain investors who are authorized to exit the American legal system. Only foreign investors may bring claims under ISDS provisions. The option is not offered to nations, domestic investors, or civil society groups alleging violations of treaty obligations. Under ISDS regimes, foreign investors are granted legal rights unavailable to others—freed from the ruling and procedures of domestic courts."

This undermining of legal protection afforded to all Americans by the Constitution clearly stacks the deck even further to corporate interests and establishes a perfect opportunity for utilizing this tool during an era marked by irresponsibility in leadership. This has already been evidenced by the lawsuits brought against the members of NAFTA.

A case from Canada offers one of best examples of the ISDS utilized to place the wishes of business over the needs of public safety. As the authors of the letter detailed, "In the third ISDS proceeding brought under NAFTA, Ethyl Corporation brought an ISDS proceeding against Canada for $251 million for implementing a ban on a toxic gasoline additive. The proceeding took place not in a court, but before an arbitration panel of the International Centre for the Settlement of Investment Disputes (ICSID). After the arbitration panel rejected Canada's argument that Ethyl lacked standing to bring the challenge, Canada settled the suit for $13 million. Moreover, Canada lifted the ban on [the] toxic additive as part of the settlement."

When reading about this successful lawsuit, one can't help but think of Flint, Michigan, where financial concerns seem to have also led to gross negligence for profit at the expense of the people. What would the outrage be if a similar lawsuit had been successfully argued by a foreign company responsible for managing the water supply? More importantly, how would those lawmakers who supported the passage of the trade agreement that opened the door to such abuses defend themselves against the people?

Despite the power within this system that was recognized by public watchdogs early in the process to be clearly contradictory to the rights and privileges guaranteed by the Constitution, this does not appear to have been the center of debate among members of Congress. For many Democrats, their support for granting the President the Promotion Authority revolved almost entirely around the inclusion of Trade Adjustment Assistance (TAA), a form of aid which has actually been around since the Kennedy administration. Jonathan Weisman detailed the benefits of TAA:

> "The bill extends assistance through June 2022, with an expansion of the program through June of 2021. That includes $2.7 billion in funds for worker retraining and education, while making workers in service industries eligible for a program once reserved for out-of-work manufacturing workers. The bill extends and expands tax credit for the purchase of health insurance, and it includes subsides for the wages of workers 50 years of age or older forced to find lower-paid jobs than the ones they lost to international competition."

This form of assistance serving as the bargaining chip for passage definitely plays into the argument that Democrats are always fine with building further dependency, but beyond the "more than 845,000 U.S. workers in the manufacturing sector [that have] been certified for Trade Adjustment Assistance (TAA) since NAFTA," it even threw in the service industry workers. In looking at the entire situation, Rep. Stephen Lynch (D-MA) summed up things best by saying, "I would rather have my representative fighting for my job than coming up with a public assistance program after I lost my job."

On a broader scale, although the American worker should not be punished with the loss of this protection from the poor policy decisions of those who represent them, these types of long-term extensions in benefits display one of the root causes of why the U.S. can never seem to begin proactively addressing the national debt. Future obligations from past failures in leadership is something that is consistent in legislatures nationwide.

Senator Orin Hatch (R-UT), chairman of the Senate Finance Committee, who singlehandedly killed the Trade Transparency Act offered by Elizabeth Warren and Joe Manchin, publically seems to have more concern for pharmaceutical companies than for the broader negative consequences these deals have always had on the American worker. In June 2015, during a debate over granting President Obama the Trade Promotion Authority, Rep. Luke Messer (R-IN) said, "I think Orin Hatch was the one who said TAA (Trade Adjustment Assistance) is the price to get TPA." To refer to protecting workers in America as some sort of "price" is more than disheartening. However, this statement seems in line with the narrow-minded approach Senator Hatch seems to be utilizing.

While the long-term Senator from Utah may not consider the drug patents having gone far enough, apparently the length of time is already enough for Doctors Without Borders to call TTP "the most damaging trade agreement we have ever seen in terms of access to medicines for poor people'—a response to leaded drafts of the deal, which [revealed] that it would grant pharmaceutical companies long-term monopolies on prescription drugs, thus dramatically driving up prices." Although drug patents are utilized to a degree for covering the enormous costs of innovation, attempts to resolve the concern should not be valued to such an extent that it overshadows the logic that places people before profit.

With how vital trade has been to Utah, one has to wonder if Senator Orin Hatch has been blinded by short-term profits. While NAFTA may have been bad for the American worker, the trade accord has been good for Utah and its estimated $7 to $8 billion in overall trade. As Doug Gibson of the *Standard Examiner* wrote in November 2015, "After the North American Free Trade Agreement was ratified in the early 1990s, the state's exports to Mexico rose from only $51 million in 1995 to $515 million in 2011. In the second quarter of 2013, exports to Mexico were tallied in Utah at $261 million."

No one should be so naïve as to disregard all the responsibilities, considerations, and pressures involved with each decision by a United States Senator—highlighted in *Profiles in Courage*, the 1957 Pulitzer-

Prize-winning book by then-Senator John F. Kennedy. One of those pressures is to discover the proper balance between state and national interests. However, when looking at the public deliberation by Orin Hatch in regards to the TPP, what Gary Hart wrote in his 2015 book comes to mind. In *The Republic of Conscience*, the former two-term U.S. Senator (D-CO) wrote, "Contrary to prevailing opinion in Washington's permanent professional political class, there is something called 'the national interest.' This is not a phrase from a political-science textbook. The national interest is tangible and it is real. It is separate from and superior to the conglomeration of special group interests that dominates our politics today."

Only time will tell whether TTP will become law through ratification. However, what is rather astonishing is that the party that presents itself as the one that protects the interests and well-being of the poor and middle class against the overriding power of Big Business has actually produced the presidents who have pushed to finalize the most extensive trade deals. Although lower prices in consumer products have resulted, many of the good-paying jobs for these groups have vanished. While President George H.W. Bush began the trade negotiations, President Clinton oversaw NAFTA. While President George W. Bush chose not to renegotiate NAFTA, President Obama has taken the aims a step forward in expanding upon it with TTP and TTIP.

Although the current administration may have its trade secretary, Michael Froman, publically come out as early as April 2014 and offer confirmation that the President was keeping the promise he made as a candidate to aggressively re-open NAFTA, Canada has remained consistent in their denial that TPP has ever served in this capacity. However, even if this is accepted as an attempt to keep his campaign promise, the accord reveals that Obama failed to protect the government from being sued by foreign countries with the Investor-State Dispute Settlements provisions remaining.

Just as Senator Hillary Clinton, in the 2008 Debate, said she would lead the government in "[taking] out the ability of foreign companies to sue," Laura Calsen, columnist for Foreign Policy In Focus, in 2009 used her coverage of a phone call from the White House to Mexican President Felipe Calderon to remind us that the President also made the same promise to "end the ability of corporations to sue governments."

Presidential motives aside, at a time when distrust in government has reached an all-time level, those delegated to represent the people have decided to hand over more power to the executive branch for unilaterally establishing trade agreements; agreements that if ratified will fundamentally change America. The Founders designed our government with checks and balances within the three branches of government as a hopeful deterrent.

If Congress regularly polls in the teens on job approval ratings and already displays a complete ineptness in service, why would any member of the legislature believe their constituency would want them to further diminish their power to check the executive branch? Why grant a president this "fast-track authority" for the next six years? How could this not be understood as merely offering another slap in the face of Americans who will only feel more alienated from their leaders? This is especially true when considering that President Obama regularly circumvents the general legislative process through consequential executive authority, much to the dismay of the majority.

As Elizabeth Warren said in her attempt to pass her Trade Transparency Bill, "Before Congress ties its hands on trade deals, the American people should be allowed to see for themselves whether these agreements are good for them." The long-term consequences in establishing a routine limitation of influence on trade within Congress could be fatal to the nation. However, for the typical politician in Washington who is clouded by appeasing special interest and Big Business to preserve political longevity, rarely is any great value placed on anything beyond securing the next election victory.

The results of not assessing the long-term ramifications of current trade policies could be devastating to America in terms of the economic and national security. The desire of the President and his advocates for advancing similar, flawed principles of free trade used with NAFTA goes well beyond the Trans-Pacific Partnership Trade Accord.

Many, if not all, of the exact same methods and ideology can be expected from the negotiations already underway with the European Union concerning the Transatlantic Trade and Investment Partnership (TTIP); a trade accord that if realized "would encompass a third of world trade and nearly half of global GDP." With the backdrop of the trade and global GDP the TPP would bring, this would mean that President Obama is attempting to almost singlehandedly lead America into trade deals that would, in effect, set the rules and standards for 90% of trade and two-thirds of the global GDP.

The negative effects of NAFTA would seem small in comparison to the extreme consequences this could foster. Groups within America, Canada, and Mexico are not alone in their fear of the inevitable repercussions. Sensing that the passage of the TTP might ultimately facilitate a resolution to finalizing the TTIP, "protestors organized by the Confederation of German Trade Union, known by its acronym DGB, worry that an agreement could lower food safety standards and undermine local regulations by giving international arbitration panels the power to rule over disputes." This group, as with the others opposed, realize that while it is true that any country can opt out of a trade accord with six months' notice, the politics surrounding the move would make the process slow (if it happened at all). As with their counterparts across the Atlantic, groups such as these also wonder why this conglomeration of concentrated power is necessary.

The better question for Americans should revolve around the timing of such a trade accord, especially when considering a May 2016 jobs report showed that only 38,000 new jobs were added to the economy. Although unsuccessful in his effort to thwart the Fast-Track Authority, Senator Jeff Sessions (in his previously mentioned interview with Breitbart) specifically addressed these employment concerns by saying, "They're not even asserting that it will create jobs in America, raise wages in America, or reduce trade deficits because these agreements in the past have been bad for all three."

At a time when America has the lowest participation level since the end of WWII, over 92 million people not working according the Bureau of Labor Statistics as of January 2015, more families on welfare, rising healthcare costs, additional obstacles for full-time employment as a result of the Affordable Care Act, stagnant wages, and a shrinking middle class, the government believes in basically taking the risk of placing all of the chips on the trade principles that have already lowered the stability of the economy and cost the American worker so much.

How could this be viewed as logical?

Following the same path to proven failures seems about as ill-advised as the allegedly fake story of a woman, who despite the unrealistic odds, was so convinced she would win the $1.6 billion Powerball jackpot from January 2015 that she was compelled to spend all of the money her family had on tickets. Although she was forced to set up a Go Fund Me page as a result of her loss, America would once again be left to look to the Chinese to further bankroll their poor judgment, despite the claims that at the center of this trade agreement is the desire to strengthen our economic check on the Chinese.

Statistics can be deceiving, especially in regards to the unemployment numbers, which do not account for those no longer seeking work. However, setting this reality aside, a report from February 2015 put the unemployment at "5.5%" and confirmed a year's worth of growth, but most of these additional jobs came from retail. Although reliable in providing the most new jobs each month, this does not go a long way in bringing Americans more sustainable levels of income, in that "retail tends to have a higher concentration of low-wage jobs than other sectors." A lower unemployment number throughout 2016 may have been heralded, but provided the same empty victory.

Then you have the insurance requirement of the Affordable Care Act, which results in many workers having to work two or three jobs to make ends meet—with full-time employment hard to secure from an employer anxious to dodge this additional monetary responsibility. In just considering these factors alone, one can understand how the statistics being celebrated at parties inside the Beltway are by no measure actually representative of what the American people are experiencing on the outside.

In an article from September 2015 entitled, "Anxiety pervasive in both parties," Cynthia Tucker wrote, "In mid-September, the U.S. Census Bureau issued its annual report on wages, poverty, and health insurance. Its findings come as no surprise: Though the official unemployment rate is down to its lowest level in seven years, the percentage of people living in poverty—around 14 percent—hasn't budged in four years." Yet none of these current obstacles kept Congress from using the end-of-the-year Omnibus Bill to "[quadruple] the number of low-skilled workers brought in under the [H-2B] program, ignoring the cries of Americans while doing the bidding of the K Street lobbyists."

Recall the Disney workers in 2015 who, from all reports, were forced to train their foreign replacements. Sara Blackwell is the attorney for those workers. In an interview, she highlighted the "1,200" Americans experiencing a similar fate in New York alone and summarized how costly the level of abuse within the program could be in the future for *Breitbart Daily News* by saying, "The purpose of H-1B is if there is no qualified American, then the H-1B person can come over and fill that position because we need them. Well, there are qualified Americans because they're being fired, but guess what, if this keeps going there aren't going to be any qualified Americans because we're training all our knowledge—sending it overseas and we're training all the H-1B workers here and we're not giving Americans the opportunity to make a decent wage or have a job so America has no future in technology, at this point."

Unfortunately, these workers only serve as a microcosm of the problems that extend across the country and stem directly from the H

-1B program, which brings in more foreigners for employment in technology. It is a practice that will only continue to grow as those in the heights of the American tech industry consistently push for more visas.

Rachel Maddow, a political commentator with her own weeknight show on MSNBC, served as the moderator for a Democratic Presidential forum in November of 2015. In asking Former Secretary of State Hillary Clinton about the influence of the tech industry, she perfectly captured the rationale of why most Americans should be concerned with general special interests and the endless revolving door in D.C.

> "I am freaked out by the influence, by the political influence of the tech industry has [sic] right now, particularly in the Democratic Party, because the Democratic Party is the more liberal of the two parties and I feel like if they're going to be captured by this hugely rich and powerful tech industry, I don't know who will ever stand up to them. And there is a big revolving door in the tech industry and the highest fliers in the Democratic Party: David Plouffe to Uber, Jay Carney to Amazon, Chris Lehane to Airbnb. You have speaking fees from companies like eBay, Qualcomm, and Salesforce.com, and I'm not saying any of those companies is a bad thing, but the tech industry you know rivals Wall Street in terms of money and influence. What is the protection that the American people have that those industries aren't just going to keep getting what they want, even when it hurts the rest of us, especially if the democrats are so in bed with them?"

The Democratic Presidential frontrunner responded by saying she supported a bill that was currently being proposed to help end the revolving door. Whether one is satisfied with her answer is irrelevant. What is of extreme significance to recognize is that beyond the various political motives of individuals involved in setting our national policy, the characteristics of the process itself should be of equal concern.

It seems to have become a common theme that in all the major decisions on extensive measures that will fundamentally affect the American people, the government has relied almost entirely on producing the minimum amount of timely transparency, while at the same time demeaning the democratic process with methods that shortchange adequate representation of the people. Beyond the executive orders and actions of the President over the last 7 years, this pattern is similar to the process that has led us to the brink of drastically overhauling trade. Even if you are still convinced that creating one governing body to correspond with a uniform set of free trade rules across the world is a worthwhile endeavor, a brief examination of some of the results of placing limitations on the role of representation in the process is vital to understand.

One of the greatest examples may be the money that was flooded back into the market by the Federal Reserve following the Great Recession. Michael Gray of *The Washington Post* describes the years from 2008 to 2015 as the "Great Fleecing," based on the unprecedented transfer of "some $4.5 trillion [being] given to Wall Street banks through its Quantitative Easing Program, with the American people picking up the IOU."

In his article entitled "Obama orchestrated the massive transfer to the 1 percent" from this past January (2015), he goes on to describe the results to the middle class, which basically got left out of the equation. "The Obama administration is the first two-term presidency that has not posted a 3% GDP growth on an annualized basis for 8 years"; he goes on to describe the environment created for the sector of the population so often disregarded. "The middle class has seen the wholesale export of good-paying jobs, while on the hook for crushing mortgages and higher taxes to pay down the growing U.S. debt to fund the banks." Somehow, there is actually a debate going on among our representatives about whether or not it is an ideal time for additional competition from low-wage foreign workers to maximize corporate profits.

A vote on TTP will likely come at a time of little growth, as "the gross domestic product sputtered to grow only 0.7 percent in the fourth quarter of 2015." Originally, most assumed that it would come in the spring or summer of 2016, but a weak economy, inner party fighting, and opposition from the GOP nominee Donald J. Trump might ultimately delay the attempt at passage until after the 2016 elections.

President Obama entered office committed to the policy initiatives of healthcare and climate change. The healthcare debate may hold no greater lasting characteristic than Nancy Pelosi's infamous, "We have to pass the bill so that you can find out what is in it." Whether her words were actually misinterpreted does not change the reality that the bill was rammed down the throats of the American people. The Affordable Care Act that resulted, much like almost all other government-run programs, has not come close to living up to the expectations of its advocates. A majority of the state-run Obamacare exchanges have closed, expansion of Medicaid within states has added additional budgeting uncertainties, doubling or tripling of premiums has occurred, and heightened difficulties in obtaining full-time employment have remained. However, as if the employment picture wasn't damaged enough through uncertainty, the Obama administration decided to unilaterally add an additional set of regulations through the use of the Environmental Protection Agency (EPA) to further compound overregulation.

Regardless of previous actions taken by the EPA, nothing in terms of climate change commitments compares to the Paris climate accord signed in December 2015. This "landmark" climate accord was literally cheered on by members of the press corps through enthusiastic jumps and shouts of acclamation. If enacted, the result would be a new level of extensive and crushing controls, regulations, taxes, and fees on American businesses, while China would be allowed to wait five years to implement the agreement.

Although Congress will likely never approve the additional pledge to provide the most foreign aid to developing countries for these environmental aims, President Obama can only be stopped by lawsuits from advancing his domestic measures. Even though the Supreme Court temporarily blocked the Obama administration from implementing regulations on carbon emissions through the E.P.A., Chief Justice Roberts chose only a month later not to grant a similar stay on the devastating mercury pollution standards.

Just as with healthcare, the successful goal of moving forward on climate concerns lacked transparency and made a complete mockery of our representation. It didn't seem to matter that in both instances a majority of the American people rejected these policies. Neither addressed the immediate need of stabilizing the economy, but instead only added more obstacles for growth that would facilitate a genuine recovery.

While a staggering economy and the rising cost of healthcare have increased the national debt and lead us further down the road of unsustainability, nothing may prove more consequential to our long-term national security than the Iran Nuclear Deal. In reaching the agreement, the Obama administration was once again given an advantage through a set of parliamentary procedures that helped circumvent any significant influence the people's representatives might have had in the process.

As a result of the negotiations, the Iranians agreed to, among other things, send most of their uranium to Russia, remove centrifuges, and allow for heightened inspections in exchange for a lifting of oil and financial sanctions that would free up over $100 billion in frozen assets. However, the United States also decided to pay Iran $1.3 billion and 400 million in debt to settle a dispute that stemmed from an ongoing 1979 dispute, despite "Republican lawmakers saying Iran owes $46 billion to American victims of the Beirut bombing and a range of suicide attacks in Israel and elsewhere."

This additional $1.7 billion unilaterally decided upon by the Obama administration without the approval of congressional lawmakers also coincided with the release of American hostages (although Iran still denied specifically paying the $1.75 billion a U.S. court had ordered them to pay in regards to the Beirut bombing alone). Regardless, the Obama administration denied that this payment had anything to do with the hostage release and also openly rationalized that future legal proceedings could ultimately cost billions more than the reached settlement.

While the House of Representatives attempted to bring restitution to families in the United States before any money could be given to Iran through the successful passage of the Justice for Victims of Iranian Terrorism Act, it had little support from Democrats, with some articulating the mindboggling notion that Iran needed the money from the nuclear deal to even be able to possibly pay the victims. The idea that the Iranians may consider the need to provide restitution to these families they have denied since the Beirut bombing because of having more money is about as plausible as the additional money from the White House not being a bribe for the release of hostages.

While every American celebrates their return, the truth is important in analyzing future foreign implications. However, in this case, the point is moot, as the bill never made it out of committee in the Senate, with an uphill battle against the Democrats that had already filibustered to preserve the Iran Deal for the President early in 2015. Fortunately for the families of the victims of the Beirut bombing and other terrorist attacks at the hands of Iran, the Supreme Court, in April 2016, upheld the Iran Threat Reduction and Syria Human Rights Act passed by Congress in 2012. This law directs around 2 billion dollars of frozen Iran assets to finally be distributed to the victims.

Whether the Iran deal ultimately results in countless American lives being put at risk in the future, we could potentially already be seeing threats as a result of ambiguities in resolve and discipline that have emboldened our enemies. While some may use the broad strokes of diplomacy for describing the recent hostage trade for five Americans, as well as the controversial one involving Bowe Berdahl, even the hint of money playing a factor in the outcome is damaging. While America now allows families to negotiate with terrorists without fear of prosecution, it has always maintained a policy that it will not negotiate with terrorists out of the fear of opening up a Pandora's box involving kidnappings. Those fears may have been confirmed with not only a college student being taken by officials in North Korea, but three Americans also disappearing in Iraq.

Following the hostage exchange, the Iraqi defense minister pointed to an abduction of Americans as being the work of an "organized gang that carries out abductions for blackmail." Unfortunately, he was right, with the "Iraqi Intelligence and U.S. government officials [confirming] the Iranian-backed Shi'ite militia was responsible."

Of course, more abductions from emboldened enemies was something almost everyone knew could happen, including those in the highest levels of our government. Current Secretary of State John Kerry appeared on "Morning Joe" following the sanctions formally being lifted on Iran. Although Secretary Kerry spent some of his time clarifying that more like $55 billion was being released to the Iranians, what was more telling was that he seemed to believe that he could provide a sense of confidence in the deal by saying the government could track the money for safeguarding against abuse. This is the same government that fails to root out the waste and inefficiencies from within. Now it would suddenly discover some new level of accountability? That seems very naïve and improbable.

Despite his initial words, Kerry admitted less than a week later that some of the money would most likely go toward terrorism. His prognostication seems to have come true quicker than the detractors even thought possible. While the Americans taken in Iraq were ultimately returned safe and sound, it could just be the beginning with future outcomes not being as small in scale or without great human sacrifice. The Iranians have already chosen to funnel some of their money toward terrorism, as they continue to take advantage of the similar desperation shown by U.S. officials in obtaining the agreement.

A probe was even launched into whether the Obama administration misled Congress in securing the deal, with reports surfacing in late March 2016 that said the White House was planning to open the U.S. financial system to Iran, despite originally saying it would not. This newfound scrutiny only gained steam in May 2016, with the revelation from President Obama's Deputy National Security Advisor Ben Rhodes that a "narrative" was sold through primarily a young, gullible, and unknowledgeable set of reporters. Only a month before this telling article, the Obama administration had decided unilaterally to help Iran fulfill its part of the agreement by purchasing "32 metric tons of heavy water, a key component of nuclear reactors" at around

$9 million. Putting this move all on the administration might be unfair when considering some Democrats might believe this will finally give Iran more than enough money to pay off American victims of world terror. The lack of common sense is truly baffling.

Then there are Iran's numerous provocations that would more than signal to almost anyone that whatever was agreed upon means nothing to them. Their launching of ballistic missiles in October 2015 looked to violate two United Nations Security Council Resolutions until we learned it was acceptable, as the agreement wasn't legally binding. Add to that the December 2015 firing of rockets toward U.S. ships in the Persian Gulf. However, maybe the most disturbing was in January 2016 when ten U.S. Navy soldiers were taken into custody after mysteriously entering into Iranian waters because of alleged mechanical problems on one of the two boats.

While it may be understandable how the PT boat under John F. Kennedy's command could have easily drifted unknowingly into a Japanese destroyer in 1943, questions must be asked as to how this could happen with today's technology. Despite U.S. officials downplaying how much was actually taken, it does not take away from the fact that the Iranians had full access to scour the boat for the newest strides in technology.

This latest incident involving American sailors actually makes twice that Iran has had their hands on U.S. military possessions, when recounting the drone that was initially reported as being shot down in Iran. Later, it was clarified that Iran's cyberwarfare unit "commandeered the aircraft and safely landed it." More importantly, in the broader scheme of things, one can't help but think about the revelation that also came from January 2016, when it was confirmed that a hellfire missile was sitting in Cuba after mysteriously being lost from an earlier routine training exercise in Europe.

Although eventually returned to the United States, this missile type just happens to contain the advanced technology that could be used with a drone; apparently, there's no need for concern, as "misshipments happen all the time because of the amount of volume of the defense trade," a State Department official said, according to the *Wall Street Journal*. Of course, never to shy away from following the lead of the Commander-in-Chief in attempting to pass the buck to someone else, at least one "U.S. official told the Associated Press the government is blaming the manufacturer Lockheed-Martin's freight forwarders." The lackadaisical culture that permeates from these type stories makes one wonder if anyone within the State Department was able to move beyond the overwhelming aim of avoiding criticism to offer adequate attention to the genuine threat an Iranian drone could have posed when it flew over a U.S. aircraft carrier positioned in the Persian Gulf in January 2016. It seems highly doubtful that anyone could.

As Israeli Prime Minister Benjamin Netanyahu said this past July (2015) when negotiations on the Iran deal were ongoing, "I would like to say here and now—when you are willing to make an agreement at any cost, this is the result." Clearly, instances of carelessness with technology have given an emboldened Iran the capabilities to strike.

One additional source of technology may have been discovered within the controversial, unsecured emails of former Secretary of State Hillary Clinton that are known to have contained "beyond top secret" information that include drone technology. Terrorists who are hell-bent on destroying America could also seek the services of one of al-Qaida's most skilled bomb experts, who was released from Gitmo in January 2016. Despite some detainees returning to the battlefield and actually resulting in the needless deaths of Americans, the White House once again unilaterally decided to release him.

Taking directly from the executive summary found within the "Recommendation for Transfer" form released by the Department of Defense, Tariq Mahmoud Ahmed al Sawah "is an admitted member of al-Qaida who developed specialized improvised explosive devices (IEDs) for use against U.S. military forces and civilians. The IEDs included the limpet mine to sink U.S. naval vessels and the prototype for the shoe-bomb used in a failed attack on a civilian transatlantic flight. Prior to detention, detainee admitted teaching explosives at the al-Qaida advanced training camp at Tamak Farm, aka (Abu Ubaydah Camp), where Usama Bin Laden (UBL) personally praised detainee for his 'good work.' Detainee is associated with numerous explosives experts including some who remain at large. Detainee also associated with the planners and perpetrators of international terrorist attacks and other senior al-Qaida members, and may have had advanced knowledge of the 11 September 2001 attacks. Detainee participated in hostilities against U.S. and Coalition forces, and is a veteran extremist combatant." It's obvious the chance for ever creating an incentive for future accountability is lost forever.

Despite the implications of negative outcomes that have become commonplace with the unilateral policy decisions of the Obama administration, much of the liberal press and a majority of Democrats will maintain a zombie-like state in falling lockstep behind the agenda. Very little can actually cause either party on Capitol Hill to place the people over their party and is why most Americans consistently reject the leadership in Washington. Having a set of core principles is one thing, but lacking an ability to offer any pragmatism is another—and is unhealthy for democracy. This commitment to party unison at all costs is why many knew the Justice for Victims of Iranian Terrorism Act (mentioned earlier) would not garner the support of the Democrats, with gov.track.us actually listing it with "a 2% chance of passage."

This percentage isn't much lower than the 11% of the time that most Americans attributed to congressmen actually choosing to place an emphasis on what the voters are saying when setting trade policy. From the Rasmussen national telephone survey, 43% chose "whoever makes the biggest contribution"; and 30% chose "business leaders" when specifically asked, "Who do politicians listen to the most on trade issues?" It is clear the American people realize that the overriding themes of partisan politics and special interests drive the policies of our lawmakers, allowing them, in terms of trade, to disregard the American worker and reward more power to Big Business that supplies hundreds of millions of dollars in lobbying and campaign contributions.

Most of the 2016 presidential field is opposed to the Trans-Pacific Partnership Trade Accord out of policy differences or concerns revolving around the leadership in Washington. Donald Trump and Bernie Sanders have been the most vocal candidates in opposition, ironically displaying just one of the ways different candidates are actually similar in the populist theme they project for garnering supporters.

In a statement to Breitbart in October 2015, Donald Trump asked, "Why are we striking trade agreements with countries we already have agreements with? Why is there no effort to make sure we have fair trade instead of 'free trade' that isn't free to Americans? Why do we not have accompanying legislation that will punish countries that manipulate their currencies to seek unfair advantage in trade arrangements? Why has the Congress not addressed prohibitive corporate tax rates and trade agreements that continue to drain dollars and jobs from America's shores?" Although consideration for these basic questions seem like they would be standard for any trade agreement, very few in Washington seem to have gone beyond the Big Business and special interests they serve to have placed much emphasis on such questions for the good of the people.

Although the elimination of thousands of tariffs was presented by the President as one of the major achievements of the deal, Heather

Gautney, associate professor of sociology at Fordham University and senior researcher for the Bernie Sanders campaign, offered a different perspective in February 2015. In an article for *The Huffington Post*, she wrote, "Economists vary widely in their assessments of the TPP, but there's general agreement across ideological stripes that tariffs are already low. In fact, some reports claim that only five of the 29 draft chapters in the agreement actually relate to lowering tariffs." Her work coincides with the findings of Don Lee, a reporter for the *Los Angeles Times*, who informed us that among the countries involved in TPP "a provision on enforceable currency rules was not seriously considered in negotiations."

It seems that despite all their claims, American leaders are about as committed to placing a check on the Chinese for influencing the market with this trade deal as they are for actually addressing the national debt which landed the Chinese power to begin with. The Chinese are simply opportunistic and rely on U.S. lawmakers to continue producing trade policies that display no true emphasis in correcting past behavior; feeling confident that they will not be losing this advantage. Imagine where the U.S. could currently be if the leadership in D.C. had remained as steadfast in solving the national debt as they have been in consistently blaming the Chinese for decades of hardships.

When asked to provide details of how he could take the middle class to new heights in June 2015 by co-host Mika Brzezinski during an appearance on "Morning Joe," the current Republican presidential frontrunner Donald Trump began his response by simply saying, without hesitation, "The biggest thing we have to do is new trade agreements." He advanced his ideas on correcting trade during the sixth Republican debate almost seven months later when he pointed to placing a 45% tariff on Chinese goods coming into the country to put an end to their practice of devaluing their currency.

His words were denounced.

In defending against criticism from others at the debate to his idea, Donald Trump said, "They do whatever what they do, okay. When we do business with China, they tax us. You don't know it, they tax us." He went on to say, "I'm saying, absolutely, we don't have to continue to lose 505 billion dollars as a trade deficit for the privilege of dealing with China." Although other candidates joined one of the moderators in implying that it would simply lead to higher prices being passed on to the American consumer if enacted, an iconic Republican may have proved otherwise.

In a 2008 piece for *The New York Times* entitled "The venerable history of protectionism, Robert E. Lihgthizer wrote, "Reagan often broke with free-trade dogma. He arranged for voluntary restraint agreements to limit imports of automobiles and steel (an industry whose interests, by the way, I have represented). He provided temporary import relief for Harley-Davidson. He limited imports of sugar and textiles. His administration pushed for the 'Plaza accord' of 1985, an agreement that made Japanese imports more expensive by raising the value of the yen." More importantly, Lighthizer, a former deputy trade representative for President Reagan, went on to write, "Each of these measures prompted vociferous criticism from free traders. But they worked. By the early 1990s, doubts about Americans' ability to compete had been impressively reduced."

Reagan clearly understood there should be flexibility within trade policies to implement some form of protectionism (if necessary). Yet many, including Republicans, are convinced that a strict adherence to free trade is actually the best policy to follow with more demands from further globalization. Although some jobs are lost as a result, the consistent advantage offered by those in favor of free trade is that overall it benefits everyone. Lower prices on consumer products are usually the anchors of this argument.

Various articles in favor of free trade have been written in 2016 alone. Rick Newman of Yahoo Finance argued that the trade deficits often referred to are actually not hurting the economy when compared to the world stage and should be taken lightly when considering that they account for only a small portion of the U.S. GDP. Ben Casselman, chief economics writer for *FiveThirtyEight*, argued that many of the manufacturing jobs that have been lost overseas are actually never coming back. Chelsea German, managing editor for HumanProgress.org, addressed the popular concerns of those against free trade. From the actual advantage of Chinese currency manipulation to how "comparative advantage" and "specialization" keep both countries, in all reality, from competing for the same jobs, the arguments she makes are thought-provoking and compelling.

However, among all those presenting the argument for the benefits of free trade, Daniel R. Pearson, a senior fellow at the Cato Institute, offers the most unique assessment. He doesn't believe the approach of using an anti-dumping and countervailing duty (AD/CVD) would be the strategy for success. In considering a number of factors, which include those U.S. companies that actually continue to benefit from cheap steel, he believes in flipping the script entirely on any arguments of imposing tariffs. Instead, Pearson advocates for an encouragement of the Chinese to send more, arguing this will chiefly lead them to re-evaluate and eventually cutback on production.

An underlying factor behind his logic is that regardless of the remedy, the U.S. can't tariff its way out of a world market where cheap steel can always be found. Pearson concludes, "The optimal policy response would be to reform U.S. trade remedy statues by adding a new requirement: AD/CVD duties only should be imposed if economic analysis indicates that doing so would increase economic welfare in this country."

Even if these writers are correct in their assessments, it would not change the underlying need to address the formulation and composition of trade deals moving forward. There should be recognition that there are some areas in which interaction is justified, even within a limited government; the lack of regulations within Wall Street should have proven this. Just as with government and the free market, there is a proper balance to be found within free trade and protectionism.

Trusting the current leadership in D.C., which lacks an adequate degree of representation and is owned by special interests, is unwise. Their answer has been, unsurprisingly, an attempt to make the debate an all-or-nothing choice that pens America into another free-trade deal tailored after the similar principles of NAFTA. A deal that resulted in the loss of "over 5 million manufacturing jobs since 2000."

An inequality in representation has led to an inequality in both foreign and domestic policies. Only when the people have reasserted more fairness in representation should any trade accord be considered, especially in regards to those on a massive scale. To move forward under the current circumstances could be disastrous for generations.

When will our leaders understand that if they desire to move the country in a profound direction, whether it is in regards to foreign or domestic policy, such a move requires a foundation of trust, accountability, and achievement to create the appropriate environment for embracing and facilitating it with confidence and optimism?

If our leaders desire for America to lead the world on renewable energy and climate change, then they should create a strong economy conducive to achieving it, which certainly doesn't begin by promising jobs and then using the 2009 stimulus to "set aside $80 billion to subsidize politically preferred energy projects"; a move that resulted in numerous failures and, as of 2012, close to 600 convictions from almost 2,000 investigations launched to investigate the predictable misuse of the stimulus funds.

Similarly, if there is a hope to lead the country into trade deals, then first we need to create an environment conducive to it through a strong economy that can compete with business-friendly taxation and regulation, especially in terms of easing the burdens on entrepreneurs and small businesses. Leaders certainly don't add an additional burden of regulation and attempt to sign another trade deal based on principles of the past that have consistently led to massive trade deficits and extreme loss of jobs in America. This is especially true if the hope is to lead America into a massive trade deal that could encompass almost half, if not two-thirds, of the world's Gross Domestic Product (GDP).

Any American president, regardless of party affiliation, should realize that the people he or she represents deserve to see that the government can actually bring positive results from negotiating small trade deals for some sense of trust before even attempting to enter into an extensive trade endeavor—one that would fundamentally change the world economy. However, as Jeff Sessions (R-AL) indicated in his letter to the White House over his concern for TPP, the most recent record lacks such achievements for any justified trust.

In the letter from May 2015, the Republican Senator from Alabama wrote, "The U.S. ran a record $51.4 billion trade deficit in March, the highest-level recorded in six years. This is especially troubling since assurances were made from the Administration that the recent South Korea free-trade deal would 'increase exports of American goods by $10 billion to $11 billion.' But, in fact, American domestic exports to Korea increased by only $0.8 billion, an increase of 1.8 percent, while imports from Korea increased $12.6 billion, an increase of 22.5 percent. Our trade deficit with Korea increased 11.8 billion between 2011 and 2014, an increase of 80.4 percent, nearly doubling in the three years since the deal was ratified." While those empty promises have been costly, imagine what the consequences could be with TPP and TTIP?

How long can the American people allow the current system to produce the same characteristics in leadership to their detriment? It is a political system that centers entirely on money and is built on (and protected) by career politicians, seniority leadership, substantial lobbying power, and the predominant motivation of self-interest. This atmosphere results in rewards for a few, while the rest of the people are left to decide between the less of two evils on almost every issue, including those of significance.

Representation within such an environment is merely a façade that is insulated with a lack of transparency for genuine accountability, but those who lead under this guise still desire for others to willingly follow them into trade. In specific regards to trade, globalization demands aggressive action as countries like China continue to expand their influence through all means, including their governmental support of "economic espionage" which "cost U.S. corporations hundreds of billions of dollars and more than two million jobs." However, Americans should never be forced into accepting a deal that has been forged at the expense of some of the fundamental rights and principles that the Founders established and countless men and women have fought and died to protect.

What can't be lost among the chaos of the times is what has been accomplished in the past by the American people when they chose to come together. The common purpose should now be to rein in the government. Unity across party lines will produce a golden opportunity for the people to re-establish their ownership of the country by creating a degree of representation that can establish a new and genuine political arena. Unity will drive a newfound debate and dialogue that can foster more equality in policies. Maybe then the country can move forward on decisions that face the nation, such as trade policy, and have a body of leaders who can produce a set of deals that will provide a greater chance in reaching what is actually best for America.

Policies might contain some degree of common sense, such as found in the words of Charles Evers in relation to trade. The 93-year-old brother of iconic civil rights leader Medgar Evers, who was tragically struck down outside his home in 1963 and the "first black mayor of a Mississippi town or city since reconstruction," simply stated in March 2016: "Our catfish is shipped to China and brought back for us to buy. Put a catfish farm here."

If President Kennedy had not pushed those around him for more options during the Cuban Missile Crisis that led to his decision for a blockade, one of the more aggressive options may have resulted in the destruction of the world. He had learned from the failure of the Bay of Pigs never to allow others to force him into a bad decision by convincing him to go against his better judgment and accept what was presented. It may be a slower decline, but unless the American people come together to demand more accountability and efficiency from our leaders, a similar tragic fate is just as certain.

In *America the Beautiful: Rediscovering What Makes America Great*, Ben Carson demonstrated how traits of common sense can be found to a degree in some of the most complicated of issues when people are truly striving for answers without all the other variables that blind judgment.

> "A friend of mine who lives in Connecticut is a self-made multimillionaire who owns many businesses and has a very keen

business mind. In order to instantly create many more jobs in the United States, he has proposed that we place a stiff tariff on products that are manufactured in other countries and are shipped here fully assembled, while reducing tariffs on products that will require assembly once they reach our shores. In order to assemble the latter group of products, many workers would have to be hired. Given the severe trade balance that we are already experiencing, such a policy would have a dramatic impact on the American job market."

One can only imagine how politicians, political pundits, and the mainstream media must have scoffed at such a simplistic idea. It's impossible to estimate the number of needless pages that would be written around the idea for accomplishing nothing more than self-interest. Of course, Senator Jeff Sessions (R-AL) may provide some insight into how many pages it may take from his November 2015 tweet of the stacked pages of the TPP on his desk with the description, "Photo of 5,554pg TPP on Sessions' desk. B/C of Fast-Track, it can't be filibustered, amended or given a treaty vote." The American people deserve better; they can obtain it by coming together.

Those Who Govern

There are only a few who will be given the privilege of serving in the most powerful position in the world. Upon being elected, each must swear to "faithfully execute the Office of President of the United States, and will to the best of their ability, preserve, protect and defend the Constitution of the United States." This is understood to extend the "against all enemies, foreign and domestic" wording specifically included within the oath of office taken by federal employees, military personnel, and the Vice President.

In what some cite as the real reason that John F. Kennedy was assassinated, he delivered a speech to the American Newspaper Publishers Association shortly before his death and spoke about the magnitude of threats the nation faced. In his speech, President Kennedy emphasized the vital role the media must play in safeguarding against such forces by utilizing their unique protection to faithfully keep the public well informed.

> "For we are opposed around the world by a monolithic and ruthless conspiracy that relies primarily on covert means for expanding its sphere of influence—on infiltration instead of invasion, on subversion instead of elections, on intimidation instead of free choice, on guerrilla by night instead of armies by day. It is a system which has conscripted vast human and material resources into the building of a tightly knit, highly efficient machine that combines military, diplomatic, intelligence, economic, scientific and political operations. Its preparations are concealed, not published. Its mistakes are buried, not headlined. Its dissenters are silenced, not praised. No expenditure is questioned, no rumor is printed, no secret is revealed. It conducts the Cold War, in short, with a war-time discipline no democracy would ever hope or wish to match."

Some people believe that President Kennedy was talking about forces of opposition well beyond Communism. They are convinced that he was also addressing secret societies such as the Illuminati—a small group of powerful individuals who are believed to actually control the world through successful infiltration of every influential sector of society, from government to entertainment. Other conspiracy theorists specifically point to organizations (such as the Bohemian Club, Skull and Bones, and the Carlyle Group) that utilize similar methods to form a culpable relationship among business, government, and the media—influencing everything from the stock market to when, where, and by whom wars will be fought. If you were to ask anyone who believes in the overwhelming power of these groups, they would emphatically tell you that one, if not all, played a role in the death of President Kennedy that fateful day in Dallas; his warnings simply too dangerous to their ultimate plans of establishing a new world order.

There are others who say that President Kennedy fell at the hands of the mob, believing the death had been orchestrated as sheer retaliation for the relentless pursuit of them by his bother Bobby Kennedy, in his role as the Attorney General. And finally, there are broader reasons such as the preservation of power within the Federal Reserve that some believe Kennedy's Executive Order 11110 was aimed at reining in, which would have been just as influential to history as those that view the war in Vietnam being in doubt had he been allowed to live. They believe President Kennedy posed a risk to a group of individuals who already had financial stakes in both (specifically in the case of Vietnam). Many scholars agree the President clearly demonstrated through private conversations and definite actions that he had no intention of allowing such an escalation.

While the debate will go on forever, most likely without any definite answer, what can be certain is that there was then and will always be powerful forces that often work behind the scenes to distort the tenants of legitimate democracy for their own self-interest. When combined with the general greed that clearly drives our current political system, it is clear the nation needs a president who is committed to establishing a foundation of transparency within the Oval Office that will set the tone for the rest of those involved in government. This role should be embraced and valued, as President Kennedy so eloquently alluded to in his speech.

> "No President should fear public scrutiny of his program. For from that scrutiny comes understanding; and from that understanding comes support or opposition. And both are necessary. I am not asking your newspapers to support the Administra-

tion, but I am asking your help in the tremendous task of informing and alerting the American people. For I have complete confidence in the response and dedication of our citizens whenever they are fully informed. I not only could not stifle controversy among your readers—I welcome it. This Administration intends to be candid about its errors; for as a wise man once said: 'An error does not become a mistake until you refuse to correct it.' We intend to accept full responsibility for our errors; and we expect you to point them out when we miss them."

It should be of little surprise that President Kennedy felt this way about the attributes of genuine debate a degree of openness would bring. He always welcomed a diversity of opinions within the decision-making process that led his administration. Unfortunately, not all presidents have felt the same, with the current president quite possibly being among the worst in possessing such a commitment to transparency.

Kirsten Powers, a well-respected columnist and frequent Fox News contributor, in her book *The Silencing: How the Left is Killing Free Speech*, writes, "By the end of 2013, dozens of America's leading news organizations had become so frustrated they signed a letter hand-delivered to then-Press Secretary Jay Carney to complain about 'limits on press access' so pervasive as to 'raise constitutional concerns.' The letter signed by outlets such as ABC, CBS, NBC, Bloomberg, CNN, Fox News, Reuters, and thirty others said in part, 'Journalists are routinely being denied the right to photograph or videotape the President while he is performing his official duties.'" Clearly the Obama administration has not produced the unprecedented level of transparency he promised.

Though troubling, the current administration is not unique in recent memory for drawing the condemnation of the media for what was viewed as an attempt to deny the press legitimate access. Beyond the typical tradeoffs for greater access that unfortunately have occurred to a degree with every administration, Carl Pope and Paul Rauber utilized their book, *Strategic Ignorance: Why the Bush Administration is Recklessly Destroying a Century of Environmental Progress*, to specifically discuss how they believed the Bush administration had gone well beyond these practices. They contend what resulted was a decline in the valuable candidness that had been created through legislative measures of the 60s and 70s. In documenting some of how widespread the response of the media had been to the Bush endeavor, the authors wrote, "Not everyone is going along quietly with the return to secret government. Many newspapers, including *The New York Times*,

Seattle Post-Intelligencer, and Atlanta Journal Constitution all editorialized against it."

However, when specifically asked to compare our last two presidents on degree of transparency, AP Washington Bureau Chief Sally Buzzbee, at a gathering of journalists, said, "The (Obama) administration is significantly worse than previous administrations." Much of what led her to this conclusion certainly revolved around the manner with which reporters were routinely bullied by the Obama administration, something she described as "extremely chilling." The claims she makes have been corroborated by a number of reporters, which included a warning Bob Woodward detailed from a "senior advisor" in the White House regarding his criticism of President Obama on the subject of sequestration. Woodward told host Wolf Blitzer on CNN in a February 2013 interview that the email "said very clearly, you will regret doing this." In that same interview, the legendary reporter went on to say, "It makes me very uncomfortable to have the White House telling reporters, you're going to regret doing something that you believe in."

Though there have been clear lapses of judgment by other former presidents, from the personal indiscretions of Kennedy and Clinton to the policy cover-ups of Nixon with Watergate and Reagan with the Iran Contra, the words of Bob Woodward provide a clear contrast to the debate welcomed by President Kennedy almost forty years before either of the last two presidents would assume office. Though there could be a debate as to whether the media of today would have ended the presidency of John F. Kennedy based on lapses of judgment within his private life, it does not take away from the words of wisdom he offered concerning the role of the media; just as it does not diminish his level of brilliance or passion that will continue to inspire generations. While a commitment to greater transparency is vital to maintaining an appropriate degree of accountability, the question of what fundamentally guides an administration should receive the most scrutiny. As Joe Scarborough, a former congressman from Florida and current co-host of "Morning Joe," noted, "Across the spectrum, money changed votes. Money certainly drove policy at the White House during the Clinton administration, and I'm sure it has in every other administration too."

As Mike Needham and Jim DeMint cited in a 2014 piece from the *Weekly Standard* entitled "The Crony Capital: Capitalism, Washington, D.C., style":

"President Obama's stimulus package, supposedly passed to

address unemployment, functioned primarily to line the pockets of well-connected unions and firms like Solyndra rather than to build a foundation for a broad based recovery."

Beyond the "38 billion in tax breaks and subsidies" that Carl Pope and Paul Rauber also highlighted in *Strategic Ignorance* as going in large part to some of the most influential members of industry who contributed to George W. Bush's campaign for the White House, a 2012 article from Scott Horton of *Harper's* demonstrated the profound effect political favors truly have on the country. The consequences he writes about are rooted in money and, in the case of former President George W. Bush, are centered on the work of his senior advisor, Karl Rove.

The main intent behind writing "Boss Rove's Justice" was actually to draw a clear connection between the successful prosecutions of former Alabama Governor Don Siegelman on corruption charges to the work of Mark. E. Fuller, the man who played a heavy hand in the outcome; someone who has actively supported and benefited from the Republican Party. As part of his argument, Scott Horton documented information to support his belief that much of this partisan direction comes from similar scheming at the top. He wrote, "Though it may be distasteful, the appointment of campaign donors to high offices belongs to the rough-and-tumble of American electoral politics. Karl Rove is the undisputed master of this practice; under his Pioneer and Ranger programs, donors who could raise or bundle $100,000 or $200,000 for the campaign were entitled to special benefits. According to Texans for Public Justice, 146 of the 548 Bush Pioneers and Rangers received political appointments within the administration."

Beyond specifically alluding to President Obama's ambassadorial appointments, which Mary Bruce of ABC News concluded required raising "upwards of a half a million dollars" to receive, as just one method in which the Democrats are just as guilty of such preferential practices, Scott Horton more importantly utilized his article to emphasize, "The Justice Department never lifted the covers to examine any of these appointments. There was a reason for that: the upper echelons of the Justice Department itself are populated with political players who raise campaign cash for the party of their choice."

During his run for president, Senator Marco Rubio said in one of his nationally televised political ads from February 2016, "Washington is broken and both parties are to blame, but it will never get better if we keep sending people to Washington who will say or do anything to get elected. It's time for a president who will stand up to runaway government and fight Washington special interests in both parties." Although the country will always be about more than one individual, there is also a limit to the amount of positive influence that can be brought singlehandedly to the culture of Washington. However, the President can be uniquely instrumental in persuading others to move. Average American citizens across the country are hoping for such a leader to emerge.

Ted Cruz added to this broad frustration during a speech from the Senate floor in July 2015 by saying, "You know who doesn't have lobbyists? A single mom waiting tables. You know who doesn't have lobbyists? A teenage immigrant like my father was washing dishes making fifty cents an hour struggling to achieve the American dream. You know who doesn't have lobbyists? A factory worker who just wants to work and provide for his or her children. They don't have lobbyists and so what happens? Career politicians in both parties gang up with giant corporations to loot their taxes to make it harder for people who are struggling to achieve the American dream."

While remaining consistent to the simplicity within his speech, Harry S. Truman's words were nonetheless profound when he said, "The President is the only person in government who represents the whole people. There are some who can afford to hire lobbyists and others to represent their special interests, but the President isn't elected to pull strings for anybody. He's elected. I've said it before, to be the lobbyist for everybody in the United States." The importance of those words may be clearer today than at any other time in history. The level of threats to America consistently grows in strength and complexity, from military means to covert political methods, such as funneling foreign campaign donations through dummy corporations, social advocacy groups, speaking fees, or other loopholes that demean the tenants of true democracy.

While the country has always faced challenges from within, such as the general concentration of wealth and corruption that was present during the Gilded Age, today special interests and Big Business have made an unprecedented gain in power and influence. Through the use of modern tools, such as super PACs, the wealthy elite have been allowed to take further advantage of the growing political and economic inequality to insulate more politicians willing to surrender their decision making for longevity.

Although it may receive less attention from the general public, unlimited corporate money, secret money, and foreign money introduced within the current political system threaten the country just as much as armed conflicts.

The people must have a trusted advocate in the Oval Office to create the new level of accountability expected in government; a necessity for better determining who will maintain the honor and integrity essential to genuine service throughout government. In the absence of sufficient resolve and discipline within leadership from the top, the status quo will remain acceptable to others. Agencies and representatives of government will produce the same inefficiencies that have continued to plague the nation.

In the United States Congress, many candidates and their supporters vying for successful election results will continue to be led by the "win at all cost" mentality that has consistently undermined the political process. As Kirsten Powers documented in her book *The Silencing*, "In a burst of refreshing honesty, Mary Frances Berry, an African American and former chairwoman of the U.S. Commission on Civil Rights under President Bill Clinton, wrote in a Politico online discussion: 'Tainting the tea party movement with the charge of racism is proving to be an effective strategy for Democrats.' Berry, a professor at the University of Pennsylvania, added, 'There is no evidence that the party adherents are any more racist than other Republicans, and indeed many other Americans. But getting them to spend their time purging their ranks and having candidates distance themselves should help Democrats win in December. Having one's opponent rebut charges of racism is far better than discussing joblessness.'"

Of course the type of electoral manipulation perpetrated on the people at the hands of Mary Frances Berry on behalf of the Democrats is by no means limited to the work of one political party, with Allen Raymond possibly providing one of the best examples of how some Republicans prescribe to the same methodology. In the case of Raymond, it may not have actually been the politician committing the act, but, instead, a surrogate working underneath them with the same incentive of being elected.

In his *Huffington Post* article "Allen Raymond: confessions of a Republican Smear Artist," Joseph A. Palermo tells us, "Raymond hired an African-American actor to record a message for 'robotic' phone calls where he affected an 'inner city' accent. The calls went out to voters in white precincts urging them to remember to vote for the Democratic Party. Raymond's goal was to identify in the mind of these white voters that the Democrats only served the needs of 'inner city' blacks." Palermo also utilized his article to underscore how similar tactics of racism were also perpetrated by Raymond on the electorate in an attempt to secure the votes of those fearing a loss of jobs to Hispanics.

Although Joseph A. Palermo's critique of Allen Raymond's book was more than insightful, going directly to the original text may actually provide the best sense of just how committed many will most likely remain to distorting the democratic process. In the actual book, *How to Rig an Election: Confessions of a Republican Operative*, the former party proxy, who was ultimately sentenced to federal prison for his atrocious actions, writes, "The RNC brought me its next generation of press secretaries, campaign managers, and political directors and I taught them all the great things I'd learned during my five years in politics—namely, how to use phones, direct mail, and the press to reconstruct reality to your own specifications. I happily taught eager young souls how to, for lack of a better phrase, corrupt the system. Or was I teaching them that the system is corrupt and that they'd better learn how to use it to their advantage? Semantics."

The current system certainly allows for rampant deceit and corruption, with no way of truly knowing how many new contributors to such practices were created from the despicable work of Allen Raymond. Just as it is impossible to know how the "Allen Raymond types" of the world within the Democratic Party have negatively influenced some of their up and rising followers. What is certain is that all the diverse obstacles to democracy demand a new foundation of accountability within the political process.

Common characteristics associated to the debate and dialogue within the arena of politics is one thing and actually separates our country from the rest of the world. Fraud, manipulation, and the overwhelming power and influence of special interests groups and lobbyists are yet another discussion. The American people deserve better, especially in regards to adequate representation, the lifeblood of democracy and catalyst for a revolution that was led by individuals committed to placing their differences aside and banning together to demand the government they deserved. Utilizing a similar unity for creating better curators to the vision of the Founders could provide the same results.

Although the American people have not united to create more equality through genuine representation, few seem to believe that the character of our leaders in Washington have not been negatively affected by all the forces that are counterproductive to accomplishing this endeavor. According to a Pew Research Poll from as recent as November 2015, "only 19% of Americans [at the time said] they [could] trust the government in Washington to do what is right 'just about always' (3%) or 'most of the time'(16%)"; a loss in faith many members of Congress are more than aware of, but often disregard. However, shortly before leaving the United States Senate at the end of 2014, in large part due to his diagnosis with cancer, Tom Coburn spoke with Leslie Stahl for "60 minutes" and said, "I see them make decisions every day that benefit their career rather than the country. And that's what's so sickening about Washington. To me, it's about our future. It's not about the politicians and we've switched things around where now it's about the politicians and not the future of the country."

Robert Reich, Chancellor's Professor at the Goldman School of Public Policy at the University of California, Berkeley and a previous cabinet member within both Republican and Democratic administrations, wrote in an article from August 2015, "We've witnessed self-dealing on a monumental scale—starting with the junk bond takeovers of the 1980s, followed by the Savings and Loan crisis, the corporate scandals of the early 2000s (Enron, Adelphia, Global Crossing, Tyco, Worldcom) and culminating in the near meltdown of Wall Street in 2008 and the taxpayer financed bailout."

In the same article by the Chancellor entitled "We're witnessing a revolt against the ruling class," the long-time political activist and scholar informed us, "In 1964, Americans agreed by 64 percent to 29 percent that government was run for the benefit of all the people. By 2012, the response had reversed, with voters saying by 79 percent to 19 percent that the government was 'run by a few big interests looking after themselves.'" As revealing as his comparison and the routine negative public opinion polls on the job performance of Congress may be, the words of Leslie Stahl quite possibly summed up the present level of discontent best. In responding to the previously mentioned perspective of former Oklahoma Senator Tom Coburn as to what was driving the Senate in his interview for "60 Minutes," she said, "It seems the public agrees with him. One poll showed that Americans have a higher opinion of witches, the IRS, and hemorrhoids than Congress."

More and more Americans are beginning to realize, and with a sense of urgency, that a fundamental change to our current political system must be found. It can be seen in the middle-class parents who were forced to learn how best to maneuver through the system of shelters to house their children or a college-aged child placing a strain on the family due to debt and lack of employment opportunities. It can be heard in the level of fear and hopelessness more often attributed to the voices of callers to radio programs, regardless of party affiliation. And more importantly, it is being felt by a majority of Americans, regardless of whether each individual actually attributes their economic hardship to the same variable of politics.

As part of a discussion as to what was fueling the popularity of outsiders in the 2016 presidential race, Chuck Todd referenced a devastating chart on income inequality composed by Steve Rattner, a financial expert and lead advisor on the 2009 Presidential Task Force on the Auto Industry. The numbers displayed that only those among the top 10 percent of Americans by wealth had actually seen their wages increase. As for those composing the remaining 90% of the country, they have witnessed their wages decrease, with those at the bottom actually seeing wages decrease the most.

Despite the broad unrest in inequality, which is no doubt driving the unprecedented 2016 elections, the longest lasting and influential theatrical production in the history of the country will most likely remain alive and well on the floors of the United States House and Senate. Democrats and Republicans publicly presenting passionate debate on certain issues will privately remain unified to the genuine commitment to maintaining the practices and procedures that retain the status quo.

Comparable to professional wrestling, many of our leaders portray themselves publicly one way and privately another way. Though they may present themselves as champions for their various constituencies, willing to be adversaries to those opposed to the greater good—even if it requires placing the people over their party—few are actually interested or willing in doing so. Their firm commitment truly remains guided by the underlying theme of working in coordination with other members to maintain the established order of Washington that profits them.

Opposition to such tactics in unison is not based around a desire for our leaders to demonstrate less civility or be unwilling to compromise in certain areas for progress; it's about not wanting this determination of when to do so to come within the similar practices and procedures that rule D.C. and legislative bodies across the country. It is obvious that such an environment corrupts the entire process and provides the expected results of serving to benefit a select few—to the detriment of the country as a whole.

The senior leadership within both parties is always composed of career politicians who are basically rewarded for their long-term ability to maneuver through this established system of operations; in turn, gladly offering their commitment to upholding what has rewarded them and those they truly serve so well. They simply attempt to put forth an agenda within these confines that results in producing the same half-measured deals that are led by special interests, often even written by lobbyists, leaving the rest of America people without a viable voice. As former 2016 presidential candidate Ben Carson posted on his Facebook page during the days of his campaign, "Speaking of serving in Congress. I constantly get asked how could I possibly become president when I have no political experience. Here is what I say. The current members of Congress have a combined 8,788 years of political experience. How is that working out?"

While political pundits and the establishment of both major parties continue to pretend that the key to proper change simply lies in a replacement of the dominant party, a number of Americans are finally deciding they have been fooled too many times by the quick talk and empty promises of campaigns from those clinging to an old system that will breed further incompetence. Republicans have felt the most recent sting of this truth, rising to the polls to secure control of Congress for their party with substantial victories in the last three election cycles starting from 2010, while seeing nothing really change. Yet, even before that time, the argument could be made that the empowered leaders within the Republican Party had not facilitated a means to live up to the ideas of small government and fiscal conservatism, two of the major principles that help form the bedrock of their platform. ₁

Republicans have also maintained that their party is the one to rein in spending, as well as stimulate the economy by getting government out of the way and relieving the burden of overregulation on businesses. They commonly refer to the negative actions of the Obama administration on the economy through the use of governmental agencies such as the Environmental Protection Agency. One wouldn't have to look closely to see the truth in the claims of a negative impact on the economy, with a low estimate of $80 billion in regulatory fees being added to U.S. businesses each year according to the "Red Tap Rising" report from Diane Katz and James Gattuso of the Heritage Foundation. However, Republicans seem pretty hypocritical in their condemnations if Charles Murray is correct in his book, *By the People: Rebuilding Liberty Without Permission.*

In what could only surprise many Republicans, Charles Murray wrote, "The Republicans controlled both houses of Congress from 1995 through 2006, and the White House as well for the last six of those years. During that period, government expanded on every dimension. The Medicare drug entitlement was just one of the legislative expansions. Even after excluding entitlements (Medicare and Social Security), unemployment insurance (directly affected by the economy), law enforcement and border security expenditures (directly affected by 9/11), domestic spending during the six years from 2000 to 2006 when Republicans had nobody to blame but themselves grew by $38.9 billion per year, more in constant dollars than under any other administration except those of Barack Obama and another Republican, George H. W. Bush. The number of pages in the Code of Federal Regulations during 2000-2009 grew more per year than at any time since Jimmy Carter's administration, except the administration of Bush Sr."

The description of the play, the lead and supporting actors of the cast, and the words of the script may change in the chambers of the U.S. Congress, but the theatrical production remains the same—with an anemic economy and approaching fiscal cliff of $21 trillion as just a few of the results produced from the charade. Unless the leads of the play change—and with a sense of urgency—the final act will be a tragedy.

In describing what lies at the source of the status quo that breeds such a level of broad restlessness, Senator Ted Cruz further took time on the Senate floor in July 2015 to tell his fellow senators, "This Senate operates exactly the same; the same priorities. And I tell you why. It's not that this majority doesn't' get things done. It does get things done. It listens to one and only one voice: that is the voice of the Washington Cartel of the lobbyists on K-street of the big money and big corporations." Of course, these words incensed most of his colleagues and drew the ire of the media, which so often seem to revel in discrediting anyone who attempts to change the "business as usual" standards.

Blindly distributing corporate welfare, placing a mountain of regulation on businesses, and increasing the corporate tax code are viewed by some as par for the course. Burying more of these type inconveniences within the thousands of pages routinely attached to bills are accepted by both parties as reasonable, despite the implications to how such actions will continue to hamper American businesses in competing with foreign companies. Unemployment will persist as small businesses, which have always created the most jobs, continue to fail in providing them.

Any representative of government, regardless of party, who stands on principle and fights the common ways of Washington should wear any disapproval from colleagues as a badge of honor, as Ted Cruz has chosen to embrace for most of his bid for the White House. In the U.S. Senate, his behavior often placed him at odds with other members because he remains committed to keeping specific promises to the constituency, regardless of how those insulated inside of the Beltway or the mainstream media react. Then again, Sen. Cruz seems to have shared the practices of his colleagues he routinely rails against by his actions at the Republican National Convention. While many might accept that his conservative principles and bitter instances over the course of the campaign between the Republican nominee and himself would warrant not holding true to his pledge, it was still a pledge. No one forced him to take it; just as no one forced him to show up at the convention and give a speech centered almost entirely on himself.

Of course, he is not alone in remaining true to what has become a novel idea of keeping promises, with the same degree of pushback applying to anyone who dares attempt to buck the system and call out those who have decided to disregard the people. U.S. Democratic Representative Tulsi Gabbard from Hawaii received a rebuke from her party for displaying the nerve to dare question the DNC and specifically the chairwoman, Debbie Wasserman Schultz, over the initial decision to limit presidential debates.

The fear of overburdening candidates was originally given by the Democratic National Committee as the rationale behind their decision to limit debates, although more were eventually added following Hillary Clinton's unexpected decline in the polls. Unfortunately, it was only after Hillary had secured the nomination that an email hack from Wikileaks confirmed that a fix was in play from the very beginning. It should come as no surprise that many people are so fed up with the system.

From John Boehner's emphasis on "protecting the institution" during his resignation speech as Speaker in September 2015 to the effort Rep. Charlie Dent launched on "Meet the Press" the following month, maintaining the order in Washington is blatant and unapologetic. Rep. Charlie Dent, a Republican, utilized his appearance to label any member of Congress who simply questions some of the counterproductive processes of the body as being part of "people that don't know how to govern."

A fellow member of his own party, David Bratt (R-Va), was also on the program and received this criticism. For Rep. Bratt's part, he simply addressed the self-serving fashion in which both parties consistently wait until the end each year to pass a multitude of deals within an Omnibus Bill by saying, "The Left is going to throw in all their toys they want into this thing. The Right's going to throw it in. This was orchestrated on purpose, in my view. The budget committee finished its work back in April, May."

It didn't seem as if any of the other politicians or political pundits on the program, including Rep. Charlie Dent (R-Oh), even blinked an eye at the implications of this critique. Instead, the attention was simply given to how the wheels of government would stop turning as a result of such beliefs, attempting, among other things, to falsely paint Representative David Brat (R-Va) and other Tea Party members of Congress as the only ones raising such legitimate concerns. A number of Americans possessing various party affiliations, as documented in consistent negative opinion polls on congressional job approval and illuminated by the 2016 election in which outsiders are resonating with voters, are evidence most of the country is fed up with the ways of Washington.

This lack of recognition or desire from those insulated within the halls of congress to ignore such a level of dissatisfaction may have been demonstrated best by Harry Reed's defense of what he did to successfully pass the Affordable Care Act by pompously saying, "That's what legislation is all about—it's the art of compromise." Of course, labeling this as a defense may actually be misleading when considering he was very unapologetic in his tone concerning the deals and payoffs to legislators, such as the "Cornhusker Kickback," to secure the 60 votes necessary to advance one of the most fundamentally altering pieces of legislation in American history. He basically believes, as many other past and present members of congress, that these are typical practices which have and should always be acceptable in reaching a workable compromise.

It shouldn't be a surprise to anyone that Charlie Dent, John Boehner, and Harry Reid have accumulated almost 105 years of public service between them, with close to 70 of those years being through an elected office in Washington. On the other hand, David Brat, who stunned the mainstream media by defeating then-House Majority Leader Eric Canter, a poster boy for the political establishment, is only in his first term. The U.S. House seat he won in 2014 is the first time he has ever been elected. Yet those in Washington and legislative bodies across the country seem to easily discount any form of voter unrest and remain committed to defending the same practices of "governing."

In February 2016, Kathie Lee Gifford and Hoda Kotb used a segment of "Today" to demonstrate how a new app from What-Dog.net allows individuals to see what breed of dog they resemble the most. In a similar spirit, while current Senate Majority Leader Mitch McConnell (R-KY) may favor the closest resemblance to a pufferfish, Harry Reid (D-NV), Nancy Pelosi (D-CA), John Boehner (R-OH), and many other former leaders of the House and Senate have been just as poisonous to the principles of true democracy.

In an October 2015 appearance during his campaign for the White House, Senator Rand Paul (R-Ky) addressed the idea of "governing" by saying, "I think the question has always been, and this is the difficulty of Washington; some Republicans say, 'Our job is to govern. Our job is to keep the government running and keep it open.' And there are those of us who say, you know what, if you keep it open and you borrow a million dollars a minute, you are going to destroy the country. So I didn't run for office because I wanted to be governing. I didn't run because I wanted to be in charge of something. I didn't need to be in charge of something. I ran for office because I was worried about our country; that we were borrowing a million dollars a minute." The plan he alluded to of "[cutting] the deficit in half, [capping] the spending, and [having] a balanced budget amendment" to alleviate much of the damage from previous behavior went nowhere in the special-interests-led Congress when he offered it for consideration.

Unfortunately, Representative Paul Ryan (R-WI), the man who ran as vice president on the 2012 Romney presidential ticket and succeeded John Boehner as Speaker of the House in late 2015, already seems to be offering more of the same devotion. Without painstakingly looking through the thousands of pages of the latest Omnibus Bill from this past December 2015, one can easily recognize that it merely serves as the usual and expected giveaway to Big Business and special interests.

Maybe nothing has ever displayed that the country is truly "of the lobbyists, by the lobbyists, and for the lobbyists" at the expense of the general American taxpayer than the words of Sen. Jeff Sessions (R-AL) from December 2015. Displaying his utter disgust for the content of the bill and the process in which it was written, Sessions told host Lars Larson, 'No member of even the House and Senate knew what was going on." Instead, he informed listeners of the radio program out of Oregon that, "special interests did because we heard from lobbyists what some things were being considered."

Senator Rand Paul (R-KY) joined Sen. Sessions in voting against the Omnibus Bill and shed light on the common sense behind his logic that seems to continue to elude the minds of almost all of his colleagues—and especially those in senior party leadership. He stated, "It was over a trillion dollars. It was all lumped together, 2,243 pages. Nobody read it, so, frankly, my biggest complaint is that I have no idea what kind of things they stuck in the bill." With members of

Congress only being given around two and half days to determine if they would actually support or reject the bill, Kaylen Tanner of Rare News explained, "For them to read the whole bill in that time, they would have had to read more than 30 pages an hour without stopping before the vote."

Obviously, few members actually took the time to read the bill themselves or value what the staff members relayed to them who did, as the results were the same. Democrats and Republicans stacked the deck with some things each desired as Rep. David Brat had predicted on "Meet the Press" two months before; spending caps were tossed aside and many of the real issues of concern on the minds of many Americans, such as the need for strengthening the oversight and regulation of the refugee program, were disregarded. When combining the $1.1 trillion appropriations bill with the $622 billion in tax breaks established only a day before, the American taxpayer further realized they would most likely continue to helplessly hold the bag on the whims of Washington indefinitely. Well beyond these two bills, the feeling originated from the blank check Congress gave itself by suspending the debt ceiling until 2017 only a month earlier.

Appropriation bills used to be voted on separately, allowing the chance for actual oversight and proper scrutiny. However, this practice of waiting to the last minute to pass almost everything into one massive bill has become commonplace, with most state legislatures across the country strategically following suit. Though some will make the argument that the wheels had already been set in motion for the Omnibus Bill long before Paul Ryan succeeded John Boehner as House Speaker, the limited debate and passage of the enormous bill provides undeniable proof that he remained true to this pattern.

During the debate surrounding Ryan's potential appointment as the new Speaker, Sen. Rand Paul actually foreshadowed this result when he said, "So you have to weigh those two things: default and shutdown vs. borrowing a million dollars a minute. I think if we continue to do the same where we 'govern,' or any Republican, Paul Ryan or others, who comes in and their main goal is to 'govern' and not to reform, then I think it'll, it won't go well." Although it is early, one has to wonder if Speaker Ryan will bring the necessary reforms moving forward, without the excuse of limited time to fall back on. As implausible as it might seem, in a place that often puts more thought into the title of a bill to the actual content, the highly speculated choice of Speaker Ryan to temporarily grow a beard may have been designed in the hopes of allowing him to remain inconspicuous in the minds of the Republican base for supporting the $2 trillion passed.

As Senator Paul alluded to in his discussion concerning the possibility of Paul Ryan becoming House Speaker, the leaders of our country consistently offer the options of either approving an end-of-the-year spending bill or defaulting on the debt. Although America has now opened the door for families to actively negotiate with terrorists for release of relatives, the government has at least publicly remained committed to the idea that the United States will never open the door to more kidnappings by negotiating with terrorists. However, some question whether both sets of negotiations that secured the release of the military deserter Bowe Bergdahl for five Taliban leaders and the most recent deal that brought home the four Iranian Americans for seven Iranian Nationals might have broken this commitment, despite carrying the label of "diplomacy."

In terms of the negotiations, regardless of what one believes concerning whether American leaders broke the long-standing pledge not to negotiate, any monetary aspect involved with the trades would be small in comparison to the money that changes hands on an annual basis in Congress. The reality is that those invested with the responsibility to represent and protect the interest of the people have begun, in a sense, holding the American people hostage each year to their demands by using the threat of shutting down the government and complete chaos. If someone was simply told about the scenario, with all labels and titles removed, and the far-reaching consequences of non-compliance were given, it is difficult to imagine how anyone would not determine that the largest blackmail known to man was taking place—most likely at the benefit of terrorists.

Using the necessity of certain bills to secure the passage of others is a tactic too often employed by both Republicans and Democrats. As Jim DeMint, the president of the right-leaning Heritage Foundation and former U.S House and Senate representative, is well aware of and wrote in July 2015, "Congress routinely attaches unrelated measures that may not be able to pass on their own to 'must pass bills' in order to pressure acceptance of it by Congress and the President. This is why year-end funding bills that prevent a government shutdown are often packed with unrelated measures." Although it is easier to hide such additions within the thousands of pages contained in an Omnibus Bill at the end of each year, it is often utilized more openly. One example is the renewal of the Export-Import Bank being attached to a massive Transportation Bill from 2015 since it could not be approved on its own otherwise, something DeMint highlighted. The bank "is a taxpayer-financed bank that loans billions of dollars to foreign companies and countries to buy products from big corporations like GE, Caterpillar, and Boeing." The fact that it had clearly been rejected by the American people a number of times made little difference to the body of men and women beholden to corporate interests.

This practice of strategically stacking bills only adds to the level of distrust many in the general public already have from the use of executive orders to pass some form of an agenda, especially in instances that are clearly unpopular with the people. Whether liked or disliked, one would be hard-pressed to deny that Senator Ted Cruz most likely summed up best what these type methods often mean for the American people.

> "You know, if you go to the American people and ask is re-authorizing the EX-IM Bank a priority for you, the standard response for most of them will be, 'the what?' They don't even know what this is. Let me tell you what it is. It is an egregious example of corporate welfare. It is the American taxpayers being on the dime for hundreds of billions of dollars in loan guarantees given out to a handful of giant corporations. It is a classic example of cronyism in corporate welfare...Every Democrat who rails against big money and corruption of Washington; every Democrat who styles himself or herself as a populist; their actions on this matter speak far louder than their words. And when it comes to Republicans, Republicans are also listening to K-street and the lobbyists. Why? It's not complicated. The giant corporations that are getting special favors from the tax payers hire an army of lobbyists that write campaign checks after campaign checks. And by the way, the checks go to both Democrats and Republicans. It is career politicians in both parties that are kept in office by looting the taxpayer to benefit the wealthy, powerful corporations.... The single largest recipient of loan guarantees from the EX-IM Bank is the Boeing Corporation. The Boeing Corporation just had an earnings call where their CEO said and I'm paraphrasing, 'But we'll be just fine without the EX-IM Bank. It's not impacting us. There are plenty of private loan alternatives out there, but you know, even though the market could provide, it's a lot easier to have compliant lawmakers.' Rob from the public first to enrich giant corporations."

Countless examples of similar results (to the detriment of the American people) were found within the Omnibus Bill, leaving many to wonder how much further punishment had been handed to future generations before the ink had even dried. This did not stop much of the mainstream press or members of Congress from patting themselves on the back for what they presented as a bipartisan success.

Similar proclamations of question—which could only reach the low benchmarks established by the lawmakers and members of the media as acceptable—can be found in the positive reactions to numerous bills. Though rarely used within the prolonged and current level of unrest and partisanship, often the label proves questionable, with the ESEA (Elementary and Secondary Education Act) Reauthorization from December 2015 providing one of the most recent examples of this type of misuse.

Heralded as a bipartisan success, the reauthorization took the terribly flawed "No Child Left Behind Act" passed under the George W. Bush administration and replaced it with the "Every Student Succeed Act." Though it alleviated some of the testing requirements that I know, as a former educator, limits genuine classroom discussion (and to a broader degree, achievement), it did not remove the overbearing intrusion of the federal government within the K-12 system. States may have retained greater ability to monitor and formulate reforms to meet requirements through additional flexibility, but no one should be fooled into believing that the federal government does not still maintain the final degree of control by holding the purse strings to what money is allocated.

If the government is not convinced that the federal standards of education are being followed, many of which originate out of the controversial "Common Core," it can withhold funding or levy fees. The lunchroom is not immune from these consequences as well, as is evident in a proposal for a fine from the U.S. Department of Agriculture's Food and Nutrition Service in March 2016 for schools that do not adequately adhere to the guidelines of the healthy lunch program passed into law in 2010—and championed by the First Lady. It is a program which indirectly led to the termination of Arnold Villalobos, an Iraq war veteran and a beloved middle school coach, who was fired for redistributing some of the fruit that would have been thrown away. "Experts estimate federal regulations that require all students to take a fruit or vegetable, whether they want it or not, has increased annual school food waste by more than $1 billion annually."

Despite many states already facing financial woes from cash-strapped agencies and the direct loss of money from a number of kids choosing to bring their lunch or not eat all together, a potentially hefty fine is seen as a wise decision by the government. The players may have changed, but the result remains the same. Policies that maintain the continued removal of a majority of autonomy away from localities stymie necessary innovation and flexibility. It makes little difference that those on the ground know best how to uniquely facilitate the desired relationship among students, parents, teachers, and administrators for success.

It is not to imply that there was not clear merit behind the school lunch program or many of the aims within the "No Child Left Behind Act," such as greater inclusion for those possessing intellectual inabilities, but the failing result is the same with both. However, during my brief time in secondary education, I never spoke with anyone who favored the bill, with various ideology and implementation concerns being rooted at the center of all the complaints. While some will disagree with my assessment as to the negative effects of what the new reauthorization means for K-12 education, little can be disputed regarding how the Congress utilized the same pattern of inadequacies in legislating for its creation—in the process, limiting what can be achieved.

Although the "No Child Left Behind Act" actually expired in 2007 and most of those in Congress were in agreement on the need for reform, genuine action did not come until eight years later. Even then, the final process involved a common routine of only allowing for a small number of legislators to actually be given time to evaluate the bill once it finally came out of committee. The practice is not unique in that the government routinely sets timetables for bills to expire to serve, in a sense, as an alarm clock to get moving; unfortunately, this seems to only result in hitting the snooze button over and over again. That it will affect the quality of education for millions of children seems to have had little bearing on whether to actually attempt to utilize a new set of methods for fostering adequate dialogue and debate. Hopefully, this bill will ultimately serve the students better than its predecessor, possessing full knowledge of the reality that it could again take eight to ten years to even begin to half-heartedly address likely failures.

Senator Marco Rubio has consistently pointed to the ineffectiveness of the United States Congress as the reason he believed that only as president could he truly have the chance of achieving the meaningful change necessary for moving the country forward. Polls routinely demonstrate that the citizens are not only unsatisfied with the results coming out of D.C., but also have disgust for the lack of leadership behind those results. As Senator Rubio alluded to in his 2016 campaign ads for president, the American people are united in the view that a new type of representative has to be discovered.

Harriett Levin Balkind, who founded HonestAds.org in an attempt to bring more truth in political advertising, cited a New York Times/ CBS News poll from September 2014 that reported "only 5% of Americans think most members of Congress deserved re-election;

87% say it's time for new people." Although a complete overhaul of Congress is somewhat simplistic in terms of believing it would fix our government, just discovering the proper balance in representation through new and retained members of Congress is impossible within the current political system. Though the major impediment to this happening is no secret, one of the best descriptions of how it is utilized by both major parties in D.C. may have come best from a beloved Republican.

In his biography, *Ronald Reagan: An American life*, the former President wrote, "As I have noted before, the Democrats have controlled the House of Representatives for most of the past six decades. In recent years, I think they managed to perpetuate their control of the House less through the popularity of their voting records than through the enormous powers of congressional incumbency. Because of their opportunities for bestowing political favors, generating publicity, and raising enormous sums of money for re-election campaigns from special interest groups that want favors from them, it is almost impossible short of a major scandal, for a member of Congress to lose his or her seat voluntarily. More than ninety-five percent of Congressional incumbents who seek re-election every two years are reelected. The dice are loaded in their favor. I don't think this is good for the democratic-with-a-small-d process, nor is it good for America." The clear advantage of incumbency remains alive and well today. However, though President Reagan was particularly addressing how the Democrats had consistently made the best use of it to retain congressional power, it seems rather obvious that Republicans went further in strengthening the tool once they finally grasped control.

After President Bill Clinton was unsuccessful in pushing a more liberal agenda during the first two years of his presidency, the Republicans won a majority of the U.S. House of Representatives by campaigning on a "Contract with America" during the 1994 midterm elections. Their pledge to enact a set of core initiatives, if given control of the House, resonated with voters and is actually a tactic Speaker Ryan seems to be attempting to follow for the 2016 elections with his June release of "A Better Way."

Only time will tell whether the policy agenda Speaker Ryan has put forth will actually mean anything. As for Paul Nehlen, Ryan's Republican primary challenger, he doesn't put much faith in the document. In a press release, he offered the following: "When you've jettisoned your principles for money and personal power, what have you got left but empty promises and marketing gimmicks? That's pretty much all anyone should expect to find in Paul Ryan's new 'Contract with

America.' For my part, I'm committed to standing by the Constitution. It's the real deal." However, what should be of most importance to Paul Ryan, or any other Republican, is how the base was satisfied with the '94 contract, but also shared a common disappointment in their party being deterred from providing more of their vision for the country due to excessive greed.

Though President Reagan had complained about the incumbency advantage, it is the Republicans that are often attributed to strengthening its role with the work of legislators by establishing a further emphasis on campaign donations. Distribution of committee assignments within the Republican Party began being more directly based on the amount of money each individual raised after they took power in the House (in 1994)—creating a trend that overtook the Democrats and has only strengthened with time. Bob Ney, a long-term U.S. Congressmen from Ohio, once said, "I was directly told, 'You want to be chairman of House Administration, you want to continue to be chairman.' They would actually put in writing that you have to raise $150,000. They still do that—Democrats and Republicans. If you want to be on a committee, it can cost you $50,000 or $100,000—you have to raise that money in most cases."

Other congressmen will most likely follow the lead of former House Speaker John Boehner in attempting to discredit anything Bob Ney says as simply coming from a disgruntled past representative who served prison time for his role in the Jack Abramoff scandal. However, in January 2015, Brian Feinstein, an attorney in Washington, wrote a piece for the *Los Angeles Times* in which he advocated for correcting the stranglehold of seniority leadership placed on the legislature by making each committee selection based on a random draw. As part of his argument, he provided direct proof of such a practice by writing, "A 2007 leaked memo from the Democratic Congressional Campaign Committee to party representatives laid bare the quid pro quo, stating that Democrats leading key committees must pay the party 'dues' reaching into the mid-six figures."

The culture of money-driven politics is alive and well, with the Citizen United ruling increasing it to an exponential degree—levels that former President Truman may not have even been able to envision. What he saw in his brief time in the U.S. Senate was enough for him to take to the floor and offer a fiery speech from December 1937 in which he said, "One of the difficulties I see is that we worship money instead of honor." A sentiment that most likely resides in the hearts of a majority of Americans who have never felt more alienation from those they entrusted to represent them.

In the summer of 2015, Megan Thee-Brenan and Nicholas Confessore of *The New York Times* referenced the results of a phone poll from May 2015 that offers one of the best insights of why Americans feel so isolated from their government. In their article entitled "Polls show Americans favor an overhaul of campaign financing," they described the results by writing, "Wearying of headlines about politicians who mix public life and personal enrichment—frequent flights on the private planes of billionaires, junkets paid for by corporate lobbyists and foreign governments, a high-end office redecoration billed to taxpayers—a number of respondents, in follow-up interviews, described political leaders as a kind of class apart." Clearly, the idea from the Founders of the citizen statesman has long been turned into a lost art in the United States Capitol.

Even if some constituents only choose to judge the United States Congress solely by the quality of fairness within the bills it produces, the sense of inequality would rather quickly become the same. Martin Gilens, a professor of politics at Princeton, and Benjamin I. Page, the Gordon S. Fulcher professor of decision-making at Northwestern University, looked at the outcomes of around 1800 policy decisions from 1981 to 2002. While the support or opposition of interests groups also shared a predominant impact in passage or failure, maybe the most telling aspect of their study discovered that "a proposed policy change with low support among economically elite Americans (one out of five in favor) is adopted only about 18% of the time, while a proposed change with high support (four out of five in favor) is adopted about 45% of the time."

While the study from Professor Gilens and Professor Page is debated by scholars as to exactly what it says about the United States as a democracy, their findings simply add another element in the scheme of things that have made many begin to assess the possibility of another form of government. As cited on "The Real Story with Gretchen Carlson" in January 2016, a New York Times/CBS News Poll from November 2015 asked Americans the question of "how they viewed socialism as a governing philosophy" and found that 56% viewed it positively, while only 29% had negative views toward it. The findings of this poll are not unique and have been routinely demonstrated, with young people typically possessing an even greater favorability of socialism; some even displaying their opposition to the current system with the #ResistCapitalism hashtag.

As crazy as it seems, the misguided rationale of young adults may be somewhat understandable when considering that many associate some of their earliest memories of capitalism revolving around events ranging from "Occupy Wall Street" demonstrations, to the tax-payer funded bailout that resulted from the "Great Recession," which most likely affected their family or someone they knew. Many have also either directly benefited from or witnessed assistance programs that provided the only lifeline during economic hardships—and falsely believe the government is the only reliable source.

When you take these personal experiences from the past and add them to the liberal prism being presented at a majority of college campuses, the polls may not be as surprising—although still just as alarming. As the words so often attributed to President Abraham Lincoln read, "The philosophy which is taught in the classroom becomes the philosophy of government in the next generation." However, no body of men and women owns the decline in the spirit and reverence for capitalism more than our representatives of government who have failed to project them through their service.

Average American citizens must help restore faith in capitalism and democracy. Everyone should remember the great opportunity they have been given. From remembering the days following the tragedy of 9/11 to thoughts associated with the loss of an American son or daughter on the battlefields abroad, the words "never forget" are routinely spoken as a rallying cry for others to conduct themselves in a manner that would never devalue or dishonor the sacrifice that has been made for the cause of freedom. However, beyond simply striving to honor these men and women by following this admonishment to remember the price that has been paid with gratitude, it often becomes more difficult for the average citizen to truly grasp what adhering to those words actually requires.

Although the answers will be more diverse, citizens should focus on utilizing the talents unique to each for pursuing the great opportunities that can enrich themselves and their country. Robert Kennedy, during his campaign for the United States Senate seat of New York, said, "We think back uh [sic] to the Greeks and what their idea really was of participation and what Pericles said in his funeral ovation. 'That we differ from the states in that we regard the individual who holds himself aloof from public affairs as being useless, and yet we yield to no one in our independence of spirit and complete self-reliance.' I think that's what has to guide us." At the least, it is obvious that each citizen should take the time to vote, understanding the price that has been paid to secure a level of freedom some will never be allowed to enjoy.

As for those in elected office, the answers should be clearer within an individual who actually values maintaining the proper level of integrity and accountability to the people. Adhering to the men and women who have sacrificed the most could never excuse partisanship that results in a failure to adequately perform critical legislative functions, which could include negligence in security that emboldens our enemies and costs additional American lives. Acting in remembrance of these words would never accept the absence or delay of general consensus as a result of placing party priorities over the well-being of the country, especially if such choices cause suffering of those depending on critical governmental services. When it comes to the principles of our democracy—the core of everything that has been sacrificed through the blood, sweat, and tears of not a few, but countless men and women from numerous generations—it is not acceptable for only a select few to be given a distinct privilege in representation.

Today, maybe the best indicator of the inefficiencies in our leadership lies in a 2016 bill introduced by Senator Richard Burr of North Carolina. "According to a report from the Treasury Inspector General for Tax Administration, of the 7,168 employees rehired by the Internal Revenue Service from Jan. 1, 2010, to Sept. 30, 2013, 824 (11.5 percent) had prior employee issues." It seems the standards of what was acceptable were so low that Senator Burr felt it was necessary to actually introduce the "Ensuring Integrity in the IRS Workforce Act of 2016." This only proves that in the absence of true leadership at the top that values honor and demands accountability, the effects of corruption begins to rapidly trickle down to every sector of the organization below.

Though the state of leadership within the country seems dim, every local, state, and federal official across the country has the power to choose another path moving forward. No contribution should be seen as too small, regardless of title or position, if the endeavor of reassessing the ownership of the people to their government is going to be successful. Maybe nothing sums up this sentiment better than the words of Robert Kennedy in 1966 to the youth of South Africa who were referenced by his brother, the late Senator Edward Kennedy, at his eulogy. The hope found in his words could resonate across the country if only our leadership would choose to follow and project it.

"Some believe there is nothing one man or one woman can do against the enormous array of the world's ills. Yet many of the world's great movements, of thought and action, have flowed from the work of a single man. A young monk began the Protestant reformation, a young general extended an empire from Macedonia to the borders of the earth, and a young woman reclaimed the territory of France. It was a young Italian explorer who discovered the New World, and the thirty-two-year-old Thomas Jefferson who proclaimed that all men are created equal. These men moved the world, and so can we all."

Unfortunately, the sad reality is that for many elected officials to truly place the people at the center of their service, it will require that they courageously place themselves at odds against the political elite found within their parties. As Thomas Jefferson once said, "Whenever our affairs go obviously wrong, the good sense of the people will interpose and set them to right." While members of both major parties may profess to wholeheartedly believe in the words of Jefferson, their actions say otherwise and will produce one of the greatest impediments to members doing the right thing. While Robert Kennedy's words concerning the power of one individual must be utilized by a number of Americans, current representatives who choose to oppose those desperate to keep things the same could discover few words that could offer as much comfort. The pushback and alienation they will receive will require great resolve.

As far as presidential elections are concerned, the 2016 contest has shown that the political elite in both parties will actually only entertain the thought of what Jefferson said to a degree, but have no intention of allowing the general public to actually determine who should represent them. Political outsiders have only been tolerated in the past because the actual chance of them winning seemed impossible. The candidate outside of the establishment would ruffle a few feathers and, at the most, maybe redirect some of the policy focus, but the actual party nominees would always still be chosen by those deemed superior to the commoners. The super-delegates of the Democrats and unbound delegates of the Republicans would provide some security. Any remaining nuisance would surely be rooted out with backroom deals, guidelines to brokered conventions, allocation of delegates within each state regardless of voting, media coverage, and, above all, the overwhelming power of money to buy and manipulate votes.

Although an array of diversity in political positions exist between the supporters of Bernie Sanders and Donald Trump, much of their support still hinges on the common desire for a political outsider. Many also view Ted Cruz in a similar light. These voters are expressing the desire from an overwhelming majority of the electorate to end the status quo in D.C. The predominant characteristic of most of the campaign contributions Sen. Sanders received provides some of the best evidence. As Sanders indicated in a January 2016 appearance on "Morning Joe," his campaign had the support of "over 2 million individual donors averaging around $27 a donation."

Even those supporting establishment candidates like Hillary Clinton compose this underlying desire for change if polling is correct. Despite her fundraising practices, pre-loyalty of super-delegates, and pro-media coverage, some may still view her as an outsider in that she would be the first female President. However, many likely view her as the practical choice to maneuver through the realities they believe will remain in D.C.

However, Judge Jeanine believes the rationale for the choice of former Secretary of State Hillary Clinton as president by the party establishment would not be as admirable. In analyzing the expressed willingness of those within the Republican establishment to actually lose an election to the Democrats in their commitment to stop an outsider like Donald Trump she stated, "The Republican establishment, elected officials, and party leaders are in bed with the Democrats!"

Maintaining the current order is the most important thing to this group of influential figures and legislators who rarely feel the negative effects attributed to others on Main Street as long as someone is elected who will keep the traditional wheels spinning. "The lobbyists keep their offices on K Street," Judge Jeanine said, "the pharmaceutical companies keep paying them, the unions keep adding to their pensions and the lawmakers get their re-election bribes—I mean contributions—while we the underclass work two and three jobs and rack up a debt our children and grandchildren will have to pay for generations."

Obviously, the task of reestablishing the proper voice of the people in the government they own is not going to be an easy endeavor. However, in specific terms of current and future representatives, if we had half the level of dedication from our leaders as the soldiers of Arlington Cemetery (who remain dedicated to guarding the Tomb of the Unknown Soldier regardless of the weather), law enforcement officers (who suit up every day and often run toward danger to shield citizens from harm's way), the first responders (who placed their fears aside and darted up the stairs of the Twin Towers over fifteen years ago), the heroic passengers of United Airlines Flight 93 (who courageously attempted to reclaim the cockpit from terrorists), our brave troops (who demonstrated the spirit that guides all our armed forces when they stormed the beaches of Normandy), the millions of women who maintained the labor force as the men went off to fight in World War II, the Rebels who kept their faith and continued to push for independence from the British despite the odds, and as the various male and female civil rights leaders of history who boldly fought for justice despite the personal sacrifice it brought, the drastic change necessary would happen. The People's Clearing House could be instrumental in helping the people assess which individuals are willing to embrace a new level of accountability for reclaiming and securing greater equality in representation.

The Example of Alabama

In an episode from "The Rachel Maddow Show" near the end of May 2016, the lively host led into a segment on Alabama with some questions and a wealth of advice that perfectly underscored the dismal degree of current leadership within the state. "Do you live in the great state of Alabama? If so, are you a decent and honest person? If so, would you please consider running for office? Your state needs you. I mean honestly, everybody out there, even if you don't live in Alabama. If you have decent and honest and patriotic friends or relatives who live in Alabama, would you please do Alabama a favor and call that person who you know in that state and tell them to run for office."

At the time of her comments, a dark cloud had formed over the state, with the heads of all three branches of government facing legal troubles over possible ethics violations. Few outside the state would have ever believed all the statements of confidence Republicans offered concerning their ability to restore trust and integrity into government after securing both chambers of the legislature from the Democrats in 2010.

Upon being elected that year on a message in part aimed at continuing the fight against corruption in Montgomery, Charles Dean, a long-time political reporter in Alabama, documented the words of Robert Bentley shortly after being elected governor. "I know of no more effective way to clean up the corruption we have seen than to pass the toughest set of ethics laws in the country." Mike Hubbard, a prominent Republican who would later be forced to step down as Speaker of the House, had also echoed this sentiment before leading the charge on the ethics reforms. "We have said for years to the people of Alabama that if you give Republicans a majority of the seats in the Legislature, we could pass new and tougher ethics laws. And, we're going to keep that promise."

Despite their lofty words and ambitions, Alabama remains just as corrupt today. While the laws may have changed, a similar unwarranted influence is being utilized by those inside the state who do not have the best interest of the people of Alabama at heart. Alabama places no limits on campaign contributions, allowing candidates to receive unlimited amounts of money from individuals, state parties, PACs, corporations, and unions. Corporations were actually limited to directly giving a candidate more than $500, until the Republicans led an effort in 2013 to remove the last limit to donations.

As of May 2015, Alabama is one of only six states in the entire country that have chosen not to place limits on campaign donations of any distinction. However, the lack of effort from state lawmakers to enact ample campaign finance allows for other methods of peddling influence. Being able to give an unlimited amount of money directly to a candidate is just one advantage within a system ripe for corruption.

To truly understand why the state faces a crisis in leadership, a look at the useless revolution of campaign finance within Alabama is necessary. If only the bills produced are considered, at no time, past or present, have those entrusted to represent the people of their state demonstrated a genuine commitment to transparency and accountability. The Fair Campaign Practices Act of 1988 basically sat idle for years with no actual ability to change the counterproductive ways of lawmakers. It was more powerful in name than in practice. Leading into the ethics reforms Republicans brought after taking control in 2010, the writers of AL.com and the *Press-Register* editorial board described the method those behind PACs, or Political Action Committees, had utilized to essentially hide their identity. "PAC-to-PAC transfers are the closest thing yet to legalized money laundering. This is how the scheme works: Say a special interest in Alabama wants to give a candidate money but wants to keep it out of sight for voters. The special interest gives money to a PAC, which gives it to another PAC and another PAC and so on, until the donation arrives in the hands of the targeted candidate."

In an article from the Alabama Policy Institute entitled "Strengthening Alabama's PAC-to-PAC transfer," the organization documented the opportunistic approach some within Alabama took: "Between 2006 and 2010, more than $100 million were funneled to candidates in the Alabama House and Senate and other statewide offices, much of it though PAC-to-PAC transfers. The use of PAC-to-PAC transfers to hide the source of campaign support resulted in the formation of over 1100 PACs during the fall 2010 election cycle." Nevertheless, many remained in the dark.

A 2010 ban on these PAC transfers wasn't worth the paper it was written on. It allowed special interests and politicians from both sides of the political aisle to continue them without consequence. As AL.com and the *Birmingham News* editorial board detailed at the time, "The grand jury report said: The law holds no individual responsible and subject to prosecution for violations; the law doesn't make it a crime for a PAC to solicit or receive an illegal donation from another PAC; the law provides no time limit for returning a contribution; the law authorizes no office or agency to monitor and review records, ensure they are filed on time and are complete and accurate. Nor is there any agency with subpoena power to investigate and levy administrative fines and to refer prosecution to the state attorney general's office or the appropriate district attorney."

Despite a legislature composed of able lawyers from across the state, the 2010 ban of PAC-to-PAC transfers definitely disregarded a number of crucial components for any beneficial outcome. The result was no indictments from the Grand Jury in 2012, allowing Republicans and Democrats to entertain the routine practice of merely pointing the finger of wrongdoing at the other side. While lawmakers played the tired game of politics, the people they were supposed to represent continued to remain unprotected. Lawmakers and those behind Political Action Committees continued to wield influence through PAC transfers and an unwillingness to self-report donations.

Mike Cason of Alabama Media Group reported on the decision of the committee put together in 2013 to address the problems of campaign finance with civil penalties. However, as part of his 2015 summary of campaign finance demonstrated, this solution held a familiar problem. Cason wrote, "But an attorney general's opinion later found that the updated law failed to specifically authorize the Secretary of State, the state's chief election official, to assess the fines." The solution advanced by a host of legislators possessing law degrees had once again created a void in the necessary authority.

In 2015, the Alabama legislature passed bill 241, which introduced a "non-partisan entity—the Alabama Ethics Commission—to serve as the authority that had been absent in previous "efforts." However, an extensive look at the "Summary of Fair Campaign Practices Act" video, provided by the state's Secretary of State in 2013, demonstrates that the bill will do little to raise accountability. Not only did it remove the right of the state to withhold the certificate of election on any winner until they correct their fines, the new parameters operate on a two-tier misdemeanor system that practically mocks providing a true deterrent. Offenders encounter empty civil fines before actually reaching a potential criminal charge; although, now even "intent" must be proven for a successful conviction.

As is so often the case, while heralded by lawmakers as a victory for the people, what is actually produced is another method for maintaining the status quo under the veil of accepted misrepresentation. Few within the general public have the time or resources to follow such matters, so what is presented is taken at face value. Making contributions more readily accessible online, as the legislature also did, will not alleviate the situation. Most Alabamians have little incentive for attempting to correct the mistakes of the state, when those in leadership produce a bleak outlook for any success.

As far as the use of civil fines, the most telling aspect is the explanation Othni Lathram, director of Alabama Law Institute, offered for having these fines precede a criminal prosecution: "We want to have a law that people who want to follow the law aren't going to violate by accident." If this applied to first-time candidates, his statement might hold credibility. However, an assessment of the bill reveals that the two-tier system, which includes civil fines, provides all lawmakers this buffer.

It would seem reasonable that those legislators who have served in the state houses of government would be capable of following the laws they pass and would not be in need of such protection. However, just as with other ideas for obtaining heightened accountability—which often include the ideas surrounding term limits advanced for consideration by Alabama and other states—the legislation produced always protects those in power. As in the case of term limits, previous service rarely applies to the bill.

Campaign finance legislation, for all intents and purposes, remained idle for over twenty years without any real attempt at compliance. Starting in 2010, it took numerous attempts by the legislature to finally provide an actual body of authority capable of enacting punishment, despite the same problem existing in each of the previous iterations. Then, when an enforcement mechanism was finally created, the penalties were watered down. Considering the number of attorneys within the state legislature, either there was a lack of incentive to provide the necessary components for actual results or the chambers of government contain the most inept lawyers in the entire country. The answer may lie in the new system of fines, which do not take effect until 2018.

As part of the 2010 ethics reforms, state legislators did place some restraints on the money for influence venue that was operating daily, without remorse, in Montgomery. However, among the rules passed on lobbying, there were "18 separately enumerated exceptions to the restriction on things of value." While it's reasonable that some exceptions might be necessary, a 2011 article from Kim Chandler, a veteran reporter, detailed how at the time, "The Alabama Ethics Commission [had] received nearly 200 requests to certify dinners, trips and conferences as allowable exemptions."

In offering an assessment of the work the Alabama Ethics Commission has conducted since receiving such requests for years, reporter Kyle Whitmire concluded in September 2015, "Far from being a watchdog with subpoena power, the commission has been a paid accomplice. Instead of scrutinizing the business of public officials and holding them accountable, the commission has repeatedly given approval for things that just don't pass the smell test." An ethics commission is what the Republicans are hanging their hats on to bring the necessary oversight for actual accountability in 2018.

In 2011, when Kim Chandler looked at the hundreds of requests submitted to the Ethics Commission for approval, she concluded, "Politicians and lobbyists do not have to get Ethics Commission approval before sponsoring events, but the requests that have been made offer a glimpse at the wining and dining that still is going on in Montgomery."

If you ask politicians if their actions are ethical, most will likely simply point to remaining inside the rules as being the determining indicator, regardless of the loopholes and exceptions strategically written into almost every bill. For Alabama, this means an open arena for the close to 900 PACs (as of 2012 alone), as well as the over 600 lobbyists as of 2015, to swindle the people out of genuine representation without much recourse.

The practice of only focusing on the legality of actions in analyzing whether one's actions are ethical, without any consideration of being morally corrupt, is too common. Few Alabama lawmakers are offering true leadership necessary for progress. However, the state is not unique in having public officials who disregard broader principles.

For example, the Texas Attn. General Ken Paxton, a Republican, took $100,000 to pay for his own legal fees from a company his department and the U.S. Justice Department were investigating. Sen. Tim Kaine, Hillary Clinton's running mate, took "$160,000 in gifts from 2001 to 2009" while in the roles of Lt. Governor and Governor of Virginia. The Democratic V.P. nominee not only didn't work to establish a higher standard for current and future representatives of government within his state, but he also rejected taking this action in style, with a June 2016 report from the *Politico*'s Isaac Arnsdorf, revealing that Kaine had received "$5,500 in clothes."

Beyond taking full advantage of the laws often tailored with themselves in mind, other politicians are more brazen in demonstrating the common misconception among lawmakers that the rules don't apply to them. Upon being indicted on "23 felony ethics counts, alleging that he used his position as speaker and former position as state chairman of the Republican Party to benefit himself and his businesses," Mike Hubbard challenged the charges by citing freedom of speech. While there should always be an endeavor to protect this fundamental right, his use of it as a defense reveals more about his character.

As the Associated Press reported, Alabama prosecutors quickly demonstrated their intolerance to the Alabama Speaker of the House at the time by saying, "Boiled down to its essence, Hubbard's argument is that he has a constitutional right to be a legislator lobbyist, or perhaps a lobbyist legislator, who earns an extremely handsome living by catering to the interests of his powerful lobbying clients and using his public position to advance their goals ahead of those of the average citizen who elected him to that position." Hubbard's arguments are similar to the arguments of those supporting Hillary's decision to grant certain donors to the Clinton Foundation access to the State Department, with the only difference being that Hubbard was eventually convicted.

Republican Mike Hubbard clearly demonstrated major shortcomings. Republican Governor Robert Bentley still faces potential impeachment over his actions related to misuse of certain funds. The campaign finance system remains riddled with various opportunities for dodging true accountability. There is routinely a fight for public records requests vital to raising the bar of transparency beyond the realm of campaign finance. Yet, despite all of these circumstances, Republicans within the state can often be heard confidently making the argument that they have produced far better results than what the Democrats did during their 136 years of power, before losing control in 2010.

It's true that it was practically a free-for-all in Alabama before the Republicans took over power from the Democrats. In August 2010, Dan Lieberman, who was at the time a reporter for ABC News, wrote, "Alabama allows lobbyists to spend up to $250 a day on an individual legislator without disclosure—or more than $90,000 a year, an amount that Ellen Miller of government watchdog The Sunlight

Foundation calls 'outrageous.'" Lieberman's article came off the heels of a report from his network a few months earlier that discovered a number of lawmakers on the golf course with lobbyists, instead of appearing at a conference they had allegedly made the trip to attend!

While it might be important to politicians, Alabamians do not care about political comparisons. Making one on the state level is about as bad as the Democratic nominee for president, Hillary Clinton, saying that she will only release the transcripts of her speeches to Wall Street when other candidates follow the same standard. Alabamians, as with most other citizens, care little about the past. They simply want leadership moving forward. A true leader does not make comparisons or merely attempt to function within established parameters; instead, they take the initiative to create new ones when needed.

Real leaders determine their success or failure by asking themselves whether they have personally lived up to the power entrusted to them. A mirror, not the actions of others around them, provides their only measuring stick for evaluation. The leadership they offer can go beyond each new challenge and is like a trip planner who demonstrates a vision for a certain path moving forward with each decision; today's leadership seems only capable of handling each pothole in the road as they come along.

Their guidance is rarely composed of long-term thoughts.

Campaign finance will always offer new challenges to necessary oversight and accountability, as wealthy donors and politicians will consistently attempt to circumvent the laws in place. Taking over five years to produce a body with the authority to investigate and impose fines should be unacceptable to anyone who truly loves Alabama.

The inability to adjust to the latest methods some use to unduly dictate representation is leaving Alabama residents open to the influence of social welfare groups, or 501(c)(4)s, which are nonprofits that share a similar characteristic to foundations—in that neither entity has to disclose their donors. While some states have passed laws for heightened transparency on donors, a bill from Sen. Orr (R-Decatur), to do the same in Alabama never received a vote. Many of the real power players within the state remain securely insulated under secrecy directly provided by their lawmakers.

Kyle Whitmire highlighted in his September 2015 article how the Republican state legislators wasted little time upon taking power in removing some important restrictions on foundations. "Initially the law prohibited foundations from making donations to other foundations, political action committees and other candidates." The use of these groups that do not disclose their donations, or "dark money," has become prevalent nationally as the new method for hiding their actions. Much of the trouble Alabama Governor Bentley faces involve the payment of an advisor he allegedly had an affair with from funds to his non-profit—the Alabama Council for Elective Government—supposedly set up by him "to promote his political agenda."

In April 2016, *The Tuscaloosa News* looked at the unwarranted impact "dark money" is having in further undermining the integrity of state government. The paper cited the "F" grade Alabama received from the analysis of the Center for Public Integrity and highlighted how lawmakers hold little enthusiasm for advancing legislation to remove various campaign cows within the flawed system that provides incumbents the upper hand. The paper summed up the matter in writing, "While the voters aren't informed as to who is pouring money into 'nonprofits' that make donations, you better believe the politicians benefiting from the donations know. And they're influenced."

Social welfare groups and the PACs that receive money from them are allowing money from outside the state to easily influence elections. While some states do not permit PACs outside the state to give money directly to candidates, Alabama has no such restriction. However, beyond legislation within Alabama that allows parties outside the state to have undue influence on decisions facing the state, a failure in leadership continues to make Alabama more beholden to the whims of the federal government.

Katherine Green Robertson, VP of the Alabama Policy Institute, described the larger impact of failed leadership on the state level in her May 2016 article for the Yellowhammer News. She wrote, "Alabama landed at number three this year in a report ranking the federal dependency of the states. Largely blamed on the state's poverty rates, Alabama's dependency on the federal government has reached dangerously high levels."

Although troubling, Robertson described the reason this dependency will most likely continue being acceptable to lawmakers by pointing out, "In the short term, this 'free' money means free political points; in other words, politicians can reap the rewards of the spending without making tough budgetary decisions or facing any real opposition."

Faced with a shortfall similar to many other states when attempting to balance the budget, Alabama state lawmakers take the money from the federal government without concern for the strings attached.

While many Republicans consistently rail against the overreach of the federal government and cry out for more autonomy, the leadership in Alabama hasn't done much in creating an opportunity for demonstrating more independence in governing. The 10th Amendment solidifying state's rights is not that useful when the federal government is routinely being used as a crutch to provide political cover on difficult issues.

Of course, this dependency (created in part by the actions of state lawmakers) does not keep them from blaming the federal government for their own failures in leadership. In speaking on the complexities that would be found in establishing the 2017 budget the following year, Sen. Arthur Orr (R-Decatur) said in October 2015, 'That's what's so frustrating about the whole budgeting scenario, the uncontrollable cost of Medicaid, this federal program that we have very little say in how it's run and the expenditures of it." While most governmental agencies are out of control and in need of more oversight, the waste and abuse found within them is not the main reason for Alabama's fiscal woes.

Even if all federal programs were introduced into the state with complete efficiency, it is unlikely to change the inability of state lawmakers to effectively budget. It would also not keep members of whichever party is in power from always trying to place a positive spin on any outcome, regardless of how dismal it might be. Speaking of the budget passed in 2015, Sen. Arthur Orr, chairman of the Senate General Fund budget committee, highlighted the mere safeguarding of vital state programs in saying, "All those services being level funded was a great achievement by the legislature."

In speaking of the same budget that pleased very few beyond sitting state legislators and actually took three special sessions to even reach—"which "cost taxpayers nearly $100,000 a week according to the Legislative Fiscal Office"—Kimble Forrister, the executive director of Alabama Arise, a non-profit which advocates for low-income individuals, offered a strikingly different take on the budget: "Barely scraping by for another year is no cause for celebration. Alabama is still shortchanging needed investments in education, healthcare, child care, public safety, and other services that make our state a better place to live and work." He may be an individual who specifically advocates for the poor, but most Alabamians agreed with his assessment.

The entire state suffers in the absence of leadership, from limited opportunities to difficulty in long-term planning—but none more than the poor, especially the children. According to the 2015 Kids Count Data Book cited in *The Times Daily* article entitled "Rise of poverty among our children is a moral failure," from December of that year, "Nearly 300,000, or 27% of the state's children live in poverty, with about half of them living in extreme poverty, where income is less than $12,000 a year."

This outlook for the future of our children looks even bleaker when considering that in "rural counties [where] half of women live in poverty" jobs are often scarce. Even the jobs more readily available typically provide the type of low wages that keep women in poverty, where certain wages result in the loss of some needed welfare assistance.

Coming off governmental dependency is difficult in that there are not adequate safeguards during that time period where people are attempting to move to self-reliance. The transitional period is when benefits need to be sustained. Still being in poverty and needing assistance during this time, often individuals become hopeless and ultimately conclude that they must settle to provide for their family. Though some may settle for it, anyone who has known someone in poverty realizes no one wants to be poor. Someone once said to me that as a child she only truly looked forward to school because she knew a meal would be available. She was a member of a poor family that saw both parents consistently absent at home due to work. Yet, despite the circumstances, especially in the failure to provide needed benefits during the period of transitioning to self-sufficiency, many demonize, misrepresent, or blame those living in poverty instead of searching for answers and creating opportunities.

While all across the state there are individuals and families experiencing these hardships, maybe no group of residents understands it better than those residing in the Black Belt. Located across the southern part of Alabama, it is one of the poorest areas in the country and is predominantly comprised of African Americans. Access to adequate healthcare, education, and job opportunities are virtually nonexistent. The people of this area need more advocates within government, but instead of aiding them in harnessing a powerful voice, lawmakers made the endeavor more difficult by making it harder to vote.

With the characteristic inability of state legislators to properly manage the budget came the decision to close certain offices to obtain drivers' licenses. A driver's license is necessary for voting in Alabama. At the time of the decision in September 2015, John Archibald of *The Birmingham News* wrote, "Every single county in which blacks make up more than 75 percent of registered voters will see their driver's license office closed."

While making cuts to save money is important, there are certain aspects that have to be protected, like maintaining proper access to voting. However, even if this was the argument from lawmakers for cutting driver's license offices in areas of low income, local political reporter Kyle Whitmire shed even further light on why using the guise of savings would be illegitimate. "The state [had] closed the driver's license office in 28 counties to save $100,000." However, Whitmire followed that information by writing, "At the same time, the state will keep open one liquor store in one county, Bibb, at a cost of $75,000 a year, so that folks there won't have to drive too far for a bottle of booze."

All the people of Alabama deserve better. In relation to those specifically living in the Black Belt region, it looks as if, for now, they are basically left to hope that more men like Steve Harvey will come into the region and produce hundreds of jobs within an area of the state most of those in Montgomery have forgotten. As Erin Edgemon reported in September 2015, "Comedian Steve Harvey and Montgomery businessman Greg Calhoun have purchased a former latex glove and condom factory in Eufaula."

While extraordinary for Eufaula, Alabama state residents merit having leaders more committed to efforts in finding solutions to that of serving special interests. Issues are complex. Not having a foundation of leadership built on a reliable electoral process of integrity causes undue hardships. In relation to the youth, beyond the negative impact easier to identify on the outside, failed leadership stunts necessary growth on the inside.

In 2009, state legislators passed the Student Harassment Prevention Act, which basically amounted to a set of generalities that has essentially allowed schools to continue clinging to the same failed practices in handling bullying. As parents and students continue to suffer through the trauma associated with the harassment that too often goes unanswered, the legislature most likely still pats themselves on the back for producing what was actually a lackluster bill. The measly requirements that were passed are not even followed by every school.

In 2012, Trisha Powell Cain of Alabama School Connection looked at whether the bill had accomplished the small aims laid out. "Alabama contained 132 school districts during the 2011-2012 school year. The ASC (Alabama School Connection), through district website review and specific information requests, verified that 88 (67%) of Alabama 132 school districts had enacted the mandated policy. The remaining 44 districts did not respond to our request nor could the policy be located on their district website." She also discovered "66 (50%) districts mandated reporting forms were either posted on their district website or provided in response to the ASC's request." However, more revealing, was that in both times she looked at the number of reports of bullying being submitted on the middle school or high school level, the results "[indicated] that either the national data [was] unreliable or that the incidents [were] going unreported."

The numbers didn't add up, because the bill was useless. Almost any teacher or student in Alabama could attest to the bill's inefficiency. The legislation simply provided a formal method for schools to check some boxes and remain true to the same practices of the past, with no intention of solving problems that can't be seen from the capital.

If anything, the bill made attempting to adequately address bullying more difficult, in that it actually made it harder for a victim or the teacher to make a formal complaint against a student, as well as protected the accused from anonymous accusations. While there has to be a consideration for those potentially wrongly accused, this virtually means all the methods routinely used by schools in Alabama for receiving anonymous reports of bullying in fact result in them being out of compliance with the bill. This truth alone should reflect how ill-conceived the suggestions were for schools to follow.

On a personal note, for over a year I worked to implement an anti-bullying plan. While working at a college, I rediscovered my love for writing and problem solving, much as a result of the Director of Education, Bob Faver, who took a chance in hiring me. Despite not having the desired experience on a resume, he saw fit to make me the Director of Career Services and encouraged me to put my passion for problem solving to use within the college. Working together, we were able to achieve a number of significant initiatives and I am confident that he will have the same success in his new role as Director of vetsvilleUSA, positively impacting the lives of veterans nationwide.

My achievements at the college created a desire to look beyond the school for challenges, which is when I began writing my anti-bullying plan, pausing along the way to obtain feedback from others within my teaching field that held more knowledge and teaching experience. However, the most influential assessment came from Jill Moore. She is the mother of Alex Moore, a former student at Jemison High School, who tragically lost her life as a result of the endless amount of harassment she received.

I had made a promise to myself that I would only proceed with my endeavor if someone who had actually lost a child to bullying believed in my plan, which is also why I attempted to contact the family of Ka'shaad Hurts, another teen from Alabama who is suspected to have died as a result of bullying. A "gifted orator" was one of the characteristics his grandmother used to describe her beloved grandson. Though I was unsuccessful in reaching the family, his story always remained a motivator for my work.

I have never been as nervous as when I met with Jill Moore. I explained to her each aspect of my plan and then intently listened to all of her feedback. She decided that day to support my work, eventually signing a letter of support and also continuing to pray daily for my success. She has spoken at schools and honors Alex every day by displaying her faith and resilience to move forward with courage.

I was excited when I left and somewhat naively believed that her support and my heart being in the right place would move others to act when I talked with them. However, when I met with some legislators in Alabama, I quickly discovered that few would be as receptive as I had hoped. Although an endorsement of my plan would have been welcomed, I simply met with them to see if they could guide me in the right direction. However, only one public servant offered a meaningful suggestion, which was reflective of the differences in the type of treatment I received. Anyone outside of government, as well as many of those on the staff of politicians, projected nothing but excitement and admiration for my ideas.

Politicians displayed consistent disinterest.

Regardless of the merits of a particular idea, with today's economic hardships and complex social issues, I was confident any representative of government would have a list of possible resources for those either seeking employment or attempting to help strengthen the community through new ideas. However, more than anything, I was truly surprised at how I was treated by a third-term state senator. I was only four words into summarizing my plan when he said in the most cynical tone, "How can I help you?" Anyone who heard it would recognize it was meant to quickly get me out of his office.

He wasn't the only one who conveyed to me that bullying was not politically expedient enough for them. One state senator I met with had been instrumental in attempting to advance other bullying measures, but it seems I must have scared him off with an email that contained a quote from Robert Kennedy at the end. He took my number, but never set up a meeting to listen to my plan. At no time during either interaction did one of the state senators ever reference the 2009 bill as already providing the answer on bullying. Both obviously knew it had not. What they did both display is the arrogance and sense of entitlement so common within government.

There was also the conversation I had with the Lt. Governor of

Alabama, Kay Ivey. I was honored to speak with her and thanked her for her service. However, I was also disappointed in her inability to direct me to resources, as well as in the advice she offered me as to how to precede. She said I needed to get a number of principals and superintendents on board before attempting to start the non-profit I had spoken of to her. She was obviously unaware of what response a number of superintendents gave Mrs. Moore at a hearing on bullying when she attempted to pass a bill named after her daughter. Mrs. Moore had told me that when she viewed the reaction on the faces of the superintendents at the hearing held by lawmakers on bullying, she realized that no additional piece of anti-bullying legislation was going to be passed.

While some individuals have taken negative interactions with others and turned them into motivators for success, how much good has been lost in the world as a direct result of the treatment some have received at the hands of those in levels of authority? Individuals who had the drive and innovation to truly make a difference in their various communities, but ultimately decided to never pursue endeavors out of discouragement.

Bill Kristol wrote an article in *The New York Times* following Tim Russert's death in 2008, in which he described how Tim received his initial chance to gain influential access. "Pat asked Tim to come to Washington as his press aide and counselor. Tim claimed to be worried that he wouldn't be as good as the Ivy League hotshots Pat was assembling on his staff. Pat responded, 'What they know, you can learn. What you know, they can't learn.'" Though Tim Russert definitely held the drive and intellect to likely succeed regardless, the words of recognition and encouragement from the late Democratic senator from New York, Patrick Moynihan, served to propel his career.

Some of the greatest leaders in history weren't always easily identifiable early in life. Take George Washington and his failed marriage proposal to Betsy Fauntleroy, highlighted by Bliss Isely in his 1962 book *The Horseman of the Shenandoah*. Privately, he sought a parental blessing, "but Betsy and her father saw in the tall, young horseman nothing more than a frontier surveyor, who was accustomed to sleep in a half-faced camp or on a floor of a cabin with the family and dogs. She could not know that her name would be remembered only because she could have been Mrs. George Washington."

Obviously, not everyone will hold the significance of Washington, but if a federal or state legislator truly values the Constitution, it is not for him or her to decide when people are worthy of being granted the courtesy of being given the type representation that strives to provide everyone the same opportunity to succeed. The job of a representative of the people is to create an equal arena that rewards those who take the initiative to earn success through their talents and available resources. As it specifically relates to school, every student deserves an equal effort in guidance and protection.

In specific relation to Lt. Governor Kay Ivey, she has built a career around her dedication to providing better education and employment opportunities for Alabamians. In 2011, she personally provided the students of Alabama with the chance to take part in the Real World Design Challenge. It's a competition designed to create more future workers in science, technology, engineering, and mathematics. In a press release from her office in September 2012: "This is a level playing field. The school budget or size matters not because participation is free!" While the program is important, it only impacts a small number of students. The equality of opportunity she expresses to possible participants reflects the type of spirit that should tell any representative the same amount of passion should be put into a genuine anti-bullying effort to protect everyone.

Her press release also ended by saying, "Alabamians need to channel the same enthusiasm we have for sports to high-tech education that leads to high-paying careers," highlighting another area that provides a distinct effort that should be matched. A quick look at a program from most, if not all, football games in Alabama will somewhere reveal the passage of Senate Bill 16 in 2001. With only one vote in the entire Alabama legislature against it, the bill not only "[created] new crimes of harassing, menacing and assaulting sports officials, coaches, and administrators," but also added some teeth to the consequences of choosing to break them. "A second-degree assault can carry a sentence of up to 10 years in prison, but under the new law, a second-degree assault of a sports official, coach and administrator could result in a sentence of up to 20 years."

Although the law applies to all sporting events, it only offers a protection to a select group of students within a school. There were already laws in place, but the legislature wanted to send a firm message to deter those considering breaking the laws. It is amazing how easy it is to get something done when there is actual resolve and incentive within a group. Where is the same demonstrated commitment to all the students in passing anti-bullying legislation, instead of providing a half-hearted effort that only looked good on paper and provided deceitful talking points for the next election?

How can any educator or legislator expect every student to recognize their true worth and value when a distinct difference in effort has been provided to only protect certain students with very little argument? Clinging to the status quo was clearly seen as insufficient when it came to protecting those participating in sports. All students deserve a similar understanding and any legislator who happens to have provided a vote on Senate Bill 16 in 2001, and the Student Harassment Prevention Act in 2009, would seem very disingenuous going inside any Alabama school and offering a speech on the worth of each individual. Less talk, more action: that is what those who have lost a child due to an absence of moral courage demand.

Martin Luther King Jr. once wrote, "Intelligence plus character—that is the goal of true education." Academic instructional time is important, especially in relation to math and science, which are often highlighted as the subjects that hold the key to the future. However, what has always separated America from the rest of the world on and off the battlefield is the spirit that guides its people. A quick look at history will reveal that many of the most successful people held the similar characteristic of being able to reinvent themselves, as things rarely went as planned. Success wasn't always about who was the most gifted, but instead about who was able to master their social development.

At a time when racial tension and a sense of heightened inequality still persists, more people are trying to survive in a struggling economy and the world is only growing more complex; the need for unity of ideas and perspectives in solving problems and addressing challenges is vital. Although typical politicians can rarely look beyond the chaotic fog of the present challenges, it even seems amazing for them not to recognize the necessity of taking proactive steps in teaching developing youth how to work beyond their differences in respectfully finding answers. Future generations should not be limited by what they can achieve due to the divisiveness of partisan and identity politics.

An instruction on the true meaning of unity, service, and accountability could begin with an example from the leaders in government. Those in Alabama need the leadership to start demonstrating the type of behavior to emulate with a sense of urgency. This would require not continuing to follow the lead of the federal government in waiting until the end of each year to attempt passing a flurry of bills to thwart oversight, just as excuses for why state agencies cannot be held accountable for waste must be eliminated. This is especially true when considering most of the excuses they offer are not credible.

In April 2015, a number of legislators determined the best way to motivate the heads of agencies to eliminate waste with warranted cuts was to essentially bribe them. In explaining the rationale behind the practice of offering them bonuses for their effort, Rep. Ed Henry (R-Hartselle) said, "Not to say that some of them aren't doing it, but there is nothing the state does to motivate them to run as lean as possible."

Less than five months later, he gave an interview with Cliff Sims of the Yellowhamer News. An article from Elizabeth BeShears, a writer for the Yellowhammer at the time, documented Henry saying, "So you've got a number of great people who are reform-minded but they are concerned about how the bureaucracy is going to hurt the very people they were sent there to serve... What I say is, let's take out the bureaucracy. If it takes massive reforms, then let's do massive reforms... We can beat them. But I promise you, giving them more money and doing what they want is never going to change anything." Although the circumstance he was addressing was different, it is this type of contradiction—in this instance, using money as an incentive—that breeds distrust. While situations are rarely the same, citizens want consistency in leadership.

Taking into account his entire record of service, Rep. Henry still seems like the type of public servant who can be trusted to lead such reforms. However, in specific relation to his claims and concerns surrounding reform, the Public Service Commission proved him wrong in his assertions. The agency proved that, in many cases, it will come down to whether the ones in leadership are dedicated to simply doing the right thing.

The same source of news, the Yellowhammer, highlighted the work of the agency in a July 2015 article by Cliff Sims entitled "As Ala. Lawmakers fret over budgets, one agency 'very easily' slashed its budget by one-third." Comm. Jeremy Oden, Comm. Chris "Chip" Beeker, and Comm. President Twinkle Cavanaugh ignored the tendencies from others to offer numerous excuses and complaints and instead got down to work.

Cliff Sims detailed the extraordinary results in writing, "The PSC maintained 59 state vehicles in 2010. They've cut that number by more than half, down to 24. The agency also consolidated its office space from an eye-popping 67,000 square feet to a more manageable 42,000, cutting its annual lease from $1.1 million to just under $700,000 in the process. Cavanaugh's office is now only one-third the size it was when she was first elected. But the most impressive cut may have been to staff, which has gone from a bloated 120 down to 75." Beyond the money that was saved, Comm. President Cavanaugh also reported only positive feedback from the community. The "backlash" concerns Rep. Henry cited were absent; the people expressed the desire for more cuts.

While the state budget in Alabama is divided into two parts, the general fund and the education fund, the ability of the leadership at the Public Service Commission to successfully oversee a transfer of almost 9 million more dollars annually to the general fund than in previous years is telling within the broader picture. While taking from one does not necessarily mean giving to another, it cannot be lost that state legislators chose to cut $7.5 million from the Alabama Reading Initiative (ARI) in the 2016 budget. Waste, fraud, and inefficiency always hurt unforeseen growth; in this case, affecting kids.

While the legislature was busy making cuts to a beneficial reading program, one Alabama high school student was working to create a summer program to help students retain and build on the skills they had already learned in reading and math. Annisha Borah of Florence High School successfully started "Each One Teach One" after recognizing a problem, conducting the research, securing the necessary funding, and assembling an able staff. More than instructing the children in valuable lessons, Annisha is clearly teaching lawmakers a number of lessons as well. Once again, in the absence of leadership in government, the private sector stepped up in an attempt to fill the void. Imagine how wonderful the economic and educational results could be if each side of the equation were equally pulling their weight in effort, commitment, leadership, and vision.

The 2016 budget also displayed a shortfall of $85 million to Medicaid, placing children and the elderly, who depend on it the most, on the front lines of those being adversely impacted by the general mismanagement and fiscal incompetence of legislators. A billion-dollar settlement from BP for the 2010 oil spill was one of the main assets being tossed around to fix Alabama's fiscal woes, with Medicaid being presented as one of the main beneficiaries in eliminating the gap. Some lawmakers even pushed at one time for taking a lump sum to eliminate the almost twenty-year time period they cited for receiving increments, with the state finance director saying, "We think if we got the $500 million and invested it, we would be better off." While it might sound reasonable to someone outside the state, Alabamians cannot trust this logic.

Distrust can most certainly be found in families of recent college graduates. At one time, Alabama ran the PACT, or Prepaid Affordable College Tuition Plan, to help parents get an early start in paying for their child's college education. It was entirely run through state management and investment. After the funds were eventually squandered, parents who had paid into it were forced to take the state to court in 2012 to protect their investment. Before the settlement, Patti Lambert, co-founder of Save Alabama PACT, was quoted as saying, "We need to do what we told them we would do to some extent, or we are going to be the biggest glorified Ponzi scheme in the history of America."

Despite state leaders apparently expecting the people of Alabama to blindly have faith in any future management and investment of funds, they themselves have proven they also possess some doubts. Alabama now promotes College Counts, an out-of-state savings program, to parents looking to save in advance of their child's future. Unlike PACT, the Alabama state treasury obviously holds no control of it. Decisions are instead left to the individual owners of each account. Out of all the product features advertised on the website of the bank and trust company in Nebraska, a line at the bottom revealed the most. In fine print, it reads:

> "Accounts and investments under the College Counts 529 Fund are not insured or guaranteed by the FDIC, the State of Alabama, the State of Alabama Treasurer, The Board, The Trust, The Program, Union Bank & Trust Company or any other entity. Investment returns are not guaranteed, and you could lose money by investing."

Other than the BP settlement being presented as the lifeline that could solve Alabama's immediate problems, Governor Bentley has also been advocating for lawmakers to provide residents with the opportunity to vote on a state lottery. Although previously against the lottery, the estimated $225 million is being presented by the governor as the best option for helping replace the $85 million deducted from Medicaid. He advocates for what could be short-term benefits, disregarding that a lottery would take some time to bring in any substantial revenue.

More importantly, Governor Bentley's conclusion concerning the positive impact to Medicaid moving forward relies on a discipline in lawmakers that is rarely demonstrated. As Dr. Kenneth Elmer, a Birmingham physician, pointed out, "If the legislature passes a lottery now there is money that can fund Medicaid and then they decrease the General Fund budget for Medicaid by the same amount, then nothing really happens." The words of Dr. Elmer were part of the report by Alan Collins of WBRC on the reaction to the cuts in Medicaid by those specifically associated with the healthcare of children.

The children of Alabama have already been forced to make some difficult cuts.

In a video from the Alabama Policy Institute, radio host Rick Burgess of the popular "Rick and Bubba Show" cited other states that have instituted the lottery as examples of how it never quite fits up to expectations. However, what is most significant is his articulation of the real root of Alabama's problems by alluding to a lack of trust, echoing the same sentiments as Dr. Elmer:

> "Well the lottery starts making money; because it will. And then the money is available now to the same people that corrupted the other tax revenue they had coming in. So magically, because it's lottery money, they now have become great with money and they manage well and they do a great job. But you know what? It doesn't matter if the money comes from tax revenue. It doesn't matter if the money comes from a lottery. If they mismanage the money they got now, they just gonna mismanage that as well. And any politician that is telling you or me, 'Look, if we want to solve our budget problems, we got to have more revenue, the answer is gambling;' that's lazy. You know what they're telling me, 'I won't take the time nor do I have the expertise to buckle down, look at the tax revenues that are coming in, and balance a budget. It's a lazy plan."

The past record of legislators managing the budget does not warrant much trust. Beyond the money routinely taken from the Education Fund—80 million with the 2016 budget—lawmakers continue to build upon a legacy of governing that relies on consistent use of IOUs. In reporting on the discussions of how to spend the $1 billion BP settlement, Mary Sell from *The Decatur Daily* reminded readers of the $161.5 million the state still had to pay back to the General Fund Rainy Day account, as well as the $437 million that Alabama legislators borrowed from the Trust Fund in 2012.

Sell documented the response of Sen. Arthur Orr to the money still specifically owed to the Trust Fund that in 2013 lawmakers committed to repay: "Orr said when the money was borrowed and the commitment to pay it back was made, the expectation was that General Fund revenues would increase, but so far, they've stayed flat." Despite being set in law, it seems some are looking for a way to abandon the 2013 commitment.

Alabama is one among only three states with a budget composed of two parts, the General Fund and the Education Trust Fund. Katherine Green Robertson of the Alabama Policy Institute further detailed the restrictions to discretionary spending found within the budget:

"Alabama's Constitution requires the diversion of certain categories of revenue to specific purposes, without those funds ever passing through the hands of the Legislature" with "88% of Alabama's general tax revenue [being] earmarked this way, while the national average is about 25%. The Education Trust Fund (ETF) receives 52% of Alabama's total state funds, while the General Fund (GF) receives only 16%."

Clearly, there is a need for more flexibility within the budget, especially when considering the uncertainty attached to the continued expansion of Medicaid each year—but where is the groundwork from lawmakers for needed credibility in changing the design of the budget? With one failed budget after another—as well as a tendency to rely on special sessions to govern, a pattern of already taking from the Education Trust Fund, a proven inability to protect public investments, a "spend it or lose it" mentality in regards to zero-based budgeting, a desperate attempt of bribery to bring desired reforms, and the elimination of funding for critical services—no lawmaker should believe necessary trust is imminent. Ultimately ending yet another required special session with the decision to use the B.P. settlement to shore up Medicaid and pay down some debt does little to raise confidence.

The problem in Alabama is not the people; it is the leadership.

An opinion poll from the *Montgomery Advertiser* found that "a majority of poll respondents said they'd be willing to pay higher taxes to protect education and healthcare from more budget cuts." The paper also highlighted the desire of most respondents to raise revenue through some degree of higher taxes on the wealthy. Speaking of those polled, the paper wrote, "They recognize Alabama's regressive tax system, with its heavy reliance on sales taxes, unfairly burdens the poor and gives more affluent, including property owners and farming and timber concerns, a sweet deal." In no place is this difference more profound than in the Black Belt region of the state, where timber and farming rule the taxation policy.

Continuing to select those who will lead in Alabama from the same political process is about as likely to produce capable representation as it is to win the lottery (if one is ever established in Alabama). It will continue to produce the type of results that will keep Alabama at the very bottom in "the health of democracy," as was shown from an examination of all states and the District of Colombia in 2015. It will result in the same political arena that makes a mockery of ethics, as the House Chairman of the Ethics and Campaign Finance Committee demonstrated in September 2016 when he pointed to "confusion among lawmakers" concerning legalities and "ambiguities" within the law. It will continue to celebrate failure, as in the case of Governor Bentley when he reacted to the signing of the dismal 2016 budget by saying, "I want to say to those that stood strong and stood tall and put people over politics and voted for a cigarette tax, I want to commend them." If anything, he only highlighted how in trouble the state would be if people quit smoking, since taxing vices is the common answer for raising revenue.

What Montgomery needs is more individuals who possess the political courage of Alex Smith, a student at the University of Alabama. In October 2015, she utilized the university newspaper, *The Crimson White*, to publicly reject the status quo mentality she had quickly discovered within her first year of service on the SGA. What has been labeled as "The Machine" by some, simply describes a powerful voting block of Greek members within the Student Governmental Associations on college campuses across the country. It essentially controls the agenda of the school by selecting a choice or preference and pressuring every member to follow suit.

In the paper, Alex explained that she became a senator because she "wanted to represent all areas of campus" and especially "give a voice to the voiceless." Impressive in its own right when considering the short-term and long-term rewards and benefits that would have resulted from simply following the crowd; it's what she wrote at the end of her article that truly exemplifies the type of character Alabamians need in their state representatives:

> "I was going to ask my fellow senators to join me, to refuse to support a system that helps the few at the expense of many. But as much as I'd like one, I don't need a revolution. Even if no one joins me, even if people who once spoke to me turn their backs to me, even if no one whose mind can be changed reads this article, I won't regret writing it. Because I'm finally doing the right thing. I'm finally free."

Some may say the decisions of a college student in no way holds the level of significance or complexity to the decisions that face those in government, and any comparison for understanding would be naïve. However, in *Profiles in Courage*, John F. Kennedy, at the time a U.S. Senator, wrote, "To be courageous requires no exceptional qualifications, no magic formula, no special combination of time, place, and circumstance. It is an opportunity that sooner or later is presented to us all."

Alex Smith displayed courage in the opportunity that was presented to her. She understood the enormous responsibility of being entrusted by others to represent them. Her conscience would not allow her to place votes under the guise of good faith, while knowing they would actually be driven entirely by an agenda tailored for a select few. She placed the needs of others above any personal short-term or long-term ambitions. Alex offered the characteristics of leadership to believe in, providing a blueprint of the type of considerations that should drive anyone, regardless of title or position.

The people of Alabama do not have to accept continuing to place at the bottom in almost every indicator of state health; consistently fighting among the states at the bottom for simply remaining above last place. The type of change necessary will never come from the same political system that consistently rewards special interests—special interests that are often given the desired camouflage by lawmakers. Nor will it come from the one party leadership that has always dominated Alabama. The People's Clearing House could be instrumental in determining which state residents are likely to lead with a heart of a servant, providing a measuring stick that requires a consistent demonstration of integrity. Alabama can lead the nation beyond football, especially in areas of social change. With the right leadership, almost anything is possible with the good people of the great state of Alabama.

The People Must Set the Standards

Appearing on the first episode of Stephen Colbert's Late Show from September 2015, Vice President Joe Biden talked about how his late and beloved son Bo "abhorred people who had a sense of entitlement." In explaining the foundation behind his son's humble nature, the Vice President remarked, "My mom used to say, remember, no one is better than you, but you are better than nobody; everybody is equal." I think someone today would be hard-pressed to discover many within the country who actually believed the bulk of Congress remembers this truth, much less allow it to guide their service.

A vast majority of legislators are unfortunately already suffering from a case of irreversible "Potomac Fever." In an interview with Merle Miller for his book, *Plain Speaking: An Oral Biography of Harry S. Truman*, Truman described "Potomac Fever" by saying, "It was Woodrow Wilson who coined the phrase. He said some people came to Washington and grew with their jobs, but he said a lot of other people came, and all they did was swell up. Those that swell up are the ones that have Potomac Fever. They're the people who forgot who they are and who sent them there."

In the book *The Autobiography of Theodore Roosevelt*, Wayne Andrews documented Theodore Roosevelt as saying, "I at one period began to believe that I had a future before me, and that it behooved me to be very far-sighted and scan each action carefully with a view to its possible effect on that future." His initial logic is not unique and seems all too familiar in D.C. and legislative bodies across the country. Presidential candidate Rand Paul called for term limits in Congress, while at the same time, advocating for a change in Kentucky law that would allow him to appear on the ballot twice for preserving his place in the

Senate. President Obama voted against raising the debt ceiling and citing it as a failure in leadership as a senator, but consistently calls for Congress to heighten it as president. Hillary Clinton once called the Trans-Pacific Trade agreement "the gold standard in trade deals"; she now opposes it in her bid for the White House.

The motivation of self-interest that initially drove Theodore Roosevelt can so often be credited with the policy decisions past and present of many who have served as representatives "for the people." However, Theodore Roosevelt ultimately, and rather quickly, recognized his mistake: "This speedily made me useless to the public and an object of aversion to myself; and I then made up my mind that I would try not to think of the future at all, but would proceed on the assumption that each office I held would be the last I ever should hold and that I would confine myself to trying to do my work as well as possible while I held that office. I found that for me personally this was the only way in which I could either enjoy myself or render good service to the country, and I never afterword deviated from the plan." Unfortunately, very few politicians today seem to reach or value such a significant conclusion.

So often, the American people are scratching their heads as to how many more times their leaders can fail tests that emphasize more willpower in doing what is right. Though a periodic review of the headlines would routinely provide more than enough examples in this regard, one of the most egregious betrayals in the name of self-interest has to be that of insider trading. For a long time, it seemed as if this unfair practice would remain legal. "A 2004 study of the results of stock trading by United States Senators during the 1990s found that senators on average beat the market by 12% a year. In sharp contrast, U.S. households on average underperformed the market by 1.4% a year and even corporate insiders on average beat the market by only about 6% a year during that period." This study may go a long way in explaining how "members of Congress had a collective net worth of more than $2 billion in 2010, a nearly 25 percent increase over the 2008 total." One can only imagine how high this number will climb in the future.

Despite clear questions of integrity revolving around the correlation of insider trading to drastic rises in income, members of Congress still took the opportunity to admonish employees within the fantasy football industry for using insider information. "There's absolutely scandalous conduct taking place through those programs, fantasy sports," Senate Democratic Leader Harry Reid told reporters. Although most would clearly agree the public should be protected against corruption, it is ironic that Congress perceives itself as the moral authority to provide such a resolution. However, in the end, the gaming industry should be fine considering "the Fantasy Sports Trade Association has spent $80,000 in 2015 to defend its interests in Washington." Money talks and this push for an investigation most likely stemmed from greed more than patriotism—with the government feeling short-changed any time it does not receive a piece of the financial pie.

Fairly recently, some members of Congress seemed as if they had finally taken a long look in the mirror, attempting to correct their own oversight in relation to insider trading with the passage of the Stop Trading on Congressional Knowledge Act. As Tamar Keith of NPR wrote in 2012, the bill, passed under President Obama's watch, "wouldn't just outlaw trading on nonpublic information by members of Congress, the executive branch, and their staffs. It would greatly expand financial disclosures and make all of the data searchable so insider trading and conflicts of interest would be easier to detect."

Despite the positives of added transparency, the teeth of the bill were stripped away due to theoretical "concerns, especially among the 28,000 executive branch staff, [which] would be required to post their financial disclosures online." Washington has a way of becoming very focused and efficient when it comes to matters of self-preservation. Both parties had good reason to raise these particular security apprehensions with "at least 72 aides on both sides of the aisle [trading] shares of companies that their bosses help oversee; according to a Wall Street Journal analysis of more than 3,000 disclosure forms covering trading activity by Capitol Hill staffers for 2008 and 2009."

Ultimately, privacy concerns were used as an excuse to circumvent any modifications and instead choose to entirely remove the most important tool for enforcing the insider trading bill; although, the government relentlessly emphasizes the need for the American people to simply trust the National Security Agency's monitoring of private information in the name of national security. With priorities evident, the Republican-led Houses of Congress utilized the "fast-track" procedure known as "unanimous consent" to quickly garner the votes necessary for passing the removal. This, of course, took place before the weekend and at a time known for receiving the least attention from the public.

Regardless, whether read or heard about publically, the American people are feeling the effects of inequality as a result of greed-driven representation. "While Americans median wealth is down 43% since 2007, Congress members' net worth has jumped 28%"; this is happening while the middle class disappears before our very eyes. In his article "The Shrinking Middle Class, Mapped State by State," Tim Henderson writes, "A new Stateline analysis shows that in all 50 states, the percentage of 'middle class' households—those making between 67 percent and 200 percent of the state's median income—shrunk between 2000 and 2013." This continues today. He goes on to write, "In most states, the growing percentage of households paying 30 percent (the federal standard of housing affordability) or more of their income on housing illustrates that it is increasingly difficult for many American families to make ends meet."

Sadly, few American families have the time or resources to make the trek to Washington, complete all the registration procedures, and search through all the individual records and codes within the documents housed in the basement to try and assemble a "Woodward and Bernstein"-type undercover story on insider trading. Families are simply trying to survive, wondering how they will provide sufficient daily resources—while fearing how they will overcome any unforeseen occurrences. They cannot possibly grasp how to defeat the corrupt system in Washington; much less begin taking the actions necessary when living paycheck to paycheck. Much of Congress is either blind to these common realities preventing Americans from focusing on holding them accountable—or celebrate in knowing they exist. Regardless, all legislators had to be more than aware that by voting to eliminate the requirement to post financial transactions of staff members online directly helped members not only to conceal any past wrongdoing, but also further maintained the atmosphere of secrecy which would allow the future theft of the American people.

Despite the attempt of Congress to limit the chances of being held responsible for their egregious behavior regarding insider trading by average American citizens, an investigation was launched by The U.S. Securities and Exchange Commission involving "44 investment funds [that] may be involved in a suspected healthcare insider trading scandal." However, the investigation was stymied nearly a year and a half by the House Ways and Means Committee that used the U.S. Constitution as the centerpiece of their refusal to produce the requested information. This irony is just another example of those in D.C. placing themselves above the people.

Although ordered by a federal judge to comply with the SEC subpoenas in early November 2015, the House won a delay in producing the requested information, having appealed the original order to comply from November. Unlike most middle class and poor Americans, the members of Congress have the luxury of being able to fight prosecution by launching as many appeals as money can buy, often provided by the taxpayers.

The rules seem to only apply to those outside of Washington. Attempting to bring a member of government to justice concerning questionable behavior consistently meets strenuous opposition. This is even the case in instances that are well known and troubling to the general public, such as the behavior of the IRS and former director Lois Lerner in possibly targeting groups for political purposes. Ms. Lerner chose to take the Fifth and not offer any testimony at the House hearings, which often indicates guilt. Either way, the Justice Department not only chose to clear her of any wrongdoing, but also took the time to send a letter to the senior members of the House Committee on Oversight and Government Reform to "praise Lerner for being the first IRS official to spot the problem in the determinations division and for taking prompt action to bring it to a halt."

Not surprisingly, the decision to formally exonerate the shameful employee took place late in the afternoon on a Friday to receive the least amount of notice. However, even the few Americans who happened to see the story were probably not surprised, as Congress is known for spending millions on hearings that often result in more political points than it does in actually holding anyone accountable for their actions.

Senator Ted Cruz took to the senate floor in July 2015 and summarized the entitlement that drives D.C.—regardless of their ineptness in leadership. In a speech that would receive criticism from both sides of the aisle, the Texas senator called Republican Majority Leader Mitch McConnell a liar and described how the voice of the American people is consistently disregarded in setting agenda regardless of which party is in power:

> "He brought up his Obamacare amendment as a smokescreen [because] it's intended to fail. But you know what he didn't bring up is my amendment to end the Congressional exemption from Obamacare; the corrupt deal that Harry Reid cut with President Obama to exempt members of Congress. We ought to live under the same rules as everyone else. Majority Leader doesn't want to vote on that because he doesn't want to end the cronyism for members of congress any more than end the cronyism for giant corporations who enrich themselves at the expense of the American people… Sadly today, we have government of the lobbyist, by the lobbyist, and for the lobbyist."

Of course, this consistent pattern of projecting entitlement and offering clear contradictions to providing true service to the entire constituency is seen as acceptable behavior. It has also been a common practice to display a belief that the institution is above reproach by simply maintaining a sense of civility within the chambers of Congress, regardless of whether any useful legislation is being passed.

One of the most significant examples may come from the documentation of David P. Schippers, chief investigative counsel for the Clinton impeachment. In describing the proceedings in his book entitled, *Sellout: The Inside Story of President Clinton's Impeachment*, David wrote, "It was obvious from the onset that the Republican leadership was totally at the mercy of the polls. As long as the President's approval rating remained high, the Republican leaders were not about to rock the boat. They were more interested in preserving the self-proclaimed 'dignity' of the Senate than in performing the constitutional duty imposed upon them by the electorate." David believes that the unwillingness of the GOP to courageously cast a light on all the information available, as well as the methods of evasion advanced by the Clinton Administration and their allies, allowed the President to successfully avoid an impeachment by the Senate.

When asked about the moment he left the limelight in Washington and whether it was difficult, former President Truman said, "Never gave me any trouble at all. I always kept in mind something old Ben Franklin said at that meeting in Philadelphia we were talking about. They had a big discussion about what should be done about ex-Presidents, and Alexander Hamilton I think it was said that it would be a terrible thing to degrade them by putting them back among the common people after they'd had all that power." Beyond the presidency, many of our past legislators share a similar view and have always planned to utilize their previous power in Congress to remain in the realm of politics or secure high-paying jobs from benefactors of past policy decisions that were favorable.

One of the best examples is former Nebraska Senator Ben Nelson, the recipient of the "Cornhusker Kickback" Medicaid provision from Harry Reid to advance Obamacare, who upon retirement "almost immediately boosted his salary over five times" by becoming the CEO of the National Association of Insurance Commissions. Although, this could actually only compose a small fraction of what he truly made that year alone when considering he also took a senior advisor position for Agenda, a public affair firm, for an undisclosed amount. While not allowed to lobby on behalf of the National Association of Insurance Commissions to the legislative branch for two years, he has already used his influence in Washington to gain the ear of the President.

Of course, this practice of simply switching roles within the arena of Washington politics is also shared by many staffers in Washington, "as former government employees accounted for 44 percent of all registered, active firm lobbyists in 2012, up from 18 percent in 1998, according to a recent study by the Sunlight Foundation." For some staffers in Washington, they seem to be taking maximizing to a whole new level. First, they help conceal questionable insider trading practices. Then, they move to K-Street as lobbyists after learning the ins and outs of how to effectively maneuver governmental treatment of the industry they will represent to further cheat the American people.

The power and luxury representatives of government enjoy at the expense of average taxpayers is just too addictive for many to ever consider exiting the arena of politics for the common existence of everyday Americans. As for Harry Truman, he didn't agree with Hamilton, but instead sided with Franklin: "But old Ben Franklin didn't agree... Franklin said, 'In free governments the rulers are the servants and the people their superiors and sovereigns. For the former therefore to return among the latter is not to degrade them but to promote them." Few legislators in state governments across the country are different than those in D.C. who fail to hold a similar conviction.

The problem of the "revolving door" of bureaucrats and former politicians became so prevalent in D.C. that the U.S. Congress acted in 2007 to curb it through laws. However, as expected, the measures were half-hearted and ultimately lacked the proper tools for oversight, allowing those who would be adversely affected through sufficient enforcement to merely rely on loopholes to successfully skirt the laws.

It seems not enough legislators agree with Teddy Roosevelt's conclusion that "it is a dreadful misfortune for a man to grow to feel that his livelihood and whole happiness depend upon his staying in office," nor take heed to his advice that "a man should have some other occupation—[he] had several occupations—to which he can resort it at any time he is being thrown out, unless he is willing to stay in at the cost of his conscience."

The legislation initially put forth by Congress began with some degree of promise. In their article "Law Doesn't End Revolving Door on Capitol Hill," Eric Lipton and Ben Protess of *The New York Times* wrote, "When Congress updated the ethics rules in 2007 in the wake of the Jack Abramoff lobbying scandal, which included illegal influence peddling between a lawmaker and a former aide, it initially drafted tighter restrictions on the revolving door, arguing that a broader

ban lasting two years might curb conflicts of interest in Washington."
More importantly, their article went on to inform us that "with protests from some lawmakers—including Representative John Conyers,
Democrat of Michigan, and Representative Lamar Smith, Republican
of Texas, then the top two members of the House Judiciary Committee—the proposal was watered down to remove the two-year 'cooling
off' period for the House and other restrictions."

Both of those representatives leading that protest had around 55
years of combined service, with Representative Smith serving since
1987 and Representative Conyers serving since 1965. Both men are
still serving in the House of Representatives today, with many of the
loopholes they helped create being actively utilized; although, the lack
of effort from the Justice Department in the enforcement of the rules
in place that remained may not require using them. "Unless the violation is brought to our attention, it is hard to enforce," said Michael P.
Kortan, the chief spokesman of the FBI.

For America to move forward, the culture found within our legislative bodies across the country and in D.C. must be drastically al-
tered, beginning with a new foundation of leadership built on accountability and responsibility that will allow it to lead from power.
Unfortunately, the current mechanisms in place are inadequate in
achieving such an endeavor, much of which clearly comes as a result
of the legislators themselves writing the rules, guidelines for enforcement, and set of punishments.

Federal elections are monitored by the Federal Elections Commission, or FEC, an "independent regulatory agency" established in 1975
"to disclose campaign finance information, to enforce the provisions
of the law such as the limits and prohibitions on contributions, and to
oversee the public funding of presidential elections." However, it's far
from independent and serves as merely a buffer for the status quo in
Washington in having a balanced committee of six members, being
composed of three Republicans and three Democrats, which thwarts
any attempt for meaningful oversight and enforcement.

"From 2008 to August 2014, the FEC has had over 200 tie votes,
accounting for approximately 14 percent of all votes in enforcement
matters," which may go a long way in explaining why Ann Ravel, the
Democratic chairwoman of the FEC, actually suggested to fix the
agency by firing everyone but herself. However, it's doubtful anyone
would label her as non-partisan, considering her support for outland-
ish requests by outdoing Sen. Minority Leader Harry Reid. "On January 4, the Washington Examiner first reported that the Senator from
Nevada made a two-pronged request to the Federal Elections Com-

mission (FEC), seeking allowance to use campaign cash to hire an administrative assistant to help with the Senator's post-office activities, and to use money from Reid's leadership PAC to fund the costs associated with transitioning out of his Senate role and into what would be his new role as a 'former officeholder.'"

Either way, even if broken, as with Alabama, there is always time to simply fix it and forget it, with no meaningful punishment in order to create a deterrent. Regardless, I do believe Ann Ravel in one respect. "She's largely given up hope of reining in abuses in raising and spending money in the 2016 presidential campaign and calls the agency she oversees 'worse than dysfunctional.'"

Although the Citizens United decision opened up the door to unlimited amounts of money being spent indirectly on campaigns, each state is still unique in determining their own campaign financing practices in regard to direct contributions, as well as establishing their own bodies of oversight and enforcement. However, as seen with Alabama, where laws were left without the proper agency to enforce them for over twenty years, this is not always something that is taken very seriously by legislators. Regardless of whether it is the FEC or another agency in charge of oversight within a state, one of the major issues lies in enforcement, where the delay in action often results in lack of meaningful punishment within the time period that could make it actually impact an election.

This is especially true in terms of Political Action Committees, or PACs, which often are disbanded before any action could be taken against them for violations (such as disclosure oversights). On the federal level, "the response time problem may be endemic to the enforcement procedures established by Congress. To complete steps necessary to resolve a complaint—including time for defendants to respond to the complaint, time to investigate and engage in legal analysis, and finally, where warranted, prosecution—necessarily takes far longer than the comparatively brief period of a political campaign." Campaign finance is no different than any other ethical matters in which Congress and state legislatures have established methods and procedures that will help make any attempt to truly enforce them against any member a very long and uphill task.

The People's Clearing House must be an independent agency that enforces the legal standards established by the people. While tougher House and Senate ethics could help carry out or coincide with the People's Clearing House penalties, it should be completely separate from the ethics committees existing in Washington and state legislatures across the country. Independence will allow the People's Clearing House the necessary authority to act in real time against new attempts to create loopholes within the system.

Beyond actively addressing efforts to undermine the integrity of the system through assigning additional deductions as necessary, the People's Clearing House will also be positioned to proactively put forth new restrictions to adequately address new threats to transparency and compliance in the future. The system has the body of oversight to quickly address non-compliance through additional deductions to set a precedent in real time—or at least establish the stage for the necessary deductions in the near future. Every aspect builds on a foundation of protection for the entire constituency from manipulation and abuse that weakens the level of equal representation.

Ethical standards in relation to other aspects of governing (such as insider trading and revolving doors) should naturally rise once the proper foundation of representation has been established through supervision and enforcement of the People's Clearing House. However, even in terms of existing ethics, true autonomy is vital to success, which President Obama tried to advocate for in a 2008 Presidential Debate:

> "I supported an office of public integrity, an independent office that would be able to monitor ethics investigations in the Senate, because I thought it was important for the public to know that if there were any ethical violations in the Senate, that they weren't being investigated by the Senators themselves, but there was somebody independent who would do it."

His attempt to merely strengthen the structures currently in place was predictably unsuccessful and only provides another example of how change is truly necessary and how difficult it will always be.

Just as the Alabama legislature strengthened the laws pertaining to harassment of school athletes and officials to demonstrate it was a priority, a clear message must be sent for a set of penalties for securing representation through compliance. Any additional percentage added to deductions for TPCH as a result of non-compliance must be measured, but effective. Beyond deductions for future donations or the current war chest an incumbent representative or candidate from office already possesses, future loss or lessening of future pensions must also be on the table as possible punishments. While some may disagree, one must ask why there is outrage from members of Congress concerning the golden parachute provided for CEOs of companies, but not a word is said about basically offering the same to members of Congress.

Members such as current U.S. Representative Charlie Rangel (D-NY), former U.S. Representative Jesse Jackson, Jr. (D-IL), and former U.S. Representative Michael Grimm (R-NY) all broke the trust of the people, but to my knowledge only Representative Grimm was stripped of his pension. Charlie Rangel remains in the House of Representatives today and merely received a slap on the wrist through formal censorship despite violating eleven of the thirteen ethics rules; although, if you go by the reaction of others in Washington who actually cried at such a perceived travesty by some inside the Beltway, you would have thought someone had died.

The punishments of TPCH must contain the teeth necessary to genuinely provide the additional incentive for a deterrent beyond the consequences of having to explain to the public why they directly chose themselves over the people. Then, the people can begin helping many in Congress do what the judge recognized U.S. Representative Grimm must do when she said, "Your moral compass, Mr. Grimm, needs some reorientation."

THE TIME FOR ACTION IS NOW.

Inaction simply creates opportunities for legislators to further entrench themselves with laws and procedures designed to make the task of fundamentally changing the counterproductive culture that lacks accountability more difficult (if not eventually impossible). Candidates such as Jeb Bush will simply continue to point to playing by the rules currently in place when taking advantage of them, such as how he raised money for the super PAC Right to Rise that supported him before officially announcing—getting around the rule which bars coordination between the two. In responding to a reporter about his assistance in raising this money for the super PAC, the former Florida Governor said, "I'm playing the rules of the game, the way it's laid out. And if the people don't like it, that's just tough luck."

Supporters of the 2016 Democratic frontrunner Hillary Clinton shouldn't feel much better if they are honest, as her campaign is "collaborating directly with Correct the Record, a super PAC providing the Democratic frontrunner's team with opposition research," despite federal law forbidding any coordination between candidates and PACs. However, what is more troubling is the fact that less than a month after telling supporters "the endless flow of secret, unaccountable money" has to be halted, the "main super PAC backing her bid for the Democratic presidential nomination accepted a $1 million contribution that cannot be traced."

Unfortunately, the line in how candidates interact with these "independent" groups will now only further be blurred in relation to super PAC involvement with campaigns by the recent ruling of the FEC to open the door for candidates and some of their campaign staff to solicit contributions—with donations of unrestricted amounts being acceptable through staffers "as long as they make clear that they are not making the request at the direction of the candidate." I mean, why wouldn't the American people trust these campaign surrogates to hold true to this behind closed doors? This meaningless specification within the ruling further mocks the electorate.

Although Republicans are often the ones fighting campaign reform the most, these latest changes in relation to coordination with super PACs were brought on by the requests of Democrats, which only further displays that neither party can be trusted in doing what is right in terms of the people. Former Republican Speaker of the House Mike Hubbard of Alabama, a chief architect of the ethics reform aimed at ending corruption within the state, unsuccessfully fought felony charges on ethics violations. He utilized previous campaign funds to base his defense on First Amendment protections.

Then you have state senator John Schickel (R-KY) who also utilized the 1st Amendment as the crux for his argument when he "filed a federal suit to overturn state limits on campaign contributions and lobbying gifts, saying they are unconstitutional and violate free speech laws." And, of course, you always have Republican Senate Majority Leader Mitch McConnell's annual effort to increase contributions to political parties by inserting provisions within spending bills at the end of each year. These are just a few examples of how the GOP earn their anti-campaign finance reform label.

Yet, Democratic National Committee Chairwoman Debbie Wasserman Schultz may have demonstrated best in the 2016 race that neither party seeks to eliminate money from campaigns. She believed taxpayers should provide around 20 million dollars to each party for their national conventions. This idea came on the brink of passing a 1.1 trillion dollar Omnibus Spending Bill. The insanity among legislators is almost laughable.

President Truman once said, "My father used to say that a man ought to leave the world a little better than it was when he came into it, and if that can be said about me, I guess you'll have to say I lived a successful life." History will continue to provide the final judgment on each of our contributions to the world; although, as it specifically relates to politics, most of the men and women who serve will be long forgotten.

Headlines will simply provide the names of former representatives who have recently passed for possibly a brief moment of being remembered by those who love them. Few can name the prominent congressmen who presided over some of the most famous instances in our government, such as the Watergate and Clinton impeachment hearings. An overwhelming majority of the general public today cannot even name those directly representing them in their home state, much less those on the federal level.

Taking all this into account, what meaningful reward is there to advocate for policies of self-interest? Any materialistic possessions or specific contributions will not be remembered, but the decisions they make will produce long-lasting consequences.

Thomas Jefferson once said, "Unless the mass retains sufficient control over those entrusted with the powers of their government, these will be perverted to their own oppression, and to the perpetuation of wealth and power in the individuals and their families selected for the trust." While Americans can wish that those endowed with the responsibility of representing them would share the characteristics of men and women from the past who demonstrated integrity in their service, it seems very unlikely when looking at current behavior. No amount of longing for our leaders to take inventory of themselves and those around them, and bring the necessary accountability to reform for our current state of cronyism and corruption, seems to compare to the overriding wish of many to remain true to the comfort and safety of maintaining the status quo.

As President Kennedy once said, "The stories of past courage can define that ingredient—they can teach, they can offer hope, they can provide inspiration. But they cannot supply courage itself. For this each [individual] must look into their own soul."

While some will ultimately choose to cling to the counterproductive ways found in Washington, the People's Clearing House could finally provide the perfect measuring stick for determining which leaders are truly committed to the people in re-establishing the degree of equality in representation the Founders originally envisioned. Their willingness to adhere and advocate for greater accountability will identify them.

Problems with Past Reform Efforts

One of the most popular reform ideas is term limits. However, success or failure often depends on whether those advocating for reform can be effective in persuading voters to choose term limits as the defining issue of the election. For an opportunity to even occur, reform advocates have to somehow convince the electorate to become personally interested in the issue, when most Americans are already overwhelmed from just addressing routine daily concerns. Most people support a candidate who shares their views on a number of political topics, ranging in varying levels of importance, such as national security. Asking a majority of the electorate to set aside party affiliation and other issues of importance to focus on one issue alone has proven virtually impossible.

Although eventual positive outcomes from establishing more equal representation could be stressed to voters, what degree of genuine enthusiasm could be generated without the promise of how their lives would improve? Even if term limits were successful in helping reestablish the citizen statesmen of the Founders, people routinely desire instant gratification that would not be met through a long process.

A number of races would have to be won to establish term limits legislation. The sustained effort necessary would depend on the willingness of politicians to remain committed to instituting term limits. Each election would also have to provide voters with an available option of a term limit candidate, many of whom would have to come from incumbents who commonly have little desire to implement a rule against self-interest. Assuming an adequate choice was actually presented, what if the voter supporting term limits was more in line with the Republican seeking office, with only the Democrat in the race favoring term limits (or vice versa)? Just achieving an effective coordination of all these variables to elect a pro-reformer has proven daunting.

Despite all obstacles, suppose a few pro-reform candidates were elected. Could these new legislators actually display the necessary discipline to remain true to their pledges on term limit legislation and effectively build a coalition against an opposition led by a swarm of career politicians? The common culture of politics has routinely changed the hearts of many individuals who entered public service for the first time.

The methods and arguments against term limits have long been perfected by those opposed and could very easily become too enticing to new members, with term limits being only one issue among many on the agendas of legislatures nationwide. More importantly, changes in congressional leadership, unexpected defeats and deaths of supportive politicians, and the attention given to the consistent growth of pressing issues and challenges facing the country daily are all inconsistencies that make even the most dedicated of efforts almost impossible.

Those currently embedded have the high ground.

In relation to campaign finance reform, many of the efforts today are also plagued with similar types of obstacles in building the necessary alliances that those trying to advance term limits encountered. What seems consistent is the absence of an instrument for unity, especially when assessing that each reform strategy hinges on creating an enduring focus from representatives and a weary (and skeptical) electorate.

Almost certainly the most well-known of these reform efforts comes from Lawrence Lessig, a Harvard law professor, who in May of 2014 formed the Mayday PAC in an attempt to change the influence of big money on elections. Professor Lessig believes that success in reform revolves around public financing; on his website, mayday.us, he refers to five plans he would support for changing how money negatively impacts elections. Those plans (which are listed on repswith.us) all contain an aspect of public financing, but vary in their matching fund schemes. Many other characteristics separate one proposal from the next, from a push for additional levels of transparency to reinforcement of judicial review—but all are designed to raise the bar of accountability.

Larry Lessig chose to direct the funds he raised from his Mayday PAC to a select number of 2014 federal midterm elections in the hopes of discovering what messaging was effective with voters in making campaign finance reform a major issue. The data was taken in the hopes of setting the stage for great strides in the current 2016 election.

As for the races of 2014, the Mayday PAC was unfortunately only two for eight in the elections it had targeted, with both of those victories virtually guaranteed before the election. The wins most likely had nothing to do with the money given by Mayday. What Professor Lessig and his supporters did learn was that partisan loyalty was more significant in ultimately determining who most people supported, revealing the unlikelihood that campaign finance reform could ever stand alone. Mayday also discovered that candidates must have a passion and willingness to make the issue one of the main focuses of their campaigns for success, something that only incumbents already possessing a safe seat in Congress seemed open to embracing. Unfortunately for candidates facing a difficult election, too much pressure dictated that their focus be placed on other major issues. Utilizing time on a cause that might actually result in alienating some voters proved too risky for most of them.

Shortly following the 2014 elections, a press release from the super PAC Mayday read: "Our aims in this election cycle were A) To send a signal to members of Congress that opposing reform could have real electoral consequences and supporting reform could have electoral benefits, B) To demonstrate that the issue of money in politics moves voters, and C) To learn lessons about campaigning on our issue this cycle to set ourselves up for 2016." The group then went on to list a number of ways in which it had accomplished these aims to a degree, specifically seeming to celebrate the effect of making incumbents spend more money than expected to fend off pro-reform challengers.

While successful, moral victories that heighten the discussion of campaign finance reform will not provide the American people anything of substance for sustaining a long battle to eventual success. It is hard enough to garner the focus of voters for just one election, something Professor Lessig has admitted to as being a great obstacle. Ben Woodford of Politico highlighted the difficulty in keeping voter attention by referencing Trump's easy access to legislators through campaign contributions, "Trump may have unlocked a riddle that has vexed reformers for years: how to stir up sex appeal around an issue about as titillating as watching paint peel on the side of a Wisconsin barn."

Being victorious in a few races and forcing incumbents to spend more money that will easily be replenished through reliable lobbyists and campaign contributors once back in office is not going to be sufficient in eliminating the apathy of the electorate. Some may be mad and frustrated shortly after the election, but then the machinations of daily life return.

Reform efforts will not come as a result of choosing to seek the highest office in the land as a one-issue candidate. This is certainly true if done as a Democrat, the party most supportive of reform—with Republicans offering the most consistent resistance. Although this is no secret, additional evidence can be found at repswith.us, which "tracks Congressional candidates' support for specific legislation that would affect fundamental reform to reduce cronyism and the corrupting influence of money in politics."

Even someone with no previous knowledge on campaign finance reform could view the findings from the support behind these proposals, personally endorsed by Larry Lessig, and understand how irrational a strategy for reform would be if it involved party affiliation. The Government by the People Act sponsored by Rep. John Sarbanes (D-MD) is listed as being supported by 140 Democrats and 1 Republican; the Empowering Citizens Act sponsored by Rep. David Price (D-NC) has the listed support of 4 Democrats and no Republicans; the Political Money Reform Proposal sponsored by former Rep. Jim Rubens (R-NH) and the Taxation Only With Representation Act written by former ethics czar for President George W. Bush, Richard W. Painter, are both listed without any recognized support. Just among these the tally is 144 Dems and 1 GOP.

The American Anticorruption Act, the lone remaining reform listed on the site, is an effort brought by Represent.us, a non-partisan movement that has had success in establishing enough support for reform through citizen initiatives at the local level. Their group recognizes that building an alliance that extends across party lines provides the only true scenario for actually winning on campaign finance reform.

Democratic presidential candidate and current Vermont senator Bernie Sanders also understands that the corruption surrounding the current political system cannot be undone by one candidate or one party, but is something that will take a revolution full of diversity. In a speech from August 2015 in which he informed the public that he would be offering campaign finance reform legislation at the beginning of the next congressional session, Senator Sanders said, "The need for real campaign finance reform is not a progressive issue. It is not a conservative issue. It is an American issue."

Senator Sanders' view is shared by Democratic Senator Tom Udall who still hopes Congress will vote on his amendment, which would grant power to the U.S. Congress and state legislatures for regulating and limiting the raising and spending of money in elections. The Disclose Act sponsored by Democratic Senator Sheldon Whitehouse from Rhode Island is more targeted in functioning to alleviate the power of "dark money" by revealing their donors. Not surprisingly, his push for reform legislation only found limited backing from predominantly fellow Democrats, similar to Sanders.

However, even when Republican legislators attempt to pass some type of reform legislation to address the fundamental problems with current campaign finance, they receive very little support from fellow Republicans. The Citizens Involvement in Campaigns (CIVIC) Act from Rep. Thomas Petri (R-WI) or the Stop Act introduced by Rep. David Jolly (R-FL) are good examples as they both barely registered in the percentage estimated for passage.

None of these previous outcomes in partisan politics that continue to help routinely deflect any potential attempt for reform kept Professor Lessig from choosing to run as a Democratic candidate for president in what he described as an attempt to "hack" the current political system. Either way, he was basically shunned by the Democratic National Convention, something Senator Sanders can more than relate to, and his campaign failed to last even a month before ending well short of the first presidential primary. Democrats consistently present the notion of living more within the mantra of "one person, one vote," but the actions of the Democratic establishment in 2016 only proved their hypocrisy in calling out Republicans for being for the elites.

Similar to the unbound delegates of Republicans, but on a much larger scale, Democrats utilize super-delegates, which are not directly tied to votes in the primary process—but instead are able to vote for whichever candidate they desire at the Democratic National Convention. Once again, the voice of the people is disregarded for the belief that those in the political elite ultimately know better what is best for America.

Although direct contributions to candidates and parties are still limited on the federal level and at the discretion of each state government, attempting to advance legislation for placing limits on money spent by outside groups, such as PACs, will always meet arguments concerning freedom of speech. Even before the famous ruling by the Supreme Court which opened the door to unlimited spending on campaigns in Citizens United v. Federal Election Commission, the Buckley v. Valeo case had already laid the groundwork by "[striking] down on First Amendment grounds several provisions in the 1974 Amendments to the Federal Election Campaign Act. The most prominent portions of the case struck down limits on spending in campaigns, but upheld the provision limiting the size of individual contributions to campaigns."

Even attempting to limit some direct contributions may eventually be in jeopardy if we are to believe the article published in the *New York University Law Review* entitled "McCutcheon Could Lead to No Limits for Political Parties—With What Implications for Parties and Interest Groups?" written by Michael J. Malbin, executive director of Campaign Finance Institute in October 2014. With the current and unpredictable nature of future court rulings paired with an ever-decreasing lack of trust in government, the mere suggestion that reform could possibly take away any aspect of speech is enough to make people question how far their leaders may try to control dialogue if given an opening. These apprehensions fall squarely on the shoulders of our leaders who have created such an atmosphere of legitimate fear via overreaching.

The self-interest that drives many legislators serves to dilute the rules that are on the books concerning money in politics by routinely choosing to manipulate them through loopholes, leaving one to wonder whether any current reform would still not require more of the same (chasing the money). In November 2013, Rep. Andy Harris (R-MD), Mo Brooks (R-AL), Mark Amodei (R-NV), and Rep. Walter Jones (R-NC) unsuccessfully attempted to "close the personal use loophole" of money to some degree in relation to political action committees. Predictably, this effort failed miserably.

It seems few politicians living off the comfort of the status quo are willing to reflect on words of former President Nixon concerning what true sacrifice offers. In his book *In the Arena: A Memoir of Victory, Defeat, and Renewal*, former President Nixon (after leaving the White House and much later in life) wrote, "We can get more fulfillment from struggling for a good cause beyond ourselves than living a life of strictly fun for ourselves. Struggle is not fun. But it is better than fun. Those who welcome and enjoy it will get something out of life far more rewarding than those who do not."

With the genuine efforts of our legislators obviously in doubt, the people must find a method to come together and harness this kind of spirit to bring meaningful change. However, this is currently unlikely considering most Americans are not engaged in solving something they only feel affected by indirectly. Other issues are too pressing.

Although most Americans have not chosen to actively become

involved in implementing any of the current reform efforts, the majority is well aware the current system needs substantial reform. As John Schwarz of *The Intercept* explained in June 2015, a poll displayed that "85 percent of Americans say we need to either 'completely rebuild' or make 'fundamental changes' to the campaign finance system. Just 13 percent think 'only minor changes are necessary,' less than the 18 percent of Americans who believe they've been in the presence of a ghost." People are also listening to individuals like former President Jimmy Carter, who appeared on the Thom Hartmann Program in July of 2015 and expressed his beliefs about what the recent court decisions to allow unlimited spending on campaigns meant to our country.

> "It violates the essence of what makes America a great country in its political system. Now, it's just an oligarchy with unlimited political bribery being at the essence of getting the nominations for president, or to elect the president. And same thing applies to governors and U.S. senators and Congress members. Now, we've seen a complete subversion of our political system, as a pay-off to major contributors who want, and expect, and sometimes get favors for themselves after the election is over. It's going to take either a horrible, disgraceful series of acts in our country that turn the public against [the status quo] and eventually, maybe even the Congress or the Supreme Court. But at the present time, the incumbents, Democrats and Republicans, look upon this unlimited money as a great benefit to themselves. Because somebody who's already in Congress has a lot more to sell to an avid contributor than somebody who's just a challenger."

In June 2015, Nicholas Confessore and Megan Thee-Brenan of *The New York Times* co-authored an article entitled "Poll Shows Americans Favor an Overhaul of Campaign Financing" and cited a New York Times/CBS News poll that displayed "deep support among Republicans and Democrats alike for new measures to restrict the influence of wealthy givers, including the amount of money that can be spent by super PACs and forcing more public disclosure on organizations now permitted to intervene in elections without disclosing the names of their donors." The divisiveness on the subject commonly found among our legislators does not appear to be as prevalent among the people and seems to indicate that great support could be formed around the right reform.

While an opportunity is there, "more than half of those surveyed said they were pessimistic that campaign finance rules would be improved," highlighting the major hurdle to any reform effort today.

This also may go a long way in explaining why a seasoned politician like former President Carter articulated that major public corruption would be necessary to garner enough resolve from the people for reform.

Americans basically have a hard time believing that anything can actually change the current political system. The task seems overwhelming when imagining the depth and reach of the tentacles of government alone, much less the power found within the special interests so committed to maintaining the present order. However, as President Kennedy once articulated, "We sometimes chafe at the burden of our obligations, the complexity of our decisions, the agony of our choices. But there is no comfort or security for us in evasion, no solution in abdication, no relief in irresponsibility."

While most Americans realize this burden can no longer be simply passed down, there is so much frustration about what to do when no current tool of reform seems promising, no individual effort feels adequate, and no choice of candidates within the current system seems powerful enough to change the inept culture of weak leadership.

While the people feel the nation crumbling around them under the chronic weight of incompetence and self-indulgence that drives our policies, they witness their current leaders act with no sense of shared urgency. Just as some hopelessly viewed a resolution to other issues in the past (such as the denial of voting rights to women and African Americans), the current system of corruption has almost become accepted as simply the way things will always be—even if it does lack any merit. The populace seeking change carries similar disillusionments of the past. However, fellow citizens no longer provide the major impediment to progress; it is instead being supplied by a corrupt government.

The hopelessness of the American people was displayed in the low level of participation in the electoral process. Shortly following the last elections in 2014, in an article entitled, "Voter turnout in 2014 the lowest since WWII," Jose A. DelReal of the *Washington Times* wrote, "Just 36.4 percent of the voting-eligible population cast ballots as of last Tuesday, continuing the steady decline in midterm voter participation that has spanned several decades. The results are dismal, but not surprising—participation has been dropping since the 1964 election, when voter turnout was at nearly 49 percent."

To put this participation into greater context, FairVote, "a nonpartisan non-profit organization that seeks to makes democracy fair, functional, and fully representative" reported that "in countries with compulsory voting (mandated voting with penalties through fines or community service for choosing not to participate) like Australia, Belgium, and Chile, voter turnout hovered near 90% in the 2000s." Although no one is advocating for punishments attached to non-participation, it's tragic that most Americans have simply given up in greater numbers on a process and, at most, only around "60% of the voting eligible population votes during presidential election years."

A majority of Americans are not just choosing to abandon the voting booth; they are also opting not to spend as much as a nickel toward a campaign system that already seems determined by a select few. "Only a quarter of 1% of the U.S. population made itemized contributions in 2010 and yet they [supplied] 2/3 of all contributions. Less than one out of 400 Americans, most of them affiliated with major corporate interests, made itemized donations of $200 or more to federal candidates or PACs."

Much of this overall picture remained true as of 2013, with "fewer than 1 in 10 Americans [having] ever made a political donation." Not surprisingly, as we have moved further and further away from the Citizens United ruling in 2010 (which basically unleashed Pandora's box in the realm of campaign spending), the statistics have been stretched even further. On August 1, 2015, *The New York Times* reported that "fewer than four hundred families [were] responsible for almost half the money risen in the 2016 presidential campaign, a concentration of political donors that is unprecedented in the modern era." In an attempt to clarify further the immense influence this group of contributors possesses, one must realize that "the 67 biggest donors, each of whom gave $1 million or more, donated more than three times as much as the 508,000 smallest donors combined, according to a POLITICO analysis of reports filed with the Federal Election Commission and the Internal Revenue Service."

Robert Kuttner, founder and coeditor of *The American Prospect*, as well as a regular columnist and contributor for multiple news outlets, wrote, "When politics does not deliver for the people, the people give up on politics. Or they see politics as a realm mainly for cultural warfare, for battles over patriotism, or as something for other people. People internalize economic reversals. Pocketbook troubles seem to be private failures rather than the consequence of political choices. The very citizens most exposed to the most severe economic stress have been deserting politics at the most accelerating rate."

While there may be a debate as to what is actually driving the most voters away, there can be no question as to the truth that nothing in reform to date has been very successful in presenting a reason to return. Some states have taken the lead in campaign finance reform by offering alternatives revolving around the common theme of public financing. The documentary "PRICELE$$" highlights the state of Arizona, where a majority of the legislature had been won through the utilization of public financing.

Though somewhat successful, the voluntary aspect of public financing continues to create a set of stipulations that result in some candidates facing an overwhelming disadvantage to candidates continuing to accept the typical outside contributions. Arizona reformers attempted to address this by creating a similar process later in each election for adding more public financing, but the court rejected the legality of this addition. This remained consistent to legal cases challenging, reducing, or eliminating reforms containing public financing that initially obtained greater success.

As far as the revenue for all this public financing, some form of indirect or direct surcharge on the people is often cited. However, with the ever-increasing debt and common instability in the economy, it will always remain a tough sell to provide public financing for elections. This is especially evident when considering past minor attempts aimed at directly enticing the electorate to be involved have been unsuccessful.

As Robert E. Mutch writes in his book, *Buying the Vote: A History of Campaign Finance Reform*, "Congress had tried to attract small contributions to House and Senate campaigns by offering tax incentives, but these measures had little success and were eventually repealed. David W. Adamany wrote decades ago that tax incentives alone could not make political activists out of the apathetic and uninformed. People who make campaign contributions tend to be well-off and well-informed about politics; people who do not contribute tend not to be, and tax incentives did little to change that pattern." A sense of excitement in participation is lacking in current reform efforts and no method has been provided for adequately addressing the advantage of campaigns that reject public financing in favor of accepting unlimited amounts of outside funding.

Time and again, the American people have proven that with proper leadership they can rise to the occasion and can meet any challenge with a united front. One only needs to remember the feelings in our nation after September 11th, where almost every American chose to put aside any differences in personal beliefs or party affiliations and came together to take care of our own. This natural inclination and desire to come together for healing is what has always separated America from the rest of the world.

Shortly following 9/11, *America Out of the Ashes: True Stories of Cour-*

age and Heroism was published. Taken from a section entitled "You have to help," an unnamed author writes, "One of the greatest frustrations for Americans watching the news and hearing about the tragedy at the World Trade Towers and at the Pentagon was the desire to do something to help. So many volunteers showed up in New York that many had to be turned away. In some cities, people overwhelmed the blood banks. They stood in long lines to give blood and to satisfy that longing to do something, anything to help."

Regardless of the potential for amassing support, in the absence of guidance for harnessing such a strong desire to strengthen our country, most Americans will simply choose to pre-occupy themselves with other things like family, sports, and television, instead of thinking about the true consequences of the inevitable current corruption. Focusing time and energy on something that seems insurmountable will be rejected.

Thomas Jefferson feared a loss of proper representation within the republic as a result of inevitable future growth and a common complacency among the American people. Something that will only further grow if we continue to rely on the current political system that has only fed more special interests since the limits of money in politics was first unregulated in the 1970s at the cost of the American people. Jefferson's concerns were so great he actually advocated in a letter to John Adams the possibility of eventually allowing localities to have more autonomy to protect against this. Although the idea was not advanced by him formally, other writings clearly confirm his apprehensions remained as to what could result:

> "The spirit of the times may alter, will alter. Our rulers will become corrupt, our people careless. A single zealot may commence persecutor, and better men be his victims. It can never be too often repeated that the time for fixing every essential right on a legal basis is while our rulers are honest and ourselves united. From the conclusion of [their] war [for independence, a nation begins] going downhill. It will not be necessary to resort every moment to the people for support. They will be forgotten, therefore and their rights disregarded. They will forget themselves but in the sole faculty of making money, and will never think of uniting to effect a due respect of rights. The shackles, therefore, which shall not be knocked off at the conclusion of [that] war will remain on [them] long, will be made heavier and heavier, till [their] rights shall revive or expire in a convulsion."

While the need for reforming the hyper-dysfunctional political system is obviously recognized by many, others pay little attention to the indirect effects of the current status quo. Although the decisions our representatives make place our overall well-being and national security at risk through outcomes such as raising the level of debt, the need to unite against a threat from within does not commonly draw the same reaction of urgency that clear threats from the outside receive.

Gary Hart, former U.S. Senator and Democratic presidential candidate, wrote about the fears Thomas Jefferson held concerning possible inadequacies in future representation and the idea he offered for the possible creation of "local (elementary) republics" to safeguard against this possible abuse in his book, *The Republic of Conscience*. More importantly, he confirmed that Jefferson was correct in his assumption of how difficult it would prove for citizens to come together for preserving their rights by writing, "We come closest to the ideal our founders established for renewal of our Republic during times of justifiable war abroad or threat of economic depression at home, but we find it difficult to unite around a positive agenda of renewal of our political faith absent a foreign or domestic crisis. Indeed, we are as far from uniting around a national renewal of principle as we have ever been."

The People's Clearing House offers a stark contrast to present reforms in campaign finance by offering a consistent renewal of recognizable results and tangible incentives for creating and sustaining a sense of optimism and desire for unity in purpose. It is designed to successfully maneuver through the common pitfalls that have limited the effectiveness of previous efforts and provides a tool for determining which politicians are committed to joining the people in reaffirming their ownership of the country.

Unlike the reformers of the past, this system revolves around the idea of giving back, as opposed to taking away, and incentives for participation will no longer seem small and insignificant, but constant and worthwhile. No longer will outcomes of elections be seen as the only hope for placing our country on the right path, but participation in the process of elections alone will provide more resources in moving the country further down the path of progress for all. Every aspect of selecting and maintaining proper representation will be utilized to strengthen the resolve and hope of our communities. With common sense standards not limiting candidates to one political party and being free to always challenge anyone committed to the status quo, each new election cycle will bring us closer to reestablishing the greater equality in representation necessary for soundly addressing current and future challenges.

The People's Clearing House

INTRODUCTION

The American Revolution, at its very core, was driven by the desire for proper representation. The Founders understood the adverse consequences of allowing a centralized power to remain inadequately challenged or scrutinized. Originally living under the rule of a monarchy instilled within the Founders a profound fear for allowing great power to remain in the hands of one individual or a select few, especially for an extended period of time. Regardless of whether one or more individuals come to possess power through birth or achievement, the Founders never desired to create an environment where a select few held the influence that could distort sacred representation. They clearly recognized how dangerous this would be to a democratic society reliant on genuine representation within a republic. When the interests of a small group comes to dominate the political landscape, such as within an oligarchy, very little reason or value remains for authentically attempting to achieve a genuine consensus on the issues.

The Founders knew the potential pitfalls of human nature and placed a necessity on establishing a sturdy foundation of checks and balances. They fashioned representation to meet the fundamental need of creating and maintaining a structure of fairness—with the House of Representatives based on population, while the Senate was uniformly distributed. Each branch of government was designed to adequately challenge the possible overreach of another, with the recognition that government would only function appropriately when all three branches held the ability to provide a check. States, through the Articles of Confederation and then the Tenth Amendment, were granted irrefutable authority to defend legitimate rights of autonomy and rein in any attempt of the federal government to centralize those powers not within its discretion. Although the Founders were unable to foresee how wealth and advances in technology would offer individuals the ability to influence a multitude of elections, I am confident they would have acted to determine a method for mitigating this ability, without infringing on rights.

Reinserting democratic principles to correct the mistakes of leaders within each branch of government has occurred throughout the history of our nation. From the repudiation of the "Sedition Acts" applied under President John Adams that illegitimately infringed on freedom of speech to the rejection of the false premise behind believing equality could be found within the "Separate but Equal Clause," the nation has proven it is possible to correct certain impediments toward the aim of equality. The same type of resolve is once again needed to root out the improper influence of money in politics. Disenfranchisement with inadequate representation fueled the revolution for establishing a new government. It should be implicit that a concerted effort is justified in effectively addressing any instrument that threatens to silence the rightful voice of the people. The principle found within "no taxation without representation" has become more meaningful to Americans of all political stripes who are fed up with special-interests-led legislatures.

The current political system often rewards those in pursuit of elected office to practice many of the same attributes that the people do not desire in those that will lead them, from false portrayal of core principles to developing a counterproductive dependency on others. The distrust in the political process to sufficiently screen and access which candidates possess the ability and desire to actually serve the people has consistently resulted in low voter turnouts. Feelings of bitterness, resentment, and hopelessness are heightened with each election. Very few Americans who already feel they have no voice in government are reassured by the partisan process rooted in money. Americans recognize that the current political system is broken. As former President Truman revealed to Merle Miller, "I was always very particular about where my money came from. Very few people are going to give you large sums of money if they don't expect to get something from it, and you've got to keep that in mind."

The American people have long recognized that inadequacies in government are due, in some part, to the electoral process itself, with prolonged failures in government merely garnering more attention to this truth. Host Chuck Todd utilized an episode of "Meet the Press" in June 2015 to highlight that "people [were] much more worried about how the campaigns [would] be conducted and paid for, not who's running," according to a NBC News-Wall Street Journal poll at the time. He went on to note that among those polled, "33% were concerned that wealthy people and companies will have too much influence. That was number one. Number two issue with 25% was the idea that there will be more negativity in the campaign instead of actual debate about solutions to problems." In summarizing these findings, the host concluded, "That was a big surprise, that both issues were process issues that the country was concerned about."

The permanent status quo in D.C., when paired with the year of political outsiders Donald Trump and Bernie Sanders, has only led more Americans to reject the argument from candidates that the end justifies the means. Constituents have grown weary of empty promises articulated by those campaigning on the idea that large donations and lobbyists will not affect their judgment, only to see otherwise. In an article from July 2015, Paul Blumenthal from *The Huffington Post* wrote, "As an oligarchy of campaign contributors has begun to dominate political fundraising, opposition is mounting, with activists calling for campaign finance reform and a rejection of super PAC politics."

Blumenthal also pointed out that "while the big-money race on the Republican side of the presidential campaign is most intense it's not absent from the Democratic Party. Frontrunner Hillary Clinton's super PAC, Priorities USA Action, a hand-me-down from President Barack Obama, raised $15.6 million, with 99 percent of it coming from $100,000-plus donors." George Soros was among the donors who gave $1 million to the super PAC. Whether in successfully funding a party, or individual candidates who compose them, the people have become awakened to the reality that select donors who create reliance from politicians, reap the benefits of their investment.

The American people, especially among the middle class and poor, long for a system that will invoke representatives to genuinely consider their common needs. Brooklyn Borough President Eric Adams told CNN correspondent Sara Ganim that the candidates were "out of touch" with many of the obstacles people encounter within his community. His assessment came less than a week before the April Democratic primary debate between Bernie Sanders and Hillary Clinton in Brooklyn, New York. He was very direct in saying that "Communities like Brownsville have been left behind," before posing the question of "Why are we focusing on places that is [sic] a success story? Why not go to the heart of areas that needs [sic] to be successful?" His desire was for the debate to be held in Brownsville, where a community that consistently faces high rates of poverty, crime, and unemployment could desperately use a shot of hope.

Sadly, the current reality is that any attention given to communities like Brownsville would be short-lived and confined to the election, as money and influence are found elsewhere. Taking on common concerns of voters in underprivileged communities for immediate gain at the election booth cannot compare to the priority of most politicians for maintaining a mutually beneficial relationship with lobbyists and major donors who almost certainly assure their political and economic longevity. While specific stories of forgotten communities like Brownsville, or numerous references to votes reeking of a "pay to play" offer proof to the great faults within the current political system, maybe the greatest evidence comes from the words of Donald Trump. In the first presidential debate, the eventual party nominee described his previous relationship with many politicians by saying, "I will tell you that our system is broken. I gave to many people. Before this, before two months ago, I was a businessman. I give to everybody. When they call, I give. And do you know what? When I need something from them two years later, three years later, I call them. They are there for me."

Money rules politics, too often dictating legislative decisions and determining the outcomes of elections. Enigmas such as Donald Trump securing the Republican nomination, despite spending much less than his opponents, should not be misunderstood to represent proof that money is no longer a significant factor in elections. The ability to outspend opponents by building a reliable source of heavy donors is a tool utilized to win a number of state and federal elections. On the federal level, despite the anti-establishment sentiment within much of the electorate, only one congressional incumbent lost in the 2016 primaries through April and he faced a multitude of corruption charges.

The overriding belief expressed so often is that anyone who enters politics will eventually become corrupt or at the least change in their original optimism. In his 1990 memoir, *In the Arena*, Richard Nixon described one of the facilitators of this common disillusionment in writing, "Except for the first six months of his two-year term, a congressman from a close district today must spend over half his time raising money for his reelection. The results of the non-stop campaign hustle are inevitable. Idealistic young congressmen are disenchanted by the grind." While the country desperately needs dreamers who enter office bright-eyed and possessing a hope to make a genuine difference in government, the current system in place often breaks them upon arrival. Even those that remain true to their principles become more susceptible to ultimately becoming one of the career politicians they originally entered office to defeat.

Legislators on both sides of the political aisle in Washington are consistently being pressured by their party establishment to raise more and more money. This is especially expected during "call time," a designated period each day where congressional members are expected to concentrate entirely on reaching out to constituents for money. Although this characteristic of money-driven politics can be equally attributed to both parties, a January 2013 article in *The Huffington Post* from Ryan Grim and Sabrina Siddiqui highlighted the work of the Democrats. They wrote, "A PowerPoint presentation to incoming freshman by the Democratic Congressional Campaign Committee, obtained by *The Huffington Post,* lays out the dreary existence awaiting these new backbenchers. The daily schedule prescribed by the Democratic leadership contemplates a nine or 10-hour day while in Washington. Of that, four hours are to be spent in 'call time' and another hour is blocked off for 'strategic outreach,' which includes fundraisers and press work. An hour is walled off to 'recharge,' and three to four hours are designed for the actual work of being a member of Congress—hearings, votes, and meeting with constituents. If the constituents are donors, all the better."

Ezra Klein, founder of Vox.com, questioned whether the findings within the DCCC PowerPoint presentation actually paint an accurate picture of how much time members of Congress spend fundraising. He was especially skeptical about the notion that there would be uniformity across the board in how new and old members raise money and explained, "That DCCC schedule might hold true for a new members [sic] from a contested district. But House incumbents typically have a 90 percent reelection rate. Most of them are in safe districts. A lot of money they raise goes to the party rather than to them. They're not going to spend most of their day doing something they hate."

The conclusions Ezra Klein reached and documented in his article from *The Washington Post* in July 2013 heavily relied on congressional surveying done by Brad Finch and his organization, the Congressional Management Foundation. However, should congressional staff really be trusted to provide the details of how their bosses routinely raise money? Even if the members of congress they serve do indeed follow the suggested daily schedule from the DCCC, what likelihood would there be for staff members to confirm such an unpopular truth, especially when considering that almost every action is politically calculated? Congressmen and women so concerned with image routinely rely on polls or surveys to make decisions related to public relations.

Assuming Ezra Klein is correct, should it make the general public feel any better? Of course, incumbents shouldn't have to spend as much time fundraising. Most are career politicians who have established a well-tuned political machine composed of staffers dedicated to joining their bosses in prioritizing re-election concerns above all else.

Though the political landscape has changed with the expanding role of super PACs, the use and maintenance of political machines have remained consistent. One of the best insights pertaining to these structures still comes from Sara Fritz and Dwight Morris in their 1992 book, *Gold-Plated Politics*. The former *Los Angeles Times* reporters took up the task of analyzing documentation and transactions often avoided by others overwhelmed at the magnitude to put together a genuine view of the D.C. culture.

In referring to the "political machine" that most incumbents had established, Fritz and Morris enlightened readers on the price of this consistent operation by writing, "To maintain these high-tech, personal political machines, incumbents spend hundreds of thousands—even million—of dollars on elections in which they have little or no opposition." In referring to the 1990 elections, they actually cited "three unopposed senators [spending] an average of $668,000, most of it simply to maintain their personal organizations." An ongoing ability for representatives to replenish their coffers feeds the impulse to consistently spend, regardless of circumstance. Spending as described on elections facing no opposition provides stable work for consultants, pollsters, and aides.

Most campaign finance reforms today center around public financing and limitations on campaign contributions. Yet public financing has proven inadequate to bring the change necessary. Although some have run successfully as publicly financed candidates, the choice has proven it has limitations. The court's rejection of allowing an additional round of public financing later in the election cycle to compete with the money raised by typical candidates highlighted this truth most accurately. This disadvantage in direct contributions has only further strengthened the power of independent expenditures from social advocacy groups and super PACs to determine the outcome of many elections.

The elections in Great Britain have been referenced by some reformists as an applicable resource of policies the U.S. should attempt to implement within its electoral system. Britain has a much shorter campaign season, which lasts around four weeks. While their laws do not place restrictions on how much money outside sources can donate, they do place limits on what individual candidates or parties can spend on the elections. However, potential candidates are free to spend before the "dissolution of Parliament," as the restrictions on what can be spent only applies during the official weeks of the campaign. As expected, parties and candidates often seek to use loopholes, with those committed to fairness forced to consistently oppose them.

Americans face a similar fight in securing a level arena for establishing genuine representation, with a number of lawmakers consistently seeking to gain an unfair advantage by discovering new methods to circumvent current laws. The most common tactic of legislators is to support laws that aid in avoiding needed transparency. The result is the non-disclosure of donors to 501(c)(4) nonprofits and the use of shell corporations to better allow shadow donors to give to super PACs. Difficult money trails are also formed when 501(c)(4)s, or social welfare groups, make contributions to super PACs. All of these practices guarantee the American people are denied pertinent information in a timely manner; votes have long been cast before abuses are revealed and verified.

Current allegations of illegal activity launched against the sitting mayor of New York City also highlights ways in which politicians aim to get around campaign finance laws. As Rick Leventhal of Fox News reported in May 2016, a portion of the FBI probe of Mayor de Blasio involves the possible coordination of "straw donors." This illegal activity involves individuals giving others money so that they can then formally make the contribution to a campaign; therefore, effectively evading state or federal limits on the maximum amount one individual is allowed to directly donate. Accusations against the mayor also involve his participation in a "pay to play" scenario, which refers to a situation in which campaign donors are given political favors for their investment.

While "pay to play" obviously occurs informally and formally all across the country as a result of a political system so driven by money, in the specific case of Mayor de Blasio, his charge concerns potential rewards to those who donated to the non-profit he established to help implement some of his policy agenda. Reporter Rick Leventhal of Fox News particularly referenced the case of a janitorial supply company making a $100,000 contribution to de Blasio's non-profit, "Campaign for One New York," and subsequently receiving a city contract. It was the type of contract that the owner had been unsuccessful in obtaining until that time, despite a decade of previous lobbying attempts.

Robert Bentley, the governor of Alabama, also established a nonprofit to supposedly support his policy initiatives. John Archibald, a seasoned columnist for the *Birmingham News*, highlighted another way nonprofits side-step accountability in writing, "Rebekah Caldwell Mason, a chief advisor to the governor of the state of Alabama, is paid by unknown entities with money funneled through an opaque nonprofit. And that shadowy operation—it doesn't have to reveal its donors—is set up by people connected to the state's most powerful and politically aggressive institutions."

Rebekah Mason, nationally known for allegations of having an inappropriate relationship with Bentley, isn't the only top advisor to the governor being paid through a foundation that effectively circumvents any safeguards in lobbying. As Alabama consistently fights for mere dominance among the states ranked at the bottom of almost every economic and social measure, the current system in place continues, at a minimum, to provide an opening for the morally corrupt to abuse. Neither major party in Alabama has proven they possess the resolve to change this truth.

Politicians have displayed an inclination to misuse any group or organization, including nonprofits and foundations, to their advantage. Greater oversight and restrictions must be placed on the role sitting representatives can have on these groups. The greatest tragedy, as it relates to foundations and nonprofits, is that the good work most are doing will face greater challenges as a result of a few selfish individuals. However, maybe no one person owns this blame more than Hillary Clinton. Whether she is ever convicted of any crime, nothing could sound the alarm bell more than the former Secretary of State's relationship to her powerful family foundation while serving.

Deroy Murdock, the contributing editor of the *National Review Online*, in an article from June 2016, offered a description of the questionable individuals who actually compose the Clinton Foundation by writing, "The Clinton Foundation, Bill and Hillary's elaborate slush fund, includes numerous donors and even one-time board members with dodgy backgrounds, shady dealings, and even criminal convictions that should repel rather than lure a once and perhaps future president of the United States."

Murdock then cited a 2015 book from Peter Schweitzer, *Clinton Cash*, which provides a fascinating in-depth look at the money trail surrounding the Clintons. Schweitzer's book, which has now been made into a movie, centers on an in-depth argument that many of her decisions as Secretary of State were influenced by this money. Sadly, regardless of the information provided, which seems to indicate a meticulous effort by the Clintons to sell out people around the world for personal gain, the reality is that many—including African-American voters—will still offer her support in November. Accusations surrounding the specific mistreatment of Haitians will not make a difference.

Surrounded by the negative assertions and accusations of others, no newfound faith was created when the foundation lifted its ban on accepting donations from foreign governments and entities; something of even greater concern when considering "the foundation also set up a Canadian subsidiary that effectively shielded some donors from disclosure requirements." Nor could any degree of faith be achieved from the 2015 report from Sean Davis, co-founder of *The Federalist*, who analyzed financial records and concluded only a minute percentage of money was actually being utilized for charity.

While the Clinton Foundation has obviously changed some lives for the better, reporters like Sean Davis are not the only ones questioning what the predominant driving force is behind the foundation's extensive work. In March 2015, a number of Haitians made their displeasure known by "[protesting] outside the Clinton Foundation."

The *Washington Free Beacon* reported on the 2015 protest: "The activists are claiming the money was stolen through the Haiti Reconstruction Commission that was headed by Bill Clinton. In January 2015, the Clinton Foundation was the target of protests for wasting more than $10 billion and awarding contracts to non-Haitian companies." In that earlier protest, writers from the *Washington Free Beacon* had also pointed out that "the country [was] still in ruin. Only 900 homes [had] been built in [those] last five years even though over $10 billion was donated from the international community to help rebuild Haiti." While troubling specifically in terms of Haiti, the overriding question remains: what could all these connections mean for America?

In a February 2015 article for *The Washington Post*, Jennifer Rubin highlighted what a vulnerable position she believed the American people would be placed in if someone like former Secretary Hillary Clinton—who was tied to a foundation that received millions from foreign governments and entities—was allowed to dictate policy abroad moving forward. Rubin may have summed up the entire relationship best when she wrote, "No presidential candidate can justify a conflict of interest of this magnitude; it is not merely the appearance of conflict but actual conflict of interest. Much of the concern clearly revolves around money given to the Clinton Foundation from the Middle East." Rubin alludes to this in her final thoughts by concluding, "It is Arab states that lavishly fund universities and think tanks. And now they are buying a president."

In contrast to the Clinton Foundation's decision to lower standards for allowing contributions to come in from governments that routinely continue to trample on human rights (most debilitating to women, children, and homosexuals), the Germans ironically provide the example of how these groups should be protected against their oppressors. After taking in an influx of migrants for a time and allowing culture to supersede law, the German justice minister, Heiko Maas, took decisive action. He clearly informed everyone that polygamy would no longer be tolerated, and in particular focused his attention on protecting the children in saying, "We need to look very carefully. Forced marriages, we cannot tolerate, and certainly not when underage girls are involved."

While feminists and human rights activists across the country remain firmly committed in lockstep behind Hillary Clinton in her bid for the White House, an official in Germany actually sent a firm message to oppressors. While the former First Lady, U.S. Senator, and Secretary of State often reminds the American people that she was vital in securing health insurance for millions of children, the foundation took money from countries that too often look the other way as mental and physical abuse occurs.

No amount of healthcare can help those killed by the culture the Clinton Foundation chose to align itself with. A report out of Pakistan on the rise of "honor" killings from July 2016 should supply anyone debating supporting Secretary Clinton with a sobering reminder of what heinous acts of violence are often allowed under extreme Islamic culture. From cutting throats to burning individuals alive, a warped rationale tells some they must kill a family member in this fashion to restore their good name. Choosing to marry for love causes many to receive such an unimaginable fate.

An article from the Associated Press reported, "The numbers of such killings have climbed in lockstep with their sometimes-public spectacle. Last year, three people a day were killed in 'honor' crimes in Pakistan: a total of 1,096 women and 88 men, according to the independent Human Rights Commission of Pakistan. In 2014, the number was 1,005 women, including 82 children, up from 869 women killed a year earlier. The true numbers are believed to be higher, with many cases going unreported, activists say." Healthcare for American children is important and necessary, but a focus placed on this achievement should not be utilized by some to deflect from the choice to abandon others.

From the "dark money" of nonprofits that avoid transparency to the abuse of foundations, the political process currently in place will always be about chasing the money, which makes the emphasis commonly placed on overturning the Supreme Court's Citizens United decision extremely puzzling. Focusing on the Citizens United ruling seems to completely disregard past history in campaign finance, which witnessed representatives of government always looking for new methods to maintain their incumbent advantage.

Politicians will always remain focused in areas of self-interest and self-preservation. Even if Citizens United is overturned to rein in the current spending of outside groups, legislators will simply seek new ways to get around campaign laws or continue passing new ones that weaken those in place. If nonprofits and foundations, which seem to currently provide political cover for expanding influence where restricted, they will simply be replaced by creating new loopholes through legislation purposely written with vagueness. While any legislature will look good on the surface for appeasing an apathetic constituency, very small emphasis will be placed on meaningful reform efforts.

Only when reform is designed to address the expected tendencies of lawmakers will it have a chance to succeed. From the distinctions in "hard money" and "soft money" to the cry of freedom of speech concerns, attempting to solve campaign finance by placing limits on what can be spent will always prove inadequate. The same outcome of failure can be expected from any attempt to persuade the public to act on reforms based solely within the context of changing an electoral process they feel isolated from. Reform needs to uniquely place those opposed front and center within the confines of the rules they have strategically established to shield them from unwanted change; meet them on their turf, so to speak. The American people need to see incentives (well beyond the election cycle) of holding incumbents and those seeking office to a higher standard of accountability. When Americans begin to be directly affected by those exploiting the system, a newfound motivation to act will be established.

With chronic issues in governance only being further emphasized through the unprecedented challenges America currently faces, citizens and legislators alike should recognize the necessity for facilitating more responsibility from those that serve. This conclusion is obvious if only financial considerations were taken into account. Waste, fraud, and abuse consistently expand the debt and increase the challenge of the ensuing entitlement crisis. Future leaders must know how to budget and make every dollar count.

However, our electoral process often results in politicians actually going into debt while campaigning. They essentially feverishly spend, despite their limited resources, with the idea that throwing more money at the problem to achieve a short-term victory should be their focus. Does this seem familiar? Should anyone be shocked that there are few representatives who actually understand how to think outside the box in solving issues, especially in finances, that at the most basic level requires discipline?

Bear Bryant, the legendary football coach who won six national championships at the University of Alabama, prided himself on making his practices tougher than the games. He was a master at getting the best from his players and understood this type of preparation gave them an advantage. More importantly, he used this process to discover which players were actually worthy of suiting up for Saturdays.

Just like Coach Bryant, The People's Clearing House has to provide a genuine test of worthiness. Although not everyone seeking public office contributed to the current financial shortfall, there must be an understanding that past failures on local, state, and federal levels demand that a higher standard of assessing those seeking to be our future leaders must be implemented; one which includes a specific emphasis on greater scrutiny of financial management skills. Not creating a true measuring stick is accepting defeat.

You can't give someone free reign to a buffet with little consequence—actually rewarding them for eating more—and then wonder why they face difficulties later in immediately going on the desired diet. Elections must be designed to help potential lawmakers learn early in the political process that actual consequences are attached to the decisions they make, providing the necessary emphasis on accountability in leadership.

America has the best and brightest, with a unique spirit that still produces unmatched potential. However, just as any great team discovers, there is only a certain amount of time that talent alone can be depended on to provide a win. When things begin going wrong and adversity must be overcome for victory, a team quickly recognizes the result of merely pointing fingers and working to protect self-interest.

There has to be a powerful force to bring them together. The People's Clearing House provides that adhesion and is designed to effectively take on those areas of common opposition—while at the same time working to bring communities across the country together. Unlike other areas of reform built around public financing, which only operate by taking away, the People's Clearing House solves issues, while giving back.

OVERVIEW

The People's Clearing House (TPCH) provides a structure for establishing a new type of representative who actually recognizes the necessity for maintaining a greater accountability to the people. It will be evident that this individual clearly welcomes the opportunity to consistently demonstrate his or her dedication to the people. Within the newly established confines of TPCH, the electoral process itself will serve as the initial step in building a newfound confidence within the constituency as to the integrity of those who are selected to lead them. This foundation of genuine faith will only be strengthened through a demonstrated commitment to abide by campaign pledges concerning fundraising, future elections, and general transparency. While human nature will always produce a component of self-interest in the decisions anyone makes, this system is tailored to better identify those individuals attempting to place the people first.

Chris Cillizza of *The Washington Post* reported that there had already been $1.2 billion in contributions for the 2016 election by the end of March. Those numbers alone provide convincing evidence that breaking the $7 billion given to the 2012 presidential election is not improbable. In an article from Politico in January 2013 following the elections, Tarini Parti provided further insight as to what was spent: "The FEC estimates that candidates spent about $3.2 billion of the total $7 billion, parties spent another $2 billion and other outside political committees made up more than $2.1 billion." However, any figure given is simply a guess. No number reached through the filings of the FEC should be taken at face value, with the only certainty being that an exorbitant amount of money is consistently being utilized in the game of politics alone.

The premise of The People's Clearing House revolves around the belief that when it comes to matters of representation, everything belongs to the people. If elections are held with the hope of creating a body of men and women who will place the country on the right path, why not allow the electoral process itself to always provide a guaranteed boost in this endeavor for true progress?

TPCH facilitates this enhancement.

It alleviates the frustrations of most Americans who view the elections as offering another example of excess being perpetrated on the people for creating nothing more than a new set of representatives that ignore them post-election. The People's Clearing House incentivizes involvement from an electorate who will witness meaningful results from their individual participation in each election, regardless of their party affiliation or receiving the results they want. Greater opportunity is given for ideas to be the deciding factor in the minds of voters, instead of the current system that seems to routinely reward the most efficient fundraiser.

Under The People's Clearing House, a percentage of each contribution to elections will be deducted and given back to the corresponding constituency. Each contribution is broken down by the local, state, or federal office being sought by the recipient. Contributions to federal elections would be processed through a National People's Clearing House, while contributions to state and local elections would be processed through The People's Clearing House established in each state.

Campaign contributors choose from a number of causes and initiatives selected by the corresponding governing body to uniquely meet the needs within their community for facilitating positive growth. City officials, such as a city council, will provide options for contributors to local candidates, just as the State House of Representatives or Senate will provide choices to state elections, and the U.S. House of Representatives or Senate will provide the same for federal elections. Just as with other aspects concerning the clearing house system, each level of government maintains power over determining specifics. Contributions to presidential candidates will choose from the same options assigned to those contributing to federal elections, although it's possible they could also choose from their state causes as well. U.S. Senate races and presidential elections offer a practical argument to possibly include national and state constituency options to donors. Here's an example of how The People's Clearing House would function on its most basic level:

Contribution	Recipient	Body that provides choices
$2,100	Candidate for State Supreme Court	State House of Representatives
$1,500	Candidate for United States House	U.S. House of Representatives
$1,000	Candidate for Mayor	City Council

Charles makes a campaign contribution of $2,100 to a candidate running for Justice of the Alabama Supreme Court. His contribution is processed through the People's Clearing House established in Alabama. The state has established the base rate of 30% to be deducted from contributions directed toward state races, meaning that $630 will be deducted from the $2,100 given. Charles now views the state causes and initiatives provided by the Alabama House of Representatives to decide how he wants his $630 taken out by TPCH to be spent. Charles decides to allocate $100 to the K-12 Greater Financial Education initiative, $200 to the New Emphasis Program for Veterans, $200 to the Black Belt Region Economic Stimulus, and $130 to the Proactive Resource and Poverty initiative. By simply participating, Charles has helped his state move forward before the first vote is cast.

Alabama is one state that does not place a limit on how much one individual can directly contribute to a candidate. This is unlike federal elections, which currently limit individuals to giving no more than $2,700. Ideally, whether limits are present or not, contributions would be assessed by the amount given for determining the proper deduction. Slightly higher deductions would apply based on certain benchmarks that have been established. However, a standard deduction for all contributions will most likely have to be applied. The federal limit of $2,700 on direct individual contributions to candidates provides the easiest example of what benchmarks for Clearing House deductions could possibly look like.

Contri-bution	Benchmarks	% to be de-ducted	Money to TPCH
$250	$0-500	10%	$25
$900	$500-1,500	20%	$180
$2,000	$1,500-2,700	30%	$600

The People's Clearing House will serve as an ongoing morale builder for uniting communities, no longer leaving individuals to feel powerless in making a difference or questioning why all of this money is simply being spent on elections instead of going toward causes and initiatives, which could include charities, nonprofits, veteran's affairs, education, medical research, and poverty. Autonomy as the Founders envisioned is maintained by allowing elected officials on local, state, and federal levels to choose the set of options contributors are offered to direct the deduction taken from their campaign contribution by the designated People's Clearing House.

While the federal government would establish the level of deduction, each state is unique in their campaign finance laws and each would be allowed to determine how the system works within their state. City and town officials could do the same or simply adopt the same level of deductions established on the state or federal level. Towns and cities maintain their autonomy in all aspects within certain guidelines. A city or town may be so small that it allows their residents to possibly pick from state options to direct their deductions. However, regardless of the money raised through deductions, the unique symbolism will remain. Any money redirected to the community instead of simply being spent on the game of politics will help unite the people and lower partisanship.

Those within their own communities understand best the unique issues and challenges they face. Very few Americans would reject the opportunity to experience the feeling of empowerment in individually determining how deductions will be utilized. Most citizens are routinely annoyed by what happens once the "people's" representatives within state legislatures and the U.S. Congress get their hands on actual taxes.

Witnessing general initiatives centered on education, small business, job training, trade promotion, entrepreneurship, lowering poverty, resource centers, and a host of other common variables essential to community building (continually being facilitated) will provide tangible reasons to remain invested in the political process. Elections will provide the spark that ignites an emphasis on holding representatives more accountable.

TRACKING FOR COMPLETE AND CONSISTENT TRANSPARENCY

Obviously, there are current procedures in place for someone to formally become a candidate for public office. Beyond all the paperwork that is commonly required, which ranges from petitions to authorization forms, the potential candidate will register with The People's Clearing House that coincides with the office sought. TPCH will assign each candidate a number of monetary cards to document all political transactions. Every contribution will be accounted for and face a deduction, regardless of the amount. Just as every transaction made with political donations will be tracked for ease in scrutinizing.

The People's Clearing House remains throughout the entirety of a political career, whether it ends on the campaign trail or after time spent in office. Greater accountability will be maintained while in office, as TPCH continues making the appropriate deductions of contributions in the ongoing process of giving back. The public will know how much money is being accumulated by the incumbent and how it is being spent.

In their 1992 book *Gold-Plated Politics*, Sara Fritz and Dwight Morris documented one of the ways members of Congress had made a complete mockery of the rules that were in place at the time by writing, "When members of Congress report thousands of dollars of unitemized expenses, they leave the impression that they are dipping into their campaign treasuries for pocket money. Under the rules, members are not required to itemize expenditures of less than $200. Using that loophole, Rep. Doug Walgreen (D-PA) failed to itemize $89,202 of his spending in reports to the FEC during the 1990 cycle. Rep. Charles B. Rangel (D-NY) failed to itemize $84,741, and Austin J. Murphy (D-PA) failed to itemize $78,250." Working within the rules, whether morally corrupt to anyone with common sense, seems to have meant nothing to these politicians.

Although Sara Fritz and Dwight Morris' book may have been written over twenty years ago, their words provide proof that the culture in D.C. remains consistently void of an ample supply of moral integrity. Just as was the case then, politicians who encounter a weak Federal Elections Committee that is unable to provide oversight of expenditures, give in to the temptation of easily claiming political purposes for questionable spending. The FEC provides the inefficiency of most federal agencies.

As Fritz and Morris wrote, "Neither the FEC or the House and Senate ethics committees attempt to verify the honesty of spending reports filed by the campaigns. There is no requirement for candidates to submit any receipts. No regular audits are conducted." Yet when it comes to those seeking welfare assistance, many of the same congressmen most likely scrutinize every penny spent by recipients.

Former Republican Illinois Rep. Aaron Schock was a gifted politician. However, his flamboyancy and dubious use of campaign funds actually sealed his fate in 2015. Among other things, Fox News reported that he had a house that "political donors built, sold, and financed," as well as thought it was a wise idea to "[decorate] his office in the theme of the PBS program 'Downtown Abbey.'" However, Rep. Aaron Schock, who seemed to revel more in boosting his persona and revealing his abs, had a short-lived political career which provided him a temporary platform that may have still been considered productive.

Being surrounded by a plentiful supply of narcissists in D.C. only fanned Rep. Shock's flame for personally disregarding the greater good—all while promoting himself. It shouldn't be surprising that a number of his colleagues were "shocked" by his announcement to resign, finding it difficult to understand how his mistakes warranted it.

After detailing a similar use of campaign contributions that former long-term U.S. Senator David L. Boren (D-OK) used to lavishly decorate his office, Sara Fritz and Dwight Morris explained, "Most of these expenditures were not even remotely improper under congressional ethic rules. While many of them appeared to be personal expenditures, most have a plausible political justification. A campaign car, for example, is usually viewed as the cheapest way for a candidate to travel around the district. Chartered airplanes are sometimes rationalized as the only logical alternative for those incumbents who represent big states or districts. Country club memberships are defended as necessities for incumbents who need to entertain political supporters and throw fund raisers." Boren, the former governor and lawmaker, who now serves as the president of the University of Oklahoma following his time in the senate from 1979-1994, was viewed as being among the good guys who recognized the need for campaign finance reform.

The ability of career politicians to consistently replenish their campaign coffers creates a sense of inevitability for frivolous spending. For some, scheming the system of the money they receive for their own personal campaigns is not enough. These politicians also utilize leadership PACs to fulfill their personal and political desires.

Award-winning journalist Andy Kroll described the fringe benefits of these PACs in writing, "Instead of raising money for a politician's own re-election bid, leadership PACs, which sprung up in the 1990s, allow members to raise money for distributing to their colleagues' reelection campaigns. By spreading money around to your pals, a lawmaker can earn some goodwill and climb the ranks within his or her own party." While not unexpected by any means, the next line Kroll wrote shows the lack of humility that permeates in D.C.: "Thanks to a loophole in the law, however, lawmakers often use their leadership PACs to pay for golf outings, tickets to NFL games and other swanky junkets that politicians can't pay for with their traditional campaign war chest."

U.S. Representative Andy Harris (R-MD) offered the Clean Campaign Contributions Act in October 2013 in hopes of closing the loophole that allowed legislators to use campaign contributions from leadership PACs on non-political activities. Only a month after his bill, Adam Smith, communications director for Public Campaign, highlighted how a few congressmen were taking advantage of the current system: "Sen. Saxby Chambliss's (R-GA) leadership PAC spent over $100,000 over the past two years on golf outings around the world. Rep. Gregory Meeks (D-N.Y.) dropped $35,000 on NFL games through his leadership PAC. This spending wasn't for official business and wasn't for getting re-elected—it was for personal use. But it's all legal."

Saxby Chambliss spent sixteen years in D.C. before retiring in 2015. He spent eight years in the House of Representatives and eight years in the Senate. Despite clear questions of integrity from past behavior, Gregory Meeks still remains in the U.S. House. He has served since 1998. "Citizens for Responsibility and Ethics in Washington (CREW) named Meeks one of the most-corrupt members of Congress in 2011."

Just as with Meeks, the loophole remains as well. The bill offered by Rep. Andy Harris (R-MD) died in the Congress like every other bill routinely does that attempts to raise the bar of accountability and common sense in service to the people. The most common attribute for these type bills when placed in the current arena is that they receive an analysis of somewhere below five percent in actual likelihood of being passed.

Though the golfing trips and football outings may have offered short-term personal gratification, most Americans would rather use money for building future communities for all. Taking the initial deduction out of contributions eliminates the ability of politicians to simply waste money that should be directed toward progress.

If anything, Saxby Chambliss and Gregory Meeks only provide evidence for establishing higher deductions for The People's Clearing House. Always having that comparison of how money that is being wasted could be utilized within the community will provide a clear perspective on what is lacking in those politicians who choose to mismanage their campaign funds. While every citizen will not follow the money regardless of the connection of directly taking from communities, the level of transparency offered by TPCH helps make presenting the information to others easy.

Any opposition from lawmakers to the heightened transparency attached with The People's Clearing House would be hypocritical. Americans are consistently asked to trust the government in their treatment of private information for maintaining national security—despite documented instances of overreach. Concerns only heightened with the routine attempt of lawmakers to place more American liberties at risk, with the most recent example being an attempt to go beyond privacy searches of phone records.

"The 2017 Intelligence Authorization Act, if enacted into law, would let the FBI obtain email records without a court order. All the agency would need is a National Security Letter, which lets the FBI get information from companies about the customers without alerting the person being investigated." This power to access private information and silence the companies that aid in the investigation, unlike a warrant, do not have to be approved through the judicial process. Fortunately, both the House and Senate bodies, as a whole, rejected amendments granting this extension of authority. However, it is only a matter of time—most likely after election season—that a renewed effort is launched.

Cases involving civil liberty concerns only serve to strengthen the understanding of how significant it has become to create a representation built on a foundation of greater accountability. TPCH provides an instrument for flipping the script on government in demanding greater scrutiny of lawmakers we are expected to trust. Without such measures, the question will always be whether any attempt to gain more information is actually rooted in national-security concerns or a further attempt at self-preservation.

As easy as it is to foreshadow the pushback of legislators concerning any attempt to raise the standard of transparency and accountability, no previous record could more firmly predict a lack of support from the next president if someone like Hillary Clinton becomes elected. She is the standard insider and represents the characteristics that are shared by a number of politicians on both sides of the political aisle, which keep them from embracing meaningful change. These members represent the common trait of publicly saying one thing, while privately working behind the scenes to conduct an agenda that is often dissimilar to what has been articulated. Hillary Clinton is just one among many other career politicians who have proven the indulgences of maintaining the status quo makes them untrustworthy in ultimately passing reform that is right for the people

As far as Hillary Clinton is concerned, although there are numerous examples for building this mistrust shared by a majority of Americans, Judge Napolitano highlighted one of the strongest reasons. During a June 2016 appearance on Fox's "Outnumbered," the former Superior Court judge said, "Mrs. Clinton, in the four years that she was Secretary of State, only used her BlackBerry. She did not use a laptop. She did not use a desktop. She didn't use a tablet. She only used her BlackBerry wherever she was. Guess where BlackBerry's don't work? They are disabled by order of the IT people on the 7th floor of the State Department. Where was her office? On the 7th floor of the State Department. So the Secretary of State of the United States, in charge of diplomatic affairs around the globe, when she wants to communicate directly with one of her ambassadors, has to leave her office, surrounded by a cordon of guards and aides, go down to the 6th floor and then respond to emails. This is this is [sic] absurd."

With the foundation of necessary information established, Judge Napolitano then explained the reason behind her persistent opposition to transparency in saying, "All of this because she refused to use—they asked her several times—a government issued Blackberry, because she knew that would be subject to the Freedom of Information Act."

The People's Clearing House does not depend on the results of one election. It places the spotlight on every race by providing a challenger to each sitting incumbent who welcomes a new standard of accountability in their service to the people. However, having allies and advocates at the heights of government could be significant in expediting the process of implementation.

TREATMENT OF PACS AND SUPER PACS

Just as there are limits on how much can be directly given to federal candidates, many states also place limits on the amount individuals and groups can directly contribute to candidates. The national average for what is allowed to be directly spent on statewide elections is $5,619 on governor's races, $2,508 on state senate races, and $2,375 on state house races. While some states, like Alabama, allow unlimited direct spending to candidates across the board, states like Montana, which place a greater value on restraining improper influence and establishing meaningful transparency, are stricter.

Regardless of the limits applied, as long as an individual remains within these guidelines, they can directly contribute to as many candidates as they choose as a result of the courts. Following the Supreme Court's decision in McCutcheon v. Federal Election Commission, 134 S.Ct. 1434 (2014) limits the total amount of money an individual can contribute during an election cycle as it violates the First Amendment and are therefore unconstitutional. Although challenged, this standard now applies to all states.

States break down their restrictions on direct campaign contributions into what individuals, party committees, corporations, unions, and PACs are allowed to donate. Some states prohibit many of these groups from contributing to candidates, as well as ban PACs (Political Action Committees) outside of their state from directly contributing. Prohibiting certain groups from giving to candidates is not new, as various groups from corporations to unions have been banned from giving directly to federal candidates beginning in the early 1900s. Limits and transparency have gone through various cycles of coming and going, just as the significance placed on it has fluctuated.

As far as PACs are concerned, while states once again vary in their restrictions, a $5,000 limit is placed on what can be directly given to a federal candidate. However, just as with the individual limit of $2,700 to federal candidates, this number of what is allowed actually doubles, as primary and general elections are counted separately, making the actual amount a PAC can give to a federal candidate $10,000 per election cycle. "After the Supreme Court's decision in Citizen United v. Federal Election Commission, 558 U.S. 310 (2010), PACs can spend unlimited amounts of money on broadcasts and communications related to an election, provided they act independently of any one candidate." Thus, super PACs were created to spend well beyond the direct $10,000.

Super PACs provide a number of services to campaigns. They aid in getting people out to vote through outreach, direct mailings, and phone calls—as well as help establish a foundation of operation within each state to advance grassroots movements of support. However, this tax-exempt organization, or "527 group," is best known for significantly impacting elections through the never-ending campaign ads. However, as with anything else political, the boundaries are consistently tested as to what the super PACs can provide to the candidate who once held the responsibility to perform the tasks.

The notion that there is no coordination between candidates and super PACs is absurd, especially when considering how inefficient the IRS is with general enforcement of other campaign laws. As an article from *The New York Times* in August 2015 brought attention to: "Many of the country's biggest donors are not only financial peers but also friends, members of the elite class of contributors who gather at events like the Club for Growth's annual Palm Beach retreat on the right, and the closed-door meetings of the Democracy Alliance on the left." It is among this subset of contributors that super PACs often arise, leaving a peer or friend to run the organization (supposedly) without any coordination with the candidate. What foundation of confidence could voters turn to for confidently believing that this level of integrity between the two is actually maintained?

The weak oversight currently provided by the FEC, IRS, and Senate and House Ethics Committees seems to have become more of a formality for appeasing voters than actually establishing a genuine deterrent. Just as with any other aspect of campaign finance, legislators consistently attempt to chip away at the laws already in place. Thanks to a ruling from late December 2015, candidates and their surrogates can now meet with super PACs as long as they make known that they are not there to solicit funds. These meetings can take place behind closed doors and consist of just a few individuals, but the FEC is convinced nothing corrupt will occur. It seems the FEC and lawmakers believe the American people are too apathetic to notice the ignorance behind this ruling—or both groups do not believe any meaningful opposition could be mounted to change things if voters were dissatisfied. The FEC has allowed legislators to again brazenly trample on what little faith the electorate held in the process.

Sen. Richard Shelby (R-AL) faced many challengers in his 2016 primary. After serving in D.C. for close to four decades, he had the war chest to secure the first step of his re-election. However, during the campaign, his record was obviously brought up against him. An article in Politico from 2010, "Shelby steers cash to ex aides," actually provided some of the ammunition. Manu Raju and John Bresnahan cited Melanie Sloan, executive director of Citizens for Responsibility and Ethics in Washington, as concluding, "Sen. Shelby, like Rep. Murtha before him, takes trading earmarks for campaign dollars to a level most members of Congress can only dream about."

While this label is troubling enough on the surface for many light readers, the two reporters from 2010 specifically pointed out the crux of the larger issue in explaining, "Shelby's earmarking doesn't appear to run afoul of Senate rules or federal ethics laws. But critics said his tactics are part of a Washington culture in which lawmakers direct money back home to narrow interests, which in turn, hire well-connected lobbyists—often former congressional aides—who enjoy special access on Capitol Hill."

As with so many others, it seems that Senator Shelby is at peace with doing anything within the realm of politics, as long as his actions remain within the rules in place, regardless of whether it clearly hurts democracy. And he's not alone in his assessment, as a media person-ality in Alabama pointed out to one of Shelby's opponents that for his corruption charge to be legitimate, it required evidence. This logic disregards moral corruption, which is subjective. A majority of aver-age Americans would determine that much of their legislators' con-duct within the rules they write are quite corrupt.

As for Senator Shelby, only he can answer to what drives his ac-tions; although, there can be little doubt that the clients his former aides lobbied for were content with whatever allowed them to receive the "more than $250 million in earmarks" as of 2010. Beyond the ri-diculous decision of the FEC to allow closer relations between cam-paigns and super PACs, candidates often display that they are guided by a similar belief in simply living within the rules for garnering the false sense of integrity it offers them.

Some lawmakers even feel it is legitimate to bypass the rules in place if they can legally do so. In his 2016 bid for the White House, Jeb Bush shamelessly raised money for a super PAC before officially becoming a candidate. He wondered why others wouldn't take ad-vantage of the same loophole. The common mantra for lawmakers is if you can maneuver in or around the rules, everything is perceived as being legitimate. Short-term success for self-interest is more im-portant than setting a higher standard.

Although the Supreme Court struck down limits on the amount of money outside groups could "independently" spend on elections, the Citizens United ruling did uphold the legitimate need for transparen-cy. Super PACs must report their expenditures and list their contributors, but just as with money laundering, donors often use shell companies to shield their actual identities. This is another rule in place that accomplishes very little.

In an August 2015 article for *The Huffington Post*, Paul Blumenthal demonstrated how this operation works. "Take Tread Standard LLC's $150,000 contribution on June 17 to Right to Rise, the super PAC that has raised $103 million to support former Florida Gov. Jeb Bush's presidential bid." Though it could seem clear to the casual observer, he then informs readers of this underlying problem often witnessed with authenticating super PAC donors in writing, "Tread Standard LLC is almost completely anonymous. Registered in Delaware on April 30, the company provided no mailing address to Right to Rise, though it was required to do so. Who's behind this group, anyway?"

The People's Clearing House raises the bar of accountability and transparency. Just as with candidates seeking office, all PACs (Political Action Committees) will register with TPCH. Each PAC, which obviously includes those designated as super PACs, will choose the distinction of being a state super PAC or a national super PAC—based on whether the organization will be contributing to races outside of the state. This declaration of being either a state or national organization will be consistently applied to all groups conducting political activity, from PACs to committees and other 527s. Every candidate, group, and organization will be appropriately assigned to the options of programs and initiatives available to direct their deductions to The People's Clearing House.

In terms of Political Action Committees, a state PAC has only been formed to give to state-wide races. Contributions to these PACs will be deducted by the State People's Clearing House, meaning choices for donors will be state-wide initiatives and causes that have been provided by the State House of Representatives or Senate. A national PAC has been formed with the intention of donating to races throughout the country, which include the presidential race. Contributions to these PACs will be deducted by the National People's Clearing House, meaning choices for donors will come from those provided by the U.S House of Representatives or Senate.

As with other individual campaign donations, in a perfect world the percentages deducted from PACs and super PACs by the State and National People's Clearing Houses would be based on a similar set of appropriate benchmarks. A separate level may be established for the entire group, such as assigning a slightly higher base set of deduction levels for groups once they reach a certain amount. For example, beyond the general deductions to the People's Clearing House, once a group had raised 5 million dollars in contributions, the percentage deducted would be lifted. However, even if the percentage of deduction is applied equally to all campaign contributions to organizations and candidates across the board, The People's Clearing House will achieve success.

The People's Clearing House immediately deducts the proper percentage from contributions. While a PAC may ultimately decide to cease activity and return money back to donors, The People's Clearing House keeps what has been deducted. As it currently stands now, the overall process of providing documentation concerning contributions is slow, which is especially detrimental to useful transparency associated with super PACs. Too much flexibility is currently given to release donor lists, allowing for the public to be in the dark until after the primary elections in some instances. PACs in the past have often disbanded before any connections could be uncovered for proper punishment, although most abuses have rarely been aggressively prosecuted initially.

The powerless Federal Elections Committee (FEC), composed equally of Democrats and Republicans, has definitely hampered meaningful oversight. Most punishments come well after the elections and are rarely more than a slap on the wrist. By The People's Clearing House proactively taking a percentage from each contribution, a second level of oversight is created within the system for quickly punishing PAC donors attempting to use shell companies as a means of hiding their true identities.

If contributions are processed by The People's Clearing House with incomplete or inadequate forms, additional percentage points of deductions can immediately be applied. The bar could be raised even higher for what is required on the forms, making the price larger for those attempting to bypass transparency, which the Supreme Court has deemed as a necessary deterrent against abuse. The foundational structure of The People's Clearing House provides flexibility for adequately addressing challenges to fairness in elections. Those driven by self-interest in their political participation will become clear.

THE "DARK MONEY" OF SOCIAL WELFARE ORGANIZATIONS OR 501(C)(4)S

Political contributions to super PACs (Political Action Committees) through the use of shell companies is not the only method donors are attempting to use to circumvent meaningful transparency. Nonprofits are the means currently receiving the most attention for their heightened impact on elections since the Citizens United ruling, which removed any limit to how much outside groups could "independently" spend on elections. Although the Supreme Court specifically emphasized the vital role of transparency in helping the people decide elections, as with politicians, special interests and Big Business will always seek new techniques to maintain their inappropriate influence in politics.

When it comes to representation—which was established for providing the level arena the Founders envisioned for facilitating the genuine debate, dialogue, and competitive principles the country was built upon—personal or professional interests should be recognized as secondary to the aim of equality in elections. Yet those individuals and special interests that eagerly seek to maintain their power and influence over those setting the rules of governing take any advantage they can get within the political arena.

In professional sports, officials who take money to influence their decisions are seen as corrupt and often face jail time if their actions are proven illegal. There are rules governing officials and players concerning attempts to seek or offer improper influence. Any player who rejects fair competition and seeks an improper advantage—even if done slightly within the current rules—would be widely branded as corrupt. Today, many profess their love for capitalism and democracy, while at the same time attempting to rig the equality of opportunity upon which it is supposed to be built. In their aim to bend the advantage more toward them, many outside of politics mirror the selfishness of the majority of legislators who currently hold office in D.C. and state legislatures nationwide.

Fair competition is not often something of significance to those driven by greed. Nonprofits are just the latest entity that was originally intended for good, but now has been exploited as reliable fronts for legally laundering money to a super PAC of choice.

In August 2015, Paul Blumenthal focused on the work of two nonprofits in Pennsylvania to provide readers with a better understanding of how this practice is utilized by donors: "The nonprofits, Rosebush Corp. and Green Orchard Inc., both appear to be associated with the Bala Cynwyd, Pennsylvania-based investment firm and its three wealthy principals: Jeffrey Yass, Joel Greenberg, and Arthur Dantchik. The two groups have dispersed at least $6.5 million to conservative nonprofits and super PACs since 2011, though the source of those funds has remained unclear because nonprofits are not subject to disclosure requirements—a phenomenon that led to those funds being known as 'dark money.'" Adequately tracing votes to the source of campaign contributions becomes much more difficult when those donors are easily shielded.

The practice of allowing donors to remain anonymous can be traced back to the Supreme Court's ruling in NAACP v Alabama, a civil-rights-era case in which the court struck down compelled disclosure of the state's NAACP's membership lists as "a violation of the Due Process Clause of the 14th Amendment." During that period of great unrest, the court understood the legitimate need to ensure that NAACP supporters would not face retaliation for their affiliation with the group. Today, nonprofits associated with political spending that face opposition to non-disclosure point to this similar need for protection.

John Riches, who serves as General Counsel for the Goldwater Institute, is an advocate for allowing nonprofit donors to remain hidden. Among other things, he points to instances where the works of the Founders were shrouded in accepted secrecy. As part of his piece entitled "The victims of 'dark money' disclosure: how government reporting requirements suppress speech and limit charitable giving" from August 2015, he notes, "Donor identities must be disclosed when they specifically earmark their donations to nonprofit organizations to be used for electioneering communications."

While John Riches believes current legislation and additional transparency requirements would limit the effectiveness of these groups even further, others contend this stipulation in earmarking highlights the means for allowing nonprofits to spend millions more on elections by having their contributors not earmark donations. This would seem to have been demonstrated with the election following the Citizens United decision, as "spending by organizations that do not disclose their donors [had] increased from less than $5.2 million in 2006 to well over $300 million in the 2012 election." While many nonprofits are established only with the desire to perform admirable works, those seeking to disguise their political power embrace this newfound method.

Emma Schwartz, as part of the "Big Sky, Big Money" documentary for Frontline, summarized the origins of these social welfare organizations through which "dark money" is being given in writing, "Nearly a century ago, Congress created the complicated legal framework that governs these tax-exempt nonprofits, also known as 501(c)(4) for the part of the tax code they fall under. The rule said they were supposed to operate 'exclusively for the promotion of social welfare'—a definition that includes groups ranging from local fire departments to the Sierra Club to the National Right to Life Committee." She went on to explain, "While these nonprofits have always been allowed to lobby for change, in 1959, regulators opened the door to political activity by interpreting 'exclusively' to mean that groups had to be 'primarily' engaged in social welfare and helping the community." Of course, the standard created was left ambiguous.

A similar concern is given to general 501(c)(3) nonprofits when it comes to lobbying. "In contrast to the prohibition on political campaign interventions by all section 501(c)(3) organizations, public charities (but not private foundations) may conduct a limited amount of lobbying to influence legislation. Although the law states that 'No substantial part…' of a public charity's activities can go to lobbying, charities with large budgets may lawfully expend a million dollars (under the 'expenditure' test), or more (under the 'substantial part' test) per year on lobbying." Even with lobbying, the rules are not written in a fashion that blurs the lines. Keeping things as vague as possible is a governmental trademark that has consistently facilitated abuse. Selling the people out for gain should never be easy, although it probably is for those legislators heavily backed by trial lawyers who receive a steady hand of work as a result.

In specific relation to the 501(c)(4)s, or social welfare organizations, one woman in particular articulated a powerful message directly to Congress. "During a July 29, 2015 Senate Judiciary subcommittee hearing focused on IRS oversight of exempt organizations with political activity, Independent Sector President and CEO Diana Aviv called for clearer rules surrounding such activities, including specific permissible levels and disclosure of donors whose contributions are intended to be used to influence the outcome of elections." The Treasury Department flirted with new rules in 2013 designed to rein in the improper political activity of these groups, but, of course, nothing came of it.

Diana Aviv called for clarity in what these social welfare organizations can spend on elections by assigning a specific "dollar amount." She rejected these groups operating further under the guidelines currently in place, which allow them to assume that as long as they spend no more than 49% of money towards political activity, they remain legal.

In considering the other nonprofits, such as 501(c)(6)s (business leagues and trade associations) and 501(c)(5)s (labor unions), also being utilized for political activity, Aviv called for a "universal definition of political activity across 501(c) organizations in order to provide clarity and consistency for the consideration of tax-exempt status applications and to prevent the shifting of political activity to tax-exempt organizations not covered under the current proposed guidance." Unlike lawmakers, Aviv understands the commitment of those who circumvent the laws and recognizes that regulations, to succeed, must not only address the current issues in transparency and abuse, but also be pro-active in closing the path that some will always use to create the next loopholes.

The clear distinction the Independent Sector President and CEO advocates for social welfare organizations, as to which funds will be utilized for political/electioneering activity and which funds will be utilized for non-partisan activities to promote their message, is implemented through The People's Clearing House. Each contribution received will require the donor to clearly identify whether to direct the money to the general social welfare account or whether to direct it toward the partisan purposes account. Any contribution designated to the non-partisan sector of the nonprofit will obviously not face a deduction from The People's Clearing House.

This separation will be deducted through The People's Clearing House, as social welfare groups will join the ranks of all candidates and organizations involved with political activity. The same initial procedure always applies. The group will first register as either a state or national nonprofit, aligning itself with the proper causes and initiatives for donors to select from. Contributions directed by donors to the political/electioneering sector of the organization will be deducted by the appropriate People's Clearing House. However, contributions to nonprofits conducting political activity will face a higher deduction for remaining anonymous. While it may be possible to provide an exception if the donor specifies that he is allowing his name to be revealed, it would have to be written with clear wording. Any opportunity to circumvent the law through a slight opening created through the wording of legislature is guaranteed to be manipulated.

An example of how a contribution to a social welfare organization would be treated: Assuming that only one standard of deduction by The People's Clearing House is applied to all other contributions to political organizations and candidates that must be transparent, such as 30%, a contribution made to the political/electioneering activity sector of a social welfare group would face a deduction of 35% or higher for maintaining their anonymity. The actual percentage taken by TPCH will depend on the standard of deduction established at the state or federal level.

Just as with other political entities, such super PACs, contributions will receive an adequate level of scrutiny. Any forms missing required information will result in an additional deduction, if not rejected entirely. Although The People's Clearing House is built on the hope of providing new causes and initiatives to meet the demands of the community, any chance of a nonprofit receiving funds from TPCH are eliminated once participation in partisan politics has occurred beyond general lobbying. If any subgroup of nonprofits received funds, it would most likely be those within the 501(c)(3) allotment.

Social welfare organizations are currently allowed to spend directly on elections, such as with placing their own ads on television. However, beyond the consistent lack of transparency, regardless of whether partisan activities are direct or indirect, the most significant issue has been the lack of transparency surrounding contributions made from 501(c)(4)s to super PACs. Just as with the intent behind the use of shell companies, money sent from social welfare groups to super PACs circumvents the small degree of transparency required of other donors to super PACs. Only the name of the nonprofit is being listed as the contributor to the super PAC. Funneling money through these social welfare organizations in no way provides voters with the transparency recognized by the Supreme Court as essential in making the Citizens United decision work in democracy.

The People's Clearing House establishes a foundation for addressing potential abuse; in a sense, separating the superficial pretenders from those of good will. Those in the past who actually sought methods for getting around transparency will no longer have the instrument of a 501(c)(4) at their disposal to do so. Instead, money that travels through this process will face two deductions—a heightened one on the money originally given to the nonprofit, before another deduction that is standard for all contributions to super PACs. These two deductions will serve as a powerful deterrent to those who only followed this process in the past to keep their donor identity disclosed. If a social welfare group rejects being the middleman to super PACS and instead chooses to directly spend on political activities, only one deduction will occur. However, donors so driven by secrecy in contributing that they are willing to accept two deductions will only serve to give more back to the community.

An example of how a donor could choose between having one deduction or two: Andy desires to give $100,000 to a super PAC, but does not want his name to be disclosed. With this in mind, he decides to give to a social welfare organization instead, allowing it to then give the money to the super PAC (so he can remain anonymous). His initial $100,000 donation to the social welfare organization is first deducted at a heightened rate determined at the federal or state level. Assuming the percentage of deduction is 38%, his initial contribution to the social welfare group would be $62,000, with $38,000 to The People's Clearing House. Let's say the social welfare organization adds $300,000 from contributions that have already been reduced once from TPCH to Andy's $62,000, and makes a contribution of $362,000 to a super PAC. Just as with any other contribution to a political organization or candidate, the $362,000 to the super PAC will be deducted by TPCH. In this case, if the rate were 30%, the super PAC would receive $253,400, while $108,600 would be directed to TPCH. The initial $100,000 donation has now faced two deductions through the process of having a middle entity. If Andy had given his $100,000 directly to the super PAC and abided by disclosure, the committee would have received $70,000 from the one deduction of 30% by The People's Clearing House. The choice remains his (as the donor). Either way the community wins, with the 30% still meaning $30,000 to TPCH.

Higher percentages deducted from donors to social welfare groups for partisan purposes should be seen as reasonable considering there are so many other methods to contribute money that only receive a standard deduction. Individuals, especially those within the social welfare group, can give directly to candidates and super PACs. General non-partisan activities to promote the nonprofit can be given without any deduction. Under TPCH system, these donors are making the decision to unnecessarily face two deductions. Other nonprofits of good will that abide by these rules will be establishing a new level of accountability to punish those who do not share their integrity.

The federal government should raise the general requirements for allowing nonprofits to conduct any partisan activity. The People's Clearing House will go a long way in aiding these groups in discovering the proper balance in any current and possible future heightened standards. Any 501(c)(4) that questions whether they can still be effective in reaching their goals without the old system that allowed them to funnel unmarked contributions into elections needs to reevaluate whether their intentions are aligned with the legitimate goals of nonprofits. Their endeavors may be better suited for an entity actually formed for politics, such as a PAC.

The Internal Revenue Service already possesses some means within the flawed system to punish nonprofits that the agency deems have improperly used their preferred status. Stephen Fishman, accomplished author and attorney, who has published a number of books designed to aid individuals in taxes and business, wrote, "Social welfare organizations that spend money on political activity can become subject to a special tax on the lesser of the organization's net investment income or the total amount spent on political activity. The applicable amount is taxed at the highest corporate tax rate—35%."

Groups can also lose their tax-exempt status at the hands of the IRS as punishment; although, anyone could guess this rarely occurs. However, even if the IRS desired to become more active in attempting to keep these organizations more accountable through the tools currently available, the agency faces the same obstacle presented when attempts have been made to rein in other entities (such as PACs).

In 2012, Emma Schwartz spelled out this difficulty in writing, "As a recent ProPublica investigation found: 'One reason the IRS struggles is that it can't match the speed of politics.' In other words, by the time these groups submit tax returns, they have often stopped operating or created new groups under new names." Just as it accounts for the disbanding of PACs and super PACs before any actions can be taken against abuses, The People's Clearing House makes a deduction immediately upon receiving a contribution; therefore, raising accountability, while building communities. It lays the foundation for timely and meaningful punishment for those abusing the system.

Regardless of the current options available to the IRS for restraining these groups, no punishment or tax deduction will serve as a direct facilitator of growth within communities. Unlike The People's Clearing House, any money deducted by these means will simply be placed in the hands of untrustworthy bureaucrats or politicians to allocate. No tool currently in place will empower communities more than The People's Clearing House, which offers constituents across the country a method for directly taking a hand in choosing from causes and initiatives for strengthening their cities and states nationwide.

Though agencies such as the Internal Revenue Service, Securities and Exchange Commission, and Federal Elections Commission could take a more aggressive role in rooting out abuses that are undermining the integrity of elections, federal legislators could take the lead in the endeavor. Beyond the realities of those within America attempting to circumvent laws intended to protect the all-important process of choosing those that will serve as representatives to the people, many foreign governments and entities also revel in loopholes that may allow them to manipulate the system.

To only view loopholes as methods for politicians and special interests groups within America to gain an improper advantage within the political system would be short-sighted. It must be understood that an absence of transparency, especially in nonprofits and foundations, provides foreigners a possible avenue for more easily joining the ranks of other "dark money" contributors. No foreign government or entity should influence elections, especially those who have demonstrated a consistent track record of ignoring human rights and practicing discrimination. Yet, none of these foreign or domestic threats to elections have persuaded the U.S. Congress to take meaningful action.

While certain states have attempted to work within the current confines of the Supreme Court's ruling by passing laws aimed at heightening the legitimate need for transparency that was upheld, federal legislators and agencies basically remain nothing more than spectators. In so doing, more of these nonprofits take full advantage, such as "Freedom Partners" [using] its status as a 501(c)(6) organization to raise and distribute over $250 million during the 2012 election campaigns without disclosing its donors." Disclose Acts, which were intended, in part, to shed light on the secret money in politics, always die in Congress. These bills join the ranks of numerous pieces of legislation that began with promise before being placed in congressional committees to remain idle.

Although some may assume that Republican voters would be more opposed to additional disclosure requirements based on the pushback often received from Republican lawmakers to any campaign finance legislation, support actually comes from across the political spectrum. As an article from Reclaim the American Dream, a nonprofit informational website, revealed, "Full disclosure is what most of the voting public wants, right, center, left. Opinion polls show that the public favors clear rules and a level playing field. In one poll, nearly two-thirds wanted disclosure on political funding and spending—66% of Democrats, 62% of independents, and 61% of Republicans." And these numbers could only rise as voters become more educated on the means of abuse.

While inaction on the matter from the federal government would be bad enough, it's the concerted effort to thwart any consequential legislation from being passed onto these organizations, which should be most troubling to citizens. "As enacted into law in December 2015, the FY2016 spending bill included a provision preventing the IRS from issuing new regulations governing political activity by 501(c)(4) social welfare organizations for the rest of the current year." Having the ability to insert small additions like these in enormous spending bills each year greatly serves the interests of lawmakers.

Focusing on all the major pieces of legislation being passed within gigantic bills is time consuming and difficult for political pundits, much less the general public. Few Americans have the time or legal expertise to sift through thousands of pages to assess what is consequential. It is a perfectly planned outcome for self-centered legislators. In this case, enough members in both major parties accepted a provision that guaranteed another election would be spared from any IRS actions on nonprofits—business as usual.

Potential voters in the 2016 presidential race have indicated that they have deep skepticism concerning some of the campaign promises from both of the major party nominees. In the case of Democratic presidential nominee Hillary Clinton, most of the distrust specifically revolves around whether she will raise the bar of accountability in elections and on Wall Street. During an episode of "Morning Joe" on MSNBC from early June 2016, co-host Mika Brzezinski referenced a Quinnipiac University National Poll that displayed "just 9% believe she can get secret money out of politics." However, even more significant and revealing, that same poll from May 2016 discovered that 63% held the belief that "Clinton would not even try to remove secret money from politics."

If the results from this Quinnipiac University Poll alone are any indication of whether Americans would trust someone like former Secretary of State Hillary Clinton to support meaningful campaign finance reform, a clear majority would not. The lack of faith from the 63% who specifically doubt she would even make an effort in rooting out the "dark money" of elections has to be based (to some degree) on her background and a campaign that was built upon, and benefited from, establishment politics. They obviously assess her as exemplifying the typical politician, who offers lip service during campaigns, committee hearings, general public statements, and speeches before working privately to conduct an agenda tailored for special interests and influential donors.

Democrats around the country may ultimately learn to distrust Hillary Clinton even more than Republicans to address campaign finance reform, considering her questionable fundraising practices, highlighted most effectively by the Bernie Sanders campaign. She definitely did not seem to live up to her pledge to strengthen democratic efforts in states across the country, according to Kenneth P. Vogel and Isaac Amsdorf. In evaluating the Hillary Victory Fund, the two Politico writers pointed out that, "Less than 1 percent of the $61 million raised by that effort has stayed in the state parties' coffers, according to a POLITICO analysis of the latest Federal Election Commission filings." Vogel and Amsdorf explained that Hillary Clinton had been able to secure big money from donors at parties and events, held by the likes of George Clooney, with her fundraising committee, in that it was designed to questionably allow her to work in correlation with the Democratic National Committee and state party committees.

Their article also enlightened readers on one of the methods the Clinton campaign used to keep some of these immense funds: "The victory fund has transferred $3.8 million to the state parties, but almost all of that cash (3.3 million, or 88 percent) was quickly transferred to the DNC, usually within a day or two, by the Clinton staffer who controls the committee, POLITICO's analysis of the FEC records found." Beyond any legality concerns to her actions, Hillary Clinton only cements her place within the ranks of other politicians who always seek to dance around the standard in place for fairness, instead of setting a new one out of personal integrity and love of country.

The practices highlighted by Vogel and Amsdorf only add to a list of other ways in which the Democratic nominee for president debatably conducts her campaign. In a June 2016 article entitled "This is the Hillary Clinton Scandal No One's Talking About" from *Paste Magazine*, Walker Bragman demonstrates how the Hillary Clinton campaign has met the testing standard of the FEC in determining that a candidate has violated federal campaign finance laws with inappropriate communication with independent expenditure groups (like super PACs). Her relationship with the Correct the Record is the point of contention; although not surprisingly, ambiguous rules exist.

As Walker Bragman wrote, "Even many of the people I spoke to who work for the FEC seemed to have a hard time explaining them. With so much confusion, it is not difficult to see how enforcement might be difficult"; a difficulty within the sham of a government someone like Hillary would seem to have disqualified herself to correct.

Beyond aiding in distinguishing between those driven by self-interest to that of service founded in the best interests of the people, The People's Clearing House would effectively get to the heart of why a social welfare group is formed. If the general cause behind the 501(c)(4) is to create an advantage for partisan purposes, donors have the option of giving to the non-political activity sector of the group and face no deductions. If the main objective is political, then a heightened deduction will occur on donations to the political activity/

electioneering activity of the group, with a possible second deduction if a contribution is made by the 501(c)(4) to a super PAC.

It seems pretty straightforward.

When it comes to 501(c)(4)s, "an organization is considered by the IRS to be operated exclusively for the promotion of social welfare if it is primarily engaged in promoting the common good and general welfare of the people and the community." If the spirit to form these groups is driven by the endeavor of common good and general welfare, then a process of providing greater scrutiny to contributions for partisan purposes should be welcomed. The People's Clearing House gives back to the entire community, while implementing greater transparency and fairness within the significant electoral process that is designated to provide genuine representatives vital to a republic.

As far as the all-important tax-exempt status at the center of what these organizations seek from the IRS, The People's Clearing House would eliminate the need for those engaging in partisan activities altogether. No process that already makes deductions and gives back to the community to such an extent would be applicable for taxation. Any time the IRS is involved, partisan politics and general corruption should be expected, as the agency is absent of trusted integrity—best demonstrated through questionable re-hiring practices and targeting of certain groups seeking tax-exempt status. The authoritarian Internal Revenue Service, a political and economic bully, should have a diminished role in everything; ideally, it would be eliminated altogether. Any method that paves the way for these results should be welcomed.

DEDUCTIONS FROM CONTRIBUTIONS ARE DETERMINED BY THE TIME IN WHICH THEY ARE GIVEN

Representation belongs to the people. Every aspect involving service should, to some degree, reveal this truth to constituents. Under TPCH, the electoral process only serves as the initial phase of strengthening communities through processes associated with representation. The tracking established at the beginning by TPCH for making appropriate deductions and maintaining accountability over the duration of a political career creates a foundation for legislators to consistently give back to their constituency.

There is a wide range of federal and state rules and regulations concerning lobbying. However, regardless of the differences, any amount of money or gifts allowed to directly be given to federal or state legislators should also face some form of deduction to TPCH. Each lobbying group and its associates would also be registered with TPCH, just as any other individual or organization that is formally involved in politics. As far as lobbying, one example would be a $110 limit placed on how much money could directly be spent during a certain time period on wooing a state representative. Another would be the money spent by a nonprofit organization like ALEC, or the American Legislative Exchange Council, for one of its routine conferences legislators are allowed to attend. To some extent, any money that is being spent to lobby state and federal legislators should face a deduction to The People's Clearing House.

Although each trip, gift, and perk associated with lobbying would ideally also face a TPCH deduction, the steady focus of the system remains on tracking and deducting campaign contributions for greater accountability and efficiency in representation. In 2012, NPR aired a documentary series entitled "Money in Politics," which provided citizens a behind-the-scenes view of what occurs in D.C. As NPR's Andrea Seabrook, along with Alex Blumberg, discovered, it was actually the members of the U.S. Congress fervently seeking the lobbyists, not vice versa, as voters commonly envision.

Much of the report from NPR centered around the insights of Jimmy Williams, a former lobbyist on Capitol Hill. Williams described the undesirable task of helping U.S. legislators raise money once they called him, merely because he desired to secure their votes on legislation. The NPR correspondents learned from him how things were routinely placed into motion after receiving such a call. "'So I call up my buddies down on K street,' Williams says. 'I'm gonna do this event for this guy, and he sits on the House Financial Services committee. You guys have any money for this person?'"

The following day, Andrea Seabrook and Alex Blumberg's next report described how these events actually looked once they had been manifested. As detailed in the article highlighting their radio segment, "At a typical event, there's a member of Congress and a member of his or her staff who is in charge of collecting the checks. This person is known as the fundraiser." Of course, the men and women of Congress will emphatically tell the American people that their votes are not dictated by money.

"'The fundraiser is standing in the room, and the fundraiser has $35,000 in checks sitting in her pocket right now,' says Jimmy Williams, a former lobbyist for the real estate industry. 'And we're going to talk about public policy while we take the checks." It seems as if this is the service with a smile that all Americans, from struggling families to hopeful entrepreneurs, are supposed to resign themselves to accept as being the best and brightest the country can produce to represent and lead them. The establishments within the U.S. Congress and state legislatures have essentially promoted the notion that they are too big to fail—confident the people will never unite for change.

Apathy will cause some to want to just believe in the current system and give the men and women who serve as representatives the benefit of the doubt regardless of the burden of proof against them. However, the frustration of an entitled congressman Williams was attempting to introduce some of his clients to should provide anyone clarity for the need to change things. Williams had apparently not been maintaining what the congressmen believed was a sufficient amount of contributions. "'I've put in two calls to your PAC director, and I haven't received any return calls," the congressmen said, according to Williams. 'Now why am I taking this meeting?'"

With the arrogant and cynical attitude of the congressman (a mindset obviously held by many federal and state legislators) it can be safely assumed that a heartfelt letter from a constituent—without a check attached—would not be granted much, if any, attention. However, individuals who don't produce a reliable and consistent flow of checks to legislators are told they should remain confident that their representative will work diligently to provide them an ample voice in government. To simply listen to those in power and hold faith would be absurd and explains why so many citizens currently feel hopeless. U.S. Senator Jeff Sessions of Alabama may have summed up things best in September 2015, when he stated, "We have too many people that are in denial. They spend too much time in fundraisers with rich people and they don't deeply understand the pain of middle-class, salaried Americans."

The consistency of money-raising events dictating the daily schedule of legislators has remained a consistent theme, where once again past history is reflective of current behavior. As former *Los Angeles Times* reporters Sara Fritz and Dwight Morris painstakingly discovered from their work in 1992. "While challengers were scrambling for cash—often spending their own money to mount campaigns—most incumbents had no trouble meeting whatever fund-raising goal they set for themselves. Virtually every weeknight in Washington D.C., the National Democratic Club, the Ronald Reagan Center, the Capital Hill Club, and various popular restaurants near the Capital were booked with an endless schedule of fund-raising parties held by members of Congress."

Beyond taking the opportunistic approach of commandeering willing lobbyists to serve as able fundraisers, incumbents utilize accumulated campaign funds to staff and maintain their ever-increasing political machine with PAC consultants. Nate Thames, Political Director at ActBlue, summarized how these consultants follow the similar practices of lobbyists. "A PAC consultant throws a party, handles all of the planning, invites all of the attendees, and the candidate just has to show up and collect the checks. Easy and efficient, but you'll pay the PAC consultant thousands of dollars a month in retainer. This is a method only available to incumbents, since PACs are interested in buying influence and aren't going to throw money at a challenger that will likely lose."

Clearly, the money being spent by incumbents on these endeavors offers just another reason why the electorate would be happy with the proactive functionality of The People's Clearing House. Spending campaign money to add more PAC consultants to an ever-growing political machine is about as irritating as when legislators use excess campaign money to mount legal defenses. The Associated Press reported in February 2015 that the Alabama House Speaker at the time, Republican Mike Hubbard, had used close to $300,000 from past campaign contributions since 2013. Although it was all legal, not even a blessing from the Attorney General's office to use campaign funds for legal fees would be enough to save Hubbard from multiple felony ethics convictions.

By having deductions from original contributions to The People's Clearing House made immediately, money is given back to the community long before there is a chance it will end up instead in the hands of consultants or attorneys. Any money spent from the war chests of incumbents will only be coming from what remains after this process. Under The People's Clearing House system, incumbents will no longer possess the same power to utilize excessive funds for self-interest over that of strengthening communities.

Beyond the standard rate of deduction(s) applied to contributions within the election cycle, The People's Clearing House addresses the never-ending grind of legislators, organizations, nonprofits, and other politically engaged individuals and entities to raise campaign money. Under TPCH, every group follows a fundraising schedule that assigns a differing rate(s) to contributions received outside of elections.

At the conclusion of each election, all these politically active groups and organizations, which are already registered with The People's Clearing House as required, will be reset within the system. This makes the rate(s) of deduction(s) applied reflective of being outside the official election cycle. The U.S. currently does not follow an official election season, so specifics on deduction rates would fall on guidelines at the federal and state level. Once again, autonomy would remain in deciding the question of how to treat contributions received outside of the official election cycle that is instituted.

Members of the U.S. House of Representatives serve two-year terms. Let's assume the federal government established an official election cycle that was twelve months. During those designated twelve months for official campaigning, the standard rates of deductions to TPCH are applied. However, whatever time—in this case a full year—that precedes the campaign season, will be deducted at a higher rate back to The National People's Clearing House. These deductions would apply to House incumbents and their challengers, as well as those political organizations, such as super PACs and nonprofits, registered as national political organizations with the National People's Clearing House.

An example of how deductions could be applied to contributions received outside of the official election cycle by House incumbents, any potential challengers, and organizations and committees registered with The National People's Clearing House: In this scenario, the 2016 elections have come to an end. All House candidates and groups and organizations registered with The National People's Clearing house to make or receive contributions will have their status reset. An 85% deduction will apply to contributions during this time before the official election cycle. Incumbents, potential challengers, organizations, and committees will have the standards of deductions applied to any contributions received.

The Contributions	Given Rate of Deduction	What is actually received by the recipient	What goes to The National People's Clearing House
A lobbyist hosts an event and raises $35,000 for a House incumbent from other registered attendees	85%	$5,250	$29,750
A 501(c)(4) organization receives a $2,200 contribution to the partisan purposes account	85%	$330	$1,870
A nationally registered super PAC receives a $10,000 contribution	85%	$1,500	$8,500

Another scenario would be where the rate of deduction to The People's Clearing House on those contributions given during the time period preceding the official election cycle may be broken down by intervals of month—instead of having one standard deduction for the entire period.

Months	Rate of Deduction
November 2016 until end of March 2017	85%
April 2017 until end of June 2017	80%
July 2017 until end of August 2017	75%
September 2017 until end of October 2017	70%

The heightened rate(s) of deduction to The People's Clearing House established on contributions received outside the election cycle would obviously need to be adjusted according to whether it was a presidential election or midterm election year. During midterm elections, deductions could simply be applied to the first year following the previous elections without any issues concerning primary dates. The official election season could allow six months of campaigning for both the primary and general election if the primaries were all held in May. Having six months of campaigning under standard deductions for both primary and general elections should be considered as reasonable.

With presidential elections, some adjustments would have to be made to account for differing primary dates. What is considered the official election season and rates of deductions on money received outside of this time period would have to be changed. This would especially be true for states that hold their primaries and caucuses early, such as New Hampshire and Iowa. If the heightened deductions were only ten months, two more months could be designated to the official election season. This change provides flexibility for states to have the desired time before primaries and general elections. With the type of adjustment described for presidential election years, the option of a standard deduction could again apply to all contributions. This would last for ten months preceding the election cycle; or instead of a deduction such as 85% on all, it could again be broken down into percentages by months. The following chart represents how rates might differentiate within the months of November 2016 to August 2017. The official election season for standard deductions would be October 2017 to November 2018. Even if a New Hampshire primary was held during the first week of February 2017, five months would be provided for standard campaigning.

Months	Rate of Deduction
November 2016 to until end of January 2017	85%
February 2017 to until end of April 2017	80%
May 2017 to until end of June 2017	75%
July 2017 to until end of August 2017	70%

National nonprofits and committees, such as 501(c)(4)s and super PACs which are registered with the National People's Clearing House, will always follow this two-year schedule, with U.S. House elections every two years. However, the autonomy of states to form their own campaign finance laws allows for adjustments to be made. Just as each state is currently unique in guidelines, such as the timeframe allowed for a state representative to raise money in and out of session, the state will control The People's Clearing House it creates for its state.

The system is a testament to democratic principles.

A state sets the rate of deductions to be applied to state incumbents, potential challengers, and political entities registered with the State People's Clearing House. While most states follow the example of the U.S. House of Representatives in having two-year terms, some states are distinctly different. For example, Massachusetts has two-year terms for state senate and house members. Nebraska on the other hand is unicameral, being the only single-house state government––having one body composed of senators. The structure of the People's Clearing House provides flexibility for states to tailor the rates of deductions and lengths of official state campaign seasons to be most effective.

Alabama is only one among a handful of states which has house and senate members elected to four-year terms. While the federal incumbents, candidates, and national political entities would consistently remain adhered to the two-year schedule of deductions established at the federal level, Alabama would utilize its autonomy to set different rates of deductions on contributions directed toward state incumbents and candidates who would be registered with the state People's Clearing House. The state will establish rates of deductions to the People's Clearing House for the additional time an incumbent has before he faces another re-election bid four years upon being elected.

While state incumbents and any of their potential challengers will face the four-year deduction schedule, political entities such as state PACs would remain on the two-year schedule of contributions determined by the states. This makes sense when considering staggered terms create an election every two years, just as on the federal level. National and state political entities, such as PACs and 501(c)(4)s, will always remain true to the two-year deduction schedule established with rates at the federal or state level. Only candidates and challengers could face an alternative deduction schedule. In this scenario, Alabama has established a level of deductions by years for state incumbents and their challengers. In the year preceding the official election season designated by the state, Alabama has decided on the option of simply applying an 85% deduction on all contributions, as opposed to assigning various levels of deductions to certain months within that

12-month period. An incoming state senator or house member would face the following contribution deduction schedule over the three-year period preceding the official election cycle set by the state.

Years	Rate of Deduction
November 2016 until end of October 2017	95%
November 2017 until end of October 2018	90%
November 2018 until end of October 2019	85%
November 2019 Until Election Day	Deduction Standard(s) for official Election Cycle Contributions

U.S. senators are elected to six-year terms. As with states like Alabama with additional years before the official election cycle, senators would also need to be assigned a standard level of deduction on contributions received by incumbents and any challengers. This would be the deductions a senator would face upon being elected.

Years	Rate of Deduction
November 2016 until end of October 2017	95%
November 2017 until end of October 2018	95%
November 2018 until end of October 2019	95%
November 2019 until end of October 2020	90%
November 2020 until end of October 2021	85%
November 2021 Until Election Day	Deduction Standard(s) for official Election Cycle Contributions

As can be witnessed with terms lasting four to six years, having more time provides more flexibility in establishing standards of deductions. These longer terms also effectively provide more time to adequately eliminate the emphasis of fundraising being the central theme of the "people's" representatives. While the two-year terms of U.S. house representatives shared with many state house representatives can still be effectively broken down into various rates of deductions, longer terms would be ideal.

Long before the considerations of more flexibility in deductions, former President Nixon addressed the ever-present fundraising that impedes meaningful service in writing, "There is one change that all those interested in better government should support. The terms of members of the House should be extended to four years, with one half being in the Presidential year and the other half in the off year. This would mean that for at least two years of his four-year term, a congressman could be a congressman rather than a perpetual candidate spending 75 percent of his time raising campaign funds and campaigning for re-election." Whether terms are ever extended as Richard Nixon suggested in his memoir from 1990, deductions based on time found within The People's Clearing House could effectively remove incentive for members to constantly raise funds.

With deductions to The People's Clearing House being universally applied to money being spent outside and inside the election cycle, every individual and group participating in politics will be held to the same standard. Just as with incumbents, candidates challenging them for their seats will be forced to campaign within the same parameters. If a candidate for office attempts to follow Jeb Bush's example from the 2016 presidential election of working to raise money with a super PAC before officially announcing his candidacy, contributions will face steep deductions if done outside the election season. The design of the system raises the level of expected accountability for anyone involved in politics, but especially serving to limit the incumbent advantage.

A system of deductions based on time will make drawing correlations between special interests money and voting records easier to assess. Instead of everything in lobbying moving so fast and at such a magnitude, The People's Clearing House helps identify which senators and representatives are most likely to receive the attention of lobbyists. A U.S. senator serving in the first or second year is not going to see as many lobbyists as a member of Congress a year or two out from re-election. So other than serving as a powerful deterrent against constant fundraising, having higher deductions on contributions outside the official campaign season will serve as the easiest predictor of where the emphasis of tracking should be directed. An enhanced scrutiny of contributions as a result of having this reliable compass should serve as a game-changer.

Some may say that lobbyists will simply make promises to politicians that they will be giving them money closer to election season. However, most lawmakers are unlikely to meet with lobbyists for simple promises, just as lobbyists are probably not going to spend much time on a representative they can't quickly buy. Without the willingness of the members of Congress to attend events, any fundraising will be marginalized. A short time period is a lifetime in politics, and very few lobbyists are likely going to use time and resources on nothing more than a question mark of influence.

Between the heightened deductions and lower enthusiasm that would be brought from a PAC consultant attending an event alone, the legislator will quickly recognize the most productive way to spend their time is actually in being a congressman or congresswoman. While a novel idea for a number of lawmakers in D.C. and state legislatures across the country, constituents often wonder whether it is a lack of common sense or absence of integrity that could allow representatives to ignore them in service. Regardless, only a system that forces this change can prevail over greed and self-interest.

Becoming an expert on sponsored bills instead of relying on aides, actually reading bills before voting, making a greater effort to listen to the constituency, pushing hard to meet new demands on chronic issues with unique solutions, and choosing to attend congressional events over fundraisers could be the new norm for members of Congress who spend more time and effort doing their job than keeping their job. Teddy Roosevelt accepted that the only way he could be of genuine service to the people was by not concerning himself with his political future, but instead only focusing on doing the best job he could each day. The challenges the country faces demands this type service.

Lobbying of federal and state legislators will still occur, just without money being a predominant variable in leading and instituting the discussion. How could lobbyists, special interests, and politicians complain about the deduction schedule of The People's Clearing House when these groups have always assured the general public that money is not what provides them with power? Opposing efforts to essentially remove money as a predominant variable of influence on those actively representing the people would only be admitting to what everyone else already knows: money currently rules politics.

Opposition to higher deductions on campaign contributions received outside of the official election cycle would indicate a clear acknowledgement that money exchanged earlier in the process has actually lowered the speech of others who give closer to elections, which would be unconstitutional. Anthony Corrado highlighted this truth in his 1997 book *Campaign Finance Reform: A Sourcebook*, in which he wrote, "The Court announced that 'the concept that government may restrict the speech of some elements of our society in order to enhance the relative voice of others is wholly foreign to the First Amendment.' It added that the 'First Amendment's protection against governmental abridgement of free expression cannot properly be made to depend on a person's financial ability to engage in public discussion.' The Buckley Court therefore saw campaign expenditure limits as a kind of 'taking,' or compulsory exaction from some for the benefit of others. The limits were unconstitutional for this very reason."

The Buckley Court, which served as the catalyst for the Citizens United ruling that opened up Pandora's box on campaign contributions, said under certain conditions one group's speech could not be lowered to benefit another group. It would seem rather obvious that early contributions currently allowed clearly give some individuals greater speech in maintaining the beneficial status quo. This ruling also dealt with limits, which The People's Clearing House is not imposing, nor is it a restriction that benefits one group over the other—as all participants compose the constituency. Deductions to The People's Clearing House go back to the entire constituency, with the emphasis of the regulations placed on raising the bar of accountability and strengthening communities. Any leveling of the political arena as a result is only a byproduct of these endeavors.

The only way a candidate or political entity would face a higher percentage deducted from a contribution to The People's Clearing House would be if they choose one. The same contribution given outside the official election season and receiving a higher percentage of deduction to The People's Clearing House can be donated within the official campaign season and receive the standard deduction, which is much less. Any argument regarding limits to speech would seem to depend on time being determined as a limiting factor. It would also seem a difficult argument to make considering that a universal standard is being applied, with everyone having the same options in how their contributions are treated—regulating them for the common good.

Another consideration in relation to the restriction placed on the time an individual can even actually vote, which some would argue was the highest expression of speech. Early voters can only begin voting at a certain time before elections, not immediately following the previous election, even if they were already convinced that they will be voting again for the newly elected member of Congress. It is easy to see how ridiculous this would be without having a record of service, as well as how unfair this would be to a potential challenger. Regardless of a vote and campaign contributions offering a voice to the political arena, it is deemed acceptable for incumbents to have an advantage in fundraising almost immediately upon taking office.

The People's Clearing House will better distinguish the motives behind service and policy. As a result, the American people will have an easier time deciphering which individuals can be trusted to lead them with a servant's heart insulated by acts of honor.

AN ALTERNATIVE TO THE VIRTUALLY IMPOSSIBLE TASK OF IMPOSING TERM LIMITS

In an address to the Midwest Republican Leadership Conference, Fred Thompson spoke about the predominant national security threats that continued to plague the nation. From terrorism concerns to the debt crisis associated with rising healthcare costs and a shrinking social security fund, he effectively articulated the extent of demands the inept culture in D.C. remained unwilling to adapt in resolving. Although the speech came from the former U.S. Senator from Tennessee in 2007, it could have easily been given today.

Specifically, Thompson, a man best known for his acting roles and significant questioning from the Watergate Hearings, offered insights as to why he ultimately decided to remain committed to his pledge of only serving two terms. While many respected a congressman who actually held true to his word, it didn't stop some from second-guessing him. During his speech, Thompson told the crowd that he would always respond to those seeking clarification by saying, "After eight years in Washington, I just longed for the realism and sincerity of Hollywood again." Few politicians are as willing to walk away from the life of entitlement they have grown to treasure above all else.

In his memoir, former President Richard Nixon addressed the consistent permanence of members in D.C. by writing, "Unless the incumbency is broken by eliminating gerrymandering and allowing challengers to compete with incumbents on a more level playing field, we will have completely impaired the Founders' goal of a Congress that renews itself constantly to reflect the changing views of the voters." While Nixon was very particular in the words he chose to present his argument, Mark Twain seems to have taken an opposite path to that of caution, as he is often attributed with the distinct phrase, "Politicians and diapers must be changed often, and for the same reason."

George Washington chose to walk away from the presidency after two terms despite the pleas from many for him to remain. As is so often taught in history classes across the country, the first president of the United States recognized the necessity of setting a two-term precedent for future occupants of the Oval Office. Though Washington, the battle-worn general and proven leader, most likely trusted his own personal discipline for serving with integrity beyond eight years, he could not predict the judgment of others to come.

Many good men have given way to the sense of power.

The assessment of President Washington has proven to be wise. Some of those who followed him have definitely demonstrated the need for an additional check on attempts to extend the power of the executive branch. Despite all of his positive attributes of service, it cannot be forgotten that President Franklin D. Roosevelt attempted to pack the Supreme Court in his second of four terms to obtain the rulings he wanted on his New Deal initiatives. Just as it can't be overlooked how power has leaned more to the executive over time, with some highlights being: Lyndon Johnson's obtainment of war powers in Vietnam; Richard Nixon's conduct surrounding his handling of Watergate; George W. Bush's expansion of authority for emergency contingency planning; and Barrack Obama's attempt to replace the legislative branch in writing immigration laws. A limit of two terms has provided confidence in the possibility of exercising restraint.

All of these former presidents were viewed by the electorate as some of the country's greatest leaders. If it is confirmed that even those who have been chosen to lead the free world require an additional safeguard against abuse of power, how could legislators be immune to such a similar necessity. Those incumbents serving multiple terms—even if their service remains dedicated to the people—are creating an opportunity for other members of less character to also stay in office. If instead they adhere to a universal standard of greater accountability and fairness, citizens will be supplied with a protection against the abuses of others absent of genuine virtue. However, this will require a decision to place "country before self" in service to the people.

Although term limits have remained the major focus of those seeking to take on career politicians, one has to wonder how effective it would be in bringing more equality to representation. Even if passed, it would do very little within the current political system to fundamentally change the ineffective and corrupt culture of D.C. and state legislatures that sabotage representation. Lobbyists remain almost entirely in control, while special interests continue to own former politicians and governmental staffers with promises of golden parachutes. Instead of focusing on term limits, which are questionable in outcomes and have proven unlikely to gain the necessary support from self-serving politicians, The People's Clearing House utilizes the structure in place to apply an additional measure on incumbents necessary for short and long-term resolutions.

Every other aspect of The People's Clearing House remains the same, with special treatment to incumbents only serving as another tool in regaining and securing authentic representation. State and federal political entities will remain on the two-year deduction schedule. U. S. house incumbents and their challengers face similar deductions from having an election every two years. State candidates will face a unique deduction schedule on inside and outside contributions as a result of variances in term lengths within their prospective states—for the same reason U.S. senators face an alternative deduction schedule to TPCH due to a six-year term. The difference is that incumbents seeking an additional term will face a higher level of base deduction(s) on direct contributions, supplying a crucial feature in discovering those worthy of leading.

The following are examples of how the higher level of base deductions could work. Each example depends on whether or not contributions can face a deduction scale based on the amount given. Ideally, direct contributions could be broken down into benchmarks, while contributions to outside political organizations (such as super PACs) would face a standard 30%. However, most likely, all contributions would have to face the same standard(s).

> a. In this scenario, unlike contributions to political organizations facing a standard 30% deduction, direct contributions to candidates are allowed to be broken down into benchmarks. Federal candidates are currently allowed to receive $2,700 in both the primary and general elections. Using this figure, this is how a higher base of deductions to TPCH could look.

Contribution Received	Standard Candidate Base Deductions	Incumbent Heightened Base Deductions
Below $1000	10%	25%
$1001-$1,900	20%	35%
$1,901-2,700	30%	45%

b. If a standard deduction must apply to all contributions received by candidates and political entities, incumbents would face something above this percentage on all direct contributions.

Standard Candidate Base Deductions	Incumbent Heightened Base Deductions
30%	45%

As with all other aspects of The People's Clearing House, autonomy remains, as higher baseline rates of deductions assigned to incumbents will be established at the federal and state level, with localities choosing to either follow those established by the state or set their own. On the federal level, since U.S. house members only serve two-year terms, they may face a higher baseline deduction after three terms. U.S. senators may face a higher baseline deduction after one term, since each term is six years in length. Variances in lengths of terms, as with the state level, could provide differences in whether the 2nd or 3rd term being sought will begin receiving the higher deduction levels.

Some states already have term limit legislation, which are either consecutive (must have time period between when someone is eligible to run again for office) or lifetime (never again can they hold office). However, the same pattern is routinely witnessed, with legislation never being written to count the years of service the current legislators have already served. Only at a future date do the rules they write ever actually apply. In fairness, some of this commonality revolves around previous court decisions. Initiatives and statutes have received mixed reviews from judges. The courts have said that because term limits constituted a qualification for office, any rules must be found in the state constitution. A statute was ruled as unconstitutional on this basis. In the specific case of Oregon, the state Supreme Court ruled that the legislation imposing state term limits violated the single-subject requirement for acceptable initiatives.

In looking at these outcomes, it's obvious there are a number of perplexities to consider when attempting to tailor and enact new campaign finance legislation. However, all of these attempts involved imposing concrete term limits, to that of process-oriented changes that TPCH would bring. It is not a firm qualification set in stone, but instead a unique collection of parameters within which incumbents accept in campaigning.

The most common argument for successfully killing the plea for term limits is that states will lose their influence in D.C. if they replace a long-term congressman. However, what proof from this system can actually be pointed to as helping the country move forward with progress, especially on chronic issues that have consistently plagued the nation? What has this permanent political arrangement really produced beyond decades of crippling partisan politics, strengthened from special interests effectively building lasting relationships with seasoned senators and representatives who serve as committee chairs? Entrenchment of career politicians, regardless of the state they represent, hurts the nation as a whole. Familiarity with the system only favors them.

The heightened baseline of deductions will only go further in strengthening the defense against distortion of equal representation. Special interests and Big Business will no longer possess the ease of investing in a particular politician for creating favorable access to a decision-maker for the long-term. The level playing field places incumbents and lobbyists on notice that previous loopholes are no longer available.

Incumbents already have name recognition and a voting record. Why would they need to have the advantage in fundraising? The People's Clearing House serves as a facilitator in making elections more about ideas again. Unlike the old practices of frivolously spending on unnecessary luxuries and unopposed elections with a confidence that the political system currently in place would always remain, incumbents will be forced to re-evaluate these decisions. Mitigating the power of fundraising outside of elections, when coupled with the higher baseline deductions on direct contributions within the election cycle, should humble any representative. A more level political arena will help answer whether an incumbent has only remained in office as a result of this unfair advantage, as opposed to their talent and the quality of their service to the people.

Grassroots campaigning could once again be the emphasis of elections. The direct investment to communities will provide a more engaged electorate to produce not only voters, but challengers with a newfound hope of winning within a fair arena. Every state encompasses numerous men and women of proven integrity and intelligence. It is arrogant for current politicians to assume that they are the only ones from their respective states who can serve effectively, especially considering the record of failure attached to most incumbents. When political machines and special interests no longer determine election outcomes, an able representation can be established. Incumbents will no longer be able to coast to re-election by providing a reliable sounding board of recycled political rhetoric narrowed for special interests.

The question should not be whether higher baseline deductions are applied to incumbents, but instead "how high these measures could eventually reach?" Would new percentage points be added to baselines with each additional term? Would a ceiling be established for deductions? All these questions of specifics would again be decided at the federal and state level; although, the key is that no current representative of government is grandfathered into the new system. The People's Clearing House would be retroactive, with current terms counted in determining appropriate deduction levels.

Major pushback can be expected from incumbents, with The People's Clearing House almost certainly providing the one thing self-serving career politicians from both sides of the political aisle would attempt to join in defeating. Why would a fair arena be something to oppose, especially considering that all deductions to TPCH are going back to the communities each state and federal legislator is currently representing? It seems a higher baseline of deductions would be welcomed in giving more back to the entire constituency for furthering efforts in community building. Under The People's Clearing House, it would quickly become evident which politicians place the people first in their service. Any member who rejects fair competition that raises the bar of accountability in representation, while strengthening communities, will be left to explain their opposition. Even those incumbents successfully re-elected by their constituency under these conditions will not serve within the same failed culture.

Opposition from incumbents only offers more reason for replacing them with new legislators who can begin their careers of service separate from the current facade of representation. Fights over making terms retroactive, as well as the task of defending against the foundation of reliable special interests already held by current members, would be removed. A political career founded on the values of accountability, transparency, and equality of elections would create an environment for consistently renewing government with the citizen statesman originally envisioned by the nation's Founding Fathers.

A personal moral code should be the guiding light for each politician. Unfortunately, too many of these individual codes are being manipulated through greed. In the absence of such a compass, the people will not be placed first in service. Only when a commitment is demonstrated to remain true to the ideal of public service will decisions be trusted and accepted—even ones the constituency disagrees with. In *Profiles of Courage*, John F. Kennedy shed light on this necessary ingredient to able service: "It is when the politician loves neither the public good nor himself, or when his love for himself is limited and is satisfied by the trappings of office, that the public interest is badly served. And it is when his own self-respect demands he follow the path of courage and conscience that all benefit." The People's Clearing House facilitates a service driven and sustained by commitments to acts of personal integrity.

SIGNIFICANT CHARACTERISTICS OF THE PEOPLE'S CLEARING HOUSE

The People's Clearing House must be independent and non-partisan. While possibly being a department of government on the state and federal level, the composition should be a mixture from the private and public sector. Remaining citizen-driven is vital. Members from the community, possibly from some aspect of civil service appointments through corresponding legislatures, could potentially be suitable. Fights concerning general implementation and potential legal obstacles could lead to a non-profit structure.

An able body of trusted men and women with the greatest possible autonomy from government would produce the most beneficial results in securing genuine representation. The people must lead for any hope of instituting meaningful change. Some will look at the system—especially the political elite, campaign hacks, and media pundits —and sneer at its simplicity. However, one must remember that the entire Constitution was written on less than a handful of pages. The politicians, mostly composed of lawyers, have convinced the people that everything must be written in lengthy and complex legal jargon. This practice of unnecessarily adding to legislation has demonstrated the greater likelihood for abuse, typically by those that have a hand in composing it. Loopholes integrated within legislation are what most incumbent's careers are built upon.

While it would be naïve to believe that those with greater knowledge and experience would not need to provide more details concerning the makeup and functionality of TPCH, the premise on which it is founded is sound. A willingness to put forth unique ideas serves to provide more encouragement for others within the private sector to demonstrate the same courage in offering solutions. Bold ideas built around democratic principles can overcome any legal or political challenge through the resolve of the people. The greatness of America resides in the ability to freely offer ideas, as well as scrutinize and challenge any representative of government, including the President.

A 1988 speech delivered by President Ronald Reagan to Moscow State University following the signing of a nuclear disarmament agreement between the U.S. and Russia (less than a year before) captures the necessity for this individual spirit. With the elegance that only "The Great Communicator" could articulate, Reagan powerfully stated:

> "Freedom is the right to question and change the established way of doing things. It is the continuing revolution of the marketplace. It is the understanding that allows us to recognize shortcomings and seek solutions. It is the right to put forth an idea, scoffed at by the experts, and watch it catch fire among the people. It is the right to dream—follow your dream or stick to your conscience, even if you're the only one in a sea of doubters. Freedom is the recognition that no single person, no single authority or government has a monopoly on the truth, but that every individual life is infinitely precious, that every one of us put on this world has been put there for a reason and has something to offer."

The People's Clearing House needs the expertise of others more familiar with the inner workings of the political culture through firsthand experiences. While The People's Clearing House lays a foundation designed to place all political entities and individuals in a fair arena, previous loopholes demand the attention of others who can be a step ahead of future attempts to circumvent greater accountability. The fact that the deductions within The People's Clearing House will directly benefit community building will not stop some from attempting to exploit the system.

In regards to the use of PACs, Scott Heins of *Gothamist* detailed the improprieties New York Mayor Bill de Blasio was being accused of in writing, "In the report, the Board of Election's enforcement counsel Risa S. Suggarman alleged that de Blasio's fundraising team deliberately sought donations larger than the permitted $10,300 limit, instructing donors to instead send checks to the Ulster County and Putman County Democratic committees, as well as the Senate Democratic Campaign Committee. Those committees then quickly transferred funds to the campaigns of Sen. Terry Gipson, Senate hopeful Justin Wagner, and Sen. Cecilia Thaczke, said Sugarman."

Although The People's Clearing House provides uniform treatment of all PACs, past scheming of contributions—from conference committees to party committees—only indicate a small degree of how politicians will always seek new methods to circumvent the system. When you add the questionable use of foundations, nonprofits, and organizations like ALEC to currently influence legislators, the necessity of having seasoned individuals to strengthen the mechanisms of The People's Clearing House becomes apparent. Having rules that adequately create a base of transparency and accountability will remove the false impression candidates project in pointing to their adherence to the rules in place—rules designed in most cases to only look good on paper.

Tom Coburn, the former U.S. senator from Oklahoma, has always been a strong advocate for more accountability from government. Beyond the frequent reports he released on governmental waste and inefficiency, Coburn informed readers in a 2015 article for the *Wall Street Journal* about "the law [he] helped pass in 2006, the Federal Funding Accountability and Transparency Act, aka 'Google Your Government,' [which] was an important marker in establishing transparency as a new norm in American politics." Coburn's sentiments for greater transparency and accountability are echoed by Libertarian candidate for president Gary Johnson and his running mate William Weld, who as governors especially demonstrated a commitment to fiscal responsibility. Each, as Republicans at the time, displayed a willingness and ability to work with all sides.

Howard Dean, the former DNC Chairman and governor of Vermont, appeared on MSNBC's "All in with Chris Hayes" in June 2016 and spoke about the need of having adequate voices on both sides of the political debate in producing legislation. Gary Hart, the former U.S. senator from Colorado in his 2015 book, *The Republic of Conscience*, emphasizes the need to be willing to place country above party. Few former politicians are blameless, but there are some who could aid The People's Clearing House.

Men and women of stature exist in every segment of the country. From their work within each community, regardless of whether it was done as a politician, there is an ample supply of individuals who have earned the trust and respect of their peers. These are the figures who must form the leadership of The People's Clearing House. These are the individuals who could proactively address instances of abuse in real time, possessing the foundation of trust and integrity to secure genuine representation.

Real-time treatment of campaign abuses would offer a significant variance from the current system, which often results in meaningless punishments that come well beyond elections. If the Supreme Court is going to trust citizens in wading through all the information offered by opposing candidates and their supporters in a campaign, a deterrent is vital. Under The People's Clearing House, punishments could revolve around additional percentage points added immediately to the deduction of a candidate's contributions moving forward—for a set period of time. The transparent design of TPCH will provide most candidates with a confidence in avoiding any unwarranted violations.

Only those attempting to circumvent the system will face consequences, with the citizen-driven and non-partisan TPCH supplying a necessary faith in the decisions reached. Current legislators, a stalemated Federal Elections Commission, and the useless, partisan Internal Revenue Service have proven they cannot be relied upon to perform this duty. Nor can the decisions these current groups make be taken as trustworthy.

United States citizens offer some of the greatest minds in the world. Men have been put on the moon, cures for diseases have been created, the NSA has unprecedented tracking capabilities, sophisticated weaponry can hit a target thousands of miles away, autonomous cars are a reality, and so much more in technological advancements—which prove virtually anything can be achieved. A system like The People's Clearing House can be created to run efficiently, if only the right amount of emphasis is applied.

The private sector must be challenged to create it. Systems of tracking for campaign finance are already utilized, and much of the work may be to simply modify these current structures when possible to form The People's Clearing House. IBM, Apple, and small tech companies and startups could compete or collaborate in establishing the technology. Some might focus on operating systems for localities and states, while others may work to create the programming for The National Clearing House. It is difficult to imagine any company not wanting the positive publicity attached to creating a system that helps bring direct aid to communities while raising desired accountability of elected officials.

An appreciative general public wouldn't forget this.

Recent issues in cybersecurity and the Obamacare rollout through a federally sponsored website provide just a few of the reasons government should not be trusted to supply the lead in writing the programming for the system. Another reason lies within the budgetary component. The People's Clearing House, beyond offering direct money to causes and initiatives chosen by campaign contributors, also utilizes a small percentage (1% or so) out of each donation to pay for the program. Unlike a governmental program, the system pays for itself. Once the preset budgeted price is met, all deductions go back toward the communities. This is also where competition within the private sector to create a system will provide an incentive to establish the lowest price. Government rarely, if ever, has such an incentive and will always run over an already bloated budget.

So many individuals and organizations have already demonstrated a commitment to achieving meaningful transparency. Nicholas Rubin, at seventeen years old, created his "Greenhouse" browser extension to spotlight money tied to members of Congress. In his *Wall Street Journal* piece, Tom Coburn recognized the power of "citizen activists who use technology to reshape the status quo" and specifically highlighted his role as honorary chairman of American Transparency founded by Adam Andrzejewski. The group utilizes "Open the Books" in an attempt to account for what government spends.

Groups focusing on technology only account for a small amount of the work being done to raise accountability. When combined with the insights of other committed groups and individuals like the Sunlight Foundation, Judicial Watch, Take Back Our Republic, The Center for Responsive Politics, Common Cause, and Larry Lessig (to name a few), it seems virtually impossible to fail in creating a people-driven deterrent. The People's Clearing House provides the rallying cry for uniting these various efforts. More importantly, the direct tie of money to communities should replace the apathy often encountered by these individuals and entities seeking change with a more engaged and invested populous. The vital elements of hope and excitement will no longer be absent from the process.

Beyond typical methods of sending in campaign contributions through the mail or online, The People's Clearing House could be offered through ATM/kiosk machines. Just like every other option in making contributions, these machines would provide selections of initiatives and causes that correspond with the appropriate national or state clearing house. In all instances, the feeling of being able to select which causes to direct individual deductions will provide instant gratification and empowerment. Verification codes and other security measures could be used to better secure the process.

Providing a foundation of strengthening and uniting communities across the country through more engagement is actually being proactive in addressing what young people have displayed that they already seek. While millennials are often legitimately associated with negative characteristics, the failure in leadership they are receiving may be the cause behind their stunted growth in attempting to contribute their full abilities.

Frustration within this subgroup of Americans is high. As Michael D. Hais and Morley Winograd wrote in their book from 2011, *Millennial Momentum*, "The way members of Congress now use social network technologies, the unwillingness of Congress to introduce new levels of transparency, and its members' continued dependence on large campaign contributions from those with the most at stake in congressional decision-making suggest that the institution is far from adopting the participatory and collaborative elements of open government that Millennials favor."

Catherine Rampell, opinion columnist at *The Washington Post*, in an article from 2015, discussed the unprecedented low turnout of young voters in the 2014 midterm elections. Among other things, a lack of faith in those currently governing them or valuing their input caused most to invest more time instead in directly helping their communities through local initiatives. Millennials clearly seek something to believe in and frustration with leadership is causing them to disengage from what seems pointless.

Millennials and other young people, who are often called the "the future," simply need meaningful direction. In *Millennial Momentum*, Hais and Winograd wrote, "In February 2010, only 22 percent of the public chose 'honest' as a word to describe Congress. Yet 81 percent of those responding to the same CNN/Opinion Research Corp. survey expressed the Millennial-like optimistic belief that 'Our system of government is broken but can be fixed.' Creating a new connection between citizens and their representatives by using the Millennial's favorite technologies to build a more transparent, open, and participatory legislative process is the essential first step in reversing the decline in the credibility in Congress." TPCH lays the foundation of accountability, transparency, and unity for future generations to further build upon.

THE PEOPLE'S CLEARING HOUSE CANDIDATE

As part of his introduction of Donald Trump at an April 2016 campaign rally, legendary Indiana basketball coach Bobby Knight stated, "I'm not here to represent the Republican Party. Quite frankly, I could give a d**n about the Republicans. And on the other hand I don't give a d**n about the Democrats, either." Though possibly choosing to phrase it differently, Americans by and large have proven they share his sentiments.

For far too long the American people have longed to change the status quo in D.C. and state legislatures across the country. Time and time again individual politicians or major parties have promised to do things differently, only to prove otherwise upon being elected. Attempts at past reform efforts in campaign finance have done little to change this pattern. Current efforts are all centered on success in the long term, relying on future loyalties from politicians that are far from certain. A plan that takes time for success also depends on an enduring focus from the general public, which daily evidence alone proves improbable. This is especially true if reform efforts are partisan in nature.

The People's Clearing House is not about winning moral victories or simply making life more difficult for incumbents in winning re-election. It is designed to make great strides in reasserting more equality in representation with each new election cycle. Although ideally it would be a newfound standard of transparency and accountability all incumbents and challengers adhere to, TPCH can infiltrate both major parties if need be.

Assuming becoming a People's Clearing House candidate is optional, if a Republican incumbent decided not to become one, another Republican challenger could offer a contrast in accepting the standard. Just like a Democratic incumbent could face a TPCH challenger in the party primary. As long as one candidate within each race accepts the universal/non-partisan standard of The People's Clearing House, voters can always choose a candidate committed to actual representation. If the two major parties fail to supply the choice of The People's Clearing House candidate, an opportunity will be created for independents, libertarians, and other parties that display the willingness.

It's not about Republicans. It's not about Democrats. It's about choosing to commit one's self to serving the people in making government more efficient, transparent, and equal—with the ultimate aim of providing more opportunity for all, regardless of differences in policies. All parties benefit from less waste, inefficiency, and fraud in government. All parties benefit from a culture that produces a more equal arena for debate and dialogue. All parties benefit from ending a status quo in governance that rewarded a few and led many to easily misinterpret personal gain for public service.

In deciding to become The People's Clearing House candidate, an individual says: I reject the advancement of the current charade of representation currently found in our elected bodies of men and women nationwide. I will not join the theatrical performances presently taking place in governing chambers nationwide, in which the leads of the play are given to lobbyists, mid-level roles are given to those masquerading as representatives, and the American people are delegated to nothing more than extras.

As The People's Clearing House candidate, I am dedicating myself to a higher standard of service that will allow the people to judge me more on my merits as a representative, to that of a fundraiser. Everything about my interactions within the political process will be about the people. This commitment will remain, regardless of whether it is as an actual representative—or only during a short-lived campaign for office.

Identifying as The People's Clearing House candidate is an acknowledgement of the necessity to consistently demonstrate a trusted level of integrity in service. This label is not to be confused with the practice of "fusion," where a candidate receives the nomination of several parties on a ballot. Fusion is currently only allowed by law in eight states, with the Working Families Party being an example of one party utilizing this power in states like New York to rally support for a particular major party candidate. The People's Clearing House is not a party, but instead a distinction that verifies a commitment to higher standards of accountability and transparency in representation.

> The People's Clearing House candidate's pledge:
>
> *a. Full disclosure/tracking of campaign contributions for established deductions to directly fund the causes and initiatives selected by constituents for community building*
> *b. Continued disclosure/tracking of remaining campaign funds for greater accountability*
> *c. Acceptance of higher deductions of campaign contributions according to time in which they are received; the state or federal deduction schedule will set the appropriate rate of deduction on contributions received inside and outside of the official election cycle.*

d. Acceptance of an increased base of deductions on direct contributions when seeking the designated term for the heightened rates determined at the state or federal level.

The Clearing House provides a representative the ability to lead from a place of strength, a characteristic which is lacking today and results in discontent and suspicion of motives. With this foundation of demonstrated integrity that will only become more strengthened through continued adherence, a representative of the people will maintain the trust of the constituency in tackling difficult and controversial issues.

If not implemented for all candidates and instead is only offered as an option, The People's Clearing House candidate will present quite the contrast to other candidates. The Clearing House candidates reject business as usual in campaign contributions that only serve to feed the game of politics—instead of strengthening communities. They reject becoming a representative of government and spending the majority of their time attempting to figure out how to best raise more money for re-election. They value staying invested with their communities, remembering their campaign promises, and placing their focus/energy on doing their best in performing actual duties of their office.

This renewed emphasis on actually serving as a representative before that of a fundraiser places The People's Clearing House candidate above the rest from the beginning. Other than highlighting how the current schedule of endless fundraising causes new legislators to follow the lead of seasoned members in building an early reliance on staff in an article for *The Huffington Post*, Ryan Grim and Sabrina Siddiqui also wrote, "Working a schedule like that as a freshman teaches a member of Congress about the institution's priorities. 'It really does affect how members of Congress behave if the most important thing they think about is fundraising,' Rep. Brad Miller (D-NC), said. 'You end up being nice to people that probably somebody needs to be questioning skeptically. It's a fairly disturbing suggested schedule. You won't ask tough questions in hearings that might displease potential contributors, won't support amendments that might anger them, will tend to vote the way contributors want you to vote.'"

The People's Clearing House candidate's adherence to the system helps them never forget the people who saw a leader in them as they attempt to make the right choices with their entire constituency in mind, instead of just a select few. These candidates can debunk the long-standing belief that all those who enter politics become corrupt over time. TPCH candidate answers the call of the American people who are yearning for such a leader to emerge from the current atmosphere of corruption; offering actual hope of genuine representation. Any incumbents who reject The People's Clearing House will be forced to explain to the people the reasons behind their opposition.

CONCLUSION

People around the world have grown weary of elitism and cronyism, especially in terms of global organizations, as best demonstrated in Britain's decision to leave the European Union. Regardless of the additional security the governing body was seen as providing with NATO, the deceit of the EU became clear as a set of faceless, unelected bureaucrats and technocrats in Brussels shredded the national sovereignty of member countries by imposing more regulations and migration demands.

Frederick Forsyth, highly acclaimed English author and former spy, traced the origins of the EU in an article for the *Sunday Express*. Forsyth placed the most emphasis on Jean Monnet, who he identified as "the French intellectual now seen as the founding father." He explained the problem Monnet faced in fulfilling his vision of selling the idea of an EU and how deception provided a solution. He wrote, "How could the various peoples ever be persuaded to hand over their countries from democracy to oligarchy, the government of the elite? Let me quote from what [Monnet] wrote: 'Europe's nations should be guided towards the Super-state without their people understanding what is happening. This can be accomplished by successive steps, each disguised as having an economic purpose, but which will eventually and irreversibly lead to federation.'"

Appearing on "Lou Dobbs Tonight" the day the British voted to leave the EU, Steve Hilton, former advisor to Prime Minister Cameron said, "I think the thing for our American viewers to understand is really what this whole um [sic] referendum is about and it's not just about individual issues uh [sic] like immigration or the economy. It's a fundamental question about how the country is governed and who makes the decisions. When I worked in government uh [sic] with Prime Minister Cameron in Downing Street I was shocked to discover that over half of all the legislation and regulation that that [sic] we had to apply actually originated in the EU. Now I live now [sic] in California. I run a business out there, a tech business, and so I understand how frustrated and angry Americans are with the federal government in Washington and in a way the EU is like a federal government for Europe, but the difference is at least in Washington the President is elected! Congress is elected! The people churning out all the regulation and legislation in the EU are not elected by anybody. And none of the member state governments can actually stop this stuff and so it's fundamentally undemocratic."

Other countries share the sentiments of those in Britain who joined together to leave the power vacuum of the EU. "The Pew Research Center survey [found] that in six of ten countries more people want devolution of the EU power than support the status quo or favor giving more power to the Brussels-based institution." As Bruce Stokes, director of global economic attitudes at Pew Research Center, went on to summarize, "Roughly two-thirds of Greeks (68%) and British (65%) want some EU power returned to Athens and London." Other countries demonstrated "pluralities" of similar support.

Although organizations such as the EU only add an additional layer of bureaucracy to highlight the lack of control citizens actually have in holding their leaders accountable, Americans already experience this feeling at home. Even if President Obama is unsuccessful in entering America into governing blocs of trade that essentially set 2/3 of global GDP, most Americans already detest governmental overreach. The U.S. has over 320 million people. Even Vermont, the smallest state, has a population of around 626,000—more than sufficient to provide a host of able state and federal legislators capable of rejecting the current corruption and cronyism tied to the status quo.

In a speech from his last year in office, President Reagan offered an amusing depiction of governmental frustration. As only he could, he said, "There's an old story about a town—it could be anywhere—with a bureaucrat who is known to be a good-for-nothing, but he somehow had always hung on to power. So one day, in a town meeting, an old woman got up and said to him: 'There is a folk legend here where I come from that when a baby is born, an angel comes down from heaven and kisses it on one part of its body. If the angel kisses him on his hand, he becomes a handyman. If he kisses him on his forehead, he becomes bright and clever. And I've been trying to figure out where the angel kissed you so that you should sit there for so long and do nothing."

Although President Reagan's analogy is amusing, there is nothing laughable about the degree to which representatives of government have abused their authority. In the New Testament of the Bible, the apostles tell the story of how Jesus, the son of God, reacted to those men who chose to desecrate the sanctity of his Father's temple. As written in John 2: 15-16, "And He made a scourge of cords, and drove them all out of the temple, with the sheep and the oxen; and He poured out the coins of the money changers and overturned their tables; and to those who were selling the doves He said, 'Take these things away; stop making My Father's house a place of business.'" With a controlled anger, Jesus, who would later peacefully allow those to take him to the cross to die for man's salvation, remained without sin in his legitimate endeavor to set things right.

In the same spirit, American legislators have made a complete mockery out of the governing chambers nationwide and have more than earned being figuratively and civilly turned upside down by the people. Members from both major parties on the state and federal level have demonstrated the ability to routinely discover faults in others, while rarely taking personal inventory. While many Republican and Democratic lawmakers denounce the words or practices of their party nominees for president in 2016, few relinquish their self-imposed moral stature to explain how they have consistently overseen the waste, corruption, and abuse in government that stifles opportunities for all; how they have almost silently continued to accept practices and procedures in governing that virtually guarantee nothing will change as they themselves "live high off the hog."

The parallels between the methods men used to defile the temple and the manner in which "representatives of the people" corrupt the houses of government are striking. Those in the temple turned the buying period for sacrifices into a marketplace for profit. Those in the highest level of leadership—the priests in this instance—used their influence to corrupt the system for the gain of themselves and those that worked with them. Today, lawmakers often place themselves above the rules and market off influence for personal gain. They routinely trade off their duty of equal representation for all to the highest bidders, who ultimately receive great returns on their investment. The political arena they have created within the walls of government is driven by the same variable found in the temple that day: greed dictates almost everything in each case.

In a "60 minutes" interview with Norah O'Donnell from April 2016, Rep. David Jolly (R-FL) explained how he has refused to take part in what he described as "a cult-like boiler room on Capitol Hill." He has not resigned himself to the common procedure of personally involving himself in reaching a certain party-recommended quote of money each day from campaign contributions for being re-elected. Rep. Jolly places the duties he was elected to perform above this aim of being a party-preferred money collector.

During an interview from MSNBC's "Morning Joe" on the Monday morning following his appearance on "60 Minutes," Rep. Jolly pointed to the thirty hours some members of the U.S. Congress were spending each week on the phones for fundraising. The frustrated congressman followed his words by telling hosts Mika Brzezinski and Joe Scarborough, "You're paying them $174,000 a year and they're spending half their time shirking, shaking down the American people for money instead of doing their job."

Although Jolly has attempted to change the culture with his "Stop Act" bill, which would remove the politician from the process of directly soliciting campaign contributions, it was dead on arrival. While it could help in keeping representatives of government more dedicated to their actual jobs, enforcement would be difficult and ripe for loopholes. The deduction schedule of The People's Clearing House, which is dictated by the time in which donations are received, provides a trusted solution.

Representation built on the current political system will always produce the failed leadership of today, characteristic of lackadaisical pieces of legislation and debate and dialogue solely designed to achieve the main endeavor of being re-elected. Partisanship will continue to grow, influence will come with a price tag, and an analysis with paralysis will remain—causing the vast majority of Americans to be unrepresented and left behind. The American people must unite and tell current and future representatives of government that moving forward they will basically be judged under the standard articulated by Alec Baldwin's character, Blake, in the movie "Glengarry, Glen Ross." He was sent by the company to inform the sales team that they should already consider themselves fired, with only an ability to prove a value to the company as a way to earn back their jobs. Although some may view his profanity-driven speech in a different way, most everyone would pay to see this character give a similar speech to useless legislators.

Those individuals who survive the baptism by fire from The People's Clearing House will be more likely to adequately represent the American people in changing the inept and unaccountable culture that is characteristic of government. Recent public scandals within the IRS and the VA have only served to highlight a small degree of the counterproductive culture that is widely accepted in state and federal agencies.

Mike Huckabee, the former Gov. of Arkansas and 2016 presidential candidate, may have summarized the current situation best in May

2016. In comparing the $182 million spent by Hillary Clinton to employ 732 individuals with that of Donald Trump who had only spent $57 million on 70 employees, Huckabee said, "I think a lot of people would like to see the American government look a lot more like Donald Trump's campaign than Hillary Clinton's campaign: bloated, overblown, and still losing."

Not only do the American people need a new type of representative to take this message of newfound accountability and transparency to agencies, but they also need men and women who are capable of implementing the change effectively. Half-hearted efforts from the past reveal a massive web of bureaucracy. Any true change will require trusted men and women to bring civil service reform to address those strategically embedding themselves in government. True representation will produce a leadership unwilling to simply accept moving troubling employees around within the bureaucratic system, or allow a nice early retirement as a form of punishment. TPCH representatives can be trusted to clean up the system and set an enduring tone of hope for the future.

Genuine representatives committed to the people will definitely not follow the recent example of the military in attempting to bring accountability. The Army National Guard created a poorly managed recruiting program to meet the essential need of replenishing the military and barely attached any oversight. The focus was clearly on the numbers alone and few demonstrated a concern about the possible abuse of the program, which not surprisingly came out of soldiers pressured into being part-time recruiters.

According to "60 Minutes" correspondent David Martin, at one time close to $28 million was spent by the Army alone just in discovering that around $10 million was most likely inappropriately given to soldier recruits. While some investigations are ongoing, more than 1000 soldiers the Army attempted to "scapegoat" for its complicity in design and mismanagement did not result in convictions.

As is so often the case, first the government creates the problem; then, the government attempts to correct the problem, but ultimately only creates more problems. Yet none of the past failures from incompetence keep bureaucrats from believing they are in the best position to make future decisions or call out others for similar wrongdoing. As the army's lead attorney, Lt. General Flora Darpino, explained to David Martin, "When it comes to crime it isn't really about the cost of what it takes to investigate. It's making sure that people are held accountable for criminal misconduct." Most viewers probably ask where is the mirror for governmental officials who never seem to see their own transgressions. Speaking of accountability as you waste taxpayer money on failed investigations, created out of earlier mistakes, offers an accurate portrayal of government.

During a town hall from February 2016 in South Carolina, Republican presidential candidate John Kasich told CNN's Anderson Cooper, "You know the strength of America is not some guy or woman coming in on a white charger here to solve all of our problems. It's…Anderson, America, the glue of America is right here in this room. It's in our communities, in our families. We need to slow down and then we've got to carry out our God-given destinies, potentials and gifts." After Kasich listed a few of the programs he could envision himself sending to the states as president, he told the crowd, "It's up to us. It's up to us to rebuild this country and renew our spirit."

Critics of the current political system are undermined by those pointing out that no alternative is actually given to change things. The People's Clearing House doesn't just explain the problems of government, offer the characteristics future representatives should possess, or create yet another system requiring the meaningless chase of money with little public interest; instead, it provides a measuring stick for determining who can be trusted to remain dedicated to their communities. It utilizes the founding principles of democracy to create a true sense of hope for actual success in implementing measured accountability, as well as provides a uniting cause for strengthening communities to establish the necessary incentive for more to become invested in the political process. More significantly, The People's Clearing House effectively addresses the previous obstacles to reform, especially in creating a potent deterrent to any opposition or attempt to circumvent the process, with the direct link of taking away from the people. Beyond any possible monetary penalties, this link alone makes public scrutiny powerful.

In a Republican presidential debate from November 2015, Carly Fiorina addressed government and regulations by explaining to potential voters, "This government has been growing bigger and bigger, more corrupt, less effective, crushing the engine of economic growth for a very long time. This isn't about just replacing a Democrat with a Republican now. It's about actually challenging the status quo of big government."

Fiorina took some of her time to list reasons a status quo built on faulty representation must be overcome. "We need to actually reform the tax code. Go to a three-page tax code. Yes, there are plans that would reform our tax code to three pages. In addition to rolling back what President Obama has done, we need to do a top-to-bottom re-view of every single regulation on the books. That hasn't been done in 50 years. We need to pass the REINS Act so Congress is in charge of regulation, not nameless, faceless bureaucrats accountable to no one. We've become a nation of rules, not a nation of laws."

U.S. House Republicans seemed to have held the spirit of Fiorina's message when composing its recent tax proposal from June 2016. It would reduce the tax-filing burden most Americans face when attempting to work through the current tax code; it would eliminate pages of regulation that many IRS workers don't even understand. Beyond helping those unable to afford outside help in filing their taxes become less disadvantaged by the system, the plan also puts the IRS in its place through reform.

Brufke Juliegrace of the *Daily Caller* informed readers, "Republican lawmakers promised, if the proposal is implemented, the tax code would be simplified to the point where the majority of Americans could do their taxes on a form as simple as a postcard."

As part of her description of the tax proposal, Ali Meyers wrote, "The plan would repeal the death tax, eliminate the alternative mini-mum tax, cut taxes on small businesses to 25 percent, and cut taxes on savings and investment, just to name a few of the reforms includ-ed in the proposal." The well-respected journalist from the *Washington Free Beacon* also cited the statements of Ways and Means Chairman Kevin Brady at the press conference introducing the tax proposal. "For the first time we'll end penalties in the current tax code that too often force American companies to move their jobs, technologies, and headquarters overseas," Brady said. "No longer will we be the only major country that still taxes its own exports. No longer will American products lose out to foreign competitors, simply because they're proudly stamped 'Made in America.'"

While the possible end results of a smaller tax code seem promis-ing, the current representation built from the money-driven political system requires Ronald Reagan's caution of "trust, but verify." Be-yond the expected differences that will occur between lawmakers on the specific rates that should be imposed, questions must always be asked concerning what actually drives lawmakers. Much of what they do is only designed to create a stalemate that allows each side to argue favorable talking points for re-election. Often, as possibly with this tax proposal, poison pills like the "repeal of the death tax" are at-tached to the entire bill by Republicans, knowing the Democrats will never support its actual passage. The "open process" routinely uti-lized by congressional leadership allows amendments from the other side of the aisle to be added, virtually guaranteeing nothing gets passed. Standalone bills to establish core legislation to build upon through a piecemeal approach on differences is rarely chosen. Common sense ideas are lost in the shuffle, but this procedure allows congressmen to protect their voting records. An avoidance of votes on key issues can always be blamed on the other side. Each side essentially contributes to a murkiness of the process that results in re-election.

Of course, there is maneuvering for passage of bills; and, of course, the legislative chambers of American politics are characterized with the civil dialogue and debate that separates it from the rest of the world. No one should undervalue these enduring truths. However, an absence of trust within those establishing the procedures surrounding the debate must be inserted. Only then can there be a faith in what priorities are setting the tone of the dialogue used to decide what is best for constituents, which, in many cases, will include compromise. By offering ample scrutiny of those seeking to lead the people, The People's Clearing House creates a representation to actually believe in moving forward.

Billions of dollars are spent on the game of politics, with the 2016 cycle projected to pass the "estimated 5.8 billion spent on 2012 elections." Excess campaign money can currently be reinserted in the electoral process, cover certain office holder expenses, be used on gifts to others, returned to donors, or spent on charities. The People's Clearing House takes some discretionary power out of the politician's hands and places it in those of the constituents to decide how to use the deduction taken from the original donation.

The billions of dollars currently spent on elections may only represent a fraction of what can be expected once more people become invested in the process through the inclusion of The People's Clearing House. This is especially true when considering that the system design creates an opportunity for rewarding participation from previous elections. For example, if more people than before turn out for the midterm elections, a decision on the state or federal level could be to start with a slightly higher percentage of baseline deductions within TPCH in the following presidential election cycle. Regardless of the amount of money that is returned to the local, state, and national communities, The People's Clearing House would create a symbol of hope. Election days could raise unity over division, renew faith instead of adding more skepticism, and create optimism instead of fear for moving forward. There will certainly be differences in which causes and initiatives are selected for meeting the unique demands of each community. However, these inclusive seeds of progress, planted by The People's Clearing House, are meant to strengthen the entire community, regardless of race, creed, religion, ethnicity, gender, sexual orientation, or socioeconomic status. The People's Clearing House presents an opportunity for constituents to demonstrate greater empowerment in offering insight to their leaders through the causes and initiatives receiving the most selections, as well as the impact these programs prove to have on the community. Leaders on the state level could also provide an option among choices for purposely offering a stimulus to the most struggling region(s) within the state.

One example would be the Alabama House of Representatives or Senate—which would be the governing body responsible for creating the choices of causes and initiatives for campaign contributors to state candidates—choosing to provide an option related to aiding the Black Belt Region. This area, located in the southern part of the state and predominantly populated by African Americans, could use additional attention. Access to quality education and economic hardships continue to plague the area, with a recent decision of the state to limit operating hours of DMVs only serving to further limit the residents' voice in the political process by making voter registration more difficult.

If a patient comes into the emergency room with a number of cuts and scratches covering their entire body and one major wound around their heart, common sense would tell anyone which area must receive the most immediate attention. While it may be easy to become distracted by the appearance and severity of other wounds, the heart must be addressed first or everything else will suffer. Any doctor, who chooses to simply add additional patches to this crucial area, while giving more attention to the rest of the body, will eventually produce unnecessary hardship and the eventual demise of the patient. If not for the moral obligation alone, consistently failing to proactively address the underlying root causes of impoverished areas will cost a state more in the long run. While money can initially be saved by ignoring this commitment, future costs associated with an increase in general governmental aid programs, crime, and medical care will serve to reveal the foolishness of failing to instill earlier hope and opportunity. By beginning with a prioritization of investment into these communities through education, economic, and social initiatives, a state will emerge with true promise for the future. The People's Clearing House allows citizens to teach this unwavering truth to their leaders.

Some may desperately argue that The People's Clearing House

merely opens the door for more regulation and deductions on other things, as fear mongering is the preferred practice of most legislators when the status quo is threatened. However, representation has a unique distinction in that it serves as the lifeblood of the republic, setting the entire agenda and direction of the country through laws and priority decisions.

Nothing in a democratic government, based from a republic, comes close to holding the significance of representation. As Merle Miller wrote of his interview with former President Harry S. Truman, "As nearly as he could remember, Harry's last act in the White House was returning a pencil or maybe it was a pen to the desk of the man he had borrowed it from. 'Everything,' he said, 'all of it belongs to the people. I was just privileged to use it for a while.'" Any concern presented by those politicians for possible overreach can be traced to the current lack of faith in government many of them personally helped create through practices The People's Clearing House helps eliminate.

Those opposed may reason that this would be nothing more than just another tax on a citizenry already possessing the frustration of the Founders regarding its overuse. However, even if it was thought of in these terms, it is already a tax in a sense. Money from campaign contributions and lobbying activities ultimately feeds the coffers of the media to run political ads and allows politicians to disseminate further to the political arena or add additional luxuries to themselves and others. The People's Clearing House takes this "tax" and reinvests it directly back into the community, according to the people's voice.

A misunderstanding of the populism behind The People's Clearing House may also be used as a tool of opposition. However, a college provides a setting to demonstrate the role of TPCH. Students choose their instructors through the classes they select each semester. However, regardless of the professors chosen, there should be a confidence in the system that each teacher will follow a set of guidelines in creating an environment of equal opportunity. While the students may not know which methods are best to achieve this endeavor, they do expect each of their professors to implement the best policies when considering everyone, as opposed to being dictated by a select group of students. Just as the dean functions as an advocate for the students in holding each instructor accountable, TPCH provides a reliable voice for the people in holding representatives accountable.

Others looking to discredit The People's Clearing House may present the notion that while the system is good, in that it strengthens communities, it will actually do nothing to change the reliance of candidates on big donors; if anything, it might even make these contributors more significant. However, this reasoning would be too simplistic as it presumes all other variables remain the same. This type of conclusion assumes that the level of participation and interest in politics would not change.

Such an analysis disregards the higher participation that will result from a newfound hope of equality in representation and excitement of having a direct voice in how to strengthen local, state, and federal communities with contributions. Greater participation led by the youth, first-time voters, and independents will offset this influence by creating a more engaged body of citizens invested in raising accountability. Voices within the poor and middle class will rise as they no longer feel forgotten.

As best witnessed with discussions concerning a possible change in the tax code, which would result in the rich paying more, some may point to the risk of more corporate inversion in reaction to having a more equal political arena. However, it is one thing for an environment of ill-conceived policies and regulations to be used by American businesses as justification for moving their companies overseas. It's an entirely different scenario to leave because money no longer dictates representation to the same extent.

Capitalism is built upon competition, but a rejection of more equality in the voices setting the rules of the game will not settle well with Americans whose country is the world's largest consumer. The fear of lost revenue, as a result of bad publicity attached to opposing a more level arena, will provide a firm restraint against businesses doing so. The idea that America would possibly crumble as a result of a revolt by the rich to leave in large droves and take their companies with them is absurd. America is built upon small businesses, which provide the majority of employment opportunities. A fairer arena through more equal representation will allow more startups, current small businesses, and entrepreneurs to flourish and innovate. In the age of technological advancement, great ideas do not always require as much investment up front, allowing new companies and individuals to replace lost capital if the environment of competition is balanced and not smothered with regulations and rules. Companies born from a more equal arena, as a result of more genuine representation, would be preferred and respected.

In his first inaugural address, President Ronald Reagan said, "We hear much of special interest groups. Our concern must be for a special interest group that has been too long neglected. It knows no sectional boundaries or ethnic and racial divisions, and it crosses political party lines. It is made up of men and women who raise our food, patrol our streets, man our mines and our factories, teach our children, keep our homes, and heal us when we are sick- professionals, industrialists, shopkeepers, clerks, cabbies, and truck drivers. They are, in short, 'We the people,' this breed called Americans."

Unfortunately, the current political system built upon campaign contributions and extreme party loyalties will continue to leave the interests of most Americans behind. One of the most recent examples is the reaction of relief and celebration from many Democrats to FBI Director James Comey's recommendation not to indict their party nominee for her lies and casual handling of classified information. Many of these same members routinely champion the causes of criminal justice reform and legitimately rail against the inequality of access and representation within the judicial system. Yet, at a time of deep frustrations with inequality, party ambitions dominate their responses.

In an article for the *Washington Times* following the press conference in which this recommendation was made, Stephen Dinan wrote, "Hillary Clinton wasn't 'sophisticated enough' to know she was risking national security when she sent and received classified information, so it was impossible to make a criminal case against her, FBI Director James B. Comey told Congress on Thursday." For many Democrats, especially those who have said that Hillary Clinton is "the most qualified candidate to ever run for President," marginalizing the severity of her actions has been the decision.

Regardless of the current level of distrust in government and further tarnishing of any faith in the judicial system, presenting a false narrative of a political witch-hunt was acceptable. For a legislator to talk against injustice in the system—for some, practically build a career off it—while demonstrating that certain individuals are, in fact, above the law, is mind-boggling. The consequences could be far reaching, as it is not unreasonable to assume the "Hillary Defense" couldn't be used in other scenarios regardless of whether intent is required or not. As with laws concerning healthcare and immigration, the government has now added "general intent" as something it has discretion in following or rewriting to fit its needs. This pattern breeds even more chaos to already troubling times.

Why couldn't any individual who drinks two beers that place him in a buzzed state while driving use the same argument? Although arrested, his lawyer explains to the local prosecutor that it was the lack of eating which led his client to misjudge his level of sobriety. Since he didn't intend to purposely do anything wrong, his lawyer asks the prosecutor not to move forward with charges. Although the charge of driving under the influence is similar to Clinton's potential charges, in that it does not require intent, it seems doubtful he will obtain the same favorable outcome. Of course, none of this means anything to many Democrats, who remain blinded by obtaining short-term political glory.

At a U.S. house congressional hearing with FBI Director Comey shortly following his announcement recommending no indictment for the former secretary, Rep. Will Hurd said, "I'm offended by my friends on the other side of the political aisle saying this is political theatre. This is not political theatre. For me this is serious. I spent 9½ years as an undercover officer in the C.I.A. I was the guy in the back alleys collecting intelligence; passing it to lawmakers. I've seen my friends killed. I've seen assets put themselves in harm's way. And this is about ca [sic] protecting information; the most sensitive information the American government has. I wish my colleagues would take this a little bit more seriously."

You can be sure it helped the freshman congressman and first African American elected to Congress from Texas actually come from the trenches to that of those firmly insulated inside the bubble and alternative reality of Capitol Hill.

The people are not receiving proper representation because of the excessive influence of party loyalty, personal ambition, and worship of money and power—which manipulates genuine dedication to performing duty. Opportunity continues to be limited as a result, with those being denied coming from all races and ethnicities. Although the reaction to FBI. Director Comey's decision not to recommend an indictment for Clinton provides an example of how party ambition incorrectly dictated the decisions of Democrats, Republicans also routinely pick their party over the people. Congressional hearings, confirmation hearings, and access of outside influences are commonly driven by what's best for the party, while most other decisions are driven by select donors. One view of a general congressional hearing would easily reveal this lasting truth. Each party routinely characterizes any investigation against a member of their party as partisan in nature. The effort the people deserve for a search for the truth is casually disregarded. Few decisions are principled, though always presented as such.

In his book *Hamilton*, award-winning author Ron Chernow wrote, "Today we cherish the two-party system as a cornerstone of American democracy. The founders, however, viewed parties, or 'factions' as they termed them, as monarchical vestiges that had no legitimate place in a true republic. Hamilton dreaded parties as 'the most fatal disease' of popular governments and hoped America could dispense with such groups. James Kent later wrote, 'Hamilton said in The Federalist, in his speeches, and a hundred times to me that factions would ruin us and our government had no sufficient energy and balance to resist the propensity to them and to control their tyranny and their profligacy." One of the legal greats, Kent served as the first professor of law at Colombia University.

Failures in leadership will continue to keep America from fulfilling its full potential if the political system remains the same. While all organizations will be flawed to some degree (in that they are run by humans), achieving the closest thing to genuine representation will remain an unachievable dream within the current parameters. Only under a system of actual accountability, transparency, and heightened public engagement will the two fronts of party loyalty and consistent fundraising—which are currently manipulating representation—be adequately confronted. The People's Clearing House breaks the stranglehold and offers a path for creating a true "party of accountability" within each major party—or opens the door for independents and third-party candidates. With a 2013 poll discovering a record 42% of the electorate now identifying as independents, there is definitely an opportunity for a major party exodus.

Following the senseless tragedy that wounded twelve people and claimed the lives of five law enforcement officers at what began as a mostly peaceful protest, Dallas Police Chief David Brown said, "This must stop: this divisiveness between our police and our citizens," before detailing the displayed courage and his hopes for future understanding. "Let me just say just uh [sic] some closing comments about Dallas police officers and DART (Dallas Area Rapid Transit); some of the bravest men and women you'd ever wanta [sic] be associated with. You see video footage after video footage of them running toward gun fire from an elevated position with no chance to protect themselves. And to put themselves in harm's way to make sure citizens can get to a place of security. So please join me in applauding these brave men and women who do this job under great scrutiny; under great vulnerability; who literally risk their lives to protect our democracy. We don't feel much support most days. Let's not make today most days. Please. We need your support to be able to protect you from men like these who carried out this tragic, tragic, event."

It's amazing how easy it can be to identify genuine leadership, something that has almost been entirely absent from D.C. for a long time. Although his statement to the press did not require him to offer anything that controversial, there was a confidence he wouldn't shy away from where the truth directed him. His heartfelt message resonated against the backdrop of recycled political rhetoric and reminded many of how it felt to watch a public servant speak and actually believe their actions were guided by the right motives. It is an amazing feat when considering his message was to a general public numbed from politicians offering rigid ideological talking points from both ends of the political spectrum.

Authenticity has truly become a rarity these days.

Not surprisingly, Chief David Brown's words to Jake Tapper of CNN a few days following the Dallas attacks only seemed to have confirmed the genuine nature many had already concluded led his service. "'I'm a servant at my core. I enjoy serving people,' he said. 'I'm a person of faith… I'm a Christian… Service is part of my direction and loving people, despite themselves, is something I aspire to… I'm flawed, though, like many of us.'"

Of course, the words of an individual not dictated by teams of pollsters, tax-funded studies on when to be ambiguous, and a staff of public relations experts is telling, but can only offer a degree of clarity in assessing the presence of moral integrity. It is the fruit someone bears that provides confirmation. In regards to the police, though the mainstream media and politicians routinely place their focus on the negative and controversial stories concerning law enforcement that fit the narrative for advancing their agenda, the unwavering courage of the officers during tragic events like San Bernardino, Orlando, Dallas, and Baton Rogue offers a reflection of the true leadership at the top.

It shouldn't take tragic events such as these to recognize and appreciate the heroic characteristic of most first responders; just as it shouldn't take events of great human loss to bring the country toward unity. Once the people set a newfound standard of accountability for those seeking to become future representatives of government, they will begin receiving the type of leadership they deserve. Individuals will then possess a greater chance of allowing commitment to community to guide their words and actions. Coming together now to raise the bar of accountability in our leaders not only enriches current circumstances, but it is also proactive in establishing an environment conducive to creating future leaders who will value true service and building community. These individuals will most likely never forget where they came from or who they are entrusted to serve. Being principled, but pragmatic, is a likely outcome, as these future leaders will not allow party ambitions to blind them of their larger duty to remain loyal to constituents. Directly or indirectly benefiting from programs of The People's Clearing House will help keep these leaders dedicated to creating more opportunities for upward mobility, holding lasting memories of communities with hope.

In an interview with Kevin Corke of Fox News from January 2016, Rep. Tulsi Gabbard (D-HA) stated, "Aloha is something that um [sic] is universal in that we need more of especially in Washington. If people would lead with Aloha, lead with a heart of a servant, um [sic] treating others truly with respect, sincerity, then I know that we could get so much more done." While no politician will ever be perfect, Rep. Gabbard, a U.S. military combat veteran and first elected American Samoan and follower of Hinduism, consistently seems to demonstrate her commitment to placing the interests of her district and national constituency at the center of her decisions. In remaining true to this guide, she has displayed a willingness to criticize her own party, not falling victim to the partisan political machine that transforms others into nothing more than voting zombies.

A leadership more committed to the people can lead from a place of strength for facilitating the same heart of a servant so desperately needed in local and state communities across the country. In summarizing the underlying need from others within the community to aid organizations to address the growing demand of poverty, Beth Haddock, executive director for the United Way of northwest Alabama, said, "There has to be a commitment on everyone's part of helping better the lives of those who've lost jobs or have suffered other setbacks. Then, we can start turning this poverty problem around." The People's Clearing House could provide the spark of unity nonprofit leaders seek; in this case, providing a ray of light to some of the 300,000 children Lisa Singleton-Rickman of the *Times Daily* detailed as living in poverty statewide.

When you build a cause that seems winnable through trusted leadership and well-planned strategies, it's amazing what can be achieved as more individuals are excited to become a part of it. The city of Lynn, MA successfully housed all of their homeless veterans by making a no-excuse commitment and then backing it up with a highly coordinated partnership among agencies built on respect and communication.

When people start feeling hope, especially in terms of economics, many of the social divisions will become greatly alleviated, creating an environment of less stress and tension for working through issues as one. An America united can boldly take on any domestic challenge with optimism, as well as fulfill its enduring role of providing a beacon of light to the rest of the world; something that may be in more desperate need at the present time than ever before. The People's Clearing House makes all this possible.

"But Goethe tells us in his greatest poem that Faust lost the liberty of his soul when he said to the passing moment: 'Stay, thou art so fair.' And our liberty, too, is endangered if we pause for the passing moment, if we rest on our achievements, if we resist the pace of progress. For time and the world do not stand still. Change is the law of life. And those who look only to the past or the present are certain to miss the future." –John F. Kennedy

"For the future belongs to those who believe in the beauty of their dreams." –Eleanor Roosevelt

Paths for Implementation of the People's Clearing House

Campaign finance has gone through numerous reforms and court rulings that have reshaped who could give donations and how much could be given. As with so many other questions before the courts regarding the means by which a citizen chooses to practice a fundamental right, the judicial opinions have drastically changed over time. What has remained consistent with these rulings concerning campaign finance has been the close voting of the Supreme Court, with one voice possibly capable of changing the outcome in the future. More importantly, although the most recent rulings of the high court have upheld unlimited independent expenditures from outside groups, the justices have indicated through their rulings what parameters the right reform must follow.

The origins of the court's treatment of campaign contributions actually began with the Buckley v. Valeo ruling, which identified money as being a form of speech, essentially leaving the door open to remove limits formally placed on outside spending. Following the Citizens United ruling, which rejected the ability to regulate, came SpeechNow.org v. FEC—which was meant to strengthen the deterrent against limits. "The court of appeals held that when the government attempts to regulate the financing of political campaigns and express advocacy through contribution limits, it must have a countervailing interest that outweighs the limit's burden on the exercise of First Amendment rights."

Under the current rulings of the court, for any reform to be constitutional, it must not be designed to: limit one group to benefit another, place limits on what can be given and received by independent groups, or contain the sole purpose of equalizing elections based on monetary standing. The Supreme Court's Citizens United ruling also closed the door on reforms built around the argument that unlimited spending breeds corruption, as Justice Anthony Kennedy spelled out in the majority opinion he composed for the court.

Justice John Paul Stevens differed greatly with Justice Kennedy's assessment that a system based around the power of unfettered spending could not be corrupt. He led the other dissenters of the Supreme Court, believing "that in the electoral context, unlimited speech (ad spending) from some people could drown out the speech of others, and effectively trample on their own First Amendment rights." Most Americans agree with Justice Stevens that unlimited spending serves as a limiting factor to others' speech.

Almost fifteen years before, Dr. Anthony Corrado, Chair of the Board of Trustees of the Campaign Finance Institute, articulated a similar view when analyzing the Buckley v. Valeo ruling. In his book, *Campaign Finance: A Sourcebook*, the respected campaign finance expert compared the Buckley decision with the 1905 Lochner vs. New York ruling that basically removed government regulation from the economic market.

In comparing the decisions that removed political and economic regulation, Dr. Corrado wrote, "On the view reflected in both Buckley and Lochner, reliance on free market is government neutrality and government inaction. But in the New Deal period, it became clear that reliance on markets simply entailed another—if in many ways good—regulatory system, made possible and constituted through law. We cannot have a system of market ordering without an elaborate body of law. For all the beneficial qualities, markets are legitimately subject to democratic restructuring—at least within certain limits—if the restructuring promise to deliver sufficient benefits. This is a constitutional truism in the post—New Deal era. What is perhaps not sufficiently appreciated, but what is equally true, is that elections based on existing distributions of wealth and entitlements also embody a regulatory system, made possible and constituted through law."

Wealthy individuals are given an advantage through the current laws dictating elections. However, as is seen from the decision in Citizens United, attempting to correct this inequality through limits will not withstand the constitutional test of the court. Any form of regulation must have a "countervailing interest" that doesn't impose a burden beyond what is acceptable under the court's discretion, as with the U.S. Court of Appeals for the District of Columbia Circuit's explanation for allowing aspects of transparency in March 2010. "The appeals court held that, while disclosure and reporting requirements do impose a burden on the First Amendment interests, they 'impose no ceiling on campaign-related activities' and 'do not prevent anyone from speaking.'"

In his 1994 analysis of the laws at the time pertaining to campaign finance, one of the questions Dr. Anthony Corrado offered readers to consider is: why couldn't the U.S Congress act to change the system? He wrote, "A system of unlimited campaign expenditures should be seen as a regulatory decision to allow disparities in resources to be turned into disparities in political influence. That may be the best decision, all things considered; but why is it unconstitutional for government to attempt to replace the system with an alternative? The court offered no answer." Later, the U.S. Congress did attempt to make some changes through the McCain-Feingold reforms, which ultimately proved inadequate and unconstitutional. The People's Clearing House takes the lessons of past reforms and court rulings and creates a regulatory system able to withstand tests.

From the Tillman Act to McCain-Feingold legislation, numerous measures have already been taken with the direct aim of limiting the power of monetary influence on elections. However, reform must evolve, as the public financing options or attempts to limit what can be spent on elections have provided consistent failures within the new legal and technological landscape. If reform is instead designed around democratic principles that protect rights while promoting mutual causes—raising accountability, lowering partisanship, strengthening communities, and promoting unity—a prevailing hope can be created for moving the country forward with genuine optimism and promise.

An analysis of regulation deemed constitutional on other fundamental rights provides clarity on what should be considered with any campaign finance reform. While Americans are guaranteed the right to bear arms under the 2nd Amendment, the means by which they practice this right has faced regulation. Congress temporarily banned certain weapons and ammunitions with the 1994 Assault Weapons Ban. Living up to Supreme Court Justice Louis Brandeis' popular description of serving as the "laboratories of democracy," the states led this endeavor by passing laws prohibiting the sale, purchase, or transfer of various weapons and gun-related items.

Washington D.C. faced legal challenges for its decision to ban handguns. As Paul Duggan of *The Washington Post* wrote of a decision in 2011, "A federal appeals court panel on Tuesday upheld the District's authority to impose a system of handgun registration and rejected a challenge to the city's ban on semiautomatic assault rifles and large-capacity ammunition clips." This decision came over three years after the 2008 Supreme Court ruling that overturned the prohibition of handguns by the city. In terms of the federal court's view toward the registration aspect for heightened transparency, "the panel ordered the District Court to hold more hearings on those provisions and others to determine whether they are necessary for public safety."

The Supreme Court has typically remained out of lawsuits regarding gun regulation. In the ruling from 2008, the court "[declared] that the constitution's Second Amendment protects a right of individuals to have commonly available firearms—including handguns—in their home for self-defense." Beyond this decision that cut down the ban on "commonly available firearms" and later upholding a ban on "straw gun purchases" in 2014, the Supreme Court has showed restraint in taking up cases related to state bans and restrictions placed on residents in practicing their 2nd Amendment rights.

So while the courts have protected the 2nd Amendment right of Americans to bear arms, it has chosen to regulate the means of carrying out that right. To own a gun, an individual has to go through certain procedures such as background checks and purchasing a license to carry. However, most of the regulation is based on the means that could lead to unwanted inequality, with restrictions placed on the legal amount of ammunition and types of firearms that average citizens can purchase to prevent this.

If most citizens possess a common handgun, they would be put at a drastic disadvantage to those carrying a high-powered weapon. The Founders had no way of knowing the damage one future weapon could cause, so it is easy to see that having restrictions on these means for practicing the 2nd Amendment is in the public's best interest. As Gary Hart wrote in his book *The Republic of Conscience*, "So the Founders would be the first to advise that we adapt our systems and our policies to the realities of the current age." Common sense allowed the Supreme Court to facilitate this aim by upholding bans or restrictions on certain methods of practicing the right to bear arms, while the court refuses to use the same component of logic on campaign finance reform.

In a different set of circumstances, but in the same spirit, the courts have ruled some methods of the death penalty as "cruel and unusual" with advances in more humane executions. In response, the states have proactively changed the means of execution to remain constitutional. In regards to gun control, there are two distinctions that seem to be utilized in reaching conclusions concerning policy. Commonly purchased firearms provide an arena that would be level to everyone, while powerful semi-automatic weaponry establishes an uneven arena worthy of a degree of limitation. While the fundamental right remains protected, the means is scrutinized for possible regulation.

Campaign finance could be thought of in a similar fashion, with the means of practicing the 1st Amendment right of freedom of speech being broken down in three distinctions. Direct contributions are level, in that everyone faces the same regulations in giving. Indirect contributions to outside groups are not level, in that they face no regulation and are unlimited. And the third category is other informal means of speech that do not involve monetary contributions, such as social media. This means of speech is obviously considered level in that they are cheap and readily available to almost anyone. However, outside of regulations on direct contributions, the court has only upheld that transparency on all groups does not place an undue burden on speech.

The Supreme Court rejected applying regulation to the uneven aspect of indirect contributions from outside organizations, and instead reduced the regulation on direct contributions. Although limits still remain on how much can directly be given to individual candidates, the court reduced regulation on direct contributions by removing the limit on how much one contributor could give overall in the election cycle in 2014. In McCutcheon v. Federal Election Commission from 2015, the court struck down the "limits capped at $48,600 the amount an individual could spend on contributions to candidates, plus $74,600 total on contributions to political parties and committees."

From the majority opinion for the McCutcheon v. FEC composed by Chief Justice John Roberts: "We have made clear that Congress may not regulate contributions simply to reduce the amount of money in politics, or to restrict the political participation of some in order to enhance the relative influence of others." In a dissenting opinion, Justice Breyer once again provided a powerful contrast, in writing, "The First Amendment advances not only the individual's right to engage in political speech, but also the public's interest in preserving a democratic order in which collective speech matters." He continued, "Where enough money calls the tune, the general public will not be heard... And a cynical public can lose interest in political participation altogether."

The important thing to remember is that The People's Clearing House does not impose limits on what can be spent by any individual or group on elections. While a variance in percentages being taken out will depend on a deduction schedule that controls donations inside and outside of the official election cycle, at no time are contributors ever limited in what they can chose to donate on elections by TPCH. Only current limits placed on direct contributions remain within the system. All the discussions about when it would be constitutional to regulate contributions through limits provide something to consider, but do not apply to the deductions found within The People's Clearing House.

Beyond limits currently placed on direct contributions, all citizens are allowed unlimited spending on elections. Any donor would be within their rights to contribute more if they desire to offset the deductions of The People's Clearing House. However, it would seem extremely illegitimate for wealthier donors to claim that deductions to The People's Clearing House, which are commonly shared by all donors, were limiting their voice. Any limit on political speech due to any monetary deficiency is shared by all.

Chief Justice Roberts, in his majority opinion from the McCutcheon's case, stated, "No matter how desirable it may seem, it is not an acceptable governmental objective to 'level the playing field,' or to 'level electoral opportunities,' or to 'equaliz[e] the financial resources to candidates.'" If the differences in socioeconomic status were not recognized by the court as limiting the speech of those unable to contribute large donations, how could the court accept an argument that the wealthy would be limited by having to spend more to possibly achieve the same impact? The elements are the same. There is no re-inventing of the wheel. Accepting the argument of a wealthy donor, despite past rejections revolving around the same factor of money, would seem corrupt.

As with the expensive political ads of today, most Americans cannot individually afford to place an ad on television that wealthy donors can afford, although everyone possesses the opportunity. However, this lack of monetary means is not something the Supreme Court recognizes as a limiting factor on their speech. All Americans are able to spend an unlimited amount of money on elections; however, the deductions of The People's Clearing House might not allow someone to spend as much toward elections as originally planned. In both instances, lack of monetary means—something the Supreme Court does not recognize as a legitimate endeavor in leveling—

reduces their contribution.

No attempt is being made to reduce the amount of money contributed in elections. No attempt is being made to lower the participation of some. More money spent will only further build communities, as well as create more hope for increasing participation.

Beyond contributions and grassroots efforts through volunteering, with today's technology and social media, anyone can offer their political views for little to nothing on certain platforms. This is a reality used by the Supreme Court to uphold the constitutionality of unlimited spending.

While the means of practicing the right is regulated, freedom of speech is never limited. The deductions of The People's Clearing House being universally applied to all contributions do not in any way limit one voice over another beyond what already is occurring. Just like with current transparency on political donations and restrictions as part of gun control, the deductions of TPCH serve a public interest while not infringing on the fundamental right. The aim of transparency is even strengthened through TPCH by supplying additional measures and incentives to properly hold donors accountable. While a leveling of the playing field may occur, it is only a byproduct of the reform.

The People's Clearing House does not serve to take away from one group to benefit another, as money is going back to the entire constituency. All donors share the same characteristic of being a part of a constituency. Greater transparency, accountability, economic growth, and heightened unity benefit everyone in the community, regardless of any individual characteristic or socioeconomic status. What could be more democratic than utilizing the principle of autonomy to restructure the electoral process for garnering the genuine representation and mutual effort in building the community the Founders originally envisioned over two hundred years ago?

In speaking in 2014 on the unhealthy influence of unlimited spending within the current political system, Sen. Elizabeth Warren (D-MA) said, "Democracy can survive for a while, but it can't survive forever under this kind of onslaught. The problem we've got is the U.S. Supreme Court, and the Supreme Court famously brought us to the point of corporations being people that seem to have better rights than our own people do."

While most Americans agree with Sen. Warren, the Supreme Court's decision to treat a corporation—"associations of citizens," as referred to by the Justices—as a person only demonstrates further why groups with independent expenditures are justified in facing deductions from The People's Clearing House. All are clearly part of the constituency.

When considering the past court decisions and campaign finance reforms, it would seem constitutional if The People's Clearing House had a uniform percentage, such as 30%, deducted from all transparent donations. Applying a higher deduction on non-disclosure contributors with organizations like 501(c)(4)s would be questionable. However, donors always possess the choice of simply giving a donation directly to candidates, PACs, or super PACs and face a standard deduction. In choosing to shield their identity by using a 501(c)(4) to funnel donations, a higher rate should be justified.

A similar ambiguity applies to variances in deductions based on benchmarks within direct contributions, as demonstrated with the federal contribution limit of $2,700. Allowing contributions from $500 and below to face a 10% deduction, while contributions above $500 faced higher deductions, is not vital to overall success. While differences in deductions based on amount given would be ideal, it could be doubtful in regards to the scrutiny the court has shown in taking from one group to benefit another. If The People's Clearing House is applied uniformly by the deduction schedule of contributions inside and outside of the election cycle, all the aims of the campaign finance reform could be achieved, allowing the people to reclaim their government. However, even if the court does not agree with the ideas of The People's Clearing House, the people possess the power to pass a new law or constitutional amendment to achieve it.

In terms of corruption, if the Supreme Court did not see the chance of it when allowing a select group of contributors the influence of giving large campaign contributions, how could it rule against something that benefits all constituents, regardless of race, gender, ethnicity, religion, sexual orientation, or socioeconomic status. The endeavors of The People's Clearing House are all in the public's interest.

SUCCESS THROUGH LEGISLATION

Politicians have consistently operated under the assumption that the people could never unite, confidently exploiting the political system without fear of ever being held accountable. With reliable division, consistent apathy, and an ebb and flow within the economy, few lawmakers, special interests fat cats, or political pundits are capable of envisioning a successful movement to challenge the current status quo. However, The People's Clearing House can produce the level of unity once unimaginable, quickly demonstrating to lawmakers that the days of abusing their power are numbered.

As is so often the case, the states will once again produce environments most conducive to reforms through legislation. While state constitutions vary on which ballot measures are available for passing a new law, some statutes place the power directly in the hands of the people. "In 21 states, citizens can start an initiated state statute," which only requires a certain number of signatures to place the measure on the ballot for a vote. This method entirely bypasses legislators, making it easy for the people to set the proper tone.

Other states offer the option of an indirect initiated state statute, in which signatures are still gathered to begin the process, but the measure must then go to the state legislature before it can move forward. Typically, a state legislature has some options, but none take away the power of residents to vote on the law that was originally submitted, which is crucial. As witnessed, when left to the discretion of state or federal legislators to write bills, too often the needs of the people are left out of the final draft.

"In 24 states and one unincorporated organized territory, legislatures can employ a legislatively referred state statute," in which the legislature puts a measure on the ballot and the citizens of the state "can only approve or reject it." Again, the problem with this form of ballot measure is that it leaves too much discretion with legislatures. Regardless of where the reform originates, the people must always take the lead in establishing the desired legislation. Consequential transparency and accountability will not result from efforts that allow legislators to tailor something less than what is actually necessary.

Montana would be the most likely to consider a reform like The People's Clearing House. Despite the Citizens United ruling that removed limits on corporate spending in elections, Montanans held true to their Corrupt Practices Act from 1912. It was originally passed to take back the state government from the Copper Kings. The Supreme Court ruled against the constitutionality of their act, making the elimination of limits found in the Citizens United decision extend to state elections. In response to this infringement of the federal government into matters of state sovereignty, Montana passed stricter requirements on campaign donors. Other states have joined suit in passing laws to strengthen the transparency the court upheld.

On the local level, a group like represent.us has demonstrated what can be achieved through reform initiatives when a movement is built around a common cause that unites across party lines. Josh Silver, the organization's director, learned that emphasizing the need to root out corruption was the most effective method for laying a foundation of strong support. In an article for *The Huffington Post* from March 2014, he wrote, "And here's the key thing: comprehensive reform proposals that overhaul ethics, lobbying, transparency and provide public financing in one fell swoop enjoy over 80% voter approval, and they are constitutional, even under the current Supreme Court."

The reform efforts of represent.us center on a number of common themes found in The People's Clearing House, with the most significant being the emphasis of citizens within the community taking the lead to create the representation they deserve. Tallahassee answered the call and "made history by approving the first city Anti-Corruption Act in the United States by an overwhelming 2-1 margin," with other cities discovering a similar success through the empowerment facilitated by represent.us.

Although The People's Clearing House offers something completely different than public financing, the fight for greater accountability, transparency, and independent oversight are mutually shared. The work of organizations like this, which have been in the weeds of victorious legislation, could be vital in strengthening any reform attempt. The people must take the lead for any chance of meaningful reform. The federal government is not unique in possessing restrictions to transparency, lax rules concerning discretionary use of campaign money, and inadequacies for proper oversight and control of lobbying. While states offer a diversity of rules concerning these matters, most all produce a similar corrupt culture that denies the people a true republic.

The same cesspool of greed and manipulation demands that citizens remain vigilant concerning the role of legislators in crafting any reform legislation. Like any other bad habit, giving up the practice of strategically designing laws with loopholes will be difficult for many career politicians. However, the people must remain resolved in achieving this vital cause. As Gary Hart wrote in 2015, "Until we have the courage to punish the corrupt and rid ourselves of a system that entwines interest groups, the lobbying octopus, and campaign coffers, we will continue to fall far short of our national expectations and promise, and our government will be corrupt and corrupted."

The task will not be easy.

Although Alabama has received the most attention in regards to political corruption on the state level, there are other members of the union that has distorted representation as a result of no current limits on lobbying activities. For years Missouri supposedly attempted to add some legislation to strengthen campaign finance and eliminate the revolving door of government, but to date has not actually taken any steps to place something significant on the books. Those embedded within government, by the support of special interests, have proven too strong.

Jon Swedien, a political reporter for the *Springfield News-Leader*, detailed the political arena that has endured as a result of passing new ethics laws. In a 2015 article, he wrote, "The Show Me State has no limits on campaign donations, no restrictions on the gifts legislators can accept from lobbyists, no rule preventing lawmakers from immediately becoming lobbyists after leaving office." Jon went on to explain, "This stands in contrast to Missouri's eight neighboring states; all limit at least one of those activities. Arkansas, Kentucky, Oklahoma, and Tennessee limit all three. Illinois, Iowa, and Kansas each limit two of the activities, and Nebraska limits lobbyists' gifts."

While these states have demonstrated a greater effort in constraining lawmakers, there is actually nothing to celebrate once the entire picture of the country is actually put into context. The State Integrity Investigation thoroughly assesses each state to determine the level of commitment each exhibits to deter corruption. Nicholas Kusnetz, formally of The Center of Public Integrity, detailed the 2015 report in an article that revealed almost everything someone would need to know in the title alone, which read: "Only three states score higher than D+ in State Integrity Investigation; 11 flunk."

The in-depth investigation revealed many of the ways in which representation is commonly being undermined. Many of the methods identified in the report are not easily correlated by citizens to corruption, but the impact is being felt in the substandard representation most all are receiving.

"The comprehensive probe found that in state after state, open records laws are laced with exemptions and part-time legislatures and agency officials engage in glaring conflicts of interests and cozy relationships with lobbyists." While some may attempt to discredit the validity of the report, the conclusions reached were based on a number of documented factors. As Nicholas Kusnetz specified, "The 2015 grades are based on 245 questions that ask about key indicators of transparency and accountability, looking not only at what the laws say, but also how well they're enforced or implemented."

Unfortunately, the study revealed that public financing has not proven sufficient in changing the culture and raising the bar of accountability. "As of October 2015, 13 states provided some form of public campaign financing." It is true that many of these states are very limited in which races they offer the public option. However, Arizona chose to make public financing available statewide and still earned a D grade.

Within these thirteen states, the grades earned were: one C-, four D(-)s, three Ds, 2 D(+)s, and 2 Fs. However, Arizona, Maine, Massachusetts, and Michigan are among the twenty-one states offering the people-initiated state statutes, making them ripe for genuine reform. Residents must take the lead in creating the type of state government that would be reflective of American values. While the absence of leadership behind the present condition is shameful, an opening has been created for the people to once again restore patriotism.

While some will always be skeptical of the people actually being persuaded to become engaged enough in the process to bring the necessary change, it can be done. Beyond the hope found within the structure of The People's Clearing House, most citizens are simply unaware of how current governmental processes are limiting them. As with the federal level, the issues are rooted in special interests and bureaucrats. Local governments have begun creating more special districts, which are "independent governmental units that exist separately from, and with substantial administrative and fiscal independence from, general purpose local governments such as county, municipal, and township governments." The state of Texas should provide a cautionary example of how this additional instrument is undermining representation.

Despite the attempt of former Texas Comptroller Susan Combs in 2012 to bring more attention to their rapid development, special districts continued to grow basically unnoticed. In 2015, Denna Winter described Comb's efforts by writing, "She sounded the alarm, waved the flag and irritated a few people in the process. But the special purpose districts continued to sprout up all over the state, now growing to about 2,000."

In the same article Winter penned for Watchdog.org, she demonstrated the crux of what dangers these extra governmental bodies present with a set of significant figures: "Combs' 2012 report found that while the number of cities, counties and school districts charging property taxes was relatively unchanged in two decades, the number of special districts increased by 500—over 45 percent—since 1992. They accounted for 87 percent of the growth in local entities charging property taxes." While some of these units provide various public services, the question of why they are necessary remains.

The answer to this question of why these units really exist most likely lies within a research paper written almost twenty years ago at the University of Texas LBJ School. The graduate students concluded that these independent entities are designed to "preserve the myth of limited government while insulating local public officials from citizen complaints about inadequate service performance or mandatory taxes." Legislators on the federal level are clearly not the only ones who hide behind bureaucrats when possible.

Politicians also too often provide a path for outside organizations to have more influence on legislation that again a majority of citizens remain unaware of; it goes beyond the use of nonprofits, foundations, and flimsy loopholes to subtly achieve this. Lawmakers in various states will actually exempt certain groups under the radar, knowing busy constituents, who have enough trouble following general legislation and individual voting records for future scrutiny, will not even notice. The American Legislative Exchange, or ALEC, basically makes puppets out of lawmakers across the country. From writing laws to tailoring the selling points to communicate to others in persuading them to accept a certain piece of legislation, ALEC works to be as much a part of the process as legally allowed. Lobbying laws meant to produce a degree of fairness make little difference on this organization—despite the access ALEC has to lawmakers who often receive aid in attending the meetings the group hosts.

Lisa Graves, executive director of the Center for Media and Democracy, wrote an article from 2011 that compared the National Conference of State Legislators, or NCSL, with ALEC. While NCSL is bipartisan in composition, ALEC remains almost entirely composed of Republican lawmakers and membership extends to the federal level. Both meet to discuss bills, but meetings of the NCSL are only attended by legislators and funded by tax dollars. ALEC, on the other hand, also houses corporations, which provide most of the funding and share a similar influence in designing new legislation to be introduced by members once they return to their home state.

In 2012, Mike McIntire from *The New York Times* described the process of how new legislation is created before being piggybacked to state legislatures. "ALEC says that its lawmaker members have the ultimate say over its policy deliberations and that no model bills are adopted unless its governing board, made up entirely of legislators, approves it. But the organization's rules give corporations a great deal of influence on the task forces, where model legislation must first clear a preliminary vote before going to the board. As a result, meeting minutes show, draft bills that are preferred by a majority of lawmakers are sometimes killed by the corporate members at the table."

When a former member of the South Carolina House of Representatives, Boyd Brown, uncovered a law that had specifically protected ALEC from proper oversight for some time, he immediately took action. Unfortunately, Republicans declined to join the Democratic lawmaker in seeing that all groups lobby on the same footing. Investigative journalist Paul Abowd detailed Brown's reaction to the law that had casually offered ease of access for around nine years. "'I can't get in a car with a lobbyist and drive up the street,' Brown said. 'But ALEC can give me a scholarship to fly across the country.'"

A decision on whether to hold a lobbying group to equal accountability shouldn't be dictated by whether their advocated ideas correlate with the political ideology of the lawmaker. In relation to ALEC, by allowing ideology and identity politics to form an opposition to reform, GOP lawmakers joined the ranks of others who have opened the government up to the potential abuse of foreign interests, which have no place in politics. Bob Sloan, award-winning journalist and executive director of the Votes Legislative Transparency Project, took a hard look at the processes of ALEC. He placed specific interest on the bylaws guiding the organization and reached a chilling conclusion when witnessing the direct role foreign politicians are actually able to play on decision making. He wrote, "Most of us have the belief that our U.S. State Department is the agency responsible for foreign policy determinations. We are unaware that ALEC was involved in helping set U.S. policy by giving foreign nations a voice in our legislative processes." Essentially, in opening membership to the world, the American Legislative Exchange Council gives foreign interests the access to legislation denied by federal law.

From the loopholes and discreet giveaways commonly found within legislation to the outside influences routinely overlooked by most of the general population, failing to adequately scrutinize the decisions of lawmakers will lead to failures in any reform. The people must lead the process and not allow similar practices of deceit and manipulation to dictate the outcome. An even higher level of skepticism must apply to the federal level. Sam Levine of *The Huffington Post* reported in July 2016 on Hillary Clinton's promise to "introduce a constitutional amendment within the first 30 days of her presidency to overturn the Supreme Court's 2010 Citizens United decision." Along with this popular (but lofty) aim, he informed readers that "Clinton has also pledged to issue an executive order to require government contractors to disclose campaign contributions, and has said she would push the Securities and Exchange Commission to require all publicly traded companies to disclose political contributions to their stockholders."

Although the legislation could have a profoundly positive impact on strengthening democracy, Hillary Clinton has proven from her past interactions with federal contractors and donors to the Clinton Foundation that her words or actions should never be taken at face value. Where was this push for disclosure during her time as Secretary of State, especially from those who met with her and subsequently earned federal contracts? A number of other questions surround why the Democratic nominee for president waited until now to offer these plans. Why didn't she attach her name to one of the multiple letters sent by legislators urging the President to sign a similar executive order in June 2015—or write her own letter if she viewed the issue with such urgency? More importantly, if the legislation is so favorable, why doesn't the President sign it today? While the idea of an executive order may be effective in earning votes for Hillary Clinton in 2016, it seems rather clear that nothing would actually result from it, allowing federal contractors to continue to buy influence in D.C. and produce the same governmental waste, fraud, and abuse. This failure to actually take significant action as promised will maintain a culture where contractors within the military segment alone will continue to produce the same dismal headlines as that from CNN's Zachary Cohen in July 2016, which read: "U.S. Navy's new $13B aircraft carrier can't fight."

As for a constitutional amendment, someone with a political career like Hillary Clinton obviously knows how difficult the process is for actual passage. Then again, although it is unlikely to pass or actually change the corrupt culture found in governing chambers even if it does, her public intention gains some political points for offering a contrast to the Republican lawmakers who likely support Citizens United. Regardless of the intentions, the threat of an amendment can be effective in getting lawmakers to act. Senator Marco Rubio joined the chorus of others in calling for a constitutional convention to offer new amendments to protect the people from the overreach of government. As with others, the senator is aware of how the people secured the 17th amendment allowing them to vote on U.S. senators by placing pressure on Congress.

In December 2015, Phillip Bump of *The Washington Post* described how the general public forced the hand of the U.S. Congress by writing, "By 1912, faced with calls for a constitutional convention from a wide swath of existing states, Congress passed the new amendment and sent it to the states for ratification, which happened the next year.

Like Scalia, Congress almost certainly didn't want to see a group of citizens get together and start proposing other amendments." Although it is unlikely that such a constitutional convention would lead to the free-for-all chaotic debate some believe, a people united on campaign finance reform across party lines can force decisive action.

Hopefully, legislators on the state and federal level will act with courage and conviction to implement meaningful campaign finance built around the ideas of The People's Clearing House. However, if, and when, a fight reaches the level of a constitutional amendment, anything less than TPCH should be emphatically rejected.

SUCCESS THROUGH OPTIONS

In a perfect world, The People's Clearing House would simply be passed into law. However, the more likely scenario in D.C. and statehouses across the country is an exceedingly bitter fight against those extremely desperate to keep grasp of the status quo. From the McCain-Feingold Reform to the public financing component found within the Clean Elections Act from Maine, the key has been offering each candidate an option of campaigning under a uniform set of guidelines that will apply to all who accept. In the case of Maine, an individual who chose the public financing option (attached with running as a clean candidate) had to almost entirely reject receiving private contributions.

As acknowledged in a 2008 article from the Institute for Local Self Reliance, it was the Maine electorate that created the public option through a 1999 state referendum after learning from the Buckley v. Valeo case that an effort to impose limits would fail. As the author of the article points out, "But in the case of the Maine Clean Election law the federal judge found that spending limits on candidates who accept public funding is not a free speech violation. This is because the system is voluntary, and while it provides 'incentives to make the public financing route attractive,' these incentives are not 'overwhelmingly or of an order that can be said to create profound disparities.'"

The People's Clearing House candidate demonstrates a similar desire to build a representation upon a foundation of accountability and fairness, but does not impose any limits on the process. The conditions candidates accept also go well beyond the elections. A constant commitment to the deduction schedule remains present over an entire career.

In the absence of laws in each state and on the federal level to formally establish The People's Clearing House, candidates could always simply run on the idea of supporting the formation of one upon being elected. As powerful as this contrast would be to typical major party candidates or sitting incumbents, hopefully the courts will allow more definite action to be taken by those individuals who desire to actually run as TPCH candidates. Campaigning on the idea alone would not likely create enough excitement to build a successful movement and a nonprofit-styled organization could offer the solution. Under the original and desired design of The People's Clearing House, it would be the leading bodies on each level of government that would—in correlation with local community leaders—utilize their autonomy to form the causes and initiatives for constituents who contribute. However, without a willingness of lawmakers to supply these choices, a citizen-driven nonprofit could work with local, state, and federal leaders to supply them. While conventional candidates without deductions may be seen as having an advantage in fundraising—as was often the case against public-financed candidates—the assertion underestimates the power behind the principles of TPCH. Beginning a career with a heart of a servant will be priceless to a forgotten electorate.

Candidates could also publically reject supporting any independent expenditure groups—such as super PACs—who do not become a People's Clearing House organization. More importantly, the general public could be able to easily distinguish which candidates and political organizations are a part of The People's Clearing House through the use of a seal. From nonprofits to super PACS, organizations which accept the transparency requirements and deduction schedule of TPCH will receive a seal. One example would be a social welfare organization, or 504(c)(4), that desires to become a member of The People's Clearing House. In registering with the proper state or national PCH, the group is voluntarily accepting: tracking and deductions of contributions according to the deduction schedule in place, scrutiny of donations for additional deductions for missing information on forms, and a detailed breakdown in money being used for partisan activities or non-partisan endeavors. Any 504(c)(4) that accepts these standards would receive a seal from TPCH, denoting their commitment. The seals of The People's Clearing House do not hold the characteristics that led to the failed attempts of residents to place labels on candidates. The courts ruled that the "Scarlet Letter" provisions from Colorado and Missouri were unconstitutional. In both of those incidents, the "amendment required ballots to list Congressional candidates' stands on term limits. Incumbent candidates who failed to support congressional term limits would have the words 'disregarded voters instructions on term limits' printed next to their names. 'Declined to pledge to support term limits' would appear next to the names of non-incumbent candidates who refused to take a term limits pledge."

Coloradans wanted to lock their representatives into voting for a constitutional amendment and their Supreme Court said, "Our holding should not be read as a condemnation of the congressional term limits. Instead, we conclude that the manner in which Amendment 12 seeks to accomplish that objective violates Article V of the United States Constitution because it attempts to usurp our elected representatives' exclusive authority to amend the United States Constitution using explicit mandate and coercion."

A seal from The People's Clearing House signifies a voluntary acceptance of higher standards of accountability. It is process-oriented and does not require any candidate to pledge to support certain legislation or not serve past a number of terms. There is no attempt to place the seal on the actual ballot, as constituents will know long before elections where each individual candidate stands on The People's Clearing House. Making The People's Clearing House an available choice to all individual candidates and political entities would be momentous to the cause of the people reclaiming the ownership of their country. However, nothing may strengthen this effort more than utilizing TCPH to raise the bar of accountability on the media as well.

In speaking at the 28th Annual News and Documentary Emmy Award Ceremony in September 2007, the late Tim Russert addressed his colleagues concerning the necessity for properly scrutinizing each candidate's messengers: "It's a whole new era where the landscape is filled with pamphleteers who have a strong ideology and they want to call foul every time a reporter asks a tough question and we know that is the reality, but we must resist any temptation to pull our punches or to try and placate people who have already chosen up sides. They are trying to get their candidate elected, not trying to allow a free and vigorous press to scrutinize their candidate."

Although there are staffers on both sides of the political aisle who often become so invested in the ascension of themselves and their candidates that they lose focus of what's important; former Republican operative Allen Raymond provided the greatest insights in his 2008 book, *How to Rig an Election: Confessions of a Republican Operative.* Raymond detailed the thoughts that ran through his head upon realizing he would soon be talking to the FBI regarding the criminal offenses he had undertaken in his aim to secure political victories for himself and others. "I had gotten a lot of people elected to a lot of powerful positions—for what? What had they done for the country? What had I expected them to do? The fact was, I'd never really cared. Every time someone talked policy, to me it was just more campaign propaganda, just some more of the old blah-blah-blah. My thoughts on policy had always been: if I listened this long, then whoever is speaking owes me a pizza; now let me get back to spinning. If they won, I gained more clout; if they lost, I found another campaign—and then I gained more clout."

Obviously, the media must present the facts and protect the people from false claims, especially with elections. Presidents Kennedy, Eisenhower, and Jefferson are just a few who specifically stressed how vital this role was in assuring the people have the information to make the proper decisions each of these men had faith in them to make. The Supreme Court also places a lot of faith in people's ability to wade through all the information and make sensible judgments. However, most would argue the press has been failing in their duty for some time, specifically in relation to covering elections. News organizations make billions each new election cycle on political ads. However, just as many politicians are ruled by greed and self-interest, the mainstream media is owned by private interests dictated by ratings and revenue. The atmosphere created is reminiscent of the description Harry S. Truman offered to Merle Miller: "Newspapermen, and they're all a bunch of lazy cusses, once one of them writes something, the others rewrite it, and they keep right on doing it without ever stopping to find out if the first fellow was telling the truth or not."

Although the decisions Americans make as to who represents them has almost immeasurable consequences on millions of lives within the country and worldwide, there is very little fact-checking of ads taking place. Money is exchanged and the ad is aired. Justin Peters, editor-at-large of the *Columbia Journalism Review*, wrote an article following the 2012 elections on the work of the Annenberg Public Policy Center, which found that stations often did not fact-check despite a reliable demand of revenue. "Of the 206 station managers surveyed by Annenberg, only 56 percent said they screen the accuracy of third-party ads. And just thirteen percent of the respondents said their stations had refused to air at least one third-party ad during the past 12 months."

Brian Stelter, senior media correspondent for CNN, looked at the amount of money involved with ads and wondered if it affected the incentive to help change the current political system built on money. In 2014, he asked, "Station owners are the ones benefiting from the status quo, so might their newsrooms be a little less likely to cover proposals to reduce the amount of money in politics?" Later in his article, he spoke of a discussion that likely provides the answer. He wrote, "When I recently asked a political reporter in one market if the money her station makes from campaign ads gets reinvested into fact-checks of those same ads, she laughed and said, 'The answer is a loud no.'"

As valuable as the work of others is in offering an accurate portrayal of the current failure within the press, Timothy Karr's look at the priorities behind what receives airtime was enlightening. In 2012, the senior director of strategy for Free Press wrote, "The hundreds of local news that aired in two weeks prior to Wisconsin's June 5 recall election included no stories on the 17 groups most actively buying time on Milwaukee's ABC, CBS, Fox and NBC affiliates. While these stations were ignoring the impact of political ads, they found time to air 53 local news segments on Justin Bieber."

While federal law may prohibit news organizations in vetting and rejecting untruthful ads directly from federal candidates, the decision to question and reject those from third parties is at their discretion. Their common refusal to hold these third parties to a higher standard continues to hurt democracy. Most Americans do not have the time or incentive to put aside their daily routine to conduct a fact-checking expedition. While the Internet has somewhat helped with ease of access to information, many still rely on local and national news organizations to present them the truth through daily television programs.

Harriet Levin Balkind, founder of HonestAds.org, is a tireless advocate for truth in political advertising. She informed readers that exposure to information is enough for many people to believe it, regardless of the truth. She refers to Brooks Jackson, who has articulated that many people simply have a false sense of faith in the screening process to provide truthful ads on TV because of the notion of "truth in advertising." However, the assumption that this FTC laws protect against the airing of false political information is incorrect and dangerous.

With the unwillingness of most news organizations to only air verified ads, it is basically a free-for-all for third parties to air whatever they desire. In 2004, Brooks Jackson provided a perfect representation of how the government uses "truth in advertising" to control the mundane, while giving political advertising a free pass. In the article written for Factcheck.org, where Brooks serves as director, the long-time, award-winning journalist wrote, "Laws protecting consumers from false advertising of products are enforced pretty vigorously. For example, the Federal Trade Commission took action in 2002 to protect the public from the self-proclaimed psychic 'Miss Cleo,' who the FTC said promised free readings over the phone and then socked her gullible clients with enormous telephone charges. The FTC even forced a toy company a while back to stop running ads showing its 'Bouncin' Kid Ballerina" doll standing alone and twirling gracefully without human assistance, which the FTC said was video hokum."

The Federal Communications Committee places more ad information online today regarding the political ads being played in major markets. Before, someone seeking more information was required to individually approach each station and attempt to dig though countless amounts of paper just to begin the process. There are groups (like the Sunlight Foundation and Free Press) that are working to try and make this more transparent through their site, politicaladsleuth.com, but the task is overwhelming.

The process seems to purposely be structured in a fashion that will always make it complex and time-consuming for concerned citizens and truth-seeking organizations to achieve their goal of accountability through heightened transparency. As Sharon McNary of Southern California Public Radio explained in July 2014, "The Ad Sleuth website is still a work in progress. It can be difficult to compile summaries on a single candidate because every TV station names its candidate files something different." Beyond not demonstrating an internal commitment to fact-checking, news organizations are also not displaying recognition for at least providing better aid to those on the outside who will.

The People's Clearing House offers the news media the opportunity to actually take a stand with the American people in reaffirming their ownership to the country. By joining the cause, journalists can serve as advocates on the frontlines of communication, as the Founders intended and President Kennedy reiterated over half a century ago. Addressing the American Newspaper Publishers Association, President Kennedy said, "Without debate, without criticism, no Administration and no country can   succeed—and no republic can survive. That is why the Athenian lawmaker Solon decreed it a crime for any citizen to shrink from controversy. And that is why our press was protected by the First Amendment—the only business in America specifically protected by the Constitution—not primarily to amuse and entertain, not to emphasize the trivial and the sentimental, not to simply 'give the public what it wants'—but to inform, to arouse, to reflect, to state our dangers and our opportunities, to indicate our crises and our choices, to lead, mold, educate and sometimes even anger public opinion."

The genuine debate President Kennedy advocated for in his speech will only be created if the press scrutinizes political ads. Transparency and accountability should be a mutual endeavor in terms of political ads, regardless of media bias, as the representation produced determines the path moving forward. As Tim Russert told that same crowd in 2007, "As competitive as our industry is, I ask that all of us lock arms, brothers and sisters, as journalists, to respect one another when we are aggressive in going after these candidates, in the interest of the First Amendment and all of us are in that together."

Although it is not a necessary component for The People's Clearing House to succeed, in the desire to achieve this mutual endeavor of keeping the American public well-informed, news organizations could follow the lead of candidates and political entities in becoming members of TPCH. The ad money received from candidates and third party groups would also face TPCH deductions for strengthening communities. Becoming members of The People's Clearing House would help strengthen the resolve of fulfilling current disclosure requirements that are unfortunately not always being followed. Just as with penalties on forms submitted to groups such as super PACs, any third party that submits money to a news organization, without attaching the required advertiser information, would face a higher price. Any news organization that is found to run a false political ad would also face higher deductions to TPCH moving forward. Obviously, participation creates similar methods for incentivizing news organizations to become the trusted gatekeepers of information vital to voters making the best decisions.

Just as with TPCH political entities, participation would allow each news organization to have the distinction of being either a state or national group. It is a little different with local affiliates of larger organizations, but the right distinctions could still be made. Under such conditions, local news stations could help alleviate the flow of money from third parties outside the state by assigning a higher deduction to TPCH. States already regulate whether individuals, parties, corporations, political action committees, and unions outside the state can offer contributions directly to candidates.

Third-party organizations paying national news organizations like NBC, ABC, CBS, and FOX for a nationally televised advertisement would select from national causes and initiatives. Contributions for local advertisements made to local stations would face a deduction and set of choices according to whether it is a state or outside group. If a state super PAC buys an ad on a news station inside the state, the deduction and choices of cause and initiatives would be determined by the state. However, if a national super PAC from outside the state bought an ad, it would most likely face a higher deduction from the local affiliate. The deduction to TPCH would be halved. With half of the money from the TPCH deduction, the leadership of the super PAC who bought the ad would choose from national programs. The other half of the TPCH deduction would belong to the local station management to select from among state options. The division of the deduction from TPCH allows both constituencies to benefit. A few examples of how advertisers would buy ads and select from the available choices:

> **State political organization purchasing from a local affiliate inside the same state:** The state super PAC "Americans Who Care" buys airtime for a political ad to be played in Texas. They contact "WFXZ," a local NBC affiliate, and discover it will be $100,000 for the ad to be played that number of times statewide. In setting the price, the station takes into account the 15% that will be deducted to TPCH established by the state. The station receives $85,000. The leadership of "Americans Who Care" determines what state causes to support with their $15,000 deduction to TPCH.

> **National political organization purchasing from a national news organization:** "Building for a Plentiful Tomorrow," a national super PAC, purchases airtime from ABC for a nationally televised ad for $2.5 million dollars, with 8% going back to TPCH. ABC receives $2,300,000, while the leadership of "Building for a Plentiful Tomorrow" selects the national causes to support with the $200,000 deduction.

> **National political organization purchasing from a local affiliate inside a state:** A national social welfare organization "Global is Real" buys airtime from a local station, "WRSV," in the state of Mississippi. The price is $1.2 million for the ad space, with 25% being deducted to TPCH. The total deduction is $300,000, which will be divided equally for both sides to choose how to spend the deduction. "Global is Real," being registered with The National People's Clearing House, will take their $150,000 and choose from among the national causes and initiatives. The leadership at "WRSV" will take their $150,000 and select from among the state programs they wish to support. Both national and state constituencies benefit.

Heightened competition, in general, was already witnessed at the beginning of the 2016 election cycle through the flooding of the mar-

ket by more super PACs. As an article in *The New York Times* at the
end of 2015 from Nick Corasaniti and Matt Flegenheimer indicated,
"in some parts of Iowa and New Hampshire, super PACs [were] paying almost nine times what a campaign would pay." While candidates
obviously must receive a reasonable and better price, news organizations should use their discretion with third-party advertisers to help
reshape the media landscape and build communities.

Few citizens will complain about the possibility of more ads from
candidates than super PACS through strengthened regulation on outside influences—all while building their communities. The Supreme
Court has already indicated that super PACs have the option of using
their money to emphasize other means for getting out their message.
As *The New York Times* reporters explained, super PACs are already
doing more for candidates. "They are overseeing extensive field operations, data-collection programs, digital advertising, email lists, opposition research, and voter registration efforts." Elections built more
around grassroots campaigning would be welcomed by most Americans. It's doubtful that too many citizens would mind the profit-
driven mainstream media using elections as a time it can give back
more to communities. The news industry—especially the major networks—have the power to set the tone when it comes to the depth
and influence of televised advertisements during elections. In choosing to join The People's Clearing House, a news organization will be
better able to raise the bar of accountability and transparency from a
greater position of moral high ground. This demonstrated commitment could also be signified by a unique seal only given to the media,
allowing the general public the ability to watch a political ad and make
two important distinctions. Is the political organization behind the ad
identified as a member of The People's Clearing House with the seal
given to candidates and political entities who are members? Does the
ad possess a seal earned by those news organizations that are TPCH
members? If so, the viewer can have greater assurance that the information presented in the advertisement has most likely faced proper
scrutiny.

Just as with other aspects of The People's Clearing House, choosing to not take a stand with the American people could be costly. Politicians could lose their political career for choosing to oppose the
measure. Businesses that reject the greater representation could lose
customers; news organizations that disregard participation in the effort could simply push more individuals to replace the mainstream
media with alternatives. Americans realize that all the endeavors of
TPCH should be shared by all.

A study released from the AP-NORC Center for Public Affairs Research and the American Press Institute in April 2016 found that "just 6 percent of people say they have a lot of confidence in the media." Just as most politicians are subservient to campaign contributions, the news media is often ruled by greed and the quest for ratings.

Bias within the media is consistently evident. It does not necessarily mean what is being presented isn't factual. Instead, it is what a particular journalist or news division chooses to focus their time and energy on, how the content is edited, and the time scale in which the information is being distributed that demonstrates partiality. Some of the prejudice even comes from incidents involving the media receiving their talking points directly from the politicians they clearly favor. In her article from November, 2015, "CNN reporter caught red handed coordinating with Hillary aide to smear this GOP candidate," Colleen Conley of TNN News cited tweets before concluding, "Here we have evidence that a foreign relations reporter from one of the world's major news outlets colluded with a top Clinton aide regarding a critically important hearing in order to disparage a conservative demanding answers from the former secretary of state concerning a notorious terror attack on Americans." The hearing was on Benghazi and the conservative she speaks of was Sen. Rand Paul, who dared push Clinton for answers.

In her reference to Sen. Rand Paul's candidacy for president in 2016, Colleen Conley actually highlights the most recent area of extreme media bias. Reporting in presidential elections routinely receives the ire of the general public, but the unfair coverage being offered for the 2016 election is unprecedented. Americans have always demonstrated a disgust for many within the media attempting to frame an election based on soundbites. The practice has almost become acceptable, especially in regards to helping defeat the conservative in the race. However, even some of the most seasoned political pundits are appalled at the failure within the news business today.

Pat Caddell, a long-time Democratic pollster, is shocked by those within the sector to which he's committed most of his adult life. He is a member of "The Political Insiders" on Fox News. In July 2016, his frustrations were visible as he questioned Reuters by saying, "The polling real clear average was dead even 43.7% until Reuters went back and re-allocated their numbers. I've never seen anything like this. I've read carefully the methodological statement and essentially what they decided was people who said "neither," in an election where attitudes are volatile, they just simply decided that there were too many Clinton people who were really going to be for Clinton and they basically—it appears to me—just allocated them to her. And what it produced is a result that is uh uh [sic] that is frankly [sic] it was not tweaking as they said, it was cooking the polls. And I'm a little tired of what's happening in the media, including using every instrument they can to try and put their thumb on the election. And I call on the American Association of Public Opinion, which is supposed to monitor our industry, and ask them to intervene in this. This is outrageous!"

Routinely many of those within the mainstream media can be heard asking supporters of Donald Trump how they feel knowing they are aligned with bigots like David Duke in their shared support of him. The belief is projected that no one could simply be choosing to vote for the Republican presidential nominee based on a number of reasons, such as his recognition of the debt crisis, trade position, or commitment to restoring law and order that has been absent the last eight years. Beyond those on the left who were arguing that everyone should understand that their mutual support of Barack Obama did not represent their agreement with the President's controversial minister, Rev. Jeremiah Wright, few today are willing to promote the same logic.

If some within the mainstream media are going to quiz Trump supporters about the correlation between those on the fringes offering support, where is the same preponderance of similar questions being asked of those supporting other candidates? Did anyone within the mainstream media ask someone supporting Bernie Sanders how they felt having a fellow supporter among their ranks who shot a high -powered weapon in the air at a Trump rally and later bragged about looting during a celebration?

What about similar questions to supporters of the Democratic nominee for president? Wilmot Proviso of the *Conservative Tribune* highlighted the tweets from Clinton campaign worker, Ms. Pinky Stanseski, which supported the Milwaukee uprising following the shooting of Sylville K. Smith. He summarized the contents by writing, "She supports the rioting and looting in Milwaukee, but she wants the whistleblowers who managed to prove the billionaire liberal George Soros was helping manipulate elections in the United States put behind bars?" An absence of comparison prevails; with those favoring Clinton not asked such ridiculous questions regarding other supporters.

Regardless of where their support lies for any particular Democratic candidate, were any questions asked by the mainstream media concerning the affiliation of those present at the 2016 Democratic Convention with others in attendance who demonstrated acts of disrespect? How do others feel about another crowd member yelling "Black Lives Matter" during what was supposed to be a moment of silence for the fallen police officers? How do they respond to being among others who turned their backs on retired four-star General John Allen and Medal of Honor recipient Capt. Florent Groberg?

A eulogy for fallen soldiers—which should have been solemn, regardless of one's individual views on the definite need for greater debate concerning U.S. foreign policy—was interrupted by chants of "no more war." However, chants of "USA" filled the arena, quickly drowning out those chants and proving that few in attendance approved the lack of respect shown; just as a majority in both major parties undoubtedly cheered when Tim Russert put an idiot like David Duke in his place in a 1991 "Meet the Press" appearance.

Running for Governor of Louisiana, the former Grand Wizard of the KKK made an appearance on the program that year and was easily obliterated by Tim Russert's methodical questioning. Russert's condescending demeanor was perfect. In a time of rising tensions, the proclivity of identity politics, and concerted efforts by some to always divide the country, the last thing the people need is the media aiding in useless division.

Although Donald Trump received legitimate criticism for his questioning the ability of Judge Gonzalo Curiel to provide fair rulings in the case involving Trump University, much of the backlash should have been based around the manner in which he raised concerns. With Trump's highly publicized stance against illegal immigration, it is reasonable to ask whether the judge's direct advocacy for the undocumented could affect his judgment; questions of concern which should have instead been raised by his lawyers.

Prof. Victor Williams of Catholic University's Columbus School of Law cited Curiel's tie to La Raza Lawyers Association in supplying the "appearance of a conflict of interest." *The Washington Times* S.A. Miller wrote, "He has specifically participated in events where illegal aliens were celebrated, where illegal aliens were promoted with scholarships." Mr. Williams said of the judge, "On a human basis I say, God bless [illegal immigrants]. But it is clear that from his association with La Raza Lawyers that he has political and ideological affiliation with illegal immigration proponents."

In a speech at the University of California, Berkeley in 2001, now sitting Associate Justice of the Supreme Court, Sonia Sotomayor, said, "I would hope that a wise Latina woman, with the richness of her experiences, would more often than not reach a better conclusion than a white male who hasn't lived that life." The 2009 CNN article also listed the other excerpts from that speech which served as the emphasis of her confirmation hearings. "'Personal experiences affect the facts that judges choose to see,' she said. 'My hope is that I will take the good from my experiences and extrapolate them further into areas with which I am unfamiliar. I simply do not know exactly what the difference will be in my judging. But I accept there will be some based on my gender and my Latina heritage.'" Clearly, she acknowledges race plays a factor in decisions.

Believing that a judge might not follow the law based on differences of opinion on one of the biggest challenges facing the nation is not racist. This is especially true considering the United States allows a wide range of opportunities for judicial activism from the bench. If race alone was the reason someone said an individual in any occupation could not perform their duty, it would be blatantly racist. It all comes down to whether or not someone believes Trump simply misrepresented his actual concern. However, presenting any discussion on how matters involving race may affect someone's judgment as racist is unfounded and counterproductive to dialogue, as even the court has shown it believes that race and gender can play a role in someone's decisions.

A young white male dodged a felony conviction in a traffic incident that tragically resulted in the lost life of an African American female in Alabama. Despite evidence that seemed to have clearly indicated that he was under the influence of a controlled substance as he ran a red light at a rate of speed well above the legal limit, an all-white, male jury ultimately decided to charge him with a misdemeanor. The judge, whose hands were tied by the verdict, was not pleased with the decision of the jury and expressed his desire to give the young man significant jail time for the crime he committed at nineteen years old.

Benie Delinski of *The Times Daily* detailed how Brian Peden, the young man convicted, has consistently projected himself as an individual unable to learn from his mistakes. Clearly, more diversity should have been on the jury and few would call it racist to question the verdict of the jury based on their limited composition. Camille Bennett of Project Say Something provided the family a strong voice for judicial fairness at the sentencing. "She said the all-white, all-male jury did not represent the makeup of the county. She issued a plea that the courts avoid such a situation in the future."

In May 2016, the Supreme Court almost unanimously threw out the conviction of an African-American man in Georgia after it was discovered in convincing notes from 1987 that Blacks were purposely kept off the jury by the prosecution. Although it routinely happens under the disguise of false pretenses by lawyers every day across the country, it is actually illegal to dismiss a juror based specifically on their race or sex.

The result of this decision gives Timothy Tyrone Foster a new trial that might allow him to go free for a murder he already admitted thirty years ago to committing. As *The Washington Post*'s Robert Barnes detailed, "Foster, then 18, was arrested in the killing of Queen Madge White, a 79-year old widow and former elementary school teacher in Rome, GA. According to prosecutors, 'Foster broke into White's home. He broke her jaw, coated her face with talcum powder, sexually molested her with a salad dressing bottle and strangled her to death, all before taking items from her home."

Some political pundits and politicians used the words of Donald Trump regarding Judge Curiel to say that it was a troubling threat to the entire judicial system. However, even if someone agrees with this assessment, how can his words alone be utilized by many of the same individuals to just now begin questioning if the integrity of the judicial branch is in danger of being undermined? The entire lot of U.S. attorneys were assigned ethics courses. President Obama took the unprecedented step of attempting to replace the legislative branch in writing a new law. The Supreme Court, which is supposed to be neutral politically, received the direct ire of President Obama during his State of the Union address. To disregard these actual acts and just now begin questioning whether the court is possibly under siege, based on words alone, has to involve partisan analysis.

Many within the mainstream media almost completely ignored the racist, bigoted, and homophobic rhetoric found within the leaked communications from the Democratic National Committee. Yet, they had no issue continuing to attack Donald Trump over his exchange with the Khans. Whatever the differences, offering anything but gratitude and condolences to Khizr and Ghazala Khan over the loss of their son, U.S. Army Captain Humayun Khan, who was tragically killed in Iraq, is absurd. Questioning whether or not Ghazala Khan could not speak during a time of grief due to her culture was done in extremely poor taste and should have been followed with an immediate apology. However, where is the similar vigor within the press for holding Clinton accountable?

Patricia Smith is the mother of Sean Smith. He was the former Navy Seal and U.S. diplomat who was killed in the attack in Benghazi. On a January 2016 episode of "The Kelly File," she joined Jeremiah and Charles Woods, the brother and father of Tyrone Woods, another former Navy Seal who was killed in the attack, to discuss how Democratic presidential nominee Hillary Clinton had lied to them as Secretary of State.

Before the families spoke, host Megan Kelly had Ed Henry, the Senior White House correspondent for Fox News at the time, lead into the segment with the up-to-date information concerning the former Secretary's reaction to the families' claims. "She did an editorial board meeting with The Daily Sun, that's a newspaper in rural New Hampshire. She said that the families' grief may have clouded their memories saying she can't recall the details when people were sobbing in front of her at Andrews. She was pressed by a columnist for that newspaper who said, 'Look, somebody is lying here, who is it?' Clinton replied, 'Not me, that's all I can tell you.'" Patricia Smith displayed anger and frustration at Henry's update, adamant that Clinton had blamed a video for the attack.

Charles Woods not only disputed Clinton's latest claims, but also read from a notebook he had used to document the words the Secretary had used to comfort him on the loss of his son that day at Andrews. He began by telling Megan Kelly, "Okay, first of all, we have some honorable people here. The members of three other families; they are honorable people. And I don't want to be political. To politicize the death of my son would be dishonoring Ty. All I can do and I did bring my notebook that I carry every year. I've carried these for years. And I'll just read what I said and then I will let people, whether you're Democrat or Republican or Independent, draw your own conclusions."

The words in the notebook were visible on the television screen for everyone at home to view as he read aloud, "I gave Hillary a hug and shook her hand and she said, 'We are going to have the filmmaker arrested who was responsible for the death of your son.'" Despite this documentation from the father of a fallen hero, the press chooses to either once again believe Hillary Clinton or instead decline to offer her a similar rebuke for her disparagement of the families. She actually pointed to them as being liars. The families are one group Clinton cannot label as part of the right-wing conspiracy she conveniently blames for her own lapses in character; though, the media would probably let her.

In speaking to the graduates of Loyal University in New Orleans in November 2015, legendary journalist Bob Woodward said, "It is said that the media is sleeping, lost its investigative zeal, and does not have the patience to dig. There is some truth to that."

Carl Bernstein, who teamed with Bob Woodard in uncovering Watergate, has offered the same bleak assessment of journalism. In a July 2016 appearance on CNN's "Smerconish," he said of the 2016 presidential coverage, "I think that these two candidates represent the most egregious failure by the press in the history [of] modern political reporting. They're the two greatest celebrities in our culture today, worldwide. And yet no major network, no cable network, no major of the three old networks, has done a single investigative biography of either of the candidates up to this point. Not even a documentary about their real existing lives. Only recently have The New York Times, The Washington Post, and The Wall Street Journal started to do really great reporting, which they're doing finally on Trump especially, and a little bit on Hillary Clinton. These two candidates, the most famous people in the world, are un-vetted."

While some may argue that a 2008 candidate named Barack Hussein Obama may not have received any more in-depth vetting than the 2016 candidates for president, Bernstein's point is still valid. It cannot be overlooked that the missing component in each is the absence of Tim Russert, who offered a presence within journalism that led others to raise the quality of their work. More journalists must strive to honor his legacy. One of the issues Carl Bernstein specifically highlighted in hampering the quality of the 2016 coverage was the tendency for journalists to get too caught up in the happenings of the day without much thought regarding the larger picture. In 2013, Bob Dotson, a long-time, award-wining, national correspondent for NBC news, perfectly described some of this in his book *American Story*: "Journalists have little time these days for in-depth reporting. Most are expected to constantly tell what they know as soon as it happens. If reporters are riding in a car and the right front tire goes flat, they typically hop out, glance at the tire, and then start tweeting. Maybe they come back a few months later to lament the fact that the right tire is still flat."

When it comes to the nominees for president, tax information, previous or ongoing lawsuits, business practices, past associations, outcomes from leadership, paid speeches to tech companies and Wall Street, and ties to foreign governments should all be on the table. Americans deserve to be given this information without self-serving bias.

During the 2016 Democratic Convention, Bill O'Reilly brought Kimberly Guilfoyle and Lis Weil of Fox News onto his show to provide an analysis of Trump lawsuits. On www.billoreilly.com, the host offers daily recaps of his "O'Reilly Factor."

As part of his summary of what the two attorneys found in their July 2016 analysis, he documented Weil as saying, "He's been victorious in 451, he has lost 38, while 500 lawsuits were dismissed and 175 were settled. We were able to discover only 60 ordinary Americans who sued him in 30 years." The summary continues, "Guilfoyle opined that Trump's history is not unusual for a billionaire tycoon. 'He isn't afraid to use the court system to defend himself, which is his right. A majority of the cases have come from casinos, and there you often have to use the court system if someone owes you money.' As for Hillary Clinton's claim that Trump has routinely stiffed working men and women, Guilfoyle declared, 'That is a false and misleading statement.'"

Obviously, other attorneys should offer an analysis, but at least it is an effort to go beyond airing just the talking points that only offer a view from the surface. Reporters should dig deep into each of their pasts with the same level of passion for informing the American people. That is not happening. Differences in the amount of focus placed on previous ties to educational institutions offer one of the most striking areas of partiality. While the mainstream media ridiculed Donald Trump over the claims of those who were suing him over their experience with Trump University, few took time to mention the Bill and Hillary Clinton association with Laureate Education. As the piece from Guy Benson of townhall.com clearly spelled out, the school is very similar to Trump University in the criticisms and lawsuits filed. Treatment from the State Department through the extent of grants is questionable, just as Bill Clinton's receiving "$16.5 million between 2010 and 2014 to serve as honorary chancellor for Laureate International University," as reported by the great legal scholar, Professor Jonathan Turley.

In his June 2016, article, Guy Benson demonstrated how Donald Trump could have dictated the media coverage of Laureate if he had only taken action. He wrote, "Much of the media is going to have to be forced into covering the story. You know who could have helped make that happen a lot sooner? Donald J. Trump and his giant megaphone. Imagine if he'd spent his time basically saying, 'I'm not going to comment on an upcoming trial, but I'm confident we'll win. But if you're so curious about alleged fraud at a university, why aren't you talking at all about Bill and Hillary Clinton and the Laureate Education scandal? That actually involved lots of money from taxpayers.'"

Within that same month, syndicated columnist Cal Thomas cited the article from Guy Benson and offered the same type of assessment as to what he believes the Trump campaign should begin doing. "Trump should ask why the media are engaging in a near total black-out of Laureate Education and the enormous flow of money to the Clintons and their foundation of governments, institutions, and individuals." He concluded his article by writing, "Speaking of qualifications, perhaps no president, or presidential candidate has been bought and paid for more than Hillary Clinton. She comes to this contest not with a long list of accomplishments, but with a trail of 'receipts' and IOUs. If she becomes president, donors might reasonably be expected to collect on their investments."

While the mainstream media places a consistent emphasis on Trump's decision not to release his tax returns and searches through old filings for answers, few reports have been made concerning the hidden transcripts of Hillary Clinton's speeches to Wall Street. In an age where almost everyone is making a recording on their individual phones, it seems hard to believe nothing can be unearthed. From documenting incidents involving the police to the secret recording that captured the 47% comment at a fundraiser that virtually ended Mitt Romney's bid for president, it is likely something exists. Either the press is not working hard enough to discover it or the event planners at the Wall Street meetings took major precautions to protect the secrecy of what Clinton told them.

Every American should be concerned with any individual or group possessing the ability to unlawfully gain access to private information—more so if it is a foreign government—but the sad reality is that the content released from WikiLeaks has brought the accountability the mainstream media and the government denied. With the release of leaked segments of communication at the DNC, as well as highlighting the actions of Hillary Clinton that the American people deserve scrutinized, WikiLeaks has promoted some fairness to the coverage of the 2016 presidential elections. It is unfortunate that it has come to this, but should anything be surprising as to the 2016 coverage leaning to Hillary, when a number of major media organizations donated to the Clinton Foundation?

An article in *The Washington Post* from 2013 provided insight into why some of the bias is undoubtedly produced, especially in terms of the media characteristically leaning left. In the article, *The Washington Post*'s Paul Farhi documented the major ties between the government and the mainstream media by writing, "The list of prominent news people with close White House relations includes ABC News President Ben Sherwood, who is the brother of Elizabeth Sherwood-Randall, a top national security advisor for President Obama. His counterpart at CBS, news division president David Rhodes, is the brother of Benjamin Rhodes, a key foreign-policy specialist. CNN's deputy Washington bureau chief, Virginia Moseley, is married to Tom Nides, who until earlier this year was deputy secretary of state under Hillary Rodham Clinton."

While obviously there are some variances in where the people Paul Farhi list are now working, the content of his article provides an accurate portrayal of the inner connections that provide the liberal bias often witnessed in the press. It starts at the top. The media—which is supposed to help the people keep their governmental officials more accountable—are insulated with similar obstacles to changing the status quo in D.C. In an article for *The Huffington Post* from August 2015, investigative historian Eric Zuesse described how the news business works with more money in politics to help promote the oligarchy. He wrote, "Already, the major 'news' media were owned and controlled by the aristocracy, and 'freedom of the press' was really just freedom of the aristocrats to control the news'—to frame public issues in the ways the owners want. The media managers who are appointed by those owners select, in turn, the editors who, in their turn, hire only reporters who produce the propaganda that's within the acceptable range for the owners, to be 'the news' as the public comes to know it."

This passing down of ideology in news-reporting explains why most of the mainstream media leans left. In 2014, an article from the Media Research Center, a nonprofit media watchdog, said, "Almost every year from 2001 through 2013, Gallup has polled American adults on the question: 'Now thinking for a moment about the news media. In general, do you think the news media is too liberal, just about right, or too conservative?' Each year, the number of Americans saying the media are too liberal outnumbered those seeing a pro-conservative bias by about a three-to-one margin."

Although much of the criticism is often directed at the liberal bias found within a majority of the media, it shouldn't be overlooked that those who lean more right obviously, to a degree, follow the same practice. Sentencing reform that led to the "largest one-time release of federal prisoners" provides one example. A guest on the Fox Business network placed the release, which could eventually see up to 46,000 inmates set free, on the shoulders of President Obama alone. As an article from the Marshall Project reveals, this misrepresentation overlooks that the decision came from the U.S. Sentencing Commission, an "independent agency of the judicial branch, made up of a bipartisan mix of seven members who vote on punishment guidelines for federal crimes."

The discussion should have instead been on why "the People's" representatives consistently create a void in which the President feels compelled to provide some type of action on the issue at hand. Not only did the U.S. Congress display an inability to put the brakes on the ruling of the Sentencing Commission when it came down in 2014—no action for a year—but it also did nothing to help build an atmosphere for such a release.

At a time of heightened crime and tension, thousands of dangerous convicts—both citizens and illegals included among them—were released. Though the President may have impacted the agency to follow a certain agenda that many within the general public did not agree with, the truth is that those designated to provide the voice of the people in shaping decisions failed to act. Members of the U.S. Congress own the results just as much as the President. Other pertinent information should have been presented by those on the Fox News networks for fairness. Blaming the President was disingenuous.

The negative impact of the greater politicization of the media to the quality of journalism is only enhanced further by the all-important aim for ratings. Funding for in-depth reporting is often cut for other stories that will keep the wheels of the news business going. Almost everyone has heard of the old tale about the news station that remained committed to only airing positive stories that quickly went under from low viewership. Taking into account all the obstacles to genuine journalism, the most ideal method for helping achieve the desired results of The People's Clearing House may exist within the creation of a news division specifically designed to report on the endeavor without prejudice. This aspect is not necessary for success, but would be beneficial. With the transparency found within the structure of The People's Clearing House, this news division could report on all aspects involving campaign finance, from how an incumbent spends their money to where certain lobbyists have a tendency to make campaign donations in relation to the contribution schedule. It will only strengthen the effort being made by groups now to track votes and campaign contributions for building a meaningful correlation, with the enthusiasm of The People's Clearing House for resolve. Having a trusted source could provide a boost to creating and maintaining accountability. More importantly, the news division could serve as a source of inspiration by highlighting the seeds of progress that are occurring as the direct result of new programs and initiatives that resulted from The People's Clearing House. It also highlights the areas where work continues to be needed, as well as keeps those recipients of funds accountable by continuing to cover how the money is being spent. Keeping people informed and invested in the community is the key to successful unity for progress.

Too often within today's news business, the truth has become nothing more than an inconvenience. American citizens need journalists who will begin choosing intellectual honesty over personal propaganda. The People's Clearing House News could create the perfect training ground for future reporters by beginning to install this truth with college interns. They could consistently form the bedrock of the staff at each station. Every state has a plentiful supply of colleges to partner with for proactively producing a greater foundation of service within future reporters before they form a particular bias. Just as with the concept of Teach for America or the Peace Corps, working "for the people" before actually getting into the typical news industry could be priceless in creating a value for remaining committed to the task of simply informing.

If The People's Clearing House was formed within a number of states, creating the news division to accompany it might simply come down to discovering another individual like Ted Turner. Based on an interview from "Your World with Neil Cavuto" in January 2016, this individual may not be as difficult to find as one might think. Appearing on the show that day, Teddy Turner, son of the media mogul who founded CNN, discussed why he estimated the former neurosurgeon was truly unique to the rest of the 2016 presidential field:

> "I love Ben Carson because he's not a politician. Um [sic] we have 9,000 years of collective experience in Washington and we've screwed it up hugely. We owe 20 trillion dollars; no reason, no way to pay it back. You're talking about China and the 4 trillion we owe them. We're in trouble. We're in really deep trouble... From what I've realized running for office and working around politics now, it's not about common sense anymore in Washington. It's about getting elected, getting re-elected and telling the base what they want to hear and most of all these candidates do that. Ben doesn't do that. He's like sitting with your grandfather talking about common sense things the way they should be. That I love about him."

While the mainstream media scrambles for ratings, Americans will embrace a non-partisan outlet that works to keep all politicians more accountable. While bias and the all-mighty dollar will lead many within the media to spin issues or opt instead for entertainment stories, The People's Clearing House News could work diligently to live up to the distinct protection within the Constitution that President Kennedy highlighted for aiding them in living up to the vital duty of keeping the general public well-informed. Individuals and small businesses of all political stripes would support the mutual endeavor of creating more equality in representation for raising the genuine diversity of voices deciding the laws governing the country. Any revenue from advertisement could also be used to further strengthen the united effort. What business would not want the distinction of helping the people reclaim ownership of the country entrusted to them? The People's Clearing News provides an opportunity for people inside and outside of the news industry to play a significant role in shaping the quality of coverage being offered.

What Can Be Achieved Once Genuine Leadership Is in Place

With current issues, from stagnant wages and civil unrest at home to the complexities of globalization and the rise of ISIS abroad, what President Kennedy said over half a century ago still applies today. "America faces challenges greater than any which it has faced before. This is no time for complacency. This is no time to abandon the drive and the optimism and the imaginative creativity which have characterized this country since its birth. This is no time for timidity or doubt. This is a time for boldness and energy. This is a time for stouthearted men who can turn dreams into reality."

The characteristics of the citizenry that John F. Kennedy so eloquently described have remained, but the leadership needed to harness those attributes has been almost entirely absent for some time. Money is exchanged for votes. Bills are laden with giveaways and non -related measures of self-interest, paid for with budgetary gimmicks and future IOUs that rely on a level of fiscal restraint consistently rejected. These are just a few of the ways government is a resistor, as opposed to a facilitator, of actual progress.

An unidentified Hispanic American who was part of a Frank Luntz focus group following the 2016 State of the Union clearly understood that only in addressing the foundation of our representation will genuine achievement become possible. As he spoke, you could hear that resolve in his voice, so often present when someone feels they are speaking the truth. He stood and confidently said, "Let me be very clear about this, is [sic] that um [sic] we are living in an oligarchy form of government and I believe that once that is taken care of, that we will be able to tackle, you know, the real issues."

Unfortunately, until the people unite and reform the current political system to demand more accountability and transparency from those that lead, representatives will continue to offer the choice of picking between the least of two evils. Crony capitalism and extreme ideology that garners reliable votes will keep the status quo securely in place. No chance will exist for pragmatism and compromise for solving chronic issues. The need for infrastructure investment, growth in renewable/alternative energy, balance between fracking and environmental concerns, better community and police relations, urban renovation and revitalization, and reforms in campaign finance, immigration, prisons, criminal justice, regulation, civil asset forfeiture, Wall Street, and the Federal Reserve are just a few areas in which legislation will remain idle. Leadership must be capable of producing answers from a place of strength and based on a vision.

All throughout government are examples of what happens when there is an inadequacy in leadership. Many are shocked to learn that the Environmental Protection Agency, or EPA, was actually established under President Nixon. The Republican took a page from the passion of Teddy Roosevelt for conservation. However, as with so many other governmental endeavors, while the initial aim was admirable, it transformed into something never intended. Under a supportive president, an unpredictable court, and a weak legislative branch, the EPA has been allowed to blatantly overextend its power. Beyond the detrimental effect to businesses as a result of unnecessary regulation, with a deficiency in proper restraint often comes a culture of inefficiency, waste, and fraud—as currently being witnessed at the Environmental Protection Agency. The Hill's Devin Henry detailed a House Oversight Committee from April 2015 that discussed the sexual harassment, watching of porn, and falsification of records that had taken place. Yet, regardless of the infraction, bringing accountability is virtually impossible; most workers are either moved to another sector or retire before any true punishment can be given as a future deterrent. The mantra seems to be: keep the earth clean while spreading filth everywhere else. However, none of these failures in character likely kept EPA officials from being self-righteous in the fines they imposed on others.

In a speech from late June 2016, Sen. Elizabeth Warren (D-MA) stated, "Anyone who loves markets knows that for markets to work, there has to be competition." She went on to explain, "But today, in America, competition is dying. Consolidation and concentration are on the rise in sector after sector. Concentration threatens our markets, threatens our economy, and threatens our democracy."

Noticeably absent from her specific rebuke of large tech companies like Apple, Google, and Amazon was the more pertinent issue of these companies always seeking the expansion of visas that result in the loss of American jobs. The senator may also find a more welcoming reception when it comes to competition if she began by taking on the daughter of her friend Sen. Joe Manchin, who practically seems to be running a monopoly on EpiPens. As CEO of Mylan, Heather Bresch, his daughter, earns $19 million, while the price of the lifesaving device has gone to over $600. And Republicans are presented as heartless. Nevertheless, in a 2015 republican debate, Carly Fiorina offered words that perfectly undermine the premise Warren offered months later.

As part of her answer on how to address Obamacare moving forward, the former candidate for president said, "Who helped write the bill? Drug companies, insurance companies, pharmaceutical companies. Every single one of those kinds of companies are [sic] bulking up to deal with big government. See that's what happens. As government gets bigger, and bigger—and it has been for 50 years under republicans and democrats alike—and [sic] business have [sic] to bulk up to deal with big government."

Small businesses are the driving force of the American economy, but the last thing the country needs is the government further attempting to pick winners and losers. Adequate representation, good tax policy, and less regulation is the key. Fiorina highlighted these points in saying, "The truth is the secret sauce of America is innovation and entrepreneurship. It is why we must cut our government down to size and hold it accountable. It's why we have to take our government back, because innovation and entrepreneurship is crushed by the crushing load of a 73,000-page tax code."

In referencing healthcare, Carly Fiorina actually brings up what should serve as another cautionary tale in what poor representation can produce. Of course healthcare needed reform, but the legislation that was passed was built on lies, manipulation, and giveaways to special interests. The true interests of the people were barely considered. The orchestrated photo op of doctors at the White House was a foreshadowing of failure.

In his book *America the Beautiful*, former 2016 presidential candidate and retired neurosurgeon Ben Carson wrote, "Providing basic healthcare for every citizen can be done quite easily without increasing our national debt one penny. If we address our inefficient and wasteful billing and collections procedures, move to a national electronic medical record, provide people with incentives to use clinics instead of emergency rooms for primary care, and engage in meaningful tort reform to limit costly lawsuits, we would have plenty of money to provide basic health care to all citizens of this country."

While numerous aspects of the Affordable Care Act could be pointed to in making a correlation between its inclusion and the desire of special interests, Dr. Carson provided an interesting interaction with Howard Dean shortly before the bill was passed. The former DNC chair was speaking on healthcare. Carson wrote, "Someone asked [Dean] the question, 'Why is tort reform not included in the healthcare bill?' 'It's really quite simple,' he replied. The Trial Lawyers Association gives us [the Democratic Party] a great deal of money, and they don't want it in there."

Democratic lawmakers rarely go beyond their tired rhetoric concerning all the individuals they added to the rolls of healthcare to draw any correlations between the direct and indirect effects of a poorly written bill. Republicans, on the other hand, attempt to place themselves on a moral high ground, despite not offering much of anything that would actually alleviate the waste and inefficiencies still present today. Either way, American families are feeling the effects of higher premiums, as well as stressing over whether their healthcare exchange will join the list of closures. The corrupt culture the bill was built upon remains characteristic in realization, according to Doug Badger. He wrote an article in July 2016 informing readers on the deliberate mismanagement of Obamacare. The House Ways and Means committee released a report that same month on "how the administration came to unlawfully funnel $7 billion in unappropriated money to insurers through a single Obamacare program."

Of course, bypassing the House of Representatives and unilaterally deciding how to spend federal funds could be called a trademark of the Obama administration, with a September 2016 article from George Will highlighting the allocation of fines imposed on the big banks as just one of the other instances. "Justice allows banks to meet some of their settlement obligations by directing 'donations' to various nongovernmental advocacy organizations that serve Democratic constituencies and objectives—organizations that were neither parties to the case nor victims of the banks' behaviors."

In regards to the funds involved with Obamacare, Doug Badger, a senior fellow with the Galen Institute, offered congressional testimony in July 2016. In his testimony, the former White House and U.S. senate policy advisor utilized his past knowledge and experience to "show how the government's unlawful spending on the CSR program fits into a broader pattern of malfeasance in Obamacare implementation. That malfeasance included decisions made during the first half of 2014 to unlawfully divert $3.5 billion to $4.5 billion from the Treasury to insurance companies through the 'reinsurance' program. It also involves the attempt by the government to turn the law's 'risk corridor' program into a new version of the Troubled Asset Relief Program (TARP), forcing taxpayers to cover losses resulting from bad business decisions made by insurance executives."

As if picking up the tab for those who recklessly speculate wasn't already enough for the taxpayer, some in government join the ranks of those on Wall Street they routinely rail against in taking advantage of the people. In both instances there is very little recourse for the people, as the Justice Department can't be counted on to hold anyone accountable in the private or public sector unless it is politically driven. A report that the Justice Department essentially told the FBI to stand down on its desire to investigate the Clinton Foundation for corruption—an instance involving the public and private sector—may demonstrate best the absence of a genuine moral compass.

Just as with the foundation of character being vital to the type of legislation you can expect from a representative, poorly written policies built on crony capitalism and special interests will lead to a domino effect of negative outcomes. Few Democrats will stop defending the healthcare bill long enough to acknowledge the reality that many within the forgotten middle class are now going into Mexico for cheaper medical care. In November 2015, Alexa D'Angelo of Cronkite News wrote an article on the specific driving forces behind U.S. citizens crossing the border for care. However, the only line necessary for clarity on the matter: "A new study from the Common Wealth Fund, a private foundation that aims to promote a high-performance healthcare system, revealed about 23 percent of Americans with coverage are considered underinsured—up from 12 percent in 2003 since the inception of Obamacare in 2012."

Healthcare must be reformed with genuine leadership. While there will always be good people and organizations in the world, others will unfortunately follow politicians in being driven by the money that can be made from the flawed system. On his HBO show "Last Week Tonight," John Oliver forgave the $15 million in medical bills accumulated by thousands of people by purchasing their debt for only $60,000. Not only did he display the type of humanity the world could use more of, but he also shed light on how failures in governmental policy create a vacuum for new problems that few consider.

The AP's David Bauder detailed Oliver's account of the situation: "Institutions often sell their debt for pennies on the dollar to companies who then attempt to collect on the bills. These companies operate with little regulation and sometimes employ shady and abusive collectors who try to intimidate people into paying."

While terrible, nothing can compare to the level that drug companies will stoop in shamelessly taking advantage of a broken medical system; a system in which few are advocates for the American people. As Harris Gardiner of *The New York Times* reported in March 2016, "The federal Medicare program and private health insurers waste nearly $3 billion every year buying cancer medicines that are thrown out because many drug makers distribute the drugs only in vials that hold too much for most patients." While over 80% of the waste could be eliminated by offering individualized doses, lost revenue is too precious. In borrowing from Obama's historic campaign: "We can do better."

Representatives create subpar legislation that limits achievement and routinely results in unnecessary hardships for many, but neither of these characteristics keep many within government from believing that they are still the best suited to solve issues. Failures in legislation are blamed on those carrying it out, not on the ones who wrote it. The reaction of lawmakers to corporate inversion, or the decision of a company to relocate their operations to another country for better tax treatment, might provide the best insight. Reforming the tax code and creating a pro-business environment through less regulation is the answer, but members of Congress commonly place the blame on companies only acting in their best business interests. While Gov. Chris Christie suggested addressing the effects of corporate inversion by possibly placing a one-time tax on the estimated 2 trillion dollars currently overseas, he and most others realize the most productive method for handling the matter is not to try and force businesses back, but instead to create an arena that entices them. Yet, the government once again disregards any responsibility and seeks to poison the market.

The White House, despite lacking a record worthy of any credibility, weighed in on the problem of tax evasion by proposing more rules regarding disclosure. However, the administration also encouraged lawmakers to ratify a number of tax treaties that Sen. Rand Paul (R-KY) soundly rejected. The senator was concerned, with good reason. Detailed tax information widely distributed to foreign governments would be unwise.

Although the Obama administration was correctly put in its place by Senator Paul, House Republicans demonstrated a similar belief that they were the ones best positioned to control regulations despite the record for mistrust they have created. The Reins Act, or Regulations from the Executive in Need of Scrutiny Act, would allow them to approve or reject some regulations. At the time, former Speaker of the House John Boehner (R-OH) said, "The REINS Act will help by giving Congress—the people's representatives—the opportunity to stop new rules that will hurt the economy or raise costs for hardworking families." While few like being at the mercy of bureaucrats, representatives shouldn't be mistaken to believe they offer any greater faith in fairness.

What is most striking is the confidence legislators try to project when attempting to pass new legislation, as if the government has not proven from one failure after another that actual efficiency is either non-existent or rarely sought. Either they truly believe that each piece of new legislation has the potential to be different from previous results or lawmakers simply don't care as long as the wheels of the status quo keep spinning. In a discussion from May 2016 concerning the unsuccessful attempt to fund Zika prevention, Andrew Taylor of the Associate Press wrote, "The Senate is moving ahead this week with a $1.1 billion plan and agreed with Obama that the money should be added to the budget deficit rather than be 'offset' with cuts to other programs." Of course, adding it to the deficit was chosen. Why make difficult decisions around elections when a lawmaker can simply place more debt on the backs of future generations?

Until genuine leadership exists, how can anyone trust any number given? From past history, it seems obvious a number of people merely sit in a room and throw around stats and figures that sound good and include all the desired handouts to special interests. There are never any consequences to fear from the process. There is always the opportunity to allocate more. Finding someone in America who actually believes $1.1 billion would be properly spent by the government on Zika would be virtually impossible.

It would be like Abraham asking God to spare the wicked people of Sodom and Gomorrah if he were able to discover 50 righteous individuals within the city's walls. Though God was willing, Abraham could not discover these 50. Abraham continued bargaining with God to ten people, but was still as unsuccessful.

Beyond the ongoing inefficiency, there's always the potential attempt of the man or woman in the Oval Office to take advantage of power if unchecked. In specific relation to Zika, who's to say that President Obama won't just seek more vagueness in future legislation from allies in Congress to again offer him the opportunity to quietly send more funds to his prized United Nations Green Climate Fund. According to Senator James Lankford (R-OK), President Obama took $500 million from State Department funds that had been allocated for "fighting infectious diseases" and instead gave them to the Climate Fund. It seems the President was determined to chip away at the $3 billion he unilaterally promised the U.N., despite not ever receiving the necessary approval of the U.S. Congress to make such a payment. Once again, a failure in leadership in the legislature provided the President an opening he was more than willing to exploit. At this point, D.C. could legitimately be named "King Obama and his court of useless subjects." Moral courage is virtually non-existent.

While many liberals may revel in the current power of the executive branch to basically rewrite the Constitution, it could always work both ways. A future Republican president could take the same opportunistic approach. A powerless legislative branch, unable to provide the intended check, should be worrisome to those who believe in democracy. The legislative branch must begin fulfilling its duty. Other than *The Washington Journal*'s estimate of "18 trillion in new spending over a decade" that Bernie Sanders' proposals would have brought, the failure of the legislative branch to effectively hold the executive branch accountable is actually the main reason electing him would be so dangerous. America was never supposed to be a country built on unilateral executive orders and actions. Unlike orders, executive actions can be put into motion behind the scenes before the general public is ever made aware of them.

Senator Sanders made clear through his words as a candidate that he would provide more of the same in terms of executive orders. The consequential impact of just a few of Obama's executive orders cannot be lost on Americans in choosing a successor. Four to eight more years of orders with no recourse from the legislative branch would be disastrous. Attempting to rein in representatives and agencies that blindly follow self-serving practices without considering how citizens are impacted is daunting enough. The people need an ally at 1600 Pennsylvania Avenue, not a facilitator of business as usual.

Career politicians who have consistently remained within this culture drift further and further from the reality of government inefficiency, remaining confident in the ability of government to provide reliable service. Being out of touch with what is actually happening on Main Street is unfortunate; being out of touch with reality in terms of policies that directly enhance the threats to national security is reckless and dangerous.

At a rally in Buena Park, California, in May 2016, the future Democratic nominee for president, Hillary Clinton, told the crowd, "And I want you to compare this. See, I [sic] want to fix our schools, our bridges, our roads, our ports, our airports, our water systems. Donald Trump wants to build a wall. A great big wall as he says, a huge wall. And he says he is going to make Mexico pay for it. Now the best estimates I've seen is that this wall would cost, oh, at least $25 billion. That is enough to build 16 Golden Gate Bridges, or 1,500 new elementary schools. It is enough to send more than 300,000 veterans to college or install enough renewable energy to power 5 million homes. We sure could help a lot of hardworking Americans if we took the money and invested it here and made a real difference in the lives, and the jobs, and schools, and the opportunities that Americans have. So we have a real choice in this election."

On the surface, her words on more infrastructure investment obviously resonate with almost all Americans. However, though the $25 billion may seem wasteful to spend on more border security within the context Clinton offers, there are other pertinent estimates that should be considered. As Fox New's Brian Kilmeade revealed in 2016, "More than 100 billion dollars a year is spent to house and feed illegal immigrants."

In June 2016, Michelle Malkin, a well-known conservative, provided insight on just a few of the governmental programs that illegals are benefitting from. She penned an article on the routine abuse of the earned income tax credit (EITC), racking up $15 ½ billion in 2015 alone, with the undocumented being among those consistently subverting the system. She also pointed out, "Illegal immigrants using individual taxpayer identification numbers have scammed another refundable tax credit program, the Additional Child Tax Credit, to the tune of $4.2 billion a year, according to tax watchdogs." Just another program with admirable intentions of producing upward mobility, morphing into a dependency never intended to be; your government at work.

The confidence Hillary Clinton exudes in what could be accomplished with the estimates she offers is absurd. Just as with the Zika funding, almost every American can already predict what would happen with a bulk of the money if allocated toward the projects mentioned at her rally. Abandoned schools, half-constructed bridges, equipment deteriorating, multiple workers standing idle, and officials explaining the need for additional funds are just a few of the images that come to mind. Any citizen doubting this expected inefficiency need only look at the U.S. Capitol dome still under renovation.

Though Hillary Clinton (in her speech) rejected the notion of a more secure border with a false confidence in governmental efficiency that is similar to other long-term lawmakers, career bureaucrats, and political insiders, her view is more dangerous because it puts national security at risk. Anyone who believes government could actually achieve her proposals with the $25 billion blindly believes agencies are doing adequate work. Then again, should the confidence Clinton articulated in the federal government be a surprise considering she is the same woman who downplayed the intensity of the problems at the V.A. in an interview to MSNBC's Rachel Maddow from October 2015?

Clinton's words at the rally only confirm that current practices and ideology leading federal agencies are acceptable to her and many others inside the Beltway who function within an alternative universe. Citizens outside the protective walls she and others in government enjoy have little chance to be acknowledged under her leadership. Following President Obama's directive that opened access to all bathrooms for transgendered individuals, Attorney General Loretta Lynch held a news conference and emotionally stated, "But no matter how isolated or scared you may feel today, the Department of Justice and the entire Obama administration wants you to know that we see you; we stand with you; and we will do everything we can to protect you going forward. Please know that history is on your side. This country was founded on a promise of equal rights for all, and we have always managed to move closer to that promise, little by little, one day at a time. It may not be easy—but we'll get there together."

For many American families, watching the Attorney General offer these words must have been difficult and it has nothing to do with the people she chose to support that day. Instead, her words of acknowledgement and encouragement are something individuals who continue to suffer from the loss of family members to the undocumented have been longing to hear for some time. Regardless of what is being offered, it should be recognized from her own reference to the "promise of equal rights for all" that every American deserves the same amount of passion and vigor in affording them protection. Laura Wilkerson, whose son was savagely murdered by an undocumented immigrant, reminded Congress and the Attorney General at a hearing from April 2016 that if she actually took the time to listen, then they would see that the rule of law is meant to protect all citizens. "The thing that you can do is enforce laws. How do you pick and choose a law? I don't understand it—how you pick and choose a law. The laws are here to be enforced by who? By you, and they're not being enforced, and my kid suffered terribly for it."

Melanie Hunter of CNSnews.com also detailed Laura Wilkerson courageously and unapologetically telling lawmakers that day, "I did not put my kid in harm's way when he went to school that day. You did. Every one of you is elected by an American. It is time for you to stand in the gap for Americans. I'm so tired of being up here and going over the same thing. You're elected by Americans. Do something. It is your job."

This same balance of consideration has been demonstrated with the treatment of those killed by terrorist acts. The Justice Department is so driven to protect Muslims living within America from any potential backlash that the Attorney General even shied away from releasing the transcript from the terror attack at the Pulse nightclub in Orlando without editing out the attacker's confirmation of being affiliated with ISIS.

Once again, while the endeavor to protect the majority of American Muslims and undocumented immigrants from backlash is admirable, the absence of a similar effort in protecting other Americans in order to protect a policy agenda through a certain narrative is unconscionable. All Americans deserve better. It is not the AG's job to decide who to protect if the words of the Constitution actually mean as much to her as she articulates. The grieving mother, who the President, the Attorney General, and a host of Democratic lawmakers have placed at the bottom of their priority list through their words and policy decisions, also detailed the method the killer admitted to using in Josh's murder; at one point, he became frustrated because her son wouldn't die. There were plans for a night out at the movies and everything involved in killing Josh—such as disposing of the body by taking the young American to a "field and [setting] his body on fire"—threatened his planned night out. American citizens deserve better.

The United States Attorney General doesn't have to blindly follow the President, as Nixon's Attorney General proved when he courageously decided to resign over principle. Loretta Lynch has the same opportunity, but the chances are dim, as she has obviously forgotten the words of John Adams from 1775, when he wrote, "The dignity and stability of government in all its branches, the morals of the people, and every blessing of society depend on an upright and skillful administration of justice."

The integrity of the Justice Department has been in question for some time. Who could forget District Judge Andrew Hanen's rebuke of DOJ attorneys, under the Attorney General's watch, who blatantly lied to the judge about operations of a program in which "more than 100,000 immigrants who qualified as parents of American born children were granted protective status." The order to stop the ongoing proceedings had been ignored.

Attorney General Lynch should sit in the front row of the ethics training the judge assigned the U.S. attorneys after citing how the lesson of truth was learned in the movie "Miracle on 34th Street." Analyzing their actions, the judge said, "Clearly, there seems to be a lack of knowledge about or adherence to the duties of professional responsibility in the halls of the Justice Department." From these words, it's obvious if the judge taught the class, he would certainly explain to the Attorney General why it was unethical to meet with former President Clinton while still deciding on whether or not to indict his wife.

Failed leadership, built upon career politicians and partisan politics, created much of the mess we're in today. Those same characteristics also keep them from correcting it. And so the Attorney General continues the common practice of government in selecting winners and losers, mostly through the act of bullying. By late March 2016, "Attorney General Lynch [had] issued a warning to municipal and state judges across the country that their courts could lose federal funding if they don't ease up on fines and arrest warrants for minor crimes involving poor offenders, indigent minorities in particular."

Lynch's message to judges was sent through the old trusted "guidance letters," or blackmail letters, for advancing her threats. As Paul Sperry of the *New York Post* noted, "This is the same dubious legal threat the administration is using to force the nation's public schools to back off suspending unruly—even violent—black students, and to force cops to avoid stopping, frisking and arresting minority offenders." Not surprisingly, the Attorney General, the President, and few Democrats in Congress point out that much of the abuse in monetary penalties come at the hands of cities run by Democrats who simply need the additional revenue in attempting to fund their massive social welfare.

Here again, in the endeavor to protect one group, the rest of the country is forgotten. California Proposition 47 provides the perfect example of what can result from being lax on crime. Voters approved a measure that made $950 the benchmark for stolen items in order for it to be considered a misdemeanor and actually carry meaningful penalties to serve as a deterrent. "The ballot measure also lowered penalties for forgery, fraud, petty theft, and drug possession."

As a result of this ill-advised policy, crime predictably rose almost immediately, making it even harder for small businesses—as if they needed any other obstacles—to find success. Practically every day business owners are being forced to spend vital time protecting their merchandise from thieves. Attorney General Lynch, who lives behind rank and money, would conclude using a threat to blindly protect a narrow interest would be the most logical approach. The needless hardship it brings to the majority of hardworking, law-abiding citizens clearly carries little value in her decisions.

Should future questionable actions from the U.S. Attorney General's office ever come as a surprise? Regardless of any past history, this department under her watch proved it couldn't even handle a social media account. Then again, maybe the tweet from the U.S. Department of Justice's official account attacking Melania Trump over her speech at the Republican National Convention was one of the most honest reflections of how partisan the department has truly become under President Obama and his minions.

While it was eventually blamed on a staffer, one can't help but wonder whether in the course of texting each other about their grandkids while watching the convention, former President Bill Clinton didn't suggest the idea to Attorney General Lynch. This is mere speculation, as no proof exists of such a conversation. And even if one had occurred, the tweet being sent would have had nothing to do with their chitchat. The decisions that come from her department continue to put Americans lives at great risk. If it wasn't bad enough that Americans were simply suffering from policies related to domestic issues without a peep from the Justice Department, the Attorney General seems to believe that showering the world with more love will be the answer to preventing terrorism from the outside. Placing aside those needlessly killed by the undocumented, speaking to the LGBT community following the shooting at the Pulse nightclub that took the lives of 49 innocent people and wounded fifty: "Our common humanity transcends our differences, and our most effective response to terror is compassion, it's unity and it's love." This couldn't have been said any better even if someone were to believe that ISIS was nothing more than a JV team.

If someone were to analyze State Department spokeswoman Marie Harf's statements from February 2015 that pointed to creating jobs for ISIS as offering the solution, President Obama's predominant focus on relieving any anti-Muslim backlash, and the theme of "love is the answer" found in the rhetoric from Attorney General Lynch, convincing conclusions can be drawn regarding their desired treatment of ISIS. The consensus on defeating ISIS would be in offering economic support, avoiding the terrorist label, and sending the terrorist savages the love necessary for a change of heart.

In a broader sense, this ill-advised plan for addressing a worldwide terrorist organization like ISIS is exactly what has been followed in dealing with a state that sponsors terrorism like Iran. The nuclear deal stimulated their economy. The President essentially disregarded their ties to terrorism and provided the terrorists able recruits with his unilateral decision to release detainees from Gitmo. As if that wasn't enough, the 100 million in an unmarked aircraft to Iran provided the money to purchase those recruits. It definitely seems ridiculous on the surface; but then again, according to the State Department spokeswoman, your average citizen is too dumb to understand it. This is the same State Department that relies on the perceived stupidity of the American people to actually believe the $400 million secretly sent to Iran through a disguised flight around the same time the hostages were released was only coincidental and not a ransom.

This is also the same flawed agency that believes buying advanced microchips for all U.S. security devices and weaponry from the Middle East is wise. As Wilmot Proviso of the *Conservative Tribune* documented of the Pentagon in June 2016, "'Our goal is to look globally,' said Andre Gudger, the Pentagon's deputy assistant secretary for manufacturing and industrial base policy. 'We want access to the latest and the greatest.'" Either the Pentagon heavily recruited within some of the misinformed Americans they apparently routinely rely upon or State Department officials aren't as smart as they think.

Rob O'Neill, the former Navy SEAL credited with killing Osama bin Laden, is one man who couldn't allow the words of State Department spokeswoman Marie Harf concerning a winning economic strategy to go unchallenged. He told Fox News, "They get paid to cut off heads—to crucify children, to sell slaves and cut off heads—and I don't think that a change in career path is what's going to stop them."

An article from Mark Finkelstein, contributing editor of NewsBusters, documented how MSNBC's Chris Matthews joined in on the rebuke of Marie Harf's articulated assessment by saying, "This sounds like we're going to get rid of juvenile delinquency in America over time by erasing poverty and improving education. Sure, over time. But the American people, I think, are getting humiliated morally by this."

Upon hearing the same type of failed rhetoric following an ISIS attack in Dhaka, Bangladesh, which killed over 20 people, Taslima Nasreen responded to these explanations of poverty being at the root of effective radicalization by tweeting, "All Dhaka terrorists were from rich families, studied in elite schools. Pl (please) do not say poverty & illiteracy make people Islamic terrorists." Taslima should know, as the Bangladeshi author and human rights activist was forced to leave the country due to her views on women's rights. Unlike those behind the secure walls of Washington, she has firsthand knowledge of what people living among hate actually have to experience.

Beyond the general threat to the safety of every American from outside forces, poor leadership continues to trickle down to agencies and politicians, threatening the inalienable rights of all citizens to liberty and the pursuit of happiness. Though many in the heights of government have gone out of their way to protect the due process of federal employees—highlighted best as the central obstacle to reforming the Veterans Affairs Agency—few on either side of the major political aisle have spoken up in outrage over the due process that is shockingly being disregarded on a number of college campuses. George Will wrote an article in May 2016 that addressed the falsehood of the "one-in-five" statistic given by certain advocates as representative of those actually being raped on college campuses, as well as demonstrated how the government is advancing its desired partisan agenda through pressure. The well-respected, syndicated columnist wrote, "In 2011, the Education Department's civil rights office sent 'dear colleague' letters to schools directing them to convict accused persons on a mere 'preponderance' of evidence. Schools were instructed not to allow accused students to cross-examine their accusers, but to allow accusers to appeal non-guilty verdicts, a form of double jeopardy."

Title IX, which protects students from being discriminated against due to gender, is the catalyst being used by the government to overextend its hand in threatening schools with the removal of allocated funds. In speaking of federal funds—beyond even the slightest chance of removal to sanctuary cities—the Obama administration has remained consistent in the practice of bullying those to comply on issues it cannot enforce through actual law or convince by debate; in this case, even with the clear removal of rights. Legal representation and the idea of "innocent until proven guilty" are absent from the proceedings routinely taking place on college campuses. Innocent lives are being ruined.

As referenced in the article from George Will, Grant Neal, who was at one time a student at Colorado State University-Pueblo, is one of those lives that has been unjustly affected. He is suing his former school for expelling him over a sexual encounter with a woman who agrees it was completely consensual. The words of another girl who knew his sexual partner and assumed the worse after spotting a "hickey on her neck" served as the driving force in the proceedings that disregarded the words of the two parties involved. Along with his lawsuit against the school, Grant is also taking the federal Education Department to court for virtually ordering the school to deprive him of his rights.

There is always a need for more effort to be placed in the protection of women. The long-term effect to victims of sexual abuse or rape cannot be understated. One look at the headlines of rape convictions ending in probation or short-sentencing reveals the necessity for continued emphasis. However, although the Justice Department commonly disregards the basic notion that one group of citizens does not deserve a level of protection that results in the removal of fundamental rights to others, there must be a fight for all. Those in government need to recognize that very few issues involve an all-or-nothing choice. In the zeal to establish an atmosphere of greater trust and safety for women, new victims of men possessing similar innocence need not be created. Countless numbers of men and women who are innocent—most likely composed of African Americans—currently sit in 6x8 prison cells because the accuser was believed. Organizations such as the California Innocence Project are specifically designed to set those wrongly accused free. In the case of the California Innocence Project, one of its most publicized cases was that of Brian Banks, who spent five years in prison instead of being able to pursue the football dreams he had earned.

Brian Banks' false accuser of kidnap and rape said she was fearful her admission of lying might have resulted in losing the "1.5 million" her family received from a civil lawsuit. Colleges should not be pressured into side-stepping protections afforded to all Americans in the judicial system, especially when considering that even under the most ideal conditions of fairness a court can still get things wrong.

Bloggers, commentators, and private citizens make judgments all the time regarding the guilt or innocence of individuals regardless of court decisions. However, when a representative of government begins advocating for the removal of due process and offers support for questionable victims, the entire system of justice becomes at risk. Unfortunately, that is what Senator Kirsten Gillibrand (D-NY)—someone who deserves nothing but admiration for her role in securing the renewal of more funding for the victims of 9/11—is doing in her desire to further protect women, an endeavor all support. Despite legitimate questions concerning the rape case, Gillibrand chose to bring Emma Sulkowicz, the alleged victim, to the State of the Union in 2015. In a Fox News special, "The Truth about Sex and College," Martha MacCallum asked about the selection. Sen. Gillibrand explained she was to "represent the victims of sexual assault on campus." She also labeled Emma a "survivor" and added that she had been "moved by her story."

Martha MacCallum then went on to ask, "What message did you want to send by bringing her?" Sen. Gillibrand gave a response of encouragement that will hopefully serve as a tool of empowerment for actual victims of rape and sexual abuse. However, she ended in a troubling way by presenting the notion that all accusers "should know they're not alone and that people will believe them." In pressing for further clarification, Martha MacCallum asked, "What about the fact that they went through the process and he was found to be 'not responsible' by the campus and then by law enforcement?" Senator Gillibrand responded by saying, "Well, I believe Emma and for all these cases, for all these survivors, sometimes the case doesn't result in a conviction."

Of course some that are guilty dodge accountability for their actions. No legal system is perfect and hearts go out to the victims who are denied. However, a public servant is entrusted to protect the rights of all individuals and must be extremely careful with the message their actions are sending to constituents. Although the men and women of congress have proven their detest for even reading proposed pieces of legislation, I would challenge all to read the texts and messages found within the lawsuit filed against Colombia University by the male victim of Emma's disproven allegations.

However, just as with the sex tape that Emma—better known as "Mattress Girl" for carrying the mattress the supposed rape occurred on across campus—made following the incident, it is highly suggested that the material is viewed outside the presence of children due to its explicit content. Regardless of any conclusions, doubts should be raised concerning the true motives of bringing Emma to the State of the Union.

One has to wonder how many other state or federal legislators are willing to take an endeavor supported by all—in this case the greater protection of women—and use it to blindly advance a practice of taking away fundamental rights with little reservation. Martha MacCallum highlighted a bill entitled "The Campus Accountability and Safety Act" currently being considered by the U.S. Congress. If passed, the guidelines that cost Grant Neal and others wrongly accused of rape would be applied nationwide.

Martha MacCallum also cited the signing of the "Yes Means Yes" law by Governors Andrew Cuomo (D-NY) and Jerry Brown (D-CA), which demonstrates once again that governmental officials think they need to overextend their authority over citizens. Many have reacted to the law by saying individuals will basically be forced to have an ongoing contract in relation to every move of a sexual encounter. Hans Bader, a Harvard grad and practicing attorney in Washington D.C., wrote an article in October 2015 that cited a story from *The New York Times* which "[quoted] the developer of the 'Yes Means Yes' curriculum admitting that under 'Yes Means Yes,' 'you have to say 'yes' every 10 minutes' during a sexual encounter to avoid sexual assault charges."

A legitimate question for Sen. Gillibrand is why has she not been as vocal in her unwavering support of all accusers, especially when it comes to those who have spoken out in response to the abuse they claim to have received at the hands of Bill Clinton. Where does she stand in regards to the woman in New Hampshire who challenged Hillary Clinton on her then documented stance "that all women should be believed?" As for Hillary Clinton, she responded to the woman in the crowd by saying, "Well, I would say that everybody should be believed at first, until they are disbelieved by evidence."

Kathleen Wiley accused Bill Clinton of sexually assaulting her. I doubt she is on the shortlist to be taken as Sen. Gillibrand's guest to the next State of the Union address. In January 2016, Kathleen spoke on "Aaron Klein Investigative Radio" and encouraged others to confidently come forward without fear and tell the truth about how Bill Clinton abused them. She thanked Republican presidential nominee Donald Trump for bringing up Bill's alleged past and hoped one day he would pose the following two-part question to the Democratic nominee. "Mrs. Clinton, is it okay with you that your husband flies around in private jets with a convicted pedophile to a private island called 'Orgy Island" and be entertained by underage girls? The real word for that is pedophilia and human trafficking. Is that okay with you?

Former President Clinton has obviously denied ever sexually assaulting Kathleen Wiley and she did display some inconsistencies in her testimony. On more than one occasion she was caught lying to the FBI. However, Kathleen Wiley insists a lie detector should be the final judge concerning the bullying to remain silent that she claims to have received at the direction of Hillary Clinton. Clinton has never taken that test.

Alana Goodman conducted an interview with Kathy Shelton—another woman who is doubtful to get a future invitation from Sen.

Gillibrand—for the DailyMail.com in August 2016. She is the woman who was tragically left barren after being sexually assaulted at the tender age of twelve by a man who a young lawyer named Hillary Clinton was able to successfully keep from a rape conviction. In speaking on the "unlawful fondling of a minor" charge he received that allowed him to escape serving more than a year in jail, Kathy Shelton said, "I don't think [Clinton's] for women or girls. I think she's lying. I think she said anything she can to get in the campaign and win."

Alana Goodman reported, "During the case, Clinton accused the 12-year-old of 'seek[ing] out older men' and 'engag[ing] in fantasizing' in court affidavits, and later laughed while discussing aspects of the case in a recently unearthed audiotape from the 1980s." However, as usual, significant events from Hillary Clinton's past history are understood by the mainstream media as off-limits in helping the public make a decision.

Though Hillary Clinton may not have publically laughed in regards to Bill's accusers, the decision of her campaign to remove the words "have the right to be believed" in regards to those who make the claim of having suffered from sexual assault or rape speaks volumes. The *Washington Examiner*'s Ashe Snow placed the change as occurring in February 2016, shortly following renewed emphasis on Bill Clinton's past.

The problem with inconsistencies in leadership that allows equal application of the law to be dictated by a certain political agenda of self-interest is that it undermines the faith Americans could have in the judicial system. Representatives should never push for fundamental rights to be lost as part of advancing a cause, regardless of how just it may be. Equal protection applies to everyone and no individual characteristic or circumstance should be used as part of a rationale for denying the aim of seeking equal justice. The people must take the lead in establishing a newfound trust in the judicial system by holding representatives more accountable to the principles the country was founded upon. Unbridled representatives and unelected bureaucrats left to their own devices will create an undesirable influence buried beneath the surface of legislative policies, appointments, and general rule changes that are often difficult to recognize. Accountability is the only method for protecting the people from abuse of authority.

Beyond negatively impacting the faith citizens have on the outcome of proceedings inside the courtroom, questionable leadership from the top is also causing a crisis in trust for those on the front lines entrusted to upholding law and order. As Lawrence Brown of Salon.com wrote in July 2015, "When a higher percentage of people in communities don't trust police, violent criminals are emboldened because they know that police-community relations are essential to effective law enforcement." Working to build this better relationship requires mutual work on both sides.

A few speeches in support of law enforcement from President Obama have not repaired the damage his administration has caused by too often inserting itself in questionable police altercations, as in the case of Professor Henry Gates Jr. No amount of recommendation from taskforces on building the desired coalition between the community and the police will mean anything if the President and his administration undermine law enforcement through silence or ambiguity. In response to Obama's assertion that the Cambridge officers "acted stupidly" when arresting Harvard professor Henry Gates Jr., the Associated Press reported from Boston that "many police officers across the country have a message for President Obama: get all the facts before criticizing one of our own." The men and women in blue have to know the President and other elected officials stand with them, so together they can work to root out the few who abuse their authority. Law enforcement deserves the benefit of the doubt, as most suit up every day and serve with honor and integrity. More importantly, officers deserve to receive the utmost support in training and equipment for protecting themselves and those they serve from danger as they perform their vital duties.

The notion of providing this level of support to law enforcement has been rejected by President Obama. As with gun control, the belief being offered is that in removing one variable alone from an equation, a solution will result. He assumes that riots involving looting and destroying of buildings will be less likely if the individual's feelings are protected. In a May 2015, speech, the President stated, "We've seen how militarized gear can sometimes give people a feeling like there's an occupying force as opposed to a force that's part of the community that's protecting and serving them." He continued, "It can alienate and intimidate local residents and send the wrong message."

Though the President is obviously acting on the recommendation from some, a leader is still responsible for the decision. The President has chosen to go against the recommendations of others in issues ranging from the military to migration. Correcting the problem of unnecessary force through the militarization of the police is a legitimate aim that requires greater oversight and legislation. However, placing all officers in greater danger by choosing to tie their hands behind their backs is short-sighted, especially when it is being done on the premise of "better feelings producing less crime."

Despite valid arguments against doing so, President Obama continues to enforce his decision following Ferguson to end "federal 1033 program, [a program that had] distributed equipment like armored vehicles for use by SWAT teams facing well-armed criminals and for other purposes like crowd control or even search and rescue efforts in hard to reach locations." Police departments can still purchase this equipment, but most are already cash-strapped. As far back as the "North Hollywood shootout" of 1987, the public has seen what happens when the police are underequipped to take on heavily armed assailants. In that instance, "eleven police officers and seven civilians were injured, and numerous vehicles and other property were damaged or destroyed by the approximately 1,750 rounds of ammunition fired by the robbers and police."

Anyone watching the San Bernardino terrorist attack actually witnessed firsthand the vital role the militarized vehicle played in protecting officers as they ended the crisis. Unfortunately, Dallas law enforcement officers did not possess this same level of enhanced equipment for protection. In the July 2016, ambush, five police officers joined the ranks of others who have heroically fallen in the line of duty. As MSNBC's Brian Williams mentioned, "They were not kitted up in Kevlar. They were not in the kind of gear that police have been criticized since Ferguson for wearing in an urban setting."

As important as the physical equipment is to the well-being of an officer, nothing replaces the significance of each possessing a positive and resolute mentality. Crime has spiked in major cities over the past few years and many believe it comes as a result of officers being inhibited from performing their duties in fear of backlash from the news media following Ferguson. Speaking to the University of Chicago Law School in October 2015, FBI Director James Comey described the "Ferguson Effect" by pointing to a "chill wind that has blown through American law enforcement over the last year."

Whether one acknowledges there is a correlation between the rise of crime and a newfound inhibition among law enforcement is a moot point. Practically doing nothing consequential from a role of leadership as cities like Chicago tragically produce a consistent flow of new African Americans killed from inner city violence is unconscionable. Elected officials, starting with the President, must place preconceived ideas and policy agendas aside and allow the data to guide their decisions for a solution.

Just as additional training, body cameras, and higher consequences for abuse of authority are vital in creating greater accountability from officers; this need should also be the endeavor for the general public on the other side of the equation. Taking into account the combative atmosphere officers are encountering more often, those resisting or interfering with arrests, offering taunts, and filing false lawsuits should face a higher level of penalties, fines, and scrutiny—providing a meaningful deterrent. Social media should not embolden citizens to misbehave. A mutual effort is necessary for progress.

Unfortunately, Baltimore State Attorney Marilyn Mosby certainly looks to have chosen to spend her time on maligning police officers, which results in more distrust. She is the woman who questionably chose to bring charges against the officers involved in the death of Freddie Gray. Despite garnering no convictions, a judge practically laughing from the lack of evidence she had in bringing a murder charge, and a lawsuit pending against her from two of the officers charged, Mosby decided to offer self-serving and counterproductive rhetoric that essentially placed her ego and desired agenda above the people at a press conference announcing that all the charges would be dropped against the three remaining officers. Three other officers had to stand trial, but all were acquitted.

Addressing the media on July 26, 2016, Mosby chose to throw the police and the judicial process under the bus in questioning the integrity of both in a clear desire to deflect attention from her own failures in conduct and judgment. Some believe she should actually face potential disbarment over what they characterize as prosecutorial misconduct, not only in bringing the charges to begin with, but also in how her department knowingly withheld evidence from the defense in trial.

While some may disagree with the assessment of her misconduct and ultimately choose to support the actions she took, it cannot be lost that in her office's questionable conduct in suppression of evidence, she practically demonstrated the unwarranted bias many within her community are protesting against. If it is a genuine fight for equal justice, then all should be against such misconduct. If movements are centered instead on equality for just one race, then selecting when a bias is acceptable is not that surprising. The death of Freddie Gray is tragic, but Marilyn Mosby's unethical decisions only made positive growth more difficult by flaming the fire of distrust. Some may ask why she would possibly follow a personal political agenda that could result in the loss of her law license instead of performing her duties with a sense of equal justice. The answer may lie in the safety net George Soros could provide her. If documents confirm that his Open Society organization approved $650,000 to Black Lives Matter following Freddie Gray's death, it's more than reasonable that the billionaire could take care of her.

In discussing the "alarming" rise of homicides in Baltimore in 2016, Greta Van Susteren asked her regular panel of attorneys to explain the effect Mosby was having on the ability of officers to fervently perform their duties to the community they serve. Former homicide detective and now criminal defense attorney, Ted Williams, said, "The criminals own the streets of Baltimore. Uh [sic] look, Police officers want to make arrests of these criminals, but these criminals are not dumb. They know that the state's attorney's office and the uh [sic] Police Department is [sic] at loggerheads with each other. And when you think about it, if a cop puts his hand on one of those criminals and Marilyn Mosby decides to prosecute him, why should a cop be that dumb and put his hands on any criminal. Criminals are not dumb people."

Katie Phang, a trial lawyer and former prosecutor, followed Ted by saying, "Well 105 homicides this year alone is nothing to be sneering at whatsoever. I I [sic] kind of intend to agree with Ted. I mean Marilyn Mosby, is this not some type of of [sic] condemnation of how she's basically running her office? If the cops think that they're not going to get an effective prosecution out of this office, this is a vote of no confidence from these cops. And it's basically the criminals saying, 'I can run around with zero compunction because I don't have to worry about anything that's going to happen to me because the cops aren't going to arrest me because they're going to get prosecuted by Marilyn Mosby and Mosby's office is going to strip the prosecution any way. So it's like a 'win, win' for the criminals in Baltimore right now."

Many have pointed to Marilyn Mosby's desire for those supposedly rioting for justice to know that it was "their day" when initially handing down the indictments; many of whom may have ultimately become a figure among the 105 killed in Baltimore referenced by Katie Phang. However, despite all of the black lives that matter continuing to die, President Obama and his vast number of cronies who file behind his ideology in lockstep continue to downplay the "Ferguson Effect" on the abilities of law enforcement. Milwaukee County Sheriff David Clark has been a consistent critic of the Obama administration's treatment of law enforcement. In addressing the President's refusal to acknowledge the "Viral Video Effect" as playing a significant factor, Fox's "Outnumbered" ran a clip of Clark telling Greta Van Susteren, "Cops are not afraid to do their job. What they are afraid of, I got a different effect, it's called 'the cop hating United States Department of Justice,' led by a race-obsessed Attorney General. The President of the United States has been leading the chorus in slandering and maligning the character, the integrity, the service, and the sacrifice of our nation's law enforcement officers. What officers fear is some witch-hunt; this this [sic] on-going witch-hunt by the Civil Rights division taking over law enforcement agencies all across the nation."

Whether one agrees or disagrees with the assessment of Sheriff David Clark, it is rather clear that at least some within law enforcement are second-guessing decisions that often must be made in a split second. Any football player knows that the easiest way to get injured is to not play to the whistle. Letting up places both your personal safety and that of your opponent at higher risk. The same is true with an officer. Loss of focus and avoidance of effort in technique and procedures due to an overbearing fear results in mistakes, which can lead to an escalation that is detrimental to everyone.

One officer in Birmingham, Alabama, narrowly escaped death after being beaten with his service revolver. He hesitated to act out of fear of being disparaged in the media, which is too often willing to ruin lives for a chosen narrative. Chris Pleasance of the Dailymail.com reported in August 2015 that the six-year veteran told CNN, "A lot of officers are being too cautious because of what's going on in the media." Pleasance also indicated that the officer had been mocked online for the incident and actually displayed a portion of a tweet that had multiple emojis of smiley faces crying and read: "Pistol whipped his a** to sleep." Among the hashtags, one read: "#FckDaPolice."

Another incident potentially involving some indecision regarding following certain procedures did not end as well. Sophie Faulkner, a teenager, witnessed the tragedy that took place inside a restaurant in Maryland a few booths from where she and her mother sat. CBS News reported that Officer Patrick Dailey attempted to approach a man whose erratic behavior was troubling to everyone else. "The deputy tried to talk to the man, who was apparently known to workers. The deputy sat down beside him, asked how he was doing, and the man shot him in the head."

The more restrained approach most likely preferred by the media in almost every incident, regardless of the unique circumstances, could have certainly played a role in lowering the officer's guard. As a result, two law enforcement officers with families at home waiting anxiously for their daily safe return lost their lives on February 10, 2016. Senior Deputy Patrick Dailey and Senior Deputy Mark Logsdon were both long-term officers, as well as military veterans.

Hearing taps at a funeral is excruciating, as anyone who has lost a family member in the military or law enforcement knows all too well.

As Ann Marimow, Justin Jouvenal, and Dana Hedgpeth of *The Washington Post* reported, "Logsdon's daughter offered a tribute to her father on her Facebook page: 'To say I'm proud of you is a complete understatement,' Bethany Logsdon wrote, 'I am so happy for the time I had with you. I am so thankful for all of the people that you protected. You are my best friend. You are my hero. I will love you forever. I am so sad our time got cut short. I am so angry that someone took this from us. I love you.'"

While most Americans of all races and ethnicities appropriately respond to tragedy by offering condolences, the rhetoric coming from Black Lives Matter is winking and nodding at extremists to wage war on the police. Beyond the looting of a 7-11 following the Dallas shooting that resulted in the death of five officers or the absurd gestures of individuals at that same station taking selfies, dancing, and taunting police, the hateful words from numerous groups on social media is the most disturbing.

The Black Power Political Organization, or at least a Facebook page claiming to represent the group, added to the documented threats against the police by taking credit for the Dallas attack. In the Facebook Post, they wrote: "BlackPower! #Black Knights! Sniper Assassins Take Down Five Police Officers! And More Will Be Assassinated in the Coming Days! Do you Like The Work of Our Assassins? Get Your Own Sniper Rifle and Join Our Thousands of Sniper Assassins Worldwide in the Fight Against Oppression!" Officers were ambushed in places across the country following the Dallas attack and continue to face threats from individuals possessing this deranged logic.

Much of the same disconcerting behavior could be seen following the attack that took the lives of officers in Baton Rouge, Louisiana. Clayton Morris of Fox News reported on more tweets from those who feel emboldened to write messages of hate on social media. Each tweet contained at least one reference to Black Lives Matter, although much of the mainstream media refuses to dig deep in assessing the group. These tweets provide an accurate snapshot of those on the fringes of this organization.

The first inhumane tweet was from "Maryland X," who wrote "Armed pigs meet political consequences in #Baton Rouge" before placing three emojis of smiling facing with tears to symbolize laughing so hard that he is crying at the murder of these officers. The rest of the contents beyond the hashtags were too vile for television.[68]

What Can Be Achieved—339

The second was from "@Tarahitense," who wrote: "Good cops need to start snitchin on their racist coworkers TO-DAY. Only yall can stop this. #BatonRouge #Dallas #Black Lives Matter." Clearly, the user believes the shootings were justified.

Not to be outdone by either of the first two highlighted by Clayton Morris, user "DrShiro TM@bvanished" placed eleven emojis of smiling facing laughing so hard they were crying before writing, "No sympathy whatsoever for these pigs. I hope #BatonRouge won't be the last;" an unimaginable level of indefensible ignorance.

Individuals like Ebony Dickens from Georgia should be in jail for making terrorist threats and inciting violence. An apology shouldn't be enough for the type of rhetoric she used over two months before the tragic incidents in Dallas and Louisiana. At that time, in a Facebook post, she "called for black people to rise up and shoot every white cop" before going on a curse-laden tirade to describe her desire and planning for the killing of cops and how confident she was that the First Amendment protected her words.

Dallas, Baton Rouge, and other places where incidents resulted in the loss of life possibly brought her satisfaction. Tobias Salinger of *The New York Times* documented the press conference that she gave in exchange for her "get out of jail free" card by writing, "She wanted to write something preposterous in hopes of starting a conversation during protests and riots in Baltimore after the death of 25-year-old Freddie Gray."

Should the words of individuals like Ebony Dickens really be surprising? Joseph Watson of Infowars posted a video of a Black Lives Matter leader calling for violence against police at a rally that coincided with the Dallas lone gunman. Watson wrote, "'If they go about their burden of whatever they said you're doing, you pull your pistol out and you f**king bust that,' says the BLM protestor, described in the video as a 'passionate speaker.'" As noted, that same speaker later said, "I don't give a f**k whether you knock 'em over, whether you run up on them, whatever you do, you better f**king take action!"

Despite the rhetoric coming from some within or affiliated with the Black Lives Matter movement, Jesse Jackson blamed Donald Trump for the Dallas shooting a few days after the senseless attack. While few would argue that Trump hasn't made some statements that have definitely raised the tension within certain groups, the "Reverend" Jesse Jackson is misguided and blatantly hypocritical in his claim. Only a day before Dallas police were ambushed as they protected those protesting against them, Jackson called the death of Alton Sterling a "legal lynching;" going as far as to say something to the extent of, "In my day it was from behind white sheets they killed us, now it's blue."

While it will be up to Jesse Jackson to look in the mirror and ask himself if the divisive rhetoric he offered fueled violence—especially in terms of the Dallas attack—to my knowledge he hasn't actually called for the murders of others (as his counterpart with the label of "Reverend.") In a 1992 tape that is clearly audible, the Rev. Al Sharpton can be heard encouraging an audience to go beyond their words and take action in murdering white officers. As part of his statements, he said, "'I'll off the man,' Well off him. Plenty of crackers walking right around here tonight." Sharpton is in his second MSNBC show and has been welcomed to the White House on numerous occasions.

In his speech at the Republican National Convention, former Speaker of the House Newt Gingrich offered clarity to where the priority should be in protecting law enforcement by saying, "Think about this. If anyone publicly threatens the life of the President of the United States, the Secret Service is on them in an instant. Our law enforcement officers deserve the same respect as the President of the United States." However, it is likely that those in the heights of the Obama administration paid as little attention to what went on inside the convention as they did to what happened outside.

In covering the convention, Ben Marquis of the *Conservative Tribune* wrote, "According to a few media reports, largely derived from witnesses on scene and overheard transmissions on police radios, it appears that the protestors have been utilizing squirt guns and balloons filled with urine and feces to attack the police."

Unfortunately, what can be expected from the U.S. Justice Department in relation to threats against law enforcement is actually probably best indicated in a U.S. attorney's reaction to an incident involving migrants. The logic of placing the focus on a certain agenda while disregarding almost everyone else comes directly from the top. After a girl was sexually assaulted by a group of refugee boys ranging from ages seven to fourteen, the U.S. Attorney Wendy Olsen cautioned residents to wait on the facts before saying, "The spread of false information or inflammatory or threatening statements about the perpetrators or the crime itself reduces public safety and may violate federal law."

Whether U.S. Attorney Olsen made this statement in regard to a specific threat or not, where is this same vigor and passion for going after those who threaten law enforcement officers? Where is her passion in defending against this type of quick judgment that often plagues the administration she works for and groups like Black Lives

Matter? Focusing attention on protection of all citizens should be the endeavor of government. Law enforcement needs an advocate it can depend upon, and many within the media have too often proven they cannot be relied upon to present an unbiased view. In an April 2016, article for the *Conservative Review*, Michelle Malkin discussed the social media posts celebrating the violence against the police and reminded readers of the CNN panel discussion from 2013 concerning Christopher Dorner. The ex-LAPD officer waged war against the LAPD that resulted in the death of civilians and officers.

As part of the discussion, Marc Lamont Hill offered this mindboggling assessment. "This has been an important public conversation that we've had about police brutality, about police corruption, about state violence. As far as Dorner himself goes, he's been like a real-life superhero to many people. Now, don't get me wrong: What he did was awful, killing innocent people. He's just bad. But when you read his manifesto, when you read the message that he left, he wasn't entirely crazy. He had a plan and a mission here. And many people aren't rooting for him to kill innocent people. They're rooting for somebody who was wronged to get a kind of revenge against the system. It's like almost watching Django Unchained in real life. It's kind of exciting."

None of the other panelists took him to task for his words. It was only after those watching, which obviously included the families of the victims, expressed outrage at his insensitivity that he offered a half-hearted apology. Just as with the U.S. State Department, he basically presented the notion that the general public was just too dumb to understand the profound statements he was actually making in his absurd analysis that day. He can still be seen regularly on CNN, as the network especially values his take on what the focus should be following race-driven incidents where cops are gunned down. The "starting a conversation" factor is what too many use to determine if an action is just.

Despite an officer possessing the body camera for more accountability and actually demonstrating that the officer was justified in firing his weapon at Sylville Smith—the African-American man in Milwaukee who unfortunately lost his life as a result—protestors chose to destroy their own community. In August 2016, Randy DeSoto reported on CNN's choice to present the victim's sister as a peacemaker by editing a video where she actually encouraged rioters to cause havoc in other areas. In the part not seen, she actually says, "Burning down s--t ain't going to help nothing. Y'all burning down s--t we need in our community. Take that s--t to the suburbs. Burn that sh-t down."

Those words must have been contrary to the desired narrative of CNN.

Although rather irresponsible in covering up the call of violent rioting by someone else, no one on the staff of CNN actually directly called for rioting, as Emmett Rensin did while serving as an editor at Vox. Placing aside the safety of everyone, including law enforcement, he wrote a number of tweets encouraging those on the ground to take action at upcoming Trump rallies. The *Washington Examiner*'s T. Beckett Adams documented one tweet saying, "It's very simple: All violence against human lives and bodies is categorically immoral. Property destruction is vastly more negotiable." As with so many others, he scoffed at those who said he was illegally inciting violence.

As if tensions were not already at a boiling point, on the day a judge decided to acquit the driver in the Freddie Gray incident, the "Rachel Maddow Show" incorrectly displayed a headline which read in huge letters, "JURY ACQUITS POLICE DRIVER IN FREDDIE GRAY CASE," as part of Rachel Maddow's recap of the day's events. Only the first trial was decided by a jury; all others, including this case, were a "bench trial," absent of a jury and involving an African-American judge making the sole decision based on the evidence presented. While likely a mistake, the timing couldn't have been worse.

In what became a cover story on Yahoo, Snenequa Golding essentially gave credence to the repugnant ideas of rapper Kevin Gates in regards to what he said would be the punishment for law enforcement if they messed with his kids. Beyond advancing his generalization through reporting the story, she actually ended her article by asking, "Think Gates is on to something?" She was questioning readers as to whether Gates was somehow being profound in his curse-ridden threat to murder an officer's entire family if he disagreed with how his kids were treated by them. Then again, maybe she was just seeking to "start the conversation" that seems to be the sole driving force of so many.

The business community also does not always offer the type of respect and support to those who deserve it the most, starting with the revelation that the NFL and MLB were actually charging the government to unite soldiers with their family members. Big corporations like Walmart refusing to take expedited action against employees who chose not to serve a police officer in uniform should be unacceptable, just as decisions from the NFL not to end the career of a player who advocates violence against police officers.

An "Instagram post depicting a police officer being stabbed in the neck by a person in a black hood" was what Cleveland Brown's running back Isaiah Crowell decided was an acceptable method for venting his frustrations. While Walmart eventually decided to remove the employee from her job, neither the Browns nor the NFL have been willing to truly stand up for officers by kicking Crowell out of the league.

Just as with leaders who guide the nation politically, businesses must fight intimidation to do the right thing. Unlike the tape that clearly shows Al Sharpton calling for the audience to kill white police officers, he deserves to be thought of as innocent until proven guilty in other matters. However, it seems almost certain that he is guilty of taking $16,000 from Reggie Anders Sr., who allegedly sought assistance from Sharpton in addressing a problem with Verizon involving discrimination. In a July 2016 article in the *New York Post*, Kathlanne Boniello and Laura Itallano detailed how Reggie Anders Sr. labeled Reverend Al Sharpton as being nothing but "a fraud" and "a crook."

Al Sharpton seems to have dangled him along without any intention of ever helping him. "Anders said he was shocked to read a Post exclusive in August 2015 about how companies paid Sharpton what amounted to 'protection' money, and companies that didn't donate, such as GM, were threatened with bad press or NAN (National Action Network)-promoted boycotts." Despite having a minister actually attend the meetings Anders Sr. speaks of for convincing verification, when asked about him, Sharpton said, "Who? I have no idea what you're talking about." Whether it be Al Sharpton or any other individual or group providing pressure, those who are in leadership positions in businesses and politics must speak with respect, admiration, and support.

This need also extends to those within the education community, considering that they are the ones playing a significant role in molding the minds of future adults. Dorthy Bland serves as "the dean of the Frank W. and Sue Mayborn School of Journalism and the director for the Frank W. Mayborn Graduate Institute of Journalism" at the University of North Texas. In October 2015 she indicated that her race (African American) had been used against her and took her grievances to the pages of the *Dallas Morning News*. However, a video from the incident—which she apparently failed to account for—was later used by multiple media outlets to discredit her claims of police acting improperly.

Ron Kirk, an African American who once served as the Dallas mayor, as well as the trade representative for the Obama administration until 2013, was having none of it. He sat down with Keven Ann Willey of the *Dallas Morning News* shortly after the incident. On the question posed as to "why he thinks this is a nonstory," he said, "There's nothing wrong here. It was a proper, polite encounter. I read her piece. I read the police chief's response. I watched the video. I was angry…I got in the shower before calling." Her impact on the general public and future journalists was definitely not lost on him.

When Kirk was asked "what's wrong with her describing how she felt," he passionately responded, "As a person of color, this upsets me. Particularly against what happened in South Carolina. Particularly as this country is wrestling with very real concerns regarding the police treatment of African-American youth. She took advantage of a very innocent and thoughtful police response—walk on the right side of the street—she's just looking for her Skip Gates moment. There's a real danger here."

When asked to elaborate further on the "danger" he spoke of, he concluded by saying, "To me, they behaved the way we're asking police to treat people. To demonize people for trying to do the right thing…it makes it easier for whites to say, 'Oh, my gosh, everything's about race now. This is all about politics and not about a very real and difficult issue.' That's the danger. And that makes me downright mad."

Two steps forward and one step back is the result of what Kirk describes. While the belief in the necessity for greater race relations remains, motivation from a broader group of people to actively participate in the endeavor becomes diminished. Many will still believe in the cause, but the irresponsible actions from some leading a movement will cause many to delay becoming involved until the true integrity of intentions are clear. Only with proper guidance from community leaders and elected officials can the proper tone be established for moving the country forward as one. It starts at the top. Many on the political right argued that the National Democratic Convention spurned the families of law enforcement killed by anti-cop haters. However, regardless of whether one believes this to be true, the decision of Hillary Clinton to reject taking the necessary steps in possibly securing an endorsement from the Fraternal Order of Police does very little to persuade many in blue uniforms to confidently believe she has their backs.

Even without documenting a single questionable decision from a specific politician or agency within recent years, any individual could recognize the poor state of the country by listening to the words of the Attorney General from mid-July 2016. In a congressional hearing following the Justice Department's decision not to indict Hillary Clinton over her misconduct with classified information, the Attorney

General—who is entrusted to serve as the chief law enforcement officer and defender of the rule of law in the United States—"declined to say whether it was legal or illegal to lie under oath."

The American people are desperate for leadership and advocacy. Seeing Loretta Lynch's words are insightful, but not necessary for those suffering under the weight of poor decisions. A Rasmussen poll from July 2016 found that "just 24% of voters think the country is headed in the right direction."

A Quinnipiac University poll from swing states in early July 2016 displayed how much Americans feel their government is out of sync with them. When asked if they agree with the statement "public officials don't care much what people like me think," voters in all three states polled, to some degree, overwhelmingly agreed. With Floridians agreeing at 80%, Ohio at 79%, and Pennsylvania at 78%, the message is clear.

So often people ask why can't the U.S. Congress pass meaningful legislation on common sense factors concerning reforms to immigration and gun control that a majority of the general public supports. In regards to gun control, having a universal background check and denying weapons to terrorists is obviously more than reasonable. However, where is the record to justify a legitimate trust from citizens? Casually talking about removing due process from gun owners is definitely not a way to begin earning it. The growth of America has been stunted for some time. If there had been proactive measures taken on immigration, the complex catastrophe of today could have been avoided altogether. If there had been an actual emphasis placed on financial education to K-12 students in the 70s and 80s, a different electorate and potential set of leaders would have been created that understands the need for fiscal responsibility. Yet, too many within all aspects of society are more invested in maintaining the status quo. Americans can no longer live in the past, but instead must push for a future that will only come from visionary leadership, built and insulated with accountability and transparency.

Addressing the Governors Club Dinner in 1988, President Reagan offered some words to the crowd that has continued to gain in popularity with each new generation:

> "When I was out in Missouri just a few weeks back, I told some students down in Cape Girardeau—and they seemed to enjoy the story—about the fellow who was running for office as a Republican in a heavily Democratic state. He stopped by a farm to do some campaigning. And when the farmer heard he was a Republican, his jaw dropped, and he said, 'You wait

right here while I get Ma. She's never seen a Republican.' So he got Ma, and while they were gone, the candidate looked around for a podium from which to give his speech. And the only thing he could find was a pile of that stuff that Bess Truman took 35 years trying to get Harry to call fertilizer. So, he got up on that mound, and when they came back, he gave his speech. At the end of it, the farmer said, 'That's the first time I ever heard a Republican speech.' The candidate said, 'That's the first time I've ever given a Republican speech from a Democratic platform.'"

Consistent lighthearted badgering will always exist between opposing parties. Just as fierce dialogue and debate will always occur within the chambers of government, as it should. What should never be forgotten is that every member is an American. If there is any chance for the country to move forward with progress, those selected to lead are going to have to start exhibiting what can be achieved through genuine unity. Yelling insults at the State of the Union or causing a disruption on the House or Senate floor does little in providing a foundation of respect and communication necessary for making meaningful decisions for the future. Nor does it provide an example to those outside of government who are filled with frustration and disillusionment about the process that denies them the voice they seek. Winning battles on legislation is important, but what can never be lost on a representative is the vital responsibility to set the proper tone through their interactions. No loss on any piece of legislation is more important than a lesson of civility for colleagues, civilians, foreign governments, and developing youth. We need more politicians that not only understand this need for civility, but who are also willing to publicly acknowledge it. In a 1960 interview on NBC's "Meet the Press" only a month before the presidential election, which all indications pointed as to being close, John F. Kennedy answered as to why he was not being as hard in his rebuke on sitting President Eisenhower as previous Republican predecessors by saying, "I have a high regard for President Eisenhower personally. I've been critical of the leadership of this administration. I feel that our power, vigor, prestige, has not kept up with the requirements of our times in the last eight years. I've been very critical in every speech I've made of that. President Eisenhower has been the President. He must bear his measure of responsibility. I'm not involved in a personal dispute. I admire the President personally, but I do disagree with the policies that his administration has followed."

In writing about what drove Lincoln in his 2002 book, *Lincoln's Virtues*, William E. Miller explained, "As a politician, Lincoln was principled and conservative but not ideological or rigid. Historian T. Harry Williams argued that 'Lincoln would not have been able to comprehend the attempts of modern writers to classify his ideas into an ideology. Indeed, he would not have known what an ideology was.'" Lincoln formulated his ideas on what was right and principled by reading from a diversity of literature, from the Bible to scientific and political writings from the greatest minds.

This open-minded nature and recognition of the great value in utilizing a diversity of opinions in reaching the best conclusions is something that Senator Kennedy echoed even before his decision to run for president. In a speech to the Loyola College Alumni Banquet from 1958, the young Sen. Kennedy said, "Let us not despair but act. Let us not seek the Republican answer or the Democratic answer but the right answer. Let us not seek to fix the blame for the past—let us accept our own responsibility for the future."

Legislators have the choice of allowing special interest and parliamentary gimmicks to always offer the most extreme positions—which also serve to embolden those on the fringes in each party on every issue—or whether to make an effort to discover the best compromise on what is best for the country. However, to even begin down that road of reaching a legitimate and acceptable consensus, each party is going to have to stop thinking in terms of having the silver bullet to success for all ideas. Insights from both sides are necessary in shaping the most beneficial policies. Tax policy provides one of the best examples. While Republican lawmakers might cite a state like Vermont where high taxation has led to a growing exodus, very few talk about Minnesota. In an article from *The Huffington Post*, Robert C. Gibson detailed how Governor Mark Dayton successfully dealt with the high unemployment rate and a 6 billion dollar budget deficit upon taking office. He wrote, "During his first four years in office, Gov. Dayton raised the state income tax from 7.85 to 9.85 percent on individuals earning over $150,000, and on couples earning over $250,000 when filing jointly—a tax increase of $2.1 billion. He's also agreed to raise Minnesota's minimum wage to $9.50 an hour by 2018, and passed a law guaranteeing equal pay for women."

The results of the moves the Republican governor made outside the norms of his party were staggering. "Between 2011 and 2015, Gov. Dayton added 172,000 new jobs to Minnesota's economy—that's 165,000 more jobs in Dayton's first term than Pawlenty added in both his terms combined." Obviously, some may not agree with the logic behind his moves and only time will tell whether his actions will continue to be favorable. His willingness to deviate from the Republican who preceded him in terms of taxation and a slight incremental increase to the minimum wage laid a foundation for success through possible compromise. He has proven rigid ideology will not rule his policy decisions.

Investment in infrastructure and education, less regulation, a livable minimum wage, and advances in medical care are all areas ripe for shared purpose. Of course, considerations must be vocalized by Republicans in terms of the minimum wage, as places that have raised the minimum wage without incremental increases have seen unhealthy consequences of business closures and fewer employment opportunities. Healthy input from various viewpoints is necessary for molding the proper legislation. No government will be perfect or immune from mistakes in judgment, as Richard Brookhiser reminded us in his book, *Founding Fathers*: "Certainly the talent level in America at the end of the eighteenth century was high. When one reflects that Washington, as President, in preparing his third annual message to Congress, took suggestions from Jefferson and James Madison, sent them to Alexander Hamilton to be worked up, and finally gave the draft to Madison for a rewrite, one then turns to any presidential speech-writing team of the last sixty years (including Nixon's) and weeps. But talent isn't everything. Even the best can fail, because the best are men."

Americans have to accept the truth that leaders will always be flawed. The Founders, in all their brilliance, still failed to reach the right conclusion on slavery. They also had bitter fights and dissention over issues, unlike the portrayal in the minds of Americans who long for the Founders to return and set things right. Too often citizens forget that even the greatest of men and women, with the most admirable ideas of justice and equality, have always faced boisterous opposition. Instead, without the fanciful imagery surrounding those who founded the nation, we can see them as men who were flawed, but dedicated to something much greater than themselves. The enduring legacy was forged out of discussions born of passion and authenticity. While imperfect, they taught us what can be achieved through leadership. Americans must strive as one to protect those who lead them from the common pitfalls of deceit, greed, and entitlement, but consistently raise the bar of accountability.

The problem with leadership today is that few recognize the value of earning and maintaining the trust of the people by consistently providing something worthy of believing in. From the salary and extreme fringe benefits received to an unwillingness to live by the same set of laws being passed, lawmakers aren't demonstrating their adherence to the higher ideas—such as equality for all—as it relates to those they serve. Ed Klein, a long-time columnist and *New York Time*'s bestselling author, addressed this disconnect in his 2006 book, *Politics Lost*, in writing, "If you're going to ask them to make a sacrifice—to pay higher taxes, or go to war—you'd best have your act together. If you're going to lead, you'd best be willing to show them something of yourself, something that hasn't been pureed by pollsters. If you want them to take a risk, you're going to have to take one yourself. Sadly, most politicians are neither risk-takers nor leaders. They are followers—of convention, of public opinion—and while leadership is art, fellowship has become a science, measured in polls and focus groups."

When I had a good friend of mine come out as being gay, he went through a very difficult time with his family. Initially, I offered him nothing but support. However, being a Christian, I felt the need to be honest with him on how I felt the Bible spoke about homosexuality, not because I sought to offer him a condemnation, but because I truly cared about my friend's eternity. I spoke with him and told him that I was not perfect by any means, but I wanted to discuss with him what I believed the Bible said about those that practice homosexuality. I told him being truthful with him was important for me, but that he was one of my best friends, I loved and cared about him, and if he took what I told him and still decided to move forward with his chosen lifestyle, I would support him. Although he was initially confused and upset, he ultimately concluded that I had demonstrated to him that I was indeed a true friend by caring about him enough to be honest with him. The reason this ultimately worked out was because I had a solid foundation of trust long before the discussion by putting in the time to build a friendship. I then utilized our mutual respect and trust to bring him my concerns and then listen to his feedback, valuing his words to reach an outcome founded in truth. This foundation of necessary trust to move forward with success is something most lawmakers have entirely ignored or overlooked despite routinely questioning why few have faith in their decisions.

Beyond the need for demonstrating the characteristics Joe Klein details for actually becoming a legitimate servant of the people, many representatives also display a basic lack of understanding as to what makes a leader. A leader isn't someone who believes he or she possesses all the answers. In fact, it's quite the opposite. It is actually someone who values the alternative viewpoints of others and is humble enough to admit when they are wrong. More importantly, what separates genuine leaders from the rest is the ability to take all the diverse information and make the best decision. Preconceived ideas have little place with this principled, but open-minded and pragmatic individual, who recognizes a candid nature is something that people will relate to and respect. With true leadership, the country can take on chronic and future challenges with optimism and promise.

The answers are out there.

The American people just need the right individuals to discover them. Only after an adequate body of men and women are in place can the country begin addressing the issues that have remained elusive. From the proper balance between interventionism and isolationism to the appropriate allocations attached to domestic spending, the best choices are there. Anemic economic growth, lack of new business investment, and an absence of upward mobility will no longer be accepted as the new norm. America is better than that and no politician, media talking head, or foreign competitor should be allowed to tell the people anything otherwise. Social security is one of the issues that has remained in dire need of true leadership. In an article for the Associated Press from May 2016, Adam Allington discussed the "4 in 10 Americans who are 50 and older" opting to begin drawing their social security due to limited income, although the result is that their benefits are permanently reduced "by up to 30 percent." Very few retirees have much money saved as well, according to the Pew Charitable Trusts report highlighted by the *Pittsburgh Post-Gazette* in June 2016. "The Pew study of 104 metropolitan areas found more than 40 percent of full-time workers have neither a pension nor a 401(k)." Yet, a government composed of individuals who can't look past the next election chooses to do nothing.

In his 2015 book, *American Dreams*, Marco Rubio, former 2016 Presidential candidate and current senator from Florida, addressed this unwillingness of lawmakers to address the entitlement programs. He wrote, "It may help a politician defeat an opponent at the ballot box, but the ultimate price of inaction will be paid by future retirees. What many in politics seem to have forgotten is that we are here to serve the public interest, not posture politically. Yet so many politicians are unable—or unwilling—to acknowledge that their lack of action dooms the very programs they claim they are committed to preserving." Again, the answers can be found through ingenuity; it just requires leaders not held to rigid ideas, but instead able to conform to the circumstances of the time.

Adam Allington noted that the decisions of the elderly would not affect the fund that is placed aside. "Gary Burtless, a Brookings Institution economist, said that people taking benefits early—or late—

should have no impact on the trust fund. 'It cost the government roughly the same amount,' he said." With the likelihood that this analysis is true, why not take advantage of the baby boomers who will be retiring *en masse* over the next few years to establish a new method for enriching both young and old at the same time.

A common obstacle for many people today to pursue an education is finding reliable childcare. Obviously, the idea of nationalized childcare has been tossed around in the past, but not by attempting to utilize those who are close to retirement and often facing reduced options. Why not create a method for allowing those that are willing and need work to bridge the gap between the last few years of receiving their full retirement to serve in the role of childcare provider at new institutions established nationwide. Harnessing the strength of this aging segment of the population would alleviate the permanent reduction in their social security payment, offer youth the wisdom of an older generation so rarely sought, provide those seeking an education a path moving forward to better the lives for themselves and their family, and create more openings for graduates entering an employment market that remains bleak. With proper oversight, the elderly who seek to remain useful and purposeful could have the choice of spending time helping the young people they often crave attention from, while removing the penalty for early payments; thus, the elderly can receive their full social security benefit at age 65 or 66.

While the answer may not ultimately offer a viable solution, it is different than the same tired rhetoric often given by politicians of all stripes unable to get beyond the talking points for re-election. The state of analysis with paralysis that has remained in government must be fundamentally changed. The People's Clearing House can provide the missing component for stimulating the growth of actual leaders, allowing citizens to witness what bills can look like from a place of greater trust and integrity. No reform or degree of renewed oversight can replace the significance of having this solid foundation. With true leadership, a balanced budget amendment for keeping members of Congress more fiscally sound could face less opposition. A push for automatic recalls could also be applied to failures in this regard for certain members of Congress—such as those in their second terms or seniority leadership—with deductions from elections only further strengthening communities across the country. Whether it is a preferred constitutional amendment, a rule change that allows committee assignments to be assigned through a draw, or any other method for intensifying the voice of the people, The People's Clearing House provides an arena for actually becoming a possible reality.

Although many U.S. and State legislators would prefer the luxury of simply erasing past mistakes in judgment from the record in a similar fashion to the attempt made by the State Department in regards to the misrepresentations surrounding the Iran Deal, it is an impossible endeavor. A vast number of Americans are personally continuing to suffer from the results of their inept leadership highlighted by failed budgets and special interests giveaways characteristic of a foundation that lacks integrity. The People's Clearing House can produce the leadership Americans desire for progress.

Conclusion

As part of his bid to become a U.S. senator from New York, Robert Kennedy spoke at Colombia University in 1964. He emphasized his positive outlook for the future by referencing Archimedes' description of the lever. Kennedy stated, "And he said show me where I can stand and I can move the world. And I think that we can."

The lever is an object that has remained mired and buried beneath the negative forces of career politicians, crony capitalists, special interests, partisan factions, and the consistent expansion in depth and width of the governmental bureaucracy. Though most may believe otherwise, moving the lever for profoundly changing the world is possible. For one class, those doubting the ability to bring a significant change would be right; just as their assessment would be correct for one race or ethnicity. Only with a united front that rejects the dividers and ignores the detractors can a change in the world occur. Such a concerted effort begins with the American people reasserting their ownership of the country through faith and resolve. Then, and only then, can the lever be reached, allowing for a diverse set of hands to work as one in positively moving it. The lines of the country go well beyond the influence peddled within the Capitol, Wall Street, and Silicon Valley. The people will decide if efforts to restore this fundamental truth will remain mere footnotes in history or moments in time in which meaningful steps in campaign finance reform were taken to create genuine representation.

The People's Clearing House could ultimately provide the type of legitimacy Americans yearn for in government. Leadership from a place of strength can provide the proper framework for progress, but the success or failure of any movement will depend on the quality of information presented. Issues are complex and the media has to begin doing a better job in reporting to help the public evaluate and determine which groups and individuals demonstrate they can be trusted through their words and actions. Whether in the public or private sector, making these type distinctions is a necessity if the American people are going to actually solve present and future challenges and issues.

Creating better race relations is one endeavor that has been stifled by the work of politicians and the mainstream media. Earning political points or ratings too often determines what, when, and how information is presented or omitted. The result is an additional layer of complexity being added to attempts to bring greater unity, as the general public remains unable to determine the facts for making decisions. The truth should never become something only applied when beneficial or convenient, regardless of the cause. Only upon a foundation of integrity will long-lasting progress be formed. Anything built on a lack of truth might bring short-term success, but it will eventually fail. In the desire to further the cause of strengthening race relations, some Americans have decided to wholeheartedly support the Black Lives Matter (BLM) organization. A September 2016 article from Jesse J. Holland and Emily Swanson of the AP highlighted the growth in support among youth. "Fifty-one percent of white adults between the ages of 18 and 30 say in a GenForward poll they now strongly or somewhat support Black Lives Matter;" adding to the majority of support witnessed among minorities. However, in the desire to further the universal cause of unity hopefully shared by all Americans, some have chosen to put forth a blanket level of support for BLM. Offering categorical legitimacy continues to hinder forming the necessary coalition for progress.

DeRay McKesson, a prominent leader of Black Lives Matter, has been with the group since its inception following the unfortunate death of Michael Brown in Ferguson, Missouri. Just as with Ferguson, he has remained a recognized voice of the group. *Fortune* magazine placed him on its list of "The Worlds 50 Greatest Leaders" from the 2015 edition. In March of that year, he was deemed to be one of the "new civil rights leaders" by the *Los Angeles Times*. As part of the profile presented, the paper highlighted him as co-winner of the PEN New England 2015 Howard Zinn Freedom to Write Award.

Despite all of the accolades, almost six months later McKesson attempted to take a horrible tragedy and turn it into an opportunity to attack another race. Following the senseless murder of WDBJ7 reporter Alison Parker and her cameraman Adam Ward on live television, McKesson took to twitter and wrote, "Some say 'disgruntled employee,' others say 'terrorist.' Whiteness will explain away nearly anything." His tweet was based around false information that the gunman was white, when later it was discovered that he was actually African American. DeRay McKesson's choice to make split-second assumptions before receiving the facts actually reflects the fault that routinely plagues the entire group. So often the desired narrative to advance the cause is substituted for the facts.

The gunman was black, two were killed and one was wounded: all the victims were white, but none of these specifics should have been used as the determining factor in how to react. In regards to McKesson, how could such a reckless tweet come from a man thought of by some as a civil rights leader? He completely disregarded the suffering of those involved in the tragedy that day and instead immediately viewed it as a chance to diminish an entire race. Not that it would serve to make it any less disturbing or understandable, but his words were not simply off the cuff in the heat of the moment. His response was calculated before being posted to his twitter feed. The mainstream media ignored it, as did others in very high places. The horrific shooting took place in August 2015. The following month McKesson secured a role as guest lecturer for the "Transformation Leadership for Church and Society lecture series" offered at Yale. He then ended the month of September 2015 with a trip to D.C., where he met with members of the U.S. Congress—which included Sen. Bernie Sanders (I-VT) and Sen. Elizabeth Warren (D-MA)—to discuss his and other supporters desired police reforms found within the Campaign Zero platform. However, just as he finished the first week of October 2015 with his lectures at Yale, he was given the opportunity to sit directly across from the Democratic presidential frontrunner, Hillary Clinton, and also inform her about how police should be reformed in the eyes of Campaign Zero.

The meeting was most likely attended by Hillary Clinton as nothing more than a photo op, as a member of Black Lives Matter (BLM) had rejected any advice from her at a rally the previous month by saying, "I say this as respectfully as I can, but you don't tell Black people what we need to do." However, regardless of the reason, why didn't former Secretary of State Clinton take the opportunity to bring together a diversity of perspectives within the African-American community for enhancing the discussion?

Nowhere in the picture of those at the table is Rep. John Lewis (D-GA), who stood with Dr. Martin Luther King, Jr. as he tailored a successful civil rights movement. Bernice King, who daily promotes a commitment to achieving progress through the nonviolent approach her father championed, was also not in attendance. Nor it seems was a single member from Project 21 or The National Leadership Network of Black Conservatives to offer a different vision for achieving the mutual desire to see African Americans move forward. Seasoned L.A. Civil Rights activists such as Rev. Cecil "Chip" Murray, Najee Ali, and Earl Ofari would have offered insight for conducting the movement, as Angel Jennings of the *Los Angeles Times* reported on their dismay regarding the group's hostile actions; yet, none of these individuals were present for the discussion.

Regardless of the questions surrounding why the meeting took place or who was allowed to attend, one has to wonder if Hillary Clinton asked DeRay McKesson about his highly insensitive tweet pertaining to the tragic murders approximately a month and a half before. It would also be nice to know whether she asked him about his general views toward law enforcement and the rule of law before denoting his ideas on police reform. It is significant when considering McKesson had just finished his lectures on "In Defense of Looting" to Yale only days before meeting with the former Secretary of State. "In Defense of Looting" was an essay written during the Ferguson unrest and basically looks to present the argument that the entire crux of racial tension is centered on property, with white supremacists relying on the police and mainstream media to serve as their henchman for maintaining control of it. This is the foundation of thought utilized by the author, Willie Osterweil, for asking whether any attention would be given to places like Ferguson if it were not for the destruction of property. It is a question that few business owners in Ferguson were considering as they saw their livelihoods decimated.

While there was diversity within those owners affected by the looting, Natalie DuBose, an African American and mother of two, witnessed her bakery reflect the wrath of looters. Cavan Sieczkowski of *The Huffington Post* recounted DuBose's experiences in her article from December 2014: "'Everything that I invested, it came from me saving money through bake sales,' she told NBC News. 'Sometimes I couldn't buy a pair of tennis shoes because I wanted to make sure I had enough money to buy a bucket of icing. It was an investment all around. I always had to work at least two jobs. I never just had just one job because my dream was always to have my own bakery.'"

The unwarranted hardships placed on Natalie DuBose and other business owners mean nothing to some within BLM. As Willie Osterweil wrote in his "In Defense of Looting" essay for *The New Inquiry*, "Whenever people worry about looting, there is an implicit sense that the looter must necessarily be acting selfishly, 'opportunistically,' and in excess. But why is it bad to grab an opportunity to improve well-being, to make life better, easier, or more comfortable? Or, as Hannah Black put it on Twitter, 'Cops exist so people can't loot ie have nice things for free so idk why it's so confusing that people loot when they protest against the cops' [sic]. Only if you believe that having nice things for free is amoral, if you believe, in short, that the current (white-supremacist, settler-colonialist) regime of property is just, can you believe that looting is amoral in itself."

As some entertained a debate around the practice of looting, a number of strangers helped provide Natalie DuBose and her family hope for the future by donating over $270,000, easily surpassing her GoFundMe goal of simply raising $20,000. The donors to the single mother displayed diversity in race and ethnicity. Apparently, no one took time to evaluate what message choosing to give or not give might send in relation to a particular movement, but instead just longed to do the right thing.

It seems safe to assume that DeRay McKesson holds the work of Willie Osterweil in high regard, considering he utilized his essay to teach a class at Yale. Osterweil is listed at *The New Inquiry* as a "writer, editor, and member of the punk band Vulture Sh**t," and has written numerous articles. A quick review of his work basically foreshadowed some of the future strategy of the Black Lives Matter movement.

A few months after Ferguson, Osterweil wrote an article for *Al Jazeera America* entitled "The political potential of party riots: Can frat bros help oppose arbitrary police violence?" He partially offers an answer to his own question in writing, "In this country, where police forces have their historical roots in fugitive slave patrols, few institutions represent and maintain white supremacy more than the police. In order to support black freedom struggles, white people will have to learn to oppose the police on an institutional level. Party riots may push white college students in that direction." The month after DeRay McKesson's lectures at Yale, the students successfully gained national headlines by protesting over Halloween costumes, with more protests to follow from other colleges and universities. The University of Missouri was also in the midst of unrest at the time. While there are many peaceful protests genuinely designed to bring needed reform, those being staged at college campuses too often display the troubling characteristics of BLM.

Impediments to building broad support from a reliable foundation of truth seem consistently self-inflicted by those offering some of the loudest voices to the BLM movement. According to the article from Rober Gehl of the *Federalist Papers*, many of the circumstances surrounding the protests in Missouri were questionable. Jonathan Butler, the central figure of the campus protests, was presented as "a young, black, angry victim of a racist country determined to keep African Americans mired in crime and poverty." However, despite consistent images from the mainstream media regarding Butler's hunger strike, Gehl cited information from Steven Crowder of "Louder with Crowder" that revealed "[Butler's] dad makes 8.4 million per year."

Jonathan Butler definitely seems disingenuous in how he presented himself. However, Payton Head, the student body president, was actually caught purposely lying and forced to apologize over his post to twitter which read, "Students please take precaution. Stay away from windows in residence halls. The KKK has been confirmed to be sighted on campus. I'm working with MUPD, the state troopers, and the National Guard." While few believe racism does not exist to a certain extent, one must ask how legitimate the extent of his other claims may be. If he is an openly homosexual African-American male, how could he have become student body president if the school was as racist as he claims? Obviously, there is a degree of unfortunate racism on almost every college campus from all diversities, but based on school figures, it seems virtually impossible that Head could become president without receiving a number of white votes.

A November 2015 article entitled "Eyes Wide Open at the Protest" from *The Dartmouth Review* provided details the mainstream media casually overlooked regarding the protests on campus that centered on Berry Library. After describing how the group of BLM protestors began the march by gathering in front of Dartmouth Hall and chanting curse words in unison, the rest of their piece focused on what took place in the library itself. "The flood of demonstrators self-consciously overstepped every boundary, opening the doors of study spaces with students reviewing for exams. Those who tried to close their doors were harassed further. One student abandoned the study room and ran out of the library. The protestors followed her out of the library, shouting obscenities the whole way. Students who refused to listen to or join their outbursts were shouted down. 'Stand the f*** up!' You filthy racist white piece of s***!'"

Despite many forms of intimidation, the school administration chose to offer its support of those protesting. Beyond defending *The Dartmouth Review* only three days later from criticism, Brian Chen highlighted how Vice Provost for Student Affairs Inge-Lise Ameer utilized the "emergency community meeting" that followed to "[express] unqualified support for the protestors, not only with respect to their safety and right to protest but also their demands and actions." She said "the protest was a "wonderful, beautiful thing" and "[the] new Provost [was] very much in support of all this." Any discussion concerning the harassment inside the library was denied preference.

A number of important things could have been discussed at that meeting. So often those outside the headlines and flashing glare of the media lights are simply forgotten. What about the students who applied to college and were not chosen; or the students working two and three jobs to simply pay for the first step in the difficult path to obtaining an education? Are the tests they face ever considered by those sitting on a college campus, especially major ones? What would countless individuals give for the same opportunity? Would they undervalue the privilege of going to a school like Yale over an argument with a professor telling people it's acceptable to dress like characters from Disney? These types of questions could come from individuals of all races and seem to receive little consideration. It is clear that a number of educational institutions are missing teaching opportunities that could lead to the positive development of minds.

The administration of Dartmouth again saw the event revisited following the destruction of a memorial for fallen police officers on campus. Beyond describing how members of BLM attempted to defend against this latest decision, Back Neff from *The Daily Caller* also described how the 566-word response from the group also addressed the violence inside the library six months earlier. They wrote, "'F**k your comfort, there is no such thing as neutral existence,' it says. 'Sitting in the library with your headphones in intensifies this violence against people of color, muting the voices of the movement, the cries of our peers, and the history of inequality.'"

Regardless of the questions of accountability that schools should be asking concerning protests, the demands of college protestors often seem puzzling. Despite a diverse coalition of Americans working together to end segregation, some African Americans today look at the practice as something that could positively affect their lives. In a September 2016 article from *The Daily Caller* entitled, "Taxpayer-funded California University offers segregated black-only housing," Annabel Scott wrote, "The Halsi Scholars Black Living-Learning Community has opened approximately nine months after the CSULA Black Student Union issued a list of demands to the university, including a 'Black student only' living space with a 'full time Resident Director who can cater to the needs of Black students.'" The cost of living that deters other students of all races and ethnicities from an education seem unimportant to the group, which shouldn't be surprising considering the one-sided rhetoric commonly attached to their demands.

The endeavor for change solely based on the advancement of one race may have been demonstrated best at a Black Lives Matter rally from November 2016 at Claremont McKenna College in California. A video from the event displays an Asian woman offering the message that no one should be judged by their race, but by the heart that is shown through their actions. Her story was about how a car containing African Americans had harassed her before a white woman had eventually come to her aid. The awkwardness from the lack of support and discontent among the crowd to her echoing of Dr. King's sentiments on character was met by the next speaker who callously said, "Ya'll, we're getting derailed, alright. You're losing sight of the movement."

The list of demands being presented by BLM activists on college campuses also include aspects of Affirmative Action that have already been consistently challenged by the court. "Racial quotas are considered unconstitutional by the U.S. Supreme Court," with race only allowed as one factor of consideration in determining which students are ultimately admitted. However, in terms of the faculty, even if quotas were utilized to produce more African-American professors, it would not guarantee better instruction. Once again, the premise of Black Lives Matter activists is that race alone should determine someone's worthiness, as opposed to judging everyone equally by their actions.

Saida Grundy was ultimately hired as a professor at Boston University despite some questionable acts of racism before the decision was finalized. She did not shy away from offering controversial tweets, with one tweet in which she called "white, college-aged males a 'problem population.'" She also allegedly belittled a past child sexual assault victim with a line of ridicule that centered on the woman essentially being white and unworthy of crying over a difference of opinion the two held in relation to a speech of empowerment. Although her parents were civil rights activists, Grundy also thought it was clever in January 2015 to tweet, "Every MLK week i [sic] commit myself to not spending a dime in a white-owned business and every year i [sic] find it nearly impossible."

Having more African-American professors would be wonderful and ideal, but giving them the job over someone else based on their race undermines equality. There are plenty of worthy candidates from every race who can simply earn the position, including African Americans, who need no special requirement for success. Presenting themes of victimhood and division is impacting Americans well beyond the classroom, as many young people are actually embracing ideas that serve as impediments to progress. In covering the Black Lives Matter protests from July 2016, Sean Hannity of Fox News had a field reporter conduct interviews with a number of those protesting. After explaining how the root cause of the grievances facing African Americans was their dependence on the "white dollar," one protestor added, "We have to start putting [sic] bringing the 'black dollar' back into our community, start building our own schools, start building start building (sic) our own stores, our own banks; things that we've always had. We've had our banks. We had the black market before. We've had the black stores before. It's time for us to start fighting for something that we need to do for ourselves."

Few would doubt the need for all Americans to strive to contribute more to their communities, but being driven by a mentality that denies certain individuals a chance at possibly building a relationship due to their race makes little sense. When a local store becomes threatened by a larger corporation from outside the community, those in the area who value the trust of a familiar face in the neighborhood should come out in droves to support them. The makeup of customers has the possibility of being diverse, as many Americans still value a "mom and pop" store. However, while diverse support could potentially be found through communication, opportunities are lost from a closed mind. Community leaders have to take a stand against identity politics and those advancing the ideas that breed division.

There is no room for ambiguity.

As part of his work in 1966 on the CBS Reports documentary, "Black Power, White Backlash," legendary journalist Mike Wallace interviewed Dr. Martin Luther King, Jr. In referring to his most cherished interview in his 2005 memoir, Wallace wrote, "In our interview, I brought up a speech King had recently given in which he reaffirmed his commitment to nonviolence; 'I would like for all of us to believe in nonviolence,' he declared. 'But I'm here to say tonight that if every Negro in the United States turns against nonviolence I'm going to stand up as a lone voice and say, 'This is the wrong way!'"

Following the horrific Dallas shooting from July 2016, Black Lives Matter released a statement that, in part, read, "Black activists have raised the call for an end to violence, not an escalation of it. Yesterday's attack was the result of the actions of a lone gunman. To assign the actions of one person to an entire movement is dangerous and irresponsible. We continue our efforts to bring about a better world for all of us."

The President has offered similar sentiments regarding the fault in making generalizations. However, where have the voices of peace been in directly opposing specific rhetoric from groups that essentially condone violence and division? This is especially true when it comes to the protection of young hearts and minds. Despite the height of the protests on college campuses, there were apparently few, if any, who felt the need to thoroughly investigate the stated goals of various groups and speak out against them when needed. Then again, regardless of what they say publicly, some may actually support the "black power"-themed rhetoric reminiscent of the 60s.

The Black Liberation Collective website provides the list of demands for 86 colleges and universities, which includes all of the highly publicized schools. The group describes itself as "a collective consisting of Black students who are dedicated to transforming institutions of higher education through unity, coalition building, direct action and political education." They are anti-capitalistic. "Instead, [they] propose a cooperative form of economics that works on shared resources and shared means of production to uplift [themselves] out of poverty." However, regardless of any debate concerning the endeavors of the group, it is their stance on the use of violence that continues to demand attention from those advocating for peace.

While not representative of all BLM, the troubling words found within the principle the Black Liberation Collective lists highlight the failure of adequate voices for direction, allowing dangerous ideas to surge. The organization writes, "We understand that continuing to remain peaceful and encouraging others to remain peaceful at the hands of white supremacist [sic] oppressive violence is illogical and immoral. We support those who believe that nonviolence is a tactic, but we are aware that this is not the only way to dismantle the system that has humiliated, physically and literally enslaved, unjustly murdered, and continues to devalue black people in America. We will strive for liberation by any means necessary, including but not limited to: armed self-defense." After these words, sitting alone beneath this paragraph, the sentence read, "We condone whatever methods Black people adopt to liberate themselves and their kin.

Skepticism regarding the announcements against violence only after an event occurs seems legitimate to raise, especially considering the blind eye essentially being given to separatist endeavors commonly advocated and backed by divisive rhetoric and words that specifically "condone whatever methods." However, radical speech is not just being heard in isolated rallies or written on websites, it is being advocated by those in the heights of Black Lives Matter, with an attorney for the group offering a striking example.

In an article from July 2016, Walter Hudson, the president of the Minority Liberty Alliance, wrote, "Black Lives Matter and their Marxist supporters don't want to trim a few laws here and tweak a few fines there. They want to abolish the established legal order. Black Lives Matter attorney Nana Gyamfi called for just that during an interview with a California Station." He then listed her saying, "I see the police as part of the state and part of state sanctioned violence against our people, and so for me, I'm not concerned about blue lives, I'm concerned about black lives. In fact, I want the police to be abolished. I think we should be pushing the police out of our community. I think that we should be defunding the police. I think that we should be demilitarizing the police and finally dismantling the police." Where are the voices of thoughtful opposition?

Some would say the police have already been pulled out of the communities in areas like Chicago due to hesitation as a result of the "Ferguson Effect." Crime has skyrocketed there as law-abiding citizens are left to watch helplessly as the gangs have practically been given an easier path to impose their will. However, instead of the media holding all accountable by asking tough questions and presenting the information without the filter of their own personal bias, many have chosen to maintain a particular narrative regardless of circumstance. As many within the heights of business, government, and entertainment either fuel those forces against the spirit of unity and inclusion or refuse to soundly reject them, the path to solving race relations continues to remain elusive. One of the greatest impediments to positive change is stereotyping, where many of the same individuals asking for one not to be used on supporters of BLM, turn right around and casually label all police as corrupt based on the actions of a few. Railing against stereotypes while consistently projecting them in your own life is disingenuous, hypocritical, and counterproductive; yet, many never seem to value this fact. Rev. Jesse Jackson's comments following the tragic death of Alton Sterling, in which he basically offered a broad generalization of the police now being representative of the Ku Klux Klan, were reprehensible. It would be unjust to judge or make assumptions about all African-American politicians as a result of the actions of a few.

Consider the son of Rev. Jesse Jackson. Jesse Jackson Jr. served himself and his wife more than any of his constituents in his "service" as a congressman from Illinois, unlawfully spending over $700,000 of campaign money to fulfill their desires. Kim Bellware detailed his acts for *The Huffington Post* in 2015. "Prosecutors said Jackson and his wife, former Chicago Councilwoman Sandi Jackson, used the funds as their personal piggy bank, spending the cash on luxury items that included vacations, furs, Rolex watches, and pricey Bruce Lee and Michael Jackson memorabilia."

There is also the more recent case of congresswoman Corrine Brown (D-FL) who was accused in July 2016 of misusing money designated for goodwill. "According to the indictment, Brown and her chief of staff are accused of using Brown's position to bring $800,000 in donations to a fraudulent education charity. Prosecutors said the organization gave out two scholarships totaling $1,200. The rest, they said, was used as 'a personal slush fund.'" The actions of a few cannot be used to judge others bearing a similar distinction. To do so would be unjust and counterproductive.

Of course, Rev. Jackson is far from alone in advancing generalizations. In explaining to the viewers of MSNBC's "The Rachel Maddow Show" why she believed Marco Rubio decided to pull out of campaigning for the 2016 presidential primary in Louisiana, Joy Ann Reid of the same network also referenced Alabama and Mississisipi before saying, "He's competing for what he knows it is, if you look at that map of the old slave states of the Union." The context and tone of the discussion is in line with her routine behavior to take almost any opportunity to paint white voters as essentially only being driven by race in the decisions they make concerning elections. Whether her comments were only aimed at the bigots and racists who can actually be found among every race, her words left the impression that she did not mind using a broad stroke in painting the entire population of white voters within each of those states as being racist.

Unfortunately, host Rachel Maddow did not offer any pushback to Joy Ann Reid on her comments. In fact, she praised her for them. No one should make generalizations about African Americans or members of the LGBT community. Yet two individuals associated with these particular distinctions did not appear to have any reservations about painting entire populations as racist. It would actually take Joy Ann Reid's continued ridicule of Melania Trump over using some words from First Lady Michelle Obama in the speech she gave at the 2016 Republican National Convention to finally receive some criticism. At one point, Chris Matthews, one of MSNBC's co-hosts for the Republican convention coverage, actually acknowledged all of her "generalizing" in the rebuke she remained determined to launch. It is very disappointing that Maddow did not take her own opportunity to do the same, as her show is one of the most thought provoking on the air.

The fear of following their lead in forming stereotypes definitely

prevents some within politics and the mainstream media from reporting or placing an emphasis on certain events. The assault of Christopher Marquez may demonstrate this best. He is the Marine who was
accosted by a group of African American teens allegedly because he
would not answer them when they approached his restaurant table
and asked about his support of Black Lives Matter. He was hit in the
back of the head with an object as he left the restaurant, only to
awake without his possessions, including his VA medical card.

The Daily Caller's Steve Birr provided some background on the
decorated Marine in writing, "Marquez served eight years active duty
in the Marines between 2003 and 2011 in Iraq and Afghanistan as a
Rifleman and Scout Sniper. He received the Bronze Star for valor
during his first deployment after he carried the body of his slain team
leader from combat following an ambush during the Battle of Fallu-
jah." A statue memorializing the event sits at Camp Pendleton and
represents the courage of all the military. This is who was attacked for
not answering a question. As he told "Fox and Friends" co-host Brian Kilmeade following his recovery, "It was a hate crime because they
did target me because of my skin color."

Despite the attempts of the mainstream media and others to present two distinct narratives when it comes to their common treatment
of Black Lives Matter and law enforcement, the general public, by
and large, still has faith in the police. If anything, the bias of the media has created a backlash. Rasmussen polls from late July 2016 reported that "Only 14% think most deaths that involve the police are
the fault of the policeman. More Americans than ever (72%) rate the
performance of the police in the area where they live as good or ex-
cellent." Fairness in reporting is what law enforcement desires so that
their jobs are not made more difficult through innuendo and mis-
truths.

Although it is not scientific by any means, a routine glance at the
comments attached to stories involving race highlighted by Yahoo
could be revealing. It is very difficult to discover many posts that are
positive. Most of the comments instead express reservations about
the media once again misleading through their choice of headlines
and writing style. Other topics that are commonly mentioned are the
absence of discussion on personal responsibility—or dismay with one
or both major parties. In responding to a story posted on Yahoo
News about the unfortunate death of Korryn Gaines at the hands of
an officer who was allegedly forced to shoot as a result of her pointing a shotgun at him, one random commenter (Jeffrey) expressed
what he believed the media should be doing as they cover these type

events. He wrote, "The best way to view all of these instances is to first remove any and all references to race. The story/case would be present [sic] differently and the cops [sic] judgment would be reviewed simply on the facts and if they used the correct amount of force. In our country, we pride ourselves on innocent until PROVEN guilty. In today's media, the exact opposite is occurring and very few are addressing it. The media does not want to attack the media… If she was truly a caring parent, she would have surrendered to the police to protect the children from the exposure to violence and potential harm. Her actions were selfish and placed her child in harms [sic] way in addition to her neighbors and the police trying to arrest her. This should be the focus of the media, not the color of her skin…."

It is unconscionable that the mainstream media very selectively chooses which individuals and entities to blindly defend, allowing the questionable actions from a few who have been given unwarranted legitimacy to undermine the real potential for progress. In the fight for better race relations and an end to the police misconduct associated with a minority of officers, it is a disservice to those genuinely seeking change when a journalist or politician out of fear or bias fails to hold all equally accountable. Disregarding uniformity in evaluating all individuals and groups seeking influence is dangerous, and also allows others to be unduly discredited by mere association. One has to wonder whether many within the media ever consider that in allowing certain individuals a pass from accountability, they are in effect hindering other figures of sound heart and true intentions to emerge and fill the void for necessary change. Within our country—which includes every segment, race, ethnicity, and gender—these leaders do exist. Medgar Evers was such an individual. His wife, also a prominent civil rights activist, described the work of her husband on the 50th anniversary of his senseless murder, by saying, "Medgar was a man who never wanted adoration, who never wanted to be in the limelight. He was a man who saw a job that needed to be done and he answered the call and the fight for freedom, dignity, and justice not just for his people but all people." The press has to do better in helping Americans discover more leaders like him.

In August 2016, it was announced that DeRay McKesson would be suing over his arrest at the Baton Rouge protests for Alton Sterling, just days before the murder of cops by a disgruntled African American. He disagrees with the police version of events that led to the arrest and contends it was unwarranted. However, Kevin Rector of *The Baltimore Sun* wrote, "In a statement released Sunday titled 'A Tale of Two Protests' Baton Rouge Police Sgt. Don Coppola Jr. said a locally organized protest on Saturday was peaceful, and resulted in zero arrests. But then, he wrote, the protest McKesson was at on Saturday night near police headquarters turned violent after 'individuals from outside our Baton Rouge community' arrived. In all, 102 people were arrested, and three rifles, three shotguns, and two pistols were confiscated,' Coppola wrote."

Yet despite his past tweets, questionable influence at protests, and dismal showing of support in his bid to become the mayor of Baltimore, the press still works to present him as offering a valued and trusted voice for progress. In that mayoral election, despite the support of certain celebrities and various members of the press, tech industry, and politics, McKesson still only earned around 2.5% of the vote. Following his arrest in Baton Rouge, Katie Couric apparently believed a softball interview was necessary, as she welcomed him for a sit down to be aired on Yahoo Global News. Unlike her gun rights documentary, this interview was likely perceived as one that would not need editing to produce the narrative she desired. Of course, Couric is far from alone in giving this man debatable attention, as McKesson is routinely given opportunities to spread his divisive rhetoric through various platforms and would have been on CBS's "Face the Nation" if he had not been in jail, according to an article from the *Observer* written by Joe Lapointe.

Though the press may be beneficial to him, DeRay McKesson also has the favor of the most powerful man in the world, as President Obama welcomed him to the White House in February 2016. In an article discussing McKesson's invitation, Kevin Whitson of *Western Journalism* wrote, "Kevin Jackson, from The Black Sphere, concluded McKesson is simply a 'race baiter' and a 'race pimp' who only goes around the country starting problems and then leaves, forcing someone else to clean up his mess."

Similar sentiments of Kevin Jackson could be heard from residents of Baton Rouge, Louisiana, who experienced unprecedented flooding only to annoyingly witness an absence in BLM activists offering aid. Valerie Richardson of *The Washington Times* posted the video and cited the words of Jerry L. Washington, an African American who caught the attention of millions online as he asked why members of Black Lives Matter and the Black Panthers were nowhere to be found. The words she documented from another resident perfectly mimicked the theme that Kevin Jackson had offered months before. "'This is the most you have done after you [came] and raised hell and stirred up [a] mess... Where are the donations from your organization?' asked Manolo Espinal of Louisiana. 'Boats to rescue people? Food for the hungry? Where are the marches and protests for the homeless and those who lost everything?'"

The only group to quite possibly draw a larger condemnation for their absence after the flooding was the mainstream media. There was a stark difference to the sustained presence that the media offered during the protests. The lack of media coverage was one of the topics Heather Cross, a resident of Baton Rouge, Louisiana, actually addressed in a Facebook post that went viral. She wrote, "I believe you people are stone cold silent about this flood, because really, there's no agenda to push. There's no side to take. There's nobody to blame," referring to her early criticism of how the media had little problem coming in during the previous unrest and offering nothing but rebuke for a community that was simply attempting to stabilize the ship to move forward.

Heather Cross also described the unity displayed by the residents during the flooding. "While it was still raining, a spontaneous, private, and well-meaning navy of ordinary people assembled themselves. They were black, white, Asian, and otherwise. They weren't protesting anything. They got into their own boats, spent their own money, spent their own time, risked their own lives. Black people saved white people. White people saved black people. Nobody asked what color you were before knocking on your door." Obviously, the memo sent out from the Obama administration warning against discriminating with aid assistance was unnecessary; but in the President's defense, this might have been difficult to comprehend from a golf course 1600 miles away!

As for McKesson, unfortunately his opportunities for influence will likely continue considering his affiliates. Kelly Riddell of *The Washington Times* wrote a January 2015 article entitled "George Soros funds Ferguson protests, hopes to spur civil action," in which she detailed the extent of the liberal billionaire's involvement. "In all, Mr. Soros gave at least $33 million in one year to support already-established groups that emboldened the grass-roots, on-the-ground activists in Ferguson, according to the most recent tax filings of his non-profit Open Society Foundation." Riddell then reflected on the impact of possessing such monetary power in writing, "The financial tether from Mr. Soros to the activist groups gave rise to a combustible protest movement that transformed a one-day criminal event in Missouri into a 24-hour-a-day national cause celebre."

An article in *The American Mirror* by Ryan Girdusky entitled "BLM leader lives in home owned by Soros' Open Society board member" highlighted the perks of selling out to the elites. In providing a correlation to confirm his claims about DeRay McKesson living in the home of Open Society donors James and Robin Wood, he posted an image of an address on a document and wrote, "It's the same address [DeRay] used when declaring his residency on his campaign committee registration form for his failed mayoral run in the city's Democratic primary earlier this year." Between the residence and the $165,000 DeRay makes as a high-ranking official in the Baltimore City School System, it would seem the sky is the limit for how much influence McKesson can bring.

Working within a school system provides easy access to recruiting for causes and poisoning young minds, but it seems his questionable tactics in protesting is not a concern for the school. Having a billionaire for possible political influence couldn't hurt. Just as having the monetary means to pay for protestors could never be a bad thing for building a team of loyal followers, if that was what someone chose to do. Only those behind the scenes know what is truly happening. But in the case of DeRay McKesson, he seems to have an ally in George Soros, who donated a million dollars to a super PAC that supported Obama in his run for President; the same was done for Hillary Clinton.

Communities have to come together so no individual or group is given the opportunity to come in and add to the complexities of solving problems that can only be adequately addressed through unity. Without this safeguard, outside influence will be used to essentially pimp out youth to a road to nowhere, whether it be through the seduction of money, power, peer-pressure, or drugs. Although these manipulations come from numerous sources, certain factions of BLM are either directly leading individuals to unwise decisions or indirectly affecting them with hostile and divisive rhetoric. One mom of a young man from Pennsylvania who joined his friend in attempting to kill a police officer with multiple gunshots said, "They are in jail for doing what Black Lives Matter wanted them to do: shoot at cops." As Kim Smith of the *Conservative Tribune* further documented from the mom of one of the boys now facing an unknown and bleak future existence, "The truth is that these are two punk kids following the orders of an irresponsible organization and now they're gonna pay for it," she said.

Research can offer insights. "In a year-long study, *The Washington Post* found that the kind of incidents that have ignited protests in many U.S. communities—most often, white police officers killing unarmed black men—represent less than 4 percent of fatal police shootings." However, the same study from reporters Kimberly Kindy, Mark Fisher, Julie Tate, and Jennifer Jenkins also found, "In the majority of cases in which police shot and killed a person who had attacked someone with a weapon or brandished a gun, the person who was shot was white. But a hugely disproportionate number—3 in 5—of those killed after exhibiting less threatening behavior were black or Hispanic."

As beneficial as this information may be in forming a more accurate picture of what is going on in the streets of America, relying on figures is about as useful in solving the problem as is the government relying on unemployment numbers to measure success or failure of the economy. Each side can pick and choose certain aspects to build a defense for proving the other side wrong, instead of working together to resolve the underlying issues that no amount of reports will ever reveal through stats alone. In August, 2015, Jamilah Nasheed, a Missouri State representative, discussed the ongoing effort to rejuvenate Ferguson and the Northern County area. She spoke of the willingness she had witnessed from the private sector to aid in the meaningful process. However, when asked by MSNBC host Craig Melvin about whether this investment had changed the atmosphere of isolation and distrust that helped fuel the 2014 riots, her response reflected that many of the components for actual recovery were still missing.

In responding, she said, "I think that when we look at the systematic problem that has plagued these individuals for so long [such as] economic and political oppression, [we can conclude] that once we change these dynamics, I think only then will we change the mindset and the hearts of these people that are in poverty along the Ferguson and the Northern County." Nasheed also said, "And I do believe that one thing that we haven't changed is the police and the community relationship. I think that we are going to have to get there and we are not there yet, but we will get there because everyone in the state of Missouri and the city of St. Louis are looking to move this city and state forward."

A number of African Americans have been hurting for some time. As with so many other issues facing the country, the idea of simply throwing more money at the situation is not going to bring solutions. Answers will never be discovered by a reliance on closed-door meetings, polls on progress, campaign visits, and standard economic numbers. Demonstrated integrity is required to alleviate the frustrations of those who feel forgotten. Only with a confidence that someone authentically cares can hope be created—a vital ingredient for individuals to possess to obtain successful upward mobility.

Former President Harry S. Truman displayed the authentic leadership needed today. As Merle Miller wrote in his book detailing his interviews with Truman, "And we remember that at the 1953 inaugural blacks were invited to all the social events for the first time in American history. But that was public, that was politics; people were watching, and the black vote was getting to be important." Miller continued, "But in 1940 in Sedalia, Missouri, before an audience mostly of farmers, many of them ex-Ku Kluxers, and not a black face anywhere, Harry S. Truman spoke out on civil rights."

After Merle Miller detailed some of the words President Truman offered to the crowd that day and then expressed his belief that such a speech from the time period was "very courageous," Truman responded, "I don't know why. That sort of thing, whether what I was saying was courageous or not, never did occur to me. And you have to understand what I said out there at Sedalia wasn't anything new for me to say. All those Southern fellas were very much surprised by my program for civil rights in 1948. What they didn't understand was that I'd been for things like that all the time I was in politics. I believe in the Constitution, and if you do that, then everybody's got to have their rights, and that means everybody, doesn't matter a d**n who they are or what color they are."

The People's Clearing House could help citizens discover which individuals would most likely demonstrate a similar political courage; actions that are not designed for the cameras, but that come from the heart of a servant. With men and women truly invested in solving the issues, life-changing alterations could occur in communities. Political leaders have the ability to set the proper tone for progress if they reject the old and counterproductive ways of conducting business, and instead embrace accountability. What could genuine representation and a true commitment to community investment have meant to a place like Ferguson, Missouri? What could it mean now? How could it possibly alter Baltimore, Maryland, where discovering employment remains bleak, sub-par educational services are being offered and an estimated "17,000" homes remain deserted within some of the areas with the lowest socioeconomic status? Following the same failed politics of today guarantees that the people located in numerous communities across the country will never be allowed to discover their true potential.

In his 2002 book, *Robert Kennedy: His Life*, Evan Thomas described the understanding the former U.S. Attorney General held for those on the ground actually planning for successful urban development. Finding a solution to helping the poor was obviously one focus of his stint in the U.S. Senate. As Thomas described, "Kennedy had a group of businessmen who were willing to invest some capital and know-how or find others to do it for them, but they knew little about the needs and wants of a Brooklyn slum. It wouldn't do for white businessman to simply dictate to black community leaders in any event." The People's Clearing House empowers the community to take a greater lead in setting the direction for solving issues. Priceless knowledge can be gained from the chosen initiatives of The People's Clearing House.

Creating this type of leadership that is more in tune with the realities of the demands and hardships facing those they represent is important, but the people in each community must take a more active role in setting the tone of unity necessary for success. Reggie Ross is one man who demonstrates that type of initiative. He is the owner of Royal Touch Barbershop in Palm Beach County, Florida, and is determined to use his interactions with young African-American men as teaching moments for success. By having each of them choose a book from his library to read and analyze while in the shop, Reggie hopes to place a dent in the current county graduation rate that has only been witnessing half of its student body actually earn a diploma. Reggie told a local new station, WPTV, "The barbershop is based on men coming together grooming each other to become better men, and I think books and education is a fundamental part of that."

The work of Reggie has not gone unnoticed. After seeing the story, Michelle King, a former Floridian, contributed an article to The Airship blog and offered a better sense of the impact his decision has had on the children that come to his shop. She wrote, "I would be lying if I said I was familiar with Royal Touch [Barbershop], but I am very familiar with the neighborhood its [sic] located in. It's 30 minutes from my childhood home, 15 from my high school and just 5 from the healthcare clinic where I volunteered. During my time at the clinic, I met many young people who had dropped out of high school. The criticism often launched at them was that they were stupid, lazy or both—but I never saw that. What I did see were young men and women who had been discouraged by their own communities. Ross's [barbershop] is fighting that."

In his final year of study at Alabama A&M, an African-American college student named Rodney Smith Jr. decided he was going to take the lead in personally strengthening his community. Anna Clair Vollers wrote in her April 2016 article for al.com, "Part lawncare company and part youth program, the service now has about 20 young men, ages 7-17, who cut lawns at no charge for the elderly, disabled, and for single mothers who don't have the time or resources to keep their yards freshly manicured."

Beyond teaching youth the satisfaction found in helping others, he is instilling valuable life lessons within each child. With "Raising Men Lawn Care Service," the Bermuda native and his business partner, Terrence Story, "take them on outings and work with them on developing self-esteem, a strong work ethic, and high moral standards." The type of work they are doing, as with that of Reggie Ross, does a hundred times more for advancing the lives of those within their community than any national anthem protest, race-baiting speech, act of violence, or hateful rhetoric designed around the idea of "us vs. them." These men are focused on positively redefining the future rather than living in the past, and know that building up young men with character and vision is the key.

It is impossible for men like Reggie Ross, Rodney Smith Jr., and Terrence Story to know what the results will be for some of the men they are profoundly affecting each day. However, Chris Redlitz may provide a hint at what their acts of kindness could produce. He has founded two programs for prisoners in the hopes of lowering recidivism, which would save billions to taxpayers over time. The program he recently launched, Code.7370, teaches prisoners to code for greater opportunity when released. His other program, The Last Mile, teaches prisoners about business. It has been around for six years and has shown exceptional results, displaying what can happen with hope. In a February, 2016 article, Redlitz described the story of one former student in writing, "In one of the early graduating classes, James Houston developed a nonprofit business plan that would positively impact at-risk youth in his old neighborhood. James created Teen Tech Hub, an afterschool program, teaching app development and basic coding instruction for kids 10 to 14 years old. After serving 18 years in prison, James returned to Richmond, California, to pursue his dream. He was hired by the City of Richmond and he plans to launch Teen Tech Hub in the fall of 2016." It's amazing what can be achieved when people work together without the burden of preconceptions.

In Paulo Coelho's acclaimed book *The Alchemist*, he wrote, "No matter what he does, every person on earth plays a central role in the history of the world. And normally he doesn't know it." Everyone has a role to play. When more Americans begin coming out of the shadows and teaching others the power of personal responsibility, sacrifice, and unity of purpose, a genuine movement for progress will be formed.

Former Boston Police Commissioner Ed Davis highlighted how

community policing had kept Boston form joining the ranks of other major cities in witnessing a recent increase in violent crime. In a June 2016 interview, he told Fox News, "We instituted an early program of community policing here in the early 90s. It's continued. Our relationship with the community is really strong. We are using data to drive our decisions. And it's it's [sic] all based upon academically proven uh [sic] strategies that reduce those causal factors. And if you continue to do that and stay close to the community, you can make a difference. I had a twenty-year stretch where we reduced crime every year in the police departments that I led. It can be done."

When members of the community begin coming together, a realization will occur that they each seek the same things from their community and government. It is whether there is a willingness to unite to achieve it. As John F. Kennedy wrote, "In a democracy, every citizen, regardless of his interest in politics, 'holds office'; every one of us is in a position of responsibility; and, in the final analysis, the kind of government we get depends upon how we fulfill those responsibilities. We, the people, are the boss, and we will get the kind of political leadership, be it good or bad, that we demand and deserve."

Greater fairness under the law is a good place to begin. Unlike those who possess the wealth to hire a team of attorneys to mount a defense, most Americans simply have to hope the eyes of Lady Justice will prevail. Nothing highlights this discrepancy more than the lack of accountability following the 2008 financial crisis that hurt so many citizens. Ben Bernanke, former Federal Reserve Chairman, published a book after the crisis in which he revealed his desire that more focus had been placed on holding those personably responsible for the event. In responding to this proclamation only coming after the fact, Shepard Smith of Fox News said, "The Great Recession began in December 2007 and ended in June of 2009, making it the longest recession since WWII. Analysts say more than 7 million people lost their jobs. The net-worth of U.S. households plunged trillions of dollars. Home prices fell 30% and the Gross Domestic Product, which measures all the goods and services in our economy, plummeted more than 4%. Tens of thousands of businesses also filed for bankruptcy and still to this day, one Wall Street executive, a guy from Credits Swill, sits in jail because of it; just one."

No greater indictment could exist between the power and influence Wall Street possesses over lawmakers of all political stripes. Some indication of the true cost may be best reflected in the tragic numbers presented by Michelle Castillo of CBS News. In September 2013 she highlighted research which found that "the overall male suicide rate in 2009 increased by 3.3 percent from the baseline estimate, which accounted for an additional 5,000 suicides per country studied." While there is no method for truly measuring the lasting toll the crisis has had on families, the loss of a family member guarantees that for some, no recovery would be sufficient in returning life to normal.

Appearing on "Shepard Smith Reporting" the same day the host ridiculed Ben Bernanke for his book, Fox News Senior Judicial Analyst, Judge Andrew Napolitano, blasted the recovery by saying, "You and I sat here while the Congress was voting on TARP (Troubled Asset Relief Program), and we sat here while they first defeated it. And then they tweaked it a little bit and then we sat here while they passed it. And we talked about where is the money going to. It's not going to the people that lost it. It's not going to Main Street. It went to AIG and it went to the big banks so that they could be made whole again. Is that the job of the federal government? Or is it the federal government's job to provide an atmosphere of freedom in which nobody can commit fraud against anyone else and get away with it?" Ordinary citizens definitely know the answer.

Beyond the typical fight to defend against criminal or civil charges, money and influence also protects a certain class from hardships even associated to the innocent under the current judicial system. Civil asset forfeiture gives law enforcement the right to seize property that is deemed to have possibly been used in a crime. While it was designed to aid law enforcement in confiscating resources for use against other criminals, the money being made behind the practice has obviously led to abuse. Ordinary citizens among the middle class and poor are often unable to recover their assets, regardless of whether they are innocent, because of the court costs associated. While some states have taken a lead in stopping the practice, the U.S. Congress has remained unsurprisingly idle. With the facade of representation, there is also a wide gap in advantages being given to those that are able to earn favor with lawmakers due to the power and wealth they possess. Tax treatment attests to this in the best manner. Noam Scheiber and Patricia Cohen of *The New York Times* described the advantage in 2015 by writing, "Some call it the 'income defense industry,' consisting of high-priced phalanx of lawyers, estate planners, lobbyists and anti-tax activists who exploit and defend a dizzying array of tax maneuvers, virtually none of them available to taxpayers of modest means."

Beyond the "private tax system" that the two reporters from the *Times* described, there are also the investors on Wall Street who are making the most of loopholes. As Alex Lazar explained in an article for OpenSecrets.org, "Hedge funds managers receive their compensation through what's known as carried interest—a share of profits made on an investment. Classified as capital gains, the proceeds are taxed at a top rate of around 23.8 percent, which sure beats the 39.6 percent top income tax rate." One can only wonder what the Founders' view would be, although Ron Chernow may have provided some insight. In his 2004 book, *Alexander Hamilton*, Chernow wrote, "Both Jefferson and Adams detested people who earned a living shuffling financial paper, and when Adams launched a bitter tirade in later years against the iniquitous banking system, Jefferson agreed that the business was 'an infinity of successive felonious larcenies.'"

The results are staggering. In 2013, over $24 billion was the combined earnings of the 25 most successful hedge fund managers. In September 2015, Lindsey Koshgarian, research director at National Priorities Project, said that "ending tax breaks for hedge fund managers would save about 1.4 billion a year…nearly enough to find 1.5 billion to cover full day, full year program for all children in Head Start." David Lebedoff, a lawyer and writer in Minneapolis, argued President Obama has always held the power to end this special taxation, since it is a rule under the discretion of the I.R.S. If Lebedoff is correct in his assertion, maybe the President can explain why he didn't end this practice the same day he explained why he rejected ever signing an executive order that would have made federal contractors disclose campaign donations.

A fine-tuning of the treatment of the poor would also most likely be welcomed by most Americans, so that citizens can be treated more like individuals instead of pawns. In the endeavor to root out the waste associated with those who abuse governmental assistance, what cannot be lost is that a number of Americans are only one event away from joining the ranks of those needing assistance. From a sudden illness to the mounting weight of student debt, many Americans face an uncertain financial future and need some pragmatism from lawmakers in finding solutions instead of demonizing them. While a properly tailored work requirement could be substantial in rooting out abuse and sparking more initiative, it should be combined with a similar effort in eliminating the corporate welfare that consistently receives billions upon billions. Legislators need to also be as driven in eliminating the bureaucratic waste that has been linked with the distribution of welfare since its inception. Those in need should be the largest beneficiaries for upward mobility, instead of those in government distributing it.

The assessment Ronald Reagan provided in 1964 concerning the problems of welfare mismanagement has remained accurate. In his famous "A Time for Choosing" speech, Reagan said, "We're spending 45 billion dollars on welfare. Now do a little arithmetic, and you'll find that if we divided the 45 billion dollars up equally among those 9 million poor families, we'd be able to give each family 4,600 dollars a year. And this added to their present income should eliminate poverty. Direct aid to the poor, however, is only running only about 600 dollars per family. It would seem that someplace there must be some overhead... Now do they honestly expect us to believe that if we add 1 billion dollars to the 45 billion we're spending, one more program to the 30-odd we have—and remember, this new program doesn't replace any, it just duplicates existing programs—do they believe that poverty is suddenly going to disappear by magic?"

Not only does the management and distribution of aid have to be held more accountable, but the actual realities facing Americans struggling to rise out of poverty has to be used in forming policy. Initiative alone cannot help someone get off welfare if millions of jobs are being lost in trade. Part-time jobs that pay at or just above minimum wage are also insufficient for most to succeed, especially if there is a punishment attached to a certain increase in wages. The editors of Zero Hedge, under their pseudonym of "Tyler Durden," described how this variable actually impedes growth.

"The 'welfare cliff' [is the point] beyond which families will literally become poorer the higher the wages, as the drop off in entitlements more than offsets the increase in earnings." According to a study from the Illinois Policy Institute, "if a single mother raising two children were to accept a pay raise from $12 to $18 per hour, her total resources would fall by nearly 33%." Disregarding the "welfare cliff" in creating policy is as misguided as attacking single mothers in the endeavor to have more people recognize the need to rebuild the family unit which would place a child of any race at an advantage. However, having two parents in a home doesn't guarantee that there is actually any parenting going on there. Some of the best guidance has come from a single-parent home as well. Effort should be placed on policy instead of unjust demonization.

Writing empty policies that have no thought for the future awaiting those affected by the changes is immoral. Of course, lawmakers most likely don't care as long as they receive the immediate result of winning political points. As Barbara Ehrenreich highlighted in her fascinating book *Nickel and Dimed*, "Very little is known about the fate of former welfare recipients because the 1996 welfare reform legislation [carelessly] failed to include any provision for monitoring their postwelfare economic condition."

It's going to require a great effort to go beneath the surface and actually address the underlying root causes of poverty. Some states have been more proactive in addressing the drug epidemic or providing more aid toward helping the mentally ill. Kelly McEvers of NPR reported on Utah successfully "reducing chronic homelessness by 91 percent." She highlighted how the leadership recognized that someone consistently living in the streets cost more money than if they were housed, when accounting for services such as medical treatment and incarceration. "Housing First," the centerpiece of the strategy used in Utah and other areas, values this reality and understands that the security found within four walls is crucial to beginning any process for actual success.

A similar proactive approach needs to be used within education. The debt crisis demands that a greater emphasis be placed on finances; something that should have happened long ago. Children need to learn about finances all throughout school. One semester in high school or college is not enough. From short-term and long-term budgeting to investing, a newfound focus has to be placed on equipping future citizens with the skills for achieving financial independence. With knowledge, a passion for this endeavor can come early, which is desperately needed. In May 2016, Bill O'Reilly of Fox News demonstrated this best by discussing the common inability of American households to sufficiently save for an unforeseen emergency equaling $1000.

By taking the numbers from the census, O'Reilly demonstrated how the poverty rate in 2014 was actually better than that of the rate in 1965 by two and a half percentage points. He then revealed the true basis for much of the problem in saying, "And here's the key stat, 50 years ago personal disposable income—that is the money you have on hand to spend, in your wallet, in your purse to spend—was just $14,000 bucks. In 2015, it was $38,000 per year; a vast improvement in spending power. The problem is we spend it all. We don't save. We're not frugal. We want immediate gratification."

Banks should be doing more for communities, which might begin by no longer soliciting students on college campuses to obtain a credit card. This is unlikely since an executive of a bank is usually on the board of educational institutions. Of course, the incentive for greater financial education is lacking, considering "America's three biggest banks—JP Morgan Chase (JPM), Bank of America (BAC) and Wells Fargo (WFC)—made more than $1.1 billion on overdraft fees in the first three months (of 2013)." Learning about financing during K-12 would begin placing future adults at an advantage.

Much of the difficulty today in instituting a solution for welfare is the absence of a foundation of knowledge on even the basics of finance, such as the IDAs from Michael Sherraden, founder and director of the Center for Social Development. In an article from May 1998, Linda Tucci wrote, "Michael Sherraden is the inventor of individual development accounts (IDAs), which allow low-income people to save money for certain investments, including a first home, higher education, job training or capitalization of a small business. Every dollar put into an IDA account is matched by at least $1—and in some programs by as much as $9—through public sources, private sources or both."

Citizens possessing a sound financial mind could produce the leaders needed in the public and private sector. However, if unforeseen life circumstances create obstacles, having a base of sustained financial education would allow more Americans to take advantage of programs like the IDAs. More importantly, by being proactive in instilling a commitment within young people for creating and maintaining financial health, the common impediment of accumulating unnecessary debts through credit cards, overcharges, and falling victim to predatory lenders will occur at a much lower rate. There is also the immigration policy, where a more united front could push leaders to finally act in addressing the issue, which a majority of Americans desire. Roy Beck, executive director of Numbers USA, highlighted some statistics that demand attention. As he noted, around 250,000 legal immigrants were allowed into the country from 1770-1970. That number is around a million today. As he pointed out, "The American people never asked for any of these increases. Polls show that there was never a time when much more than 10% of the American people wanted higher immigration."

Instead of stabilization at around 260 million if the 250,000 level had been followed, Beck argued that the increases put the number at 437 million by 2050. While future projections should only be taken with a grain of salt, it is something that deserves consideration. Congress rarely thinks beyond the short-term, but Beck placed the population at 625 million at the end of the century if the current track is followed.

Roy Beck's estimations are not an attack on immigrants. They only highlight the necessity for addressing illegal immigration, when legal immigration policy already poses serious questions in terms of resources for future generations of Americans. One general solution in terms of numbers alone may be to simply tweak the method used to determine how many immigrants can legally enter the country each year. Regardless of the calculation performed today; the number allowed could be more closely tied to the unemployment number, with an established percentage leading to lowering the rate of immigration. At that point, only when a required number of benchmarks are met would the rate of immigration be allowed to return to the previous rate utilized. In terms of illegal immigration, any genuine discussion for answers must begin with those overstaying their visas, which is actually the largest problem within the issue. In a December 2015 congressional hearing, an official from the Department of Homeland Security could not provide the number of how many had illegally overstayed.

Another aspect that is rarely mentioned due to the emphasis placed on those illegally coming across the southern border is the practice of "birth tourism," with "an estimated 40,000 babes [being] born to couples posing as tourists each year." When you add this aspect to the fraud and abuse within the H-1B program, definite action must be taken by the U.S. Congress; a step which must account for all these components and go well beyond simply addressing the issue of illegals flowing across the southern border.

America is a nation of immigrants, but an absence of discipline in following the law has led to more complexities. John Adams believed in adhering to the law, despite the immediate backlash he received. Following the Boston Massacre many longed to inflict their own form of justice on the soldiers who had tragically killed or wounded some Bostonians who had been fired upon outside the Custom House on King Street. However, Adams did not allow emotions to dictate his decisions in regards to the British soldiers in question, allowing him to serve as their attorney for the trial they were afforded under the law. He understood that following the rule of law was significant.

While many believed John Adams was essentially committing political suicide by standing on principle, he proved them wrong. The character and courage he demonstrated were two characteristics that are now attributed to him, as a man who served as a Founding Father and 2nd President of the United States. Concerning other Presidents, Bill Clinton advocated for the rule of law, stating in his 1995 State of the Union address, "We are a nation of immigrants. But we are also a nation of laws. It is wrong and ultimately self-defeating for a nation of immigrants to permit the kind of abuse of our immigration laws we have seen in recent years, and we must do more to stop it." His words were met by a standing ovation, which included both major parties.

There are concessions that could create a solution that would allow citizens to build a meaningful partnership with many of the undocumented for tackling future challenges. Taking a page from the idea behind Veterans Preference, in which veterans are given an advantage in the hiring process, ordinary citizens could possess a similar protection. The undocumented could possess a form of identification—possibly a driver's license—which has icons that symbolize the years they have been in the country. This would help locate the small criminal faction who will obviously not attempt to obtain the mandated identification, as well as reduce the incentive of crossing the border by making employment more difficult. It would also offer a protection for current undocumented workers from wage abuse. E-verify could be used to eliminate the chance of hiring anyone else who comes across the border after the legislation is passed.

Another aspect could be an additional tax of 2 to 3 percent placed on the undocumented beyond the standard taxes paid by American citizens. This money could be used to strengthen the border, hire additional immigration judges, and expedite the process for those who are currently attempting to legally become American citizens. Such an additional tax has already been suggested in Sweden, a historically open-border country. However, after informing the people in October 2015 how dire the situation had become in finances due to migration, an additional tax was going to be directed on its citizens. As Sean Adl-Tabtabai documented, "On October 8, the Swedish Association of Local Authorities and Regions (SKL) warned that municipalities need to increase the tax rate by 2%." In the U.S., the alternative is to possibly receive a ruling from the Supreme Court that allows a President to bypass the legislative branch in allowing the undocumented to earn federal earned-benefit programs beyond the social services they already receive. President Obama failed in this regard, but a future President, with the right Supreme Court, could drastically raise the cost of additional taxes.

A reassessment of foreign aid, especially to countries with questionable human rights records, could possibly help alleviate future immigration issues on the southern border. Sixty percent of Americans in 2013 supported reducing the amount. The U.S. is always contributing the most to international organizations. Almost every nation in the U.N. receives some aid, including Russia and China. Even a slight reduction across the board to numerous countries currently receiving aid could help, especially by reallocating that money to countries closer to home like Guatemala, Honduras, El Salvador, and Mexico.

Investing in these countries could be a legitimate part of homeland security. Why not spend more money closer to home for protection by proactively strengthening these countries with investment? Adding money to what the U.S. is currently giving these countries to the south could raise the standard of living for those who might look to migrate, as well as keep the fight with gangs like MS-13 well below the southern border. For any of this to happen, political leaders must remember the words of John F. Kennedy, "Compromise need not mean cowardice." More importantly, this needs to be recognized by those leaders within the undocumented, who could push the discussion by putting together their own package of compromises for moving forward on legislation, as the American people consistently demonstrate they are for some form of pathway. In June 2015, "a survey conducted by Pew Research Center found that 72 percent of Americans support legal status for such immigrants"; support is present for it.

Placing a reasonable alternative in front of the people to rally around in contrast to the stalemate found within the U.S. Congress could be successful. Neither major party has taken the chance to use their power before. The first two years of Obama's term provided the latest example, when Democrats prioritized healthcare over immigration with their control over both chambers of Congress. As Dana Perino, former press secretary to President George W. Bush, highlighted, "every single month in America, 50,000 Hispanics turn eighteen years old." Beyond these Hispanics, if the undocumented create a reasonable compromise that a majority of Americans support, the choice of a lawmaker or major party to reject it could cost them votes in their own base.

The undocumented suffer from the same failure in leadership that Americans do. Beyond the violence some experienced, many came to America due to the economic conditions caused from poor trade deals such as NAFTA, which displaced over a million campesinos (farmers). Rallying around legislation that actually offers compromises would end the state of limbo that both major parties have left the undocumented in. A compromise that adheres to laws removes the likelihood of more illegal immigrants facing long-term uncertainty in detention centers. However, the only chance for this type of movement is if the undocumented can unite around a compromise, requiring some to drop the idea of migration as a right. Holding out for full citizenship on all the terms they desire will keep things stagnant.

One possible aspect of a compromise could be for Dreamers (those brought illegally as a child by their parents to America) to have a path to citizenship, while adults could only gain legal status. An AP-FFK poll from the end of 2015 found that, "Six in 10 Americans, including three-quarters of Democrats and nearly half of Republicans, favor providing immigrants who were brought to the country illegally as children with a way to stay in the country." Americans, especially those with children, can empathize with parents who do something positive for the well-being of their family. This would further demonstrate the fact that most immigrants come to the U.S. for their children. My friend Elizabeth, a Dreamer, demonstrates daily the commitment to family her parents instilled in her.

Americans can relate to someone who admits fault and takes responsibility, as everyone has made mistakes. After the Bay of Pigs fiasco, President Kennedy at a press conference said, "There's an old saying that victory has 100 fathers and defeat is an orphan," before ultimately following that line with, "Further statements, detailed discussions, are not to conceal responsibility because I'm the responsible officer of the government." President Kennedy could have made excuses or blamed a lower-level official. Instead, he chose to take full responsibility for the failure. His approval ratings went to the highest level of his presidency following that speech.

It will be difficult for the undocumented to gain empathy without humility. The choice of some within the community to post videos cursing America or involving themselves in riots that burn the American flag or commit acts of violence against citizens is only counterproductive to gaining support; just as refusing to demonstrate any empathy following the murder of Americans at the hands of illegals. It's legitimate to believe that a golden opportunity was lost by the decision of many within the undocumented in refusing to support legislation named after Kate Steinle, the 32-year-old woman who was sadly killed by an illegal immigrant, who later admitted to shooting her.

"Kate's Law" was aimed at ridding the streets of illegal felons. While there is obviously a similar fear among the undocumented for governmental officials to go beyond legislation passed and target more than felons, the symbolism of displaying the type of empathy they hope to receive from American citizens would be priceless. The expression of compassion could also open the dialogue for other areas of mutual concern. One of those concerns around the issue of immigration that should draw a shared endeavor in solving is the horrific fate that has been awaiting a number of the children who cross the southern border. Mostly likely at the hands of the drug cartels, children will continue to be sold into sex slavery, if not pressured by violence to become drug runners. The longer all sides related to the debate continue to ponder on the issue without providing a workable path to solving it, the more children will suffer as a result of the failure.

Regardless of the path ultimately taken on the issue of illegal immigration, the U.S. has to remain committed to the high principles upon which the nation was founded. No nation is perfect, and the U.S. is not immune to some questionable decisions on the world stage, but the people can never lose sight of the unique hope America will always offer the world. We need more men like Sgt. 1st Class Charles Martland, a Massachusetts native who disregarded the debatable alliance with some in Afghanistan and defended a boy who was allegedly raped by a police commander who was a friendly with the U.S. Although the U.S. government initially punished his admirable act, the officer, who has a distinguished military career, was eventually reinstated for thinking beyond himself.

Many within the heights of the U.S. government should take note, as the spirit that has always defined America should be found in domestic and foreign policy. A review of the past to rediscover some of what made America great should be reviewed by all those in government; though, it appears many are clearly unaware or indifferent to it. Author Donald Robinson detailed one of the best examples of what America should always stand for if the world is going to survive. In his 1958 book, *The Day I Was Proudest To Be An American*, he documented the recording from Major General Charles I. Carpenter, the first Chief of Chaplains for the U.S. Air Force. The Major General described his 1951 Easter Sunday from Korea, where a number of the Korean children from an orphanage took part in the celebration. "Most of them were wearing blouses that had been concocted out of G.I. shirts—shirts that some American soldiers had taken off their own back to give them."

As the recording of Major General Carpenter revealed, "They knew G.I. Joe. He was an American soldier who'd come in through the beleaguered port of Pusan and fought his way north, pushing back the Communist invaders who'd slaughter their parents. This G.I. Joe was the fellow who moved into a town with his tanks, his rifles, and his grenades and dislodged the enemy. While he was doing it, he would spy some frightened, little tyke, all alone, cowering in a corner or hiding in a barrel. He'd pause long enough to take the child in his arms, pet her a bit, and give her a bar of chocolate. Then he'd hunt up a chaplain, slip him a few bills, and say, 'Chappie, you take care of this child, and when I get a chance, I'll see that you get some money.'"

And the men did follow up on that promise. As documented by Donald Robinson in his chapter dedicated to the insightful recording, "On this basis, orphanages had sprung up all over Korea. Through G.I. generosity, tens of thousands of war-made orphans, from whose lives love and security had vanished, found new homes and a new affection."

Just as the past can provide a reminder to Americans of the broader moral fiber that should always define our country, it can also supply an individualized idea of what to aspire to be. In the first GOP undercard debate from August 2015, moderator Martha MacCallum framed this question to candidate Carly Fiorina, "Carly, you were CEO of Hewlett-Packard. You ran for Senate and lost in California in 2010. This week, you said, 'Margaret Thatcher was not content to manage a great nation in decline, and neither am I.' Given your current standings in the polls, is the Iron Lady comparison a stretch?"

Fiorina responded by listing some of the candidates who had started off low in the polls before ultimately picking up enough momentum to become president, as well as took the rest of her time to summarize her record of various achievements. Though Carly Fiorina was running for President of the United States and deserved close scrutiny, all Americans should hope that the country has not become so elitist in thinking that now only a few, once their resumes have been padded, will be deemed worthy enough to claim the similar resolve of certain pivotal figures in history. Much of the problem in society today is that not enough believe in the power of the individual to bring change. Cynicism in the world today should not deter those who seek strength by looking at the past for examples of courage and triumph. As Robert Kennedy believed, "Few will have the greatness to bend history itself, but each of us can work to change a small portion of events, and in the total of all those acts will be written the history of this generation." He knew, as did President Kennedy, that the only hope for achieving true progress would come down to the individual, as was evident in his challenge to the audience at Colombia University in which he said, "President Kennedy's favorite quote was really from Dante. 'The hottest places in Hell are reserved for those who in time of morale crisis preserved their neutrality.'" If the people are going to reassess their ownership of the country, a number of Americans are going have to recognize that everyone possesses a role in strengthening their communities and providing a voice for the forgotten.

The past can also provide clear indications of who the people should be wary of. In June 2014, CNN's S.E. Cupp of "Crossfire" reminded a long-time Hillary Clinton advisor and surrogate, Tracy

Sefl, of the "over 50% of people" who desired for someone other than the former Secretary of State to run for president. The "Crossfire" co-host also presented the words of former Gov. of Montana, Brian Schweitzer, who was on the record as saying, "You can't be a candidate that shakes down more money on Wall Street than anybody since, I don't know, Woodrow Wilson, and be a populist."

Sefl, the leader behind the Ready for Hillary independent super PAC that operated for years to build support for Clinton's eventual run, took aim at Schweitzer by responding, "Well, Governor Schweitzer and his sort of folksiness is an interesting line for him to go to and this isn't the first time he's said something like this." Folksy, "sometimes used derogatorily to describe affected simplicity," was how she chose to describe him. If she was berating the former governor as it appeared, her attitude would reflect the type of elitism demonstrated in Hillary Clinton's labeling 50% of those supporting Donald Trump as a "basket of deplorables" some two years later.

One can only imagine what former Governor Schweitzer's true assessment would be of the Democratic nominee for president now, with the Center for Responsive Politics, as of July 2016, putting Hillary Clinton at $48.5 million in campaign contributions from Wall Street hedge funders to Donald Trump's $19,000. Despite even the latest numbers from the campaign, Sen. Elizabeth Warren (D-MA), who fancies herself as a populist, continues to offer support for the Democratic nominee.

Senator Warren has even witnessed firsthand how Hillary Clinton is ultimately beholden to donors. In a 2004 interview, Sen. Warren explained how Clinton, serving as First Lady at the time, met with her for a lengthy discussion before expressing her support for defeating a bankruptcy bill under consideration. However, once Clinton became a New York Senator, one of her first acts was voting in favor of a similar bill.

A small clip of the interview clearly displays Sen. Warren pointing to Hillary simply caving on the bill to stay in good favor with donors vital to re-election. This assessment of her actions are similar to what the 2008 Presidential candidate Barack Obama perceived drove her words, with an opening from one of his ads saying, "It's what's wrong with politics today. Hillary Clinton will say anything to get elected." However, any reservations Warren should have regarding Hillary Clinton based on the previous behavior of question did not impact her decision to support her for President.

Elizabeth Warren's support is especially troubling considering the amount of power she knows a President Hillary Clinton would have if the "We the People Act," for campaign finance she and other Democrats are championing, was passed. Michael Sainato, in an article from the *Observer*, displayed this inconceivable level of trust in Hillary Clinton by writing, "According to a press release from the Democratic Policy & Communications Center, the bill calls for the Federal Election Commission to be absolved and replaced by a new agency, whose five commissioners would be appointed by the President and confirmed by the Senate." Although it seems impossible for oversight to be any more pathetic than what is currently happening under the FEC, giving Hillary Clinton that much power over any alternative would pose a much greater threat.

Unlike Senator Warren, anyone left to decide on whether or not to take Hillary Clinton at her word on the campaign trail, need only to review her 2008 bid for the presidency. In a debate from February of that year, NBC News Washington Bureau Chief Tim Russert offered the following question, "Senator Clinton, on the issue of jobs. I watched you the other day with your economic blueprint in Wisconsin saying, 'This is my plan, hold me accountable.' I've had a chance to read it very carefully. It does say that you pledge to create five million new jobs over ten years, and I was reminded of your campaign in 2000 in Buffalo, my hometown, just three hours down Route 90. You pledged 200,000 new jobs for upstate New York. There's been a net loss of 30,000 jobs. And when you were asked about your pledge, your commitment, you told the Buffalo news, 'I might have been a little exuberant.' Tonight will you say that the pledge of five million jobs might be a little exuberant?"

Politicians like Hillary Clinton will continue to be produced from both sides of the political aisle if the current electoral process is maintained. Empty promises and the status quo will continue, with little or no recourse for the American people. This truth may have been highlighted best by the recent decision of the Supreme Court to toss out the conviction of former Republican Governor of Virginia, Bob McDonnell. The decision essentially paved the way for others to disregard most attempts for accountability within current campaign finance laws with little fear of ever facing consequences. Without a new measuring stick for determining the type of integrity needed in future politicians to reject the negative ways of the past, most citizens will remain voiceless. Without a foundation of reliable representation to authentically attempt to represent and protect the interests of the people, men like George Soros can continue to wreak havoc on the principles of democracy; to sit back and use his influence to pit

Americans against one another as if we were mere rats in his elaborate maze. Beyond the money he gives to campaigns, which includes millions to Hillary Clinton and Barack Obama, thanks to WikiLeaks, the American public can see Soros as the unelected puppet master he appears to be. Soros gave Secretary of State Clinton advice on the Albania unrest and the decision was made to pick an individual he believed was best.

Predictably, both Hillary Clinton and President Obama supported Prime Minister Cameron in his effort to stop Brexit—or Britain's decision to leave the European Union. President Obama even traveled to London to try and dissuade the people not to vote for exiting through a subtle threat on trade. The UK Independence Party revealed in its "EU Rich List" that "the top 200 EU officials were all paid more than the UK Prime Minister" and "the average Rich List official receives 10 times more money every year than the average UK worker." Although this power dynamic clearly did not bother some leaders, it should serve as a cautionary tale to Americans who truly value democracy.

In a town hall debate leading up to the referendum, members of the audience offered questions to Prime Minister Cameron. A man named James asked Cameron a powerful question concerning national sovereignty: "Mr. Cameron, we recently celebrated the 800th anniversary of the Magna Carta, uh [sic] the United Kingdom has been built on the pillars of democracy and we have the greatest legal system in the world. Is it not shameful that since joining the EU our Parliament is no longer sovereign, our Supreme Court is no longer supreme, and our nation is no longer self-governing?"

After Prime Minister Cameron offered a response, which included his assurance that "[their] Parliament [was] sovereign," old trusty James quickly countered his remarks by saying, "Your own House of Commons Library has estimated that up to 55% of our laws are made by Europe—i.e. unelected bureaucrats—and we also are in the position that our own Supreme Court judges can be overruled by European judges, some of whom may never have even stepped foot in this country. It's a disgrace!"

Despite the fear mongering routinely associated with legislation that threatens the status quo, the British people chose to exit the EU, putting the elitist/Marxist bureaucrats and technocrats of the world on notice. Doomsday rhetoric was ignored, the stock markets bounced back quickly, and Britain can now conduct trade on its own terms once the transition from the EU is complete. "International Trade Secretary Liam Fox boasted that Britain remains the 'number one' destination in Europe for investment." While powerful men like George Soros can make things difficult within the world market, freedom and liberty should never be exchanged for any perceived economic advantages.

Any additional level of international bureaucracy is likely desirable when compared to the versions of globalization that President Obama and his surrogates like Secretary of State John Kerry espouse. In a commencement speech at Northeastern University from Boston in May 2016, John Kerry said, "The future demands from us something more than nostalgia for some rose-tinted version of the past that did not really exist in any case. You're about to graduate into a complex and borderless world."

Steve Guest of *The Daily Caller* detailed Rush Limbaugh's response to Kerry's commencement. Guest documented the popular radio host saying, "'And this will not come to a shock to anybody, this is exactly what everybody is afraid the globalists want,' Limbaugh said. 'This is exactly what people think is all tied up in these never-ending trade deals and the never-ending illegal immigration, the numbers of which just continue to expand.'" Guest also made note of Limbaugh's suggestion to Kerry regarding his "world with no borders" in saying, "Kerry needs to tell that to his European buddies who are busy putting their borders back up as fast as they can, as fast as the EU will let them."

Although broadly criticized by other countries in the region, Hungary built a wall to stop the threat officials knew migration posed to the country in August 2015, which resulted in only "41 people" crossing in a day. "The figure of 41 represents a new daily record low in 2015 Hungary, which witnessed up to 10,000 people stream across its borders daily since the summer." The U.S. is giving close to $530 million in taxpayer money to help secure the Tunisia and Jordan borders with "electronic fencing. Many Americans wish a similar commitment would be made on the southern border, where policy seems to have undermined genuine security for some time. The threat has never been higher, but many with government seem completely oblivious.

In assessing the words of one of the investigating officers at the massacre of innocent lives by Islamic terrorists at the Bataclan concert hall on November 2015, the French government covered up the degree of atrocities that actually occurred. "According to [his] testimony, Wahhabist killers apparently gouged out eyes, castrated victims, and shoved their testicles in their mouths. They may also have disemboweled some poor souls. Women were stabbed in the genitals—and the torture was, victims told police, filmed for Daesh or

Islamic State propaganda." Yet, while the U.S. government was placing more citizens at risk by essentially offering illegal immigrants an easier path across the southern border, ignoring problems in vetting migrants, and "accidentally" allowing over 800 immigrants from countries of concern to become citizens instead of being deported as planned, tax money was spent to secure foreign borders.

In a video from the last day of July 2016, well-known conservative Michelle Malkin posted a video she added to the *Conservative Review* that spotlighted the demonstrated hypocrisy of Democrats at their national convention when it comes to the border. When it actually came to their safety, there was much more emphasis on creating a stern deterrent. As Malkin described, "Jump the Democratic Convention security fence: get a jail sentence. Jump America's security fence: collect your 'get out of jail free' card and go directly to your free education, work permits, and lifetime Democratic Party membership. If the Republicans were smart, they'd force Democrats to vote on a measure making trespass across our country's borders a felony; the same standard they apply to their own convention fence." For that to occur, Republicans would have to reject the big business special interests that desire undocumented workers to remain and keep wages low to protect their bottom line. History proves the chances are slim to none.

In his 2008 book, *How to Rig an Election: Confessions of a Republican Operative*, Allen Raymond perfectly summarized how a facade of representation is consistently instituted and why true leaders are rarely created to fix it. "How did we get here? Because election operatives like myself and the kind of politicians who hire us have ensured that idealists can't win elections. Only the cynics are making the laws." He went on to say, "They get in power, they stay in power, and they keep the power. But don't the voters have some power in this mess. Sure. And they give it up every election." Something has to change, but only the people can decide to bring it.

Some would say that it is unfortunately too late, that the length of inadequacies in leadership have already sealed the demise of the country. However, these individuals underestimate the power of the people. Currently, the country is similar to a baseball stadium in which visibility is fleeting for the players. Those in charge failed to begin the process of building up the lights earlier in the day to have them ready when darkness fell, which is why few can see beyond solving the problems directly in front of them. However, it is actually not as late as it seems, with just one shifting cloud away from a new window of opportunity to use the remaining daylight to prepare for the future.

The People's Clearing House can assure that this window of opportunity is properly utilized.

In many ways, the American people find themselves in the same vulnerable position as Theodore Roosevelt when talking about those who work to distort the true tenants of democracy. Due to a childhood sickness that left him open to bullying, Teddy Roosevelt quickly learned the lesson that defeat at the hands of those who made use of his disadvantage was unacceptable when the weakness could be corrected to alter the future. As recorded in *The Autobiography of Theodore Roosevelt* and edited by Wayne Andrews, "The experience taught me what probably no amount of good advice could have taught me. I made up my mind that I must try to learn so that I would not again be put in such a helpless position; and having become quickly and bitterly conscious that I did not have the natural prowess to hold my own, I decided that I would try to supply its place by training. Accordingly, with my father's hearty approval, I started to learn to box."

It's time for the American people to unite and fight back like Roosevelt, never forgetting the present feeling of helplessness and defeat, and using it to sustain us in the painstaking endeavor to reclaim the country from the elites, crony capitalists, and career politicians. While men like Louis Farrakhan point to the pain of the country being centered on "white supremacy," the real ailment is apathy, as witnessed by an absence of men and women of sound heart uniting to reject all individuals of hate and division.

At his first inaugural address from Arlington Cemetery, President Reagan said:

> "Each one of those markers is a monument to the kinds of hero I spoke of earlier. Their lives ended in places called Belleau Wood, the Argonne, Omaha Beach, Salerno, and halfway around the world on Guadalcanal, Tarawa, Pork Chop Hill, the Chosin Reservoir, and in a hundred rice paddies and jungles of a place called Vietnam. Under one such marker lies a young man—Martin Treptow—who left his job in a small town barbershop in 1919 to go to France with the famed Rainbow Division. There on the western front, he was killed trying to carry a message between battalions under heavy artillery fire. We are told that on his body was found a diary. On the flyleaf under the header, 'My Pledge,' he had written these words, 'America must win this war. Therefore I will work, I will save, I will sacrifice, I will endure. I will fight cheerfully and do my utmost, as if the issue of the whole struggle depended on me alone.' The crisis we are facing today does not require of us the kind of sacrifice that Martin Treptow and so many thousands of others were called upon to make. It does require, however, our best effort, and our willingness to believe in our-

selves and to believe in our capacity to perform great deeds; to believe that together, with God's help, we can and will resolve the problems which now confront us."

What will your pledge be to strengthen your country? "Across 10 countries more than 130,000 Americans are buried and another 124,000 missing in action are memorialized by name in one of the 25 cemeteries overseen by the American Battle Monument Commission," according to Elizabeth Shell. Chris Dickon, historian and author of the book *Americans at War in Foreign Forces*, discovered there are an unknown number buried abroad; some lying unmarked in cemeteries among foreign soldiers. The sacrifice of all these soldiers for freedom, justice, and liberty demand definite action.

The most significant question is who will pledge to reaffirm the ownership of the country to the people? Not for one party, one race, one gender, one ethnicity, one socioeconomic class, but for all—to restore a genuine representation that safeguards freedom, liberty, and justice for all. The stakes could not be any higher. As President Kennedy said, "If we succeed in this country, if we make this a great country to live, if we reflect our vitality and energy and strength around the world, then the cause of freedom is strengthened. But if we fail, all fail. If we stand still, freedom stands still." It is up to us.

References

Introduction

1. http://www.cbsnews.com/news/anaonymous-inc-60-minutes-steve-kroft-investigation/ "Anonymous, Inc." Transcript. CBS Newtwork. Xfinity 1009 CBSHD, Correspondent Steve Kroft, Graham Messick and Kevin Livelli, producers. Jan. 31, 2016.
2. "Fox Report Weekend." The Political Insiders." Xfinity 1105 FNCHD, Host Pattie Ann Browne, July 5, 2015.
3. Lewis, Edwards and Richard Rhodes, eds. John F. Kennedy: Words to Remember. United States: Hallmark Cards Incorporated, 1967. (p.36, 28, 29, 50).
4. "Real Story with Gretchen Carlson." Xfinity, 1105 FNCHD, Aug. 20, 2015.
5. http://reason.com/blog/2016/04/30/venezuela-runs-out-of-beer. Krayewski, Ed. "Venezuela runs out of beer," Apr. 30, 2016.
6. http://www.tpnn.com/2015/10/20/whoops-bernie-sanders-just-let-spill-a-huge-secret-that-will-make -even-his-supporters-think-twice/. Conley, Colleen. "Whoops: Bernie Sanders just let spill a huge secret that will make even his supporters think twice," Oct. 20, 2015.
7. http://news.yahoo.com/60-something-socialist-britains-unlikely-political-star-094842757.html. Lawless, Jill. "60-something is Britain's unlikely political star," Sept. 6, 2015.
8. http://www.politico.com/story/2016/04/millennials-largest-generation-222448. Ehley, Brianna. "Millennials dethrone baby boomers as largest generation," Apr. 26, 2016.
9. www.finance.yahoo.com/news/here-s-where-rick-santorum-gets-his-campaign-money-144704063.html. Newman, Rick. "Here's where Rick Santorum gets his campaign money," May 17, 2015.
10. http://www.politico.com/story/2015/01/blue-billionaires-on-top-114151.html. Vogel, Kenneth P. "Blue billionaires on top: Politico's list of top 100 donors of disclosed money tilts leftward," Jan. 11, 2015.
11. *Mr. Smith Goes to Washington*. Dir. Frank Capra. Perf. James Stewart, Jean Arthur, Claude Rains, Edward Arnold. Columbia Pictures, 1939. DVD.
12. Kiernan, Stephen P. *Authentic Patriotism: Restoring America's Founding Ideals Through Selfless Action*. St Martin's Press: New York, 2010. (p.45).
13. Jackson Sr., Jesse L. Afterword. Why We Can't Wait. By Martin Luther King, Jr. Signet Classic: New York, 2000. (p.162, 163).
14. Johnson, Boris. The Churchill Factor: How one man made history. New York: Penguin Group, 2014. (p.214).
15. http://www.cbsnew.com/news/cajun-john-wayne-clay-higgins-resigns-sheriffs-department-louisiana/. "'Cajun's John Wayne' resigns sheriff's office job," Mar. 1, 2016.
16. Captain Clay Higgins. "Clay Higgins: 'America United,'" Online video clip. YouTube. YouTube, 3 May 2015. Web. May 6, 2016.

The Accepted Culture of Waste

1. https://www.conservative.com/commentay/2016/02/national-debt-reaches-19trillion. "National debt reaches $19 trillion," Feb. 2, 2016.
2. http://dailyreckoning.com/simple-math-shows-america-is-headed-for-an-economic-disaster/. Chudley, Jody. "Simple math shows that America is headed for an economic disaster," Mar. 30, 2016.
3. http://www.bloomberg.com/news/articles/2015-06-16/government-debt-to-reach-107-of-u-s-economy-in-2040-cbo-says. Klimasinska, Kasia. "Government debt to reach 107% of U.S. economy in

2040, CBO says," Jun. 16, 2015.

4. http://www.caintv.com/uh-oh-government-has-run-up-20. Cain, Herman. "Uh oh: government has run up $200 billion deficit already in FY 2016, Dec. 13, 2015.

5. "Meet the Press." Moderator Chuck Todd, NBC, Xfinity 1105 FNCH, Feb. 14, 2015.

6. Brookhiser, Richard. Founding Fathers: Rediscovering George Washington. The Free Press: New York, 1996. (p.133).

7. Feldkamp, Fred, ed. By Will Cuppy. The Decline and Fall of Practically Everybody: Great figures of history hilariously humbled. Illustrated by William Steig. Dorset Press: United States, 1992. (p.62).

8. http://endoftheamericandream.com/archives/30-stupid-things-the-government-is-spending-money-on. Snyder, Micheal. "30 stupid things the government is spending money on," Feb. 29, 2012.

9. http://freebeacon.com/issues/wastebook-2015-sen-flake-continues-coburns-tradition/. Harrington, Elizabeth. "Wastebook 2015: Flake continues Coburn's tradition," Dec. 8, 2015.

10. Dave. Dir. Ivan Reitman. Perf. Kevin Klein, Sigourney Weaver, Frank Lamgella, Kevin Dunn, Ben Kingsley. Warner Brothers, 1993. DVD.

11. http://www.heritage.org/research/reports/2014/10/eliminating-waste-and-controlling-government-spending. Boccia, Romina. "Eliminating waste and controlling government spending," Dec. 17, 2014.

12. http://www.newsmax.com/Headline/donald-trump-supports-penny-plan/2016/03/07/id/717959/. Richter, Greg. "Trump: I support across the board cuts except for military," Mar. 7, 2016.

13. "Wolf." Host Wolf Blitzer. Xfinity 1106 CNNHD, Oct. 8, 2015.

14. Thomas, Cal. "Carly Fiorina Major Leaguer." The Times Daily 23 Aug. 2015: A5. Print.

15. http://www.newsmax.com/Newsfront/Congress-spending-spree-Vermon/2013/10/07/id/529773/. Burke, Cathy. "State Dept. spent millions on embassy crystal week before shutdown," Aug. 7, 2013.

16. "Outnumbered." Xfinity, 1105 FNCHD, Oct. 23, 2015. TV.

17. Thomas, Cal. "How to reform institutions" The Times Daily 6 Mar. 2016: D1. Print.

18. http://www.dailymail.co.uk/wires/ap/article-3498271/US-govt-sets-record-failures-files-asked.html. "US govt. sets record for failures to find files when asked," Mar. 18, 2016.

19. http://dailycaller.com/2016/03/18/reid-silent-on-baffling-decision-to-block-bipartisan-ig-empowering-bill/. Watson, Kathryn. "Reid silent on baffling decision to block bipartisan IG-Empowering Bill," Mar. 18, 2016.

20. http://watchdog.org/88146/govt-workers-rack-up-29-billions-in-credit-card-charges/. Kittle, M.D. "Govt. workers rack up $29 billion in credit card charges," Jun. 3, 2013.

21. www.gao.gov/new.items/d08333.pdf. "GAO Report to the permanent subcommittee on investigations, committee on homeland security and governmental affairs, U.S. Senate," Mar. 2008.

22. https://selfgovern.org/ronald-reagan-speech-a-time-for-choosing/. "A Time for Choosing": Ronald Reagan's Self-Governance Speech," Oct. 29, 2014.

23. http://www.c-span.org/video/?407380-1/1980-republican-presidential-candidates-debate&start=804. "1980 Republican Presidential Candidates Debate," Apr. 23, 1980.

24. http://www.washingtonpost.com/wp-dyn/content/article/2010/12/03/AR2010120303160.html. Stier, Max. "Five myths about federal workers," Dec. 5, 2010.

25. http://usgovinfo.about.com/od/moneymatters/tp/5-Presidents-Who-Raised-The-Debt-Limit.htm. Murse, Tom. "5 Presidents who raised the debt ceiling," Jul. 12, 2015.

26. http://www2.deloitte.com/content/dam/Deloitte/us/Documents/process-and-operations/us-cons-zero-based-budgeting.pdf. "Zero-based budgeting: Zero or hero?"

27. http://reason.com/archives/2014/04/16/department-of-cronyism. de Rugby, Veronique. "Department of cronyism: the department of commerce's economic development administration is a favor-dispensing machine," Apr. 6, 2014.

28. "The Kelly File." Xfinity, 1105 FNCHD, Oct. 21, 2015. TV.

29. https://www.yahoo.com/tv/s/jon-stewart-makes-triumphant-return-daily-show-trevor-044512614.html. Emery, Debbie. "Jon Stewart makes triumphant return to the 'daily show with Trevor Noah,'" Dec. 7, 2015.

30. http://www.newsleader.com/story/news/local/2015/11/03/911-victims-group-critisizes-goodlatte/75080720/. "9/11 victims group criticizes Goodlatte," Nov. 3, 2015.

31. http://www.wfmynews2.com/story/news/local/2014/06/25/report-claims-one-thousand-veterans-diesd-Waiting-for-care/11344083/. "Report: 1,000 veterans die while waiting for care, VA wastes billions," Jun. 25, 2014.

32. https://www.opposingviews.com/i/politics/va-inspector-general-says-their-database-inadequate-servicing-veterans. Rubinstein, Alexander. "VA inspector general admits over 300,000 vets died waiting for healthcare," Sept. 7, 2015.

33. http://www.usatoday.com/story/news/politics/2015/11/11/veterans-affairs-pays-142-million-bonuses-amid-scandals/75537586/. Slack, Donovan and Bill Theobald. "Veterans affairs pays $142 million in bonuses amid scandals," Nov. 11, 2015.

34. http://www.military.com/daily-news/2016/03/23/va-suspends-top-official-in-relocation-scam.html.

"VA suspends top official in relocation scam," Mar. 23, 2016.
35. Colvin, Jill. "Trump releases plan aimed at improving veterans' care." The Times Daily 1 Nov. 2015: A5. Print.
36. http://freebeacon./com/issues/democrat-blocks-vote-on-va-accountability-act-in-senate/. Chalfant, Morgan. "Democrats block vote on VA accountability act in senate," Oct. 20, 2016.
37. "Fox and Friends." Xfinity, 1105 FNCHD, Apr. 8, 2016.
38. Colleen, Mastony. "At VA suicide-prevention program, loss turns to hope" The Times Daily 20 Sept. 2015: D1. Print.
39. http://guardianofvalor.com/elvin-joe-swisher-has-conviction-overturned-for-wearing-an-unearned-purple-heart/. "Elvin Joe Swisher, has conviction overturned for wearing an unearned purple heart," Jan. 14, 2016.
40. http://clerk.house.gov/evs/2013/roll61.xml#N.
41. http://usatoday30.usatoday.com/news/opinion/forum/2010-07-07-column07_ST1_N.htm. Sherk, James. "Government jobs: bloated pay, benefits cost all," Jul. 6, 2010.
42. http://www.protectingtaxpayers.org/assets/files/Congressional_Compensation.pdf. "Are taxpayers getting their money's worth: an analysis of congressional compensation," Jul. 2011.
43. http://dailycaller.com/2016/03/03/heres-why-its-all-but-impossible-to-fire-a-fed/. Watson, Kathryn. "Here's why it's all but impossible to fire a fed," Mar. 3, 2016.
44. http://www.nytimes.com/2016/04/09/us/politics/dozens-punished-by-tsa-for-whistle-blowing-are-later-exonerated.html?_r=0. Nixon, Ron. "Dozens punished by T.S.A. for whistleblowing are later exonerated," Apr. 8, 2016.
45. http://www.westernjournalism.com/watch-arizona-sheriff-cant-take-it-anymore-spills-obamas-dark-secret-he-never-wanted-out/. Davis, Jack. "Watch: Arizona sheriff can't take it anymore, spills Obama's dark secret he never wanted out," Mar. 9, 2016.
46. http://www.newsmax.com/Newsfront/policy-force-border-patrol-agents/2016/02/04/id/712787/. Burke, Cathy. "New policy forces border patrol agents to release illegal immigrants," Feb. 4, 2016.
47. http://www.washington.com/news/2016/mar/1/border-chief-chides-agents-object-obama-amnesty/?page=all. Dinan, Stephen. "Top border chief to agents who object to Obama amnesty: 'look for another job," Mar. 1, 2016.
48. http://dailycaller.com/2016/03/16/ice-director-givers-shocking-excuse-for-failure-to-detain-killer-illegal-alien-video/. Ross, Chuck. "ICE director givers shocking excuse for failure to detain killer illegal alien," Mar. 16, 2016.
49. http://www.thedailybeast.com/articles/2016/04/03/intel-analysts-we-were-punished-for-telling-the-truth-about-obama-s-isis-war.html. Harris, Shane and Nancy A. Youssef. "Intel analysts: we were forced out for telling the truth about Obama's war," Apr. 4, 2016.
50. http://www.dailymail.co.uk/news/article-3506491/Emory-president-Students-scared-Trump-2016-chalk-signs.html. Robinson, Will and (The Associate Press). "Students freak out because someone chalked Trump slogans on campus: Emory university president says students are scared and 'in pain'," Mar. 23, 2016.
51. http://thehill.com/blogs/congress-blog/homeland-security/268282-dhs-ordered-me-to-scrub-records-of-muslims-with-terror. Haney, Philip. "DHS ordered me to scrub records of Muslims with terror ties," Feb. 5, 2016.
52. http://dailycaller.com/2016/02/09/exclusive-ice-whistleblower-fired-after-refusing-dhs-hush-money/. Gahr, Evan. "Exclusive: ICE whistleblower fired after refusing DHS hush money," Feb. 9, 2016.
53. http://www.newsmax.com/Newsfront/Harry-Reid-Unspent-Campaign-Funds-Retirement/2016/01/20/id/710178. "Harry Reid wants to use $600k of unspent campaign funds for retirement," Jan 20, 2016.
54. https://www.rt.com/usa/266701-dhs-agent-whistleblower-harassed/. "DHS whistleblower 'almost loses child' for probing immigration & corruption," Jun. 12, 2015.
55. http://completecolorado.com/pagetwo/2016/01/27/u-s-homeland-security-loses-1300-badges-and-credentials-in-31-months/. Shepherd, Todd, "US Dept. of Homeland Security loses 1,300 badges, and credentials in 31 months," Jan. 27, 2016.
56. http://abcnews.go.com/TheLaw/homeland-security-lost-dozens-guns-report/story?id=9875383. Ferran, Lee. "Homeland security lost dozens of guns, according to internal report," Feb. 18, 2016.
57. http://www.foxnews.com/politics/2016/02/01/hundreds-dhs-badges-guns-cell-phones-lost-or-stolen-2012.html. Shaw, Andrew. "Hundreds of DHS badges, guns, cell phones lost or stolen since 2012," Feb. 1, 2016.
58. http://www.sonsoflibertyinternational.com/.
59. Baldor, Lolita C. and Deb Riechmann. "US general: only a handful of Syrian fighters remain in battle." The Times Daily 17 Sept. 2015. A5. Print.
60. http://www.cbsnews.com/news/ohio-boys-20-investment-in-kindness-yields-big-return/. Hartman, Steve. "Ohio boy's $20 investment in kindness yields big return," Mar. 28, 2014.

61. https://www.conservativereview.com/commentary/2016/04/whistleblower-cockroaches-served-for
-dinner-at-chicago-area-va-hospital/. Richards, Tori. "Whistleblower: cockroaches served for dinner at
Chicago-area VA hospital," Apr. 27, 2016
62. www.stripes.com/news.us-has-trained-fewer-than-100-in-syria-to-fight-islamic-state-1.416530. Copp,
Tara. "US has trained fewer than 100 in Syria to fight Islamic State," Jun. 27, 2016.
63. http://www.washingtonpost.com/politics/report-mcauliffe-asked-for-and-got-favors-at-homeland-
security/2015/03/24/00f62514-d24-ee745911a4ff_story.htm. Hamburger, Tom and Rachel Weiner.
"Report: Va. Governor received special treatment from   Homeland Security," Mar. 24, 2015.
64. https://www.washingtonpost.com/news/post-nation/wp/2016/04/22/about-200000-convicted-
felons-in-virginia-will-now-have-the-right-to-vote-in-november/. Horwitz, Sari and Jenna Portnoy.
"About 200,000 convicted felons in Virginia will now have the right to vote in November," Apr. 22,
2016.
65. http://dailycaller.com/2016/07/23/this-is-how-badly-terry-mcauliffe-wants-felons-to-vote/. Daley,
Kevin. "This is how badly Terry McAuliffe wants felons to vote," Jul. 23, 2016.
66. http://www.foxnews.com/politics/2016/05/23/virginia-gov-terry-mcauliffe-under-investigation-by-
doj-over-possible-illegal-campaign-contributions.html. "Virginia Gov. Terry McAuliffe under investigation by DOJ over possible illegal campaign contributions," May 23, 2016.

Truman Leads the Way

1. http://www.washingtonpost.com/news/the-fix/wp/2015/11/18/was-neil-cavutos-painful-interview-
with-a-college-student-activist-fair-game/. Borchers, Callum. "Was Neil Cavuto's painful interview with
a college student activist fair game," Nov. 18, 2015.
2. Fox Business. "Students want top earners to pay for their tuition." Online video clip. YouTube, 13
Nov. 2015. Web. Apr. 25, 2016.
3. Mullen, Madison. "The Privilege Project, Keely Mullen." Online video clip. YouTube. YouTube, 25
Feb. 2013. Web. Apr. 25, 2016.
4. http://www.examiner.com/article/keely-mullen-million-student-march-spokeswoman-is-the-one-
percent. Nal, Renee. "Keely Mullen: Million student march spokeswoman is in the 'one percent,'" Nov.
13, 2015.
5. Miller, Merle. Plain Speaking: An Oral Biography of Harry S. Truman. Berkley Publishing Corporation: New York, 1974. (p.147, 163-169, 392).
6. http://www.socialistalternative.org/about/. "About SA."
7. Fox Business. "Million Student March organizer: capitalism has proven itself illegitimate." Online
video clip. YouTube. YouTube, 14 Apr. 2015. Web. Apr. 25, 2016.
8. http://www.peggynoonan.com/. Noonan, Peggy. "Trump and the rise of the unprotected: why political professionals are struggling to make sense of the world they created," Feb. 25, 2016.
9. https://www.nationalpriorities.org/campaigns/military-spending-united-states/. "Military spending in
the United States."
10. http://www.thefiscaltimes.com/2015/05/08/Pentagon-s-90-Billion-Slush-Fund-Comes-Under-
Attack#sthash.mP4sRkN1.dpuf. Pianin, Eric. "Pentagon's $90 billion 'slush fund' comes under attack,"
May 8, 2015.
11. http://www.politico.com/story/2015/03/war-budget-might-be-permanent-slush-fund-116367.
Bender, Bryan and Jeremy Herb. "War budget might be permanent 'slush fund,'" Mar. 3, 2015.
12. https://www.nationalpriorities.org/blog/2015/10/28/what-if-we-spent-pentagons-2016-slush-fund-
differently/. Tucker, Jasmine. "What if we spent the Pentagon's 2016 slush fund differently," Oct. 28,
2015.
13. http://www.usneews.com/news/articles/2016-02-12/inside-the-pentagon-slush-fund-the-secret-
budget-that-just-wont-go-away. Shinkman, Paul D. "Inside the Pentagon's 'Slush Fund,'" Feb. 12, 2015.
14. https://www.nationalpriorities.org/ampaigns/overseas-contingency-operations/. "Overseas Contingency Operations: the pentagon slush fund."
15. http://news.yahoo.com/senate-vote-massive-defense-bill-143955273--politics.html#. Riechmann,
Deb. "Senate OKs massive defense bill, sends measure to Obama," Aug. 7, 2015.
16. http://www.rollcall.com/news/obama_signs_budget_deal_and_debt_limit_suspension-244552-
1.html. Krawzack, Paul M. "Obama signs budget deal and debt limit suspension," Nov. 2, 2015.
17. http://news.yahoo.com/senate-vote-massive-defense-bill-143955273--politics.html#. Riechmann,
Deb. "Senate OKs massive defense bill, sends measure to Obama," Aug. 7, 2015.
18. http://www.thefiscaltimes.com/2015/03/19/85-Trillion-Unaccounted-Should-Congress-Increase-
Defense-Budget. Leo, Jacqueline and Brianna Ehley. "With $8.5 Trillion Unaccounted for, Why Should

Congress Increase the Defense Budget," Mar. 19, 2015.

19. http://www.reuters.com/investigates/pentagon/#article/part1. Paltrows, Scot J. And Kelly Carr. "How the Pentagon's payroll quagmire traps American troops," Jul. 2, 2013.

20. http://www.reuters.com/investigates/pentagon/#article/part3. Paltrow, Scott J. "Why the pentagon's many campaigns to clean up its accounts are failing," Dec. 23, 2013.

21. http://www.thefiscaltimes.com/2015/11/09/Outrageous-500-million-Post-One-Form-Immigration-Site. Pianin, Eric. "Outrageous! $1 Billion to Post One Form on Immigration Site," Nov. 9, 2015.

22. http://thehill.com/homenews/administration/257798-obama-vetoes-defense-bill. Fabian, Jordan. "Obama vetoes defense bill," Oct. 22, 2015.

23. http://www.factcheck.org/2011/07/obama-inflates-defense-cut/. "Obama inflates defense cut," Jul. 22, 2011.

24. http://www.scragged.com/articles/yes-virginia-a-298-hammer-really-costs-our-government-100. Offensicht, Will. "Yes, Virginia, A $2.98 Hammer REALLY Costs Our Government $100," Jan 15, 2010.

25. http://truth-out.org/archive/component/k2/item/93261:solution-the-pentagon-continues-to-overpay-for-everything-lets-fix-it. Rasor, Dina. "Solution: The Pentagon Continues to Overpay for Everything; Let's Fix It," Dec. 9, 2010.

26. http://www.cnn.com/2015/07/16/politics/f-35-jsf-operational-costs/. Cohen, Zachary. "The F-35: Is the world's most expensive weapons program worth it," Jul. 16, 2015.

27. http://truth-out.org/archive/component/k2/itemlist/user/37625?Itemid=252

28. http://articles.latimes.com/1986-07-30/news/vw-18804_1_nut. Smith, Jack. "$37 screws, a $7,622 coffee makers, $640 toilet seats; suppliers to our military just won't be oversold," Jul. 30, 1986.

29. https://en.wikipedia.org/wiki/Commission_on_Wartime_Contracting_in_Iraq_and_Afghanistan. "Commission on Wartime Contracting in Iraq and Afghanistan," May 29, 2015

30. http://cybercemetery.unt.edu/archive/cwc/20110929230444/http://www.wartimecontracting.gov/index.php/pressroom/pressreleases/209-cwc-nr-50. "CWC-NR-50: Wartime Contracting Commission closes its doors September 30," Sep. 28, 2011.

31. http://freebeacon.com/issues/government-owe-money-entire-economy/. Meyer, Ali. "Auditor: Government will owe more money than entire economy produces," Apr. 7, 2016.

32. https://en.wikipedia.org/wiki/Truman_Committee.

33. http://www.americanrhetoric.com/speeches/dwightdeisenhowerfarewell.html. "Dwight D. Eisenhower Farewell Speech," Jan. 17, 1961.

34. http://finance.yahoo.com/news/cagw-releases-2016-congressional-pig-130000799.html. "CAGW releases 2016 congressional pig book," Apr. 14, 2016.

35. http://www.thedailybeast.com/articles/2013/06/12/the-military-industrial-complex-is-real-and-it-s-bigger-than-ever.html. Avlon, John. "The Military-Industrial Complex is Real, and It's Bigger Than Ever," Jun. 12, 2013.

36. https://en.wikipedia.org/wiki/List_of_U.S._executives_branch_czars.

37. https://www.whitehouse.gov/blog/2009/09/16/truth-about-czars. Dunn, Anita. "The truth about 'czars,'" Sept. 16, 2009.

38. http://www.rollcall.com/news/policy/fight-looms-size-white-house-national-security-staff-2. Bennett, John T. "Fight looms on size over size of White House National Security Staff," Apr. 26, 2016.

39. https://cei.org/content/federal-regulation-cost-reaches-1885-trillion. "Federal Regulation Cost Reaches $1.885 Trillion," May 4, 2016.

40. http://nsarchive.gwu.edu/NSAEBB/NSAEBB101/. Prados, John. "JFK and the Diem Coup," Nov. 5, 2013.

41. http://www.jfklibrary.org/Research/Research-Aids/JFK-Speeches/American-Newspaper-Publishers- Association_19610427.aspx. John F. Kennedy Speeches: The President and the Press, Address before the American Newspaper Publishers Association, Waldorf-Astoria Hotel, New York City, April 27, 1961.

42. http://www.npr.org/templates/story/story.php?storyId=1569483. Burnett, John. "Halliburton Deals Recall Vietnam-Era Controversy," Dec. 24, 2013.

43. Pope, Carl and Paul Rauber. Strategic Ignorance: Why the Bush Administration Is Recklessly Destroying a Century of Environmental Progress. Sierra Club Books: San Francisco, 2004. (p.101).

44. http://dailycaller.com/2016/04/17/exclusive-disgraced-clinton-donor-got-13m-in-state-dept-grants-under-hillary/. Pollock, Richard. "Exclusive: Disgraced Clinton donor got $13M in state dept grants under Clinton," Apr. 17, 2016.

45. http://www.charlotteobserver.com/opinion/op-ed/article69538017.html. Jackson Jr., William E. "Congress is letting unelected bureaucrats run U.S. war effort," Arp. 2, 2016.

46. http://billmoyers.com/2014/02/21/anatomy-of-the-deep-state/. Lofgren, Mike. "Essay: Anatomy of a Deep State," Feb. 21, 2014.

47. http://www.theamericanconservative.com/articles/deep-state-america/. Giraldi, Philip. "Deep State America: Democracy is often subverted by special interests operating behind the scenes," Jul. 30, 2015.

48. http://www.pogo.org/blog/2015/02/Groups-Seek-to-Ban-Secret-Election-Support-by-Contractors.html. Amey, Scott. "Groups Seek to Ban Secret Election Support by Contractors," Mar. 2, 2015.
49. http://www.dailykos.com/story/2016/1/8/1467312/-29-Dems-Senators-Call-on-Obama-to-Take-Executive-Action-to-Limit-Anonymous-Campaign-Contributions. Liberty Equality Fraternity and Trees. "29 Dem Senators call on Obama to take executive action to Limit anonymous campaign contributions," Jan. 8, 2016.
50. https://www.yahoo.com/news/firms-paid-clinton-speeches-us-govt-interests-075043845-finance.html. Braun, Stephen. "Firms that paid for Clinton speeches have US gov't interests," Apr. 22, 2016.
51. https://en.wikipedia.org/wiki/Jorge_Scientific_Corporation.
52. http://abcnews.go.com/US/wild-drinking-drugs-sandal-cyber-security-savior/story?id=32763736. Schwartz, Rhonda and Brian Ross. "From Wild Drinking, Drugs Scandal to Cyber Security Savior," Jul. 31, 2015.
53. https://www.washingtonpost.com/news/the-switch/wp/2015/01/12/the-centcom-hack-that-wasnt/. Fung, Brian and Andrea Peterson. "The Centcom 'hack that wasn't,'" Jan. 12, 2015.
54. http://motherboard.vice.com/read/teen-who-hacked-cia-email-is-back-to-prank-us-spy-chief. Bicchierai, Lorenzo Franceschi. "Teen who hacked CIA email is back to prank US spy chief," Jan. 12, 2016.
55. https://motherboard.vice.com/read/teen-hackers-a-5-year-old-could-have-hacked-into-cia-directors-emails. Bicchierai, Lorenzo Franceschi. "The hackers: A '5 year old' could have hacked into CIA director's emails," Oct. 19, 2015.
56. Green, Charles. "A Conversation with… Ted Koppel." AARP Bulletin/Real Possibilities. Oct. 2015: Vol 56, No. 8.
57. https://www.yahoo.com/politics/gop-would-have-us-in-seven-wars-right-now-090043699.html. Knox, Oliver. "GOP would have U.S. in 'seven wars right now,'" Oct. 6, 2015.
58. https://www.washington.com/world/national-security/obama-issues-syria-red-line-warning-on-chemical-weapons/2012/08/20/ba5d26ec-eaf7-11el-b811-09036bcb182b_story.html. Ball, James. "Obama issues Syria a 'red line' warning on chemical weapons," Aug. 20, 2012.
59. http://www.cnn.com/videos/politics/2015/12/18/obama-bombing-syria-right-sot.cnn/video/playlists/-last-news-conference/. Obama on Syria: I was right [Video file]. (2015, December 12).
60. http://america.aljazeera.com/articles/2014/3/14/syrian-s-forciblydisplacedtop9million.html. "UN: 9 million Syrians now displaced as conflict ticks into fourth year," Mar. 14, 2014.
61. http://www.huffington.co.uk/2015/10/31/syrian-civil-war-death-_n_8440378.html. York, Chris and George Bowden. "Syria Civil War Death Toll Paints A Horrifying Complex Picture," Oct. 31, 2015.
62. http://www.pbs.org/wgbh/frontline/film/children-of-syria/transcript/. Filmed, produced, and directed by Marcel Mettelsiefen. Co-produced by Stephen Ellis. "Children of Syria." Apr. 19, 2016.
63. http://www.pbs.org/wgbh/americanexperience/features/primary-resource/tr-progressive/?flavour=mobile. "1912 Progressive Party Platform."
64. http://conservativetribune.com/judge-irs-ruling-then-1-demand/. Smith, Kim. "Judge Hits Obama's IRS With BRUTAL Ruling, Then Makes It Worse With 1 Demand," Mar. 24, 2016.
65. http://www.thefiscaltimes.com/2016/03/30/How-Government-Spent-86-Million-Plane-Hasn-t-Flown. Matishak, Martin. "How the Government Spent $86 Million for a Plant That Hasn't Flown, Mar. 30, 2016.
66. http://www.csmonitor.com/World/Global-News/2015/1102/Pentagon-spends-43-million-to-build-gas-station-won-t-say-why. Regan, Michael D. "Pentagon spends 43 million to build gas station, won't say why," Nov. 2, 2016.
67. http://www.stripes.com/news/middle-east/green-beret-officer-blames-moral-cowardice-for-strike-on-Doctors-without-borders-1.407056. Lamothe, Dan. "Green beret officer blames 'moral cowardice' for strike on Doctors Without Borders," Apr. 29, 2016.
68. http://www.huffingtonpost.com/2013/03/06/eric-holder-banks-too-big_n_2821741.html. Gongloff, Mark. "Eric Holder admits some banks are just too big to prosecute," Mar. 6, 2013.
69. http://democrats-armedservices.house.gov/index.cfm/files/serve?File_id=48FF2A32-DB43-4AB7-92EC-138A6D50C2D7.
70. http://thehill.com/policy/defense/231443-obamas-pentagon-request-sets-up-fight. Wong, Kristina. "Obama's DOD funding request sets up fight," Feb. 2, 2015.
71. http://www.stripes.com/news/lacking-basic-gear-special-operators-stuck-buying-their-own-equipment-1.396109. Tritten, Travis J. "Lacking basic gear, special operators stuck buying their own equipment," Feb. 25, 2016.
72. "Shepard Smith Reporting." Host Shepard Smith, Fox News, 1105 FNCHD, Xfinity, Mar. 4, 2016.
73. http://time.com/4293549/james-grant-united-states-debt/. Grant, James. "The United States of Insolvency," Apr. 14, 2016.
74. https://mises.org/blog/james-grant-points-out-us-broke-left-goes-nuts. Bishop, Tho. "James Grant points out U.S. is broke, left goes nuts," Apr. 20, 2016.

75. https://mises.org/blog/foreign-regimes-dumping-us-debt-%E2%80%94-will-fed-just-monetize-debt -instead. McMaken, Ryan. "Foreign regimes dumping U.S. debt- will the fed just Monetize the debt instead," Mar. 17, 2016.
76. http://www.breitbart.com/video/2016/04/19/obam-rips-bill-allow-911-victim-families-sue-nations-support-terrorism/. Poor, Jeff. "Obama rips bill that will allow 9/11 victims families to sue nation that support terrorism," Apr. 19, 2016.
77. http://www.philly.com/philly/business/3777890051.html. Mondics, Chris. "Senate bill would allow suits against Saudi Arabia for 9/11," May 3, 2016.
78. http://usatoday.com/story/opinion/2015/07/06/declassification-28-pages-911-saudis-column/28926283/. Bovard, James. "We need to know: Did Saudis help fund 9/11 attacks," Jul. 6, 2015.
79. http://www.foxnews.com/politics/2016/04/17/budget-cuts-leaving-marine-corps-aircraft-grounded.html. Tomlinson, Lucas and Jennifer Griffin. "Budget cuts leaving marine corps aircraft grounded," Apr. 17, 2016.
80. http://www.nola.com/politics/index.ssf/2016/07/file_17_document_reveals_info.html. "'File 17': Document reveals info on people of interest in 9/11 attacks," Jul. 2, 2016.
81. www.westernjournalism.com/obama-administration-seeks-to-delay-release-of-clinton-aides-emails-until-late-2018/. Desota, Randy. "Obama Administration seeks to delay release of Clinton aides' emails until late 2018," Jun. 30, 2016.
82. freebeacon.com/issues/state-department-grilled-75-year-wait-time-rnc-foia-request/. Heretik, Jack. "State Department grilled on 75-year wait time for RNC FOIA request," Jun. 7, 2016.
83. https://www.scribd.com/document/318415850/US-Declassifies-Secret-9-11-Documents-Known-as -the-28-Pages#from_embed.

Migration

1. http://www.nbcnews.com/meet-the-press/meet-press-transcript-january-25-2015-n297681. "Meet the Press" Transcript, Moderator Chuck Todd, Jan. 25, 2015.
2. http://www.washingtontimes.com/news/2015/nov/21/bill-maher-blasts-liberals-defending-islam-muslims/. Howell, Kellan. "Bill Maher blasts liberals for defending Islam: Muslims sharing   Western value is bull ****,' Nov. 21, 2015.
3. http://www.infowars.com/sweden-syrian-migrant-brutally-rapes-woman-while-spitting-in-her-face. Watson, Joseph. "Sweden: Syrian migrant brutally rapes woman while spitting in her face: Victim: suffers shocking double rape near refugee center," Nov. 12, 2015.
4. http://www.infowars.com/german-police-covering-up-rapes-so-as-not-to-legitimize-critics-of-mass-migration/. Watson, Joseph. "German Police covering up rapes so as 'Not to legitimize critics of mass migration: fears public knowledge of children being molested by Muslim migrants could lead to "right-wing demonstrations," Jul. 23, 2015.
5. http://www.nytimes.com/2015/12/20/world/europe/norway-offers-migrants-a-lesson-in-how-to-treat-women.html?smid=tw-nytimes&smtyp=cur&_r=1. Higgins, Andrew. "Norway offers migrants a lesson in how to treat women," Dec. 19, 2015.
6. http://www.examiner.com/article/cologne-police-chief-fired-amid-sex-attack-by-1000-muslims-german-media-coverup. Chang, Samantha. "Cologne police chief fired after sex attack by 1000 Muslims: Teens gang-raped" Jan. 8, 2016.
7. http://www.examiner.com/article/germany-mayor-blames-victims-for-sex-attack-by-1-000-muslims-media-censorship. Chang, Samantha. "German mayor blames victims for sex attacks by 1,000 Muslims: Media coverup." Jan 5, 2016 .
8. "Refugee debate should focus on facts, not fear mongering" The Times Daily 20 Nov. 2015: A5. Print.
9. http://www.nbcnews.com/meet-the-press/meet-press-december-6-2015-n475061. "Meet the Press" Transcript, Moderator Chuck Todd, Dec. 6, 2015.
10. http://newsok.com/trancript-of-president-obamas-oval-office-address/article/5465147. Casteel, Chris. "Transcript of President Obama's Oval Office address," Dec. 6, 2015.
11. http://www.bloomberg.com/politics/articles/2015-11-18/bloomberg-poll-most-americans-oppose-syrian-refugee-resettlement. Taley, Margarae. "Bloomberg Politics Poll: Most Americans oppose syrian refugee resettlement," Nov. 18, 2015.
12. http://www.npr.org/sections/thetwo-way/2015/12/01/4580003126/unprecedented-what-isis-looks -like-in-america. Chappel, Bill. "'Unprecedented': What ISIS looks like in America," Dec. 1, 2015.
13. http://www.breitbart.com/big-government/2015/12/10/sessions-senate-moves-ratify-Immigration-

foreign-muslims-civil-right/. Hahn, Julia. "Senate Judiciary Committee Votes Foreign Muslims May Not Be Banned Based on religion," Dec. 10, 2015.

14. http://dailycaller.com/2015/11/23/canada-to-no-longer-accept-single-male-refugees-from-syria/. Bojesson, Jacob. "Canada To No Longer Accept Single Male Refugees From Syria," Nov. 23, 2015.

15. http://www.ibtimes.com/european-refugee-crisis-2015-50-asylum-seekers-landing-are-syrian-Un-report-2084862. Brandan, James. "European Refugee Crisis 2015: 50% of Asylum Seekers Landing In Europe Are Syrian, UN Report Finds," Sep. 6, 2015.

16. Lewis, Edwards and Richard Rhodes, eds. John F. Kennedy: Words to Remember. United States: Hallmark Cards Incorporated, 1967. (p.13, 14).

17. http://www.buzzfeed.com/andrewkacynski/state-department-only-2-of-syrian-refugees-in-us-are-Military#.hneZV70Dx. Kacynski, Andrew. "State Department: Only 2% Of Syrian refugees in U.S. are military-aged men with no family," Nov. 26, 2015.

18. http://www.westernjournalism.com/watch-krauthammer-just-diagnosed-what-is-really-wrong-with-obama/. Agee, Christopher. "Watch: Krauthammer just diagnosed what is really wrong with Obama," Sept. 1, 2015.

19. http://www.wtvm.com/story/30551039/rep-sanford-bishop-strategizes-to-bring-the-abducted-nigerian-schoolgirls-bac-home. "GA congressman works to recover Nigerian girls abducted by Boko Haram," Nov. 18, 2015.

20. http://www.theaustralian.com.au/news/world/children-burnt-alive-by-nigerian-islamists/news-story/faa36fdddbeb823bd179f283238c9cac. "Children burnt alive by Nigerian Islamists," Feb. 2, 2016.

21. http://www.dailymail.co.uk/news/article-3279094/A-close-shave-Terrified-jihadists-leave-BEARDS-battlefield-shave-faces-dress-women-flee-Syria.html. Malm, Sara. "A Close shave? Terrified jihadists leave their BEARDS on the battlefield as they shave their faces in mass and dress as women to flee Syria," Aug. 19, 2015.

22. http://apusa.us/fbi-900-isis-probes-james-comey-900-investigations-38007. "FBI: 900 ISIS probes: James Comey 900 Investigations," Oct. 22, 2015.

23. http://www.telgraph.co.uk/news/worldnews/asia/afghanistan/9014282/Afghan-boy-sucide-bombers-tell-how-they-are-brainwashed-into-believing-they-will-survive.html. Farmer, Ben. "Afghan boy suicide bombers tell how they are brainwashed into believing they will survive," Jan. 13, 2012.

24. http://www.huffingtonpost.com./entry/lindsey-graham-visas_55a7a7bde4b0896514d06220. Kiely, Eugene. "Lindsey Graham gets it wrong on the visas of 9/11 hijackers, again: Only two of the hijackers," Jul. 16, 2015.

25. http://www.factcheck.org/2013/05/911-hijackers-and-student-visas/. Farley, Robert. "9/11 Hijackers and Student Visas," May 10, 2013.

26. Zoll, Rachel. "US religious leaders make refugee appeal" The Times Daily 22 Nov. 201: A4. Print.

27. http://whnt.com/2015/blindfolded-muslim-student-asks-for-hugs-trust-at-auburn/. Bryan, Shevaun. "Blindfolded Muslim student asks for hugs, trust at Auburn," Dec. 5, 2015.

28. http://www.reagan.utexas.edu/archives/speeches/1984/102684a.htm. "Remarks to Members of the Congregation of Temple Hillel and Jewish Community Leaders in Valley Stream, New York," Speech Transcript, October 26, 1984.

29. http://time.com3662152/kareem-abdul-jabbar-paris-charlie-hebdo-terrorist-attacks-are-not-aboutreligion/. Kareem Abdul-JabbarAbdul-Jabbar, Kareem. "These Terrorists Attacks Are Not About Religion," Jan 9, 2015.

30. http://yellowhammernews.com/faithandculture/hero-alabamaian-stormed-normandy-beach-d-day-carrying-auburn-creed/. Sims, Cliff. "Hero: this Alabamian stormed beach on D-Day carrying the Auburn Creed," Jun. 6, 2016.

31. "Varney and Company." Fox Business Network, Xfinity 1117, FBNHD, Jun. 24, 2016.

32. http://www.foxnews.com/us/2016/08/18/syrian-describe-confusing-vetting-process-uncertainty-in-america.html. McKay, Hollie. "Syrian refugees describe confusing vetting process, uncertainty in America," Aug. 18, 2016.

Trade

1. Carson, Ben and Candy Carson. America the Beautiful: Rediscovering what makes America great. Zondervan: Michigan, 2012. (p.79).

2. http://www.realclearpolitics.com/video/2015/06/18/trump_on_trade_we_dont_have_our_best_and_brightest_negotiating_for_us_were_getting_ripped_off_major_league.html. Trump on Trade: "We Don't Have Our Best and Brightest Negotiating For Us... We're getting Ripped off big league," June 18, 2015.

3. Kuttner, Robert. The Squandering of America: How the failure of our politics undermines our prosperity. New York: Alfred A. Knopf, 2007. (p.217).
4. http://www.latimes.com/business/la-fi-pacific-free-trade-20151005-story.html. Lee, Don. "Trade deal puts a U.S. stamp on Asian economy. Oct. 5, 2015.
5. https://en.wikipedia.org/wiki/North_American_Free_Trade_Agreement.
6. Dobbs, Lou. Exploring America: Why corporate greed is shipping American jobs overseas. Warner Brooks: New York, 2004. (p. 73).
7. http://www.aflcio.org/Issues/Trade/Trans-Pacific-Partnership-Free-Trade-Agreement-TTP.
8. http://www.huffingtonpost.com/laura-carlsen/obama-reaffirms-promise-t_b_157316.html. Calsen, Laura. "Obama reaffirms promise to renegotiate NAFTA," Feb. 12, 2009.
9. http://www.huffingtonpost.com/lori-wallach/nafta-at-20-one-million-u_b_4550207.html. Wallach, Lori. "NAFTA at 20: One million U.S. jobs lost, higher income inequality," Jan. 6, 2014.
10. http://www.huffingtonpost.ca/2014/02/18/barack-obama-nafta-tpp_n_4810868.html. Panetta, Alexander. "Obama's NAFTA Promise Resurfaces, Harper Spokesperson Denies Renegotiations," April 20, 2014.
11. http://blogs.wsj.com/washwire/2015/06/22/support-for-free-trade-drops-amid-raging-congressional-Debate-wsjnbc-poll/. Hook, Janet. "Support for Free Trade Drops, Amid Raging Congressional Debate- WSJ/NBC Poll," Jun. 22, 2015.
12. http://citizen.typepad.com/eyesontrade/2008/06/poll-roundup-am.html.
13. http://www.bizjournals.com/bizwomen/news/profiles-strategies/2015/05/how-tim-russerthelped-this-intern-become-the.html?page=all. Portillo, Caroline McMillan. "How Tim Russert helped this intern become the executive producer for 'Meet the Press,'" May 18, 2015.
14. http://www.slate.com/articles/news_and_politics/press_box/2003/07/how_to_beat_tim_russert.html. Shafer, Jack. "How to beat Tim Russert," July 2, 2003.
15. http://blogs.suntimes.com/sweet/2008/02/complete_transcriptdemocratic.html. Sweet, Lynn. "Complete transcript Democratic Presidential Debate." Courtesy MSNBC Cleveland, Ohio, Feb. 26, 2008.
16. http://news.yahoo.com/clinton-opposes-pacific-rim-trade-deal-breaking-obama-200914025.html. Lerer, Lisa and Catherine Lucey. "Clinton opposes Pacific trade deal in major break with Obama," Aug. 7, 2015.
17. "Fox and Friends First." Hosts Abby Huntsman and Heather Childers. Xfinity 1105 FNC, Jan. 13, 2016.
18. http://www.nytimes.com/2015/10/06/business/international/the-trans-pacific-partnership-trade-deal-explained.html?src=mv&_r=0. Granville, Kevin. "The Trans-Pacific Partnership Trade Accord Explained," Oct. 5, 2016.
19. http://fas.org/sgp/crs/misc/R43491.pdf. Fergusson, Ian F. and Richard S. Beth. "Trade Promotion Authority (TPA): Frequently Asked Questions, " July 2, 2015.
20. http://thehill.com/business-a-lobbying/245417-house-approves-fast-track-218-208-sending-bill-to-senate. Marcos, Cristina and Vicki Needham. "House approves fast-track 218-208, sending bill to senate," June 18, 2016.
21. http://www.politico.com/story/2015/06/tpa-trade-bill-democrat-vot-tally-119331. Kim, Seung Min. "13 Senate Dems vote with GOP to advance trade bill," Jun. 23, 2015.
22. http://www.waren.senate.gov/?p=press_release&id=825. "Senators Warren, Manchin introduce Trade Transparency Act to require release of trade deal text before congress grants fast track authority," May 19, 2015.
23. http://observer.com/2015/08/elizabeth-warren-slams-confidentiality-of-sputtering-trans-pacific-Partnership-deal/. Sainato, Michael. "Elizabeth Warren slams confidentiality of sputtering Trans Pacific Partnership Deal," Aug. 9, 2015.
24. http://www.dailykos.com/story/2015/05/22/1386927/-TPP-Remains-Classified-after-Trade-Transparency-Act-is-Blocked-by-Senate-Republicans#. Benavides, Stephen. "TPP remains classified after Trade Transparency Act is blocked by Senate Republicans," May 22, 2015.
25. "Fox Report Weekend: The Political Insiders." Anchor Pattie Ann Browne. Xfinity 1105 FNC, July 5, 2015.
26. http://www.huffingtonpost.com/heather-gautney/why-the-transpacific-part_1_b_6598604.html. Gautney, Heather. "Why the Trans-Pacific Partnership is bad for workers, and for democracy," Feb 3, 2015.
27. http://www.sessions.senate.gov/pulic/index.cfm/2015/5/sessions-sends-letter-to-obama-on-trad-pact-make-living-agreement-provision-public-before-fast-track-vote. Jeff, Sessions. "News Release: Sessions sends letter to Obama on trade pact: Make 'living agreement' provision public before 'fast-track' vote," May 6, 2015.
28. http://www.breitbart.com/big-government/2015/11/06/jeff-sessions-trans-pacific-trade-deal-erosion-Sovereignty/. Swoyer, Alex. "Jeff Sessions: TPP 'breathtaking… erosion of sovereignty," Nov. 6, 2015.

29. http;//www.washingtonpost.com/r/2010-2019/WashingtonPost/2015/04/30/Editorial-Opinion/Graphics/oppose_ISDS_Letter.pdf.
30. http://www.nytimes.com/2015/06/26/business/economy/house-approves-trade-bills-expansion-of-worker-aid.html. Weisman, Jonathan. "House approves trade bill's expansion of worker aid," Jun. 25, 2015.
31. http://blogs.rollcall.com/218/republicans-get-obama-trade-promotion-authority/. Dumain, Emma, Fuller, Matt, Lesniewski, Niels, and Matthew Fleming. "How Republicans could Get Obama trade promotion authority, " 16 June 2015: Video.
32. http://www.huffingtonpost.com/2015/06/24/obama-trade-win_n_7655224.html. Carter, Zack and Laura Barron-Lopez. "Senate grants Obama fast-track trade authority after contentious battle," Jun. 24, 2015.
33. http://www.standard.net/News/2015/11/29/Trade-biological-patents-among-Senate-issues-says-hatch. Gibson, Doug. "Trade, biological patents, among senate issues for Hatch," Nov. 29, 2015.
34. http://www.theguardian.com/us-news/2015/oct/08/hillary-clinton-tpp-disapproval-critical-turning-point. Greenhouse, Steven. "Hillary Clinton's TPP deal disapproval is 'a critical turning point,'" Oct. 8, 2015.
35. Kennedy, John F. Profiles in Courage: Decisive moments in the lives of celebrated Americans. HarperCollins Publisher: New York, 1955.
36. Hart, Gary. The Republic of Conscience. Penguin Random House: New York, 2015. (p. 127).
37. http://news.yahoo.com/photos/photos-of-the-day-october-10-2015-1444494796-slideshow/consumer-rights-activists-part-march-protest-against-ttip-photo-123539709.html. "Photos of the Day," Oct. 10, 2015.
38. http://news.yahoo.com/thousands-demonstrate-germany-against-eu-us-trade-deal-102955133-fiance.html. "Thousands demonstrate in Germany against EU-US trade deal," (AP) Oct. 10, 2015.
39. http://www.politifact.com/truth-o-meter/statements/2015/feb/10/ted-cruz-says-92-million-americans-aren't-working/. Jacobson, Louis. "Ted Cruz says 92 million Americans aren't working," Feb. 10, 2015.
40. https://www.yahoo.com/music/powerball-reimbursement-fund-page-created-235504618.html. Golding, Shenequa. "A Powerball reimbursement go fund me page has been created," Jan. 14, 2016.
41. http://money.cnn.com/2015/03/06/news/economy/february-jobs-295000-us-economy/index.html. Gillespie, Patrick. "Good news: Unemployment at lowest in 7 years," Mar. 6, 2015.
42. Tucker, Cynthia. "Anxiety pervasive in both parties," The Times Daily 19 Sept. 2015: A1, Print.
43. https://www.conservativereview.com/commentary/2015/12/paul-ryan-ends-the-year-with-an-omni-bust. Horowitz, Daniel. "Paul Ryan ends the year with an Omni-bust- Jail break is next," Dec. 12, 2015.
44. http://www.breitbart.com/big-government/2015/11/26/lawyer-displaced-disney-workers-1200-american-workers-n-y-training-foreign-replacements. Fields, Michelle. "Lawyer for displaced Disney workers: 1,200 American workers in N.Y. are training their foreign replacements," Nov. 26, 2015.
45. "First in the South Presidential Candidates Forum," Moderator Rachel Maddow. Xfinity 1108 MSNBC. South Carolina. 5 Nov. 2015. Television.
46. http://nypost.com/2016/01/17/occupy-obama-he-orchestrated-a-massive-transfer-of-wealth-to-the-1-percent/. Gray, Michael. "Obama orchestrated a massive transfer of wealth to the 1 percent," Jan. 17, 2016.
47. http://canadafreepress.com/article/78587. Cain, Herman. "Ouch: U.S. economy stumbles with 0.7 percent growth in 4Q 2015," Jan 31, 2016.
48. http://hotair.com/headlines/archives/2015/12/12/video-press-corps-cheers-paris-climate-accord/. Adams, Becket. "Video: Press corps cheers Paris climate accord," Dec. 12, 2015.
49. http://www.ndtv.com/world-news/us-to-pay-iran-1-7-billion-in-debt-and-interst-john-kerry-1266963. "US to pay Iran $1.7 billion in debt and interest: John Kerry," Jan. 18, 2016.
50. http://www.cnn.com/2016/01/17/politics/us-pays-iran-1-7-billion/index.html. Koran, Laura. "U.S. to pay Iran $1.7 billion in legal settlement," Jan. 17, 2016.
51. http://www.washingtontimes.com/news/2015/oct/1/house-votes-delay-iran-sanctions-relief/?page=all. Howell, Jr., Tom. "House votes to block sanctions relief until Iran pays its U.S. victims of terrorism," Oct. 1, 2015.
52. http://news.yahoo.com/iraqi-minister-says-blackmail-behind-kidnapping-u-citizens-21470947.html;_ylt=AwrSbDc11KZWvrYAUzRXNupA;_lu=X3oA;_ylu=X3oDMTByNWU4cGh1BGNvbG8DZ3ExBHBvcwMXBHZ0aWQQDBHN1YwNzYw—. "Iraqi minister says 'blackmail' behind kidnapping of U.S. citizens," Jan. 21, 2016.
53. "Morning Joe" Host Mika Brzezinski and Joe Scarborough, Xfinity 1108 MSNBC, Jan. 18, 2016.
54. http://thehill.com/policy/defense/266619-kerry-some-iran-santions-relief-will-go-to-terrorists. Kheel, Rebecca. "Kerry: Some Iran sanctions relief will go to terrorists," Jan. 21, 2016.
55. http://finance.yahoo.com/news/uani-gravely-concerned-over-reported-223100379.html. Cohen, Steven. "UANI gravely concerned Over reported plan to allow Iran access to U.S. financial system, calls on administration to continue to deny use.

56. https://www.washingtonpost.com./news/checkpoint/wp/2016/01/18/pentagon-releases-new-details-on-how-u-s-sailors-were-taken-captive-by-iran/. Lamothe, Dan. "Pentagon release new details on how U.S. sailors were taken captive by Iran," Jan. 18, 2016.

57. https://en.wikipedia.org/wiki/Iran%E2%80%93U.S._RQ-170_incident.

58. http://www.westernjournalism.com/scary-advanced-u-s-missle-went-missing-where-it-surfaced-has-officials-panicked/. Davis, Jack. "Scary: Advanced US missile went missing; Where it surfaced has officials panicked," Jan 8, 2016.

59. http://www.foxnews.com/us/2016/01/29/iran-says-it-flew-drone-over-us-aircraft-carrier.html. "Iran claims it flew drone over US aircraft carrier, snapped photos," Jan. 29, 2016.

60. https://www.washingtonpost.com/blogs/right-turn/wp/2015/07/14/critics-relieved-that-the-iran-deal-is-absurd/. Rubin, Jennifer. "Critics relieved that the Iran deal is absurd," July 14, 2015.

61. http://nypost.com/2016/01/20/hillarys-emails-were-beyond-top-secret/. Schultz, Marisa. "Hillary's emails were 'beyond to secret,'" Jan. 20, 2016.

62. http://projects.nytimes.com/Guantanamo/detainees/535-tariq-mahmoud-ahmed-al-sawah.

63. https://www.govtrack.us/congress/bills/114/s2086#.

64. https://ballotpedia.org/2016_presidential_candidates_on_the_Trans-Pacific_Partnership_trade_deal.

65. https//www.washingtonpost.com/news/the-fix/wp/2016/01/14/6th-republican-debate-transcript-annotated-who-said-what-and-what-it-means/. The Fix Team. "6th Republican debate transcript, annotated: Who said what and what it means," Jan. 14, 2016.

66. http://www.nytimes.com/2008/03/06/opinion/06iht-edlighthizer.1.10774536.html?_r=0. Lighthizer, Robert E. "The venerable history of protectionism," Mar. 6, 2008.

67. http://dailysignal.com/2012/10/18/president-obamas-taxpayer-backed-green-energy-failures/. Schow, Ashe. "President Obama's taxpayer-backed green energy failures," Aug. 18, 2012.

68. http://www.cbsnews.com/news/60-minutes-great-brain-robbery-china-cyber-espionage/. Transcript "The Great Brain Robber," Correspondent Leslie Stahl, Rich Bonin, Producer. 17 Jan 2016.

69. https://twitter.com/SenatorSessions/status/663828771959607296.

70. http://thehill.com/policy/energy-environment/271614-chief-justice-rejects-plea-to-block-air-pollution-rule-. Cama, Timothy. "Chief Justice rejects plea to block air pollution rule," Mar. 3, 1016.

71. http://www.usatoday.com/story/news/politics/onpolitics/2016/03/04/brother-slain-civil-rights-leader-medgar-evers-endorses-trump/81314234/. Harris, Bracey. "Brother of slain civil rights leader Medgar Evers endorses Trump," Mar. 4, 2016.

72. http://finance.yahoo.com/news/trump-s-bad-logic-on-%E2%80%9Cbad-trade-deals%E2%80%9D-200134642.html#. Newman, Rick. "Trump's bad logic on 'bad trade deals,'" Mar. 4, 2016.

73. http://www.cato.org/blog/why-you-shouldnt-fear-trade-china. German, Chelsea. "Why you shouldn't fear trade with China," Mar. 7, 2016.

74. http://fivethirtyeight.com/features/manufacturing-jobs-are-never-coming-back/. Casselman, Ben. "Manufacturing jobs are never coming back," Mar. 18, 2016.

75. "Early Start with John Berman and Christine Romans," CNNHD 1106, Apr. 8, 2016.

76. http://www.ktbs.com/story/31771957/high-court-sides-with-families-of-83-beirut-bombing-victims. Sherman, Mark. "High Court sides with families of '83 Beirut bombing victims," Apr. 20, 2016.

77. http://www.cnn.com/2016/04/22/politics/us-nuclear-iran-purchase/. Sciutto, Jim and Ryan Browne. "U.S. to buy nuclear material from Iran," Apr. 22, 2016.

78. http://www.nytimes.com/2016/05/08/magazine/the-aspiring-novelist-who-became-obamas-foreign-policy-guru.html?_r=0. Samuels, David. "The Aspiring Novelist Who Became Obama's Foreign-Policy Guru," May 5, 2016.

79. www.marketwatch.com/story/us-gains-just-38,000-new-jobs-in-may-2016-06-03. Bartash, Jeffry. "U.S. jobs growth in the month of May was slowest in more than five years," Jun. 3, 2016.

80. http://www.politico.com/story/2016/07/terry0mcauliffe-hillary-clinton-tpp-trade-226253. Karnie, Annie. "Clinton friend McAuliffe says Clinton will flip on TPP, then walks it back," Jun. 29, 2016.

81. http://www.cato.org/publication/free-trade-bulletin/global-steel-overcapacity-trade-remedy-cure-worse-disease. Pearson, Daniel R. "Global steel overcapacity: Trade remedy 'cure' is worse than the disease,'" Apr. 11, 2016 .

Those Who Govern

1. https://en.wikipedia.org/wiki/Oath_of_office_of_the_President_of_the_United_States.

2. http://foavc.org/file.php/1/Articles/5%20U.S.C.%203331.htm.

3. https://en.wikipedia.org/wiki/Vice_President_Oath_of_Office_%28United_States%29.

4. http://www.jfklibrary.org/Research/Research-Aids/JFK-Speeches/American-Newspaper-Publishers-Association_19610427.aspx\. "John F. Kennedy Speeches: The President and the press: Address before the American Newspaper Publishers Association." Waldorf-Astoria Hotel, New York City, Apr. 27, 1961.

5. Powers, Kirsten. The Silencing: How the left is killing free speech. Regnery Publishing: Washington, DC, 2015 (p.8, 133, 134).

6. Pope, Carl and Paul Rauber. Strategic Ignorance: Why the Bush Administration is recklessly destroying a century of environmental progress. Sierra Club Books: San Francisco, 2004 (p.106,176).

7. http://finance.yahoo.com/news/journalists-criticize-white-house-secrecy-002418926.html. Tarm, Michael. "Journalist criticize White House for 'secrecy'," Sep. 17, 2014.

8. http://www.huffingtonpost.com/2013/02/27/bob-woodward-white-house-threatened-sequestrer_n_27777681.html. Mirkinson, Jack. "Bob Woodward: 'Very Senior' White House Official Told Me I'd 'Regret' Sequester Comments." (Video) Feb. 27, 2013.

9. https://theintercept.com/2015/07/30/politicians-admitting-obvious-fact-money-affects-vote/. Schwarz, Jon. "'Yes, We're Corrupt': A list of politicians admitting that money controls politics," July 30, 2015.

10. http://www.weeklystandard.com/articles/crony-capital_794962.html?page=2. DeMint, Jim and Mike Needham. "The Crony Capital: Capitalism, Washington, D.C., style," Jun. 23, 2016.

11. http://harpers.org/blog/2012/09/boss-roves-justice/. Horton, Scott. "Boss Rove's Justice," Sept. 13, 2013.

12. "Marco Rubio Ad." Xfinity, 1105 FNCH, Feb. 2, 2016.

13. "Ted Cruz Speech on Senate Floor" Xfinity Channel 104 (C-Span 2) Jul. 24, 2015.

14. Miller, Merle. Plain Speaking: An Oral Biography of Harry S. Truman. Berkley Publishing Corporation: New York, 1974 (p. 146, 415).

15. http://www.huffingtonpost.com/joseph-a-palmero/allen-raymond-confessions_b_86039.html. Palmero, Joseph A. "Allen Raymond: Confessions of a Republican smear artist," Feb. 11, 2008.

16. Raymond, Allen with Ian Spiegelman. "Confessions of a Republican operative: how to rig an election. Simon & Schuster: New York, 2008. (p. 122).

17. http://www.people-press.org/2015/11/23/public-trust-in-government-1958-2015/. "Public Trust in Government: 1968-2015," Nov. 23, 2015.

18. "Crime Against Humanity, Senator Tom Coburn, Misty Copeland." 60 Minutes, CBS, Xfinity 1009 WHNT, Lesley Stahl as moderator, Produced by Ira Rosen and Habiba Nosheen. Aug. 23, 2015.

19. http://www.newsweek.com/were-witnessing-revolt-against-ruling-class-359168. Reich, Robert. "We're witnessing a revolt against the ruling class," Aug. 8, 2015.

20. https://www.facebook.com/realbencarson/posts/513020902197714.

21. Murray, Charles. By the PEOPLE: Rebuilding liberty without permission. New York, Crown Publishing Group, 2015. (p. 102).

22. http://abcnews.go.com/Politics/video/house-speaker-boehner-announces-resignation-34044243. "House Speaker Boehner resigning to 'protect the institution,'" Sept. 24, 2015.

23. http://www.nbcnews.com/meet-the-press/meet-press-transcript-october-11-2015-n442476. "Meet the Press" transcript. Moderator Chuck Todd. Oct. 11, 2015.

24. http://www.theoaklandpress.com/general-news/20100221/harry-reid-takes-heat-for-cornhusker-kickback. Mascaro, Lisa. "Harry Reid takes heat for 'Cornhusker Deal,'" Feb. 21, 2010.

25. "Today," Host Kathi Lee Gifford and Hoda Kotb, Xfinity 1011 WAFFD, Feb. 2, 2016.

26. "Outnumbered." Xfinity 1105 FNCHD, Oct. 23, 2015.

27. http://www.breitbart.com/big-government/2015/12/18/who-wrote-the-omnibus-four-lawmakers-many-lobbyists/. Schweizer, Peter. "Who wrote the Omnibus? Four lawmakers, many lobbyists," Dec. 18, 2015.

28. Tanner, Kaylen. "Rand Paul chews out Congress for not knowing how the government will spend its new trillion dollars," Dec. 21, 2015.

29. http://dailysignal.com/2015/07/27/gop-leadership-prioritizes-corporate-welfare-over-defunding-planned-parenthood/. DeMint, Jim. "GOP leadership prioritizes corporate welfare over defunding planned parenthood," July 29, 2015.

30. http://americanlibertypac.com/2016/03/fines-coming-schools-dont-follow-flotus-lunch-regulations/. Katie. "Fines coming for schools who don't follow FLOTUS lunch regulations," Mar. 28, 2016.

31. http://www.alternet.org/media/imagine-if-politicians-were-forced-tell-truth-their-ad-campaigns?paging=off&current_page=1#bookmark. Balkind, Harriet Levin. "Imagine if politicians were forced to tell the truth in their ad campaigns: lies distort every critical issue the U.S. faces," Aug. 14, 2014.

32. Reagan, Ronald. Ronald Reagan: An American Life. New York: Threshold Editions, 1990. (p. 482)

33. http://www.latimes.com/opinion/op-ed/la-oe-feinstein-congress-committees-random-assignment-20150105-story.html. Feinstein, Brian. "A simple way to fix gridlock in Congress -- change committee.s," Jan. 4, 2015.

34. Confessore, Nicholas and Megan Thee-Brenan. "Polls shows Americans favor an overhaul of campaign financing." The New York Times 3 June. 2015: A18. Print.

35. https://scholar.princeton.edu/sites/default/files/mgilens/files/gilens_and_page_2014_-testing_theories_of_american_politics.doc.pdf. Gilens, Martin and Benjamin I. Page. "Testing theories of American politics: Elites, interest Groups, and average citizens," Sept. 2014, Vol. 12/No. 3 (p.568, 572).

36. "The Real Story with Gretchen Carlson," Xfinity 1105 FNCH, Jan. 19, 2016.

37. http://www.barrypopik.com/index.php/new_york_city/entry/the_philosophy_of_the_class_room_inonegeneration.

38. https://www.youtube.com/watch?v=h6XB2CxZEWQ&list=PL6ZAY8frA1WcD7pb4NCaa7 XEoQPeKrslm. "Robert F. Kennedy speech at Colombia University 1963- RFK Speaking," Published Sept. 5, 2013.

39. "IRS crate of bad apples tend to keep turning up," The Times Daily 23 Feb. 2016: A4. Print.

40. http://www.jfklibrary.org/Research/Research-Aids/Ready-Reference/EMK-Speeches/Tribute-to-Senator-Robert-F-Kennedy.aspx. Kennedy, Edward M. "Tribute to Robert F. Kennedy, St. Patrick Cathedral, New York City, Jun. 8, 1968.

41. "Meet the Press." Moderator Chuck Todd, NBC, Xfinity 1105 FNCH, Jan. 10, 2016.

42. Adler, Bill, ed. America's founding fathers: The uncommon wisdom and wit. Lanham: Rowman and Littlefield, 2015. (p. 97).

43. http://www.tpnn.com/2016/03/21/judge-jeanine-just-hurled-the-most-serious-accusation-against-the-establishment-yet-wow/. Bartlett, Russell. "Judge Jeanine just hurled the most serious accusation against the establishment yet … wow," Mar. 21, 2016.

44. http://abcnews.go.com/blogs/politics/2014/02/what-does-it-cost-to-be-an-obama-ambassador/. Bruce, Mary. "What does it cost to be an Obama ambassador," Feb. 7, 2014.

45. http://eagnews.org/school-fires-coach-for-taking-discarded-cafeteria-fruit-giving-it-to-hungry-athletes/. Skinner, Victor. "School fires coach for redistributing discarded Michelle O fruit to hungry athletes," Apr. 14, 2016.

46. http://www.heritage.org/research/reports/2015/05/red-tape-rising-six-years-of-escalating-regulation-under-obama. Gattuso, James L. and Diane Katz. "Red Tape Rising: Six years of escalating regulation under Obama," May 11, 2015.

47. http://thehill.com/homenews/house/282094-ryan-previews-a-better-way-gop-agenda. Wong, Scott. "Ryan previews 'A Better Way' GOP agenda," Jun. 3, 2016.

48. www.paulnehlen.com/paul-ryans-counterfeit-contract-with-america-wont-be-worth-paper-its-printed-on-says-wisconsin-challenger/. Lombard, Kirsten. "Paul Ryan's counterfeit 'contract with America' won't be worth paper it's printed on, says Wisconsin challenger," Apr. 28, 2016.

49. observer.com/2016/07/wikileaks-proves-primary-was-rigged-dnc-undermined-democracy/. Sainato, Michael. "Wikileaks proves primary was rigged: DNC undermined democracy," Jul. 22, 2016.

50. "Morning Joe." Hosts Joe Scarborough, Mika Brzezinski, MSNBC, Xfinity 1108 MSNBC, Jan. 6, 2015.

The Example of Alabama

1. "The Rachel Maddow Show." Host Rachel Maddow. MSNBC, Xfinity 1108 MSNBC, May 25, 2016.

2. http://blog.gl.com/spotnews/2010/11/tougher_ethics_laws_top_alabam.html. Dean, Charles J. "Tougher ethics laws top Alabama GOP lawmakers' agenda," Nov. 7, 2010.

3. www.ncsl.org/research/elections-and-campaigns/campaign-contribution-limits-overview.aspx

4. https://ballotpedia.org/Camapaign_finance_requirement_in_Alabama.

5. http://blog.al.com/press-register-commentary/2010/11/editorial_campaign_finance_ref.html. "Editorial: Campaign finance reform," Nov. 27, 2010.

6. www.alabamapolicy.org/wp-content/uploads/GTI-Brief-PAC-to-PAC-Law.pdf .

7. http://blog.al.com/birmingham-news-commentary/2012/04/our_view_the_legislature_must_2.html. "Our view: The legislature must patch the Alabama Fair Campaign Practices Act to ensure it can be properly enforced," Apr. 18, 2012.

8. http://www.al.com/news/index.ssf/2015/07/alabama_lawmakers_again_try_to.html#incart_related _stories. Cason, Mike. "Alabama lawmakers again try to tighten campaign finance law," Jul. 19, 2015.

9. Sell, Mary. "Legislation puts more enforcement in campaign finance reporting laws". The Times Daily 10 Jun. 2015: Times Daily.com Web 25 Aug. 2015.

10. Alabama Secretary of State. "Summary of Fair Campaign Practices Act (FCPA) law changes." Online video clip. Youtube. Youtube. 1 Aug. 2013. Web. Sept. 2, 2016.

11. http://www.wileyrein.com/newsroom-newsletters-item-3706.html. "Alabama amends ethics, lobbying, and campaign finance," March 2011.

12. http://blog.al.com/spotnews/2011/11/alabamas_new_ethics_law_fails.html. Chandler, Kim. "Alabama's new ethics law fails to stop exemption requests from lobbyists and public officials," Nov. 6, 2011.

13. http://www.al.com/opinion/index.ssf/2015/09/it_took_alabama_democrats_136.html#incart_related_stories. Whitmire, Kyle. "It took Alabama Democrats 136 years to be this corrupt, the GOP match it in four," Sept. 10, 2015.

14. http://blog.al.com/press-register-commentary/2012/04/editorial_revisit_ethics_laws.html. "Editorial: Revisit ethics laws, then enforce law," Apr. 18, 2012.

15. http;/ethics.alabama.gov/news/2014_Lobb_List_Arch_12_31_14.pdf.

16. http://www.salon.com/2016/07/26/texas_attorney_general_took_gift_while_investigating_company/. Weber, Paul J. "Texas attorney general took gift while investigating company," Jul. 26, 2016.

17. http://www.politico.com/story/2016/06/tim-kaine-virginia-veep-mcdonnell-clinton-224888. Arnsdorf, Isaac. "Kaine accepted clothes, vacation as gifts," Jun. 30, 2016.

18. http://www.al.com/news/index.ssf/2015/09/prosecutors_denounce_speaker_m.html. Cason, Mike. "Prosecutors denounce speaker Mike Hubbard's claims that ethics law is unconstitutional," Sept. 22, 2015.

19. http://www.timesdaily.com/news/state/prosecutors-say-hubbard-challenging-ethics-law-he-championed/article_a5246f98-d13d-570d-be2f-92d4b1ae6455.html. "Prosecutors say Hubbard challenging ethics law he championed," Sept. 22, 2015.

20. http://abcnews.go.com/Blotter/caught-tape-lobbyists-golf-party-lawmakers/story?id=11921636. Lieberman, Dan. "Caught on tape: A lobbyist's golf party for lawmakers," Aug. 20, 2010.

21. "Dark money remains shrouded." The Times Daily 1 May 2016. D2. Print.

22. www.al.com/news/index.ssf/2016/03/gov_robert_bentley_rebekah_cal_1_html. Gore, Leada. "Gov. Robert Bentley, Rebekah Caldwell Mason scandal: 12 questions that remain," Mar. 31, 2016.

23. "Around the state." The Times Daily 30 Apr. 2016: A4. Print.

24. http://yellowhammernews.com/politics-2/alabamas-shrinking-sovereignty/. Robertson, Katherine. "The omnipotent federal government is devouring Alabama's sovereignty," May 18, 2016.

25. Sell, Mary. "Bentley: Budget may need more revenue." The Times Daily 4 Oct. 2015: B1. Print.

26. Sell, Mary. "General Fund include cuts to state agencies." The Times Daily 17 Sept. 2015: A1. Print.

27. http://yellowhammernews.com/politics-2/bentley-we-will-pass-a-tax-even-if-it-takes-10-special-legislative-sessions/. Beshears, Elizabeth. "Bentley: We will pass a tax hike, even if it takes 10 special sessions," Mar. 24, 2015.

28. Chandler, Kim. "Bentley signs budget: Plan is a step in the right direction, governor says." The Times Daily 18 Sept. 2015: A1. Print.

29. "Rise of poverty among our children is a moral failure." The Times Daily 6 Dec. 2015: D2. Print.

30. http://www.al.com/news/index.ssf/2015/09/report_6_out_of_10_single_moth.html#incart_most-commentd_auburnfootball. Edgemon, Erin. "Report: 6 out of 10 single mothers in rural Alabama live in poverty, 90 percent are black," Sept. 16, 2015.

31. http://www.nytimes.com/2015/10/10/us/alabama-budget-cuts-raise-concern-over-voting-rights.html?partner=rss&emc=rss&_r=2. Robertson, Campbell. "For Alabama's poor, the budget cuts trickle down, limiting access to driver's licenses," Oct. 9, 2015.

32. http://www.al.com/opinion/index.ssf/2015/09/alabama_sends_message_we_are_t.html. Archibald, John. "Alabama sends message: We are too broke to care about right and wrong," Sept. 30, 2015.

33. Whitmire, Kyle. "State closes driver's license offices, keeps mony-losing ABC stores open," The. Birmingham News 28 Oct. 2015: A17. Print.

34. http://www.al.com/business/index.ssf/2015/09/comedian_steve_harvey_montgome.html. Edgemon, Erin. "Comedian Steve Harvey, Mongomery businessman buy Eufaula latex plant, plan to hire 300," Sept. 23, 2015.

35. http://alabamaschoolconnection.org/wp-content/uploads/2012/06/Alabamas-Student-Harassment-Prevention-Act-Does-It-Do-What-It-Said-It-Would-Do.pdf. Cain, Trisha Powell. "Alabama's Student Prevention Act: Does it do what it said it would do," June 2012.

36. http://www.wsfa.com/story/24778631/sources-union-springs-boy-committed-suicide-after-being-bullied. Henry, Bryan. "Bullying led Union Springs boy to suicide, according to soruces," Mar. 22, 2014.

37. http://www.wsfa.com/story/24745505/grandmother-of-dead-union-springs-boy-speaks. Henry, Bryan. "Grandmother of dead Union Springs boy speaks," Mar. 23, 2014.

38. http://www.nytimes.com/2008/06/16/opinion/16kristol.html?_r=0. Kristol, William. "Big Tim," Jun. 16, 2008.

39. Isely, Bliss. The Horseman of the Shenandoah: A biographical account of the early days of George Washington. The Bruce Publishing Company: Milwaukee, 1962. (p.31).

40. http://ltgov.alabama.gov/PR/PressRelease.aspx?ID=7043&t=1. Sulhoff, Katy. "Lt. Governor Ivey

announces real world design challenge," Sept. 12, 2012.

41. (2015, August). Muscle Shoals Trojans vs. Memphis East. Muscle Shoals Varsity Football Program. (p.6).
42. http://www.inc.com/marla-tabaka31-martin-luther-king-jr-quotes-to-inspire-greatness-in-you.html. Tabaka, Marla. "31 Martin Luther King Jr. quotes to inspire greatness in you," Jan. 18, 2016.
43. http://www.timesdaily.com/news/bill-would-give-bonus-to-agency-leaders-to-make-cuts/ article_980b9840-1ed2-5218-802b-683de10f640b.html. Sell, Mary. "Bill would give bonus to agency leaders to make cuts," Apr. 25, 2015.
44. http://yellowhammernews.com/politics-2/alabama-lawmaker-unloads-on-tax-raisers-scandal-ridden-politicians-in-provocative-interview-audio/. Beshears, Elizabeth. "Alabama lawmaker unloads on tax-raisers & scandal ridden politicians in provocative interview (Audio)," Sept. 2, 2015.
45. http://yellowhammernews.com/politics-2/as-ala-lawmakers-fret-over-budgets-one-agency-very-easily-slashed-its-budget-by-one-third/. Sims, Cliff. "As Ala. Lawmakers fret over budgets, one agency 'very easily' slashed its budget by   one-third," Jul. 2, 2015.
46. "Reading initiative needs more funds." The Times Daily 19 May 2016: A4. Print.
47. Edwards, Jennifer. "Florence High student organizing free program." The Times Daily 16 Jul. 2016. B1. Print.
48. Sell, Mary. "Bond money sought in bill: Senators want investment of BP settlement." The Times Daily 6 Aug. 2015: A1. Print.
49. http://blog.al.com/spotnews/2012/03/alabamas_prepaid_tuition_progr_2.html. Chandler, Kim. "Alabama's prepaid tuition program will go broke in three years by one estimate," Mar. 25, 2012.
50. https://www.collegecounts529.com/529-overview/.
51. http://www.wsfa.com/story/32731791/childrens-of-alabama-discusses-impact-of-medicaid-cuts. Collins, Alan. "Children's of Alabama discusses impact of Medicaid cuts," Aug. 10, 2016.
52. Alabama Policy Institute. "Rick Burgess on Alabama Lottery." Online video clip. YouTube. YouTube, 10 Feb. 2016. Web. Aug. 27, 2016.
53. http://www.decaturdaily.com/news/other_news/state_capital/lawmakers-disagree-over-futre-of-bp -settlement-bill/article_62c4ccd702-5a13-59cd-bdfl-a331fe986922.html. Sell, Mary. "Lawmakers disagree over future BP settlement bill," Apr. 27, 2016.
54. http://www.alabamapolicy.org/budget-basics-legislatures-limitations-need-reform/. Robertson, Katherine Green. "Budget Basics: The legislature's limitations and need for reform," Sept. 20, 2014.
55. Sell, Mary. "Lawmakers end 2016 session." The Times Daily 8 Sept. 2016. A1. Print.
56. "Around the state." The Times Daily 13 Feb. 2016: A4. Print.
57. "Alabama ranks last on health of its democracy." The Times Daily 14 Jul. 2015: A6. Print.
58. Sell, Mary. "Chairman Ethics laws need updating" The Times Daily 2 Sept. 2016. A1. Print.
59. http://www.cw.ua.edu/article/2015/10/why-im-leaving-the-machine. Smith, Alex. "Why I'm leaving the machine," Oct. 26, 2015.
60. Lewis, Edwards and Richard Rhodes, eds. John F. Kennedy: Words to Remember. United States: Hallmark Cards Incorporated, 1967. (p.7).

The People Must Set the Standards

1. http://www.theverge.com/2015/9/11/9310497/stephen-colbert-joe-biden-late-show-interview. Welch, Chris. "Stephen Colbert's interview with Joe Biden is the best he's ever done," Sept. 11, 2015.
2. Miller, Merle. Plain Speaking: An Oral Biography of Harry S. Truman. Berkley Publishing Corporation: New York, 1974. (p.44, 431).
3. http://www.breitbart.com/2016-presidential-race/2015/08/22/kentucky-republican-party-allows-rand-paul-to-run-for-senate-president/. "Kentucky Republican Party allows Rand Paul to run for senate, president," Aug. 22, 2015.
4. Andrews, Wayne. The Autobiography of Theodore Roosevelt. Octagon Books: New York, 1975. (p. 55, 37).
5. https://www.rollcall.com/news/And-Congress-Rich-Get-Richer-209907-1.html Singer, Paul and Jennifer Yachnin. "And congress' rich get richer," Oct. 31, 2011.
6. http://endoftheamericandream.com/archives/insider-trading-is-legal-for-members-of-congress-and-they-refuse-to-pass-a-law-that-would-change-that. Snyder, Michael. "Insider trading is legal for members of congress- and they refuse to pass a law that would change that," Oct. 19, 2010.
7. http://news.yahoo.com/reid-u-congress-act-scandalous-fantasy-betting-225015608--sector.html. Sullivan, Andy and Diana Bartz. "Reid: U.S. Congress should act on 'scandalous' fantasy betting," Oct. 6, 2015.

8. http://www.npr.org/sections/itsallpoltics/2013/04/16/177496734/how-congress-quietly-overhauled-its-insider-trading-law. Keith, Tamara. "How Congress Quietly Overhauled Its Insider Trading Law," Apr. 16, 2013.

9. http://money.cnn.com/2015/01/12/news/economy/congress-wealth/index.html. Luhby, Tami. "Congress is getting richer," Jan. 12, 2015.

10. http://www.pewtrusts.org/en/research-and-analysis/blogs/stateline/2015/3/19/the-shrinking-middle-class-mapped-state-by-state. Henderson, Tim. "The Shrinking Middle Class, Mapped State by State" Mar. 19, 2015.

11. http://www.law360.com/articles/558483/sec-says-humana-trading-probe-involves-44-funds-entities. Teichert, Erica. "SEC Says Humana Trading Probe Involves 44 Funds, Entities," Jul. 17, 2014.

12. https://beta.finance.yahoo.com/news/u-judge-rules-sec-fight-162538112.html. Raymond, Nate. "U.S. judge rules for SEC in fight with House panel over insider trading probe," Nov. 16, 2015.

13. http://townhall.com/news/politics-elections/2015/12/07/congressional-panel-wins-delay-in-sec-insider-trading-probe-n2090486. "Congressional panel wins delay in SEC insider trading probe," Dec. 7, 2015.

14. https://beta.finance.yahoo.com/news/lois-lerner-cleared-sparking-conservative-221500733.html. Garver, Rob. "Lois Lerner is Cleared, Sparking Conservative Fury," Oct. 23, 2015.

15. "Ted Cruz Speech on Senate Floor" Xfinity Channel 104 (C-Span 2) (7/24/2015).

16. Schippers, David P. Sellout: The inside story of President Clinton's impeachment. With Alan P.. Henry. Washington, DC: Regnery Publishing, 2004. (p.260-263).

17. http://dailycaller.com/2013/11/21/cornhusker-kickback-senator-meets-with-obama-to-talk-obamacare-fix/. Conner, Paul. "'Cornhusker kickback' senator meets with Obama to talk Obamacare fix," Nov. 21, 2013.

18. http://agenda-global.com/agenda/.

19. http://dealbook.nytimes.com/2014/02/01/law-doesnt-end-revolving-door-on-capitol-hill/. Lipton, Eric and Ben Protess. "Law Doesn't End Revolving Door on Capitol Hill," Feb. 1, 2014.

20. https://en.wikipedia.org/wiki/Federal_Election_Commission.

21. http://www.huffingtonpost.com/2015/05/03/fec-ann-ravel-dysfunctinal_n_7197360.html. "FEC Chair Ann Ravel Says Agency Is 'Worse Than Dysfunctional' At Regulating Money In Politics" May 2, 2015.

22. http://www.foxnews.com/politics/2015/07/31/fec-head-suggests-fixing-agency-by-firing-everyone-Except-her-html. "EC head suggests fixing agency by firing everyone except her" Jul. 17, 2015.

23. http://blogs.suntimes.com/sweet/2008/02/complete_transriptdemocratic.html. Sweet, Lynn. "Complete transcript democratic presidential debate," Feb. 26, 2008.

24. http://www.nytimes.com/2015/07/18/nyregion/michael-grimm-former-congressman-gets-8-month-sentence.html?_r=1. Clifford, Stephanie. "Michael Grimm, Former Congressman, Is Sentenced to 8 Months," Jul. 17, 2015.

25. https://www.washingtonpost.com/politics/now-its-even-easier-for-candidates-and-their-aides-to-help-super-pacs/2015/12/24/d8d1ff4a-a989-11e5-9b92-dea7cd4b1a4d_story.html. Gold, Matea. "Now it's even easier for candidates and their aides to help super PACs," Dec. 24, 2015.

26. http://news.yahoo.com/group-backing-hillary-clinton-gets-1m-anonymous-donors-192934568-election.html. Bykowicz, Julie. "Group backing Clinton gets $1M from untraceable donors," Oct. 10, 2015.

27. http://www.washingtonpost.com/news/post-politics/wp/2015/08/02/jeb-bush-on-helping-super-pac-raise-103-million-you-might-as-well-front-load-it-if-you-can/. Gold, Matea. "Jeb Bush on helping super PAC raise $103 million: 'You might as well front load it if you can," Oct. 2, 2015.

28. http://www.cincinnati.com/story/news/politics/kentucky%20govenrment/2015/09/24/nky-senator-sues-end-campaign-donation-limits/72768196/. Pilcher, James. "NKY senator sues to end campaign donation limits," Sept. 25, 2015.

29. http://www.stetson.edu/today/2015/04/free-speech-vs-free-elections/. Salis, George. "Free Speech vs. Free Elections" Apr. 1, 2015.

30. http://www.tpnn.com/2015/12/15/what-debbie-and-the-dems-just-demanded-will-infuriate-overburdened-taxpayers/. Bartlett, Russel. "Debbie and The dems just hit a new low. They actually want people to…," Dec. 15, 2015.

31. Adler, Bill, ed. America's Founding Fathers: The Uncommon Wisdom and Wit. Lanham: Rowman and Littlefield, 2015. (p.108).

32. Lewis, Edwards and Richard Rhodes, eds. John F. Kennedy: Words to Remember. United States: Hallmark Cards Incorporated, 1967. (p.6).

33. www.huffingtonpost.com/cameron-fegers/harry-reid-makes-disturbi_b_8917016.html?ncid+txtlnkusa0lP00000592. Fegers, Cameron. "Harry Reid Makes Disturbing Request," Jan 5, 2016.

Problems with Past Reform Efforts

1. http://www.huffingtonpost.com/2014/05/15/mayone-lawrence-lessig_n_53333020.html. Blumenthal, Paul. "The super PAC to end all super PACs gets off to a super start." May 5, 2014.
2. https://mayday.us.
3. http://www.repswith.us.
4. http://www.huffingtonpost.com/2014/11/06/mayday-pac-2014_n_6109992.html. Blumenthal, Paul. "Mayday PAC lost nearly all its races this year, but refuses to concede defeat." Nov. 6, 2014.
5. http://blog.mayday.us/post/113583420335/press-release-in-2014-maydayus-moved-voters. "MAYDAY.US Press release" Nov. 7, 2015.
6. http://www.politico.com/magazine/story/2015/08/meet-the-liberals-who-love-trump-121733#.Vd494WDO6FI. Wofford, Ben. "Meet the liberals who think that Trump's good for democracy." Nov. 25, 2015.
7. http://thehill.com/blogs/ballot-box/presidential-races/250187-sanders-campaign-finance-system-amounts-to-legalized. Carney, Jordain. "Sanders: campaign finance system 'amounts to legalized bribery." Aug 4, 2015.
8. http://www.businessinsider.com/larry-lessig-wants-to-hack-politics-with-2016-campaign-2015-8. Bykowicz, Julie. "Harvard professor wants to 'hack' politics with long-shot Democratic presidential run." Aug 11, 2015.
9. http://www.newsmax.com/Newsfront/lessig-quits-race/2015/11/02/id/700180/. "Larry Lessig Ends Presidential Bid, Citing Restrictive Debate Rules." Nov. 11, 2015.
10. https://en.wikipedia.org/wiki/Buckley_v._Valeo.
11. http://www.cfinst.org/pdf/papers/Malbin_Parties-and-Groups-Post-McCutcheon_NYULRev_Final.pdf. Malbin, Michael J. "McCutcheon could lead to no limits for political parties- with what implications for parties and interest groups?" 89 N.Y.U.L. Rev. Online_(forthcoming 2014).
12. http://www.huffingtonpost.com/2013/11/22/republican-campaign-finance-reform_n_4324754.html. Blumenthal, Paul. "Start Of A Trend? Another Republican Endorses Campaign Finance Reform." Nov. 22, 2013.
13. Nixon, Richard. In the Arena: A memoir of victory, defeat, and renewal. Simon and Schuster: New York, 1990. (p. 107, 108).
14. https://theintercept.com/2015/07/30/politicians-admitting-obvious-fact-money-affects-vote/. Schwarz, Jon. "Yes, we're corrupt:" A list of politicians admitting that money control politics. July 30, 2015.
15. http://www.esquire.com/news-politics/a36856/jimmy-carter-us-oligarchy/. "Jimmy Carter Thinks the U.S. Is Really an Oligarchy" October 2, 2015.
16. http://www.nytimes.com/2015/06/03/us/politics/poll-shows-americans-favor-overhaul-of-campaign-Financing.html?_r=0. Confessore, Nicholas and Megan Thee-Brenan. "Poll shows Americans favor an overhaul of campaign financing." June 2, 2015.
17. Lewis, Edwards and Richard Rhodes, eds. John F. Kennedy: Words to Remember. United States: Hallmark Cards Incorporated, 1967. (p. 38).
18. http://www.washingtonpost.com/news/post-politics/wp/2014/11/10/voter-turnout-in-2014-was-the-Lowest-since-wwii/. DelReal, Jose A. "Voter turnout in 2014 was the lowest since WWII." Nov. 10, 2014.
19. http://www.fairvote.org/research-and-analysis/voter-turnout/.
20. http://www.pricelessmovie.org/the-issues/campaign-finance/.
21. http://billmoyers.com/2013/11/26/republicans-yes-republicans-are-joining-the-battle-against-big-money-politics// Kroll, Andy. "Republicans – Yes, Republicans – Are joining the battle against big money politics" Nov. 26, 2013.
22. Confessore, Nicholas, Cohen, Sarah and Karen Yourish. "Small pool of rich donors dominates election giving." The New York Times 1 Aug. 2015: A1. Print.
23. http://www.politico.com/story/2015/08/wealthy-donors-and-gusher-of-cash-change-2016-race-120894#Ixzz3hZ1ArGva?ml=tb. Meyer, Theodoric, Vogel, Kenneth P. and Tarini Parti. "67 donors and gusher of cash change 2016 race: Cruz, Huckabee, others gain from unprecedented political buying power of wealthy donors." Aug. 1, 2015.
24. Kuttner, Robert. The Squandering of America: How the failure of our politics undermines our prosperity. New York: Alfred A. Knopf, 2007. (p.6).
25. https://en.wikipedia.org/wiki/Publicly_funded_elections.
26. Mutch, Robert E. Buying the Vote: A history of campaign finance reform. New York: Oxford University Press, 2014. (p.168).
27. O'Leary, Jeffrey. Foreword. AMERICA Out of the Ashe: True stories of courage and heroism. Hon-

or Books: Oklahoma, 2001. (p.57).

28. Adler, Bill, ed. America's Founding Fathers: The uncommon wisdom and wit. Lantham: Rowman and Littlefield, 2015. (p.62, 63).

29. Hart, Gary. The Republic of Conscience. Penguin Random House: New York, 2015. (p.52).

The People's Clearing House

INTRODUCTION

1. Miller, Merle. Plain Speaking: An Oral Biography of Harry S. Truman. Berkley Publishing Corporation: New York, 1974. (p.159).

2. http://www.nbcnews.com/meet-the-press/meet-press-transcript-june-21-2015-n379316. "Meet the Press," Moderator Chuck Todd. Transcript. Jun. 21, 2015.

3. http://www.huffingonpost.com/entry/oligarachy-super-pac-megadonors-have-conquered-ameriacn-politics_55bc1eece4b0b23ce2f5ec. Blumenthal, Paul. "Oligarchy of super PAC mega donors have conquered American politics: the majority of money raised for the 2016 presidential race came from those giving $100,000 or more," Jul. 31, 2015.

4. "CNN Newsroom with Fredricka Whitfield." Xfinity 1106, CNNHD, Apr. 10, 2016.

5. http://time.com/3988276/republican-debate-primetime-transcript-full-text/. "Transcript: Read the full text of the primetime republican debate," Aug, 11, 2015.

6. https://www.washingtonpost.com/news/the-fix/wp/2016/04/26/the-2016-election-has-claimed-its-first-incumbent-loser-rep-chaka-fattah/. Phillips, Amber. "Meet 2016's first incumbent loser: Rep. Chaka Fattah," Apr. 26, 2016.

7. Nixon, Richard. In the Arena: A memoir of victory, defeat, and renewal. Simon and Schuster: New York, 1990. (p. 201).

8. http://www.huffingonpost.com/2013/01/08/call-time-congressional-fundraising_n_2427291.html. Grim, Ryan and Sabrina Siddiqui. "Call time for congress shows how fundraising dominates bleak work life," Jan. 8, 2013.

9. http://www.washingtonpost.com/news/wonkblog/wp/2013/07/29/congress-spends-too-much-time-fundraising-but-its-less-time-than-you-think/. Klein, Ezra. "Congress spends too much time fundraising. But it's less time than you think," Jul. 29, 2013.

10. Fritz, Sara and Dwight Morris. Gold-Plated Politics: Running for congress in the 1990s. Washington, D.C.: Congressional Quarterly Inc., 1992. (p. 3, 8).

11. http://www.loc.gov/law/help/campaign-finance/uk.php. Feikert, Clare. "Campaign Finance: United Kingdom," April 2009.

12. "America's Newsroom with Bill Hemmer and Martha MacCallum." Fox News, Xfinity 1105 FNCHD, May 16, 2016.

13. http://www.al.com/opinion/index.ssf/2015/09/a_sure_scandal_in_gov_robert_b.html. Archibald, John. "A sure scandal in Gov. Robert Bentley's Administration," Sept. 4, 2015.

14. http://www.nationalreview.com/article/41979/clinton-foundation-reeks-crooks-thieves-and-hood-deroy-murdoc.

15. http://www.newsmax.com/Politics/Hillary-Clinton-Clinton-Foundation-donations/2015/02/18/id/625535/. Devaney, Jason. "Clinton Foundation drops ban on foreign government donations," Feb. 18, 2015.

16. http://www.nytimes.com/2016/05/23/us/politics/election-clinton-foundation.html?partner=rss&emc=rss. Hunt, Albert R. "Possible conflict at heart of Clinton Foundation," May 22, 2016.

17. http://thefederalist.com/2015/04/27/in-2013-the-clinton-foundation-only-spent-10-percent-of-its-budget-on-charitable-grants/. Davis, Sean. "In 2013, the Clinton Foundation only spent ten percent of its budget on charitable grants," Apr. 27, 2015.

18. http://freebeacon.com/politics/haitians-protest-outside-hillary-clintons-office-over-billions-stolen-by-clinton-foundation. "Haitians protest outside Hillary Clinton's office over 'billions stolen' by Clinton Foundation," March 20, 2015.

19. http://freebeacon.com/issues/clinton-foundation-hq-protested-for-missing-money-in-haiti-recovery/. "Clinton Foundation HQ protested for 'missing money' in Haiti recovery," Jan. 12, 2015.

20. http://www.washingtonpost.com/blogs/right-turn/wp/2015/02/18/foreign-donations-to-hillary-clintons-foundation-raise-major-ethical-questions/. Rubin, Jennifer. "Foreign donations to foundation raise major ethical questions for Hillary Clinton," Feb. 18, 2015.

21. http://www.dailymail.co.uk/news/article-3643411/Germany-scrap-cultural-immunity-no-longer-

allows-migrants-mulitiple-marriages-child-brides.html. Linning, Stephanie. "Germany to scrap 'cultural immunity' and will no longer allow migrants to have multiple marriages or child brides," Jun. 15, 2016.

22. http://www.factcheck.org/2008/03/giving-hilary-credit-for-schip/. Jackson, Brooks. "Giving Hillary credit for SCHIP," Mar. 18, 2008.

23. https://www.yahoo.com/news/pakistan-gruesome-honor-killings-bring-backlash-060717119.html. "In Pakistan, gruesome 'honor' killings bring a new backlash," Jul. 4, 2016.

OVERVIEW

1. http://www.washingtonpost.com/news/the-fix/wp/2016/04/21/its-official-the-2016-campaign-has-passed-the-1-billion-mark-in-spending/. Cillizza, Chris. "$1.2 billion has been raised already in the 2016 race. The general election is in 201 days," Apr. 21, 2016.

2. http://www.politico.com/story/2013/01/7-billion-spent-on-2012-campaign-fec-says-087051. Parti, Tarini. "FEC: $7B spent on 2012 election," Jan. 31, 2013.

TRACKING FOR COMPLETE AND CONSISTENT TRANSPARENCY

1. Fritz, Sara and Dwight Morris. Gold-Plated Politics: Running for congress in the 1990s. Washington, D.C.: Congressional Quarterly Inc., 1992. (p. 66-69).

2. http://foxnews.com/politics/2015/03/18/report-republican-rep-schock-resigning/. "Republican Rep. Schock resigning amid ethics questions," Mar. 18, 2015.

3. https://en.wikipedia.org/wiki/Aaron_Schock.

4. https://en.wikipedia.org/wiki/David_L._Boren.

5. http://billmoyers.com/2013/11/26/republicans-yes-republicans-are-joining-the-battle-against-big-money-politics/. Kroll, Andy. "Republicans—yes Republicans—are joining the battle against big money in politics," Nov. 26, 2013.

6. https://www.govtrack.us/congress/bills/113/hr3356. "H.R. 3356 (113th): Clean Campaign Contributions Act of 2013," Oct. 28, 2013.

7. http://publicampaign.org/blog/2013/11/12/gop-rep-andy-harris-introduces-leadership-pac-bill. Smith, Adam. "GOP Rep. Andy Harris introduces Leadership PAC bill," Nov. 12, 2013.

8. https://en.wikipedia.org/wiki/Saxby_Chambliss.

9. https://en.wikipedia.org/Gregory_Meeks.

10. http://www.cnet.com/news/senat-bill-would-let-fbi-read-your-emails-wiouth-a-court-order/. Tibken, Shara. "Senate bill would let FBI read your emails without a court order," May 25, 2016.

11. https://www.eff.org/issues/national-security-letters/faq#1.

12. finance.yahoo.com/news/senate-blocks-allowing-access-online-153650637.htm. Lardner, Richard. "Senate blocks access to online data without warrant," Jun. 22, 2016.

13. "Outnumbered," Fox News, Xfinity 1105 FNCHD, Jun. 1, 2016.

TREATMENT OF PACS AND SUPER PACS

1. http://www.ncsl.org/research/elections-and-campaigns/campaign-contribution-limits-overview.aspx.

2. http://www.infoplease.com/us/history/campaign-finance-reform-timeline.html. Rowen, Beth. "Campaign-Finance Reform: history and timeline."

3. http://www.opensecrets.org/overview/limits.php. "2016 Campaign Contribution Limits."

4. https://www.opensecrets.org/527s/types.php. "Types of Advocacy Groups".

5. Confessore, Nicholas, Cohen, Sarah and Karen Yourish. "Small pool of rich donors dominates election giving." The New York Times 1 Aug. 2015: A1. Print.

6. https://www.washingtonpost.com/politics/now-its-even-easier-for-candidates-and-their-aides-to-help-super-pacs/2015/12/24/d8d1ff4a-a989-11e5-9b92-dea7cd4b1a4d_story.html. Gold, Matea. "Now it's even easier for candidates and their aides to help super PACs," Dec. 24, 2015.

7. http://www.politico.com/story/2010/07/shelby-steers-cash-to-ex-aides-040388. Raju, Manu and John Bresnahan. "Shelby steers cash to ex-aides," Jul. 29, 2010.

8. http://www.washingtonpost.com/news/post-politics/wp/2015/08/02/jeb-bush-on-helping-super-pac-raise-103-million-you-might-as-well-front-load-it-if-you-can/. Gold, Matea. "Jeb Bush on helping super PAC raise $103 million: 'You might as well front load it if you can," Oct. 2, 1015.

9. http://www.huffingtonpost.com/entry/disclosed-super-pac-donations_us_55d38968e4b07addcb445bb7. Blumenthal, Paul. "We're still in the dark about some super PAC donors: who's behind these groups, anyway?," Aug. 19, 2015.

THE "DARK MONEY" OF SOCIAL WELFARE ORGANIZATIONS OR 501(C) (4)S

1. http://www.huffingtonpost.com/entry/on-the-trail-to-find-out-who-is-behind-two-dark-money-groups_55ccfe24e4b064d5910af11e. Blumenthal, Paul. "These dark money groups shed some light on secretive megadonors,' Aug. 17, 2015.
2. http://blog.constitutioncenter.org/2015/11/supreme-court-refuses-to-hear-donor-disclosure-case/. Iannacci, Nicandro. "Supreme Court refuses to hear donor disclosure case, Nov. 11, 2015.
3. http://goldwaterinstitute.org/en/work/topics/constitutional-rights/free-speech/the-victims-of-dark-money-disclosure-how-government/. Riches, John. "The victims of 'dark money' disclosures: how government reporting requirements suppress speech and limit charitable giving," Aug. 5, 2015.
4. https://en.wikipedia.org/wiki/501%28c%29_organization.
5. http://www.pbs.org/wgbh/pages/frontline/government-elections-politics/big-sky-big-money/the-rules-that-govern-501c4s/. Schwartz, Emma. "The rules that govern 501(c)(4)s," Oct. 30, 2012.
6. https://www.independentsector.org/501c4_organizations.
7. https://www.independentsector.org/uploads/DA_IRS_Testimony_7_2015.pdf. Aviv, Diana L. Statement for the record. "Hearing on revisiting I.R.S. targeting: progress of agency reforms and congressional options," Jul. 29, 2015.
8. http://www.nolo.com/legal-encyclopedia/what-section-501c4-social-welfare-organizations.html. Fishman, Stephen. "What are section 501(c)(4) social welfare organizations?," May 2013.
9. http://reclaimtheamericandream.org/progress-disclose/. "The push to get dark money out in the open."
10. "Morning Joe" MSNBC, Xfinity 1108, Jun. 2, 2016.
11. http://www.ctpost.com/local/article/Q-Poll-Voters-don-t-believe-Trump-Clinton-7958931.php. Shay, Jim. "Q Poll: Voters don't believe Trump, Clinton promises," Jun. 2, 2013.
12. http://www.politico.com/story/2016/04/clinton-foundraising-leaves-little-for-state-parties-222670. Vogel, Kenneth P. and Isaac Arnsdorf. "Clinton fundraising leaves little for state parties," May 2, 2016.
13. https://www.pastemagazine.com/articles/2016/06/this-is-the-hillary-clinton-scandal-no-ones-talkin.html. Bragman, Walker. "This is the Hillary Clinton scandal no one's talking about," Jun. 21, 2016.

DEDUCTIONS FROM CONTRIBUTIONS ARE DETERMINED BY THE TIME IN WHICH THEY ARE GIVEN

1. http://www.npr.org/sections/money/2012/04/19/150904641/whylobbyists-dodge-calls-from-congressmen. Seabrook, Andrea and Alex Blumberg. "Why lobbyists dodge calls from congressmen," Apr. 19, 2012.
2. http://www.npr.org/sections/money/2012/04/20/150984304/when-lobbyists-pay-to-meet-with-congressmen. Seabrook, Andrea and Alex Blumberg. "When lobbyists pay to meet with congressmen," Apr. 20, 2012.
3. Dennis, Steven T. "Sessions feels vindicated by Trump's surge" The Times Daily 17 Sept. 2015: A5. Print.
4. Fritz, Sara and Dwight Morris. Gold-Plated Politics: Running for congress in the 1990s. Washington, D.C.: Congressional Quarterly Inc., 1992. (p. 4).
5. http://www.quora.com/How-much-time-do-politicians-spend-fundraising. Thames, Nate. "How much time do candidates spend fundraising," Jan. 12, 2011.
6. http//www.al.com/news/index.ssf/2015/02/indicted_alabama_house_speaker.html. "Indicted Alabama House Speaker Mike Hubbard spent $300,000 in campaign funds on legal fees," Feb. 2, 2015.
7. http://www.ncsl.org/research/about-state-legislatures/number-of-legislatures-and-length-of-terms.aspx. "Number of legislators and length of terms in years," Mar. 11, 2013.
8. http://www.nebraskalegislature.gov/about/history_unicameral.php. "History of Nebraska Unicameral."
9. Nixon, Richard. In the Arena: A memoir of victory, defeat, and renewal. New York: Simon and Schuster, 1990. (p. 202).
10. Corrado, Anthony et. al, eds. Campaign Finance Reform: A sourcebook. Washington D.C.: The Brookings Institution, 1997. (p. 116).

AN ALTERNATIVE TO THE VIRTUALLY IMPOSSIBLE TASK OF IMPOS-ING TERM LIMITS

1. "In Memoriam: Sen. Fred Thompson (R-TN) 1942-2015. Speech to Midwest Republican Leadership Conference from 8/25/07," Indian Convention Center, CSPAN, Xfinity 6, Dec. 12, 2015.
2. Nixon, Richard. In the Arena: A memoir of victory, defeat, and renewal. New York: Simon and Schuster, 1990. (p.200).
3. http://www.goodreads.com/quotes/41195-politicians-and-diapers-must-be-changed-often-and-for-the.
4. http://www.ncsl.org/research/about-state-legislatures/chart-of-term-limis-states.aspx. "The Term-Limited States."
5. Kennedy, John F. Profiles In Courage: Decisive moments in the lives of celebrated Americans. New York: HarperCollins Publishers, 1984. (p.51).

SIGNIFICANT CHARACTERISTICS OF THE PEOPLE'S CLEARING HOUSE

1. http://millercenter.org/president/speeches/speech-3416. Reagan, Ronald. "Transcript of address at Moscow State University," May 31, 1988.
2. http://gothamist.com/2016/04/24/de_blasio_investigation_continues.php. Heins, Scott. "Report: De Blasio violated campaign finance laws," Apr. 24, 2016.
3. www.openthebooks.com/wall_street_journal_editorial_by_tom_coburn_track_government_waste_there's_an_app_for_that/. Coburn, Tom. "Wall Street Journal editorial by Tom Coburn, track governmental waste – there's an app for that," Oct. 7, 2015.
4. "All in with Chris Hayes," Host Chris Hayes, MSNBC, Xfinity, 1108 MSNBC, Jun. 8, 2016.
5. Hais, Michael D. and Morley Winograd. Millennial Momentum: How a new generation is remaking America. Rutgers University Press: New Jersey, 2011. (p.100).
6. Rampell, Catherine. "Where are the young voters?" Times Daily 28 Jul. 2015. A6. Print.

THE PEOPLE'S CLEARING HOUSE CANDIDATE

1. http://www.realclearpolitics.com/video/2016/04/28/bobby_knight_trump_rally_i_could_give_a_damn_about_republicans_or_democrats_heart_great_american.html. Schwartz, Ian. "Bobby Knight at Trump Rally: I could give a damn about Republicans or   Democrats, 'At the heart he is a great Ameri-can,'" Apr. 28, 2016.
2. https://www.brennancenter.org/publication/more-choices-more-voices-primer-fusion.
3. https://en.wikipedia.org/wiki/Electoral_fusion.
4. http://www.huffingtonpost.com/2013/01/08/call-time-congressional-fundraising_n_2427291.html. Grim, Ryan and Sabrina Siddiqui. "Call time for congress shows how fundraising dominates bleak work life," Jan. 8, 2013.

CONCLUSION

1. http://www.express.co.uk/news/politics/679227/History-EU-how-burcaucrats-seized-power. For-syth, Frederick. "Birth of superstate: Frederick Forsyth on how UNELECTED Brussels   bureaucrats SEIZED power," Jun. 13, 2016.
4. https://en.wikipedia.org/3wiki/World_population.
5. https://en.wikipedia.org/wiki/List_of_U.S._states_and_terrorists_by_population.
6. http://millercenter.org/president/speeches/speech-3416. Reagan, Ronald. "Transcript of address at Moscow State University," May 31, 1988.
7. The apostle John inspired by God. "John 2: 13-16."
8. http://ww.cbsnews.com/preview-dialing-for-dollars/. "U.S. Representative says calling donors for money is a shameful distraction." CBS Network. Xfinity, 1009 CBSHD, Correspondent Norah O'Don-nell, Apr. 22, 2016.
9. http://www.newsmax.com/Politics/david-jolly-florida-stop-act-telemarketers/2016/04/25/id/725579/. Fitzgerald, Sandy. "Rep. Jolly: Congressman paid $174,000 a year to be telemarketers," Apr.

25, 2016.

10. https://www.congress.gov/bill/114th-congress/house-bill/4443?q={%22search%22%3A[%22jolly%22]}. "H.R. 4443- Stop Act, 114 Congress (2015-2016)."

11. Glengarry, Glen Ross, Dir. James Foley. Perf. Al Pacino, Jack Lemmon, Alec Baldwin, Ed Harris, Allen Arkin, Kevin Spacey. New Line Cinema, 1992. Film.

12. "Fox and Friends Sunday." Fox News, Xfinity, 1105 FNCHD, May 22, 2016.

13. http://www.cbsnews.com/news/60-minutes-backlash-from-army-largest-criminal-investigation/. Transcript: "60 Minutes: 'Backlash from Army's Largest Criminal Investigation'" S48, Ep 38. Correspondent David Martin, Producer Mary Walsh," May 22, 2016.

14. "Anderson Cooper 360 GOP Town Hall." CNN News, Xfinity 1106 CNNHD, Moderator Anderson Cooper. Television. South Carolina, Feb. 18, 2016.

15. http://www.nytimes.com/2015/11/11/us/politics/transcript-republican-presidential-debate.html?_r=0. "Transcript: Republican Presidential Debate," Nov. 11, 2015.

16. http://www.iheart.com/news/republicans-lay-out-proposal-to-majorly-14848529/. Brufke, Juliegrace. "Republicans lay out proposal to MAJORLY overhaul the tax code," Jun. 24, 2016.

17. http://freebeacon.com/issues/house-republicans-aim-reform-tax-code-fit-postcard/. Meyer, Ali. "House republicans aim to reform tax code to fit on a postcard," Jun. 24, 2016.

18. http://www.csmonitor.com/Business/Saving-Money/2012/1111/The-election-is-over-What-happens-to-all-that-campaign-cash. Ballenger, Brandon. "The election is over. What happens to all the campaign cash?," Nov. 11, 2013.

19. Miller, Merle. Plain Speak: An Oral Biography of Harry S. Truman. Berkley Publishing Corporation: New York, 1974. (p.16).

20. http://battleby.com/124/pres61.html. Reagan, Ronald. "First Inaugural Address," Jan. 20, 1981.

21. http://www.washingtontimes.com/news/2016/jul/7/fbis-comey-hillary-clinton-not-sophisticated-enough/. Dinan, Stephen. "Comey says Clinton not 'sophisticated enough' to understand classified markings," Jul. 8, 2016.

22. "The Real Story with Gretchen Carlson." Fox News, Xfinity 1105 FNCHD, Guest Host Heather Nauert, Jul. 7, 2016.

23. Ron, Chernow. Alexander Hamilton. Penguin Group, Inc: New York, 2004. (p.390).

24. http://www.britannica.com/biography/James-Kent.

25. http://www.gallup.com/poll/166763/record-high-americans-identify-independents.aspx. Jones, Jeffrey M. "Record-high 42% of Americans identify as independents," Jan. 8, 2014.

26. "Fox and Friends." Fox News, Xfinity 1105, FNCHD, Jul. 8, 2016.

27. http://observer.com/2016/07/theres-more-to-the-real-story-of-gretchen-calson-fox-firing. Lapointe, Joe. "Sunday wrap up: 'There's more to the story of Gretchen Carlson's Fox firing,'" Jul. 11, 2016.

28. https://www.yahoo.com/news/video/inroducing-hawaiis-democratic-congresswoman-tulsi-163654381.html. "Introducing Hawaii's Democratic congresswoman: Tulsi Gabbard (Fox News Videos), Jan. 3, 2016.

29. Singleton-Rickman, Lisa. "1 and 6 are in need" The Times Daily 3 Jul. 2016: A1, Print.

30. http://boston.cbslocal.com/2016/03/30/lynn-receives-attention-housing-homeless-veterans/. Lans, Chantee. "Lynn becomes first Mass. city to end veteran homelessness," Mar. 30, 2016.

31. http://www.jfklibrary.org/Research/Research-Aids/Ready-Reference/JFK-Quotations.aspx. "Address in the Assembly Hall at the Paulskirche in Frankfurt (266)," June 25, 1963, Public Papers of the Presidents: John F. Kennedy, 1963.

32. http://womenhistory.about.com/cs/quotes/a/qu_e_roosevelt.htm. Lewis, Joan Johnson. "Eleanor Roosevelt Quotes: Human Rights Advocate (1884-1962)," Feb. 20, 2015.

Paths for Implementation

LEGALITY

1. http:www.fec.gov/law/litigation/speechnow.shtml.

2. http://www.vox.com/cards/super-pacs-and-dark-money/what-is-the-citizens-united-decision-citizens-united-v-fec. Prokop, Andrew. "The Citizens United era of money in politics, explained," Jul. 15, 2015.

3. Corrado, Anthony et. al, eds. Campaign Finance Reform: A Sourcebook. Washington D.C.: The Brookings Institution, 1997. (p.116, 117).

4. https://enwikipedia.org/wiki/Lochner_v_NewYork.

5. https://en.wikipedia.org/wiki/Assault_weapons_legislation_in_the_United_States.

6. https://en.wikipedia.org/wiki/Laboratories_of_democracy.

7. https://www.washingtonpost.com/local/federal-appeals-court-panel-rules-in-favor-of-dc-gun-law/2011/10/04/gIQAWekxLL_story.html. Duggan, Paul. "Federal appeals court panel rules in favor of D.C. gun law," Aug. 4, 2011.

8. http://www.csmonitor.com/USA/Justice/2010/0301/Supreme-Court-to-take-up-landmark-gun-control-case. Richey, Warren. "Supreme Court to take up landmark gun-control case," Mar. 1, 2010.

9. http://www.npr.org/2014/06/16/322650543/supreme-court-rules-against-gun-purchases. Totenberg, Nina. "Supreme Court rules against gun 'straw purchases,'" Jun. 16, 2014.

10. Hart, Gary. The Republic of Conscience, Penguin Random House: New York, 2015. (p.5).

11. https://www.washingtonpost.com/politics/supreme-court-strikes-down-limits-on-federal-campaign-donations/2014/04/02/54e16c30-ba74-11-e3-c739f29ccb08_story.html. Barnes, Robert. "Supreme Court strikes down limits on federal campaign donations," Apr. 2, 2014.

12. http://www.motherjones.com/politics/2014/03/supreme-court-mccutcheon-citizens-untied. Kroll, Andy. "The Supreme Court just gutted another campaign finance law. Here's what happened," Apr. 2, 2014.

13. http://www.realcrealpolitics.com/video/2014/09/05/elizabeth_warren_democracy_can_survive_for_a_while_but_it_cant_survive_forever.html. Schwartz, Ian. "Elizabeth Warren: 'Democracy can survive for a while, but it can't survive forever,'" September 5, 2014. Video.

14. http://www.nytimes.com/2016/03/30/opinion/taking-n-citizens-united.html. Weintraub, Ellen L. "Taking on Citizens United," Mar. 30, 2016.

SUCCESS THROUGH LEGISLATION

1. http://ballotpedia.org/States#Initiative_.26_referendum_in_the_U.S.

2. http://www.yesmagazine.org/people-power/give-us-our-law-back-montana-fights-to-stop-corporate-corruption. Clements, Jeff and Gwen Stowe. "Give us our law back: Montana fights to stop corporate corruption, " May 24, 2011.

3. http://www.washingtonpost.com/blogs/the-fix/post/supreme-courts-montana-decision-strengthens-citizens-united/2012/06/25/gJQA8Vln1V_blog.html. Weiner, Rachel. "Supreme Court's Montana decision strengthens Citizens United," Jun. 25, 2012.

4. http://www.gazettenet.com/home/17778673-95/adam-fisher-a-big-political-idea-from-the-big-sky-country?print=true. Fisher, Adam. "A big political idea from the Big Sky country," Jul. 15, 2015.

5. http://www.huffingtonpost.com/josh-silver/all-is-not-lost-how-to-wi_b_5084786.html. Silver, Josh. "All is not lost: How to win money-in-politics reform," Mar. 4, 2014.

6. https://represent.us/action/tallahassee/.

7. Hart, Gary. The Republic of Conscience, Penguin Random House: New York, 2015. (p. 11).

8. http://www.news-leader.com/story/news/politics/2015/08/22/missouri-lags-behind-neighbors-ethics-laws/32214531/. Swedien, John. "Missouri lags behind neighbors on ethics laws," Aug. 25, 2015.

9. http://www.publicintegrity.org/2015/11/09/18693/only-three-states-score-higher-d-state-integrity-investigation-11-flunk. Kusnetz, Nicholas. "Only three states score higher than D+ in state integrity investigation; 11 flunk," Nov. 9, 2015.

10. https://ballotpedia.org/Public_financing_of_campaigns.

11. http://www.publicintegrity.org/2015/11/09/188822/how-does-your-state-rank-integrity.

12. https://en.wikipedia.org/wiki/Special-purpose_district.

13. http://www.texaswatchdog.org/2011/02/growing-governments-how-special-districts-spread-across-Texas-power-to-tax/1297796531.story.

14. http://watchdog.org/252328/special-districts/. Winter, Deena. "Special districts – with power to tax – grow like weeds in Texas," Dec. 25, 2015.

15. http://www.texaswatchdog.org/2011/02/growing-governments-how-special-districts-spread-across-Texas-power-to-tax/1297796531.story. Peebles, Jennifer. "Growing governments: How 'special districts' spread across Texas with limited oversight and accountability – but with plenty of power to tax," Feb. 15, 2011.

16. http://www.nytimes.com/2012/04/22/us/alec-a-tax-exempt-group-mixes-legislators-and-lobbyists.html?_r=0. McIntire, Mike. "Conservative nonprofit acts as a stealth business lobbyist," Apr. 21, 2012.

17. http://www.prwatch.org/news/2011/07/10882/comparison-alec-and-ncsl. Graves, Lisa. "A comparison of ALEC and NCSL," Jul. 13, 2011.

18. http://www.motherjones.com/politics/2012/05/alec-lobbyist-exemption. Abowd, Paul. "ALEC gets a break from state lobbying laws," May 8, 2012.

19. http://www.dailykos.com/story/2012/6/26/1103251/-ALEC-Hidden-Membership-EXPOSED.

Sloan, Bob. "ALEC- Hidden membership exposed," Jun. 26, 2012.
20. http://www.huffingtonpost.com/entry/hillary-clinton-citizens-united_us_578a42cfe4b08608d334c7bd. Levin, Sam. "Hillary Clinton pledges constitutional amendment to overturn citizens united in her first 30 days," Jul. 16, 2016.
21. http://www.cnn.com/2016/07/25/politics/uss-gerald-r-ford-aircraft-carrier-delay/index.html. Cohen, Zachary. "U.S. Navy's new $13B aircraft carrier can't fight," Jul. 25, 2016.
22. https://www.washingtonpost.com/news/the-fix/wp/201/09/03/tom-coburn-wants-to-convene-a-constitutional-convention-congress-wont-let-that-happen. Bump, Phillip. "Marco Rubio wants to convene a constitutional convention. It won't happen," Dec. 30, 2015.

SUCCESS THROUGH OPTIONS

1. http://www.ilsr.org/rule/campaign/2177-2/. The Public Good, Dec. 1, 2008.
2. http://www.ncsl.org/research/about-state-legislatures/summariers-of-term-limits-cases.aspx. "Term limits and the courts."
3. http://www.c-span.org/video/?201144/news-documentary-emmy-awards. "News and Documentary Emmy Awards." Sept. 24, 2007. Video.
4. Raymond, Allen with Ian Spiegelman. "Confessions of a Republican operative: how to rig an election. Simon & Schuster: New York, 2008. (p. 194, 195).
5. Miller, Merle. Plain Speaking: An Oral Biography of Harry S. Truman. Berkley Publishing Corporation: New York, 1974. (p. 251).
6. http://www.cjr.org/united_states_project/many_stations_dont_factcheck_s.php. Peters, Justin. "Many stations don't factcheck super PAC ads: survey in conference highlights differences in attitudes between industry, watchdog groups," May 24, 2012.
7. http://money.cnn.com/2014/11/04/media/political-ads-midterms/index.html. Stelter, Brian. "You won't miss those annoying political ads. Stations will miss the money," Nov. 3, 2014.
8. http://www.freepress.net/blog/2012/09/24/tv-stations-accept-political-ad-cash-and-leave-viewers-dark. Karr, Timothy. "TV stations accept political cash – and leave viewers in the dark," Sept. 24, 2012.
9. http://www.npr.org/sections/itsallpolitics/2012/10/03/162184983/should-tv-stations-refuse-to-air-political-ads-that-make-false-claims. Finn, Scott. "Should TV stations refuse to air political ads that make false claims?" Oct. 3, 2012.
10. http://www.alternet.org/media/imagine-if-politicians-were-forced-tell-truth-their-adcampaigns. Balkind, Harriet Levin. "Imagine if politicians were forced to tell the truth in their ad campaigns: Lies distort every critical issue the U.S. faces," Oct. 14, 2014.
11. http://www.factcheck.org/2004/06/false-ads-there-oughta-be-a-law-or-maybe-not/. Jackson, Brooks. "False ads: There oughta be a law! – Or maybe not," May 10, 2007.
12. http://www.scpr.org/blogs/politics/2014/07/01/16942/broadcast-tv-stations-must-now-post-political-ad-b/. McNary, Sharon. "Broadcast TV stations must now post political ad buy documents online," Jul. 1, 2014.
13. http://www.jfklibrary.org/Research/Research-Aids/JFK-Speeches/American-Newspaper-Publishers-Association_19610427.aspx\. "John F. Kennedy Speeches: The President and the press: Address before the American Newspaper Publishers Association." Waldorf-Astoria Hotel, New York City, Apr. 27, 1961.
14. http://www.ncsl.org/Portals/1/documents/legismgt/elect/ContributionLimitstoCandidates2015-2016.pdf. "State limits on contributions to candidates: 2015-2016 election cycle."
15. http://www.nytimes.com/2015/12/23/us/politics/as-tv-ad-rates-soar-super-pacs-pivot-to-core-campaign-work.html?=0. Corasaniti, Nick and Matt Flegenheimer. "As TV ad rates soar, 'super PACs' pivot to core campaign work," Dec. 23, 2015.

A NEWS ALTERNATIVE

1. http://www.activistpost.com/2016/04/death-of-mainstream-media-6-percent-trust.html. Jankowski, Joe. "New poll shows only 6% of people trust the mainstream media," Apr. 19, 2016.
2. http://www.tpnn.com/2015/11/27/cnn-reporter-caught-red-handed-coordinating-with-hillary-aide-to-smear-this-gop-candidate/. Conley, Colleen. "CNN reporter caught RED HANDED coordinating with Hillary aide to smear this GOP candidate," Nov. 27, 2015.
3. "Fox Report Sunday." The Political Insiders, Host Pattie Ann Browne, Fox News, Xfinity 1105 FNCHD, Jul. 31, 2016.
4. https://www.conservativeoutfitters.com/blogs/news/92753985-black-lives-matter-fire-guns-after-chicago-trump-rally. "Vide: Black Lives Matter protestors shoot guns and loot after forcing Donald

Trump to cancel rally in Chicago," Mar. 12, 2016.
5. http://conservativetribune.com/hillary-camp-sickened-milwaukee/. Proviso, Wilmot. "PHOTOS: Hillary camp sickened when they see who got caught supporting looting in Milwaukee," Aug. 16, 2016.
6. "Fox and Friends." Fox News, Host Brian Kilmeade, Ainsley Earhardt, and Steve Doocy, Xfinity 1105 FNCHD, Jul. 29, 2016.
7. Pontifex08. "Tim Russert SCHOOLS David Duke." Online video clip. YouTube, 18 Jun. 2008. Web. Aug. 24, 2016.
8. http://www.washingtontimes.com/news/2016/jun/8/law-professor-backs-trump-conflict-interest-judge/. Miller. S.A. "Law professor backs Donald Trump's conflict-of-interest charge against federal judge," Jun. 8, 2016.
9. http://www.cnn.com/2009/POLITICS/05/28/sotomayor.latina.remark.reax/. "Latina woman' remark may dominate Sotomayor hearings," May 28, 2009.
10. Delinski, Bernie. "Judge chastises jury in Peden trial" The Times Daily 1 Jul. 2016: A1. Print.
11. https://www.washingtonpost.com/politics/courts_law/supreme-court-finds-bias-in-jury-selection-in-condemned-georgia-mans-case/2016/05/23/5239544e-20f6-11e6-aa84-42391ba52c91_story.html. Barnes, Robert. "Justices throw out death sentence given to black man by all-white jury," May 23, 2016.
12. https://wikileaks.org/dnc-emails/.
13. "The Kelly File." Host Megan Kelly, Fox News, Xfinity 1105 FNCHD, Jan. 1, 2016.
14. http://newsbusters.org/blogs/tim-graham/2015/05/11/bob-woodward-yes-medias-sleeping-lost-its-investigative-zeal. Graham, Tim. "Bob Woodward: Yes, media's'sleeping,' Lost its 'investigative zeal,'" May 11, 2015.
15. "Smerconish." Host Michael Smerconish, CNN, Xfinity 1106 CNNHD, Jul. 23, 2016.
16. Dotson, Bob. American Story: A lifetime search for ordinary people doing extraordinary things. Penguin Group: New York, 2013.
17. http://www.billoreilly.com/show?action=latestTVShow. "Is it legal? All about Trump lawsuits," Jul. 26, 2016.
18. http://townhall.com/tipsheet/guybenson/2016/06/09/by-the-way-heres-the-clinton-university-fraud-controversy-nobodys-talking-about-n2176138. Benson, Guy. "Clinton U: Here's the other multi-million dollar fraud scandal the media isn't telling you about," Jun. 9, 2016.
19. Thomas, Cal. "Hillary Clinton: The most qualified" The Times Daily 19 Jun. 2016: D1. Print.
20. Gerstein, Josh, Parti, Tarini, Hadas, Gold and Dylan Byers. "Clinton Foundation include dozens of media organizations, individuals," May 15, 2015.
21. https://washingtonpost.com/lifestyle/style/media-administration-deal-with-conflicts/2013/06/12/e6f983-14-ca2e-11e2-8da7-d274bc611a47_story.html. Farhi, Paul. "Media, administration deal with conflicts," Jun. 12, 2013.
22. http://www.huffingtonpost.com/eric-zuesse/jimmy-carter-is-correct-t_b_7922788.html. Zuesse, Eric. "Jimmy Carter is correct that the U.S. is no longer a democracy," Aug. 3, 2015.
23. http://www.mrc.org/media-bias-101/exhibit-2-5-gallup-polls-media-bias. "Exhibit 2-5: Gallup polls on media bias," Jan. 7, 2014.
24. https://www.themarshallproject.org/2015/10/06/what-you-need-to-know-about-the-new-federal-prisoner-release?ref=hp-2-121. "What you need to know about the new federal prison release," Oct. 6, 2015.
25. Fox Business. "Sheriff Babeu: Obama has led the largest prison break in American history." Online video clip. YouTube, 7 Oct. 2015. Web. Aug. 25, 2016.
26. http://www.wnd.com/2015/10/obamas-trick-or-treat-6000-convicts-go-free/. Hohmann, Leo. "Obama's trick or treat: 6,000 convicts go free," Oct. 19, 2015.
27. "Your World with Neil Cavuto, Fox News, Xfinity 1105 FNCHD, Jan. 13, 2016.

What Can Be Achieved

1. Lewis, Edwards and Richard Rhodes, eds. John F. Kennedy: Words to Remember. United States: Hallmark Cards Incorporated, 1967. (p. 14).
2. "The Kelly File." Host Megan Kelly. Fox News, Xfinity 1105 FNCHD, Jan. 12, 2016.
3. http://thehill.com/policy/energy-environment/240645-oversight-rips-epa-on-employee-misconduct. Henry, Devin. "Oversight rips EPA on employee misconduct," Apr. 30, 2015.
4. http://www.businessinsider.com/elizabeth-warren-attacks-apple-google-amazon-over-antitrust-democracy-consiliation-competition-2016-6. Price, Rob. "Warren: Companies like Apple 'snuff out competition,' and that 'threatens our democracy,'" Jun. 30, 2016.
5. http://dailycaller.com/2016/08/25/manchins-daughter-raked-in-19-million-while-spiking-price-of-

epipen/. Brufke, Juliegrace. "Manchin's daughter raked in $19 million while spiking price of EpiPen," Aug. 25, 2016.

6. http://www.nytimes.com/2015/11/11/us/politics/transcript-republican-presidential-debate.html. "Transcript: Republican Presidential Debate," Nov. 11, 2015.

7. Carson, Ben. America the Beautiful: Rediscovering what made this nation great. Michigan: Zondervan, 2012. (p. 95, 153).

8. http://thehill.com/blogs/pundits-blog/healthcare/287906-panic-prompted-obamacare-lawlessness. Badger, Doug. "Panic prompted Obamacare lawlessness." Jul. 15, 2016.

9. Will, George. "A 'slush fund' by any other name." The Times Daily 4 Sept. 2016: D1. Print

10. http://www.washingtontimes.com/news/2016/aug/11/obama-admin-blocked-fbi-probe-clinton-foundation/. Miller, S.A. "Obama admin blocked FBI probe of Clinton Foundation corruption: Report," Aug. 11, 2016.

11. D'Angelo, Alexa. "More middle-class Americans visit Mexico for low-cost medical care" The Times Daily 1 Nov. 2015: D1. Print.

12. http://www.businessinsider.com/ap-john-oliver-buys-and-forgives-15-million-in-debt-2016-6. Bauder, David. "John Oliver bought and forgave 9,000 people's debt worth $15 million," Jun. 6, 2016.

13. http://www.nytimes.com/2016/03/01/health/waste-in-cancer-drugs-costs-3-billion-a-year-a-study-says.html?_r=0. Harris, Gardiner. "Waste in Cancer drugs costs $3 billion a year, a study says," Mar. 1, 2016.

14. http://www.washingtonpost.com/news/the-fix/wp/2016/01/14/6th-republican-debate-transcript-annotated-who-said-what-and-what-it-meant/. "6th Republican debate transcript, annotated: Who said what and what it meant," Jan. 14, 2016.

15. "White House proposes rules aimed at tax evasion" The Times Daily 6 May 2016. A3. Print.

16. http://www.yahoo.com/news/obama-calls-sen-paul-drop-objections-tax-treaties-182700096.html?ref=gs. "Obama calls on Sen. Paul to drop objections to tax treaties," May 6, 2016.

17. http://www.thefiscaltimes.com/2015/07/29/GOP-Makes-Move-Rein-Obama. Garver, Rob. "The GOP makes a move to Rein in Obama," Jul. 29, 2015.

18. Taylor, Andrew. "House GOP presses ahead with $622M Zika measure" The Times Daily 19 May 2016: A3. Print.

19. The inspired word of God. The Bible. Genesis 18: 23-33.

20. http://dailycaller.com/2016/05/23senator-obama-steals-from-zika-victims-to-fund-un-climate-programs/. Bastasch, Michael. "Senator: Obama steals from Zika victims to fund UN climate programs," May 23, 2016.

21. http://www.wsj.com/artilces/price-tag-of-bernie-sanders-proposals-18-trillion-1442271511. Meckler, Laura. "Price tag of Bernie Sanders's proposals: 18 trillion," Sept. 14, 2015.

22. http://hillaryspeeches.com/2016/05/25/hillary-clinton-campaigns-in-buena-park-and-salinas/. White, Emma. "Hillary Clinton campaigns in Buena Park and Salinas," May 25, 2016.

23. "Fox and Friends." Host Ainsley Earhardt, Brian Kilmeade, Steve Doocy, Fox News, Xfinity 1105 FNCHD, May 26, 2016.

24. https://www.conservativereview.com/commentary/2016/malkin-the-16-billion-tax-credit-black-hole. Malkin, Michelle. "Malkin: The $16 billion tax-credit black hole," Jun. 1, 2016.

25. http://www.militarytimes.com/story/veterans/2015/10/26/clinton-va-scandals/74618360/. "Clinton: VA problems not as bad as GOP suggest," Oct. 26, 2015.

26. https://www.justice.gov/opa/speech/attorney-general-loretta-e-lynch-delivers-remarks-press-conference-announcing-complaint. "Attorney general Loretta E. Lynch delivers remarks at press conference announcing complaint against the state of north Carolina to stop discrimination against transgender individuals," May 9, 2016.

27. http://www.cnsnews.com/news/article/melanie-hunter/mother-teen-murdered-illegal-immigrant-tells-congress-do-something-it. Hunter, Melanie. "Mother of teen murdered by illegal immigrant tells Congress: 'Do Something – it is your job," Apr. 20, 2016.

28. http://www.christianexaminer.com/article/ag-orders-transcripts-of-calls-between-orlando-terrorist-and-police-edited-to-remove-isis-loyalty-pledge/50810.html. Tomlin, Gregory. "AG orders transcripts of calls between Orlando terrorist and police edited to remove ISIS loyalty pledge," Jun. 20, 2016.

29. duhaime.org. "Judicial Branch Definition."

30. http://www.usatoday.com/story/news/2016/05/19/judge-orders-ethics-training-doj-lawyers/84624098/. Johnson, Kevin. "Judge orders ethics training for DOJ lawyers," May 19, 2016.

31. http://nypost.com/2016/03/27/ag-loretta-lynch-wants-to-let-nation-break-law-without-consequences/. Sperry, Paul. "AG Loretta Lynch wants to let nation break law without consequences," Mar. 27, 2016.

32. http://www.foxnews.com/us/2016/05/14/california-ballot-measure-blamed-for-shoplifting-jump.html. "California ballot measure blamed for shoplifting jump," May 14, 2016.

33. http://finance.yahoo.com/news/justice-dept-tweets-cnn-melania-150309592.html. "Justice Dept. tweets about CNN and Melania Trump in huge social media fail," Jul. 19, 2016.

34. http://www.washingtontimes.com/news/2016/jun/21/loretta-lynch-most-effective-response-to-islamic-t/. Ernst, Douglas. "Loretta Lynch: 'Most Effective' response to Islamic terrorism 'is love.'" Jun. 21, 2016.
35. http://www.foxnews.com/politics/2015/02/18/state-department-spokeswoman-call-for-using-jobs-to-combat-terror-too-nuanced.html. "State Department spokeswoman: Call for using jobs to combat terror 'too nuanced' for critics," Feb. 18, 2015.
36. http://www.breitbart.com/big-government/2016/08/02/report-obama-admin-airlifted-400000000-iran-americans-freed/. Huston, Warner Todd. "Report: Obama Administration airlifted $400,000 to Iran as Americans freed," Aug. 2, 2016.
37. http://conservativetribune.com/obamas-pentagon-middle-east/. Proviso, Wilmot. "What's Obama's pentagon just purchased from the middle east will give you chills," Jun. 7, 2016.
38. http://newsbusters.org/blogs/mark-finkelstein/2015/02/16/mad-matthews-america-getting-humiliated-sounds-we-cant-stop-isis. Finkelstein, Mark. "Mad Matthews: America 'getting humiliated, sounds like we can't stop ISIS,'" Feb. 16, 2015.
39. https://www.yahoo.com/news/stop-saying-islam-religion-peace-143200315.html. "Stop saying Islam is a religion of peace: Taslima Nasreen," Jul. 3, 2016.
40. Will, George. "Due process is being kicked off campus." The Times Daily 15 May 2016. D2. Print.
41. http://nypost.com/2016/04/23/the-lawsuit-that-might-rock-college-sexual-assault-cases/. "The lawsuit that might rock college sexual assault cases," Apr. 23, 2016.
42. http://espn.go.com/los-angeles/ncf/story/_/id/7967794/ex-usc-trojcans-recruit-exonerated-rape-conviction. "Brian Bank's rape conviction vacated," May 24, 2012.
43. http://video.foxnews.com/v/47/4711634737001/fox-news-reporting-the-truth-about-sex-amp-college#sp=show-clips. MacCallum, Martha. "Fox News Reporting: The truth about sex & college," Jan. 19, 2016.
44. https://kcjohnson.files.wordpress.com/2013/08/nungesser-complaint.pdf.
45. http://hotiar.com/archives/2015/06/06/college-rape-culture-movement-fails-again-as-mattress-girl-releases-sex-video/. Shaw, Jazz. "College 'rape culture' movement fails again as Mattress Girl releases sex video," Jul. 6, 2015.
46. http://www.cnsnews.com/commentary/hans-bader/news-york-times-reveals-stupidity-yes-means-yes-sexual-assault-policies. Bader, Hans. "New York Times reveals stupidity of 'Yes Means Yes' sexual assault policies," Oct. 19, 2016.
47. http://nypost.com/2015/12/03/hillary-asked-about-rape-claims-against-bill-at-campaign-event/. Schultz, Marisa. "Voter asks Hillary Clinton about rape claims against Bill," Dec. 3, 2015.
48. http://www.breitbart.com/2016-presidential-race/2016/01/10/exclusive-kathleen-willey-urges-clinton-s-sex-victims-to-break-silence-nobody-can-touch-you-now/. "EXCLUSIVE- Kathleen Willey thanks Donald Trump for highlighting Bill Clinton's history with women, urges more victims to come forward," Jan. 10, 2016.
49. http://www.dailymail.co.uk/news/article-3729466/Child-rape-victim-comes-forward-time-40-years-call-Hillary-Clinton-liar-defend-rapist-smearing-blocking-evidence-callously-laughing-knew-guilty.html. Goodman, Alana. "EXCLUSIVE: Child rape victim comes forward for the first time in 40 years to call Hillary Clinton a 'liar' who defended her rapist by smearing her, blocking evidence and callously laughing that she knew he was guilty," Aug. 9, 2016.
50. http://www.washingtonexaminer.com/hillary-clinton-campaign-removes-statement-about-believing-rape-accusers/article/2599338. Schow, Ashe. "Hillary Clinton campaign removes statement about believing rape accusers," Aug. 15, 2016.
51. http://www.salon.com/2015/07/20/worried_about_rising_crime_rates_then_its_time_to_get_the_police_under_control/. Brown, Lawrence. "Worried about rising crime rates? Then it's time to get the police under control," Jul. 20, 2015.
52. http://www.nydailynews.com/news/politics/obama-doesn-regret-acted-stupidly-remark-henry-gates-jr-arrest-articl-1.394423. "Obama doesn't regret 'acted stupidly' remark about Henry Gates Jr. arrest," Jul. 24, 2009.
53. http://www.cnn.com/2015/05/18/politics/bayonets-police-white-house/index.html. Perez, Evan, Liptak, Kevin, and Allison Malloy. "Obama will restrict grenade launchers, military equipment from local police," May 18, 2015.
54. http://conservativetribune.com/feds-seize-equip-bama-police/. Marquis, Ben. "Obama's feds seize equipment from Alabama police… Sheriff responds, 'People will die,'" Nov. 20, 2015.
55. https://en.wikipedia.org/wiki/North_Hollywood_shootout
56. "MSNBC News." Host Brian Williams, MSNBC, Xfinity 1108, Jul. 8, 2016.
57. http://www.nytimes.com/2015/10/24/us/politics/fbi-chief-scrutiny-of-police-with-rise-in-violent-crime.html?_r=2. Schmidt, Michael S. and Matt Apuzzo. "FBI chief links scrutiny of police with rise in violent crime," Oc. 23, 2015.
58. http://www.baltimoresun.com/news/maryland/freddie-gray/bs-md-ci-gray-officers-sue-mosby-20160525-story.html. Fenton, Justin and Kevin Rector. "Two officers in Freddie Gray case sue Marilyn

Mosby for defamation," May 15, 2016.

59. https://gma.yahoo.com/judge-finds-prosecutors-withheld-evidence-freddie-gray-officer-154226833-abc-news-topstories.html. Khan, Mariam and Morgan Winsor. "Judges find prosecutors withheld evidence in Freddie Gray officer case," Jun. 9, 2016.

60. http://www.breitbart.com/big-government/2016/08/16/hacked-soros-memo-baltimore-riots-provide-unique-opportunity-reform-police/. Klein, Aaron. "Hacked Soros memo: $650 to Black Lives Matter," Aug. 16, 2016.

61. "On the Record with Greta Van Susteren." Fox News, Xfinity 1105 FNCHD, Jun. 1, 2016.

62. "Outnumbered." Fox News, Xfinity 1105 FNCHD, May 16, 2016.

63. http://www.dailymail.co.uk/news/article-3198613/Cop-pistol-whipped-unconscious-weapon-afraid-use-force-against-unarmed-black-attacker-wak-Ferguson-shooting.html. Pleasance, Chris. "Cop who was pistol-whipped unconscious with his own weapon was afraid to use force against his unarmed black attacker in the wake of Ferguson shooting," Aug. 14, 2016.

64. http://www.cbsnews.com/news/suspect-killed-two-deputies-wounded-in-maryland-shootout/. "2 Sheriff's deputies fatally shot in Maryland," Feb. 10, 2016.

65. https://www.washingtonpost.com/local/public-safety/a-horror-panera-customer-describes-shooting-of-md-deputy/2016/02/11/bf087472-d0d0-11e5-b2bc-988409ee911b_story.html. Marimow, Ann, Jouvenal, Justin, and Dana Hedgpeth. "Witness describes chaotic Panera shooting that left two deputies dead," Feb. 11, 2016.

66. "Fox News." Xfinity 1005 FNCHD, Jul. 8, 2016.

67. http://www.mirror.co.uk/news/world-news/dallas-police-shooting-black-power-8378177. Jones, Stephen. "Dallas police shooting: 'Black Power group' claims responsibility for police killings and warns of more assassinations to come," Jul. 8, 2016.

68. "Fox and Friends." Host Abby Huntsman and Heather Childers, Fox News, Xfinity 1105 FNCHD, Jul. 18, 2016.

69. http://www.nydailynews.com/news/crime/georgia-woman-called-death-white-cops-apologizes-article-1.2628073. Salinger, Tobias. "Georgia woman who called for 'death to all white cops' apologizes publicly, charges dropped," May 6, 2016.

70. http://www.infowars.com/video-black-lives-matter-protest-leader-calls-for-shooting-running-over-cops/. Watson, Joseph. "Video: Black Lives Matter' protest leader calls for shooting, running over cops," Jul. 11, 2016.

71. http://conservativetribune.com/jesse-jackson-makes-sick-claim/. "Jesse Jackson makes sick claim about who's responsible for Dallas cop assassinations," Jul. 10, 2016.

72. "The Kelly File." Fox News, Xfinity 1105 FNCHD, Jul. 6, 2016.

73. https://pjmedia.com/video/remember-when-al-sharpton-said-to-kill-police-officers/. "Remember when Al Sharpton said to kill police officers?" Jul. 11, 2016.

74. "MSNBC Specials." Republican National Convention, MSNBC News, Xfinity 1008 MSNBC, Jul. 20, 2016.

75. http://conservativetribune.com/cleveland-cops-sick-protesters/#respond. Marquis, Ben. "Breaking: Cleveland cops under attack… sick protestors doing the unthinkable," Jul. 19, 2016.

76. http://conservativetribune.com/obama-attorney-issues/. Falkenberg, John. "Obama attorney issues outrageous statement after refugees urinate on 5-year old girl," Jun. 30, 2016.

77. https://www.conservativereview.com/commentary/2016/04/vspshooting-trooper-assassin-james-brown-iii-was-a-cop-hating-django. Malkin, Michelle. "Malkin: #VSPShooting: Trooper assassin James Brown III was a cop-hating Django," Apr. 1, 2016.

78. http://graphics.latimes.com/towergraphic-who-they-were-dorner-alleged-victims/. Pesce, Anthony. "Who they were: Victims in the Dorner case," Feb. 12, 2013.

79. http://www.rushlimbaugh.com/daily/2013/02/15/marc_lamont_hill_apologizes_for_being_misunderstood_by_all_you_stupid_people. "Mark Lamont Hill apologizes for being misunderstood by all you stupid people," Feb. 15, 2013.

80. http://www.westernjournalism.com/cnn-misrepresented-sylville-smith-sisters-call-for-peace/. Desoto, Rand. "CNN misrepresented Sylville Smith sister's call for peace," Aug. 15, 2016.

81. http://www.washingtonexaminer.com/vox.com-suspends-editor-over-pro-riot-tweets/article/2592948. Adams, T. Becket. "Vox.com suspends editor over pro-riot tweets," Jun. 3, 2016.

82. "The Rachel Maddow Show." MSNBC News, Xfinity 1108 MSNBC, Jun. 23, 2016.

83. https;//www.yahoo.com/music/kevin-gates-issues-defiant-response-160622236.html. Golding, Snenequa. "Kevin Gates issues a defiant response to any officer who harasses his children," Jul. 18, 2016.

84. http://www.teaparty.org/no-apology-from-walmart-after-police-officer-in-uniform-refused-service-by-clerks-182492/. "No APOLOGY FROM WALMART after police officer in uniform refused service by clerks," Aug. 16, 2016.

85. http://www.cleveland.com/browns/index.ssf/2016/07/browns_say_isaiah_crowells_apo.html. Cabot, Mary Kay. "Browns say Isaiah Crowell's apology for 'extremely disturbing' post is insufficient and

must back it up with positive steps," Jul. 11, 2016.

86. http://www.thegatewaypundit.com/2016/08/walmart-meets-with-st-cloud-fl-police-cashier-who-refused-to-serve-officer-out-at-store/. Taylor, Kristinn. "Walmart meets with St. Cloud, FL Police; Cashier who refused to serve officer out at store," Aug. 17, 2016.

87. http://nypost.com/2016/07/17/al-sharpton-sued-for-allegedly-swiping-16k-from-arizona-man/. Boniello, Kathlanne and Laura Itallano. "Al Sharpton sued for allegedly swiping $16K from Arizona man," Jul. 11, 2016.

88. http://thescoopblog.dallasnews.com/2015/11/dorothy-bland-my-assumptions-may-have-been-wrong-but-fears-were-real.html/. Weiss, Jeffrey. "Dorothy Bland: My assumptions may have been wrong but fears were real," Nov. 10, 2015.

89. http://www.dallasnes.com/opinion/latest-columns/20151029-qa-former-dallas-mayor-criticizes-race-claims-in-dorothy-bland-case.ece. Willey, Keven Ann. "Q&A: Former Dallas mayor criticizes race claims in Dorothy Bland case," Nov. 23, 2015.

90. http://dailycaller.com/2016/08/06/clinton-chooses-black-lives-matter-over-law-enforcement-support/. Picket, Kerry. "Clinton chooses Black Lives Matter over law enforcement support," Aug. 6, 2016.

91. http://www.mediated.com/tv/loretta-lynch-refuses-to-say-whether-its-illegal-to-lie-under-oath/. Griswold, Alex. "Loretta Lynch refuses to say whether it's illegal to lie under oath," Jul. 12, 2016.

92. http://www.rasmussenreports.com/public_content/politcs/weekly_updates/what_they_told_us_reviewing_last_week_s_key_polls2. "What they told us: Reviewing last week's key polls," Jul. 30, 2016.

93. https://www.qu.edu/news-and-events/quinnipiac-university-poll/2016-presidential-swing-state-polls/release-detail?ReleaseID=2365. "Clinton losing on honesty in Florida, Ohio, Pennsylvania, Quinnipiac University swing state poll finds," Jul. 13, 2016.

94. https://reaganlibrary.archives.gov/archives/speeches/1988/100488e.htm. "Remarks at the Republican Governors Club Dinner," Oct. 4, 1988.

95. David Von Pein's JFK Channel. "John F. Kennedy on NBC's 'Meet the Press,'" Online video clip. YouTube. YouTube, 29 Aug. 2013. Web. Aug. 23, 2016.

96. http://abarahamlincolnsclassrooom.org/abraham-lincoln-in-depth/abraham-lincolns-values-and-philosophy/. Miller, William E. Lincoln's Virtues: An ethical biography. New York: Alfred A Knopf, 2002.

97. http://www.jfklibrary.org/Research/Research-Aids/Ready-Reference/JFK-Quotations.aspx "Speech at Loyola College Alumni Banquet, Baltimore," Maryland, 18 February, 1958, Senate Files, box 899, John F. Kennedy Presidential Library.

98. http://townhall.com/tipsheet/mattvespa/2016/04/04/vermont-residents-leave-state-as-it-becomes-riddled-with-high-taxes-n2143564. Vespa, Matt. "Vermont residents leave state as it becomes riddled with high taxes," Apr. 4, 2016.

99. http://www.huffingtonpost.com/carl-gibson/mark-dayton-minnesota-economy_b_6737786.html. Gibson, Robert C. "The Billionaire governor taxed the rich and increased the minimum wage – now his state's economy is one of the best in the country," Feb. 19, 2016.

100. Brookshire, Richard. Founding Father: Rediscovering George Washington. New York: Simon and Schuster, 1997. (p. 10).

101. Klein, Joe. Politics Lost: How American democracy was trivialized by people who think your stupid. Doubleday: New York, 2006. (p. 24).

102. https://www.yahoo.com/news/ap-poll-many-social-security-full-retirement-131726304.html. Allington, Adam. "Many opt to take social security before full retirement age," May 26, 2016.

103. "The great gap in Americans' post-work lives" The Times Daily 4 Jun. 2016: A4. Print.

104. Rubio, Marco. American Dreams: Restoring economic opportunity for everyone. New York: Penguin Group, 2015. (p. 152).

Conclusion

1. Public Domain Footage. "Robert F. Kennedy speech at Coumbia University 1964- RFK speaking." Online video clip. YouTube. YouTube, 5 Nov. 2013. Web. Jul. 7, 2016.

2. Holland, Jesse J. and Emily Swanson. "Poll: Support for movement grows among white youth." The Times Daily 6 Sept. 2016. A5. Print.

3. http://fortune.com/worlds-greatest-leaders/2015/. "The World's 50 Greatest Leaders," 2015.

4. http://www.latimes.com/nation/la-na-civil-rights-leaders-br-20150304-htmlstory.html Pearce, Matt and Kurtis Lee. "The new civil rights leaders: Emerging voices in the 21st century," Mar. 5, 2015.

5. http://dailycaller.com/2015/08/26/deraymckesson-tweets-then-deletes-claim-that-virginia-shooter-was-white. Ross, Chuck. "DeRay McKesson tweets – the deletes – claim that Virginia shooter was white," Aug. 25, 2016.

6. http://www.mediaite.com/online/blacklivesmatter-protester-deray-mckesson-to-teach-at-yale/. Griswold, Alex. "#BlackLivesMatter protestor DeRay McKesson to teach at Yale," Sept. 11, 2015.

7. http://twtichy.com/2015/09/30/deray-mckesson-meets-with-sen-elizabeth-warren-to-talk-campaignzero-praises-her-sincerity/. "DeRay McKesson meets with Sen. Elizabeth Warren to talk #campaignzero, praises her incerity," Sept. 30, 2015.

8. http://news.yahoo.com/black-lives-matter-activists-bring-agenda-hillary-clinton-212732637.html. McCray, Rebecca. "Black Lives Matter activists bring their agenda to Hillary Clinton," Oct. 9, 2015.

9. http://news.yahoo.com/clinton-tells-black-lives-matter-activists-change-policies-230947473.html. "Clinton tells Black Lives Matter activists to change policies, not hearts," Aug. 18, 2015.

10. http://www.latimes.com/local/california/la-me-black-lives-matter-20151030-story.html. Jennings, Angel. "Longtime L.A. civil rights leaders dismayed by in-your-face tactics of new crop of activists," Oct. 30, 2015.

11. http://thenewinquiry.com/essays/in-defense-of-looting/. Osterweil, Willie. "In Defense of Looting," Aug. 21, 2014.

12. http//www.huffingtonpost.com/2014/12/01/ferguson-bakery-donations_n_6247708.html. Sieczkowski, Cavan. "Ferguson bakery destroyed by looters receives more than $250,000 in   donations," Dec. 2, 2014.

13. thenewinquiry.com/author/willie/.

14. http://america.aljazeera.com/opinions/2014/10/ferguson-keene-pumpkinfestpartyriotspoliceviolence.html. Osterweil, Willie. "The political potential of party riots: Can frat bros help oppose arbitrary police violence?" Oct. 28, 2014.

15. http://www.the.federalistpapers.org/us/oppressed-mizzou-student-protesting-privilege-has-a-secret. "'Oppressed' Mizzou student protesting 'privilege' has a secret," Nov. 11, 2015.

16. http://twitch.com/2015/11/11/mizzous-student-body-president-apologizes-for-scaring-everybody-with-false-kkk-on-campus-rumor-screenshot. "Mizzo's student body president apologizes for scaring everybody with false KKK on campus rumors [screenshot]," Nov. 11, 2015.

17. http://www.dartreview.com/eyes-wide-open-at-the-protest/. "Eyes wide open at the protest," Nov. 14, 2015.

18. http://www.dartreview.com/protesters-deny-physical-harassment-gain-vice-provost-ameers-endorsement/. Chen, Brian. "Protesters deny physical harassment, gain vice provost Ameer's endorsement," Nov. 17, 2015.

19. http://dailycaller.com/2016/05/15/dartmouth-students-defend-tearing-down-police-display-with-566-word-letter/. Neff, Blake. "Dartmouth students defend tearing down police with 566-word letter," May 15, 2016.

20. http://dailycaller.com/2016/09/06/taxpayer-funded-california-university-offers-segregated-black-only-housing/. Scott, Annabel. "Taxpayer-funded California University offers segregated black-only housing," Sept. 6, 2016.

21. http://100percentfedup.com/watch-blacklivesmatter-students-panic-when-asian-student-turns-tables-on-them-talks-about-racial-harassment-by-blacks/. "WATCH #BlackLivesMatter students panic when Asian student turns tables on them… talks about racial harassment by blacks," Nov. 11, 2015.

22. http://www.cnn.com/2013/11/12/us/affirmative-action-fast-facts/index.html. "Affirmative action fast facts," May 9, 2015.

23. http://www.boston.com/news/education/2015/05/21/incoming-boston-university-professor-talks-about-that-time-she-kind-catfished-another-woman/PtwqTdQDNhT0gsPc2GL8BK/story.html. Wilder, Charlotte and Allison Manning. "Incoming Boston University professor talks about the time she impersonated another woman online," May 21, 2015.

24. www.foxnews.com/us/2015/05/09/boston-university-prof-flunks-white-masculinity-in-controversial-tweets.html. Lott, Maxim. "Boston University prof flunks 'white masculinity' in controversial tweets," May 9, 2015.

25. "Hannity." Fox News, Host Sean Hannity, Xfinity 1105 FNCHD, Jul. 8, 2016.

26. Wallace, Mike. Between you and me: A memoir. With Gary Paul Gates. New York: Hyperion, 2015. (p.82).

27. http://dailycaller.com/2016/07/08/blm-statement-on-dallas-condemns-violence-a-year-ago-members-chanted-pigs-in-a-blanket-fry-em-like-bacon/. Datok, Christian. "BLM statement on Dallas condemns violence – a year ago members chanted 'Pigs in a blanket, fry 'em like bacon,'" Jul. 8, 2016.

28. http://minutemennews.com/obama-you-cant-hold-well-meaning-blm-activists-responsible-for-what-they-say/. "Obama: You can't hold well-meaning BLM activists responsible for what they say," Jul. 12, 2016.

29. http://www.blackliberationcollective.org/news/.

30. https://pjmedia.com/trending/2016/07/16/philando-castile-got-pulled-over-a-lot-and-deserved-

it/2/#comments. Hudson, Walter. "Philando Castile got pulled over a lot, and deserved it," Jul. 16, 2016.

31. "The Kelly File." Fox News, Host Megan Kelly. Xfinity 1105 FNCHD, Jul. 6, 2016.

32. http://www.huffingtonpost.com/2015/06/22/jesse-jackson-jr-released_n_7636842.html. Bellware, Kim. "Ex-Congressman Jesse Jackson Jr. released from halfway house as sentence winds down," Jun. 22, 2015.

33. http://rare.us/story/democrat-congresswoman-faces-more-than-three-lifetimes-behind-bars-for-fraud/. "Democratic congresswoman faces more than three lifetimes behind bars for fraud," Jul. 10, 2016.

34. http://www.realclearpolitics.com/video/2016/03/03/joy_ann_reid_trump_is_dog_whistling_at_the_old_south_and_they_hear_him.html. Hains, Tim. "Joy Ann Reid: The 'Old South' hears Trump's dog-whistles loud and clear : Menacing to black and Jewish voters," Mar. 3, 2016.

35. "The Place for Politics 2016." MSNBC, Xfinity 1108 MSNBC, Jul. 18, 2016.

36. http://dailycaller.com/2016/02/15/marine-allegedly-assaulted-mid-burger-at-mcdonald-as-gang-yelled-do-you-believe-black-lives-matter/. Birr, Steve. "Marine allegedly assaulted mid-burger at McDonald's, as gang yelled, 'Do you believe black lives matter," Feb. 15, 2016.

37. insider.foxnews.com/2016/02/23/donations-pour-marine-hero-christopher-marquez-who-was-attacked-dc-mcdonalds. "2 arrested in cowardly ambush attack on marine outside D.C. McDonalds," Feb. 23, 2016.

38. http://www.rasmussenreports.com/public_content/politics/weekly_updates/what_they_told_us_reviewing_last_week_s_key_polls2. "What they told us: Review last week's key polls," Jul. 30, 2016.

39. https://www.yahoo.com/news/police-officers-kill-woman-barricaded-hom-child-223306767.html. "Police officers kill armed woman barricaded in apartment," Aug. 1, 2016.

40. http://en.wikipedia.org/wiki/Medgar_Evers.

41. http://www.theblaze.com/stories/2016/08/04/black-lives-matter-activist-deray-mckesson-sues-baton-rouge-over-arrest-during-protest/. Urbanski, Dave. "Black Lives Matter activist DeRay McKesson sues Baton Rouge over arrest during protest," Aug. 4, 2016.

42. http://www.baltimoresun.com/news/maryland-baltimore-city/bs-md-deray-arrested-20160710.html. Rector, Kevin. "DeRay McKesson arrested during Baton Rouge protest," Jul. 10, 2016.

43. https://en.wikipedia.org/wiki/Baltimore_mayoral_election_2016.

44. https://www.yahoo.com/katiecouric/black-lives-matter-leaders-on-protests-and-arrests-182004725.html. Delaney, Summer. "Black Lives Matter leader DeRay McKesson on protests and his arrests," Jun. 10,2016.

45. https://www.theguardian.com/us-news/2016/may/31/katie-couric-apology-misleading-edit-under-the-gun. Beckett, Lois. "Katie Couric says sorry for 'misleading' edit in gun rights documentary," May 31, 2016.

46. http://observer.com/2016/07/theres-more-to-real-story-of-gretchen-carlsons-fox-firing/. Lapointe, Joe. "Sunday wrap up: 'There's more to the story of Gretchen Carlson's Fox firing," Jul. 11, 2016.

47. http://www.westernjournalism.com/revealed-who-obama-is-welcoming-into-the-white-house-today-speaks-louder-than-any-words. Whitson, Kevin. "Revealed: Who Obama is welcoming into the White House today speaks louder than any words," Feb. 18, 2016.

48. http://www.washingtontimes.com/news/2016/aug/21/black-lives-matter-takes-heat-louisiana-flood-reli/. Richardson, Valerie. "Black Lives Matter mobilizes in Baton Rouge for protests, passes on flood relief," Aug. 21, 2016.

49. https://www.facebook.com/heather.cross.9693/posts/619830094838374.

50. http://www.washingtontimes.com/news/2016/aug/19/obama-offends-louisiana-flood-victims-me/. Richardson, Valerie. "Obama irks La. Flood victims with memo warning them not to discriminate," Aug. 19, 2016.

51. http://www.washingtontimes.com/news/2015/jan/14/george-soros-funds-ferguson-protests-hopes-to-spur/. Riddell, Kelly. "George Soros funds Ferguson protests, hopes to spur civil action," Jan. 14, 2015.

52. http://www.theamericanmirror.com/blacklivesmatter-leader-deray-lives-home-owned-by-soros-connected/. Girdusky, Ryan. "COZY: BLM leader lives in home owned by Soros' Open Society board member," Jul. 12, 2016.

53. http://conservativetribune.com/protesters-identies-revealed/. Proviso, Wilmot. "SHOCK: Anti-Trump protestors real identities revealed when online form leaks," Jun. 7, 2016.

54. http://www.huffingtonpost.com/entry/oligarchy-super-pac-megadonors-have-conquered-american-politics_55bc1eece4b0b23e3ce2f5ec?. Blumenthal, Paul. "Oligarchy of super PAC megadonors have conquered American politics," Jul. 31, 2015.

55. http://conservativetribune.com/media-mom-cop-shooter-said/. Smith, Kim. "Media will never report what mom of cop shooter just said about black lives matter," Aug. 3, 2016.

56. http://www.washingtonpost.com/sf/investigative/2015/12/26/a-year-of-reckoning-police-fatally-

shoot-nearly-1000/. Kindy, Kimberly, Fisher, Mark, Tate, Julie and Jennifer Jenkins. "A year of reckoning: police shoot nearly 1,000," Dec. 26, 2015.

57. "MSNBC Live" MSNBC, Host Craig Melvin, Xfinity 1108 MSNBC, Aug. 7, 2015.

58. Miller, Merle. Plain Speaking: An Oral Biography of Harry S. Truman. Berkley Publishing Corporation: New York, 1974. (p.154, 155).

59. Linderman, Juliet. "Sit-in follows decades of festering ills" The Times Daily 16 Oct. 2015: A6. Print.

60. Thomas, Evan. Robert Kennedy: His Life. New York: Simon & Schuster. 2002. (p. 325).

61.http://www.theroot.com/articles/culture/2014/07/ florida_barbershop_promotes_reading_by_giving_kids_books/. Finley, Taryn. "Florida Barbershop promotes literacy by giving books to its young customers," Jul. 17, 2014.

62. http://airshipdaily.com/blog/07212014-barbershop-library. King, Michelle. "South Florida barber shop doubles as library," Jul. 21, 2014.

63. http://www.al.com/living/index.ssf/2016/04/alabama_college_student_launch.html. Vollers, Anna Claire. "How one college student uses free lawn care for elderly to teach young men about community," Apr. 27, 2016.

64. http://ideas.ted.com/why-im-teaching-prisoners-to-code. Redlitz, Chris. "Why I'm teaching prisoners to code," Feb. 18, 2016.

65. Coelho, Paulo. The Alchemist. San Francisco: HarperSanFrancisco, 1993. (p. 167).

66. "America's Newsroom with Bill Hemmer and Martha MacCallum." Fox News, Xfinity 1105 FNCHD, Jun. 6, 2016.

67. Kennedy, John F. Profiles In Courage: Decisive moments in the lives of celebrated Americans. New York: HarperCollins Publishers, 1984. (p. 18, 224)

68. "Shepard Smith reporting." Fox News, Host Shepard Smith, Xfinity 1105 FNCHD, Oct. 5, 2015.

69. http://www.cbsnews.com/news/report-2008-financial-crisis-increased-suicide-rates-in-us-europe/. Castillo, Michelle. "Report: 2008 financial crisis increased suicide rates in U.S., Europe," Sept. 18, 2013.

70. http://www.nytimes.com/2015/12/30/business/economy/for-the-weatlhiest-private-tax-system-saves-them-billions.html. Scheiber, Noam and Patricia Cohen. "For the wealthiest, a private tax system that saves them billions: The very richest are able to quietly shape tax policy that will allow them to shield billions in income," Dec. 29, 2015.

71. http://www.opensecrets.org/news/2015/09/attacks-on-low-taxes-for-hedge-fund-managers-will-face-fierce-fight/. Lazar, Alex. "Attacks on low taxes for hedge fund managers will face fierce fight," Sept. 10, 2015.

72. Chernow, Ron. Alexander Hamilton. New York: Penguin Group, 2004.

73. https://www.nationalpriorities.org/blog/2015/09/22/one-five-american-children-poverty-how-did-we-get-here/. Koshgarian, Lindsay. "One in five American children in poverty: How did we get here?" Sept. 22, 2015.

74. http://www.slate.com/articles/business/moneybox/2014/06/taxation_of_carried_interest_the_loophole_for_hedge_fund_managers_could.html. Lebedoff, David. "Why doesn't Obama end the hedge fund tax break?" Jun. 2, 2014.

75. http://www.reagan.utexas.edu/archives/reference/timechoosing.html. Reagan, Ronald. "A Time for Choosing," Oct. 27, 1964.

76. http://www.zerohedge.com/news/2015-08-07/when-work-punished-ongoing-tragedy-americas-welfare-state. Durden, Tyler. "When work is punished: The ongoing tragedy of America's welfare state," Aug. 7, 2015.

77. Ehrenreich, Barbara. Nickel and Dimed: On (not) getting by in America. Metropolitan Books: New York, 2001.

78. http://www.npr.org/2015/12/10/459100751/utah-reduced-chronic-homelessness-by-91-percent-heres-how. McEvers, Kelly. "Utah reduced chronic homelessness by 91 percent; here's how," Dec. 10, 2015.

79. "The O'Reilly Factor." Fox News, Host Bill O'Reilly, Xfinity 1105 FNCHD, May 24, 2016.

80. http://money.cnn.com/2015/05/27/investing/overdraft-fees-over-1-billion-big-banks/. Long, Heather. "Overdraft fees top $1 billion at big banks," May 27, 2013.

81. http://www.bizjournals.com/stlouis/stories/1998/06/01/focus3.html. Tucci, Linda. "Sherraden invents IDA savings plan: Matchmaker," May 31, 1998.

82. https://www.numbersusa.org/#. Beck, Roy. "Immigration by the Numbers," 2010.

83. http://www.infowars.com/video-homeland-refugee-screening-coordinator-cant-answer-basic-questions-about-program/. Skinner, Victor. "VIDEO: 'Homeland' refugee screening coordinator can't answer basic questions about program," Dec. 12, 2015.

84. http://www.foxnews.com/us/2015/03/03/feds-crack-down-on-chinese-birth-tourism-scam/. Jeunesse, William La. "Feds crack down on Chinese 'birth tourism,'" Mar. 3, 2015.

85. The Book Archive. "State of the Union Address: Speech by President Clinton." Online video clip. YouTube. YouTube, 5 May 2012. Web. Sept. 7, 2016.

86. http://yournewswire.com/sweden-on-brink-of-collapse-worrying-report/. Adl-Tabatabai, Sean.

"Sweden on brink of collapse, worrying report," Oct. 19, 2015.

87. http://www.ibtimes.com/us-foreign-aid-washington-gives-billions-is-it-money-well-spent-1625994. Keith, Ross. "US foreign aid: Washington gives billions, but is it money well spent?" Jul. 11, 2014.

88. http://news.yahoo.com/poll-most-back-legal-status-immigrants-us-illegally-140306959-election.html?nf=1. Caldwell, Alicia A., and Emily Swanson. "Poll: Most back legal status for immigrants in US illegally," Jun. 4, 2015.

89. "The Kelly File." Fox News, Host Megan Kelly, Xfinity 1105 FNCHD, Oct. 21, 2015.

90. www.huffingtonpost.com/lori-wallach/nafta-at-20-one-million-u_b_4550207.html. Wallach, Lori. "NAFTA at 20: One million U.S. jobs lost, higher income inequality," May 8, 2014.

91. http://news.yahoo.com/ap-gfk-poll-majority-americans-favor-path-citizenship-192320344-election.html. Swanson, Emily. "AP-GfK Poll: Majority of Americans favor path to citizenship," Dec. 17, 2015.

92. Jack McFile. "JFK-Press conference 21 April 1961 Enhanced 3/3" Online video clip. YouTube. `YouTube 21 Dec. 2011. Youtube Sept. 8, 2016.

93. http://www.military.com/daily-news/2016/04/29/army-reverses-decision-to-kick-out-green-beret-confronted-rapist.html. Tomlinson, Lucas. "Army reverses decision to kick out green beret who confronted rapist," Apr. 29, 2016.

94. Robinson, Donald. The day I was proudest to be an American: Sixty-nine Americans recount stirring episodes that reflect our country's greatness. New York: Doubleday and Company, Inc: New York, 1958. (p. 153, 154, 155).

95. https://www.washingtonpost.com/news/post-politics/wp/2015/08/06/transcript-gop-aug-6-undercard-debate/. "Transcript: GOP Aug. 6 undercard debate," Aug. 6, 2015.

96. http://www.jfklibrary.org/Research/Research-Aids/Ready-Reference/EMK-Speeches/Tribute-to-Senator-Robert-F-Kennedy.aspx. Kennedy, Edward M. "Tribute to Robert F. Kennedy, St Patrick Cathedral, New York City, Jun. 8, 1968.

97. America Rising PAC. "America Rising PAC's Tim Miller joins CNN's crossfire to talk about 'Failed Choices.'" Online video clip. YouTube. YouTube, 10 Jun. 2014. Web Aug. 8, 2016.

98. http://www.the.freedictionary.com/folksiness.

99. http://nypost.com/2016/09/17/almost-half-of-america-could-become-the-new-permanent-underclass/. Callahan, Maureen. "Almost half of America could become new permanent underclass," Sept. 17, 2016.

100. "Fox and Friends." Fox News, Hosts Steve Doocy, Brian Kilmeade, Guest Host Sandra Smith, Xfinity 1105 FNCHD, Aug. 1, 2016.

101. http://www.subjectpolitics.com/watch-hillary-wants-this-video-deleted-from-the-internet/. "WATCH: Hillary wants this video DELETED from the internet," Jun. 16, 2016.

102. http://usatoday30.usatoday.com/news/politics/2008-01-24-1966293725_x.htm. Kuhnhenn, Jim. "Adwatch: Dueling Obama, Clinton ads," Jan. 24, 2008.

103. http://observer.com/2016/06/after-decades-vacuuming-up-dubious-donations-clinton-suddenly-favors-campaign-finance-reform/. Sainato, Michael. "After decades vacuuming up dubious donations, Clinton suddenly favors campaign finance reform," Jun. 14, 2016.

104. http://blogs.suntimes.com/sweet/2008/02/complete_transcriptdemocratic.html. Sweet, Lynn. "Complete transcript Democratic Presidential Debate." Courtesy MSNBC Cleveland, Ohio, Feb. 26, 2008.

105. http://www.theamericanmirror.com/leaked/e-mail-shows-george-soros-urged-clinton-intervene-albania-civil-unrest/. Girdusky, Ryan. "Leaked e-mail shows Soros urged Clinton to intervene in Albania civil unrest," Aug. 11, 2016.

106. https://www.politicshome.com/news/europe/eu-policy-agenda/brexit/news/74199/hillary-clinton-warns-uk-against-brexit. Ashmore, John. "Hillary Clinton warns UK against Brexit," Apr. 24, 2016.

107. "The Real Story with Gretchen Carlson." Guest Host Martha MacCallum, Fox News, Xfinity 1105 FNCHD, Jun. 24, 2016.

108. http://www.ukip.org/ukip_release_the_eu_rich_list_2015_16. "UKIP release the EU rich list 2015/16," Dec. 26, 2015.

109. Scott Arthur. "The ITV #Brexit 'Debate'- David Cameron & Nigel Farage on the EU referendum" Online video clip. YouTube. YouTube 8 Jun. 2016. Youtube Jul. 8, 2016.

110. http://canadafreepress.com/article/foreign-investors-flocking-to-uk-as-brexit-implementation-nears. Calabrese, Dan. "Foreign investors flocking to UK as Brexit implementation nears," Sept. 2, 2016.

111. http://www.washingtontimes.com/news/2016/may/10/editorial-john-kerrys-world-without-borders/. "John Kerry's world without borders," May 10, 2016.

112. http://dailycaller.com/2016/05/09/limbaugh-kerrys-borderless-world-comment-strengthens-trumps-appeal-audio/. Guest, Steve. "Limbaugh: Kerry's 'borderless world' comment strengthens Trump's appeal," May 9, 2016.

113. http://news.yahoo.com/hungary-says-migrant-influx-stops-114617312.html. "Hungary says mi-

grant influx 'stops,'" Aug. 19, 2015.

114. http://intelligencebriefs.com/us-to-fund-24-9-million-electronic-security-surveillance-on-the-tunisia-libya-security-wall/. Muthoni, Beth. "US to fund $24.9 million electronic security surveillance on the Tunisia-Libya security wall," Mar. 29, 2016.

115. https://news.vice.com/article/the-great-wall-of-jordan-how-the-us-wants-to-keep-the-islamic-state-out. Arkin, William M. "The great wall of Jordan: How the U.S. wants to keep the Islamic state out," Feb. 24, 2016.

116. http://www.foxnews.com/world/2016/07/15/french-lawmakers-told-bataclan-terrorists-tortured-disemboweled-victims.html. Mensch, Louise. "French lawmakers told Bataclan terrorists tortured, disemboweled victims," Jul. 15, 2016.

117. https://www.yahoo.com/news/more-800-immigrants-mistakenly-granted-citizenship-130452164-politics.html. Caldwell, Alicia A. "More than 800 immigrants mistakenly granted citizenship," Sept. 19, 2016.

118. https://www.facebook.com/therightmichellemalkin/?fref=ts.

119. Raymond, Allen with Ian Spiegelman. "Confessions of a Republican operative: how to rig an election. Simon & Schuster: New York, 2008. (p. 239).

120. Andrews, Wayne. The Autobiography of Theodore Roosevelt. New York: Octagon Books, 1975.

121. http://www.nytimes.com/aponline/2015/10/09/us/politics/ap-us-ap-was-there-million-man-march.html. "AP was there: 20 years ago million man march drew many to DC," Oct. 9, 2015.

122. http://bartleby.com/124/pres61.html. Reagan, Ronald. "First inaugural address," Jan. 20, 1981.

123. http://www.pbs.newhour/updates/thousands-american-military-graves-lie-forgotten-lost-abroad/. Shell, Elizabeth. "Thousands of American military graves lie forgotten and lost abroad," May 26, 2014.

124. Lewis, Edwards and Richard Rhodes, eds. John F. Kennedy: Words to Remember. United States: Hallmark Cards Incorporated, 1967. (p. 15).